Praise for
Plain, Honest Men

"Authoritative and readable ... Beeman's work is distinguished by a gently judicious tone that allows us to appreciate, and draw some lessons from, the delicate balances that emerged out of that passion-filled Philadelphia crucible." —*The New York Times Book Review*

"The fullest and most authoritative account of the Constitutional Convention ever written."
—GORDON S. WOOD, author of *The Radicalism of the American Revolution*

"This book offers a rare treat for American history devotees. ... Beeman reveals a vast knowledge of the era. ... A bravura display of literary talent and historical insight." —*American Heritage*

"An engrossing account of the men who met in Philadelphia in 1787 to design a radically new form of government. ... [Beeman] is a fine writer and has a firm grasp on the motives, machinations, and personalities of the twenty major players." —*The Christian Science Monitor*

"A work of first-rate scholarship ... Not since Catherine Drinker Bowen's *Miracle at Philadelphia* (1966) has there been such a superb, comprehensive account of the Constitutional Convention of 1787. Beeman's lucid prose takes readers beyond the modern mythical perceptions of the founders and into a turbulent world of fierce back-room debates and deal making [providing] readers with an understanding of just how fragile the consensus emerging from Philadelphia really was. . . . Highly recommended." —*Library Journal* (starred review)

"This is a great narrative." —JON STEWART on *The Daily Show*

"Masterful . . . Beeman gives each decision, each vote, the weight it deserves and, in brief sketches, brings the delegates alive. . . . [It's] a story freighted with world-historical significance . . . well told here as can be imagined. This account is now the most authoritative, up-to-date treatment of the Constitutional Convention since Catherine Drinker Bowen's *Miracle at Philadelphia* over forty years ago. It's unlikely to be surpassed." —*Publishers Weekly* (starred review)

"A judicious history of 'one of the most important gatherings in modern history'. . . Beeman eschews the heroic version of the story in favor of a hard-eyed narrative that in no way diminishes the Framers' achievement. . . . In a motion-by-motion, day-by-day, debate-by-debate fashion, he re-creates the hard bargaining over issues. . . . Masterfully told American history for the scholar and general reader alike." —*Kirkus Reviews* (starred review)

"Genuinely new and revealing." —*The Washington Post*

"In sprightly, engaging prose and with a sure, steady scholarly hand, Richard Beeman has given us a vivid account of the most vital chapter of our early history: the making of the Constitution. This is a terrific book." —JON MEACHAM, author of *American Lion*

"Astute, dramatic and gracefully written . . . an important work from an eminent scholar that truly furthers our knowledge of the 'miracle at Philadelphia.' " —*The Providence Journal*

"Skillfully, Beeman uses character development to drive his narrative." —*The Dallas Morning News*

"In Beeman's prose, readers can visualize the scenes as delegates engage the issues on which the Constitution's compromises rest. . . . Beeman's depiction of one of chattel's champions, Charles Pinckney, underscores a primary intention of the author: to show in greater relief members of lesser historical fame . . . who had decisive effect on the Constitution. . . . Beeman's work compares well with its classic predecessor, Catherine Drinker Bowen's *Miracle at Philadelphia*."

—*Booklist*

BY RICHARD BEEMAN

The Varieties of Political Experience in Eighteenth-Century America

Beyond Confederation:
Origins of the Constitution and American National Identity (ed.)

The Evolution of the Southern Backcountry: A Case Study of Lunenburg
County, Virginia, 1746–1832

Patrick Henry: A Biography

The Old Dominion and the New Nation, 1788–1801

Plain, Honest Men: The Making of the American Constitution

The Penguin Guide to the United States Constitution: A Fully Annotated
Declaration of Independence, U.S. Constitution and Amendments,
and Selections from the Federalist Papers

Our Lives, Our Fortunes, Our Sacred Honor: Americans Choose Independence

PLAIN, HONEST MEN

PLAIN, HONEST MEN

THE MAKING OF
THE AMERICAN CONSTITUTION

Richard Beeman

RANDOM HOUSE TRADE PAPERBACKS
NEW YORK

2010 Random House Trade Paperback Edition

Published in the United States by Random House Trade Paperbacks, an imprint of The Random House Publishing Group, a division of Random House, Inc., New York.

RANDOM HOUSE TRADE PAPERBACKS and colophon are trademarks of Random House, Inc.

Originally published in hardcover in the United States by Random House, an imprint of The Random House Publishing Group, a division of Random House, Inc., in 2009.

Library of Congress Cataloging-in-Publication Data

Beeman, Richard R.
Plain, honest men : the making of the American Constitution / Richard Beeman.
p. cm.
Includes bibliographical references.
ISBN 978-0-8129-7684-7
eBook ISBN 978-1-58836-726-6
1. United States. Constitutional Convention (1787) 2. Constitutional history—United States. I. Title.
KF4510.B44 2009
342.7302'9—dc22
2008028841

Printed in the United States of America

www.atrandom.com

Book design by Christopher M. Zucker

To Mary

PREFACE

ON SEPTEMBER 18, 1787, the day following adjournment of the Constitutional Convention, an exhausted George Washington dashed off a quick note to the Marquis de Lafayette. He had promised his old comrade in arms a full account of the proceedings of the Convention, but, desperately eager to return to Mount Vernon, he could summon up only enough energy to offer a brief characterization of that summer's work. The "production of four months deliberation," Washington wrote, was "now a Child of fortune, to be fostered by some and buffeted by others. What will be the General opinion on, or the reception of it, is not for me to decide, nor shall I say any thing for or against it—if it be good, I suppose it will work its way good—if bad it will recoil on the Framers."[1]

Nearly five months later, comfortably ensconced at Mount Vernon and warmed by a fire on a bitterly cold February day, the general's optimism about the proposed new Constitution had improved considerably. Writing again to Lafayette, Washington observed that it was "little short of a miracle" that the men gathered in Philadelphia that past summer could "unite in forming a system of government so little liable to well-founded objections."[2]

Catherine Drinker Bowen began her stirring 1966 account of the making of the Constitution, *Miracle at Philadelphia*, with an evocation of Washington's more sanguine assessment of the Constitution. "Mira-cles," she wrote, "do not occur at random. . . . Every miracle has its provenance, every miracle has been prayed for." Her intention, she declared, was to celebrate the "most remarkable political document in history."[3]

Gouverneur Morris, a Convention delegate from Pennsylvania who shared Washington's hopes for the proposed Constitution, had achieved his fame and fortune by keeping his eyes fixed on worldly concerns, not on the heavens. Speaking of the document that emerged from the Assembly Room of the Pennsylvania State House, Morris noted that "while some have boasted it as a work from Heaven, others have given it a less righteous origin. I have many reasons to believe that it is the work of plain, honest men."[4]

Morris's homely description, though perhaps less inspiring than Washington's or Bowen's, brings us closer to the truth. But it takes us only a part of the way toward understanding either the individuals or the set of circumstances that brought the American Constitution into being. The Constitutional Convention of 1787 effected a revolution in the nature of the American government. That revolution occurred neither by accident nor by divine intervention. It was, in its inception, the work of a small group of men who had become convinced that America's experiment in republican liberty was in jeopardy and that bold action was necessary if that experiment was to flourish. Those men—most conspicuous among them Washington, James Madison of Virginia, and two Pennsylvania delegates—Gouverneur Morris and James Wilson—set the revolution in motion by introducing during the early days of the Convention a bold, even audacious, plan for an entirely new form of national government. But their attempt at revolutionary change, once launched, proved difficult both to sustain and to control.

This book presents a full narrative account of the work of the fifty-five men who spent the summer of 1787 in the Assembly Room of the Pennsylvania State House crafting an entirely new form of continental government. Much of their work occurred during the formal sessions of the Convention itself, running six days a week—with only Sundays off—between May 25 and September 17. But I intend also to take readers behind the scenes and beyond the debates, into the taverns and boardinghouses of the city, to present a full account of how the world's most important constitution was forged.

An important part of the story hinges on the individual and collective characters of the men responsible for the Constitution's drafting. Interspersed with the narrative of events of the Convention, I have sought to free our "Founding Fathers" from their bronze or marble likenesses and bring them to life. These men were—I state it unabashedly—extraordinary individuals. Their ultimate achievement, however difficult it may have been to come by, was magnificent. They were, however, mortals—not, as some have characterized them, "demigods."[5]

As the historian Gordon Wood has reminded us, the leaders of America's Revolutionary generation were not men of the twenty-first century. They were the product of a particular place and moment of the late eighteenth century. They were deliberating at a point in history when intellectualism and political activism could naturally, easily, coexist. The most influential of these men could lay claim to being both the intellectual and political leaders of their respective states—men confident of their ability to put their ideas about politics into practical form.[6]

For all of their ability to combine intellect and activism, however, the Founding Fathers were also products of a provincial world—one in which the perspective of even the most cosmopolitan among them was limited by the vast expanse of the American landscape and the inadequacies of the communication networks available to them in eighteenth-century America. Whether residents of Georgia or Maryland, New York or New Hampshire, the delegates of the 1787 Constitutional Convention struggled against the limitations they faced not only to envision themselves as citizens of a single nation but to forge a coalition of their individual states into a unified whole.

When viewed through the lens of the twenty-first century, the creation of a durable, democratic nation among thirteen disparate and far-flung sovereign states assumes an aura of inevitability. But when viewed from the perspective of the summer of 1787, that outcome was more improbable than inevitable. It is my hope that the readers of *Plain, Honest Men: The Making of the American Constitution* will come to appreciate not only the extraordinary achievements of the Founding Fathers, but also the conflict, contingency, and uncertainty that marked their deliberations.

While most of the delegates came to Philadelphia hoping to create a significantly strengthened continental government, none of them could have imagined the goliath of a nation that America was to become. And few of them could have imagined that this goliath would become a *democratic* nation. The vast majority of the Founding Fathers were republicans, not democrats, which is to say that they had rejected monarchy and hereditary rule and they had embraced unequivocally the idea of representative government. But there were nearly as many different answers to the question of how to define the relationship between representatives and the citizens they served as there were delegates to the Convention. At one extreme, there were those who believed that representatives had an obligation to mirror faithfully the views of their constituents. At the other, many of the Convention delegates believed that the best form of representative government was one in which the virtuous few, once elected or appointed to office, acted independently of the whims of public opinion to serve the "public good."

Just as the delegates regarded democracy with varying degrees of enthusiasm, so too did they differ in their understanding of the meaning and character of the very structures of government they were creating. As the delegates began their deliberations in late May, they most often spoke of creating a "national" government. As they ended their deliberations in mid-September they tended to describe their creation as "federal." Within a few months of their adjournment, James Madison was speaking of the proposed new government as "part national" and "part federal," but there was precious little agreement among even those who had drafted the Constitution as to the precise meaning of this new definition of federalism.

If the debate over the "national" or "federal" character of the Constitution was often confusing, the debate over the nature of the American presidency was pure torment. Although the delegates wished at all costs to avoid creating an "elective monarch," there the agreement ended. What should the relationship of the new American president to the new Congress or, more problematically, to the people of America be? Again, the delegates' answers to those questions varied enormously, and few among them had much confidence that their attempt to harmonize those differences of opinion—through the creation of an electoral college—would prove a durable and workable solution.

Democracy, federalism, and *executive power* are words that have been at the center of our political life—and our political and constitutional debate—from 1787 forward. There is yet another word—*equality*—that has come to define the very nature, the highest aspiration, of the American experience. Yet neither that word, nor its antithesis—*slavery*—is anywhere mentioned in the text of the Constitution. The seemingly anomalous existence of slavery in a nation founded on a revolutionary promise of equality was not—at least in the minds of the framers—the central issue at stake in the making of the American Constitution. But it was certainly more important than most previous histories of the Constitutional Convention have made it out to be.

This history of the Constitutional Convention of 1787 will devote more space to the delegates' inconclusive and, in the end, unsatisfactory decisions about the place of slavery in the new republic than any previous work of its kind. In dealing with this vexing subject, I have been mindful once again that the framers of the Constitution were men of the late eighteenth century, a time when the enslavement and subjugation of one group of human beings by another was more often the commonplace, rather than the exceptional, occurrence. This fact does not excuse the failure of the Founding Fathers to eradicate what historian Bernard DeVoto long ago called "the paradox at the nation's core," or, indeed, their failure even to address the moral issues associated with slavery, but it does provide a frame of reference for understanding the causes of that tragic failure.

AMERICANS BEGAN TO ARGUE about how their Constitution should be interpreted from the very moment that the new government under that Constitution commenced. Those arguments have persisted, sometimes with extraordinary vehemence, to the present day. Politicians, jurists, and ordinary citizens insist, at one extreme, that ours is a "living Constitution," intended by the founders to be interpreted in light of constantly changing circumstances. At the other extreme, the Constitution is viewed as a straightforward legal text, to be interpreted according to the "plain meaning" of the words on the page, as understood by the people of the United States at the time it was drafted. One of my hopes in writing this book is that those who profess a self-confident certainty about either the "intent" of the framers or the "original meaning" of the words written on the Constitution's four parchment pages will, as they confront the uncertainty and humility with which the framers approached their task, admit to a bit more uncertainty and humility in their own pronouncements about our nation's fundamental charter.

The most important purpose propelling this work is—dare I say it?—a patriotic one. The American experiment in liberty and constitutional governance has had its rocky moments, but our Constitution has not only proven to be the world's most durable written frame of government, but it is also, I believe, its most just and equitable. The men who drafted it knew that they had not created a "perfect" constitution, but they were nevertheless committed to continuing the quest for a "more perfect union." They knew that they were embarked on an important experiment, one that could achieve success only by a combination of conscientious stewardship and an openness to further experimentation and change.

Americans of the twenty-first century are the stewards of the United States Constitution, and perhaps we will be able to learn some valuable lessons from both the humility and the audacity of those men who came together in Philadelphia to effect the revolution of 1787.

CONTENTS

KEY TO THE FRONTISPIECE

1 Jared Ingersoll – *Pennsylvania*
2 Pierce Butler – *South Carolina*
3 John Rutledge – *South Carolina*
4 Nicholas Gilman – *New Hampshire*
5 Thomas Fitzsimons – *Pennsylvania*
6 Daniel of St. Thomas Jenifer – *Maryland*
7 Daniel Carroll – *Maryland*
8 William Samuel Johnson – *Connecticut*
9 George Clymer – *Pennsylvania*
10 Alexander Hamilton – *New York*
11 William Jackson. Secretary
12 Gunning Bedford, Jr. – *Delaware*
13 Richard Bassett – *Delaware*
14 Robert Morris – *Pennsylvania*
15 Thomas Mifflin – *Pennsylvania*
16 Hugh Williamson – *North Carolina*
17 Nathaniel Gorham – *Massachusetts*
18 James Wilson – *Pennsylvania*
19 George Washington – *Virginia*
20 Benjamin Franklin – *Pennsylvania*
21 Jacob Broom – *Delaware*
22 James Madison – *Virginia*

23 James McHenry – *Maryland*
24 William Paterson – *New Jersey*
25 William Livingston – *New Jersey*
26 Gouverneur Morris – *Pennsylvania*
27 Jonathan Dayton – *New Jersey*
28 Rufus King – *Massachusetts*
29 Charles Cotesworth Pinckney – *South Carolina*
30 George Mason – *Virginia*
31 Roger Sherman – *Connecticut*
32 John Dickinson – *Delaware*
33 David Brearly – *New Jersey*
34 Edmund Randolph – *Virginia*
35 George Read – *Delaware*
36 William Blount – *North Carolina*
37 John Langdon – *New Hampshire*
38 John Blair – *Virginia*
39 Abraham Baldwin – *Georgia*
40 Richard Dobbs Spaight, Sr. – *North Carolina*
41 Charles Pinckney – *South Carolina*
42 William Few – *Georgia*
43 Elbridge Gerry – *Massachusetts*

PRINCIPAL CHARACTERS

THE INDISPENSABLE MEN OF THE CONVENTION

JAMES MADISON: Short, sickly, and with a tendency to mumble in his speechmaking, the thirty-seven-year-old Madison was as politically and intellectually astute as he was physically unimposing. Through his diligent preparation before the Convention—embodied most dramatically in the draft of the Virginia Plan—he was able to seize the initiative from those delegates who arrived at the Convention with only the modest goal of "amending" the Articles of Confederation.

GEORGE WASHINGTON: Having agreed to attend the Convention only with the greatest reluctance, Washington did not miss a single day of the body's proceedings. And although he uttered barely a word during the debates, his prestige, dignity, and evenhandedness in presiding over the proceedings established him at the Convention—as those qualities had in other instances—as America's "indispensable man."

BENJAMIN FRANKLIN: "Dr. Franklin," wrote the Georgia delegate William Pierce, "is well known to be the greatest philosopher of his age; all of the operations of nature he seems to understand, the very heavens obey him, and the Clouds yield up their lightning to be imprisoned in his rod." Franklin's contributions to the debates in the Convention were often quirky, but his final speech, urging the delegates to put the need for a harmonious union above their own interests and ideologies, to check their egos at the door, in essence, marked a decisive moment in the process of the making of the Constitution.

MEN WHO HELPED SHAPE THE CONSTITUTION

GOUVERNEUR MORRIS: Born into a family of wealth and privilege in New York, Morris moved to Philadelphia shortly after the outbreak of independence because he thought his financial and political ambitions would be better served there. Only Madison spoke more often than he in the Convention, and Morris's contributions to the debate—always on the side of creating a vigorous national government—were forceful and eloquent, although occasionally bombastic. As chair of the Committee of Style, Morris supplied some of the necessary polish to the Constitution.

JAMES WILSON: Like Madison, Pennsylvania's James Wilson lacked the attributes of charm or oratorical eloquence that were the traditional marks of an eighteenth-century gentleman, but, like his Virginia counterpart, he made up for those deficiencies with the sharpness of his mind and the depth of his knowledge of law and political theory.

ROGER SHERMAN: "The oddest shaped character I ever remember to have met with, he is awkward, un-meaning, and unaccountably strange in his manner." Thus observed William Pierce of Georgia. But Sherman would be in the thick of every important debate in the Convention—whether on the subject of the apportionment of representation in the legislature, the powers of the chief executive, or the thorny subject of slavery—and he would play a crucial role in key compromises on all of those issues.

CHARLES PINCKNEY: The young delegate from South Carolina combined in his character high intelligence, eloquence, and an overriding vanity that caused him to claim, falsely, that he was the youngest man present in the Convention. He would also claim, with greater plausibility but nevertheless excessive grandiosity, that he—not Madison—was the true "author" of the Constitution. Pinckney would play a key role in writing into the Constitution important protections for the institution of slavery.

INFLUENTIAL CHARACTERS

WILLIAM PATERSON: The sternly moralistic Princeton graduate was the author of the so-called New Jersey Plan, the principal alternative to Madison's Virginia Plan. He was one of the Convention's strongest advocates for the interests of the "small states."

NATHANIEL GORHAM: Gorham did not play an active role in debate, but as chair of the Committee of the Whole, the Massachusetts delegate presided effectively over the Convention's early deliberations during the first half of the summer.

EDMUND RANDOLPH: Governor of Virginia in 1787, Randolph could trace his lineage back to one of the state's most distinguished families, and it was perhaps for that reason that he—not Madison—was selected to present the Virginia Plan to the Convention. In the end, however, he would join the ranks of those dissenting from the final document.

JOHN DICKINSON: A reluctant Revolutionist in 1776, Dickinson was the author of an early draft of the Articles of Confederation. Although he did not play a major role in drafting the Constitution, his speeches on a wide range of subjects—from the meaning of federalism to the importance of a separation of powers within the new government—were timely and sagacious.

OLIVER ELLSWORTH: Like his fellow delegate from Connecticut Roger Sherman, Ellsworth was involved in all of the important compromises that enabled the Convention to move forward with its agenda.

JOHN RUTLEDGE: The most powerful politician in South Carolina, Rutledge played a key role as chair of the so-called Committee of Detail, which reviewed and refined all of the confusing and conflicting proposals that had been presented to the Convention during the first two and a half months of debate. On August 6, Rutledge presented the first coherent version of the Constitution yet to appear.

ALEXANDER HAMILTON: The young and ambitious Colonel Hamilton may have been the smartest man in the Convention, but his fondness for the British Constitution and disdain for the state governments may have alienated other delegates.

ROBERT MORRIS: The "financier of the American Revolution" was among the most powerful and influential men in America. He said little on the Convention floor, but, as the patron of James Wilson and Gouverneur Morris and the host of George Washington during the summer, his behind-the-scenes influence was no doubt considerable.

THE PRINCIPAL DISSENTERS

ELBRIDGE GERRY: This Massachusetts delegate was contentious, deeply suspicious of what he believed to be the "democratic excesses" of the state governments, and equally suspicious of the dangers of unchecked central government power. Gerry may have been the most consistent naysayer at the Convention, and, in his final act of naysaying, he refused to sign the Constitution on September 17.

LUTHER MARTIN: Martin's reputation has been shaped primarily by his fondness for drink. But Luther Martin in a state of inebriation could sometimes be more shrewd than many of the delegates in states of sobriety. An advocate for keeping the essential elements of the Articles of Confederation intact, he left in a huff before the work of the Convention was complete.

ROBERT YATES and **JOHN LANSING:** These two New York delegates constituted two of the three members of their state's delegation. As long as they were present at the Convention, New York's delegation could be counted on to oppose anything that might weaken the power of their state. Their decision to leave the Convention early would leave the New York delegation without a quorum and therefore unable to participate in many of the key votes in the Convention.

GEORGE MASON: Author of Virginia's Declaration of Rights, Mason was one of the few delegates who insisted that the new Constitution contain a bill of rights. He made important contributions to the debates in the Convention, but, in the end, he refused to sign the completed document.

THE CONSTITUTIONAL CONVENTION OF 1787: A CHRONOLOGY

MARCH 25, 1785—Delegates from Virginia and Maryland meet at Mount Vernon to discuss issues of commerce.

SEPTEMBER 24, 1786—Annapolis Convention adjourns, calling for a "general convention" to meet in May 1787.

WINTER 1786-87—Shays' Rebellion breaks out in Massachusetts.

FEBRUARY 21, 1787—Continental Congress approves call for a convention.

MARCH 28, 1787—George Washington agrees to attend the convention.

MAY 3, 1787—James Madison arrives in Philadelphia.

MAY 13, 1787—George Washington arrives in Philadelphia.

MAY 14, 1787—Convention scheduled to open, but it is postponed due to lack of a quorum.

MAY 16–MAY 24, 1787—Virginia and Pennsylvania delegates meet informally to devise a new plan of government.

MAY 25, 1787—Convention opens for business. George Washington elected president of the body.

MAY 29, 1787—Edmund Randolph presents the Virginia Plan. Charles Pinckney presents his plan for a new government.

MAY 30, 1787—Delegates endorse the Gouverneur Morris resolution proposing that "a national government ought to be established consisting of a supreme legislative, executive, and judiciary."

JUNE 11, 1787—Roger Sherman proposes an early version of the so-called Connecticut Compromise. James Wilson and Charles Pinckney propose the three-fifths clause.

JUNE 15, 1787—William Paterson presents the New Jersey Plan.

JUNE 18, 1787—Alexander Hamilton proposes a government based as much as possible on the "British model."

JULY 2, 1787—Grand Committee established to seek compromise on representation in the Congress.

JULY 6, 1787—Grand Committee proposes a version of the Connecticut Compromise.

JULY 16, 1787—Delegates narrowly endorse the Connecticut Compromise, including the three-fifths clause.

JULY 17, 1787—Delegates reject Madison's proposal for congressional veto of state laws.

JULY 23, 1787—Delegates appoint a five-person Committee of Detail to "prepare and report a Constitution."

JULY 27–AUGUST 5, 1787—Convention is in recess while Committee of Detail does its work.

AUGUST 6, 1787—Committee of Detail submits its report.

AUGUST 25, 1787—Delegates agree to prohibit Congress from interfering with international slave trade until 1808.

AUGUST 28, 1787—Delegates approve fugitive slave clause.

SEPTEMBER 8, 1787—Committee of Style is appointed.

SEPTEMBER 12, 1787—Committee of Style presents its report. Delegates choose not to include a bill of rights in the Constitution.

SEPTEMBER 15, 1787—Final draft of the Constitution is approved and ordered to be engrossed.

SEPTEMBER 17, 1787—Final draft of the Constitution is signed and Convention adjourns.

SEPTEMBER 28, 1787—Continental Congress approves sending the proposed Constitution to the states for their consideration.

DECEMBER 7, 1787—Delaware ratifies the Constitution.

DECEMBER 12, 1787—Pennsylvania ratifies the Constitution.

DECEMBER 18, 1787—New Jersey ratifies the Constitution.

JANUARY 2, 1788—Georgia ratifies the Constitution.

JANUARY 9, 1788—Connecticut ratifies the Constitution.

FEBRUARY 6, 1788—Massachusetts ratifies the Constitution.

MARCH 24, 1788—Rhode Island refuses to call ratifying convention.

APRIL 28, 1788—Maryland ratifies the Constitution.

MAY 23, 1788—South Carolina ratifies the Constitution.

JUNE 21, 1788—New Hampshire ratifies the Constitution.

JUNE 25, 1788—Virginia ratifies the Constitution.

JULY 26, 1788—New York ratifies the Constitution.

MARCH 4, 1789—The Constitution goes into effect.

SEPTEMBER 25, 1789—Congress proposes the Bill of Rights.

NOVEMBER 21, 1789—North Carolina ratifies the Constitution.

MAY 29, 1790—Rhode Island ratifies the Constitution.

DECEMBER 15, 1791—States ratify the Bill of Rights.

PLAIN,
HONEST
MEN

CHAPTER ONE

THE CRISIS

IT WAS A BLUSTERY SATURDAY morning on March 15, 1783, and patches of snow still flecked the ground. General George Washington strode up a long hill toward a rocky promontory at the American army encampment seven miles southwest of Newburgh, New York. He was about to face the greatest personal challenge of his career. He was uncharacteristically nervous and uncertain, roiled by sensations of anger, frustration, and inadequacy. He had led his army to a brilliant victory over the British at Yorktown some seventeen months earlier. Yet the soldiers at Newburgh remained in the field, languishing, while peace negotiations dragged on in Paris. His troops had not been paid for many months, and the Continental Congress's promises of a generous pension seemed as empty as the coffers of the bankrupt Confederation government.

To make matters worse, a cabal of American army officers, angry over the failure of the continental government to make good on its promises, had decided to take matters into their own hands. Five days earlier, Major John Armstrong, aide-de-camp to the commander at Newburgh, General Horatio Gates (Washington's longtime rival), circulated an "address" to the soldiers, urging them to cease their meek supplications to an uncaring Congress and, if necessary, to throw off Washington's leadership and redress their grievances by force of arms. In a letter to his former aide-de-camp and protégé, Alexander Hamilton, Washington expressed his fear that the disgruntled soldiers might throw "themselves into a gulph of Civil Horror." Yet at the same time he had deep sympathy for their plight. Indeed, Hamilton had been gently nudging his mentor to throw in his lot with the discontented soldiers. As he approached his destination, Washington faced a painful choice: to remain loyal to his long-suffering troops or to honor the rule of law.[1]

America's ambitious experiment in liberty had seemed full of promise seven years earlier, in the summer of 1776, when Washington had ordered his commanders to read the Declaration of Independence aloud to their troops in order to steel them for the sacrifices ahead. And they had met the challenge. Since that time they had persevered through the cold and deprivation of Valley Forge, through nearly seven years of often dispiriting battle against the better-equipped British Army. Washington had come to understand that American liberty and American union—a strong union—were inseparable. The discontented soldiers at Newburgh threatened to put both liberty and the union at risk.[2]

When he reached the top of the promontory, Washington entered a cavernous, drafty building, one hundred ten by thirty feet, which looked down on the Continental army encampment below. The "New Building" had been constructed a few months earlier to encourage "sociability" among the officers. But as Washington walked the length of the long hall past the five hundred assembled officers toward a small stage and lectern at the far end, there was little feeling of sociability in the air. The spectacle presented by the officers, many of them with faces set in anger, deepened Washington's gloom. Everything about their appearance testified to the shameful neglect they had suffered at the hands of the continental government—from their torn and soiled uniforms to their worn-out boots and gaunt faces. And these were the privileged few, the officers. Washington knew that the enlisted men, waiting in their barracks for news of the outcome of the meeting, had suffered even greater privation. While the officers were at times reduced to making their overcoats out of blankets, they wore those overcoats, as historian Charles Royster has observed, "in the presence of men who had no blankets." Forced to endure bitterly cold winters, often clad in uniforms pieced together from an old hunting shirt, overalls, or even rags, and subsisting on a diet barely adequate to keep body and soul together, the ordinary foot soldiers in Washington's army had every reason to believe their country had betrayed them. The failure of the government to pay the soldiers their wages hit the enlisted men the hardest, and it seemed to Washington nothing short of criminal. Their wives and children back home were reduced to begging in the streets in order to avoid starvation. Was this the "liberty" for which Americans had fought?[3]

By the time Washington made his entrance, General Gates had already opened the meeting. Washington interrupted him, asking for permission to address the officers. Visibly shaken by Washington's presence, Gates had no choice but to accede to the request of his rival, who was, after all, the commander in chief of the Continental army.[4]

A man typically comfortable and confident in any public situation, Washington was visibly agitated and uneasy. He began with an apology. He had not intended to involve himself in the controversy, but upon reading the content of Major Armstrong's address, he felt it necessary to speak his mind. In a departure from his usual manner in speaking to his officers, he would not speak off-the-cuff. Instead he took from the pocket of his coat a speech he had painstakingly written out the day before. He began by vowing that he would extend every effort and power at his command "in the attainment of complete justice for all of your trials and dangers," but then, assuming a suppliant tone, he proceeded.

> Let me entreat you, gentlemen, on your part, not to take any measures which, viewed in the calm light of reason, will lessen the dignity and sully the glory you have hitherto maintained; let me request you to rely on the plighted faith of your country, and place a full confidence in the purity of the intentions of Congress. . . . You will, by the dignity of your conduct afford occasion for posterity to say, when speaking of the glorious example you have exhibited to mankind, "had this day been wanting, the world had never seen the last stage of perfection of which human nature is capable of attaining."[5]

It was an impressive ending, perhaps as impressive a speech as Washington had ever given, but looking out at his audience, he could see that many of the officers remained unmoved. At that point he pulled from his pocket a letter from one of his Virginia friends—Joseph Jones, a delegate to the Continental Congress—who had written him expressing sympathy for the plight of the soldiers and promising to work in the Congress to honor the government's obligations to them. The letter was scrawled out in barely legible form, and Washington stumbled over its first few sentences. Disoriented, he searched in the pocket of his coat once again and pulled out a pair of spectacles that had recently been sent to him by the Philadelphia scientist, David Rittenhouse. It was probably the first time anyone had ever seen Washington wear spectacles in public. "Gentlemen," he said, "you must pardon me. I have grown grey in your service, and now find myself going blind." He put on the glasses and finished reading the letter, making it clear to the officers that he would place his prestige and honor on the line in their cause, so long as that cause was served in a peaceful and lawful manner. Then, without fanfare, he left the room—and the soldiers to their deliberations.[6]

As he made his exit, tears streamed down the cheeks of some of the soldiers' faces, and a hush—a hush borne of contrition and shame—fell over the hall. When they recovered their composure, the soldiers gave him a formal vote of thanks, repudiated Major Armstrong's address, and asked their commander in chief to act as their agent in securing their just rewards for service to their country.[7]

Was it a guileless performance? It probably was not, for Washington was a man who always carefully gauged the effects of his demeanor and his words in any public situation. But one thing is certain. No other man in America could have pulled it off. And Washington was true to his word. The Continental Congress, terrified by the threat of armed revolt and grovelingly grateful to Washington for his intervention, pledged its support for a financial settlement that went at least a part of the way toward meeting the soldiers' salary and pension demands.

If one is looking for critical turning points in American history, times when the future direction of the republic might have altered course, Washington's performance at Newburgh, the Constitutional Convention, Lincoln's Gettysburg Address, and the subsequent passage of the constitutional amendments eradicating slavery from the American Constitution stand out as decisive. Washington was the only man in America who possessed the combination of charisma, political and military experience, and public support capable of converting America's experiment in republican liberty into a dictatorship—a benevolent dictatorship perhaps, but a dictatorship nevertheless. Given the financial disarray and civil disorder represented by the discontent of the soldiers at Newburgh, Washington could have convinced himself that military solutions to civil political problems were the best course of action, as did many leaders in the revolutions of Latin America in the century to come. Some, like Simón Bolívar in Venezuela, Peru, and Columbia, did so reluctantly. Others, like

Santa Anna in Mexico or Bernardo O'Higgins in Chile, did so more eagerly. All of these countries have lived with a tradition of military intru-
sion in the affairs of their governments ever since.

As he confronted the soldiers, Washington realized that his standing
with the officers might not be enough to assuage what were very reasonable grievances. His discomfort was all the more acute precisely because he
shared these grievances so deeply and, indeed, shared much of the soldiers' contempt for the weakness of the central government. How tempting it must have been to think that he—alone among all others—had it in
his power to correct the weaknesses of the Confederation by stepping in
and assuming control of the country. But he never even considered it.

WASHINGTON'S DECISIVE PERFORMANCE at Newburgh was
one of the moments in his career that help explain why he occupies such
a preeminent place in our nation's history. But the fact that he found
himself in a position in which he had to put his prestige on the line in
order to avert a military uprising reflected the weakness and fragility of
the Confederation government. We will never know all of the details of
the "Newburgh Conspiracy," for, as with most conspiracies, the planning behind the soldiers' efforts was shrouded in secrecy. But one thing
was clear to all. The soldiers' grievances cast a harsh spotlight on many
of the fundamental weaknesses of the new American union, in particular
the potentially disastrous effects of the bankruptcy of the Confederation
government's treasury. And another thing was becoming clear as well.
Certain politicians in America were eager to leverage the soldiers' discontents to further their own plans to strengthen the continental union.

It is hardly surprising that Americans had been wary about giving too
much power to a new continental government. One of the logical conclusions to be drawn from the struggles with Great Britain leading to the
Revolutionary War was that government should be small, weak, and,
whenever possible, local. How else could lawmakers be sensitive to the
effects—good and bad—of the laws they had enacted? And how else
could the people express their displeasure when things went wrong?

Yet the imperatives of fighting and winning a war would clarify the
need for a government that was neither purely local nor provincial. It was
one thing to *declare* independence. It was quite another to *secure* it. Military victory required a sizeable army drawn from all of the colonies. And
the financing of that effort required a measure of sacrifice and a degree

of cohesiveness far greater than any the British had ever demanded of them. Securing independence would require Americans to act not as individual states but as "united states."

How would the former British colonies in America, often ignorant and suspicious of one another, overcome their provincialism and unite in a continental union? On the eve of independence, residents of the thirteen colonies were more likely to be familiar with events and fashions back in England than they were with those of a neighboring colony, and the representatives of those colonies, when they first gathered in Philadelphia in the fall of 1774 to consider common action against the British, were just as often struck by the differences as the similarities among them. The resolutely provincial John Adams, surveying his fellow delegates to the Continental Congress, exclaimed that "the art and address of Ambassadors from a dozen belligerent Powers of Europe, nay, of a Conclave of Cardinals at the Election of a Pope . . . would not exceed the Specimens We have seen [in the Congress]."[8]

America's patriot leaders knew, however, that some form of union was essential if they were to succeed in their quest for independence. Just a week after they had adopted the Declaration of Independence, America's representatives in the Continental Congress began work on a new frame of government, the Articles of Confederation and Perpetual Union. The Articles of Confederation, America's first "constitution," was not really a proper constitution, but rather a peace treaty among thirteen separate and sovereign states. It amounted to nothing more than a league of friendship, a form of alliance in which "each state retains its sovereignty, freedom, and independence, and every power, jurisdiction and right, which is not by this Confederation expressly delegated to the United States, in Congress assembled."[9]

Faced with the task of fighting a war against the world's most formidable military power, the Articles of Confederation created a government with vast responsibility—but little authority. Armed with the power only to "request" contributions of men, materiel, and money from the individual states, officials in the Confederation government discovered how ephemeral public support of the war effort could be. America's commitment to liberty and independence had been accompanied by a surge of utopian idealism in the summer of 1776, with the newly established state governments pledging solemnly to contribute to the common cause. But as the optimism of 1776 confronted the reality of a protracted and bloody war, officials in the continental government struggled to persuade the individual state governments to match their words with their deeds. By the beginning of 1777, those government officials were reduced to begging the states to contribute their fair share to the war effort. When it became clear that the states themselves were too strapped for cash to contribute money to finance the war, the Continental Congress began to request that the states meet their obligations by providing supplies—food, clothing, weapons—directly to the army. Unfortunately, the economic dislocations caused by the war made it difficult for the states to do so.

The American military effort ebbed and flowed between hope and despair. America's eventual victory at Yorktown in October of 1781 seemed nearly miraculous, coming as it did in the wake of a devastating military campaign in the South, where victory in most of the savage and bloody battles—fought amidst a divided American population—went to the British. The successful outcome of the Patriot war effort owed as much to British indecisiveness as it did to American military prowess. Even after victory was secured, the leaders of the American government in Philadelphia faced the daunting task of holding their fragile continental union together.

The Articles of Confederation suffered from three fatal flaws. It didn't allow the continental government the power of the purse—the power either to levy taxes directly or to compel the states to pay their fair share of the expenses of the government. It required unanimous approval of the state legislatures for any amendment to the Articles—including any amendment that might provide a remedy for the government's inability to raise revenues independently. And it failed to provide for a chief executive capable of giving energy and direction to the new central government as it sought to carry out its essential tasks. Lacking the power to tax and unable to rely solely on voluntary contributions from the states, the Continental Congress initially issued paper currency whose value was supposedly guaranteed by the thirteen states. Those guarantees proved meaningless, and over the course of the war continental currency depreciated to the point of near worthlessness—from whence came the derisive phrase "not worth a Continental." Beginning in late 1776, the Continental Congress began to experiment with another expedient, issuing loan office certificates—government bonds—which offered a modest rate of interest, but that, like the continental currency, were quickly depreciated by rampant inflation. The results of this dubious system of public finance were predictable. Confidence in the credit of the continental government—and in the government itself—plummeted.

The events at Newburgh brought into bold relief the inadequacies of America's first experiment in union.[10]

THE CONTROVERSIAL ROBERT MORRIS

Philadelphia merchant Robert Morris, surveying the wreckage of America's finances, could not contain his dismay. Writing to Benjamin Franklin in the fall of 1781, Morris observed, "A Revolution, a war, the dissolution of government, the creating of it anew, cruelty, rapine, and devastation in the midst of our very bowels. These Sir, are circumstances by no means favorable to finance."[11]

Morris was thirteen years old when he emigrated from Liverpool to Oxford, Maryland, in 1747 to join his father, a tobacco trader of modest means. He quickly made his way to Philadelphia as an apprentice to a major shipping company. Just a few years later, at the age of twenty, he became a partner in the company, and in the process established a reputation extending well beyond Philadelphia for extraordinary financial acumen. By 1776 he was quite possibly the wealthiest man in America. He was also one of his city's most reluctant revolutionists. In the years immediately preceding independence, he consistently argued for reconciliation with Great Britain, fearing that his trade with the mother country—and the profits he derived from it—would vanish should America go to war with England. As a member of the Continental Congress, he voted against the Declaration of Independence in July of 1776, but he reconsidered in August, signing the document only when he realized that the consequences of being branded a Tory might be even worse than the risks of being identified by his British trading partners as a Patriot.[12]

A large man standing fully six feet tall, with a round, somewhat fleshy face and graying brown hair, Morris sported a stoutness of frame that bespoke a healthy appetite for both food and drink. He rarely hesitated to use either his wealth or his imposing physical presence to intimidate a business associate or a rival. Self-assured to the point of arrogance, he had little patience for those "vulgar souls," as he derisively labeled them, whom he did not consider his social or intellectual equals. Operating in an eighteenth-century world that viewed unbridled ambition with unease, Morris was, undeniably, ambitious. His critics tended to view him as a man whose single-minded devotion to the pursuit of wealth and power led to business practices that were self-serving and dishonest.

Arthur Lee and Richard Henry Lee, influential members of the Continental Congress from Virginia, positively despised Morris. They considered his conduct and character a "danger to liberty." Thomas McKean of Pennsylvania, contemplating Morris's rise to power, went so far as to suggest that Morris's ambition would lead him to become the "financial dictator" of the new republic. But however much some may have disliked his personal manner and distrusted his business practices, few doubted his financial genius.[13]

In February 1781, the Continental Congress, desperate to put the country's finances in order, offered Morris the position of superintendent of finance. But Morris drove a hard bargain before he would accept the job. He insisted not only that he be given sweeping powers over government finance, but that he be given power over virtually every other aspect of the Confederation government's operations as well—including its dealings with other nations. Morris's demands seemed outrageous to some members of the New England and Southern delegations to the Continental Congress, but his supporters—who viewed him as the only man in America capable of bringing the country back from the brink of insolvency—won the day. With the greatest reluctance, the Continental Congress acceded to Morris's demands, and on May 14, 1781, Morris accepted the job. The Articles of Confederation's third fatal flaw—the failure to provide for a chief executive or "president" within the structure of the new central government—effectively left Morris as the closest thing to a "prime minister," British style, that America has ever had. Indeed, Morris had prevailed. But at what cost? Because so much of Patriot feeling and rhetoric was driven by an intense fear of concentrations of power of the sort they had faced under the British, many in the country worried that the Morris cure might be worse than the disease.[14]

From a purely financial point of view, Morris's efforts to put the failing finances of the Confederation government in order were heroic. Using a combination of his business expertise, his own considerable wealth, the strength of his personal credit rating, and the influence of his prominent and wealthy friends in the mercantile community, he halted the spiral of inflation and introduced up-to-date management practices in the conduct of the continental government's financial business. Aided by the shrewd diplomacy of Benjamin Franklin, he was successful in securing $5.9 million in loans from France and, with the help of the American ambassador to Holland, John Adams, another $2 million from the Dutch. For all his skill and power, Morris could not remedy the central government's inability to obtain for itself a stable, permanent revenue. Without that revenue, even a man of Morris's formidable abilities found it difficult to pay and supply the troops. Moreover, the task of getting every state in the fragile new union to agree to grant the government the all-important power to impose taxes proved formidable indeed.[15]

Using a combination of his forceful personality and his extensive financial leverage, Morris relentlessly pressured the state legislatures, many of whose members included some of his mercantile associates, to ratify an amendment permitting the government to levy an impost (a tax on imported goods) of 5 percent. By the fall of 1782, it looked as if he might attain the unanimous approval required. But Morris had not reckoned on a dramatic change in the political winds in America's smallest state. Rhode Islanders had a long history of resistance to intermeddling by any outside authority, beginning in 1636 when Roger Williams, banished from Massachusetts because of his unorthodox religious views, established the colony. The fall 1782 elections for the legislature produced a strong resurgence in that independent resolve. Led by a fiery agrarian democrat, David Howell, the state legislature expressed its implacable hostility to any cession of power to the central government. In a letter to the governor of the state, Howell and his colleagues wrote that it was "as clear as the Meridian sun," that the power to levy taxes, once granted to the central government, would "add the Yoke of Tyranny fixed on all the states, and the Chains Rivotted." The opposition of that single group of Rhode Island provincial politicians was enough to sink Morris's plans to strengthen the continental government.[16]

Morris, furious that a tiny state could stand in the way of the welfare of the entire country, was quick to act when he learned of the discontent brewing among the troops at Newburgh. Morris encouraged the soldiers to press their demands, and, having fomented a more rebellious mood, he spread the word to the Congress meeting in Philadelphia that "the army have swords in their hands" and that a "most violent political storm" threatened the very existence of the union. James Madison, who was not part of the cabal with the soldiers, was nevertheless thoroughly alarmed. "The opinion seems to be well founded," he wrote, that "the arms which have secured the liberties of the country will not be laid down until justice [for the soldiers] is secured." Others openly hinted that if Congress did not act, the army would be "ripe for annihilating them."[17]

This was the point at which Washington made his fateful appearance before the soldiers at Newburgh, after which he managed to prod the

Continental Congress into fulfilling at least part of their obligations to the soldiers. Robert Morris and his nationalist aims did not fare so well. The Continental Congress refused to act on Morris's demand for a permanent source of revenue for the government. Moreover, Washington, long a supporter of Morris, was infuriated by the financier's role in fomenting the unrest at Newburgh and broke off relations with him. (Although, as we will see, they would eventually reconcile.) On September 3, 1783, American and British diplomats reached final agreement on terms of a Treaty of Peace in Paris, and when news of the signing of the treaty reached America in late October, the Continental army began quietly to disband. Morris, left with little support either in Congress or in the military, had no choice but to resign as superintendent of finance.[18]

Washington, for his part, received the news of the signing of the Treaty of Peace with an overwhelming sense of joy and relief. As the British prepared to evacuate their troops from New York in November 1783, Washington issued a proclamation to his troops declaring the achievement of American independence "little short of a standing miracle." At last, America's citizen-soldiers, and their commander in chief, could lay down their arms.[19]

INTERLUDE

On December 4, 1783, Washington bade an emotional farewell to his officers at Fraunces Tavern, on Pearl Street, in what is now lower Manhattan. He then made his way to Annapolis, Maryland, the temporary home of the Continental Congress, where he attended a dinner and dance in his honor on the evening of December 22. Washington loved to dance, and, even at the age of fifty-one, the six-foot-two-inch general continued to display unusual grace on the ballroom floor. One of those present reported that "the General danced every set, that all the ladies might have the pleasure of dancing with him, or as it since has been handsomely expressed, get a touch of him." The next day he appeared before the Congress of the Confederation and formally resigned his commission as commander in chief of the American army. He had served his country for eight and a half years—a service far longer and more arduous than anything he could have imagined when he accepted the commission. As soon as the ceremony was over—about midday—he set off on the final leg of his journey. After a day and a half of hard riding, he ascended the circular driveway of his beloved Mount Vernon on Christmas Eve as the sun was setting. His wife, Martha, awaited him at the door.[20]

An unusual cold spell, accompanied by snow and ice, would bring to the retired general a splendid isolation for the next six weeks. He wrote few letters, and, as the roads were impassable, he received no visitors. During the first few weeks of his solitude he continued to worry about the effects of the fragile state of public finance on the welfare of the men who had served with him in the Continental army, but, gradually, he began to feel a sense of peace. When the snow and ice lifted, Washington threw himself into the business of being a farmer once again, overseeing every aspect of the management of his multiple plantations. Writing to the Marquis de Lafayette, he expressed perfect contentment at being

> a private citizen on the banks of the Potomac, and under the shadow of my own vine and my own fig tree. Free from the bustle of the camp and the busy scenes of public life, . . . I am not only retired from all public employments, but I am retiring within myself, and shall be able to view the solitary walk and tread the paths of private life with heartfelt satisfaction.[21]

But it was not to be. While Washington was enjoying his retirement, the threads holding the fragile union together were unraveling, and by the late fall of 1786 the general would be forced to confront an end to his idyll.

THE COLLAPSE OF THE CONFEDERATION

Although Americans had won their war for independence, and the soldiers in the Continental army had returned peaceably to their homes, their fragile union remained in a precarious state. While Washington was reveling in his return to private life during the years 1784–86, the continental government was barely functioning. The sole branch of that government, the Congress, went for weeks at a time without the ability to attract the necessary quorum of members to allow it to do its business. The immediate cause of this inactivity and apathy was obvious. Chronically short of revenue, Congress could accomplish very little.

With the official end of the war and the disbandment of the army, some of the financial strains on the Confederation government's treasury had abated, but they did not disappear altogether. The first installments on the loans Robert Morris, Benjamin Franklin, and John Adams had negotiated with France and Holland came due in 1785, and the Confederation cupboard was bare. It was one thing for America's weak central government to default on its payments to private creditors, but it was quite another to fail to honor its obligations to powerful nations in Europe. American commercial interests in Europe depended on the stability of the American government's credit abroad. Moreover, although France and Holland had been America's allies during the Revolution, one of the painful lessons that American diplomats had learned during that Revolution was that today's allies could become tomorrow's adversaries. The American government simply could not default on its loans to France and Holland.

The 1782 success of the Rhode Island state legislature's move to quash the amendment to the Articles of Confederation that would allow the Confederation government to levy taxes on goods imported into America did not stop the Continental Congress from trying again the following year, when it presented to the states yet another proposal for a federal impost. However, the signing of the Treaty of Peace and the disbandment of the army in 1783 caused the states to lose interest in the proposal. Faced with the demands of the French and Dutch for repayment of their loans in 1785, though, they began to reconsider. The individual state governments finally began to awaken to the severity of the financial crisis and to recognize that their well-being might also be threatened by the collapse of America's public credit. By the summer of 1786, nearly all of the states, including recalcitrant Rhode Island, had ratified the impost in one form or another. But New York, already enjoying substantial revenue from its own tax on goods entering the port of New York City and fearful of the effects of imposing a federal impost on top of her own, put so many qualifications on its approval that the proposal was effectively killed.[22]

Once again, provincial interests had trumped those of the country as a whole. But the action of New York's legislature did more than threaten the financial well-being of the young American nation. It brought into bold relief an even more painful reality: the very structure of the Articles of Confederation, which required that any meaningful change in the country's federal charter receive the unanimous approval of the states, was fundamentally defective. Those who sought to strengthen the federal union knew that unanimity on any issue within the diverse confederation of American states was bound to be fraught with obstacles. They now recognized that unanimous agreement on an amendment allowing the American government even a limited power to levy taxes—an amendment vital to the government's survival—was virtually impossible.

"A PRETTY FORMIDABLE REBELLION"

At nearly the exact moment that New York was dealing a death blow to plans for a federal impost, the fabric of society in Massachusetts began to tear. The threat of violence had hung over Massachusetts like a heavy fog all during the summer and fall of 1786. The state's government, intent on shoring up its own credit rating, had implemented an aggressive policy of fiscal restraint. The practical effect of this was to place a heavy burden on cash-poor farmers in western Massachusetts, who found themselves threatened with foreclosure because they owed back taxes or had unpaid loans. Facing destitution, the discontented farmers turned to vigilante action, banding together to close the courthouses in some western counties and mobbing those unfortunate county sheriffs charged with the task of implementing the courts' edicts.[23]

Captain Daniel Shays, a farmer and former Revolutionary War officer from Pelham, was among the throng of Massachusetts men—estimates have varied from several hundred to as many as fifteen thousand—who joined the insurgency. He was only one of many local leaders of the grassroots revolt, but local law enforcement authorities apparently singled him out as one of the prime movers, and Shays' Rebellion has forever borne his name. Placing sprigs of pine needles from a metaphorical "liberty tree" in their hats, the Shaysites intensified their resistance to the government, threatening a government arsenal in Springfield and, in the process, frightening the state's political leaders in Boston out of their wits.[24]

William Cushing, chief justice of the Massachusetts Supreme Court, fell into a paroxysm of hysteria. He railed against the "ignorant, corrupt . . . and evil minded persons" who had fomented the rebellion and warned that Massachusetts was on the precipice of anarchy. Then Henry Knox weighed in. Knox was one of the largest landowners in Massachusetts in more than one sense of that word. He tipped the scales at 280 pounds. More important, he was a trusted confidant of General Washington. In the early fall of 1786, the Confederation Congress commissioned Knox to investigate reports of the disturbances in western Massachusetts, and he returned with a wildly exaggerated account of the situation. Estimating that there were upward of fifteen thousand western Massachusetts rebels under arms (in all likelihood, there were probably no more than a few thousand), he predicted that "this business must and will progress from one stage to another until it amounts to a pretty formidable rebellion." He believed that the rebels were "determined to annihilate all debts public and private. . . . The dreadful consequences which may be expected from wicked and ambitious men," Knox reported, were such that they threatened "to overturn, not only the forms, but the principles of the present constitutions."[25]

General Henry Lee, a close friend and neighbor of General Washington, had been receiving copies of Knox's overheated reports on the situation in Massachusetts. In mid-October he wrote the general an anguished letter warning that "the malcontents" in Massachusetts had as "their object . . . the abolition of debts, the division of property, and re-union with G. Britain. . . . In one word my dear General, we are all in dire apprehension that a beginning of anarchy with all its calamitys has approached." Lee entreated Washington to use his "unbounded influence" to bring the Massachusetts rebels "back to peace and reconciliation."

On October 31, 1786—a cold, raw fall day with gusts of wind and mists that turned into a hard, driving rain—Washington responded to Lee's plea with a mixture of despair and exasperation.

> The picture you have drawn . . . of the commotions & temper of numerous bodies in the Eastern states are equally to be lamented and deprecated. They exhibit a melancholy proof of what our trans-Atlantic foe have predicted; and of another thing perhaps, which is still more to be regretted, and is yet more unaccountable: that mankind, left to themselves are unfit for their own government. I am mortified beyond expression when I view the clouds which have spread over the brightest morn that ever dawned upon any country.

Washington adamantly declared that he was not the solution to his country's distress. "You talk, my good Sir, of using influence to appease the tumults in Government—I know not where that influence is to be found; and if attainable, that it would be a proper remedy for the disorders. Influence is not government. Let us have one by which our lives, liberties, and properties will be secured, or let us know the worst at once."[26]

James Madison, at that point a relatively obscure representative from

Virginia in the Continental Congress, had also begun to worry about the deficiencies of the Confederation government on the basis of his frustrating service there. When he received Henry Lee's exaggerated reports that the Massachusetts rebels greatly outnumbered those who supported the government, he wrote in a letter to his father that the rebels "profess to aim only at a reform of their constitution and of certain abuses in the public administration, but an abolition of debts public and private and a new division of property are strongly suspected to be in contemplation." Madison ended gloomily, expressing an apprehension that "an appeal to the sword is exceedingly dreaded."[27]

But while government officials in the Continental Congress were among those most terrified by the threat posed by Shays' Rebellion, they had no money with which to pay a force of federal troops to quash the insurrection. Realizing that the Confederation government was helpless to do anything about the rebellion, Massachusetts governor James Bowdoin managed to raise twenty thousand dollars from private donors, and with that sum he put together a force of 4,400 men to confront the rebels. On January 25, 1787, Bowdoin's private militia, led by General Benjamin Lincoln, marched to Springfield, Massachusetts. It was an incredibly cold day, with temperatures dipping to twenty degrees below zero and heavy snowdrifts obscuring portions of the battlefield. Bowdoin's forces overwhelmed the Shaysite insurgents, killing four of the rebels during the first volley of fire and forcing the remainder to take flight. Shays' Rebellion, such as it was, had ended.[28]

Most ordinary Americans, living and working on their farms, were as unconcerned with matters of continental finance as they were with the events of an abortive uprising of discontented debtors in western Massachusetts. But for those who cared about the fate of America, not as a loose collection of states and localities but, rather, as a single nation—particularly those who had seen firsthand the deficiencies of the continental government—the developments of late 1786 and early 1787 seemed ominous indeed. Shays' Rebellion convinced many of America's most influential people that something drastic needed to be done to save their experiment in liberty and union.

THE ANNAPOLIS CONVENTION

The twin crises of the government's financial collapse and Shays' Rebellion unfolded just as a small group of delegates was gathering in Annapolis, Maryland, on September 11, 1786, to consider ways to remedy yet another of the Confederation government's deficiencies. The Articles of Confederation lacked any provision permitting the American government to impose uniform commercial regulations among the states. As a consequence, the individual American states frequently fell into destructive competition with one another. Virginia and Maryland argued over navigation rights on the Potomac River, disputes between New York and the Vermont territory occasionally erupted into violence, and several of the states imposed onerous restrictions on interstate commerce. At times, the behavior of the American states toward one another seemed reminiscent of some of the worst examples of competition among the rival nations of Europe.

The Annapolis Convention, as it came to be known, was really not a proper convention. Although called into being by the Continental Congress, only twelve delegates from five of the thirteen states turned up and, lacking a quorum, they had no authority. But the twelve delegates who had gone to the trouble to make the trip to Annapolis—among them John Dickinson of Delaware, Alexander Hamilton of New York, Virginia's James Madison, and Virginia's governor, Edmund Randolph—all held unusually strong views about the need for a significantly stronger central government. Concluding their business, or, rather, facing the reality that they had no business to conclude, the twelve delegates directed an address to the Continental Congress—prepared by Hamilton—asking, "with the utmost deference," that the states appoint commissioners to meet in Philadelphia in May of the coming year "to devise such further provisions as should appear to them necessary to render the constitution of the federal government adequate to the exigencies of the union." What harmless-sounding words! But the men in Annapolis—Hamilton and Madison in particular—had something more ambitious in mind than a mere tinkering with the Articles of Confederation. They intended to scrap the Articles of Confederation altogether, create an entirely new government in its place, and, in the process, effect a dramatic change in the balance of power between the central government and those of the individual states.[29]

But if they were to move their plans forward, they would have to gain the approval of a somnolent—and occasionally hostile—Continental Congress in New York. Although the Congress received the address from the Annapolis Convention on September 20, 1786, it didn't get around to considering it for another three weeks, at which time it merely referred it to a Grand Committee that was supposed to consist of a delegate from

each of the thirteen states. And there the proposal for a convention lan-
guished. Some of the inactivity stemmed from the reservations of committee members, especially those from New England, who believed that
the Congress had no right to call such a convention. The more important
reason for Congress's inaction stemmed from its inability to get the requisite number of delegates together to take up the matter at all. The Congress went for seventy-two consecutive days between early November of
1786 and mid-January of 1787 without achieving a quorum.[30]

Finally, on February 20, 1787, the Grand Committee, by a majority of
only one, presented a report to the Congress recommending that a convention be held in Philadelphia in May for the purpose of considering
changes to the Articles of Confederation that would make the government "adequate to the exigencies of the union." Some of the credit for
finally getting things moving belongs to James Madison, who, overcom-
ing bouts of hypochondria, roused himself to travel to New York to urge
his colleagues to act on the Annapolis proposal. Another important factor in motivating Congress to act was the changing attitudes of some of
the representatives to the Congress from New England. Although the
Shaysite rebels in western Massachusetts had been dispersed by Governor Bowdoin's private army two weeks earlier, they continued to believe
that Massachusetts was in danger of lapsing into a state of anarchy, and
therefore felt a new sense of urgency about the need to strengthen the
federal government.[31]

The whole Congress received the report of the Grand Committee the
following day, February 21, and proceeded to wrangle over the wording
of the resolution endorsing the calling of a convention. Congress's final
approval of the proposal was carefully hedged. It stipulated that a convention of delegates be held in Philadelphia in May "for the sole and express purpose of revising the Articles of Confederation, and reporting to
Congress and the several legislatures such alterations and provisions
therein as shall when agreed to in Congress and confirmed by the States,
render the federal Constitution adequate to the exigencies of Government and the preservation of the Union."[32]

The congressional delegates, grudgingly agreeing to the idea of a convention, proceeded to make every effort to limit its authority. The authorization for the convention made it clear that anything accomplished
at the gathering would be subject to the approval of both the Confederation Congress and the states. But those strictures would soon be ignored
by a small cadre of Americans who had in mind a more ambitious idea for

a federal union. Those men—led by James Madison and Edmund Randolph of Virginia, Gouverneur Morris, James Wilson, and Robert Morris of Pennsylvania, and Alexander Hamilton of New York—had by early 1787 reached a conclusion strikingly at odds with the one initially embraced by most of the Patriots of 1776. In 1776, most Americans, embarking on a perilous war against a powerful Empire, believed that the greatest threat to liberty was to be found in the overriding power of a distant, centralized government. The men responsible for initiating the call for a constitutional convention, their hopes and fears shaped by the challenges and frustrations of fighting a long, costly war and of securing peace and public order at home, had come to believe that the continental government's lack of "energy" posed an equally formidable threat to liberty. As they prepared to meet in the Pennsylvania State House—the same building in which Americans had declared their independence in 1776—they were contemplating a second revolution in American government.

CHAPTER TWO

THE INDISPENSABLE MEN
OF THE CONVENTION

JAMES MADISON ARRIVED in Philadelphia from New York City aboard a rapid stagecoach, the New York–Philadelphia Flier, on May 3, 1787, eleven days before the Constitutional Convention was due to begin. He had hoped that other members of the Virginia delegation would follow suit. Writing to Virginia's governor, Edmund Randolph, the month before, Madison urged him to arrive at least a week before the Convention's start date in order that the Virginia delegates might take the lead in preparing "some materials for the work of the Convention."[1]

Each day for those eleven days, Madison watched eagerly for other delegates to join him, but aside from the Pennsylvanians, who were already in town, a canvass of the taverns and boardinghouses in Philadelphia yielded disappointing results. When he appeared at the State House on the morning of May 14, his fears were confirmed. Only a handful of delegates, not nearly enough for a quorum, had turned up. Madison was by nature punctual and conscientious; moreover, he felt a pressing need to get on with the business of constitutional reform. He could not have been happy about the meager turnout.

Thomas Jefferson was in Paris, and although he did not take part in the deliberations that summer, he would serve as a sounding board for his friend Madison's frustrations. Writing to Jefferson on Tuesday, May 15 (a letter Jefferson would not receive until the middle of July), Madison lamented that "the number yet assembled [is] small." He blamed "the late bad weather" for the tardy arrival of the delegates, and to some extent that was true. Heavy rainstorms up and down the East Coast during the previous two weeks had turned dirt roads, already soggy and treacherous in the springtime, into veritable rivers of mud. On a good day, a delegate traveling to Philadelphia by horseback might cover fifty miles, and by carriage he would cover considerably less. But there were few good days that spring. The crude and hazardous state of America's roads stood as a sharp reminder to men like Madison of the way in which America's infrastructure—whether in roads, bridges, schools, or public agencies capable of promoting economic development—had suffered because of the frailty of government at every level of American society. One aspect of America's Revolutionary heritage was an aversion to energetic government in any form. For that reason, Madison had every reason to fear that it was not muddy roads alone that were keeping the delegates away, but an obstacle far more serious. He had witnessed firsthand the way indolence and apathy combined among the delegates to the Confederation Congress to cause the increasingly ineffectual body to go for weeks at a time without a quorum. Would the Convention in Philadelphia suffer the same fate?[2]

The only interesting thing that happened in Philadelphia that May 14, as reported in the Pennsylvania *Herald,* occurred about a block from the Pennsylvania State House. "A young cox-comb who had made too free with the bottle," staggered up to a young "lady of delicate dress and shape," took hold of her hand, and, peeping under the large hat covering her face, exclaimed that he "did not like her so well *before* as *behind,* but notwithstanding he would be glad of the favour of a kiss." The young woman, unperturbed, coolly replied, "With all my heart, Sir, if you will do me the favour to kiss the part you like best!" Not known for his sense of humor, Madison was probably not amused.[3]

Madison would have to wait eleven more days, until May 25, for the Convention to get underway. He spent much of that time in his lodgings in Mary House's bustling boardinghouse on the corner of Fifth and Market streets, just a block's distance from the Pennsylvania State House. He had stayed there previously, from March of 1780 until the fall of 1783, while serving his first term in the Continental Congress. Mary House and her daughter, Eliza Trist, had operated one of the city's most popular and respectable boardinghouses at that location since 1778. Because Eliza was married to a Virginian, it had become particularly popular among the Virginia delegates to the Continental Congress when that body was meeting in Philadelphia during the Revolution. It was their home away from home, and they often referred to Mary and Eliza as their "family." Madison would stay at Mary House's during the summer of 1787 with a cohort of five other delegates, including James McHenry of Maryland, John Dickinson and George Read of Delaware, Charles Pinckney of South Carolina, and, for a time, Edmund Randolph of Virginia.[4]

Madison returned to Mrs. House's carrying powerful and bittersweet memories. It was there, in the winter and spring of 1783, that the resolutely cerebral Madison had found he was falling in love with a young woman less than half his age—Catherine, the fifteen-year-old daughter of the New York congressman William Floyd. Thirty-two years old at the time, Madison was extraordinarily shy in nearly all social situations, particularly ones in which attractive women were involved. Standing only a few inches over five feet tall and prematurely balding, he frequently brushed the few remaining wisps of hair at the top of his head downward to hide his bald spot. Chronically suffering from a combination of poor physical health and hypochondria, and painfully awkward in any form of public speech, Madison came across as neither a commanding nor a self-confident figure. That lack of self-confidence may well have prevented him from risking rejection from a woman his own age, but Kitty Floyd's girlish spontaneity emboldened his romantic instincts.[5]

Thomas Jefferson had boarded at Mary House's in the winter of 1783 as well and had seen proof of the mutual attraction between Kitty and Madison. On his way back to Monticello in April of 1783, he wrote a letter to his friend urging him to propose marriage. Madison replied to Jefferson with characteristic earnestness, as if he were writing about the purchase of a house or a carriage rather than an affair of the heart. "Your inference on the subject," he wrote, "was not groundless. Before you left us I had sufficiently ascertained her sentiments. Since your departure the affair has been pursued. Most preliminary arrangements, although definitive, will be postponed until the end of the year in Congress."[6] Madison's decision to focus his attention on business rather than his heart proved disastrous to his matrimonial hopes. On April 29, Kitty departed for her home in New York. Madison rode with her by carriage for about sixty miles, as far as Brunswick, New Jersey, and said good-bye, never to see her again. By late July he had an inkling that something had gone awry, noting to Edmund Randolph that his return to Virginia would be delayed "by a disappointment in some circumstances."[7]

On August 11, 1783, Madison broke the bad news in an extraordinary letter (written in code) to his friend Jefferson. Fifty years later, while going through his papers, Madison mutilated the letter so badly that one can barely read it. Kitty Floyd had fallen in love with someone else—a nineteen-year-old medical student at the College of Philadelphia, to whom she was married eighteen months later. Jefferson could offer little consolation. "Of all machines," he wrote, "ours is the most complicated and inexplicable."[8]

THE SCHOLAR

The trajectory of Madison's romance with Kitty Floyd was perhaps predictable. He was, by temperament, scholarly and introverted. He did not fit the mold of a successful politician. New Englander Fisher Ames, describing him a few years later, found him "a good man and an able man," but a man of "rather too much theory. . . . He is also very timid and seems evidently to want manly firmness and energy of character." Only in the eighteenth century, where intellect and depth of character were at least as highly valued as wit, telegenic good looks, or "manly firmness," could a person like Madison have achieved public prominence.[9]

Born in 1751, Madison was the eldest among the eleven children of James Madison, Sr., the wealthiest man in Orange County, Virginia. Even as a child, Madison had been unusually studious. As a boy, he left his father's plantation to attend an advanced school in a neighboring county. After five years studying astronomy, French, logic, mathematics, and philosophy, he returned to his family's plantation, Montpelier, to be tutored for two more years by a local minister, the Reverend Thomas Martin. At that point, in 1769, Madison moved northward to the College of New Jersey (now Princeton).[10]

Madison arrived in Princeton just as the ideas of the Scottish Enlightenment were sweeping the university. Under its new president, John Witherspoon, students imbibed the moral philosophy of Frances Hutcheson, Thomas Reid, and Lord Kames, and the political philosophy of Adam Smith and David Hume. Madison zipped through the college's undergraduate curriculum in two years rather than the usual three or four, and then stayed on for another year to study ethics and Hebrew. While it would be a mistake to draw too direct a linkage between Madison's studies at Princeton and his subsequent ideas about the American Constitution, his experience there provided an important introduction to political philosophers, especially David Hume, whose observations

James Madison: The Most Diligent Delegate. Portrait by
James Sharples, circa 1796–97, courtesy of Independence National Historical Park.

about governance in an "extended republic" would have a profound influence on Madison in later years.[11]

When Madison returned to Virginia in the fall of 1772, he was only
twenty-one years old, but in such poor health that he predicted gloomily
to a friend that he would not live either a "long or healthy life." Moreover, the prospect of following in his father's footsteps—becoming a
gentleman-farmer in what he derisively called "an obscure corner of
land" in the Virginia Piedmont—caused him to sink into a dark depres-
sion. But as America's growing conflict with England began to encroach
even on the lives of people in Virginia's backcountry counties, Madison
found he was drawn into the politics of Revolutionary America. He made
his first foray into public life in December 1774, when he was elected to
the Orange County Committee of Safety, the local agency created by Virginia's legislature to mobilize the county's residents against the British.
Madison's service in Orange County led in the spring of 1776 to a seat in
the Virginia Provincial Convention, the body that on May 15 would in-
struct its delegates to the Continental Congress to propose a declaration
of independence. Just a few years out of college, Madison was strictly a
backbencher at that convention, content to allow more established Vir-

ginia politicians such as Edmund Pendleton, George Mason, and the fiery orator Patrick Henry to dominate the proceedings.[12]

The following year, in 1777, Madison stood for election to Virginia's House of Delegates, the state's lower house of assembly. It was the first time he had to campaign for public office, and, possessed with an instinctive aversion to stooping to what he called "an electioneering appearance," he refused to provide the liberal quantities of food and liquor that Virginia voters had come to expect. His opponent, a tavern keeper as well as a planter, had no such compunctions and soundly defeated him.[13]

Keen of mind but lacking confidence in debate, Madison would bounce back from this initial rejection by his local constituents, as he was elected by the Assembly to serve on the Council of State, an advisory counsel to the governor. Virginia's political elders quickly recognized his intelligence, his judgment, and, most important, his diligence, and they selected him as one of the state's delegates to the Continental Congress. At age twenty-eight, James Madison would be the youngest member of the Congress.[14]

Men like Patrick Henry and George Mason came of age at a time when the imposition of taxes by a distant, overbearing imperial government and the unbridled exercise of power by royal governors were thought to be the greatest threats to liberty. Madison's experience as a delegate to the Continental Congress convinced him that the weakness of America's new central government posed at least an equal threat to liberty and, equally important, American unity. He watched, frustrated, as many of the independent state governments thwarted efforts to give to the Confederation government the power to levy taxes or regulate commerce. In the early spring of 1786, he began making extensive notes on the history of "ancient and modern confederacies," a project that led him across more than three thousand years of history, from ancient Greece to the cantons of Switzerland. In April 1787, he composed a private memorandum—though one he obviously intended to circulate to others—which he titled, "The Vices of the Political System of the United States." An extraordinary glimpse into both the rigor and the conservatism of Madison's mind, "Vices of the Political System" laid out in systematic fashion both his assessment of the weaknesses of the existing American governments—state and confederated—and his thoughts on the best remedies for those weaknesses.[15]

Madison identified a dozen vices he believed to be fatal to the health of the republic. Several of those vices lay in the ways the newly independent states had overreacted to prior abuses of power by British royal governors. It was not surprising that state constitution makers deprived their new governors of the power to dissolve assemblies or to exercise an absolute veto over legislation, but Madison believed they had gone too far. Most of the new state constitutions vested the legislatures with the power to elect governors and most denied the chief executive even a limited veto. The result, in Madison's view, was that states frequently enacted "vicious legislation," too often prompted by the whims of public opinion rather than sober reflection. He was horrified by the irresponsible actions of the Rhode Island legislature, which allowed its citizens to pay off their debts in depreciated state currency, and by Patrick Henry's nearly successful effort in the mid-1780s to derail the passage of Thomas Jefferson's Bill for Religious Freedom, a move that threatened to undermine one of Jefferson and Madison's most cherished principles—the separation of church and state.[16]

The problem did not lie with the irresponsibility of state legislatures alone. Much of Madison's analysis focused on weaknesses in the Confederation government that allowed the self-interests of any one state to overwhelm the public interest of the nation. He chronicled the instances in which states had ignored their obligations to the union. Indeed, many states appeared willing to contribute their share of financial support for the Revolutionary War effort only when the threat of attack within their borders seemed imminent, and, conversely, to ignore those obligations when the battle moved elsewhere. "This evil," he wrote, "has been so fully experienced both during the war and since the peace," that it might well be "fatal" to the very existence of the union. Equally serious were the frequent instances in which the states encroached on the authority of the continental government, as in the case of Georgia's brutal war against the Creek Indians—waged without the Confederation government's consent—or the routine cases in which individual states violated terms of the Treaty of Peace with England, as in the continued persecution of Loyalists, when it suited their interests.[17]

Madison was even more troubled by the tendency of "courtiers of popularity"—men like Patrick Henry, who possessed all of the oratorical skills that Madison lacked—to please their local constituencies while at the same time pursuing policies harmful to the broader interests of the Confederacy. Madison accepted the inevitability that citizens would work to promote their interests at the expense of others. But, contrary to the widely accepted view that liberty could best be protected in republics of limited geographic size, Madison argued that only in a large republic—where "society becomes broken into a greater variety of interests, of pursuits, of passions, which check each other"—could one prevent the provincialism and attendant injustice that afflicted states like Rhode Island, where, Madison believed, a small faction of self-interested politicians had gained control of the legislature and subverted the public good.[18] Only a shift in power from the smaller state governments to a larger and stronger federal government would "render [government] sufficiently neutral between the different interests and factions, to controul one part of Society from invading the rights of another, and at the same time [remain] sufficiently controuled itself, from setting up an interest adverse to that of the whole society."[19] This shift in power was essential if America was to become a unified nation rather than a chaotic assemblage of quarrelsome states.

Madison's acknowledgment of the existence of "interests" in society and his desire to create a large, energetic government designed to neutralize—but not eliminate—those interests pointed in an entirely new direction. In Madison's conception, governments were designed not to embody virtue and the public good, but, rather, to mediate among the various interests in society and, in the process, allow the public good to be served. But in other ways his vision of the virtues of an extended republic was distinctly traditional, reflecting classical republican attitudes about the importance of selecting virtuous political leaders and drawing on seventeenth- and eighteenth-century English traditions. Voters who selected their leaders from larger districts would be choosing from a much wider pool of talent, a circumstance that would encourage the voters to select only "the purest and noblest characters," thereby ensuring that their representatives would be more likely to rise above purely provincial concerns and petty self-interest, and to represent the concerns of all the people.[20]

Madison's treatise on the "Vices of the Political System" ended on that conservative note. Never an optimist about human nature, he nonetheless hoped that he could persuade the delegates to the Philadelphia Convention, who, after all, were more likely to resemble the pure and noble characters he hoped would govern the extended American republic, that it was time to transform a weak confederation into a strong, unified nation.

THE GENERAL AND DR. FRANKLIN

Madison had spent ten days at Mary House's before another out-of-state delegate turned up. Whereas Madison had arrived in Philadelphia without fanfare, the new delegate's entrance was marked by church bells ringing, cannons firing, and the cheers of the people lined up to greet him. General George Washington's trip had not been an easy one. Departing from Mount Vernon in his carriage early in the morning on May 9, he fell ill during the journey and was delayed by rain and turbulent winds. He finally arrived in Chester, just outside of Philadelphia, on May 13. He was met by a cadre of seven of his closest Revolutionary War compatriots—three generals, two colonels, and two majors—with whom he shared an afternoon meal. From there, the city's Light Horse Troop, composed of about thirty gentlemen of the "highest respectability and fortunes" and decked out in their fanciest dress uniforms, escorted him to Gray's Ferry, where he crossed the Schuylkill River over a floating bridge the British had built when they occupied Philadelphia during the Revolution. As Washington's journey progressed, Philadelphians got word of his impending arrival. So by the time he appeared, a large party of the city's residents were prepared to meet him. As the Pennsylvania *Packet* reported it, "The joy of the people on the coming of this great and good man was shewn by their acclamations and the ringing of bells."[21]

While Madison had come to Philadelphia eagerly, Washington—comfortable in retirement at Mount Vernon—was deeply ambivalent about abandoning the tranquility of his retirement. But after reading overwrought accounts from Henry Knox, John Jay, and Henry Lee about the perilous state of America's experiment in republican liberty, he was forced to consider, once again, a return to public life.[22]

The disturbing letters describing the financial crisis of the Confederation government and the tumult in Massachusetts had reached Washington in late October 1786, shortly after the small group of delegates had gathered in Annapolis to consider making significant alterations to the Articles of Confederation. James Madison, who had by this time become Washington's most reliable political informant, wasted no time communicating the results of the Annapolis meeting to the general. On his journey from Annapolis back to Virginia in early October, Madison stopped by Mount Vernon and apprised the general of the resolution reached at the meeting. Both men knew that Washington's attendance at the proposed convention in Philadelphia would greatly improve the chances of the convention's success, but at that stage, fearing rejection, Madison had not risked directly asking the general to attend. On November 8, back in Richmond serving in the Virginia Assembly, Madison wrote to Washington, again not pressing him to accept or decline a nomination as a delegate to the Convention, but noting that the mere fact of his being elected a delegate by the Virginia legislature would "assist powerfully in marking the zeal of our legislature in its opinion of the magnitude of the occasion." Between November and mid-March, Madison, Virginia's governor Edmund Randolph, Henry Knox, and New York's John Jay had joined Madison in urging Washington to attend the convention. Randolph apologized for acting like an "intruder" but implored that "every day brings forth some new crisis." Knox was quick to add that should "an energetic and judicious system . . . be proposed with Your signature, it would be a circumstance highly honorable to your fame, in the judgment of the present and future ages; and doubly entitle you to the glorious republican epithet—The Father of Your Country."[23]

These pleadings—and Knox's flattery—forced Washington to confront several dilemmas. First, he was beginning to feel all of his fifty-five years. While all of our images of Washington are uniformly heroic and show the general standing tall, forceful, and self-confident, he had in fact reached the point at which the effects of degenerative rheumatoid arthritis had made it increasingly difficult for him to effect that pose, let alone participate in the fox hunts he enjoyed. The very prospect of making the long trip to Philadelphia, with his rheumatism heightening the jarring effect of every bump along the way, filled him with dread. Moreover, he knew that once he arrived, the discussions about amending the Articles of Confederation would be protracted, requiring him to be away from Mount Vernon for an extended period of time. As he explained to Henry Knox, although he earnestly hoped the effort to amend the Articles would be successful, his fondest hope was to see this achieved while he was "gliding down the stream of life in tranquil retirement." To complicate matters further, Washington had recently told his fellow Revolutionary War officers in the Society of the Cincinnati that his health would not permit him to attend their annual meeting in Philadelphia, which was scheduled for the same month the proposed convention was to be held. The Society of the Cincinnati, founded by Knox with Washington's encouragement, was composed of all of those who had served as officers in the Continental army with Washington during the Revolution. Washington felt great affection for the Society and its members, and should he turn up at a constitutional convention after declining their invitation, he would be caught in a breach of etiquette that "might be considered disrespectful to a worthy set of men." Third, at this stage in his deliberations, before the Confederation Congress had added its approval to the call for a constitutional convention, Washington worried that "a Convention so holden may not be legal."[24]

Finally, Washington was not convinced that such a convention could be successful in achieving its aims. He was sufficiently cognizant of his own prestige to know that his failure to attend the convention might indeed spell its doom, but neither was he convinced that his presence would guarantee its success. In response to the pleas from his friends, he repeatedly expressed his doubt that the people of the nation were ready for the dramatic overhaul of their government he thought necessary. Washington himself was convinced that the country had reached a desperate state, but he feared that most of the people at large did not "feel" the government's inadequacies. Until such time as that feeling became more widespread, he doubted that success was possible. Washington was a patriot who wished the best for his country. But he was also a proud man, a man who did *not* wish his career to be associated with failure, especially at this late stage.[25]

But when Washington heard the news that the Confederation Congress had grudgingly approved the call for a convention in late February, his attitude toward the meeting began to change. Not only did the action of the Congress eliminate some of his concerns about the legality of the initiative, but it put him in a more optimistic frame of mind about its chances of success. On March 28, after much hemming and hawing, he wrote to Virginia governor Edmund Randolph saying that although he ardently desired *not* to attend the convention, the entreaties of his friends had brought him, reluctantly, "to a resolution to go if my health will permit."[26]

The next phase in the lobbying of George Washington was aimed at persuading him to support a program of thorough, rather than piecemeal, reform at the Convention. At this point, James Madison weighed in fervently. Washington had given Madison an opening to press his views when he had written his younger colleague on March 31 "that a thorough reform of the present system is indispensable." Indeed, Washington feared that the convention might adopt "temporizing expedients" instead of probing the "defects of the Constitution to the bottom, and provid[ing] radical cures." On April 16, while composing his thoughts on the "Vices of the Political System," Madison summarized in a long letter to Washington the argument he was preparing to make at the Convention. Knowing that Washington had experienced firsthand the effects

George Washington sat for this portrait during the Convention's recess for the Fourth of July holiday. Portrait by Charles Wilson Peale, 1787, courtesy of Pennsylvania Academy of Fine Arts.

of a weak central government and did not need to be reminded of the structural flaws of the Confederation, Madison devoted most of his letter to outlining a system of government that would create an energetic executive, legislature, and judiciary capable of ensuring "national supremacy."[27]

Washington read Madison's comments about the structure of the new government with care. He had received similar letters from John Jay and Henry Knox expressing their opinions about the possible framework for the new government. He took the time to sit down and write a summary of the proposals coming from each of the three men. Jay's, Knox's, and Madison's thoughts all led in the same direction, but Madison's were the most thoroughly articulated. Jay may have been the most senior statesman in terms of prestige and Knox may have been one of Washington's closest confidants, but the general's notes on Madison's letter were far more detailed than they were on those from his other two colleagues.[28]

As Washington prepared to set off for the Convention, he received other communications as well. Benjamin Franklin sent a brief note to him expressing his hope that he would see the general at the Convention, "being persuaded that your Presence will be of the greatest Importance to the Success of the Measure." Robert Morris, immensely proud of his magnificent mansion on Market Street near Sixth Street, just up the block from the Pennsylvania State House, wrote on April 23 inviting the general and Mrs. Washington to "come to our house and make it your Home" during the Convention. Washington politely declined the invitation, explaining that his wife, Martha, would not be accompanying him and, as the Convention was likely to be a protracted affair, he considered it improper to "prevail upon myself to give so much trouble to a private family." This was a diplomatic way of saying no, but Washington had another reason for declining. As much as he appreciated Morris's service as superintendent of finance, he could not have forgotten his role in encouraging rebellion among the soldiers at Newburgh, and that breach, in spite of overtures from Morris, had not fully healed.[29]

There were others eager to show their hospitality to General Washington—some for obviously self-interested reasons. Edward Moyston, the proprietor of Philadelphia's City Tavern, lost no time trying to get Washington to use his "influence with such Gentlemen of your acquaintance as may want Accomodation." Moyston would also take out advertisements in newspapers around the country proclaiming that he had "provided himself with cooks of experience, both in the French and English taste," and had "laid in a fresh supply of liquors of the very first quality" for the delectation of the Convention delegates.[30]

As Washington arrived in Philadelphia on May 13, his carriage making its way through the crowds of citizens who welcomed him, he had every intention of joining Madison at Mrs. House's. When he arrived at Mrs. House's, yet another throng of people had gathered to cheer him. Among them was Robert Morris, who would not be deterred. He intercepted the general, gathered his luggage, and persuaded him to put aside whatever concerns had prompted his earlier declination and to stay at his house for the duration of the Convention. Morris ultimately prevailed on Washington because Martha Washington and Morris's wife, Mary, were good friends, and the two couples had shared many evenings together over the years. In spite of his lingering resentment over Morris's role in the Newburgh affair, Washington was undoubtedly swayed by the memory of the convivial, gracious, and lavish manner in which Morris had hosted him on previous occasions. Morris's mansion was grand even by the standards of the wealthiest city in America. In addition to a beautiful walled garden, his property contained an icehouse, a hothouse, and a stable with room enough for twelve horses. The luxury evident inside the house was, in the words of one French visitor, equal to that of "any commercial voluptuary of London."[31]

Another advantage of staying at the Morrises' was that Washington's longtime mulatto manservant, Billy Lee, could be at his beck and call, as Morris had enough room in the servants' quarters of his mansion to accommodate the slave. Billy Lee had attended to Washington's every need day in and day out for the better part of the general's adult life, and while Washington could bear the separation from his wife, Martha, he was utterly dependent on his servant. His other two slaves—his groom, Giles, and his coach driver, Paris—stayed in far more humble quarters at a cramped workingman's boardinghouse, further up Market Street.[32]

Washington did not even unpack his bags at the Morris mansion before setting off to pay a visit to Philadelphia's first citizen, Benjamin Franklin. Franklin's home was just a few blocks from Morris's, in a pretty courtyard just off of Market Street between Third and Fourth. Though he could easily have walked to Franklin's he most likely traveled in his carriage. The rainy weather that day no doubt played some role in the decision to go by carriage, but, perhaps equally important, Washington's meeting with Franklin had the character of a formal state visit. Washington and Franklin were perceived by their countrymen as America's two most distinguished citizens, but the demands of their respective military and diplomatic duties had kept the two men apart for nearly all of their professional lives. Franklin had met the twenty-four-year-old Colonel Washington while on a postal inspection trip to Virginia in 1756, and the two met again in the fall of 1775, shortly after Washington had taken over as commander in chief of the Continental army. But aside from those brief interactions, they were essentially strangers.[33]

Although we have no record of their conversation, it is not hard to conjure a vision of the two old warriors sharing a cup of tea, or—given Franklin's well-developed French tastes—a glass of wine, under the mulberry tree in Franklin's garden. The general, though it was difficult for him to stand tall, retained his imposing physical presence. We might imagine that Washington's side of the conversation with the estimable doctor had been marked not only by a genuine cordiality, but also with reserve—a hallmark of his public persona. The general, no matter what the situation, seemed to recognize that he was always on display and that his every word and inflection needed to be carefully calculated.[34]

For his part, Franklin was a physical wreck, overweight and suffering from gout and kidney stones. None of that, however, would have dulled his boyish delight at the opportunity to entertain the general. He would have put on display for Washington the full measure of his wit and bon-homie. He had recently completed a major renovation and expansion of his home, adding a three-story wing shortly after returning from Paris, and he no doubt relished the opportunity to give his distinguished visitor a full tour. On the ground floor was an impressive new dining room, capable of seating twenty-four people, but his greatest source of pride was his new library, which took up the entire second floor. As Washington made his way to the library, Franklin could not have resisted showing him his elaborate collection of electricity equipment, his glass "armonica" (an elaborate contraption that produced a musical sound similar to that of a roomful of people moving their fingers around the rims of wineglasses), or the mechanical arm he had constructed in order to retrieve books from the top shelves of his extensive collection of 4,276 volumes. He may also have been tempted to do a subtle bit of political lobbying, bringing out the two-headed snake he had carefully preserved in a vial in his library. The snake was a gift from a friend who recalled Franklin's support for a single—rather than bicameral—legislature when Pennsylvania drafted its constitution in 1776. In arguing for a single chamber, Franklin had recounted the fable of the snake with two heads and one body. The snake "was going to a brook to drink, and in her way was to pass through a hedge, a twig of which opposed her direct course. One head chose to go on the right side of the twig, the other on the left, so that time was spent in the contest; and before the decision was completed the poor snake died with thirst."[35]

For all his reticence, Washington could display a spontaneous sense of humor, and that garden meeting may well have provided America's two most illustrious statesmen with the opportunity to form a bond that would prove immensely valuable in the months to come.

WHILE MADISON HAD developed concerns about the state of the union over years of frustrating service in the Confederation Congress and Washington had felt the weaknesses of the government while commanding the troops of the Continental army, Franklin's opinions about government had been shaped during his years of diplomatic service abroad. He had been away from his home in Philadelphia for twenty-five of the thirty years prior to the Constitutional Convention, serving as a colonial agent in England before the Revolution and, after a brief return, leaving Philadelphia once again for France on October 27, 1776. Settled in at "a fine house" with a large garden in Passy, a beautiful village of villas and chateaus about three miles from the center of Paris, Franklin loved every minute of his nearly nine years in France. He may well have been the most popular man in all of Paris. A much-sought-after celebrity among the aristocracy and literati of the city, his own dinner parties were legendary for the quality of the conversation, food, and drink (the inventory of wines in his cellar at Passy numbered more than one thousand bottles) that he provided for his distinguished guests.[36]

Franklin's puritanical diplomatic colleague in France, John Adams, could not contain his impatience with or jealousy of Dr. Franklin. "The business of our commission," he fumed,

> would never be done unless I did it. . . . The life of Dr. Franklin was a scene of continual dissipation. . . . It was late when he breakfasted, and as soon as breakfast was over, a crowd of carriages came to his levee . . . some Phylosophers, Accademicians, and Economists, some of his small tribe of humble friends in the litterary way whom he employed to translate some of his ancient compositions . . . but by far the greater part were women and children, come to have the honor to see the great Franklin, and to have the pleasure of telling stories about his simplicity, his bald head, and scattering strait hairs among their acquaintances. These visitors occupied all the time, commonly, till it was time to dress to go to dinner.[37]

Adams's hostility was misguided. The Pennsylvanian's role in the diplomacy of the Revolution was in fact crucial to America's success. His combination of tough-mindedness and bonhomie was ideally suited to the realpolitik of the French court. He was the primary negotiator of the initial Revolutionary alliance with France and of the eventual Treaty of Peace with Britain and France ending the Revolutionary War. Like Madison and Washington, his experience during the decade following independence had convinced him of the need for a central government with the requisite "energy." He had learned that American diplomats abroad operated in a world of fierce rivalries and struggles for domi-

*Although absent on the opening day of the Convention due to ill-
ness, Franklin attended every day thereafter.* Portrait by Charles
Willson Peale, 1785, courtesy of Pennsylvania Academy of
Fine Arts.

nance. France and Spain, though nominally America's allies in the struggle for independence, were ultimately guided by their sense of national
self-interest. Franklin came to realize that the new American nation
would have to present a united front if it were to hold its own in the
treacherous world of European diplomacy.

When Franklin returned to Philadelphia in September 1785, he
proudly reported that he was "received by a crowd of people with huzzas
and accompanied with acclamations quite to my door." He found the
people of Pennsylvania enjoying peace and prosperity. At the same time
Washington was receiving gloomy reports from Madison and Henry
Knox about the desperate state of government in the young nation,
Franklin remained sanguine. "Our husbandmen," he wrote to a friend in
France,

> have had plentiful crops, their produce sells at high prices and
> for hard money. . . . Our working-people are all employed and
> get high wages, are well-fed and well-clad. . . . The Laws

govern, justice is well administered and property is as secure as in any country in the globe. All among us may be happy who have [happy] dispositions; such being necessary to happiness even in Paradise.[38]

Shortly after his arrival back in Philadelphia, in September 1785, Franklin was elected to his state's Executive Council, and then to the position of president of that council. Pennsylvania's state constitution, in accordance with Franklin's preferences, provided for a single-house legislature, annual elections, and a weak executive. Franklin's title as "president" sounded grander than it was. The position of president rotated among members of the Executive Council, and that council was far less powerful than the executive branches in all of the other states in America, most of which provided for a single "governor" as chief executive. The extraordinary power of Pennsylvania's popularly elected, single-house legislature created a political culture in the state that was the most aggressively democratic and fractious of any in America. Pennsylvania was no doubt one of the states James Madison had in mind when he wrote of the "Vices of the Political System of the United States." But Franklin was well used to the turbulence of colonial Pennsylvania politics, and he was not as troubled by any perceived vices of its state government as most critics of the Pennsylvania Constitution. Similarly, the sage of Philadelphia seemed largely unfazed by the reports that he had been receiving about Shays' Rebellion. In that sense, Franklin and his young Virginia colleague, James Madison, were, if not of different minds, at least of different temperaments.[39]

Franklin's intellectual range and power were legendary, but his approach to politics had always been dictated by pragmatism and expediency. He acknowledged that there probably were "some errors in our general and particular constitutions," but he most likely had not formed any precise position with respect to the scope of powers of a new central government.

At least some of Franklin's dissatisfaction with the Confederation government was rooted in purely personal considerations. Although he had received immense adulation upon his return from France, privately Franklin expected more. As he later confided to his Philadelphia friend Charles Thomson, the Continental Congress had failed to "make some liberal provision for ministers when they return home from foreign service." The Congress could, for example, "at least have been kind enough to shew their Approbation of my Conduct by a Grant of some small Tract of Land." To make matters worse, the Congress had also replaced him as North America's postmaster general while he was serving in France, a further insult to both his dignity and his pocketbook. Franklin may have affected the persona of homespun philosopher and scientist, but he would have been among the first to admit that he was not immune to pride or vanity. He was convinced that a few "envious and malicious Persons" had soured efforts to find suitable rewards for his service. The most likely culprit in poisoning the well against him, Franklin knew, was John Adams—who remained incensed at Franklin's free-living and free-spending ways while in France.[40]

MADISON, WASHINGTON, AND FRANKLIN were three men of widely varying ages, temperaments, and talents. Madison was young, ambitious, deeply thoughtful, unprepossessing in his personal appearance and manner, and still little known except within his own state and among a few stalwart members of the Continental Congress. General Washington was middle-aged—and increasingly aware of his mortality and legacy. Benjamin Franklin was nearing the end of his life, well past worrying about his legacy, and therefore able to view the occasionally stormy debates in the Convention with a philosophical detachment.

James Madison, more than any other delegate, would provide the combination of intellectual firepower and dogged persistence that animated the Convention. Washington would contribute not merely his prestige and gravitas, but, just as importantly, his calm and deliberative leadership. Without Washington's presence, an event notable as a *deliberation* among thoughtful, public-spirited men could just as easily have become notable as a scene of acrimony and disputation among self-interested men. While Franklin's interventions in the deliberations would sometimes be off the point, even a little bizarre, he would embody the spirit of compromise necessary if the thirteen independent states were to come together in an effective and durable union. Together, these three extraordinarily different Americans would help make the revolution of 1787 possible.

CHAPTER THREE

THE DELAY THAT PRODUCED
A REVOLUTION

AS GEORGE WASHINGTON and James Madison walked to the Pennsylvania State House on the morning of May 14, they did so with a sense of foreboding. And when they arrived at the Assembly Room shortly before eleven that morning, their fears were confirmed. Aside from a few members of the Pennsylvania delegation, they were the only delegates to appear on time for the scheduled start of the Convention. They may well have wondered whether their trip to Philadelphia had been in vain, and whether the same apathy that had crippled the Congress of the Confederation would doom to failure any attempt to gather enough delegates to amend the Articles of Confederation.

The two Virginians and their Pennsylvania colleagues agreed to meet at eleven the next morning in the hopes that others might turn up. Again, they found no other delegates.

That evening, May 15, Washington joined about twenty members of the Society of the Cincinnati (with whom he had made amends once he decided to attend the Constitutional Convention) for dinner. Against the general's protestations, the members of the Society reelected him as their president. While Washington was being wined and dined by his fellow officers, Madison wrote a morose letter to Jefferson from his boardinghouse, complaining that there had been "less punctuality in the outset than was to be wished."[1]

Although it appeared to Madison an inauspicious beginning, in fact, the combination of bad weather and sloth that delayed the opening of the Convention would provide him with an invaluable opportunity to build support for the dramatic reforms that he sought.

THE VIRGINIA DELEGATES GATHER

If Madison's badgering had not managed to bring the Virginia delegates to Philadelphia on time, it did at least get them there earlier than most. The remaining five members of the delegation arrived in Philadelphia by May 17. On the same day, John Rutledge and Charles Pinckney arrived by ship from Charleston, South Carolina. Their arrival would add to the number of delegates present, but, as subsequent events would reveal, their zealous defense of the institution of slavery would further complicate the work of the Convention.[2]

Virginia's Edmund Randolph, who had arrived on May 15, had worked most closely with Madison on the advance planning for the Convention, and, although he was the youngest member of the Virginia delegation at the age of thirty-three, he was among the most influential. The Randolph family dynasty was the richest and most powerful in Virginia, and Edmund Randolph was the heir designate to his family's long tradition of leadership within the colony and state. Madison had already convinced Randolph that only a thorough overhaul of the Articles of Confederation could save the union, and he had enlisted Randolph, whose friendship with Washington was much closer than Madison's, to help persuade the general to attend the Convention. Randolph and Madison would be in constant communication during the early weeks of the Convention, as the Virginia governor lived at Mrs. House's with Madison until his wife and family arrived to join him in mid-June.[3]

The final and perhaps most respected member of the Virginia delegation next to Washington, George Mason, arrived on May 17. Mason drew respect and praise as the principal author of the Virginia Declaration of Rights, a document that had been incorporated into the state constitution when Virginia had declared its independence. The sixteen articles in the Virginia Declaration of Rights explicitly articulated those "unalienable rights" proclaimed in Thomas Jefferson's preamble to the Declaration of Independence. The Declaration of Rights served as an important model for other states as they drafted bills of rights for their own constitutions and was to provide much of the inspiration for the Bill of Rights that would eventually be incorporated into the new federal Constitution soon after the new government began its operations.[4]

Mason took his lodgings at the Indian Queen, the city's largest boardinghouse and tavern, located on Fourth Street between Market and Chestnut. Writing to his son, Mason reported that he had "a good room" to himself, at the modest charge of "twenty-five Pennsylvania currency per day, including our servants and horses, exclusive of club in liquors and extra charges." And Mason would require all of its services. In addition to the stabling of his horses and his carriage, he needed to provide lodgings for his "servants." Accustomed to a life of comfort on his plantation, which had a corps of more than three hundred slaves, Mason brought at least two slaves with him to Philadelphia, one to attend to his personal needs and the other to take care of his horses and carriage.[5]

Decidedly provincial in every aspect of his life, Mason vastly preferred the life of private citizen to that of public servant. It was only out of an old-fashioned sense of noblesse oblige that he was able to tear himself away from his beautiful plantation on the Potomac River, first to serve his colony and state during the crisis of the Revolution, and then to serve his nation at the Constitutional Convention. Indeed, Mason's service in Philadelphia would mark the only time in his life when he ventured outside of Virginia for more than a few days. It quickly became apparent that however virtuous he may have felt about his service in Philadelphia, he didn't much enjoy it. Although he seemed well satisfied with his accommodations at the Indian Queen, the Virginia country squire made no secret of his dissatisfaction with life in what was, for him, a big city. Within two weeks of his arrival, he was complaining to his son that he was "heartily tired of the etiquette and nonsense so fashionable in this city." Although Mason was accustomed to the casual gentility of Virginia's well-heeled planter class, he was unfamiliar with the ways of Philadelphia's merchant aristocracy—families headed by men like Robert Morris, William Bingham, and Samuel Powel, whose elaborate social rituals were more self-consciously fashioned on the aristocratic cultures of England and France. Whether threatened or simply repelled by the formality and stylishness of his Philadelphia hosts, Mason, like many other provincial delegates who found themselves thrust into Philadelphia high society, plainly felt uncomfortable in their midst.[6]

Mason's provincial perspective set him apart from James Madison and other continental-minded delegates in another important respect. In the years immediately following the Revolution, Mason contentedly returned to the life of a gentleman-planter in his small corner of Virginia and, as a consequence, he had not felt the inadequacies of the Confederation government as acutely as Madison. Although mildly disturbed by the reports of Shays' Rebellion, his initial willingness to support Madison's scheme for a thorough overhaul of the continental government owed less to conviction than to deference to General Washington, with whom Mason had a long and affectionate relationship. That relationship would be sorely tested in the weeks to come.

THE PENNSYLVANIA CO-CONSPIRATORS

If there was one other group at the Convention likely to be receptive to Madison's plan for scuttling the Articles of Confederation and substituting in its place a truly "national" government, it was the Pennsylvania delegation. Benjamin Franklin's service abroad had convinced him of the need for a stronger, more unified government if America were to hold its own with the nations of Europe. Although at age eighty-one he was more inclined to play the role of the dispassionate sage than to initiate a comprehensive plan for a new government, there were other extraordinarily able members of the Pennsylvania delegation whose thinking about the needs of a continental government was closely aligned with Madison's.

The most powerful of these was the same man who was providing Washington with bed and board during his stay in Philadelphia—Robert Morris. While many appreciated his role in keeping the continental government afloat during the Revolution, at least as many became alarmed by his aggressive accumulation of power during his terms of service as superintendent of finance in the Confederation government. And Morris's ethics had also come under attack. By the time Morris had resigned as superintendent of finance in March 1784, his political enemies, suspecting a conflict of interest between his role as superintendent and that as the head of the most active merchant house in Philadelphia, had launched an investigation into his official conduct. Morris did not deny that he used his official post to steer some business toward himself and his friends, but, he pointed out, he had also been willing to put his own financial resources at risk in service to the teetering Confederation government. Although he was exonerated from charges of official misconduct, the whole affair left Morris contemptuous of those members of the Confederation Congress who had not only obstructed efforts to rescue the Confederation government from insolvency, but who had also called his integrity into question. As Morris contemplated his role in the upcoming Constitutional Convention, he approached the task as a businessman, not as a politician. His hostility toward the Articles of Confederation owed more to a businessman's desire for a government that protected and promoted finance and commerce than it did to any deeply rooted feelings about the character of ancient or modern republics.[7]

There was another Morris in town that week—Gouverneur Morris. He was an imposing physical specimen, a little over six feet tall, well proportioned, with a prominent nose and a strong chin. Morris's physical appearance was sufficiently close to that of Washington that he later served as the model for the statue of the general that stands in the Virginia state capitol of Richmond and, in duplicate, in front of what we today call Independence Hall. Gouverneur Morris was a newcomer to Pennsylvania politics, but he nevertheless carried with him a distinguished colonial pedigree. He was born in 1752, just a year after Madison, and came of age at the time in which the crisis with England was coming to a boiling point. As with Madison, the advent of independence offered to him opportunities for public service in a continental, rather than a provincial, arena, a circumstance that would incline him to support bold measures to strengthen the Confederation government.[8]

Gouverneur Morris was not a native-born Pennsylvanian, but a New Yorker, and a member of one of the most affluent and politically powerful families in that colony. At the age of nine, he was sent to study at Benjamin Franklin's Academy of Philadelphia, a preparatory school for Franklin's recently established college, which would later become the University of Pennsylvania. In 1764, at the age of twelve, Morris went to King's College (now Columbia University) in New York City, where he displayed a high intelligence, if not a seriousness of purpose, as a student. Whereas Madison immersed himself in the study of political philosophy at Princeton, Morris was writing his bachelor's and master's degree essays on "Wit and Beauty" and "Love." And whereas Madison's romantic life, both as a college student and for many years thereafter, resembled that of a medieval monk, Morris's interest in topics such as wit, beauty, and love was not purely cerebral. As a young man he never passed up an opportunity for amorous adventure. As the son of a wealthy and prominent family known for its sociability, those opportunities abounded.[9]

Upon graduation, Morris apprenticed to William Smith, Jr., a family friend and one of New York's most prominent lawyers. When he began practicing law in New York City in 1771, the combination of his social connections and his intellectual and legal skills guaranteed him a rapidly growing practice, the income from which he augmented with some timely land speculation on the side. As the Revolution neared, Morris was one of those New Yorkers who, though distressed with British violations of American rights, was prospering and thus counseled reconciliation up to the end. Like many of his contemporaries, he ultimately determined that being labeled a Loyalist and a traitor in a society where public opinion was rapidly turning toward the Patriot side would be bad for both his pocketbook and his political future. By the time the colonies declared their independence, Morris was firmly in the Patriot camp, serving his constituency in Westchester County in the New York Provincial Congress.[10]

In May of 1777, the New York legislature selected Gouverneur Morris to serve in the Continental Congress in Philadelphia, where he developed a particular expertise in matters involving the supply of the Continental army. Morris witnessed firsthand the devastating effects of the government's failure to provide adequate supplies for the American troops. Two years later, in the spring of 1779, Morris learned that the New York legislature had discontinued his appointment to the Congress. His opponents in the legislature had claimed that the Tall Boy, as his enemies were inclined to call him, had neglected the interests of his home state in his zeal to serve those of the continent. Some of this resentment may have resulted from Morris's less-than-zealous defense of New York's interests in a boundary dispute with Vermont, but perhaps the greater measure owed to what many believed to be Morris's excessive arrogance. John Jay, another continental-minded New York political leader, defended Morris, claiming that his defeat was the consequence of only a few "men who envy his talents." Jay assured Morris that if he returned to New York to mend fences, he would soon be reelected to the Continental Congress, but Morris, stung by his defeat and too proud to grovel before his political adversaries, would have none of it. Although he could have returned to Westchester County and enjoyed a life of affluence and leisure at his palatial manor, "Morrisania," he decided to stay in Philadelphia, believing that he would have more success constructing a professional and political career there.[11]

Not long after his political setback in New York, Morris suffered a serious setback of another kind. In 1780, his left leg was caught in the wheel of a carriage, dislocating his ankle joint and badly breaking his leg.

The financial genius of the Revolution (standing) and his protégé (seated). Portrait of Robert Morris and Gouverneur Morris by Charles Willson Peale, 1783, courtesy of Pennsylvania Academy of Fine Arts.

Morris's regular physician was temporarily absent from the city and, acting on the advice of others, Morris agreed to have the leg amputated. When Morris's own physician returned, he was appalled at the decision. But the deed was done. For the rest of his life, Morris would walk with a simple oak peg attached to the stump of his leg, just below the knee.[12]

Gouverneur Morris put the period of his convalescence to good use, qualifying to practice law in Pennsylvania. He then began establishing a professional career in his adopted city. In May of 1781, he accepted a position as Robert Morris's assistant in the Office of Finance in the Confederation government. Through that association Gouverneur developed a more sophisticated understanding of public finance and, perhaps more importantly, took on some of his mentor's frustrations with the ineptitude of the Confederation government. While Robert Morris seldom talked publicly about his political views, his protégé was openly derisive about the ways in which provincial legislatures failed to live up to their financial obligations. Moreover, Gouverneur was equally disdainful of the democratic tendencies in both New York and Pennsylvania politics that, he believed, allowed ignorant country bumpkins to take the place of more virtuous men in their legislatures. As James Madison observed, with typical understatement, Morris did not "incline to the democratic side." Moreover, he was, as one historian has noted, "a respecter of very few persons." As an avowed elitist, he made it abundantly clear that he believed only people like himself should be entrusted with political power. His sense of his own superiority, which he did little to conceal, did not always win him friends. Nevertheless, his expertise in law and commerce made him powerful and, when combined with his association with Robert Morris, formidable. Gouverneur Morris was a man on the way up in Philadelphia society.[13]

Morris's fondness for women, developed as a young man, hardly abated during his one-legged adulthood. He remained a bachelor until he married Anne Cary Randolph, a member of the influential Virginia family, in 1809. But during the more than quarter century that led up to his matrimony he developed a reputation extending to both sides of the Atlantic as a consummate philanderer. Not allowing his peg leg to interfere with his amorous inclinations, he was a fixture at nearly all of the important events of Philadelphia high society, working his charms on married and single women alike. Morris's romantic adventures were so extensive that his friend and mentor, John Jay, was led to comment that though the loss of Gouverneur's leg was a "tax on my heart," Jay was on occasion "tempted to wish that he had lost *something* else." Indeed, although the rumor was without foundation, some in Philadelphia persisted in believing that Morris had lost his leg while leaping from a balcony to avoid being caught in one of his trysts with a married woman.[14]

Morris's tendency toward recklessness is captured in an oft-told, though disputed, story of one of the most memorable wagers in American history. In 1784, Morris bet Alexander Hamilton that he would have the courage to "take a liberty with General Washington" at a dinner with more than a dozen notables, including the Marquis de Lafayette and the generals Henry Knox, Nathaniel Greene, Baron Von Steuben, and Anthony Wayne. In the course of the dinner, after telling an inconsequential story, Morris leaned back in his chair and slapped Washington on the back, exclaiming, "Wasn't it so, my old boy!"[15]

One did not slap the general on the back. Washington sat stone-faced, not uttering a word or moving a muscle, after which a "strained silence fell over the company." Morris later commented to Hamilton, "I have won the bet, but paid dearly for it, and nothing could induce me to repeat it." As it happened, Washington was among the few people whom Morris, a "respecter of few persons," did in fact respect.

William Pierce, a delegate to the Convention from Georgia, who wrote thumbnail sketches of all of the delegates, captured Morris's combination of brilliance, arrogance, and occasional self-indulgence: "Gouverneur Morris is one of those Genius's in whom every species of talents combine to render him conspicuous and flourishing in public debate;— He winds through all the mazes of rhetoric and throws around him such a glare that he charms, captivates, and leads away the senses of all who hear him. . . . But with all these powers he is fickle and inconstant."

Pierce concluded his sketch by noting, disapprovingly, that Gouverneur, influenced by Robert Morris, had ceased to practice the law, and had turned instead to "some great mercantile matters with his namesake."[16]

When the Pennsylvania legislature balloted for delegates to the Constitutional Convention on December 30, 1786, Morris had turned his attention away from politics and was preoccupied with the management of his extensive landholdings in New York. Nevertheless, the legislature elected him to serve in the Convention—barely. Among the eight delegates selected, he received the fewest votes, and the barest of majorities—thirty-three out of sixty-three votes cast. The Pennsylvania legislature, by electing only Philadelphians as delegates, was able to avoid paying travel and expense allowances, and therefore had the luxury of sending the largest delegation of any state to the Convention. Had this not been the case, Morris likely would not have been chosen.[17]

Another member of the Pennsylvania delegation who just barely managed to be included in the proceedings was James Wilson, who received only thirty-five votes for a spot on the Pennsylvania team. A decade older than Gouverneur Morris and eleven years older than Madison, his political worldview was strikingly similar to those of his younger counterparts, and, like those two, he didn't have to be convinced that the central government needed strengthening.[18]

Born in the Scottish lowlands in 1742, Wilson was educated just a few miles to the east of his home town, at the University of St. Andrews. Wilson spent his first four years at St. Andrews studying a wide range of subjects that bore greater resemblance to the liberal arts curriculum Benjamin Franklin was implementing at his new College of Philadelphia than it did the narrower, more classical approach to learning still practiced at most British and American universities. Wilson's parents, staunch

Presbyterians, had hoped that he would become a minister. At their urging, he stayed on at St. Andrews for a fifth year to begin preparation for the clergy. Midway through that year, Wilson's father died, liberating him from a career he had not really wanted to pursue. After a brief stint in Edinburgh, where he studied bookkeeping and accounting, he set sail for America in the fall of 1765 in search of greater opportunity than that offered in Scotland to a young man from a family of only modest means.[19]

Wilson's St. Andrews education stood him in good stead. He immediately obtained a position as a tutor at Franklin's College of Philadelphia, and, in 1766, he began studying law with John Dickinson, at the time possibly the finest lawyer in America. Wilson's association with Dickinson came at a particularly propitious time, for in November 1767 Dickinson published his *Letters of a Pennsylvania Farmer*, one of the earliest and most important pamphlets arguing that England could not tax the colonies without their consent.

James Wilson was a brilliant and serious student, and he quickly proved himself an equal to his mentor. His reading in the theory and practice of the law went well beyond what was necessary for the provincial law practice he started after leaving Dickinson's office. He accepted any case that came his way in the Pennsylvania hinterland, where opportunities for a bright young attorney to find work were better than in a city already overrun with lawyers. As the Revolution neared, Wilson was elected to represent the town of Carlisle, one hundred twenty-five miles west of Philadelphia, at the Provincial Conference, the body that would lead Pennsylvania into revolution.[20]

Wilson's rise to a position of political prominence was owed in large measure to his authorship of an extraordinarily influential pamphlet, *Considerations on the Nature and Extent of the Legislative Authority of the British Parliament*, first published in 1774. In that pamphlet, Wilson emphatically rejected all parliamentary authority over the colonies, articulating a notion of America's relationship with Great Britain, based on "obedience and loyalty to the King," that was strikingly close to the voluntary relationship by which the British would govern the members of their "Commonwealth" once they had absorbed the lessons of America's secession from their empire. He allowed for a purely voluntary obedience to British trade regulations but denied subservience to Parliament in any form. It was at least in part on the strength of this formidable intellectual achievement that the still relatively unknown Carlisle attorney gained election to the Second Continental Congress.[21]

In 1778, Wilson moved from Carlisle to Philadelphia to seek his fortune. Like Gouverneur Morris, Wilson found Robert Morris the most convenient path to influence and wealth. He became Robert Morris's principal legal adviser, and, trying to imitate the Philadelphia financier's success as a merchant and speculator, he embarked on a wide range of investments—from banking to real estate to shipping to manufacturing. Unfortunately for Wilson, the timing of his investments was not always on the mark, and on the eve of the Convention his personal finances were in a state of near collapse.[22]

In spite of his financial difficulties, Wilson continued to advance his public career, serving in the Confederation Congress for four years during the 1780s. Wilson's service in the continental government, along with the powerful influence of Robert Morris, led him to the same conclusions reached by his colleagues from Pennsylvania and Virginia. He was dismayed by the failure of state legislatures to assume their fair share of support for the continental union and continually frustrated by the Confederation government's inability either to raise a revenue on its own or to coerce the states into meeting their responsibilities.

Aside from Madison, there was no one in the Convention better prepared intellectually for the task of constructing a stronger government. Gouverneur Morris, James Wilson, and James Madison shared similar views on the need to strengthen the continental government, but only Wilson and Madison had the combination of temperament and intellectual acuity capable of winning the respect even of those delegates who may have disagreed with them. The two men worked collegially with Morris, but they were his polar opposite in terms of manner and style. While Gouverneur Morris possessed great wit and revelled in purely social conversation, Wilson and Madison spoke little and were socially awkward. Whereas Gouverneur Morris delighted in oratorical pyrotechnics, Madison and Wilson preferred scholarly logic to the clever turn of phrase. William Pierce captured Wilson's great strengths, and at least hinted at some of his weaknesses.

> Mr. Wilson ranks among the foremost in legal and political knowledge. He has joined to a fine genius all that can set him off and show him to advantage. He is well acquainted with man, and understands all the passions that influence him. Government seems to have been his peculiar study, all the political institutions of the world he knows in detail,

and can trace the causes and effects of every revolution
from the earliest stages of the Grecian commonwealth
down to the present time. No man is more clear, copious,
and comprehensive than Mr. Wilson, yet he is no great
orator. He draws the attention not by his eloquence, but by
the force of his reasoning.[23]

These then were the men whose conversations and conclusions *before*
the Convention would do the most to influence the eventual outcome.
From Virginia came Washington, Randolph, Mason, and Madison. And
from Pennsylvania came Franklin and the triumvirate of Robert Morris,
Gouverneur Morris, and James Wilson. Among the Virginians, it was
clearly Madison who provided the brainpower, but, emphatically, it was
Washington who provided the political clout. The dynamic among the
Pennsylvanians was more complicated. Franklin was the titular leader of
the Pennsylvania delegation. But, weakened by age and painful kidney
stones—and less convinced of the need for dramatic change—he was
unlikely to supply either the energy or the ideas for a revolution in government. Robert Morris was at that moment the most powerful man in
Pennsylvania, and he was the mentor and patron of both Gouverneur
Morris and James Wilson. But his power and prestige were more likely
to be on display in the counting room or the drawing room, not in a public forum. Together, though, these four Pennsylvanians, each playing to
his particular strengths, would combine with the Virginians to set the
agenda for the upcoming Convention.

"TO FORM A PROPER CORRESPONDENCE
OF SENTIMENTS"

On the evening of May 16, Benjamin Franklin hosted a dinner in his
grand new dining room for what he proudly described as "the principal
people . . . of our Confederation." Of course, many of those "principal
people" had not yet arrived in Philadelphia, but we do know that most of
the delegates then present in Philadelphia—Washington, Madison, Edmund Randolph, George Wythe, John Blair, and James McClurg, the
Virginians; Franklin, Robert Morris, Gouverneur Morris, James Wilson, and Thomas Fitzsimons, the Philadelphians; and perhaps George
Read, a delegate from Delaware who had also just arrived in the city—
attended. Recounting the events of the evening in a letter to his old Lon-

don friend Thomas Jordan a few days later, Franklin described with pride having gathered "what the French call *une assemblee des notables*," and he spared no effort to lay out a lavish spread for his company. Franklin was well satisfied with the pleasure with which his guests received his hospitality. He had ordered a special cask of porter for the occasion. When that cask "was broached," he boasted, "its contents met with the most cordial and universal approbation. In short, the company agreed unanimously that it was the best porter they had ever tasted."[24]

While the Virginians and Pennsylvanians had met briefly from May 14 to 16, the dinner at Franklin's house that night, and possibly the porter in particular, enabled the delegates most committed to a dramatic overhaul of the Articles of Confederation to coalesce. It helped that the two titans of America's Revolutionary experience—Franklin and Washington—made clear their support for a reinvigorated continental government. Equally important, it provided the Virginians and the Pennsylvanians an opportunity to get to know one another in a relaxed and convivial setting and to share their ideas on not *whether*, but *how* the central government should be strengthened. Franklin, more than any delegate at the Convention, had a superb sense of the way in which good food, liquor, and conversation could lubricate the machinery of government and politics, and his dinner gathering was well designed for that purpose.

Following the dinner at Franklin's, and with the arrival of George Mason the following day, the members of the Virginia and Pennsylvania delegations began to confer in earnest. According to Mason, who reported on the meetings to his son, the gatherings served to allow the Virginians and Pennsylvanians to "grow into some acquaintance with each other" and to "form a proper correspondence of sentiments." Washington already had well-established relationships with all of the key members of the Pennsylvania delegation, and Madison, though he had probably met Franklin for the first time only that week, had worked with the two Morrises and James Wilson in the context of his earlier service in the Continental Congress. The other Virginians had only passing acquaintances with their Pennsylvania counterparts. Randolph had served briefly in the Continental Congress in Philadelphia in 1781 and 1782, and he may have worked with Robert Morris and James Wilson, but he was probably meeting Franklin and Gouverneur Morris for the first time. George Wythe had been a signer of the Declaration of Independence, so he certainly knew Franklin, but he may not have known any of the other Pennsylvanians prior to the previous evening's dinner. And Mason, having never ventured more than a few miles outside of Virginia and having missed the dinner at Franklin's, knew the Pennsylvania delegates only by reputation.[25]

The Virginia and Pennsylvania delegates would meet frequently over the next seven days prior to the opening of the Convention on May 25. They made the ceremonial trip to the State House each day, meeting informally there for a few hours, and then they continued their conversations over dinner at the City Tavern or the Indian Queen in the late afternoon. James Madison was at his best in these small, informal settings. Although he was often inept in public debate, his growing comfort with the Pennsylvanians—particularly Gouverneur Morris and James Wilson—and his extensive advance preparation allowed him to take the lead in formulating a plan to be presented to the Convention. And he did not hold back. Drawing on his earlier work on "The Vices of the Political System of the United States," the extensive memorandum he had sent to George Washington on April 16, and further refinements of those thoughts composed during his days in Philadelphia in early May, he came forward with a plan for "a total alteration of the present federal system." The most important parts of that radical alteration were

- The weak, single-house legislature of the Confederation government would be replaced by a two-house, national legislature "with full legislative powers upon all subjects of the Union."

- The national legislature would have the power to veto any law passed by a state legislature that it judged to be contrary to the best interests of the union as a whole.

- The formula of equal representation for each state in a single-house legislature would be replaced by a system in which representation in each house of the new national legislature would be apportioned according to some combination of a state's population and wealth.

The change in the formula for representation lay at the heart of Madison's radical plan, for it signified a government in which the people of the nation, rather than the state governments, were supreme. Madison also indicated the need for a stronger executive branch, as well as a national judiciary, but he had not fleshed out the structure and power of those two branches of the government at this point.[26]

Madison's specific ideas about the new government's structure did not go unchallenged. The two Morrises and James Wilson agreed with Madison that the principle of equal representation for each state in the national legislature—a central feature of government under the Articles of Confederation—needed to be overturned. But Gouverneur Morris and Robert Morris, joined by other Pennsylvanians, wished to make a *preemptive* strike against the principle of equal representation. They thought "the large states should unite in firmly refusing to the small states an equal vote" in the proceedings of the Convention. Fearing that delegates from the smaller states would block any attempt at creating a government founded on the principle of proportional representation, they wanted to weaken the power of those states in the upcoming Convention by insisting that each state's votes in the Convention be weighed according to its population.[27]

While Madison supported the principle of proportional representation in the national legislature, he feared that a "fatal altercation" with the smaller states on an issue of such importance so early in the proceedings would doom the Convention before it had even begun its work. Instead, he argued, they should attempt to convince the small states "in the course of the deliberations, to give up their equality for the sake of an effective government." With perhaps too much optimism, Madison predicted that the strategy of simply allowing the debate over representation to unfold naturally would cause a preponderance of states to see that it was in their self-interest to support the principle of proportional representation. The Northern states, he reasoned, would favor proportional representation because of "their present populousness," and the Southern states, whose populations at that time were growing more rapidly than those of the North, would be induced to support the principle because they "expected advantage in this respect" in the future. He believed that "the lesser States" would eventually yield to the "predominant will," but he correctly foresaw that an immediate confrontation on the issue would be counterproductive.[28]

Madison and the other Virginians persuaded the Pennsylvanians to hold their fire on the question of representation. The Pennsylvanians, for their part, made substantial contributions to Madison's still hazily formed notions about the character of the chief executive. When Madison shared his ideas about the shape of a new government with George Washington a month before the Convention, he admitted that he had "scarcely ventured as yet to form my own opinion either of the manner in which [the executive] ought to be constituted or of the authorities with which it ought to be cloathed." He clearly recognized that the absence of an effective executive had seriously undermined the effectiveness of the Confederation government, but when he arrived in Philadelphia, he was still uncertain about whether the new government should have a single chief executive or some form of plural executive council. And, in spite of his interest in the principle of separation of powers, he had not yet defined precisely what the powers of a chief executive might be. It would take most of the summer before the Convention delegates could come to a meeting of the minds on the character of the executive branch, but in those days before the Convention actually got under way it would be the Pennsylvanians—especially James Wilson and Gouverneur Morris—who would be most instrumental in clarifying aspects of what would become the American presidency.[29]

Outlining the sort of system that Madison had envisioned in his letter to his son, George Mason, using English institutions as his frame of reference, characterized the national legislature Madison had proposed as a "Parliament." Indeed, Madison's initial formulation, which did not specify the character of the relationship between an extraordinarily powerful legislature and a still-undefined executive, could have easily evolved into a parliamentary rather than a presidential system of government. In such a system, the executive, being primarily a creature of the legislature, would have more closely resembled an English prime minister than a president. James Wilson and Gouverneur Morris argued strongly for a single powerful executive as a means of giving energy to the central government, and their support of that idea—and likely Washington's as well—led to a decision to press for an executive "to be chosen by the National Legislature for a term of __ years." One looking for the origins of the idea of the American presidency as a strong symbol of a unified nation need look no further than the ideas of Gouverneur Morris and James Wilson, presented during those seven days of informal discussion. And it didn't hurt that George Washington, the most powerful exemplar of those ideas, was present for those discussions.[30]

AS THE VIRGINIANS and Pennsylvanians met during that week, delegates from other states trickled into town, but far too slowly in the opinion of one distinguished delegate. George Washington, writing to his neighbor Arthur Lee on May 20, complained about the lack of a quorum of state delegations. "These delays," he grumbled, "greatly impede public measures, and serve to sour the temper of the punctual members, who do not like to idle away their time." Washington, never one to idle away his time, could certainly be counted among that group. However much progress the Virginians and Pennsylvanians may have been making in achieving a coalescence of their views on a new government, it would all be for naught if the indifference of the American states were to cause the Convention to expire even before it had begun.[31]

Some of the delegates arriving between May 17 and the opening of the Convention on May 25—men like Alexander Hamilton of New York and Charles Pinckney of South Carolina—would have approved of the deliberations of the Virginians and Pennsylvanians. Others—especially Robert Yates and John Lansing of New York—may well have been appalled by what Madison and his colleagues were up to. As representatives of the state that a few months earlier had dealt a deathblow to the Confederation government's attempt to levy import taxes, and as men committed to defending the commercial advantages already enjoyed by New York, they would emerge as staunch opponents of the effort to strengthen the continental government. While the delegates who had arrived after May 16 seem to have taken part in the formal gathering of delegates at the State House each day prior to May 25, they do not appear to have been active participants in the informal meetings among the men from Virginia and Pennsylvania.[32]

The Convention finally mustered its quorum on May 25, a day on which twenty-seven delegates from seven states attended. At that point, Madison had been in town for three weeks, Washington for nearly two. Despite how much they may have complained about the delay, and despite how much they may have fretted over whether the requisite number of delegates would show up, they had in fact been given a wonderful, serendipitous gift. The eleven-day period between May 14 and May 25 formed a bond not only between the delegations of the country's two most powerful and populous states but, equally important, among some of the most active and intellectually gifted delegates who would participate in the Convention. Out of the sight of those delegates who would eventually appear in Philadelphia less prepared and less committed to the idea of a vigorous national government, they had crafted a bold plan. They were now ready to move that plan forward to a larger stage, and to a largely unsuspecting audience.

CHAPTER FOUR

THE CONVENTION
OPENS FOR BUSINESS

FRIDAY, MAY 25, 1787, didn't feel much like a late spring day, as temperatures hovered in the fifties and a cool rain fell intermittently. But with the arrival of three more delegates from just across the Delaware River in New Jersey, the Convention finally achieved the quorum of seven of thirteen states necessary to begin its business. Madison's frustration at the delay was giving way to cautious optimism. Writing Virginia State Supreme Court justice Edmund Pendleton on May 27, he speculated that the delegates at that first session "seem to accord in viewing our situation as peculiarly critical and in being averse to temporising expedients."[1]

As the delegates began to arrange themselves in the Assembly Room of the State House, Robert Yates and Alexander Hamilton of New York took their seats at the table at the back, on the north side of the room. New York's third delegate, John Lansing, would arrive a week later. Only three of New Jersey's five delegates—David Brearley, William Churchill Houston, and William Paterson—occupied the seats at the table next to New York's. The other two, Governor William Livingston and Jonathan Dayton, were busy with what they considered to be more important business within their state government. Livingston would not arrive until June 5 and Dayton would arrive more than three weeks later, on June 28.[2]

Pennsylvania's delegation, with eight members the largest in the Convention, was represented on that first day by only four men—Robert

Morris, Thomas Fitzsimons, James Wilson, and Gouverneur Morris. Three of Delaware's five delegates—George Read, Richard Bassett, and Jacob Broom—were present; Gunning Bedford, Jr., and John Dickinson would follow shortly.[3]

Thanks to Madison's entreaties, all seven of Virginia's delegates were present and accounted for on that opening day—George Washington, Edmund Randolph, John Blair, James Madison, George Mason, George Wythe, and James McClurg. Four of North Carolina's five delegates—Alexander Martin, William Richardson Davie, Richard Dobbs Spaight, and Hugh Williamson—were present; the fifth, William Blount, did not arrive until late in June. South Carolina had a strong—and strongly opinionated—delegation, and they were all present on the opening day. They constituted an unusually closely knit group. Indicative of the tight control of South Carolina politics by a small, interconnected elite, all of its members—John Rutledge, Charles Cotesworth Pinckney, Charles Pinckney, and Pierce Butler—were related by kinship to one another. More important, all four gentlemen owned slaves in large quantities, and their vigorous assertion of interest as planters and slave owners would have a profound impact on the proceedings of the Convention.[4]

While the Southern states were quite well represented, none of the New England states had managed to assemble a working delegation in Philadelphia by May 25. No doubt the bad weather had something to do with the New Englanders' absence. The heavy rains and deteriorating road conditions lengthened what would have been a five- to seven-day journey to one of as long as two weeks. But in some cases, the delegates' absence reflected the apathy with which some viewed the Convention. The New Hampshire legislature, for example, refused to pay the expenses of the delegates it had elected several months earlier. The state would remain unrepresented in the Convention until late July, when John Langdon, a wealthy merchant with close ties to Robert Morris, dipped into his own pocket and paid his own expenses and those of his Convention colleague, Nicholas Gilman. In feisty Rhode Island, a narrow majority of provincial politicians, fearful that a stronger central government would undermine the independence of their state, declined participation in the Convention altogether. Only one delegate from Massachusetts, Rufus King, was ready for business on May 25; his colleagues, Elbridge Gerry, Nathaniel Gorham, and Caleb Strong, had not yet turned up. King, who agreed that more power should be consolidated in the central government, wrote to a political associate back home that he was "mortified" to be the only New England delegate present. He was immensely relieved when his three Bay State colleagues appeared over the course of the next few days. The Connecticut delegates—Roger Sherman, William Samuel Johnson, and Oliver Ellsworth—had not yet arrived but would trickle in the following week.[5]

Among the Southern states, Maryland was notably late in getting its act together, because although the legislature elected delegates, those elected kept refusing to serve. Maryland finally managed to put a delegation together on May 26, but most of the state's five delegates were consistently tardy or absent for much of the summer. Indeed, one of Maryland's delegates, Daniel Carroll, did not bother to show up until August 6, and he then stayed only eleven days before departing. The remarkable apathy shown by many of the Marylanders elected as delegates to the Convention serves as a reminder that, though the Constitutional Convention of 1787 proved to be one of the epochal events of American history, there were many in the country at the time who held no such expectations for it.

The Maryland state legislature's instructions to its delegation were unique among all of those states present in that they allowed the delegation to cast a vote at the Convention even if only one member was in attendance. (More typically the state legislatures only permitted their delegations to vote when a majority of their members were present.) If Maryland had not adopted such a permissive rule, it would have gone without a vote in the Convention for much of the summer. William Few of Georgia was the other Southern delegate present on that opening day. The other three delegates from Georgia—Abraham Baldwin, William Houstoun, and William Pierce—would arrive by June 11.[6]

Plainly, not everyone in America shared James Madison's sense of urgency about the business of continental union. Certainly the inclement weather had something to do with the eleven-day delay in the opening of the Convention and the paucity of delegates present on that opening day, but the more likely culprit was apathy. As the Convention finally got down to business, there was ample reason to doubt whether America's political leaders really wanted to create a "more perfect union."

THE PENNSYLVANIA STATE HOUSE

Many of the delegates converging on the Pennsylvania State House, known now as Independence Hall, were already familiar with the building and its history. The State House was the obvious venue for a meeting of this importance, both practically and aesthetically. Its elegant exterior was widely admired for its marriage of dignity and simplicity, and its meeting spaces were large enough—barely—to hold contingents of delegates from each state.[7]

As the delegates entered the ground floor of the State House, they found themselves in a wide, noisy, bustling hallway. The hallway opened on the west side to the Pennsylvania State Supreme Court, and because there were no doors or partitions separating the courtroom from the hallway, there was a constant commotion of people of every sort waiting to do business with the court. As the delegates walked through the opened double doors leading into the Assembly Room (so named because it was the meeting place of the Pennsylvania Assembly), they were well aware that they were entering the room—and taking their seats at the same tables—where delegates to the Continental Congress had endorsed the Declaration of Independence eleven years earlier. Eight of the men who would eventually attend the Constitutional Convention carried particularly strong memories of the room, for they had been among the fifty-six delegates to the Continental Congress who had signed the Declaration of Independence.[8]

What greeted them was not, by the standards of modern legislative chambers, a particularly imposing space at forty feet by forty feet, with a plaster ceiling twenty feet high. Its austere, wooden, gray-paneled walls housed fourteen tables, each covered in heavy, green, woolen cloth. On each side of the front of the room was a fireplace, set in marble. Some of the gloom of the surroundings was relieved by the high, wide windows on the north and south sides of the room, which let in at least some natural light. Another small table intended for the Convention secretary stood in front of one of the fireplaces. Occupying center stage, between the two fireplaces, on a low dais, was the table on which the Declaration of Independence had been signed eleven years earlier. Behind that table sat a handsome, high-backed mahogany chair that would, after the proceedings of the summer of 1787 had been completed, become one of the most famous pieces of furniture in all of America.[9]

For those delegates unaccustomed to urban life, the building may have seemed anything but peaceful. As the delegates entered the Assembly Room on that first day, and indeed throughout the summer, they were forced to contend with the racket from the bustle of people headed to the court across the hall. If that wasn't bad enough, that summer twenty-five convicts from the Walnut Street jail were engaged in a noisy excavation of the site for the foundation of the new county courthouse a hundred feet away. Finally, there was the din of the street traffic, which led the delegates to badger the street commissioners into regraveling the streets immediately surrounding the State House.[10]

The State House's grandeur was likely diminished by its proximity to the massive Walnut Street jail, which stood immediately across the street and dwarfed the State House in size. The lucky among its more than one hundred inmates had a view of the State House yard and were known to rain insults and complaints on passersby or beg for money by means of hats affixed to the ends of long poles. Just two months before the delegates convened, the inmates made an abortive attempt at a prison break, and in July, in the midst of the Convention's deliberations, the prisoners rioted, complaining about overcrowded and harsh conditions.[11]

Inside the walled State House yard, however, the atmosphere was more bucolic. Serpentine walks ran along the east and west sides of the yard, and a variety of shrubs and trees had recently been planted to provide a naturalistic setting. George Washington pronounced himself de-

The Assembly Room of Independence Hall was restored after meticulous research in 1965. Courtesy of Independence National Historical Park.

lighted by the beauty of the landscaping, so much so that he paid Samuel Vaughan, the English merchant and amateur landscaper responsible for the design, to carry out work on the grounds of his plantation at Mount Vernon.[12]

Amid this natural beauty, near the northeast corner of the yard was a large privy, to which the delegates could gain access from a small door on the right-hand side of the front of their meeting room. By the standards of the time, it was a grand edifice. Octagonal in design, it had four chambers with glazed transoms to provide natural light for the occupants. Each side of the octagon was five feet wide and flanked by handsome stone steps to allow those using the "necessary," as it was called, easy entrance to and egress from the elevated chambers inside. Each of the four sections of the privy was a "four-holer," meaning that the lavatory could accommodate up to sixteen people at a time. Although it was primarily constructed for the use of people working for the city and state, there was nothing in the design to enforce such exclusive use. In practical terms, this meant that George Washington or Benjamin Franklin might find himself seated or standing next to a day laborer or a common seaman.[13]

The State House Yard, with a view looking toward the south entrance to the State House. Etching by Thomas Birch, circa 1800, courtesy of Independence National Historical Park.

THE DELEGATES: AGE, EDUCATION, EXPERIENCE, AND ECONOMIC INTERESTS

At no time during the summer were all fifty-five elected delegates present in the Assembly Room at the same time, but had they all gathered together, one of the striking features of the group would have been its relative youth. The members ranged in age from twenty-six—Jonathan Dayton of New Jersey—to eighty-one—the venerable Franklin. The average age was forty-four, the median forty-three. But averages do not tell the whole story. At one end of the age scale, Franklin was fifteen years older than the next oldest delegate—Roger Sherman of Connecticut. At the other end, twelve of the delegates were thirty-five or younger. Part of the explanation for the relative youth of that cohort of delegates lies in the fact that they were a product of a society where political power was just as often derived from family heritage as from hard work and experience. Men like Rufus King of Massachusetts, Gouverneur Morris of Pennsylvania, Edmund Randolph of Virginia, and Charles Pinckney of

The residents of the "gaol" facing the State House may occasionally have wondered what was going on behind closed doors. The Walnut Street Gaol by Thomas Birch, circa 1800, courtesy of Independence National Historical Park.

South Carolina were born into families where service in high public office was considered both a birthright and an important responsibility. The accident of a fortunate birth was not sufficient to gain for those men an automatic claim to power, but it certainly accelerated their rise to positions of political prominence.

Another part of the explanation is more complex and more revealing of the character of many of the delegates who found themselves in Philadelphia that summer. Many of America's older and more experienced political leaders were simply too busy with the affairs of their individual states to be bothered to make the journey to Philadelphia to attend the Convention. As a consequence, men like Patrick Henry—next to Washington, the most revered man in all of Virginia—declined their election to the Convention, leaving the field open to younger men like James Madison. Further to the north, Governor George Clinton of New York was similarly occupied with purely provincial affairs, thus enabling the thirty-year-old upstart Alexander Hamilton to play a role in the constitutional drama.

All but two or three of the Convention delegates had performed some sort of government service during their careers. But the most striking fact about the men who were to gather in Philadelphia that summer was the extent to which the vast majority of them had served in the continental government. Forty-two of the fifty-five delegates had served at one time or another in the Continental Congress, an experience that gave those men a very different perspective on the challenges, and frustrations, involved in holding the fragile American union together. Many of the men not present in Philadelphia—"old revolutionaries" like Patrick Henry, George Clinton, John Hancock, and Sam Adams—had devoted the better part of their careers to serving first the people of their colony and second their state. They were proud of that service and did not feel the same sense of urgency about the condition of the continental union felt by their younger colleagues. Of course, the "young men of the Revolution" were not the only ones worried about the state of the continental union. There were some important senior citizens—Franklin and Washington—who brought a distinctly cosmopolitan perspective to the Convention. In that sense, age was less important a factor than outlook in shaping a delegate's attitude.[14]

The more cosmopolitan cast of mind of the delegates was shaped by their educational backgrounds. By the standards of even the political elites of America, they were unusually well educated. Twenty-nine of the fifty-five had undergraduate degrees. The College of New Jersey (Princeton) could claim nine delegates among its alumni, William and Mary and Yale four each, and Harvard and King's College (Columbia) three each. Three of the delegates—South Carolina's Charles Cotesworth Pinckney, Pennsylvania's James Wilson, and North Carolina's Richard Dobbs Spaight— did their undergraduate study abroad, receiving their degrees from Oxford, Saint Andrews, and Glasgow, respectively. Twelve of the delegates had gone on to do some form of post-graduate study, and an astonishing twenty-nine of the fifty-five delegates had studied law. Six of those twenty-nine—John Blair of Virginia, John Dickinson of Delaware, William Houstoun of Georgia, Jared Ingersoll of Pennsylvania, and Charles Cotesworth Pinckney and John Rutledge of South Carolina—had completed their legal study at the prestigious Inns of Court in London.[15]

One of the important functions of the United States Constitution, both at its inception and in the present, is to protect property and to promote economic development. It is therefore not surprising that historians have devoted so much attention to the "economic interests" of the framers of that document. In fact, though, the task of identifying any one delegate with a specific set of economic interests is not an easy one. The Founding Fathers lived in an age in which many men pursued multiple careers simultaneously, or, conversely, in which some gentlemen may not have felt any need to engage in the grubby pursuits of the marketplace. Consequently, it is difficult to compile a precise list of the occupations of the delegates. While twenty-nine of the delegates had qualified for the bar, only thirteen pursued that profession as their principal means of livelihood. Fourteen of the delegates were merchants, three made their primary income through manufacturing, and ten were involved to some degree in the world of banking and finance. Although nearly all of the delegates owned substantial amounts of land, sixteen, most of them from the South, made their living chiefly as farmers or planters. At least three—William Blount of North Carolina, Jonathan Dayton of New Jersey, and Nathaniel Gorham of Massachusetts—were heavily involved in speculation in western lands, although perhaps as many as a dozen others had at one time or another also made such investments. Two of the delegates—Virginia's James McClurg and North Carolina's Hugh Williamson—had medical degrees and made their primary living as doctors. Roger Sherman, who had at various times in his life been a farmer, a surveyor, a publisher of almanacs, and, finally, a lawyer, was perhaps the only man who earned a living from the salaries he received by serving in multiple local offices in his home state of Connecticut.

Nearly all of the Founding Fathers, with the possible exceptions of Sherman and William Few of Georgia, were men of considerable wealth. Living in an age in which we distinguish between the merely rich and the super-rich, we might well wonder what it meant to be wealthy in the late eighteenth century. Such was the structure of wealth in early America that no one, either at the Convention or outside of it, ever managed to accumulate the kind of staggering wealth like that enjoyed today by a Bill Gates or a Warren Buffet, or, indeed, even a successful hedge fund manager. There were some among the merchant and financial class—John Langdon of New Hampshire, Gerry of Massachusetts, and Thomas Mifflin and Robert Morris of Pennsylvania—who had not only achieved impressive wealth but also enjoyed displaying it; but even among that group there were some—Morris, for example—who carried substantial burdens of debt at the same time that they were bringing in large sums of money. Similarly, many of the Southern delegates—Washington and Mason of Virginia, Daniel Carroll and Daniel St. Thomas Jenifer of Maryland, Charles Pinckney, Charles Cotesworth Pinckney, and John Rutledge of South Carolina—maintained a lifestyle on their slave-based plantations that suggested great comfort and affluence, but at one time or another all of those men suffered from a shortage of ready cash.

Most of the delegates in Philadelphia were accustomed to a standard of living that set them apart from the people whom they were representing. Many, perhaps most, came from families that already enjoyed wealth, but a substantial number, among them Robert Morris, Benjamin Franklin, and Alexander Hamilton, had started pretty close to the bottom of the social hierarchy and worked their way up. Indeed, although birthright and family reputation were important to economic and political success in the world of the Founding Fathers, they were not in and of themselves sufficient to a claim to political leadership. The men who came to Philadelphia, though they did not have a monopoly on merit and political experience, had by their past public service *earned* their places in the Convention. Moreover, there is no indication that those delegates whose careers had been aided by family wealth and prestige considered these to be of any importance in their relationships with those delegates who had not enjoyed similar advantages.[16]

There was, however, one set of economic interests that did intrude in a consistent fashion in the debates over the Constitution. One of the persistent sources of conflict in the Convention was the status of the institution of slavery and its future in the new republic. Twenty-five of the men who attended the Convention owned slaves, and among those twenty-five, sixteen—all of them from the South—depended on their slave labor as indispensable factors in their economic success. As we will see, the divisions in the Convention on the issue of slavery did not fall neatly along North/South lines. Indeed, there were a few moments in the Convention during which delegates with large slaveholdings expressed their concern about the perpetuation of the institution. Nevertheless, the fact that nearly half of the delegates who attended the Convention were to a greater or lesser extent dependent on slaves for their comfort or profit would play an important part in the constitutional drama that was about to unfold.[17]

GETTING DOWN TO BUSINESS

The agenda on that first day of the Convention's business was light. The first order of business was to select a president to preside over the proceedings, a secretary to record them, and finally a doorkeeper and a messenger. The delegates then presented their credentials as the official representatives of the seven states that had thus far managed to assemble.

As the proceedings commenced, and with no one officially in charge at that point, Robert Morris took the initiative and nominated his houseguest, George Washington, as presiding officer of the Convention. Benjamin Franklin, the only man in the Convention who might have been viewed as a challenger to Washington as a candidate for president of the Convention, had hoped to be the one to nominate the general. But the combination of the rainy weather and another attack of kidney stones kept him at home that day. In Franklin's absence, Morris claimed the honor. In the only speech he is known to have made during the Convention, Morris, "by instruction and in behalf of the deputation of Pennsylvania," nominated the general as president, "expressing his confidence that the choice would be unanimous."[18]

Morris's confidence was not misplaced. There was no need to go around the room to poll the seven delegations seated there. The delegates, by acclamation, immediately and unanimously endorsed his nomination. Morris and John Rutledge of South Carolina, who had seconded Morris's nomination of Washington, ceremoniously escorted Washington from the table where the Virginia delegation was seated to the highbacked chair at the front of the room. As Washington took his seat as presiding officer, there was enough of a chill in the room that fires burned in both hearths behind him.[19]

Washington's own account of the moment, recorded laconically in his diary, betrays only the slightest hint of his feelings about either the honor or the responsibility accorded him. His diary entry merely states that "by a unanimous vote I was called up to the Chair as President of the body." Delegates who witnessed the occasion commented that he seemed deeply touched by his election as the Convention's president. Although the general's public behavior was frequently marked by a self-conscious display of humility, he also possessed immense pride, and he certainly would have been chagrined had he not been offered the position.[20]

The delegates dispatched the next piece of business quickly, but without the unanimity accompanying Washington's election. The Convention's secretary was responsible for keeping a journal of each day's proceedings, including the recording of any votes. It was essentially a clerical position, but for at least a few men, who coveted the honor of playing a role in deliberations of public importance but who lacked the stature to be decision makers in those deliberations themselves, it was nevertheless a highly sought-after position. Washington, now running the show, recognized James Wilson, who nominated Benjamin Franklin's grandson, twenty-seven-year-old William Temple Franklin, as the Convention's secretary. Temple—as he was called—was something of a fop and a rogue, and Wilson may have made the nomination more out of loyalty to his senior colleague than out of any real confidence in Temple's abilities. Whereas the young Benjamin Franklin had been muscular and athletic, Temple, with his slender frame, carefully coiffed hair, and stylish European clothes, projected an image of effete languor. Temple had accompanied his grandfather to France, and, with a good deal of help from Franklin, had managed to get himself appointed as secretary to the American peace delegation. Temple's primary achievement in France, however, was to earn a reputation as a clotheshorse and a hedonist, a pursuit that led him to father an illegitimate son with a married woman, Blanchette Caillot. Franklin, whose relationships with his wife and family were in most cases marked with indifference, doted on his grandson; young Temple would never have been considered for the post of Convention secretary were it not for the stature and influence of his grandfather.[21]

But there were some who did not wish to see the young Franklin rewarded again simply because he had an illustrious grandfather. Alexander Hamilton of New York rose and nominated Major William Jackson, a South Carolinian who had served as assistant secretary of war and as personal secretary to General Washington during the Revolution. Jackson clearly coveted the post. He had spent much of the month of April beseeching Washington and any other potential Convention delegate with whom he had an acquaintance to appoint him. Jackson's great fear, he confided to one of Washington's close associates, was that the combined influence of Robert Morris and Franklin would deprive him of the position. In the end, Jackson's lobbying campaign, aided by Temple's less-than-stellar reputation, paid off, and he was elected secretary.

As is often the case in politics, those with the skills to be elected do not necessarily have the chops for the job, and Jackson turned out to be an exceptionally poor choice. Sadly, his skills as a lobbyist far surpassed those he possessed as a note taker. When Secretary of State John Quincy Adams undertook the task of organizing Jackson's notes prior to the publication of the Convention Journal in 1819, he discovered that they were a mess. They essentially consisted of random daily notes, from which, Adams complained, "the regular journal ought to have been, but never was, made out." Moreover, Jackson seems to have thrown away "all the loose scraps of paper" given to him by various delegates, leaving an already paltry Convention record even more so.[22]

The other item on the agenda was ostensibly a formality—that of reading the credentials of those delegates present. But politicians being politicians, and state pride and state jealousies being what they were, it was too much to expect that the state legislatures sending delegates to the Convention would be content merely to provide a list of the delegates representing them. Nearly all of the states prefaced their rosters of delegates with grandly worded statements expressing their reasons for participating in the Convention. All of the states acknowledged the imperfections of the Articles of Confederation. But not even Virginia and Pennsylvania, whose delegates were the boldest in proposing radical changes in the continental government, went so far as to suggest that the Convention should scrap the Articles of Confederation altogether. Nevertheless, the Virginia preamble, written by Madison, conveyed some of the exigency that at least a few delegates felt about the occasion. "The crisis is arrived," the Virginia preamble declared,

> at which the good People of America are to decide the
> solemn question whether they will by just and magnanimous
> Efforts reap the just fruits of that Independence which they
> have so gloriously acquired and of that Union which they
> have cemented with so much of their common Blood, or

whether by giving way to unmanly Jealousies and Prejudices or to partial and transitory Interests they will . . .
furnish our Enemies with cause to triumph.

The rhetoric was distinctly overheated, and uncharacteristically so in
Madison's case. Perhaps it was a mark of how deeply invested the young
Virginian was in his plans for a constitutional revolution.[23]

Whatever their differences in rhetorical style may have been, nearly all
of the states went on record in support of the effort to revise the Articles
of Confederation. But as George Read of Delaware rose to read the commission from his state, he gave a clear signal of serious trouble down the
road. For most of its history, Delaware had been simply called the "Three
Lower Counties," a mere appendage of the powerful and populous colony
of Pennsylvania. As it assumed its place among the independent states of
America, its political leaders were determined to defend the territorial integrity, the honor, and, most important, the political power of their state.
The commission from the state of Delaware specifically prohibited its
delegates from altering the part of the Articles of Confederation that established "an equality of voting among the states." The least-populous
state in the fragile union had, on the very first day of the Convention, announced its intention to obstruct a key element in what would become
one of the Virginians' and Pennsylvanians' principal goals: the call for
proportional representation.[24]

Read was fifty-three years old at the time of the Convention, and despite an appearance of physical frailty and a feeble voice that rendered his
oratorical power "fatiguing and tiresome to the last degree," he was a force
to be reckoned with. A signer of the Declaration of Independence and the
principal author of Delaware's new state constitution, Read had become
the most powerful politician in his state by 1776. In 1786, Read led his
state's delegation to the Annapolis Convention, where he had heartily endorsed the call for a new convention. Indeed, he favored an entirely new
government, believing that to patch up the old Articles of Confederation would be like "putting new cloth upon an old garment." He argued
that any new constitution ought to give the new government explicit supremacy over those governments of the individual states and that the new
national legislature should have a veto over any state laws that might conflict with those of the central government. He wished to create a strong
chief executive armed with an absolute veto.[25]

But while Read was prepared to grant the central government sover-

eign power over the individual states, he was unwilling to change the essential element of the Articles of Confederation that protected the sovereignty of those states—that giving each state, regardless of size, an equal
vote in the Congress. Read and his fellow Delaware delegates had only
one objective in mind: the aggrandizement of their own political power.
They avidly desired a stronger central government, but with equal ardor
insisted that their state of fewer than 60,000 residents be given as much
power as, for example, Virginia, with its population of 750,000.

Read knew that he could not rely on the goodwill of the larger states to
protect Delaware's independence and identity. Writing to his colleague
John Dickinson shortly before the Convention got under way, he confessed that he "would trust nothing to [the] candor, generosity, or ideas
of public justice" of the larger states. He predicted that once the Convention began, "argument or oratory . . . [would] avail little" in safe-
guarding Delaware's interests. He was prepared to scrap the whole
program of constitutional reform if it proved necessary to protect the
welfare of his home state. It was this sort of commitment to provincial
interests that had made the Confederation government ineffectual. And
it was the same provincialism that now threatened to throw the Convention off course before it had even begun.[26]

On that disquieting note, the delegates concluded their first day of business. They appointed a committee to prepare standing rules and orders for
the Convention and then adjourned until the following Monday. The real
work of the Convention—made even more difficult by Delaware's early
display of determination to protect its interests at all costs—had not yet
begun.[27]

SETTLING IN

May 26 would be the only Saturday until the end of the July on which
the delegates did not meet. For most of the summer, the Convention met
Monday through Saturday, with sessions beginning at ten or eleven
o'clock in the morning and adjourning around three or three-thirty in
the afternoon, with no break. While that work schedule may seem a bit
leisurely, in fact the delegates carried out much of their work outside of
the State House, in the taverns, coffee houses, and private homes of
Philadelphia.[28]

For those delegates who had arrived only recently, the weekend offered an opportunity to acclimate themselves to life in America's largest city. In 1787, the city's inhabitants numbered about 40,000—15,000 more than its nearest competitor, New York. And those 40,000 residents lived and worked in some 6,500 houses and 415 stores and shops. To most of the delegates to the Constitutional Convention, coming from their small towns, farms, or plantations, Philadelphia must have seemed like a huge and densely packed metropolis. But compared to European cities like London—whose population was closing in on a million by the end of the eighteenth century—it was a small market town.[29]

In 1787, most of Philadelphia's population was concentrated within eight blocks running east to west from the Delaware River to Eighth Street, with the area west of Eighth more closely resembling the countryside than a cityscape. Philadelphians—rich and poor, slave and free, English, Irish, German, and African, Quaker, Presbyterian, Lutheran, Catholic, or Jew—lived and interacted with one another in close quarters. While the city's wealthiest residents built lavish townhouses on the city's main streets, their houses sat immediately in front of mean tenements.[30]

The Delaware riverfront in Philadelphia drove the city's economic and cultural vitality. On any given day one might find a dozen or more ships loading grain and livestock bound for Europe and the West Indies or unloading molasses from the West Indies or manufactured goods from Europe. Equally important, many of those ships contained human cargo. Every year, tens of thousands of immigrants from the British Isles, Germany, and other parts of Europe poured into America through the port of Philadelphia. Although many of those immigrants would move on to the hinterland, many stayed, infusing the city with an ethnic and religious diversity unequaled anywhere in the Western world. They were joined every week by scores of former slaves from the South who had gained their emancipation in the aftermath of the Revolution and were now moving North in search of greater opportunity.[31]

By the time of the American Revolution, Philadelphia had become the center of the American Enlightenment. The American Philosophical Society, founded by Benjamin Franklin in 1743 for "the promotion of useful knowledge among the British plantations" and intended to be an American counterpart to the Royal Society of London, was just beginning to build new and larger quarters for itself on the corner of Fifth and Chestnut streets. The Library Company of Philadelphia, also founded by Franklin in 1731, had by 1787 become the largest public library in America.[32]

Arguably the most popular of Philadelphia's cultural institutions was the Repository for Natural Curiosities, which was created by the talented Philadelphia painter and intellectual, Charles Willson Peale, and visited by all of the delegates. More commonly called "Peale's Museum," this distinctly eccentric institution first served to display Peale's artwork, but in 1784 its owner began to display a collection of mastodon bones and all manner of stuffed exotic birds and animals. The public was fascinated by such "curiosities."[33]

As the delegates began the exploration of their temporary home for the summer on that first Saturday, they were immediately drawn to the city's main thoroughfare—variously called Market Street or "the High Street." There they confronted the sights, sounds, and smells of America's most diverse town in its most concentrated form, particularly as they approached the High Street Market, open for business on Wednesdays and Saturdays. As one neared the market, the first two sets of stalls, between Fourth and Second streets—the domain of the butchers and the fishmongers—greatly impacted a visitor's visual and olfactory experience. The butchers slaughtered their animals on the spot, not bothering to mop up the pools of blood in which their patrons were forced to stand. On a hot day—and there were many during the summer of 1787—it was not surprising to see the entire carcass of an animal covered thick with flies.[34]

The market was not merely a place for buying necessary provisions. Market days in eighteenth-century Philadelphia were great communal gatherings. Perhaps the most striking feature of the scene was the diversity of those who crowded into the market—people of all nationalities, races, and social classes. Intermingled in the throng were the "lower sorts," including prostitutes, who charged one or two dollars for their services, and pickpockets, of whom there were many. The market was also a good place for law enforcement officials to demonstrate their authority against the criminal element. Until the late 1780s, if one of the delegates was of a mind to do so, he could amuse himself by watching a public flogging.[35]

Contemporary engravings of late-eighteenth-century Philadelphia invariably depict a city with spotless thoroughfares and relatively few people or animals, but the reality of street life confronted by the delegates was far different. They encountered packs of dogs and pigs roaming the streets, and, no doubt, a few of them would have echoed the complaint of many of the city's townspeople over the practice of "leaving the carcasses of dead horses on the common."[36]

The delegates' olfactory senses were assaulted by a powerful array of smells, particularly as the heat of the summer mounted. Philadelphians had become accustomed to the stench, but those delegates with more delicate sensibilities would have detected almost every variety of foul odor known to man. The butchers who operated in the covered market and the tanners who ran the tanyards around Second and Third streets contributed to the stink of rotting animal carcasses. The tanners threw used carcasses into the creek (actually more of a sewer) at Dock Street, which also contained the waste products of the neighboring brewing establishments and soap boilers, not to mention the constant flow of excrement seeping into the creek from the neighboring privies.[37]

The pungent atmosphere in the streets may merely have been offensive, but the sources of those smells amounted to a real danger to the public health. Frequent contamination of the water supply was a major cause of the "bloody flux," a particularly severe form of gastrointestinal ailment. More serious, the flies and insects that bred in the stagnant pools of water were sources of contagious and potentially fatal diseases. Virtually everyone visiting the city, particularly in the summertime, complained about the flies and insects, especially mosquitoes, which caused periodic yellow fever outbreaks. One prospective delegate, Erastus Wolcott, when elected by the Connecticut General Assembly to serve in the Philadelphia Convention, wrote to the governor and assembly with his regrets, stating that, since he had never had smallpox, "a Disorder to which he would be greatly exposed in the City to which he was appointed to repair, he cannot suppose it would be prudent for him to hazard his life without the most pressing necessity."[38]

Philadelphians had a prodigious capacity for alcohol, so wherever the delegates walked in Philadelphia—day or night—they encountered the city's one truly ubiquitous institution, the tavern, of which there were more than one hundred. Most were modest establishments—no more than a room with a bar and a single table at which the patrons could sit and drink from pewter cans or tankards. Most male Philadelphians began their day with a glass of beer, and they then continued to drink beer, cider, wine, and rum all the way through the day and well into the evening.[39]

Philadelphia was such a compact city that all of the delegates, whether they stayed in boardinghouses, taverns, or private homes, lived within easy walking distance of the State House. Mrs. House's was the most popular of the boardinghouses, and six of the delegates had booked lodgings there. William Pierce of Georgia and Richard Bassett of Delaware

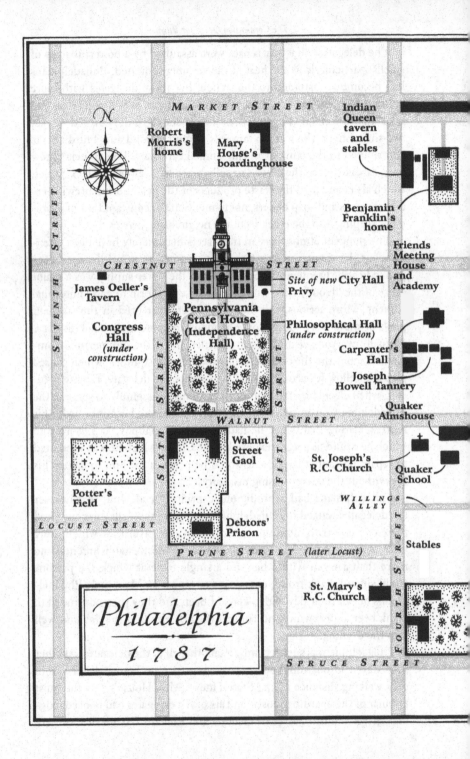

N

MARKET STREET

Robert Morris's home

Mary House's boardinghouse

Indian Queen tavern and stables

Benjamin Franklin's home

Friends Meeting House and Academy

CHESTNUT STREET

SEVENTH STREET

James Oeller's Tavern

Pennsylvania State House (Independence Hall)

Site of new City Hall
Privy

Congress Hall *(under construction)*

Philosophical Hall *(under construction)*

Carpenter's Hall

Joseph Howell Tannery

SIXTH STREET

FIFTH STREET

WALNUT STREET

Quaker Almshouse

Potter's Field

Walnut Street Gaol

St. Joseph's R.C. Church

Quaker School

WILLINGS ALLEY

LOCUST STREET

Debtors' Prison

Stables

PRUNE STREET *(later Locust)*

FOURTH STREET

St. Mary's R.C. Church

Philadelphia
— · —
1 7 8 7

SPRUCE STREET

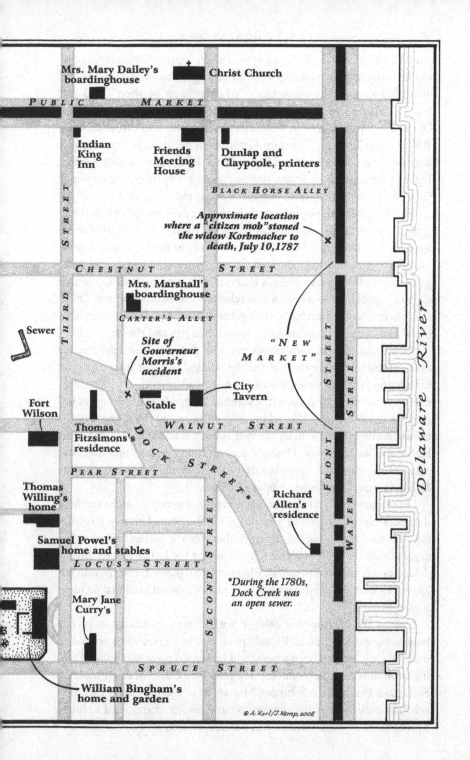

Mrs. Mary Dailey's boardinghouse

✝ Christ Church

PUBLIC MARKET

Indian King Inn

Friends Meeting House

Dunlap and Claypoole, printers

BLACK HORSE ALLEY

Approximate location where a "citizen mob" stoned the widow Korbmacher to death, July 10, 1787 →×

THIRD STREET

CHESTNUT STREET

Mrs. Marshall's boardinghouse

CARTER'S ALLEY

Sewer

Site of Gouverneur Morris's accident

"NEW MARKET"

Fort Wilson

×
Stable

City Tavern

FRONT STREET

WATER STREET

Delaware River

WALNUT STREET

Thomas Fitzsimons's residence

PEAR STREET

DOCK STREET*

Thomas Willing's home

Richard Allen's residence

Samuel Powel's home and stables

LOCUST STREET

SECOND STREET

Mary Jane Curry's

During the 1780s, Dock Creek was an open sewer.

SPRUCE STREET

William Bingham's home and garden

© A. Karl/J. Kemp, 2008

joined Virginia's George Mason at the Indian Queen. Alexander Hamilton and Massachusetts delegate Elbridge Gerry stayed at Miss Daley's boardinghouse, on the north side of Market Street between Third and Fourth streets. Two of the Connecticut delegates, Roger Sherman and Oliver Ellsworth, lodged at Mrs. Marshall's on Second Street between Walnut and Chestnut. The third Connecticut delegate, William Samuel Johnson, and Massachusetts delegate Rufus King stayed at City Tavern. Later in the summer, Johnson, worried about his finances, moved out of City Tavern to find a cheaper room at a house elsewhere in the city.[40]

The delegates also began to settle in to their daily dining rituals. They typically ate breakfast around nine o'clock in the morning. Most of them were likely to have their breakfast—usually a light meal—at their boardinghouses. While coffee and green tea were popular beverages, the delegates followed the workingmen's tradition of beginning their day with a glass of "small beer"—a beer with a relatively low alcohol content. Other than their morning beverages, they generally contented themselves with bread and butter and, occasionally, some salted fish and cheese.[41]

As was the custom throughout much of America, the delegates ate their "dinner," the big meal of the day, around three or three-thirty in the afternoon. They were invariably eager to adjourn their proceedings not long after three. Indeed, as the summer dragged on, the delegates became visibly more irritable and grouchy when one of their long-winded colleagues threatened to delay the dinner hour. Some of the larger boardinghouses, such as Mrs. House's, served dinner on the premises, but many of the delegates dined regularly at one of the city's taverns—the Indian Queen, City Tavern, Epple's, or Oeller's.

On almost every evening of the summer, a group of eight or more delegates dined together as a "club"—which denoted simply a regular but informal gathering of diners rather than a formal membership organization—usually at either City Tavern or the Indian Queen. All the delegates were invited to join in whenever they pleased, and they do not appear to have grouped themselves in any consistent sectional or ideological pattern.[42]

George Washington was deluged with dinner invitations in private homes during his time in Philadelphia, but he nevertheless tended to dine "in club" at least once a week, and he made a particular point of trying as often as possible to join the delegates for a convivial club dinner on Saturdays. On that first Saturday, May 26, he joined the club at City Tavern for a meal, and, as the summer progressed, he often joined a club at Springsbury, a country manor just outside the city.[43]

Following substantial club dinners, many delegates no doubt indulged themselves in a late afternoon nap, but others used the late afternoon and early evening hours to catch up on their correspondence or to visit with some of the principal residents of the city. Around eight or nine, most delegates enjoyed an evening "tea." This was the easiest way for many of Philadelphia's most prominent citizens to entertain the delegates, so on any given evening one could find groups of delegates scattered about the city enjoying the company of the elite of Philadelphia society.

On Sunday, May 27, General Washington chose to have a quiet day and evening. On one of only three occasions during the entire summer that he attended church, he went to a High Mass at Saint Mary's Roman Catholic Church. After attending services, he returned to the home of Robert Morris, where he spent a quiet day and evening, devoted in part to writing a long letter to his nephew, George Augustine Washington, to whom he had entrusted oversight of all of the operations of his plantation during his absence from Mount Vernon.[44]

THE RULES OF THE GAME

When the Convention resumed business at ten o'clock in the morning on Monday, May 28, nine more delegates had turned up, bringing the total number of delegates present at the Convention to thirty-eight. Oliver Ellsworth of Connecticut and James McHenry of Maryland were the first delegates from their respective states to appear, Gunning Bedford joined the Delaware delegation, and all four of the remaining Pennsylvania delegates were present. The instructions to the Massachusetts delegates from their legislature required that a majority of delegates be present in order for that state to take part in the proceedings, and come Monday, with the addition of Nathaniel Gorham and Caleb Strong, the Massachusetts delegation was ready and able to participate.[45]

The most prominent addition, though, was Dr. Franklin. The pain from his kidney stones had abated, and the onset of fair, if cool, weather made the two-block trip from his home to the State House less arduous for the aging statesman. Franklin arrived in style; he was carried to the Convention by prisoners from the jail in an ornate sedan chair he had brought home with him from Paris. With glass windows on each side, it was essentially a miniature carriage, but instead of running on wheels, it was supported by two poles, ten or twelve feet long, with just enough bend in them to ease the bumps and bounces as he was carried over

Philadelphia's cobblestone streets. The old philosopher was then helped from his chair and escorted to the Assembly Room, where he took his seat in an armchair located at the back of the room on the center aisle.[46]

All of the delegates were fully aware of his fame, but this may have been the first encounter with the legendary Dr. Franklin for at least some of them. As Georgia's William Pierce observed, "Dr. Franklin is well known to be the greatest philosopher of the present age; all the operations of nature he seems to understand,—the very heavens obey him, and the Clouds yield up their Lightning to be imprisoned in his rod." But the spectacular nature of his arrival must have reinforced their impression of the singular character of the great man. Franklin was surely cosmopolitan, but at the same time he was plainly dressed and genuinely humble as he greeted his fellow delegates. Everyone in the room could feel the presence of greatness.[47]

The seating pattern within the Assembly Room thus began to take shape. Although there was certainly some informality and fluidity in the seating arrangements, for the most part delegates from each state sat clustered together, arranging themselves in a circular pattern, with those from the Southern states sitting on the south side of the room, the delegates from the Mid-Atlantic states arranging themselves around the semicircle on the west side of the room, and the Northern delegates on the north side of the room.[48]

The chamber was large enough to accommodate all twelve state delegations, but with very little room to spare. The tables were bunched closely together, and the simple wooden Windsor chairs behind each table needed to be pushed together in a tight cluster in order for the occupant of a chair to have even a small space at the table for himself. It would be difficult that summer for any group of delegates to have a quiet conversation without being overheard by the others or, indeed, for even a grimace or meaningful glance from a delegate to go undetected. In such a situation, the practice of mutual respect was not only desirable, but, perhaps, a virtual necessity.

For the next day and a half, instead of taking up the challenge that Delaware's demand for equality of representation had posed to their plan for the new government, the Virginia and Pennsylvania delegates kept their peace while the Convention received, and then debated, the report prepared by the committee created the previous Friday to draw up the rules for the Convention's proceedings. The committee's chair, George Wythe, had been trained in law, and, in an age when most lawyers gained

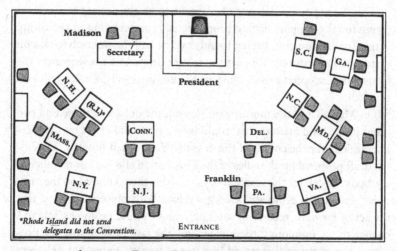

ASSEMBLY ROOM, PENNSYLVANIA STATE HOUSE
Seating Chart of State Delegations
(*The arrangement of chairs around the tables almost certainly
varied according to the delegates' shifting patterns of attendance.*)

admission to the bar after only a scant legal apprenticeship, the Virginia jurist could claim a deep and thorough understanding of his profession. Unlike John Dickinson and James Wilson, who acquired at least a portion of their impressive educations in Great Britain, Wythe's legal wisdom was entirely homegrown. Like his most famous law student, Thomas Jefferson, Wythe was neither a forceful nor a dynamic public speaker, but the weight of his intelligence—combined with a sense of righteousness owing at least in part to his Quaker upbringing—made him a forceful presence in any gathering. Portraits and descriptions of him suggest a man of considerable elegance, with a high forehead, long, silvery hair, piercing eyes, and a sharp, long nose that, in the words of historian Catherine Drinker Bowen, called to mind "a sinewy old eagle."[49]

The Rules Committee had met briefly over the weekend to formulate its recommendations. The committee's report reflected the values of an age far removed from our own intensely partisan, and frequently uncivil, political realm. As inheritors of a classical republican tradition, the delegates were deeply committed to retaining decorum in their proceedings and enforcing a code of gentlemanly respect. The rules stipulated, for example, that "a member may be called to order by any other member, as well as by the President; and may be allowed to explain his conduct or expressions supposed to be reprehensible."[50]

The Pennsylvania delegates had spent some time over the weekend trying to rally support behind proportional representation in the voting at the Convention, but, having found that few had the stomach to take on that issue immediately, they let the matter drop. As a consequence, the Convention adopted a rule giving each state equal weight in its deliberations.

On May 28 and the morning of May 29, the delegates agreed on two other procedural matters that would have a profound effect on their deliberations over the course of the next three and a half months. The initial draft proposal for the rules of the Convention allowed any member of the body "to call for the yeas and nays and have them entered on the minutes," but Rufus King and George Mason both objected, noting that the act of formally recording votes on issues "would be an obstacle to a change of . . . opinions," thereby making the task of achieving the necessary compromises that would lead to a consensus among the delegates more difficult. Later in the day, North Carolina's Richard Dobbs Spaight went even further, suggesting that any member of the Convention be allowed to request reconsideration of any motion previously discussed and voted upon. Spaight's suggestion, adopted as a formal motion the following morning, proved to have far-reaching consequences. It would enable the Convention to function not like a legislative body, with strict rules for the recording of votes and the bringing of business to the floor, but rather as an informal "committee of the whole." The parliamentary device of the committee of the whole, though not formally written into the Convention rules, had ample precedent in English and American legislative bodies. When the delegates chose to form themselves into a committee of the whole they were free to debate and vote on a wide range of issues in much the way that a committee would, with the outcome of any votes being considered merely as recommendations, and not formal decisions by the Convention. This strategy gave the delegates the opportunity to take "straw votes"—to measure the relative strength of opposing opinions on particularly contentious issues and, when appropriate, to change their minds as they groped their way toward compromise and consensus.[51]

That decision slowed the progress of the Convention at some points, but it also increased the feeling of collegiality among delegates. It allowed delegates, even when they disagreed with one another, to revisit issues that were particularly important to them. It was clear from the outset that any successful effort to amend the Articles of Confederation would not be achieved by a mere majority of the states. Something approaching unanimity, or at least a solid consensus, would be necessary if a new and stronger union were to be achieved.

The delegates added one other important stipulation to the Convention's rules. In order to protect the Convention from "licentious publication of their proceedings," Pierce Butler of South Carolina proposed that a strict rule of secrecy be observed throughout the Convention, with "nothing spoken in the house [to] be printed, or otherwise published or communicated without leave." Years later, James Madison contended that "no Constitution would ever have been adopted by the convention if the debates had been public."

One uncomfortable consequence of this decision was that the Convention would proceed throughout that Philadelphia summer—with an average daytime temperature in July and August hovering in the eighties and low nineties and the intense humidity for which Philadelphia is still famous—with its doors closed and, much of the time, its windows shut. In the first month of the Convention, the weather was cooler and wetter than usual, but by mid-July the heat and humidity arrived with a vengeance.[52]

The delegates would adhere scrupulously to the rule of secrecy. Barely a word of their deliberations, debates, or decisions leaked out of the Convention over the course of the summer. There were a few minor exceptions. Rufus King, for one, wrote several letters to his Massachusetts political confidants Nathan Dane and Henry Knox describing the general tone and tenor of the debate, but Dane and Knox for their part do not appear to have betrayed King's confidences to anyone else.[53]

The rule of secrecy, however alien to our twenty-first-century values, helped make the Constitutional Convention of 1787 an agency of deliberation rather than partisan debate. It allowed the delegates to take risks in debate, float only partially developed ideas, or disagree vehemently, but ultimately reconcile their views. As George Mason put it, the rule of secrecy was "a necessary precaution to prevent misrepresentations or mistakes; there being a material difference between the appearance of a subject in its first crude and undigested shape, and after it shall have been properly matured and arranged." All of this, in combination with the decision of the Convention not to take formal votes and instead to function as an informal committee of the whole, proved vitally important to the task of consensus building that was essential to the Convention's success.[54]

Not everyone was happy with the secrecy rule, however. When news that the Convention was operating in secret reached Thomas Jefferson in Paris, he lamented to his colleague John Adams that the delegates "began their deliberations by so abominable a precedent as that of tying up the tongues of their members. Nothing can justify this example but the innocence of their intentions, & ignorance of the value of public discussions." Jefferson was being true to the belief in the value of free debate and discussion that had guided him through his career. And he articulated that belief most forcefully in his preamble to the Virginia Statute of Religious Liberty, written in October of 1785. Jefferson wrote,

> Truth is great and will prevail if left to herself, that she is the proper and sufficient antagonist to error, and has nothing to fear from the conflict, unless by human interposition disarmed of her natural weapons, free argument and debate, errors ceasing to be dangerous when it is permitted freely to contradict them.

Jefferson surely had the best of the argument based on the principles of liberal democracy (which the American nation would eventually come to embrace), but for the moment discretion would triumph over free public argument and debate.[55]

The rule of secrecy, a blessing for the participants in the Convention, has been a curse ever since for those seeking to understand what took place in the Pennsylvania State House that summer. The Convention's secretary, William Jackson, did a miserable job of keeping track of the proceedings, doing little more than recording the outcome of the straw votes in the Convention. Several delegates—including Robert Yates of New York, Rufus King of Massachusetts, and James McHenry of Maryland—either kept very sketchy journals or made occasional comments on the proceedings in their correspondence, but their accounts amount to little more than fragments. Charles Pinckney had proposed that a committee be appointed to "superintend the Minutes," but the delegates rejected his proposal on the grounds that "a committee might have an interest & bias in moulding the entry according to their opinions and wishes."[56]

In the absence of an officially sanctioned effort at recording the debates in the Convention, and therefore unconstrained by an obligation to represent any opinion other than his own in deciding what was and was not recorded, one man stepped forward to undertake the task of keeping a full account of the Convention's proceedings. Although James Madison had no way of knowing the full extent of William Jackson's inadequacies as secretary, he was determined to preserve a record of the Convention that went beyond the bare-bones structure of a Convention journal. In the same spirit of studious determination with which he had prepared for the task attending the Convention, Madison decided that he would preserve for posterity the proceedings that were about to unfold. Describing his motives more than forty years later, Madison recalled that in trying to satisfy his own curiosity about "the History of the most distinguished Confederacies," he had been frustrated by "the deficiency" of materials relating to "the process, the principles, the reasons, & the anticipations, which prevailed in the formation of them." It was that frustration, he recalled, which "determined me to preserve as far as I could an exact account of what might pass in the Convention."[57]

Accordingly, on the opening day of the Convention, Madison chose a seat next to William Jackson in the front of the room. "In this favourable position for hearing all that passed, I noted to myself . . . what was read from the Chair or spoken by the members; and losing not a moment unnecessarily between the adjournment and reassembling of the Convention, I was enabled to write out my daily notes." Diligent student that he was, Madison did not miss a single day of the Convention nor, indeed, "more than a casual fraction of an hour in any day." Madison wanted to be confident that he would capture a complete record of the proceedings. As we will see when we take a close look at the next piece of business to come before the Convention, Madison's diligence was in some measure self-serving. The story of the proceedings that we glean from his notes must, therefore, be viewed with a critical eye.[58]

CHAPTER FIVE

A HIGH-STAKES GAMBLE

THE VIRGINIA PLAN

On the morning of May 29, as Edmund Randolph took his seat at the Virginia delegates' table, located in the back of the room right next to that of the Pennsylvania delegation, he was acutely aware of the weight of responsibility that had been thrust upon him. After the delegates had dispensed with a few procedural details, George Washington, fully prepared for what would happen next, called upon his young Virginia colleague. Randolph rose to "open the main business" of the Convention. He and his co-conspirators from Virginia and Pennsylvania were well aware they were undertaking a high-stakes gamble. Randolph began cautiously, praising the authors of the Articles of Confederation, many of whom were gathered in the Assembly Room around him, for "having done all that patriots could do, in the then infancy of the science, of constitutions and of confederacies." But the dependent clause of that same sentence suggested less caution to come. At the time the Articles of Confederation had been created,

> inefficiency of requisitions was unknown—no commercial
> discord had arisen among any states—no rebellion had
> appeared as in Massachusetts—foreign debts had not
> become urgent—the havoc of paper money had not been
> foreseen—treaties had not been violated—and perhaps

nothing better could be obtained from the jealousy of the states with regard for their sovereignty.[1]

Randolph then moved on to offer his "remedy" for those defects, the basis of which, he assured the delegates, "must be republican in principle." In his notes on the debates that day, James Madison modestly referred to the plan Randolph was about to present as the Randolph Resolutions, but as the summer progressed, the delegates began to call it the Virginia Plan. The plan was largely Madison's handiwork, although Madison himself insisted that it was the result of a "consultation among the deputies," by which he meant the collection of Virginians and Pennsylvanians who had gathered in Philadelphia before the Convention.

It was no accident that Randolph—and not Madison—presented the plan. Randolph was the governor of the most populous and powerful state in the confederated union, and he came from its most politically powerful family. Indeed, his was the most politically powerful family in perhaps all of America. His father, John Randolph, his uncle, Peyton Randolph, and his grandfather, Sir John Randolph, had been among the handful of Virginians who had guided the affairs of their colony in the years before the

Virginia's Governor Edmund Randolph introduced the Virginia Plan on May 29. The portrait, printed by Constantino Brumidi, unknown date, is from a mural hanging in the rotunda of the United States Capitol. Courtesy of the Library of Congress.

Revolution. Edmund, who had distinguished himself as one of General Washington's aides-de-camp during the Revolution, showed every sign of achieving at least equal fame. Moreover, standing only a few inches shorter than his commander in chief and with a forceful but easy manner of speaking, he possessed nearly all of the physical presence and oratorical ability that Madison lacked.[2]

The opening lines of the Virginia Plan, as presented by Randolph that day, did not immediately reveal its revolutionary character. It resolved only "that the Articles of Confederation ought to be . . . corrected and enlarged." But as Randolph delivered his speech, which took up the better part of the remainder of that day's session, the delegates began to realize that he was proposing to scrap the Articles altogether for a truly "national" government. Not everyone was surprised, for as George Mason noted in a letter to his son before the Convention got under way, many of the delegates from the "principal states" (by which he meant the delegates from Virginia, Pennsylvania, and, possibly, South Carolina) favored a "total alteration of the federal system." But those delegates present who were not representing "principal states"—men like William Paterson of New Jersey or Gunning Bedford of Delaware—may well have gasped in disbelief at the audacity of Randolph's statement of intent.

Randolph then proceeded to enumerate the specifics of his proposal. Among its most radical features was the creation of a new national legislature, or Congress. Representation in Congress would not be distributed equally among the states, as it had been in the Continental Congress, but rather it would be apportioned according either to "quotas of contribution" or "the number of free inhabitants" of a given state. This new Congress would possess the power to "legislate in all cases to which the separate States are incompetent," as well as the ability to veto any law passed by a state that the national legislature considered contrary to the interests of the country as a whole.[3]

These three proposals, out of a total of fifteen, amounted to an entirely new conception of the fledgling American government, a revolutionary step that would render the governments of the individual states distinctly inferior to that of a new "national" government. The delegates from Virginia and Pennsylvania who had drafted the plan risked drawing fire from two different sources—delegates from the less populous states who would seek to protect their right to equal weight in the National Legislature, and those from a variety of states who only eleven years after declaring their independence from Britain were wary of ceding too much power to any central government.

As Randolph spoke, William Paterson, sitting at the New Jersey table at the back of the room, scrawled animatedly in his notes six words that would sum up one of the key points of contention: "objn:—sovereignty is an integral thing." He recognized quite clearly that the intent of the Randolph Resolutions was to undermine the sovereign power of the states, and he didn't like it one bit. Robert Yates of New York was another delegate clearly shocked by the substance of what he unhappily described as Randolph's "long and elaborate speech." New York at the time had a population of 340,000—making it the fifth most populous state in the union—and therefore had little to fear from a system of proportional representation. Nonetheless, Yates was appalled by Randolph's proposals. Though he, like William Paterson, remained silent while Randolph spoke, his notes on the speech sizzle with indignation. Randolph, he scribbled, had no intention of creating a "federal" government, but, rather, "a strong *consolidated* union in which the idea of states should be nearly annihilated."[4]

Several of the resolutions presented by Randolph sought to redefine the relationship between the legislature, the states, and the people of the country at large. The single-house legislature of the Confederation government, whose representatives were elected by and answerable to their state legislatures, was clearly intended to be a creature of those state legislatures. The national legislature proposed in the Virginia Plan was to have two branches, whose members would have very different relationships both to their state governments and to the people they were supposed to serve. The people would directly elect representatives in the first branch, while those in the upper house were to be elected by those of the lower house from a pool of candidates supplied by each of the state legislatures.

The concept of bicameralism—a government with a two-house legislature—was nothing new. The English Parliament had an "upper" and a "lower" chapter—an elected House of Commons and a hereditary House of Lords. The Virginia Plan rejected the English notion of a hereditary upper chamber but nevertheless reflected a continuing belief in the traditional English idea of rule by the virtuous few. In defending his proposals, Randolph stated that many of the problems afflicting the governments of the individual states arose "from the democratic parts of our constitutions." By giving too much power to the lower houses of assembly, the state constitutions, he believed, had failed to provide "sufficient checks against democracy," and he hoped the creation of a strong Senate, elected by members of the House of Representatives, would pro-

duce an upper house composed of the country's most able and thoughtful citizens—people who would serve as a brake on the whims of the
populace. At the same time, by stipulating that representation in both
houses be apportioned according to population, the authors of the
Virginia Plan were stating their emphatic intention that this new
government—even if some of its officials were only to be elected indirectly—was to represent the people of the nation at large, not the states
as separate and sovereign entities.[5]

Randolph then went on to sketch out the components of the "national
executive" in the seventh resolution of the Virginia Plan. This resolution
stipulated that the chief executive would be indirectly elected by the national legislature, a provision similarly shaped by the Virginians' and
Pennsylvanians' concerns about an excess of democracy. The resolution
left open the question of whether the national executive would be a single person or a group of people. James Madison admitted that his thinking about the character of the executive branch had not fully gelled
before the Convention got under way, and the seventh resolution, as presented by Randolph, was sharply at odds with two central ideas that
would eventually emerge as defining characteristics of American government: democracy and separation of powers. Not only was the selection of
the executive one step removed from the people at large, but, in proposing that the Congress be given the power to select the executive, the Virginia Plan would have made the president excessively dependent on the
Congress. Over the course of the long summer to come, the delegates
would tie themselves into knots trying to find a means by which to assure
that only wise and knowledgeable people would participate in the selection of the executive, while at the same time guaranteeing the executive
some measure of independence from Congress.[6]

The eighth resolution of the Virginia Plan also reflected some of the
uncertainty of its authors about the relationship of the various branches
of the government to one another. It called for the creation of a so-called
council of revision, to be composed of the chief executive and a "convenient number of the national judiciary." The proposal for a council of revision was one of Madison's pet ideas. As he conceived it, the council
would have the authority to "examine" every act passed either by Congress or by any of the state legislatures. It would possess a form of constitutional veto over legislation emanating from any of those bodies.
Beyond its role in the council of revision, the judiciary's place in the proposed system was left vague.[7]

Randolph continued his presentation of the remainder of the fifteen resolutions of the Virginia Plan well into the afternoon, concluding with one that provided that the proposed "amendments," once approved by the Convention, "ought at a proper time . . . to be submitted to an assembly or assemblies of Representatives . . . to be expressly chosen by the people, to consider and decide thereon." In his final words that day, Randolph exhorted his fellow delegates "not to suffer the present opportunity of establishing the general peace, harmony, happiness, and liberty in the United States to pass away unimproved."[8]

Many of the delegates were stunned by the revolutionary character of the proposal so boldly laid before them. They had come to Philadelphia to revise the Articles of Confederation and were now being asked to create an entirely new kind of government. The Articles of Confederation had created a "federal" government, in the common understanding of that word. The resolutions presented by Randolph repeatedly used the word "national" rather than "federal" to describe the various branches of the proposed government, and their insistence that the powers of this government were superior to those of the states left no doubt of their intention.

THE RULE OF SECRECY in the Convention operated powerfully to the advantage of those advocating the Virginia Plan, for if news of the plan had gone beyond the Convention walls, there would have been howls of protest from a host of prominent Americans not present in Philadelphia. Thomas Jefferson, in Paris, was far less concerned about threats to public security by democratic majorities in the individual states than his friend James Madison. Sam Adams of Massachusetts, a strong proponent of state sovereignty, was lukewarm at best about the idea of a constitutional convention and had not been elected as a delegate to Philadelphia. Adams's populist leanings and pride in his ability to keep the Massachusetts government operating smoothly without interference from an overbearing central government almost certainly would have made him skeptical of many of the details of the Virginia Plan—had he known about them.

Patrick Henry, the firebrand of the Revolution in Virginia, would have been absolutely aghast at the events of May 29. Henry, more than any Virginian—including Jefferson or even Washington—was revered in his home state as the man who had led his colony to revolt against the overly centralized, overly distant government of England. Virginia's first elected governor, he had served three consecutive terms, the maximum allowed. The state's constitution stipulated that a period of four years had to elapse before a governor could serve again, and in 1784, after the four-year interval had passed, Henry was again elected to the governorship. Henry took pride both in his home state's political stability and in the economic recovery that took place there in the aftermath of the war. When the Virginia legislature had balloted for delegates to the proposed Convention in Philadelphia, Henry received more votes than any Virginian other than Washington. But he declined to attend. Henry is said to have refused to go because he "smelt a rat." In other words, he believed the Convention might propose measures harmful to the independence of the states and the liberty of the people. However, there is no convincing evidence that he ever used that phrase and, indeed, if Henry was suspicious of any mischief that might arise from the proceedings, the very best thing he could have done would have been to attend. The real problem, more likely, was that Henry didn't sufficiently smell that rat. Instead, having just retired as governor of Virginia, he was probably more concerned with personal and local matters than with continental ones.[9]

Had the Convention rules not dictated absolute secrecy about the proceedings, and had Patrick Henry been made aware of the dramatic changes proposed on May 29, he would have mounted his horse, ridden to Philadelphia, and voiced his vehement opposition to this dangerous attempt to undermine the single greatest achievement of the Revolution. As one of America's most effective spokesmen for the continuing sovereignty of the states, Henry would have been James Madison's worst nightmare.[10]

The delegates had listened to Randolph's presentation all through the morning and well into the afternoon. And they clearly needed a respite—some time to absorb the implications of the momentous proposition Randolph had placed before them. Accordingly, they agreed to adjourn for the day and to reconvene the next morning "to consider the State of the American Union." Before the delegates exited from the East Room, however, Charles Pinckney of South Carolina insisted on presenting an alternative plan of government to the Convention, asking that the delegates consider his plan, along with the Virginia Plan, when they discussed the state of the American Union the following day. The fate of Pinckney's plan remains one of the great mysteries of the Constitutional Convention of 1787.

THE "OTHER" PLAN

While James Madison's notes on Randolph's speech and on the details of the Virginia Plan are voluminous, his notes on Pinckney's proposal are surprisingly brief.

> Mr Charles Pinckney laid before the house the draught of a federal government which he had prepared to be agreed upon between the free and independent States of America. Ordered that the same be referred to the Committee of the Whole appointed to consider the state of the American Union. Adjourned.

If we were to rely solely on Madison, there would be little else to say about Pinckney's plan. But there is reason to believe that Madison, impelled by motives about which we can only speculate, was less than evenhanded in his reportage of the contributions of his South Carolina colleague to the making of the United States Constitution.[11]

Historians have not presented Charles Pinckney's claims to authorship of the Constitution in a favorable light. James Madison's biographer, Irving Brant, called him a "sponger and a plagiarist." Catherine Drinker Bowen, in her account of the Constitutional Convention, derided Pinckney's "extravagant claims" to authorship of the Constitution, and constitutional scholar Forrest McDonald has described Pinckney's subsequent desire for credit as the Constitution's author as nothing short of "pathetic." Some of Pinckney's contemporaries would not have disputed those descriptions. James Madison, late in his life, described Pinckney's claims to importance in the framing of the Constitution as essentially a figment of the South Carolinian's imagination. Even some of Pinckney's South Carolina political colleagues, familiar with the size of his ego, were disinclined to exalt his role in the Convention.

Born in 1757, Charles Pinckney was the fourth and eldest surviving son of a prominent lawyer and planter from a wealthy and well-connected South Carolina family. But at the outbreak of the Revolution, he faced challenges different from those of many of his planter-aristocracy predecessors. His father was slow to embrace the cause of independence and at one point had at least a portion of his estate confiscated. Charles had planned to study law at the Middle Temple in London, but the war, and

Author of the "Pinckney Plan" for a new constitution. Portrait of
Charles Pinckney, courtesy of New York Public Library.

perhaps his family's straitened circumstances, forced him to make do with
a legal education in the more provincial confines of Charleston. He began
service in the Revolutionary War in 1779 as a lieutenant in the Charleston
regiment of the militia, but he was soon captured in the siege of Savannah
and held prisoner by the British. Released in June 1781, Pinckney began
to build his law and political career. He had been elected to the South
Carolina legislature shortly before his capture by the British, and in November 1784 he was elected a delegate to the Continental Congress. He
served in that body continuously until just a few months before the meeting of the Constitutional Convention. As he journeyed to Philadelphia to
attend the Constitutional Convention, Pinckney, at the age of twenty-
nine, had good reason to be proud of his achievements within South Carolina and in the continental government.[12]

But Pinckney had one significant weakness, perhaps best evidenced in
an episode revealed soon after the Convention concluded its business.
William Pierce, in his character sketches of the delegates, mistakenly
recorded Pinckney's age as twenty-four, which would have made the
South Carolinian two years younger than Jonathan Dayton of New Jer-

sey, who, at age twenty-six, was the Convention's youngest delegate. Not only did Pinckney do nothing to correct the error, but in subsequent years he compounded it, going to great lengths to express "the deep diffidence and solemnity which he felt, being the youngest member of that body." Pinckney, in short, lied about his age. The same tendency toward vanity, many concluded, was also behind his spurious claim to have been the primary author of the United States Constitution.[13]

But was Pinckney's claim really spurious? He had been an early critic of the Articles of Confederation and in early 1786 had begun work on an alternative plan of government. He was among the first in the Continental Congress to call for a "general convention" to consider remedies for what he called the "weakness and inefficacy" of the Confederation government. His objections, openly expressed at the time, were essentially identical to those "defects" enumerated by Edmund Randolph when he presented the Virginia Plan. On May 3, 1786, Pinckney repeated his request for a general convention, this time proposing that a Grand Committee of the Congress review the state of the union. It took the Congress another two months to appoint the committee, but when it finally convened, Pinckney was elected the chair of a subcommittee that proposed seven important changes in the structure of the Confederation government, among them proposals to strengthen its powers over taxation and the regulation of commerce, both of which would be central features of the document that would emerge from the Philadelphia Convention. Sometime between his departure from Congress and his arrival in Philadelphia for the Convention, Pinckney had laid out his thoughts on the form of a new government in much greater detail.[14]

We have no evidence to indicate Pinckney ever shared his plan with the Virginia or the Pennsylvania delegates in advance of the Convention. It would be puzzling if he had not done so since he had taken up residence in Philadelphia on May 17, and he certainly could have joined the informal discussions among the Virginians and Pennsylvanians at the State House and the Indian Queen in the days before the Convention got under way. Moreover, he was living in the same boardinghouse as Madison and Edmund Randolph and, according to later testimony from Madison, took part in informal conversations about the upcoming convention there. Since Mary House served both breakfast and dinner at her establishment, it is hard to imagine that the three men never had an exchange of views on the important subject before them.[15]

Pinckney likely circulated his document to at least a few delegates.

George Read, also living at Mary House's, confided to his Delaware colleague John Dickinson as early as May 21—four days before the Convention opened—that he was "in possession of a copied draft of a federal
system intended to be proposed." The copy in Read's possession was
very different in format from either the Virginia Plan or the final draft of
the Constitution, and, judging from its similarity to Pinckney's subsequent descriptions of his plan, it was almost certainly a version of Pinckney's draft. It proposed a government with a bicameral legislature, a
single executive, and a supreme judiciary. Like the Virginia Plan, it called
for a significant strengthening of the national legislature, including the
power to levy imposts, regulate interstate commerce, enforce the collection of revenue from the states, and veto state laws that conflicted with
those of the national legislature.[16]

   In addition to preparing his plan for presentation to the Convention,
Pinckney composed a speech he hoped to deliver to the Convention to
accompany the presentation of his plan. Madison, who claimed never
to have missed more than a few minutes of the Convention's proceedings, failed to include any mention of Pinckney's speech in his notes,
and it is entirely possible, given the lateness of the hour, that Pinckney
never delivered the speech on May 29. Shortly after the Convention
adjourned on September 17, Pinckney published his speech under the
title "Observations on the Plan of Government Submitted to the Federal Convention In Philadelphia on the 28th of May, 1787, by Mr.
Charles Pinckney." We do not know what, if any, changes Pinckney
made in the speech between the time he intended to deliver it in May
and its publication after the Convention had adjourned, but if the substance of it was written in May and not September, then it is notable in
at least two respects. First, Pinckney was in substantial agreement with
the Virginians and the Pennsylvanians that the Articles of Confederation were fundamentally defective and in need of complete overhaul.
And he was far less restrained in his chronicle of the weaknesses of the
Confederation than was Edmund Randolph in his speech introducing
the Virginia Plan. He averred that

> our government is despised—our laws are robbed of their
> respected terrors—their inaction is a subject of ridicule—
> and their exertion, of abhorrence and opposition—rank
> and office have lost their reverence and effect—our foreign
> politics are as much deranged, as our domestic economy—

our friends are slackened in their affection—and our citizens loosened from their obedience. We know neither how to yield or how to enforce—hardly anything abroad or at home is sound and entire—disconnection and confusion in offices, in States and in parties, prevail throughout every part of the Union. These are facts, universally admitted and lamented.[17]

Pinckney's lack of restraint in his denunciation of the weaknesses of the Articles of Confederation and the absence of any reference of respect for the wisdom of the men who helped frame that government certainly would not have pleased those delegates who were already upset by Edmund Randolph's understated and respectful, if equally critical, assessment of government under the Articles. And Pinckney's proposed remedies would likely have stoked the fears of those who still wished to preserve state sovereignty. Pinckney was emphatic that a new federal government recognize the principle that "each State ought to have a weight in proportion to its importance." Indeed, he argued that the status quo offended the very principle for which Americans fought in their struggle for independence against Great Britain. "The assigning to each State its due importance," he wrote, would remedy three of the principal defects of the Articles of Confederation. The first, he argued, was "the inequality of Representation"; the second was "the alteration of the mode of doing business in Congress; that is voting individually, and not by States"; and the third was "that it would be the means of inducing the States to keep up their delegations by punctual and respectable appointments."[18]

Unfortunately, we will never know precisely which plan Pinckney presented to the Convention that day. The Convention's secretary, William Jackson, failed to keep a copy of the proposal that Pinckney submitted on May 29. When John Quincy Adams set about the task of publishing the Journal of the Convention in 1818 he wrote to Pinckney, then sixty-one years old and thirty-two years removed from the event, to see if he could obtain a copy from him; Pinckney examined all of the various notes and papers he had relating to the Convention and wrote back to Adams saying that he had "several rough draughts of the Constitution I proposed & that they are all substantially the same differing only in words & the arrangement of the Articles." He then sent to Adams "the one I believe was it."[19]

This last statement was simply untrue, for there are aspects of the plan that Pinckney sent to Adams that contradict statements he made during the course of the Convention. Some twelve years later, when James Madison began preparing his own notes of the Convention for publication, he was incensed that Pinckney had, in his view willfully, sent Adams a draft of a proposal for the Constitution that would have the effect of magnifying Pinckney's contribution to the final document.[20]

When historian Jared Sparks began compiling his history of the Constitutional Convention in the early 1830s, Madison spared no effort to persuade Sparks that Pinckney had vastly overstated his contribution. Sparks had begun his history believing that Pinckney's draft of a proposed constitution was of central importance to the subsequent proceedings, but Madison managed to persuade Sparks that Pinckney had fabricated the draft he sent to Adams in order to claim primary authorship of the Constitution. Sparks's view, which was endorsed and embellished by Madison's admirers and biographers, became the common currency. And for much of America's history, Pinckney has remained a minor footnote—indeed, an egotistical, self-aggrandizing minor footnote—to the story of the making of the Constitution.[21]

In fact, Pinckney's claims to making an important, if not *the* most important, contribution to the Constitution are far stronger than Madison was willing to admit. As historians and political scientists have analyzed the various Pinckney drafts of the Constitution, they have concluded that while the South Carolinian may have exaggerated his claim to authorship, his proposals to the Convention did constitute "a noteworthy contribution to the Constitution."[22]

It is one of the remarkable facts of history—and of historical reporting—that our record of the origins and original meanings of our nation's most revered document is so overwhelmingly dependent on the diligence, and the honor, of just one man. Much of that record was compiled contemporaneously, but it is equally clear that much of it was organized, edited, and perhaps even rewritten by Madison when he was an eighty-one-year-old veteran of more than forty years of political warfare over the nature and meaning of "his" Constitution. His many letters to friends and colleagues, and in particular to Jared Sparks during the period 1830–31, reveal how deeply engrossed Madison was in preparing— one might say constructing—his history of the Convention. Perhaps, just perhaps, Madison's diligence may have exceeded his honor as he engaged in this task.

THE CONSTITUTIONAL REVOLUTION MOVES FORWARD

Just before the delegates adjourned on the afternoon of May 29, they agreed to constitute themselves as an informal Committee of the Whole the following day to discuss both the Virginia and Pinckney plans. The decision to use the parliamentary device of the Committee of the Whole had been made possible by the Convention's adoption early on May 29 of Richard Dobbs Spaight's proposal that any member of the Convention could request reconsideration of any motion previously discussed and voted upon. As events would show, this would prove to reduce the risk of a fatal rupture in the harmony of the Convention early in the game, for it would allow those delegates who had grave misgivings about the plans presented by Randolph and Pinckney to feel some assurance that they would have ample opportunity to voice their objections and to offer alternative proposals.

From May 30 through June 13, General Washington would call the Convention to order, but he would then relinquish the chair to Nathaniel Gorham of Massachusetts, whom the delegates had elected to serve as chair of the Committee of the Whole. Gorham was a good and obvious choice. He had just completed a term as presiding officer of the Confederation Congress, and therefore he had ample experience in mediating among the interests of contending state delegations. The Virginians and Pennsylvanians may also have supported him in the hope of gaining support from his region of the country for their proposals.[23]

When the delegates reconvened at ten o'clock on the morning of May 30, the Virginians and Pennsylvanians made certain that it would be Randolph's resolutions, and not Pinckney's, that would form the main topic of business. Whether by personal preference or prearrangement, Gorham allowed the authors and principal advocates of the Virginia Plan to speak first. Gouverneur Morris did not hesitate to push forward aggressively. He suggested that before discussing the specifics of the resolutions presented by Randolph the previous day, the delegates endorse three general propositions that embodied the principles on which the Virginia Plan was based. The first of those propositions stated that a "Union of the States merely federal" was insufficient to accomplish the aims for which the Articles of Confederation were originally created, "namely, common defence, security of liberty, and general welfare." The second proposition stipulated that "no treaty or treaties among the whole

Nathaniel Gorham ably chaired the Committee of the Whole for much of the first half of the Convention. Portrait by Charles Willson Peale, circa 1793–94, courtesy of Museum of Fine Arts, Boston.

or part of the States, as individual Sovereignties, would be sufficient." The meaning of that language, though convoluted, was nevertheless clear to all of the delegates: The Articles of Confederation amounted to nothing more than a treaty among individual, sovereign states, and any such treaty, so long as the states retained their sovereignty, could never be the basis for a proper and durable union. The third proposition was wholly unambiguous. It stated "that a national government ought to be established consisting of a supreme Legislative, Executive and Judiciary."[24]

There it was—the first explicit proposal to scrap the Articles of Confederation and substitute in its place a supreme national government. The strategy of the Virginia Plan's advocates was to get the delegates to accept the basic principle of a "supreme national government" before getting bogged down in the details of the plan itself.

Perhaps unsurprisingly, it was none other than Charles Pinckney who was the first to rise and offer his opinions on the first two of Randolph's and Morris's revolutionary proposals. Was their intent, he asked, to "abolish the state governments altogether?" If that was the case, Pinckney observed, then "their business was at an end," for the charge given to the Convention by the Continental Congress had been to offer amendments to the Articles of Confederation; it had not authorized "a discussion of a System founded on different principles." According to Robert Yates (although not Madison, who once again omitted most of the details of Pinckney's speech), Pinckney's "argument had its weight," and, as a consequence, the delegates agreed to drop discussion of the first and second propositions and move on to discuss the third.[25]

The key words in that third proposition—"that a national government ought to be established consisting of a supreme Legislative, Executive and Judiciary"—were "national" and "supreme," and several of the delegates wished clarification of their meaning. Charles Pinckney again asked whether giving the central government supreme power would amount to the annihilation of the state governments. His second cousin, General Charles Cotesworth Pinckney, and Elbridge Gerry of Massachusetts expressed the same fear. Gouverneur Morris, who likely persuaded Madison and Randolph to lead with such an explicit rejection of the principles underlying the Articles of Confederation, did not pull any punches in his response. A "federal" government, he explained, was nothing more than a "mere compact resting on the good faith of the parties," whereas a supreme, national government, would possess "a compleat and compulsive" power. "In all communities," he contended, "there must be one supreme power and one only." It was essential to locate sovereign power in the national and not the state governments if America was to be a nation worthy of the name.[26]

A few in the Convention—Roger Sherman, just taking his seat that morning as a delegate from Connecticut, Robert Yates of New York, General Pinckney, and George Read of Delaware—thought this was going too far too fast. Read and Pinckney moved to postpone discussion of the third proposition and asked that the delegates take up a significantly weaker version acknowledging that "a more effective Government consisting of a Legislative, Executive and Judiciary ought to be established." Their amended version was put to a vote, and four state delegations, Massachusetts, Connecticut, Delaware, and South Carolina, voted in favor; and the other four present, New York, Pennsylvania, Virginia, and North Carolina, opposed. South Carolina's Pierce Butler then called for a vote on the original wording of Gouverneur Morris's third proposition: "that a national government ought to be established consisting of a supreme Legislative, Executive, and Judiciary." Apparently, many of those who had voted in favor of Read and General Pinckney's milder resolution decided that, whatever their misgivings about the word "supreme," they would rather support Morris's emphatic assertion of national power than sit idly by and do nothing to strengthen the government. Convention secretary William Jackson polled each of the state delegations. Massachusetts, Pennsylvania, Delaware, Virginia, North Carolina, and South Carolina voted in favor; Connecticut was the lone state to vote no; and, the New York delegation, still consisting only of the strong nationalist Alexander Hamilton and the contrary-minded Robert Yates, was divided.[27]

And thus on the third full day of business, the Convention rejected the principle of federalism on which the American republic had been founded and endorsed in its place the notion of a supreme national government. In the geographic expanse over which it would operate and in its power over the individual states, this proposed government was closer to that of the imperial British government against which the colonies had rebelled than to the confederation of sovereign states they had created in the aftermath of the Revolution.

Six of the eight states then represented in the Convention had reached agreement on that fundamental shift in principles. James Madison in particular must have felt a keen sense of satisfaction, for without his initiative, careful planning, and intellectual leadership, the push for a radical overhaul of the central government could not have reached this point. But Madison was a worrier, and he knew well that many questions remained unanswered. Did those delegates who had voted yes understand the implications of the proposal they had endorsed? Would he and his nationalist allies be able to sustain their advantage once the delegates got down to details? And what about the five states still missing from the Convention? Six states, with varying degrees of enthusiasm, had endorsed Morris's resolution, but six states did not make a nation.

The five absent states—Rhode Island, New Hampshire, New Jersey, Maryland, and Georgia—were all "small states" with relatively smaller populations, and therefore they were more likely to oppose any plan for a national government based on proportional representation. Madison knew too that even within those state delegations whose votes were counted on May 30, the delegates were not always of one mind. Elbridge Gerry of Massachusetts was instinctively opposed to an excessively strong central government, but on this—and many other occasions—he found himself outvoted by his three Massachusetts colleagues, Nathaniel

Gorham, Rufus King, and Caleb Strong. Among the South Carolinians, Charles Pinckney remained skeptical about both the Virginia Plan and Morris's resolution, and his colleague Pierce Butler was on the fence, confessing that "he had not made up his mind on the subject, and was open to the light which discussion might throw on it." The Delaware delegation initially supported the much weaker resolution calling for the creation of a "more effective government" that was proposed by its leader, George Read. It had swung around to support Morris's more aggressively nationalistic resolution, but Madison knew that Delaware's support was contingent on further concessions on the issue of that state's relative weight in the proposed national legislature. George Read in particular had made it clear that his state would oppose any feature of the Virginia Plan that threatened its interests.[28]

The New York delegation, with delegate John Lansing still among the missing, was divided in the extreme. Alexander Hamilton was not only the most vehement champion of a strong and vigorous central government of anyone present at the Convention, but he would also distinguish himself (or, in the minds of many, bring discredit on himself) as an outspoken admirer of the British government, which many delegates associated with aristocracy and monarchy. By contrast, Robert Yates went to great lengths to serve the interests of his political patron, New York governor George Clinton, who as chief executive of a state already enjoying commercial prosperity, adamantly opposed any step that might serve to strengthen the central government at the expense of his state's power.

The apparent consensus in the Convention concerning the desirability of a supreme, national government did not even extend to those delegations which seemed most spirited in their support of a total overhaul of the Articles of Confederation. While virtually all of the Pennsylvanians—and especially Gouverneur Morris, Robert Morris, and James Wilson—remained firmly committed to the idea of a national as opposed to a confederated government from the first to the last days of the Convention, the Virginians would prove to be of a more divided mind. Although George Mason and Edmund Randolph arrived at the Convention apparently committed to a substantial overhaul of the Articles of Confederation, Mason's approach was instinctively protective of the provincial interests of his home state, and both men would come to express ever-greater fears about excessive concentrations of power in the new government as the Convention progressed.

Since the rules of the Convention stated that any vote taken might be revisited subsequently if a respectable number of delegates requested it, the outcome of the vote was by no means irreversible. May 30 marked only the beginning, not the fulfilment, of the attempt to bring about a revolution in the American government. But it was a vitally important step, for it put the delegates on a course to abandon—rather than revise—the definition of federalism embodied in the Articles of Confederation.

CHAPTER SIX

"WE THE PEOPLE"
OR "WE THE STATES"?
CREATING
THE AMERICAN CONGRESS

WITHIN MINUTES AFTER SIX of the eight state delegations had endorsed the idea of a supreme national government, the fragile consensus fashioned around that proposition began to disintegrate. Immediately after the delegates acted on Morris's resolution in the midafternoon of May 30, they turned to the first substantive item in the Virginia Plan—that providing for a system of proportional representation in the national legislature. James Madison believed from the outset that the fight to create a system of representative government in which ultimate sovereignty resided in the people of the nation as a whole rather than in the states would depend on creating a national legislature based on the principle of proportional representation. He knew too that the vested interests of many of the less-populous states would lead them to oppose that method of apportioning representation. He could not have realized at the time, however, just how acrimonious and protracted the battle over that issue would be.

FOLLOWING ITS OPENING PROPOSAL that the Articles of Confederation be "corrected and enlarged," the Virginia Plan turned to the structure, composition, and authority of the "first branch" of the government—the national legislature. It was hardly surprising that the authors of the Virginia Plan gave primacy of place to the legislative branch. In the wake of their revolution against monarchical rule, all Americans embraced the idea that legislatures—composed of representatives answerable to the people—were the heart and soul of any system of truly "republican" government. But how was the legislature to be constructed? How would the people serving in the legislative branch of government be selected? And, most challenging, how could the interests of thirteen states—so extraordinarily diverse in their geography, in the range of their economic pursuits, in their size, and in the ethnic and religious makeup of their populations—be fairly represented within a single, national legislature? The struggle against British rule had given the states a common cause around which they could unite, but in the aftermath of the Revolution many of the citizens of Georgia felt less kinship with their counterparts in New England than they did with their forebears in Old England. The citizens of New Jersey, for example, looked warily at their more powerful neighbors in New York and Pennsylvania as they calculated the best means of preserving their economic independence and political autonomy. It is not surprising that the construction of the national legislature, the entity that all of the delegates believed would be the most important branch of the new government, would become a source of contention.

While preparing for the Convention, Madison was determined to do away with the provision for equal representation for each state, but he was less certain about how to best represent each state's power and population. The convoluted language of the second item in the Virginia Plan revealed this uncertainty. The "rights of suffrage in the National Legislature," it stipulated, "ought to be proportioned to the quotas of contribution, or to the number of free inhabitants, as the one or the other rule may seem best in different cases." Imbedded in this opaque language were two very real issues capable of blowing the Convention apart—the idea of scrapping equal representation in favor of some form of proportional representation, and the question of "what" or "who" was to determine the relative power of each state in the national legislature.

By proposing two alternative means of apportioning representation—based on the revenue contributed to the central government by each state or on "the number of free inhabitants"—the authors of the Virginia Plan attempted to sidestep these explosive issues. Most delegates commonly understood the phrase "free inhabitants" to mean all free men, women, and children, but the precise meaning of "quotas of contribution" was murkier. It suggested a formula by which states would be represented according to their wealth. Its logic held that if states were to be expected to pay taxes for the support of government in proportion to their wealth, their representation in the legislature should be similarly apportioned. Although individual opinions about the means of calculating wealth may have varied in some particulars, the commonly understood basis for such a calculation was "property." Included in that calculation of property would be a class of inhabitants who were decidedly not "free"—the slave population of the South.

As James Madison readied himself for the debate on apportioning representation the afternoon of May 30, he realized that any plan to institute a system of proportional representation would draw fire from at least some of the delegates from smaller, less populous states, and he wished to avoid anything that might strengthen this opposition. Fearful that a formula based on "free inhabitants" might alienate delegates from the slave-owning South and therefore torpedo his effort to change the existing formula for representation, Madison seized the initiative. Immediately after Convention secretary Jackson read aloud the resolution dealing with apportioning representation, Madison rose from his seat at the front of the room and proposed that the phrase "free inhabitants" be struck from the resolution. While Madison may have had a mild preference for slaves to be counted in the formula for representation, his primary objective was to build a strong consensus around the principle of proportional representation, for that principle was essential to his vision of a truly national government. He realized that he could not build that consensus without the support of the Southern states, and thus he wanted to send a clear signal to his more militant Southern colleagues— in particular, the delegates from South Carolina and Georgia, who would prove the most aggressive in promoting the interests of slave owners during that summer of 1787—that the new national government need not threaten their interests.[1]

Rufus King of Massachusetts, whom Madison counted as a supporter of his nationalist vision for the new union, objected to Madison's proposed new language. King, thirty-two, handsome, ambitious, and, according to one of his contemporaries, possessed of "something of a pride and hauteur in his manner," was an unusually effective public speaker who combined a melodious voice with penetrating logic. His rebuttal to Madison raised an important point. The formula of "quotas of contribution" would not provide a stable measure for apportioning representation. The means of setting those quotas of contribution, King argued, would be a constant source of controversy, for the precise wealth of any given state would be "continually varying." King's retort, however sound from a logical point of view, nevertheless reflected the interests of a delegate from a populous Northern state composed entirely of "free inhabitants." He and his Massachusetts constituents had nothing to gain and much to lose from inflating the representation of Southern states by including slaves.[2]

Alexander Hamilton, less concerned than Madison with mollifying the South, pushed his own strong nationalist vision by proposing that the resolution simply read "that the rights of suffrage in the national legislature ought to be proportioned to the number of free inhabitants." It was not merely that Hamilton, a New Yorker, had less desire than Madison to appease the delegates from the slave-owning states; by temperament, he was more likely than Madison to voice his own opinions forcefully, no matter whom he might offend in the process.

At this point, with agreement nowhere in sight, Nathaniel Gorham, still moderating the proceedings as chair of the Committee of the Whole, correctly read the mood of the delegates and ordered that discussion of the second resolution be postponed. Madison and Randolph, not to be deterred, pressed ahead, hoping at least to get the Convention's endorsement of the principle that "the rights of suffrage in the national legislature ought to be proportioned." At that point, several delegates, seeking to strengthen Madison and Randolph's proposal, suggested adding the words "and not according to the present system."[3]

This formulation left open the question of *how* representatives were to be apportioned, but it clearly rejected the system of equality of state representation used in the Articles of Confederation. The small states' delegates were unyielding, so the advocates of changing the formula for representation backtracked even further, proposing yet another resolution that left out any mention of proportional representation, but affirmed that "the rights of suffrage in the national legislature ought not to be according to the present system." Desperate to make some progress but anxious to avoid creating unnecessary division, Madison made one more attempt to get his colleagues to go on record supporting the principle of proportional representation. He proposed that "the equality of suffrage established by the Articles of Confederation ought not to prevail in the national legislature and that an equitable ratio of representation ought to be substituted."[4]

Madison rarely injected his own opinions or speculations as he recorded the debates in the Convention, but at this point he indulged himself. He noted that his own proposal was "generally relished," by the delegates, and "would have been agreed to," had not George Read of Delaware taken the floor to throw his plan off course.[5]

As much as Read may have wished to strengthen the continental government, he did not wish to do so at the expense of his tiny state. With fire in his eyes, he jumped to his feet and reminded his colleagues that "the deputies from Delaware were restrained by their commission from assenting to any change of the rule of suffrage." Moreover, he announced, should "such a change . . . be fixed on," Delaware would leave the Convention. For the first time, a palpable sense of acrimony infected the atmosphere inside the Assembly Room. Gouverneur Morris, mercurial in temperament and even more strongly committed to overthrowing the principle of representation embodied in the Articles of Confederation than Madison, rose in exasperation, protesting against "so early a proof of discord in the Convention as a secession of a state." He refused to back down in the face of Delaware's threat. The "change [in representation] proposed was . . . so fundamental an article in a national government," he insisted, "that it could not be dispensed with." Madison tried to be more conciliatory, though not without first reminding Read of the rationale for the proposed change. "Whatever reason might have existed for the equality of suffrage when the union was a federal one among sovereign states, it must cease when a national government should be put into place." Madison was still committed to a national—not a federal—government, but he was also intent on avoiding a showdown. He suggested that the delegates go ahead with a vote on the issue, but, "to save the Delaware deputies from embarrassment," the vote should be an informal one, taken in the Committee of the Whole.[6]

Madison believed that the votes were overwhelmingly on his side. If he could convince the Delaware delegates of this in an informal straw vote, he hoped they would back down. But Read would have none of it, insisting that further discussion of the matter be postponed. Madison no doubt could have forced a vote, but he chose not to. Once again engaging in a little editorializing, and some wishful thinking as well, Madison recorded in his notes that it was well understood by the delegates that "the proposed change of representation would certainly be agreed to, no objection or difficulty being stated from any other quarter than from Delaware." After that tactical retreat by the nationalists, Nathaniel Gorham declared the Convention adjourned until ten o'clock the next morning.[7]

Although the proceedings of the previous two days had been momen-

tous, the delegates, as far as we know, remained true to their pledge of secrecy. Philadelphia was filled with ambitious journalists and printers
looking for news. But the local press made no mention of the revolutionary proposals being put before the Convention. A few perfunctory articles noted that the requisite number of delegates had finally gathered,
but they included nothing of substance about their deliberations. The
delegates were equally discreet in their private correspondence. Two of
the North Carolina delegates, Richard Dobbs Spaight and William
Davie, wrote letters to political associates back home telling them that
Washington had been selected as president of the Convention but gave
no other hint of the business being conducted.[8]

General Washington was even more circumspect. Writing to Thomas
Jefferson the evening of May 30, he did not even mention his selection as
president, confining himself only to the comment that "the business of
this convention is as yet too much in embryo to form any opinion of the
conclusion." The most important event of Washington's day, at least according to his diary, was his dinner with Samuel Vaughan. Washington
had been so impressed with Vaughan's renovation of the Pennsylvania
State House yard that he sought him out and persuaded him to visit
Mount Vernon later that summer. Over the course of his time in
Philadelphia, Washington enjoyed Vaughan's company frequently, no
doubt finding conversation about gardens and trees a welcome relief
from political disputes.[9]

CREATING THE HOUSE OF REPRESENTATIVES

Having reached an impasse on the issue of proportional representation,
the delegates turned on the morning of May 31 to the less contentious
third and fourth parts of the Virginia Plan—the proposal that the Congress ought to consist of two branches, and "that members of the first
branch of the National Legislature ought to be elected by the people of
the several States." Nearly all of the delegates, with one notable exception, favored a two-house legislature. There was a strong consensus
among them that the actions of the lower house—the "popular
branch"—needed to be tempered by a smaller and more selective upper
house. All of the states except Pennsylvania had two-house legislatures,
and the delegates were not inclined to make any innovations on that
score.

The Pennsylvanians were the only delegates to raise an objection, and their dissent was purely perfunctory, meant only as a gesture of courtesy to Benjamin Franklin, who retained a fondness for the one-house legislature in his home state. The other Pennsylvania delegates, particularly Robert Morris, Gouverneur Morris, and James Wilson, strongly favored a bicameral legislature, for, unlike Franklin, they believed that the tumultuous politics of their state had often been abetted by Pennsylvania's single-house legislature. They believed that the legislature had too often fallen under the control of back-country rubes and Philadelphia radicals who had swayed the people to their side, thwarting legislation aimed at promoting the state's economic development. They knew that Franklin was not likely to regard the proposal for a bicameral system as a fatal flaw in the new constitution, and they calculated that siding gracefully with their senior colleague in defeat would ease any possible disappointment that the elder statesman might feel about having his preferences ignored.[10]

The fourth part of the Virginia Plan, which called for election of representatives in the lower house directly by the people, sparked opposition from states as far apart as Massachusetts and South Carolina. This was the first occasion on which the delegates were called to state their opinions on the role of the people—the efficacy of democracy—in the proposed new government, and their views ranged widely. The intensity of feeling on that subject was not as passionate as the feeling that divided large and small states over proportional versus equal state representation, but the long-term consequences of that debate would be in the end more momentous. Once government under a new Constitution commenced, the differing characteristics of small states and large states rarely proved a source of division in national politics, but decisions about the role of ordinary citizens in the new government—about the extent to which *democracy* would be an essential feature of our national system—provoked conflict almost immediately.

Elbridge Gerry of Massachusetts was the first of a diverse group of delegates to express his skepticism about excessive popular participation in the body politic. The son of a modestly successful sea captain and merchant, Gerry earned both a bachelor's and a master's degree at Harvard in the early 1760s. Despite cultivating his interests in political theory, philosophy, and history as a student at Harvard, Elbridge ended up running his father's business. But he never lost his interest in politics. He would serve in the Continental Congress during the Revolution, developing a particular expertise in the business of financing and equipping the Continental army. That tour of duty caused him to be particularly sensitive to the weaknesses of the Confederation government and inclined him to support efforts at strengthening the government.[11]

Gerry was respected, according to Georgia delegate William Pierce, as "a gentleman in principles and manners," with a character noted for "integrity and perseverance." But he was "a hesitating and laborious speaker," who, "though capable of delving deeply into any subject on which he spoke," did so "without respect for elegance or flower of diction." Gerry's biographer, George Billias, describes his subject as a "nervous and birdlike little person," who spoke with a stammer and developed a disconcerting habit of "contracting and expanding the muscles of his eye." When one takes the sum of these disparate images, what emerges is a man who, though respected by his colleagues, was not always pleasant company.[12]

Gerry arrived in Philadelphia on May 29, and it didn't take him long to develop a hearty dislike for the city. After the May 30 session had adjourned, he returned to his room at Miss Daley's boardinghouse to write a letter to his wife, Ann, the beautiful daughter of one of New York's

Elbridge Gerry, one of the Constitution's most persistent and caustic critics. Etching by James Bogle after John Vanderlyn, 1861, courtesy of Independence National Historical Park.

wealthiest merchants. Ann looked younger than her twenty-four years and Gerry looked much older than his forty-three, so much so that Manasseh Cutler, a minister and land speculator who visited them in Philadelphia that summer, reckoned that Ann "was not more than 17, and I believe him to be turned of 55." The two had been married for only eighteen months, and Ann had just recently delivered their first child, a son. She and the child would soon join Gerry in Philadelphia, but on that May 30 evening, Gerry, feeling homesick, complained to his wife of the "heavy, inelastic air of this city," which, he claimed, gave him headaches. Moreover, although he was a product of Puritan Boston, he nevertheless found the Quaker influence in Philadelphia to be oppressive. He likened the upper-class citizens of Philadelphia to "Monks and Nuns in a monastery" and warned his wife that when she arrived there she should not expect the gaiety and sociability that she had enjoyed in New York. While Gerry's attitude toward his personal circumstances would improve once his wife and child joined him in Philadelphia, his mood about the proceedings inside the State House grew steadily more sullen.[13]

Gerry, like many New Englanders whose political principles had been formed in the cauldron of opposition to the monarchical power of England, was driven by a nearly pathological fear of the misuse of power. During and after the Revolution, he had been among those most outspoken in denouncing the evils of any concentration of power in the hands of the "few"—whether those few be members of a British aristocracy or the collection of American Revolutionary War officers who banded together in the Society of the Cincinnati, who, Gerry was convinced, aimed to establish their own form of aristocracy in America.

Gerry's fear of concentrated power might have led him to oppose any move to strengthen the central government, but his experience as a member of the Massachusetts House of Representatives confronting the Shaysite rebels had given him an equally intense fear of the anarchy of mob rule. He railed against the "livilling spirit" of the Shaysites, and believed that only a strong use of government force could quell the "anarchy as now exists." Tyranny, Gerry believed, could come not only from the selfishness of the privileged few, but also from the impulsive and irrational behavior of the multitude. Shays' Rebellion had proven to be extremely important to the nation's future history not so much from any real danger that it posed either to Massachusetts society and government or to that of the country as a whole, but because of the way powerful men like Gerry and George Washington reacted to it.[14]

Over the course of the Constitutional Convention, Gerry would express grave concerns about the excessive power of the proposed new government, but at this early moment in the Convention's deliberations, a mere three days in, his primary concern was with an "excess of democracy"—a condition that would be abetted by popular election of members of the lower house of the national legislature. In his first speech before the Convention, in which he stated his opposition to direct election of representatives, Gerry argued that "the people do not want virtue, but are the dupes of pretended patriots." Surely referring to his experience in Massachusetts, he claimed that "it has been fully confirmed by experience that they are daily misled into the most baneful measures and opinions by the false reports circulated by designing men."[15]

From the other end of the Atlantic seaboard, Pierce Butler, the son of an Irish nobleman and the owner of a substantial plantation with 143 slaves, weighed in with a steadfast defense of the notion that property, including slave property, should be the basis for representation in the new government. He declared simply that he "thought an election by the people an impractical mode." Whereas Gerry's fear of popular passions sprang from deep reflection about the conditions necessary to preserve a republican system of government, Butler simply assumed that wealthy and well-born planter-gentry men like himself were the only people who could be trusted to make political decisions of any consequence.[16]

The most puzzling ally of those opposed to direct election of representatives was Roger Sherman of Connecticut, who shared Gerry's misgivings about an excess of democracy but added to them a concern that the Virginia Plan had gone too far in repudiating the Articles of Confederation. Sherman had cast his vote against Gouverneur Morris's resolution calling for a supreme national government the day before, and on this day he stated flatly that "the people . . . should have as little to do as may be about the government. They want information and are constantly liable to be misled."[17]

It was a peculiar position for a man in Sherman's position to take, for if there was any member of the Convention who had risen from the ranks of the common citizenry of America, it was he. Sherman, one of seven, was born in 1721 to a shoemaker of exceptionally modest means. At the time of his death, when Roger was nineteen, the inventory of the family estate consisted of seventy-three acres, three cows, two steers, a heifer, two sheep, and a small assortment of furniture, including only three beds for the nine family members. After his father's death, Roger took up his father's trade and moved to western Connecticut, reportedly carrying his cobbler's tools on his back to the town of New Milford. Once in New Milford, a new community still in the early stages of settlement, Sherman borrowed some money and bought a small plot of land. He learned the trade of a surveyor and by 1745 was appointed chief surveyor of his county, a strategically important position in a region where land development was occurring rapidly and boundary disputes between landowners were commonplace. He used his role as county surveyor as a springboard for his own modest rise to wealth, for in that position he was able to make a few timely land investments of his own, and, more important, he gained appointment to the astonishingly large number of public positions from which he earned his primary income.[18]

Sherman may be the only person among the Founding Fathers to have made a professional career of serving in public, salary-paying offices most of his life. During the forty-eight-year period between 1745 and his death in 1793 he served as a jury man, tax collector, inspector of pennies, town clerk, deacon of his Congregational church, town agent to the Assembly, justice of the peace, justice of the county court, representative in the lower house of the Connecticut Assembly, member of the upper house of the Assembly, commissary for the Connecticut militia, and judge of the Connecticut Superior Court. Along the way, he studied law and gained admission to the bar in 1754. He was also able to supplement his income by publishing a highly successful series of almanacs.[19]

As important as his service in provincial office may have been to his livelihood, Sherman was able, in the midst of all of his public duties in Connecticut, to compile a record of service to the continental government perhaps unequaled by any of the Founding Fathers. He was the only person at the Constitutional Convention to have supported the set of proposals in the First Continental Congress denying Parliamentary authority over the colonies; to have served on the drafting committee and then signed the Declaration of Independence in the Second Continental Congress; to have served on the drafting committee and then signed the Articles of Confederation; and to have served in the Continental Congress and then voted for the Treaty of Paris in 1783. Indeed, his length of service in the Continental Congress exceeded that of any other American.[20]

By the testimony of virtually everyone who recorded an impression of him, Sherman was one of the most physically ungainly specimens ever put on God's earth. John Adams, who was an extravagant admirer of Sherman's in other respects, described his appearance as "the reverse of grace; there cannot be a more striking contrast to beautiful action, than the motions of his hands; generally he stands upright, with his hands before him, the fingers of his left hand clenched into a fist, and the wrist grasped with the right." Sherman's appearance and simple manner of dress are starkly displayed in the only known portrait of him, painted by a relatively obscure artist named Ralph Earl in 1775 or 1776. Sitting somewhat uncomfortably in a Windsor chair, square jawed, wigless, wearing a suit of country clothing on which one can make out a worn spot on the right knee, Sherman seems the essence of Yankee simplicity and frugality.[21]

Sherman's diction betrayed his lack of formal schooling. William Pierce spoke of the "vulgarisms that accompany his public speaking" and, perhaps betraying his preference for the slow Georgia drawl of his own region, lamented that the "strange New England cant which runs through his public as well as his private speaking make everything that is connected with him grotesque and laughable." Yet the very people who deprecated his appearance and diction were among those who praised his intellect and public-spiritedness. John Adams thought him "a solid, sensible man" and counted him "one of the most cordial friends which I ever had in my life . . . , one of the soundest and strongest pillars of the Revolution."[22]

Sherman's intellectual abilities were such that they could be intimidating to those who found themselves on the opposite side of an issue. A political competitor in Connecticut, Jeremiah Wadsworth, wrote to Massachusetts delegate Rufus King warning him of Sherman's likely opposition to attempts to strengthen the central government. Wadsworth wrote that Sherman was "cunning as the devil, and if you attack him, you ought to know him well; he is not easily managed, but if he suspects you are trying to take him in, you may as well catch an eel by the tail."[23]

The plainly dressed, awkwardly formed but wise delegate from Connecticut would play an enormously important role in the Convention, speaking more frequently than any other delegate except Gouverneur Morris and Madison. More importantly, he would take the lead in forging some of the Convention's central compromises.

On the issue before the Convention during the afternoon of May 31,

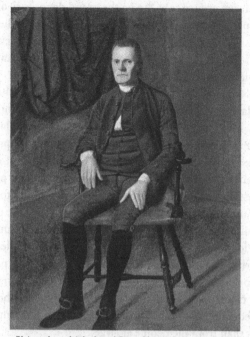

Plain-spoken, plainly dressed Roger Sherman was esteemed as a
"solid, sensible man." Portrait by Ralph Earl, 1775–76, courtesy
of Yale University Art Gallery.

Sherman found himself in a distinct minority. When the proposition considering popular election of the first branch of the national legislature was put before the Committee of the Whole, the proposition passed, with six states, Massachusetts, New York, Pennsylvania, Virginia, North Carolina, and Georgia, voting yes; two states, New Jersey and South Carolina, voting no; and Connecticut and Delaware divided.[24]

Interestingly, while two of the men who had questioned the ability of ordinary people to make intelligent decisions about government— Sherman and Elbridge Gerry—were themselves individuals of humble origins, one of the most eloquent defenders of the role of ordinary citizens in the affairs of government was by birth and present circumstance one of the most exalted. George Mason of Virginia, born to privilege and steadily enhancing his wealth over the course of his lifetime, was the one man who stood that day to give a passionate defense of direct, popular participation in the selection of representatives. The House of Representatives, Mason argued, was "to be the grand depository of the democratic principle of the government. It was, so to speak, to be our House of Commons—It ought to know and sympathize with every part of the community." Mason believed that it was the duty of government "to attend to the rights of every class of the people."[25]

James Wilson of Pennsylvania, whose social standing at birth was not as lofty as Mason's but who could certainly be counted among the patrician class by the time of the Convention, immediately followed Mason with another passionate defense of popular election of representatives. Wilson's passion was generated less by an instinctive trust of the common man than by the conviction that the only way to gain popular support for a vastly strengthened central government was by founding that government firmly on the will of the people. He wished, he told the delegates, to "raise the federal pyramid to a considerable altitude," and the only way to do that was "to give it as broad a basis as possible." Assessing the way in which state jealousies had operated during the period of the Confederation, as in the refusals to grant the Confederation government powers over commerce or taxation, he noted wryly that "the opposition of states to federal measures had proceeded much more from the officers of the states, than from the people at large."[26]

Though the delegates were clearly of a divided mind about how much power to give to ordinary citizens in the operation of the proposed new government, it did seem that the preponderance of opinion fell on the side of giving them substantial power at least in the election of members of the House of Representatives.[27]

FIRST STEPS TOWARD AN AMERICAN SENATE

If the delegates differed about how much power to give to the people in electing representatives to the lower house of the legislature, their opinions on both the composition and the mode of election of the upper house were not merely diverse, but deeply confused. The precise origins of the term "upper house" are obscure, but from the thirteenth century onward, it seems to have been applied to the legislative body in England in which the second estate—or aristocracy—sat. By the mid-seventeenth century, the English political philosopher James Harrington associated the upper house with political wisdom and prudence. That notion persisted in America well after the Revolution, and for Americans an upper house denoted a chamber of the legislature whose members were more likely to be drawn from the upper levels of society, to be "higher in place" than ordinary citizens and, above all, more knowledgeable and more deliberative.[28]

The Virginia Plan's fifth resolution called for the members of the lower house of the national legislature to choose members of the upper house from a group nominated by the state legislatures. Some of the most committed nationalists—Rufus King of Massachusetts, James Wilson and Gouverneur Morris of Pennsylvania, and James Madison of Virginia— remained steadfast in arguing that the formula for proportional representation that they had favored for the lower house should also be applied to the upper. Since the principle of proportional representation in the lower house had already drawn substantial fire from delegates from the smaller states, it was hardly a surprise that those same delegates would deem a similar formula for the upper house unacceptable.

Rather than engage the delegates in debate on that obviously controversial subject at this early stage, Madison and the other prime movers of the Virginia Plan directed the discussion toward the method of selecting members of the upper house. Here too, though, the delegates' views ranged widely. There was relatively little support for the method proposed in the Virginia Plan. Pierce Butler of South Carolina, fearful that election of the upper house by the lower house of the national legislature would take a vital power out of the hands of the states, challenged Virginia's Edmund Randolph to "explain the extent of his ideas" on that matter. Randolph responded hesitatingly, diffidently, confessing that he hadn't really thought the matter through and, upon reflection, admitted that the specific proposal contained in the Virginia Plan should perhaps not have been introduced.

Pierce Butler, Roger Sherman of Connecticut, and Richard Dobbs Spaight of North Carolina all favored some means by which the state legislatures, rather than the lower house of Congress, would select members of the upper house. Each of those delegates was, to a varying degree, beginning to feel some uneasiness about the "national" rather than the "federal" character of the proposed new government, and by giving each state legislature the right to select senators, they hoped to return at least some measure of power to the states.

Pennsylvania's James Wilson opposed selection of members of the upper house by either the state legislatures or the lower house. He was convinced that a truly national legislature ought to be chosen by direct election by the people.

Madison was the author of the proposal calling for election of the upper house by the lower. Although he may have considered direct popular election preferable to a method that ceded the power of election to state legislatures, his vision of an American Senate was that of a body that was in no way beholden to the state legislatures for its authority and whose members represented that combination of political wisdom and prudence that James Harrington had described long ago. And he could not have been happy that his Virginia colleague Edmund Randolph, who had been entrusted with presenting the Virginia Plan, was so quick to question the wisdom of the proposal. Ignoring the obvious contention over the issue, Madison pushed for a vote on the original proposal in Resolution Five of the Virginia Plan. Only three states, Massachusetts, Virginia, and South Carolina, voted yes; while the other seven states, Connecticut, New York, New Jersey, Pennsylvania, Delaware, North Carolina, and Georgia, voted no. In Madison's words, "A chasm [was] left in this part of the plan." For the first time, he found himself on the losing side.[29]

THE EXTENT OF CONGRESSIONAL POWER

With no resolution of the question of how senators were to be elected, the delegates next turned to the sixth of the Virginia Plan's proposals. That resolution, which described the extent of the new Congress's power, may well have been the most important of the lot. The delegates quickly and without debate agreed to the first two components of the resolution, which allowed each branch of the legislature to originate laws and transferred the existing powers of the Confederation Congress to the proposed Congress.

The subsequent phrases of the sixth resolution spoke to the very essence of the revolutionary plan introduced by the Virginians and Pennsylvanians. The new national legislature would not only "enjoy the Legislative Rights vested in the Congress by the Confederation," but it would also have the power

> to legislate in all cases to which the separate states are incompetent, or in which the harmony of the United States may be interrupted by the exercise of individual Legislation; to negative all laws passed by the several States, con-

travening in the opinion of the National Legislature the
articles of Union; and to call forth the force of the Union
against any member of the Union failing to fulfill its duty
under the articles thereof.[30]

The nationalists had won an important victory the previous day in
getting six of the eight states present to agree *in theory* to the establishment of a national government with a supreme legislature, executive, and
judiciary, but Resolution Six brought home with unmistakable speci-
ficity the meaning of that abstract notion of national supremacy. Although the South Carolinians had voted for the abstract proposition the
day before, they were beginning to have misgivings. Charles Pinckney
objected to the term "incompetent," describing it as too vague, and John
Rutledge agreed. Pierce Butler joined in, expressing his fear that the delegates were "running into an extreme in taking away the powers of the
States." Madison and Randolph tried to assure their South Carolina colleagues that the government they aimed to create was one of specific and
enumerated powers and promised them that concerns about excessive
vagueness would be addressed over the course of the Convention. For
the moment at least, this assurance seemed to work. In a show of near
unanimity, with nine states voting yes and Connecticut divided, the delegates agreed to the language that bestowed a lawmaking power superior
to that of the individual states on the proposed Congress, including the
power to veto any state law the new Congress considered to be contrary
to "the articles of union."[31]

The final clause of Resolution Six, and the final item of business on
the busy day of May 31, authorized the national government to use force
to compel any "delinquent state" into conformity with federal law. Although this clause was most likely Madison's handiwork, he rose in the
Convention that afternoon and asked to postpone discussion of it. His
words in the last speech on May 31 were prescient. As he contemplated
a situation in which the national government might be compelled to use
force to bring a recalcitrant state into line, he began to fear that the ultimate effect of such an action might prove catastrophic to the harmony
of the union. "The use of force against a state," he reflected, "would
look . . . like a declaration of war . . . and would probably be considered
by the party attacked as a dissolution of all previous compacts by which
it might be bound." Some seventy-four years later the American union
would face just the sort of crisis that Madison hoped to avert. In 1861,

not one but several American states would come to regard the coercive power of the national government sufficiently dangerous to justify dissolution of the union.[32]

As the delegates adjourned for the day, the Virginians and Pennsylvanians had cause for satisfaction. They had seized the initiative of the Convention and gained at least tentative endorsement of many of their most important ideas. Most of the states present at the Convention had endorsed the idea of a national government with a supreme legislative, executive, and judiciary. In the discussions of the general powers of the national legislature that day, they had gone even further, making it clear that the proposed new Congress would have the power not only to legislate in those cases in which the state legislatures were incompetent, but also to veto any state laws that seemed to contravene national law. This step amounted to a direct repudiation of the principles of the Articles of Confederation.

As they moved from May to June, the delegates also seemed prepared to endorse the idea of a bicameral legislature. At this point, their reasons for preferring a two-house legislature over a single chamber varied. To the extent that there was a consensus among the delegates on the need for a two-house legislature, it was based on the belief that the upper house should be smaller and therefore more selective than the lower house. Following the logic of that assumption, the delegates seemed to agree that the upper house—or, as it would come to be called, the Senate—should be composed of "gentlemen" elected not directly by the people, but by some other means whereby the best, brightest, and most virtuous could be identified as sufficiently qualified to serve.

THE DESIRE TO MAKE the Senate the repository of superior wisdom and virtue reflected the deep ambivalence among most of the delegates about popular election of government officials. Nearly all harbored keen misgivings about the desirability of democracy as a guiding principle for the new government. Nearly everyone in the Convention would have counted himself a "republican," which at the time meant one who stood solidly against hereditary monarchy and in favor of some form of representative government. But among the Convention's republican delegates, the advocates of an *unmediated* democracy were few and far between. The Convention delegates would debate long and inconclusively about the place of democracy in the American government over the course of the summer, struggling to find a balance between traditional— that is to say elitist—definitions of republicanism and a more explicitly democratic conception of the role of ordinary citizens in the affairs of government.

As the delegates completed their first full week of deliberations, they were far from resolving the issues relating to the scope, composition, and means of electing their national legislature, but they had at least made some progress. During the early weeks of June they would continue to struggle with those issues, but they would also confront a new set of questions that would prove even more confounding—those relating to the creation of an American president.

CHAPTER SEVEN

IMAGINING THE AMERICAN PRESIDENCY

AS THE DELEGATES took their seats at ten o'clock on an unseasonably cool and cloudy June 1 morning, Madison and his nationalist allies remained in control of the agenda. The Convention began its business for the day as George Washington once again stepped down from his chair as president of the Convention and took a seat at the Virginians' table, and Nathaniel Gorham stepped up to the chair to resume his role as chairman of the Committee of the Whole. Rather than attempting to seek agreement on the issues left unresolved the day before, Gorham directed the delegates' attention to the next item in the Virginia Plan— "that a national Executive be instituted, to be chosen by the National Legislature—for the term of __ years." The decision to move forward rather than back to tackle contentious issues like that involving the dispute between large and small states over representation was one likely reached by a consensus of the delegates. Whatever their differences, they agreed on the importance of maintaining momentum—finding common ground where common ground existed—in their enterprise.

But the challenges associated with creating a chief executive would prove at least as complicated as those associated with constructing the legislature. From the morning of June 1 until the very end of the summer, the form, powers, and mode of selection of the national executive would be a constant source of dispute. The debate over the executive did not cause sharply defined divisions between whole groups of state delegations, as had been the case between the large and small states on the subject of apportionment, but there was a greater range of individual opinion among the delegates on the character of the executive branch than on any other issue in the Convention.

AMERICANS HAVE ARGUED about the nature and extent of presidential power from the time of George Washington to the present. But it was another George, one who preceded our first president in the national consciousness, who played an even more important role in conditioning American attitudes toward the presidency—King George III.

The experience of eighteenth-century Americans with the office of the chief executive—in its monarchical form—had not been a happy one. During the years leading up to the Revolution, royal governors—acting on the instructions of the king in London—had dissolved recalcitrant colonial legislatures, preventing colonial residents from meeting to elect representatives, and they had attacked the independence of colonial courts. Indeed, in composing the Declaration of Independence, Thomas Jefferson devoted a large portion of his effort to chronicling the ways in which the British king, through his royal governors, had pursued that "long train of abuses" that compelled Americans to sever their ties with their Mother Country.

The constitutions of the newly independent states reflected Americans' profound distrust of executive power. In almost all cases, the new state constitutions relegated the powers of the executive branch—in most states a "governor" but in a few a "president"—to a distinctly subordinate role in relation to the state legislature. The Articles of Confederation neglected to provide for an executive branch altogether. The Confederation government's power, feeble as it was, rested with the Continental Congress. To the extent that the Articles of Confederation provided for any executive power at all, it was in the clause authorizing a Committee of the States to act for the government when the Continental Congress was in recess. That committee, composed of one delegate from each state, was empowered to choose "one of their number to preside," but the presiding officer of the committee was a "president" in name only. He was merely an agent for carrying out the will of Congress. The Congress itself often went weeks and months at a time without achieving a quorum, but it does not appear that the Committee of the States stepped in to take up the slack; on the few times the Committee actually met, it did not manage to transact any business of substance.[1]

Perhaps the closest the Confederation government ever came to naming a chief executive worthy of the name was during the time of Robert Morris's tenure as superintendent of finance. In his decisive—albeit controversial—exercise of the financial power of his office, he more closely resembled a powerful minister in the cabinet of King George III than a president. While his service as superintendent of finance was a key component in America's struggle for independence, the lesson most Americans probably took away from his tenure was that a power-ful minister of Robert Morris's ilk was precisely what they did *not* want.

On the other hand, when Madison composed his musings on "The Vices of the Political System of the United States" in April 1787, he pointed to the price Americans were paying for their distrust of execu-tive power. By denying state governors the power to veto laws passed by their legislatures, the state constitutions drafted in the aftermath of in-dependence too often gave legislatures the license to pass laws by which momentary majorities threatened the rights of minorities. That had been the case when a pro-debtor faction gained control of the Rhode Island legislature, passing laws rendering creditors powerless to collect the full value of the debts owed them. It had also been the case in several states where legislatures passed laws depriving returning Loyalists of the right to recover property confiscated from them during the Revolutionary War. The Confederation government, lacking an executive altogether, was powerless to do anything to restrain irresponsible behavior in the in-dividual states and was at best only a broker among the interests of the states.[2]

It was in this atmosphere of powerful memories of a tyrannical king, tempered by the realization that governments did occasionally need to speak for the people with a single voice, that the Founding Fathers began to imagine the character and authority of their new national chief execu-tive. At this early stage in the Convention, the exercise truly did require a leap of imagination, for there was little in the delegates' past experience that gave them a clear view of how the office of the chief executive should be constructed.

South Carolina's Charles Pinckney, no doubt still smarting from the way the Virginia Plan had taken center stage at the expense of his own plan, stood first to offer his views on the executive branch. Ostensibly speaking in defense of Resolution Seven of the Virginia Plan, Pinckney was in reality defending the version of the executive branch contained in the plan he presented on May 29. Pinckney's plan had explicitly referred to the chief executive as a "president" and had been far more explicit than the Virginia Plan in spelling out his powers.[3]

James Wilson weighed in next. From the first words he uttered on that June 1 morning through the remainder of the Convention, it would be Wilson, far more than Madison, Pinckney, or any other delegate, who developed a coherent and comprehensive conception of the American presidency. Wilson's initial remarks focused on the composition of the executive branch. Whereas Resolution Seven had not addressed the question of whether the chief executive should be a single person or a group of men, Wilson proposed that "the Executive consist of a single person." Only a unitary executive, he argued, could lay claim to being the sole representative of the people of the nation as a whole. The other alternative, he warned, was a multiple executive whose members, inevitably selected from different parts of the country, would act as advocates for the different interests of their regions, thus diluting the authority of the executive. Only a single executive, he insisted, could give "energy, dispatch, and responsibility" to the government.

Charles Pinckney, whose plan for the government specifically referred to a single executive, immediately seconded Wilson's motion, and then, according to Madison, "a considerable pause" ensued. As the pause lengthened, Nathaniel Gorham asked the delegates if they would like to vote on the matter. Benjamin Franklin, who had been largely silent until this moment, issued a gentle caution, noting that "it was a point of great importance." He then asked that the delegates be given an opportunity to "deliver their sentiments on it before the question was put."[4]

FRANKLIN'S INVITATION TO DISSENT immediately had its desired effect, as many of the delegates, after being recognized by Nathaniel Gorham, rose to express their misgivings. Roger Sherman of Connecticut offered a boldly contrary view. The "executive magistracy," Sherman argued, should be "nothing more than an institution for carrying the will of the Legislature into effect." Sherman believed that the members of the legislature should decide what business the executive ought to undertake, and that the person or persons in that office should be appointed by and directly accountable to the legislature. Reflecting the prevailing mistrust of executive power, Sherman asserted that the legislature—not the executive—was "the depositary of the supreme will of the society."[5]

It is hard to imagine a chief executive more unlike that of the modern American presidency than the one envisioned by Sherman. America's system of government is founded firmly on a principle of separation of powers—the relative independence of each of the branches of the government. Had Sherman and several other delegates who identified themselves with his position won the day, America would be ruled by a parliamentary, rather than a presidential model of government, with a majority of members in the legislature determining the authority of their "prime minister."

The next person to speak against the idea of a unitary executive was none other than Edmund Randolph, the man who had presented the Virginia Plan. While Randolph agreed with Wilson that the executive branch needed to have "vigor, dispatch, and responsibility," he was dead set against the accumulation of executive power in the hands of a single person. With images of King George III still imprinted on his memory, he believed that a unitary executive contained within it "the foetus of monarchy." He implored his fellow delegates to resist the temptation to use "the British Government as our prototype."[6]

Randolph delivered his speech on the corrupting effects of a single executive just a few feet from George Washington, who, having stepped aside to allow Nathaniel Gorham to chair the discussions, was seated alongside Randolph among the Virginia delegates. Washington was not only the one man whose support of a new constitution would be essential to its success, but he was also the only man in the room who could be assured of unanimous support in the role of unitary executive. Randolph's remarks about the dangers of "executive tyranny" may well have been more vehement had Washington not been present, and indeed it is likely that the debates over the character of the American presidency that whole summer were influenced by the presence of America's first citizen. Washington's very reluctance to assume power combined with his unique qualifications as the only man in America who could shape the office of the presidency such that it would prevent others from using it to subvert liberty were crucial factors in guiding the thinking of virtually everyone in the Convention. Had Washington been absent, it is entirely possible that the framers of the Constitution would have created a multiple executive. They may have followed Roger Sherman's instincts and created a chief executive whose selection and legitimacy depended upon the sentiments of a majority in the legislature. Without Washington in the Assembly Room of the Pennsylvania State House, America might well have a parliamentary, and not a presidential, system of government.[7]

THE CONTRADICTORY CHARACTER OF JAMES WILSON

Only one member of the Convention envisioned an American government, and a president, much like those we have today—vigorous and powerful, but based firmly on the will of the people. James Wilson of Pennsylvania, reacting to the inability of the Confederation government to speak with a single voice or to intervene in a forceful way to prevent quarrels among the states from undermining the strength of the nation as a whole, argued strenuously that only a president elected directly by the people of the nation at large could give the necessary energy and direction to the new national government. He wished, he explained, "to derive not only both branches of the legislature from the people, without the intervention of the state legislatures but the executive also; in order to make them as independent as possible of each other, as well as of the states." He was concerned that the Virginia Plan, in its present form, would create a system in which both the executive and judicial branches were excessively dependent on the Congress. Wilson was the first delegate to realize that the only way to create a true separation of powers, to render the Congress and president independent of one another, and to ensure their legitimacy in the eyes of the people, was to insist on direct popular election of each.[8]

As one of the most firmly committed nationalists in the Convention, Wilson also believed that a president, elected directly by the people, was essential as both the symbol and the executor of "we the people." To this day, all of the other elected officials within the federal government represent particular constituencies within the national polity; only the president stands above region or state and only the president can claim to represent the will of all of the people.

Although Wilson's colleague Gouverneur Morris occasionally, and inconsistently, argued for direct election of the president, for the most part Wilson was a minority of one. At least a few delegates—eighteenth-century men born and raised in a society in which most people still believed in a natural and, indeed, divinely sanctioned hierarchy of beings—thought the people of the nation at large were inherently incapable of making a wise selection for their chief magistrate. Those delegates—men like Elbridge Gerry of Massachusetts, Roger Sherman of Connecticut, and Pierce Butler of South Carolina—believed that the ordinary citizens of America were too gullible, and that their votes could be too easily manipulated.

In fact, only a small minority of delegates believed that the ordinary citizens of America were insufficiently intelligent to make a wise choice for their president. Rather, an overwhelming majority thought the people at large were simply too ignorant. Although the late eighteenth century was an age in the midst of its own communication revolution of sorts—with the number of newspapers being published in America increasing from thirteen in 1750, to twenty-two in 1775, to nearly one hundred by 1787—that revolution was still a highly localized one. America's communications media were overwhelmingly provincial, seldom looking at a political world beyond the borders of their own states, or even their own towns. The typical American newspaper was printed on four pages, the first and fourth devoted entirely to classified advertisements, and the second and third pages—the "inside pages"—devoted to a combination of news reports, public announcements, assorted literary efforts, and additional classified advertisements.[9]

The readers of the May 30 Pennsylvania *Gazette*, for example, would have encountered multiple advertisements for "goods at auction," including cotton and muslin fabrics, china and table linens imported from Europe, building materials, and furniture. Those seeking passage on ships leaving Philadelphia would have seen spaces available on ships bound for Jamaica, Madeira, Bristol, and London, and those looking to purchase land would have found opportunities to do so in advertisements for both raw land and farms in Bordentown, New Jersey, Maryland, and Jamaica. While many of the advertisements seem not all that different from the sort that we might find in our local newspapers today, the *Gazette* also offered opportunities to "purchase" indentured servants, who would be required to work for them for periods of one to seven years. Another offered a reward for the return of runaway slaves.[10]

The news of the day, on pages two and three, was often of dubious value. The news section of the June 1 edition of the Pennsylvania *Packet*, for example, featured a truly awful poem entitled "An Ode to the Connecticut River" and a reprinting of the official proceedings of the Continental Congress meeting in New York. Since the Congress was mostly somnolent, there was little to report, but the value of the report was further diminished by the fact that it was from a session held nearly a month earlier. The most important news report from outside of Philadelphia was a reprint of a proclamation from the Massachusetts governor on the aftermath of Shays' Rebellion, dated more than a month earlier, April 27.[11]

How would it be possible, then, for voters in Georgia to know the merits of a presidential candidate in New York, or voters in Massachusetts to be familiar with the talents of a candidate in North Carolina? By and large, it was not contempt for the people that caused the framers of the Constitution to reject what seems to us an obvious democratic method of electing a president answerable directly to the people. Rather, nearly all of the delegates—with the notable exception of Wilson—believed that the sheer expanse of America would frustrate any effort to create an informed electorate.

However much James Wilson may have embraced a theoretical belief in the wisdom of the American people, if truth be told, he did not feel any great affection for the common man. In his outward demeanor he had, in the words of his biographer, Page Smith, an "unbending stiffness" about him and took such pride in his intellect that he was often unable to hide his feelings of superiority over those ordinary citizens around him. The French chargé d'affaires stationed in America in 1787, Louis-Guillaume Otto, who genuinely admired Wilson's intellect, nevertheless described him as "haughty" and "aristocratic." Wilson's por-

James Wilson was a forceful advocate for a government based on "We the People." Portrait by Philip Fisbourne Wharton after the James Barton Longacre engraving, 1873, courtesy of Independence National Historical Park.

trait, in which he appears with a prim white wig and thick-lensed glasses, conveys the suggestion of a man who is looking down his nose at those around him.[12]

Some of that aura of arrogance was probably unintentional, merely an unfortunate mannerism of a man who had, after all, come from the sturdy middle class in Scotland and risen to his position of prominence through merit, not through birth or court patronage. But some of his discomfort with the people was the result of immediate personal experience.

Although Wilson had been an early and eloquent defender of American rights during the years leading up to independence, when the moment to take that fateful step arrived, he was among many prominent Philadelphians—including his patron, Robert Morris—who wavered. Wilson never opposed independence, but he certainly argued for delay, a posture that won him few friends among the more radical Philadelphians who successfully overthrew the old guard in the Pennsylvania Assembly in June of 1776. The radicals then moved forward not only to declare independence on their own, but also to draft a constitution for the independent state that was more radically democratic than any in America. Although Wilson ultimately endorsed independence, he detested the new Pennsylvania Constitution's weak executive branch and popularly elected unicameral legislature, the latter of which, he feared, was subject to popular convulsions.[13]

As the war progressed, and the British occupied Philadelphia, many of the radical politicians in power in the Pennsylvania government considered Wilson insufficiently zealous in his opposition to that occupation. To make matters worse, once the occupation ended, Wilson chose to defend some of his friends and neighbors who had been accused of cooperating with the British. At a time when the populace was deeply divided over the merits of the radical Pennsylvania Constitution and over the question of how to deal with those suspected of Toryism, Wilson, with his increasingly aristocratic pretensions and his haughty manner, came to be seen by many radical working-class Philadelphians as the epitome of much of what they detested.[14]

On October 4, 1779, a group of Philadelphia militiamen began to organize to drive Royalists out of the city. As they gathered at Paddy Burns's tavern on the morning of October 4, with plenty of liquor to stoke the fires, the cry went up to "Get Wilson." Wilson quickly got wind of the fact that he was one of the targets of the mob and rallied many of his friends and political supporters into a counter-militia to ward off the mob. As biographer Page Smith has observed, the band of men gathered at Wilson's house on the corner of Walnut and Third streets, dubbed by the insurgents as "Fort Wilson," made a curious picture—a group of about twenty "stout, prosperous men clutching muskets and pistols" to protect one of the city's leading citizens. The two groups—the larger group of working-class militiamen and the band of officers and gentlemen protecting Wilson—converged within a block of Wilson's house. The militiamen broke through the resistance offered by Wilson's supporters and made their way toward the house. At this point, one of the officers stationed inside Wilson's house, a Captain Campbell, yelled out the window ordering the militiamen to cease their march. The command did not have its desired effect. One of the militiamen fired a musket ball that killed Campbell instantly and precipitated a melee of confusion, gunfire, and bloodshed that only ended when the president of the state government, Joseph Reed, appeared at the head of the city's elite militia unit, the City Troop of Light Horse, and moved in to quell the riot. When it was all over, four of the militiamen were dead, along with another African American boy who had joined the mob. Fourteen were wounded. Casualties among Wilson's defenders were less severe. Though Captain Campbell died, only a few others were wounded.[15]

After this incident, Wilson, convinced that his life would come to a quick end if he stayed in Philadelphia, skulked out of the city to hide in Robert Morris's country house. When it became apparent that that might be too obvious a hiding place, Wilson relocated to another spot, somewhere across the river in New Jersey. By the middle of October, the forces of law and order in Philadelphia had arrested most of those responsible for the violence, and the popular outrage against Wilson had subsided sufficiently to allow him to slip unobtrusively back into the city and reoccupy his house. But Wilson would never forget the incident. However much he may have believed—in theory—in the principle that the people should be the source of government power, he would always retain a visceral fear of those same people when aroused by the "lower sorts."[16]

As a consequence, then, of both temperament and experience, Wilson's democratic faith was philosophical rather than instinctive. His beliefs were born of a practical understanding of the need to found a strong national government on the sovereign will of an abstracted "people" more than of any warmth of feeling for the actual people who were to make up the polity.

Given the feelings of most of his fellow delegates, however, Wilson's preferences and motivations were moot, for his plan for a directly elected president went nowhere. Not a single delegate rose to support Wilson's proposal.

The debate on the presidency dragged on through the first week of June—a week marked by cold, rainy weather and continuing disagreement over almost all aspects of the executive branch. That week also marked the arrival of more delegates—William Samuel Johnson of Connecticut, Daniel of St. Thomas Jenifer of Maryland, John Lansing of New York, and Governor William Livingston of New Jersey. With Jenifer's arrival, the state of Maryland was now able to take part in the Convention's proceedings, leaving only New Hampshire and Rhode Island unrepresented.

The delegates continued their debate on both the powers and mode of election of the chief executive on Saturday June 2 and Monday June 4, and once again they found almost nothing about which they could agree. Although a clear majority of delegates preferred a single executive, several influential delegates—led by Edmund Randolph and George Mason of Virginia—argued that a single executive would inevitably lead to tyranny. In spite of Washington's presence, they issued the dire prediction that a unitary executive would inevitably seek to gather all of the government's power in his hands, thereby transforming the presidency into an "elective monarchy," a monarchy no less dangerous, in their view, than a hereditary one.[17]

Once again, James Wilson came forward with the most compelling rejoinder. The vast extent of the country, Wilson argued, required a single executive to bring unity to the nation, and America's "republican manners" made it unthinkable that an American president could transform himself into a monarch. On June 4, with Wilson in the lead, the delegates approved the proposal for creating a single executive. Massachusetts, Connecticut, Pennsylvania, Virginia, North Carolina, South Carolina, and Georgia voted in favor; and three states, New York, Delaware, and Maryland, voted against. The seven-to-three margin was deceptive, for even within the state delegations where a majority of delegates were in favor, there were some—Randolph and Mason in the Virginia delegation, for example—who still feared that a single powerful executive would lead to autocracy.[18]

If the delegates had not achieved unanimity, they had at least approached a workable majority in favor of a single executive. But their initial discussions of how to select the chief executive revealed vast differences of opinion, with no resolution in sight.

Most of the delegates favored the Virginia Plan's call for election of the president by the national legislature. That provision had support in all regions of the country, from men of such varying political views as Madison, who hoped for a powerful, independent executive, and Roger Sherman, who wished the chief executive to be a mere servant of the legislature. But there were other proposals. John Rutledge of South Carolina wanted only the upper house of the Congress—the most select and furthest removed from the people—to choose the president. A few of the delegates—Gerry of Massachusetts, Bedford of Delaware, and several members of the South Carolina and Georgia delegations—concerned with preserving the authority of the individual states, put forth various schemes by which the state legislatures would appoint the president. Madison and other nationalists strenuously objected to this method, worrying that it would "unbalance" the government, making the president a mere power broker among the interests of the several states, rather than the symbol of a unified nation.[19]

James Wilson, having failed to win support for his plan for direct election by the people, introduced another alternative that, though it removed the people from any direct role in selecting the president, had the virtue of rendering the executive independent of the national legislature and the individual state legislatures. It was, in its basic outlines, an early version of the complicated system by which Americans elect their president today. Wilson proposed that the states be divided into districts and that within those districts "electors" would be selected by the voters; the electors would then meet to choose the chief executive. That method, Wilson reasoned, would place ultimate responsibility for selecting the president in the hands of individuals—the electors—whose superior knowledge and prominence in their communities would enable them to make a wise choice, but at the same time it would give to the people at large at least an indirect role in the selection of their president.

Without naming it, Wilson was calling for the creation of an electoral college. He still preferred his original proposal for direct election of the president by the people, but recognizing that he was unlikely to persuade the delegates to adopt that method, he thought that election of a specially designated set of presidential electors was the next best thing. It would preserve a separation of powers between the executive and legislative branches and prevent the state legislatures from interfering in the presidential selection process. Wilson was convinced that the president needed to be a creature of the national polity, not of thirteen individual and fractious states.[20]

Over the course of the next four sessions, from June 2 through June 6, the delegates took a series of straw votes on a wide range of methods for presidential selection. Wilson's proposal for direct election by the people had so little support that he never even attempted to bring it to a vote. And when Nathaniel Gorham polled the delegates on Wilson's alternative proposal for election of the president by a group of presidential electors, it too was overwhelmingly defeated, with only Pennsylvania and Maryland supporting it. When the delegates considered the Virginia Plan's original scheme for electing the president by the national legislature, the outcome was precisely the opposite. Eight states supported the original proposal, with Pennsylvania and Maryland opposing.[21] But the faces of many of those who had voted in favor of the proposal suggested a continuing uneasiness. Many viewed it as the least offensive of any of the possible alternatives, but they remained wary about lodging too much power in the hands of the national legislature. Still others—particularly from the lower South—continued to hope they could find a way to give the state legislatures some greater influence in the process. The issue was far from settled.

If the decision to have the Congress elect the president had held, the resulting system would have been antidemocratic—allowing only the "best and brightest" in the Congress to record their opinions on the nation's chief magistracy. Such a decision would also have undermined one of the hallmarks of the American constitutional system, one that would evolve over the course of that summer—the principle of separation of powers.

The delegates inherently feared concentration of power in the hands of any one individual or agency of government, but at this stage in the Convention they remained uncertain about how to construct a government with an adequate separation of powers. That uncertainty was evident in nearly every debate relating to the presidency, beginning with the president's term of service. Nearly everyone who spoke on the subject was concerned with the same two issues—ensuring that the executive could function with a reasonable amount of independence from the legislature while at the same time preventing him amassing too much power for an extended period of time. The first of many votes on the president's term came at the end of the day on June 1. Although Madison's notes simply refer to "the question for seven years," the delegates were most likely also voting on the language of the seventh of Edmund Randolph's original resolutions, which stated that the chief executive would "be ineligible a second time." The outcome of that vote was hardly decisive. Five states, New York, New Jersey, Pennsylvania, Delaware, and Virginia, voted yes; four states, Connecticut, North Carolina, South Carolina, and Georgia, voted no; and the Massachusetts delegation was divided. The Convention delegates were uncertain whether a vote of 5-4-1 could be considered an "affirmative" one. General Washington, momentarily stepping back into his role as president of the Convention, ruled that it could. While Washington may have been technically correct in his ruling, everyone present understood that such a weak affirmation hardly constituted a permanent resolution of the issue.[22]

THE EXECUTIVE VETO

The debate on the power of the president to veto a bill passed by Congress was shaped by the delegates' powerful memories of the ways in which royally appointed colonial governors, acting on instructions from the king, had abused their unconditional power to veto legislation passed by colonial assemblies. The first three grievances listed in the Declaration of Independence had been directed at the abuse of the royal governors' veto power. Most of the newly independent states, reacting to the excesses of the colonial governors, adopted constitutions that denied their elected governors a veto power. While many of the Convention delegates believed that the states had gone too far in weakening executive power, which rendered governors powerless to restrain the democratic excesses of legislatures, they held a deep antipathy toward any hint of a return to the old English system.

Resolution Eight of the Virginia Plan proposed "that the Executive and a convenient number of the National Judiciary ought to compose a Council of Revision" with the authority to examine the acts of both the national legislature and the state legislatures. The council was to have a limited veto (the precise limits were left vague) over laws passed by either the national or state legislatures.[23]

The debate on Resolution Eight revealed some of the difficulty the delegates faced in finding an appropriate mechanism for reviewing laws passed by Congress or the state legislatures. As our constitutional system has evolved, the executive branch has played at least a limited role in assessing the constitutionality of laws passed by Congress. The president may veto congressional statutes if he believes them to be unconstitu-

tional, but if two-thirds of the members of each house of Congress disagree with the president's constitutional interpretation, they may override the veto. And, beginning in 1803, when Chief Justice John Marshall
articulated a limited conception of judicial review in *Marbury v. Madison*, the Supreme Court has steadily asserted its role in judging the constitutionality of laws passed by either Congress or the various state
legislatures. Marshall's ruling had a solid foundation in English and
early American law, but the delegates in Philadelphia had a long road to
travel before they developed a clear understanding of the distinction between the executive's role in reviewing the actions of the legislature and
the ultimate responsibility of the judicial branch to review the constitutionality of federal or state laws. The initial proposal for a council of
revision—and the debate that ensued—revealed some of the delegates'
uncertainty.[24]

As the debate on Resolution Eight unfolded on June 4, James Wilson
opposed mingling the executive and judiciary in a council of revision on
the grounds that the powers of the various branches of the government
should be "distinct and independent." It was essential, Wilson insisted,
that the executive possess an "absolute negative" in order to achieve the
necessary independence and separation from the legislative branch.
"Without such a defense," he argued, "the legislature can at any moment sink it into non-existence." Alexander Hamilton, the only man in
the Convention who desired a chief executive even more powerful than
that envisioned by Wilson, emphatically supported Wilson's proposal,
predicting that the mere threat of an executive veto would probably be
sufficient to keep the legislature from overstepping its bounds. Demonstrating how out of touch he was with most Americans' intense fear of a
revival of monarchical power, he sought to assure the delegates that "the
King of Great Britain had not exerted his negative since the Revolution." Virtually no one in the room felt any comfort in that assurance.[25]

There were few others in the Convention inclined to support an absolute veto for the president. Benjamin Franklin, remaining seated in his
chair on the middle aisle, strongly opposed Wilson's proposal. Many of
Franklin's contributions to the debate over the character of the American
executive were diffuse and off the point. On June 2, for example, he
asked James Wilson to read a lengthy speech for him in which he laid out
an elaborate argument for denying the president any compensation beyond his "necessary expenses." Drawing on his knowledge of the behavior of kings and arbitrary rulers throughout human history, Franklin

argued that the office of the executive offered powerful temptations toward self-aggrandizement. The love of power and the love of money would, he was convinced, combine to corrupt the executive. It was a peculiar speech, failing to draw distinctions between individuals subject to the popular will and serving limited terms and hereditary monarchs. Franklin's personal life history and his egalitarian instincts should have worked toward an egalitarian solution to the issue. In this case, however, his proposal would have led in the opposite direction—limiting service as chief executive only to those free of the obligation to earn a living. Alexander Hamilton seconded Franklin's motion, with a wink at the other delegates to make it clear that he was doing so simply out of courtesy to the esteemed doctor. Madison noted in his journal that Franklin's proposition was "treated with great respect, but rather for the author of it, than from any apparent conviction of its expediency or practicality."[26]

Franklin would base his opposition to an absolute executive veto, registered on June 4, on the same fear of the avarice of government officials. Drawing on his memory of the stormy relationship between the Pennsylvania legislature and the colony's proprietary governors in the years before the Revolution, Franklin was convinced that an executive armed with an absolute veto would use it in order to "extort money" for his own personal gain. "No good law," Franklin claimed, "could be passed without a private bargain" aimed at padding the executive's pocketbook.[27]

Wilson, in answer to Franklin, pointed to the important differences between a governor appointed by either a king or a proprietor and an elected executive accountable to the people within a republican system, but others opposed the veto on different grounds. Elbridge Gerry, ever distrustful of democracy in any form, believed that since the members of the national legislature would be chosen from among "the best men in the community," there would be no need for the chief executive to exercise such close control over its actions. Arguing on the same side, but with a more populist bent, Roger Sherman once again opposed "enabling any one man to stop the will of the whole." "No man," he believed, "could be found so far above all the rest." Sherman, perhaps more than any delegate present, believed in a doctrine of nearly absolute legislative supremacy, wishing to limit the authority of the executive to that of carrying out the will of the legislature.[28]

It was left to James Madison to grope for a solution that lay somewhere between an unchecked legislative authority and an absolute executive veto. Although he mounted a mild defense of an absolute veto, reasoning that even if the president possessed that power he would be unlikely to use it if a substantial majority in each house of Congress held a contrary view, he signaled his willingness to compromise. Madison acknowledged reluctantly that a provision requiring a "proper proportion of each branch" to override an executive veto might serve the same purpose.[29]

But the delegates were not yet ready for compromise. Toward the end of the day on June 4, the Committee of the Whole voted on a range of possible alternatives respecting the executive veto. The first presented was that favored by Wilson and Hamilton—"an absolute negative." It failed to receive support from any of the ten state delegations present. Pierce Butler of South Carolina then proposed that the president be given the power to suspend a law, which met the same unanimous opposition.[30]

The next proposal, inspired by Elbridge Gerry, would have enabled two-thirds of each branch of the Congress to overrule any veto imposed by the proposed council of revision. That proposal seemed to find some favor among the delegates, but it was then amended to take the judiciary out of the equation. The amended version provided that the president alone would have the "revisionary control," unless overruled by two-thirds of each house of Congress. This formulation drew support from eight states, with Connecticut and Maryland opposing. This seemed like real progress and, indeed, pointed the way to the eventual language in the completed Constitution. However, Madison, still clinging to his original notion of having the national judiciary combine with the executive branch in some sort of council of revision, proposed an amendment to add "and a convenient number of the national judiciary" to share with the national executive this proposed "revisionary check." At this point the consensus collapsed, Alexander Hamilton objected on a point of order, and the whole matter of the executive veto—with or without judicial endorsement—was postponed until the Convention could take up the larger question of the extent and scope of powers of the national judiciary.[31]

REMOVING A PRESIDENT

On the few occasions since the adoption of the Constitution when Americans have confronted the choice of impeaching and removing their president from office, the ensuing debate and decision have aroused enormous conflict, rancor, and, on at least two occasions, national trauma. The first such occasion, the impeachment and acquittal (by the vote of a single senator) of President Andrew Johnson for his willful refusal to carry out the Northern-controlled plan for reconstruction of the Southern states, occurred in the aftermath of a horrific civil war. The second, the resignation of Richard Nixon in the face of likely impeachment by the House, occurred in an atmosphere of partisan rancor between Republicans and Democrats. Nevertheless, members of the House from both political parties seemed to agree that the president had abused the power of his office and that the nature of the abuse did rise to the standard, however vaguely stated, of "high crimes and misdemeanors." The impeachment of William Jefferson Clinton, based on transgressions and possible untruths respecting his personal life, certainly stirred up partisan rancor but ultimately did not lead either to national trauma or to Clinton's removal from office. They are three very different cases—one involving a bitter division over policy between members of Congress and an accidental, Southern-born president, another involving more clear-cut abuses of presidential power, and the third involving presidential lust and prevarication. Does the wisdom of the Founding Fathers teach us much about the appropriateness of the device of impeachment in any of these three cases? Alas, the delegates were as divided on this subject as on many others.

On June 2, Delaware's John Dickinson initiated the discussion of how one might remove a chief executive from office. He did so in the midst of a chaotic discussion ranging over the various ways in which the executive should be appointed or elected and immediately following Benjamin Franklin's lengthy excursion into the evils of compensating the executive. Randolph's original resolutions on the character of the executive branch said nothing about removal, and Dickinson, though he found distasteful the whole idea of "impeaching the great officers of state," nevertheless thought that "it was necessary . . . to place the power of removing somewhere." His thinking on the matter was shaped primarily by his concern about the drift in the Convention toward a national form of government. With those concerns in mind, he proposed that "the executive be made removable by the national legislature on the request of a majority of the legislatures of the individual states." Impeachment, if Dickinson had had his way, would have been a cumbersome process, requiring action by both a majority of state governments and the Congress.[32]

Roger Sherman spoke next, arguing strenuously for the principle of legislative supremacy. Again advocating what would have amounted to a parliamentary system of government in which a prime minister might be turned out of office on the basis of a vote of no confidence, Sherman contended that the national legislature "should have power to remove the executive at pleasure." George Mason, already alarmed over the idea of a single rather than a plural executive, agreed that some method for removing "an unfit magistrate" needed to be devised. However, he opposed the idea that the president would be the "mere creature of the legislature" on the grounds that it violated the principle of separation of powers. Sherman's view of total legislative supremacy, though he would argue for it again and again over the course of the summer, had little support among the delegates.[33]

Madison and James Wilson, concerned primarily about preserving the national character of their plan, strongly opposed intermingling state and national authorities in the business of the executive branch. They suggested that Dickinson's proposal be amended by striking the phrase "on request by a majority of the legislatures of the individual states." Only three states—Connecticut, South Carolina, and Georgia—supported their proposal to remove the states from the process. To confuse things further, when the delegates voted on Dickinson's original motion, they rejected it even more emphatically, with all of the states except Dickinson's home state of Delaware opposing it.[34]

With the rejection of Dickinson's proposal, the delegates were right back where they started, with no agreement either on the power of the executive to overturn congressional legislation or on the power of the state governments or the Congress to remove an executive who proved himself unfit to exercise the powers of the office. As the Convention prepared to adjourn on June 4, nearly every important aspect of the executive branch in the proposed new government remained undecided. Although a decisive majority of delegates had expressed a preference for a single executive, the strong opposition of delegates like Mason and Randolph, who otherwise had supported the nationalist agenda, surely caused unease among those who hoped to deliver a solid consensus behind a strong national government. On virtually every other important issue—the length of the executive's term and the whole range of issues relating to the relationship between the national legislature and the national executive—the delegates' sentiments seemed to be moving in every conceivable direction, except toward consensus.

AS THE CONVENTION ADJOURNED on the afternoon of June 5, nationalists like Madison, Gouverneur Morris, and James Wilson began to worry. Just a week before, they had succeeded in placing before the Convention a bold plan for a dramatically strengthened national government. Though vague on details, the plan's essential features—the call for a truly national government and the supremacy of national legislation over laws passed by the states—had effectively stolen the thunder from those delegates in the Convention who might have preferred more palliative measures in strengthening the Confederation government. But as the debate over the details unfolded during the next week, it became clear not only that there was significant disagreement over many of the details, but also that many in the Convention would use that disagreement to try to reverse, or at least weaken, the thrust of Gouverneur Morris's May 30 resolution, which called for the creation of a national government with a supreme executive, legislature, and judiciary.

Perhaps there was no avoiding this kind of backsliding. Perhaps Madison, Wilson, and Gouverneur Morris had pressed the delegates too far too fast; certainly any hopes the Virginia delegates may have had for a speedy Convention that would produce an easy consensus were evaporating. The cool days of early June would soon give way to more typical summer weather. It would be a long, hot, contentious summer in Philadelphia.

CHAPTER EIGHT

COUNTERATTACK

AS THE DELEGATES READ their morning newspapers on Friday June 8, they were no doubt surprised to learn from the Pennsylvania *Herald* that one of their actions that week had been to decree "that Rhode Island should be considered as having virtually withdrawn herself from the union." The *Herald* went on to report that the Convention had determined that the continental government should be prepared to use military force to ensure that the absent Rhode Islanders pay their fair share of the federal debt. Though many delegates were no doubt perturbed by Rhode Island's absence, and some would have liked to find a means to coerce the state to meet its financial obligations, the *Herald*'s report did not contain a single grain of truth. Indeed, to the extent that the Philadelphia press reported on the proceedings of the Convention at all, the rule of secrecy ensured that virtually all of their reporting was either erroneous or wholly fabricated.[1]

On the morning of June 8, the weather had warmed significantly, such that the delegates began their proceedings for the first time without fires in the hearths at the front of the room. Opening the proceedings, Charles Pinckney of South Carolina reintroduced Randolph's original resolution giving to Congress the "authority to negative all laws which they should judge to be improper." Pinckney now argued that "such a universality of . . . power was indispensably necessary" to render the new government effectual. Madison had long regarded such a power as

the heart and soul of his plan for a new government, and he rose in support of Pinckney's proposal. But other delegates began to express second
thoughts.[2]

Elbridge Gerry of Massachusetts, though still concerned about the
way an ill-informed populace had led to the corruption of state legislatures, now expressed equal concern about the potential for tyranny in an
all-powerful national Congress. He was willing to give a veto power to the
proposed Congress, but only in specifically enumerated circumstances—
for example, if the state legislatures proved irresponsible in issuing paper
money, as had happened in Rhode Island and other states in recent years.
Roger Sherman of Connecticut concurred, insisting that "the cases in
which the negative ought to be exercised . . . be defined." Gunning Bedford of Delaware raised an issue that had been troubling him and many
other members from the less-populous states—the possibility not only
that the new national government might lead to the destruction of the independence of the state governments, but that the biggest losers in that
process would be the small states, who, "strip[ped] . . . of their equal
right of suffrage" in the national legislature, would find themselves at the
mercy of the large states.[3]

Bedford, a man described as both "corpulent" and "handsome," had
been a classmate of James Madison's at Princeton. Indeed, in spite of
Madison's scholarly bent, it was Bedford who graduated at the head of
their class. Although born in Philadelphia and trained in the law there
after graduating from Princeton, he was, steadfastly, a "small states
man," a determined and pugnacious defender of Delaware's interests.
He calculated that under the scheme proposed by Madison, Pennsylvania and Virginia alone would have about a third of the representatives in
Congress and Delaware only about one-ninetieth. In a preview of the
rancorous language in which he would indulge in the weeks to come,
Bedford charged that the Virginians and Pennsylvanians wished "to provide a system in which they would have an enormous and monstrous influence." Pierce Butler of South Carolina, who in his earlier interjections
had seemed at least sympathetic to the general thrust of the Virginia
Plan, joined Bedford in opposing the idea of a congressional veto over
state legislation, arguing that it would cut "off all hope of equal justice in
the distant states." In Butler's case, "distant" probably referred to his
concern that the interests of a slave-owning state from the lower South
might well be threatened by the larger number of non-slave-owning
states.[4]

As the day drew to a close, and Nathaniel Gorham asked for a vote on the question of giving Congress an unlimited veto power over legislation from the state governments, Madison and his fellow nationalists could see the promise of the first days of the Convention slipping away. Delegates like Gunning Bedford from small states feared that their interests would be sacrificed to those of the large states, delegates like Butler feared that the interests of the slave-owning states might be endangered by a Congress dominated by non-slave-owning states, and delegates like Elbridge Gerry voiced a more generalized fear of centralized power. Only Massachusetts (with Gerry dissenting), Pennsylvania, and Virginia supported the proposition; Connecticut, New York, New Jersey, Maryland, North Carolina, South Carolina, and Georgia opposed it; and Delaware was divided. The devil *was* in the details, and as delegates started to take a closer look at the specifics of the Virginia Plan, they began to discover more that they did not like.[5]

The following day, Saturday June 9, dawned clear and fine, although the weather, like the mood of the Convention, would grow gloomy as the day wore on. The cantankerous, irascible Luther Martin of Maryland finally took his seat in the Convention on that day, and he would soon become one of the most ardent, tireless, and, in the view of many, tiresome opponents of the nationalist vision.

The day began with the delegates once again wrangling inconclusively about the mode of selecting the president, but then William Paterson of New Jersey took the floor to take aim at the issue on which consensus had proven the most elusive—the manner of apportioning representation in the national legislature. He emphatically registered his opposition to Madison's proposal for proportional representation in both houses of Congress and then proceeded to launch a full-scale counterattack on Madison's conception of a government based on the sovereign power of the people of the nation as a whole rather than that of the individual states.[6]

William Paterson had immigrated to America from Ireland with his family when he was two years old, settling in Princeton, New Jersey, where his father achieved modest success as a storekeeper. Short and slight of build, Paterson was determined to rise above the normal aspirations of the son of a storekeeper, entering the College at Princeton in 1759, at the age of fourteen. Among his classmates were two future Convention delegates, Luther Martin of Maryland and Oliver Ellsworth of Connecticut. Although he did not remain in close touch with them after graduation, he and Martin in particular would find themselves in com-

William Paterson was a stalwart defender of the interests of the "small states" in the Convention. Portrait by James Sharples, 1794, courtesy of New York Public Library.

mon cause at the Convention, emerging as two of the most vocal defenders of small-state interests. Paterson stayed at Princeton after graduating in 1763, first to take a master's degree and then to study law. He worked hard as a journeyman lawyer during the years leading up to the Revolution and, beginning with the advent of independence, combined his law career with public service as New Jersey's attorney general from 1776 to 1783.[7]

Paterson had spent nearly all his life and public career inside New Jersey, and from the moment he arrived in Philadelphia to serve in the Constitutional Convention he would complain about the trials and tribulations of living away from home. Paterson's combination of an unrelenting provincialism and a formidably stern moral code carried over into every aspect of his life—personal, religious, and political. Paterson was among the many Americans who viewed the Revolution against British rule not only as a constitutional struggle, but also as one that pitted virtuous, pious Americans against the extravagant excesses of the British monarchy and aristocracy—and he intended to enforce that virtue. As New Jersey's attorney general during the Revolution, Paterson had been particularly zealous in prosecuting people for fornication.

Later, as governor, he was a keen advocate of legislation outlawing the playing of billiards and reducing the number of taverns in the state. Finding himself in Philadelphia that summer of 1787, where one could not walk a hundred feet without seeing a tavern or avoid the advances of prostitutes in the public market, Paterson's well-developed sense of virtue and propriety were no doubt constantly offended.[8]

At the center of Paterson's concerns was an abiding fear of disorder—whether in his own personal life or in the behavior of others. He fervently believed that "obedience to the law is the first political maxim and duty in a republican government." Through relentless self-discipline, he led his own life in an orderly, purposeful manner. However, controlling the behavior of others proved more difficult. Everywhere he turned, Paterson saw evidence of people's susceptibility to licentiousness, and he felt that their political judgment could not be trusted.[9]

Paterson had remained silent during the first two weeks of the Convention, contenting himself with occasional, and at times rather cryptic, note taking. By June 9, though, he had a clear enough grasp on the direction the Convention was moving to speak his mind. And when he did, he didn't hold back. From the very opening of the Convention on May 25 until the moment he rose to speak on June 9, no one had questioned the legality of the proceedings. Yet Paterson opened his speech by reminding the delegates of the terms under which the Confederation Congress had agreed to call a Convention and demanding that the commission of the delegation from Massachusetts be read aloud. That commission followed the form of many other states in stipulating that the Articles of Confederation "were . . . the proper basis of all the proceedings of the Convention." Paterson charged that by endorsing the general principles enunciated in the Virginia Plan, the delegates had usurped the charge given to them by their constituents. In spite of his innate distrust of the passions of the people, Paterson, at least on this occasion, maintained that the job of a representative was to represent—indeed, to mirror—the views of his constituents. He insisted that his fellow delegates be bound by that responsibility. "The idea of a national government," Paterson claimed, "never entered into the mind" of any of the states that had sent delegates to the Convention. "We have no power to go beyond the federal scheme," he argued, "and if we had, the people are not ripe for any other. We must follow the people; the people will not follow us."[10]

According to Paterson, a confederacy, by definition, required equality

of representation of its constituent parts. It was a definition more harmonious with traditional understandings of federalism than was Madison's proposal for a radical shift in the locus of sovereignty. Indeed, the
various features of the Virginia Plan, together with Madison's frequent
use of the word "national" rather than "federal," convinced Paterson
that Madison had abandoned the principles of federalism altogether.

Paterson did agree that a new and improved form of the Articles of
Confederation should have extensive new powers, including that of co-
ercing state governments to bow to the superior will of the central
government. But he was adamant about the principle of equality of representation. Referring to a "hint" made by James Wilson of Pennsylvania that the large states might be forced to form their own union on
principles of proportional representation if the smaller states were unwilling to join, Paterson threw down the gauntlet.

> Let them [the large states] unite if they please, but let them
> remember that they have no authority to compel the others
> to unite. New Jersey will never confederate on the plan
> before the Committee. She would be swallowed up. I would
> rather submit to a monarch, to a despot, than to such a fate.
> I will not only oppose the plan here, but on my return home
> do everything in my power to defeat it there.[11]

James Wilson came right back at Paterson, warning his New Jersey
neighbor that if his state were unwilling to join a union on those terms,
then it might very well find itself confronting a powerful union of states
willing to move forward without New Jersey's participation. There was
an element of bluster in all of this. Madison, Gouverneur Morris, and
Wilson may have been able to muster a bare majority of state delegations
in support of their vision of a government in which the people of the
states, and not the states themselves, were equally represented, but they
knew they needed more than a bare majority. Nevertheless, the nationalists demanded that their views be put to a vote in the Committee of the
Whole. Paterson, observing that "much depended on it," asked that the
vote be postponed. A hush settled over the room; the nationalists realized that they had reached a critical moment in the proceedings. Without
anyone rising to contest Paterson's request, the nationalists backed off,
agreeing to the postponement. With that, the Convention adjourned for
the remainder of the weekend.[12]

ROGER SHERMAN'S ATTEMPT AT COMPROMISE

Monday, June 11, was warmer than average, the high temperature that day reaching the low eighties. The New Englanders, habitually dressed for colder weather, were beginning to feel the heat; the Southerners, well used to heat and humidity, were just beginning to feel comfortable. While the previous week had ended on a note of rancor, this week would begin with a search for compromise. Roger Sherman of Connecticut attempted to find a middle ground between the large and small states. He proposed

> that the proportion of suffrage in the first branch should be according to the respective numbers of free inhabitants; and that in the second branch or Senate, each state should have one vote and no more. . . . As the states would remain possessed of certain individual rights, each state ought to be able to protect itself; otherwise a few large states will rule the rest. The House of Lords in England . . . had certain particular rights under the Constitution, and hence they have an equal vote with the House of Commons that they may be able to defend those rights.[13]

Sherman was no supporter of a hereditary aristocracy, and he knew that the proposed Senate in the American government would differ significantly from the House of Lords, but his comparison with the House of Lords was not inapt. Like Madison, he wished to pay due deference to the wisest and most virtuous in society by creating a Senate consisting of men possessing those qualities. The upper house of Congress would be the embodiment of social and political traditions as well as state interests. But Sherman had much greater respect than Madison for the value of the colonial and state governments in guiding America's destiny. Sherman thought it not only proper but, from a pragmatic point of view, prudent to recognize the states as separate entities and to give them equal weight in at least one of the coequal branches of the legislature.

Sherman's proposal differed in only a few particulars from what would later be called the Connecticut Compromise. He would restate it in slightly altered form on June 20, and his Connecticut colleagues Oliver Ellsworth and William Samuel Johnson would endorse a similar proposal on June 29. If the delegates had been prepared to follow the advice of Connecticut's representatives, they would have saved themselves many weeks of further contention. But too many—both among the large- and small-state delegations—were simply not in a mood to embrace compromise. One by one, they rose to defend their ideas and, more importantly, the interests of their particular states.[14]

In the midst of this jockeying for advantage on June 11, Benjamin Franklin asked that his ideas on the subject of representation be read to the Convention by James Wilson. What followed was a peculiar discourse indeed, with hints of sagacity mixed with some fanciful, and dubious, statecraft. Franklin began by observing that until the subject of representation had come before the Convention, "our debates were carried on with great coolness and temper." Alas, the delegates seemed now inclined to "declarations of a fixed opinion and of determined resolution" that were unlikely to produce either enlightenment or a consensus. Invoking the classical republican ideal of "disinterested public service," Franklin hoped that "every member of Congress . . . [would] consider himself rather as a representative of the whole, than as an agent for the interests of a particular state." With that ideal in mind, he thought that "the number of representatives should bear some proportion to the number of the represented, and that the decisions should be by the majority of members, not by the majority of states." He discounted the likelihood that large states would tyrannize over small states and, in fact, thought that "in the present mode of voting by states, it is equally in the power of the lesser states to swallow up the greater."[15]

Ever the pragmatist, Franklin acknowledged that the small-state delegates were unlikely to embrace his reasoning, so he went on to offer a complicated alternative for apportioning both representation and taxation. His formula for apportioning taxation involved determining the proportion of essential government expenses that the "weakest state" would be able to pay, with all other states then being required to match that sum. Since this formula was unlikely to provide adequate revenue, Franklin proposed that the balance be made up by voluntary contributions from "the richer and more powerful states," a highly unlikely result if past history were any guide. His formula for representation, which seemed slightly more sensible, would have given to each state an equal number of delegates, but with voting in the Congress to be done by individual delegates, not by the states as units. This method, Franklin believed, would encourage members of Congress to serve the broad public good rather than merely represent the interests of their particular states.[16]

The delegates listened politely to Franklin's proposal but let it drop without comment. At that point, Rufus King of Massachusetts and

James Wilson resumed their effort to get the Convention to endorse the principle embodied in the Virginia Plan: "the right of suffrage in the first branch of the national legislature ought not to be according to the rule established in the Articles of Confederation, but according to some equitable ratio of representation." The definition of "equitable" was, of course, in the eye of the beholder. And as was to become all too clear, it varied according to the interests of different states. But on that question at least the nationalists were able to prevail. Massachusetts, Connecticut, Pennsylvania, Virginia, North Carolina, South Carolina, and Georgia voted yes; New Jersey, Delaware, and New York voted no; and the Maryland delegation was divided. The victory was ambiguous at best for the nationalists and accompanied by the ominous note of New York's opposing vote. Even at this early point in the Convention, New York's two militantly antinationalist delegates—Robert Yates and John Lansing—demonstrated their determination to outvote their state's only nationalist delegate, Alexander Hamilton. More alarmingly, such was their opposition to any effort to change the structure of the continental government that they seemed inclined to vote no on virtually any question, whether it might be in their state's interest or not.[17]

REPRESENTATION, SLAVERY, AND THE BEGINNINGS OF SECTIONAL CONFLICT

The most persistent division during the first six weeks of the Convention's deliberations was that between large and small states, and it centered on the question of proportional versus equal representation. But the issue of *who* was to be represented in any system of proportional representation would always lurk in the background, and whenever the question was raised, the issue of the status of slaves and the value of their labor in the calculation on representation would intrude on the discussion.

What was an "equitable ratio of representation"? No sooner had the resolution supporting the large-state position on representation passed on June 11 than John Rutledge, South Carolina's most powerful politician, staked his claim as the most articulate and effective advocate of the interests of the slave-holding South. Rutledge would support a vastly strengthened national government throughout the Convention, but always on terms calculated to serve the interests of his home state. Rutledge's support for a system of proportional representation in the Congress was always predicated on the assumption that South Carolina would be one of the primary beneficiaries of such a system, and he was now prepared to push forward measures that would guarantee that outcome. "Money is power," he argued, and thus "states ought to have weight in the government in proportion to their wealth." Following that line of reasoning, he and his South Carolina colleague Pierce Butler proposed that representation in the House of Representatives be apportioned "according to the quotas of contribution," a phrase that dated back to at least 1783, when members of the Continental Congress tried to work out a formula by which states would contribute to the support of the continental government in rough proportion to their wealth. But Rutledge and Butler were now breaking new ground by suggesting that not only relative rates of taxation—but also representation—be based on wealth. And in so doing, they were injecting the issue of slavery squarely into the discussion.[18]

James Wilson, well aware that the two South Carolinians intended that slaves be counted fully in apportioning representation, offered a compromise proposal, striking the phrase "quotas of contribution" and adding the words "in proportion to the whole number of white and other free Citizens and inhabitants of every age sex and condition including those bound to servitude for a term of years and three-fifths of all other persons not comprehended in the foregoing description, except Indians not paying taxes, in each state." He was immediately seconded by Charles Pinckney of South Carolina, suggesting that perhaps the Northerner and Southerner may have already agreed that this was the best way to resolve a potentially explosive issue.[19]

There it was, dressed fancily in euphemism—"three-fifths of all other persons not comprehended in the foregoing description." As shocking as this formulation may seem to twenty-first-century readers, it seemed a reasonably practical way to deal with the question of how to balance the interests of the slave-owning and non-slave-owning states to most of the delegates gathered in the Assembly Room that day. Wilson and Pinckney, though they represented states with different interests on that particular question, were both nationalists who wished to see the Convention adopt the principle of proportional representation, and they hoped that by bending a bit on the issue of counting slaves in the apportionment of representation, they could assemble a coalition of Northerners and Southerners that would be sufficient to withstand the challenge of the defenders of small-state interests such as William Paterson.[20]

The three-fifths compromise was not proposed because the delegates believed that African slaves were only 60 percent human. Rather, the fraction "three-fifths" was intended as a rough approximation of the measure of wealth that an individual slave contributed to the economy of his or her state. That formula was first proposed in 1783 when the Continental Congress, seeking some means of achieving solvency, proposed a system of requisitions in which a state's contributions would be apportioned according to its ability to pay—in other words, on wealth. The politicians in the Continental Congress charged with finding a means of calculating each state's obligations—apparently with little serious empirical analysis—estimated that the wealth-producing capacity of a slave was roughly three-fifths of that of a free person. In fact, the Congress's proposal failed to receive the unanimous approval of the states necessary for its passage. Predictably, Northern states thought it undervalued slaves, and Southern states thought it overvalued them. In that sense, although the "idea" of a three-fifths ratio may have come from the 1783 Congress, because the proposal was never implemented, it falls somewhere short of a well-established precedent. Moreover, the three-fifths proposal coming out of the Confederation Congress referred only to the means of calculating a slave's value for the purpose of calculating relative rates of taxation. Since the principle of equal representation for each state was the bedrock of the Confederation government, no one ever suggested that slaves should be counted as three-fifths of a person in apportioning representation.[21]

Nevertheless, the idea of a three-fifths ratio, however arbitrary it may have been, obviously stuck in the minds of many Convention delegates. Charles Pinckney had used the three-fifths ratio in his neglected plan for the new government he presented on May 29. Wilson had seen a copy of Pinckney's plan prior to the opening of the Convention, and he noted that it contained a provision in which the "lower House of Delegates" was to be elected by the state legislatures and was to "consist of one Member for every US thousand Inhabitants, 3/5 of Blacks included."[22]

There are two other notable aspects of the language of Wilson and Pinckney's June 11 proposal. First, the individuals to be counted in the apportioning of representation consisted of the "whole number of white and other free citizens and inhabitants of every age sex and condition," including indentured servants. The definition of who among those "inhabitants" might be considered citizens and who might not was left ambiguous, but, at least for the purposes of apportioning representation, all free people—including women, children, and indentured servants—

were to be included in the calculation. The "other persons" who were to be weighted at a three-fifths ratio were not identified. All of the delegates knew who those other persons were. They were slaves bound to service not only for their lives, but also for the lives of their descendants.

Whether out of delicacy or out of shame, most Southerners and Northerners went to great lengths *not* to identify by name those other persons who were to be the source of contention. But one individual, the bristly Elbridge Gerry, cut through the linguistic fog in blunt language when he opposed giving a three-fifths weight to slaves. Gerry noted that "blacks are property, and are used to the southward as horses and cattle are to the northward; and why should their representation be increased to the southward on account of the number of slaves, than horses or oxen to the north?" Although Gerry's mercantile business does not appear to have included trading in slaves, there is nothing in his career that suggests he felt any moral outrage over the institution. It's more likely that Gerry was merely defending the self-interests of Massachusetts, which had no slaves, in equating slaves with cattle and oxen. In William Paterson's recollection of Gerry's speech, Gerry was also voicing his resentment at having free inhabitants associated in any way with slaves. Paterson's abbreviated summary of Gerry's remarks reads, "Slaves are not to be put upon the Footing of freemen—Freeman of Massts. Not to be put upon a Footing with the Slaves of other States—Horses and Cattle ought to have the Right of Representn—Negroes—Mules—."[23]

Though Wilson and Pinckney's proposal left a lot to be desired, nine states voted in the affirmative, and only two—New Jersey and Delaware—opposed. New Jersey and Delaware, far from casting their votes against the absurdity of a three-fifths ratio, were simply reasserting their interests as small states. They were voting against the idea of proportional representation in *any* form.[24]

ALTHOUGH NEW JERSEY and Delaware appeared unreconciled to any form of proportional representation in either house of Congress, it appeared that most states were willing to endorse the idea of proportional representation in the lower house. And although Elbridge Gerry's intervention may have caused at least a few delegates to ponder the logical and moral contradictions of a formula that treated slaves as both property and human beings, most delegates—at least for the moment—seemed satisfied with the three-fifths ratio as a reasonable way to placate the interests of North and South. With that still-tenuous consensus in place, the del-

egates moved on to consider the mode of apportioning representation
in the Senate. Immediately after the delegates tentatively approved the
Wilson-Pinckney formulation, Connecticut's Roger Sherman fired the
first shot on the question of representation in the upper house, noting
that "the smaller States would never agree to the [Constitution] on any
other principle than an equality of suffrage in this branch." His colleague
Oliver Ellsworth echoed those sentiments. When the question was first
put to a vote it quickly became apparent how persistent the stalemate was
likely to be. The delegates first voted on Sherman's proposal for equality
of representation in the upper house. Five states favored the formula, six
opposed. Then, without debate, they voted on a proposal from Wilson
and Hamilton for proportional representation in the upper house—six
states in favor, five opposed. In each case, the alignment was identical:
Massachusetts, Pennsylvania, Virginia, North Carolina, South Carolina,
and Georgia insisted on proportional representation in both houses;
Connecticut, New York, New Jersey, Delaware, and Maryland supported
the principle of equality of state representation.[25]

Although the delegates themselves described the protracted debate
over proportional versus equal representation as one dividing large and
small states, the reality was more complicated. Although all of the delegates' votes on the issue were based on their perceptions of the way in
which their states' self-interest would best be served, the ways they calculated their present and future self-interest varied. Two of the four
most populous states in the union, Virginia (747,000 inhabitants) and
North Carolina (395,000 inhabitants), were located in the South. Virginia's population was fully 60 percent larger than the country's second
most populous state, Pennsylvania (433,000) and nearly twice that of the
fourth-largest state, Massachusetts (378,000). Not surprisingly, all four
of these states found themselves in the "large-state" camp in the voting
on the question of proportional representation. Those four states were
joined by South Carolina (249,000) and Georgia (82,000). South Carolina's population was slightly smaller than some of the so-called small
states, and Georgia's population exceeded that only of Rhode Island and
Delaware. The populations of South Carolina and Georgia, however,
were growing rapidly, fueled in particular by an explosive growth in the
slave population. Their delegates believed that if they could get their way
on the issue of counting slaves in the apportionment of representation
they would quickly rival states like Virginia and North Carolina in their
political power. As America's history unfolded, it would be the commercial and increasingly urbanized North that would gain in population rel-

ative to the agrarian South, but that was not the way the future looked to many of the Convention delegates from the South in 1787.[26]

The only two Southern states siding with the so-called small-state bloc in the Convention were from the upper south—Maryland (319,000) and Delaware (60,000). All of the other support for the small-state position came from the North—from Connecticut (237,000), New Jersey (154,000), and New York (340,000). The positions of Maryland and New York are particularly interesting. Maryland's population was large enough to give its delegates some confidence that their state could hold its own in a union based on a system of proportional representation, but its position on the question of representation was shaped by two factors. Maryland's most outspoken delegate, Luther Martin, opposed proportional representation because he believed that any departure from the essential features of the Articles of Confederation was not only unwise, but illegal. The position of the other Maryland delegates was more likely shaped not by ideology, but by their awareness that their state had a long history as an inferior stepchild to the more populous and economically powerful Virginia. Many Marylanders justifiably feared that Virginians would come to dominate the new union. This, more than any precise calculation of present or future population, was enough to make the Maryland delegates hold fast to the principle of equality of representation in the national legislature.[27]

New York, the fifth most populous state in the union, was growing rapidly. More important, the economic power of the port of New York City guaranteed the state an important place within any form of union. Two of New York's delegates, however, Robert Yates and John Lansing, strongly opposed any government based on nationalist principles. Yates and Lansing shared the view of their political benefactor—New York's powerful governor, George Clinton—that New York had fared well within a relatively weak confederation of states, and thus they opposed any measure aimed at changing that situation.[28]

Although the factors that caused some states to consider themselves part of either the large- or small-state bloc may have been complicated—even contrived—the reality of that division simply would not go away. For the next month, the Convention remained deadlocked on the question of how to apportion representation in the Senate. Although the large-state delegates managed to muster a bare majority in support of their position during that month, no one in the Convention believed that a bare majority on an issue so fundamental would be sufficient to command a consensus for a new constitution.

THE REVISED REPORT ON THE VIRGINIA PLAN

In the midst of this impasse, the delegates moved forward on other aspects of the new government. On June 13, Nathaniel Gorham, acting on behalf of the Committee of the Whole, issued a revised report on the original Randolph Resolutions. The purpose of the report, which contained nineteen specific provisions as opposed to the fifteen in the original Virginia Plan, was to summarize and clarify the decisions made by the delegates in the two weeks since Randolph had introduced his resolutions. The report, probably a joint effort by Gorham and Convention secretary William Jackson, reflected the extent to which the Virginia and Pennsylvania nationalists had controlled the agenda up to that point. It continued to tilt toward the nationalist vision of what the new government should look like, while slighting the concerns of those who continued to worry about the excessive centralization of power in the new government. Most important, the revised report restated the proposition that "a National Government ought to be established, consisting of a supreme Legislative, Executive & Judiciary." It called for a lower house whose members would be elected by the people of the various states and who would serve terms of three years, and an upper house whose members would be chosen by the state legislatures and who would serve terms of seven years. The report also reaffirmed the supremacy of the national legislature and reasserted the Congress's power to veto laws passed by the state legislatures. And it affirmed the nationalist position that representation in both houses should be based on some "equitable ratio of representation, namely in proportion to the whole number of white & other free citizens and inhabitants," with slaves, still described euphemistically as "all other persons," to be weighted at three-fifths of those other citizens and inhabitants.[29]

The sections of the report on the national executive reiterated the desire of nationalists like Madison to have the Congress select the president, but they also fleshed out some of the details that had been left vague in the original Virginia Plan. It called for a presidential term of seven years, with no second term, and it gave the president a veto over congressional legislation, with the stipulation that two-thirds of both houses of Congress could override the veto.[30]

The report scuttled Madison's proposal for members of the national judiciary and the president to combine in a council of revision with authority to veto laws passed by either the Congress or the state legislatures. It simply stipulated that a "national judiciary be established, to consist of one supreme tribunal," leaving open the option for the national legislature to appoint inferior courts. The justices were to hold their offices "during good behavior," and the Senate would be responsible for their appointment, a nod to those who remained suspicious of too much popular involvement in the appointment of judges.[31]

Before the Convention adjourned at the end of the day on June 13, the delegates were given permission to make handwritten copies of the revised report on the Virginia Plan. One delegate, whose identity never became known, mislaid his copy. Pennsylvania delegate Thomas Mifflin spotted it on the floor of the Assembly Room and quickly gave it to General Washington, who put it in his pocket. Washington kept his silence until the end of the session, at which time he rose from his seat and, with a sternness that plainly unsettled the delegates, expressed his displeasure "to find that some one member of this body, has been so neglectful of the secrets of the Convention as to drop in the State House a copy of their proceedings, which, by accident, was picked up and delivered to me this morning. I must entreat [the] gentlemen to be more careful, lest our transactions get into the news papers, and disturb the public repose by premature speculations. I know not whose paper it is, but there it is." At that point, he threw the document down on the presiding officer's table, exclaiming, "Let him who owns it take it."[32]

After Washington had finished with his admonishment, he bowed, picked up his hat, and strode out of the room, leaving the delegates dumbstruck. Georgia delegate William Pierce, in recalling the incident, confessed that he was sent into a state of terror by Washington's remarks, for, when he checked his coat pocket for his copy, he could not find it. He cautiously advanced to the table on which Washington had thrown the copy, and was relieved to discover that the handwriting of the draft was not his own. He was further relieved when he went back to his lodgings at the Indian Queen and found his copy in the pocket of another coat he had been wearing earlier in the day. Such was the severity of Washington's rebuke, and such was the seriousness with which the delegates took their vow of secrecy, that the offending delegate never did have the nerve to come forward to claim the mislaid document.[33]

THE NEW JERSEY PLAN

Washington's concern about disturbing the "public repose by premature speculations" was well founded. Though the Convention's nationalists may have been pleased that most of the elements of the Virginia Plan had survived intact in the report from the Committee of the Whole on June 13, within twenty-four hours they would discover that those who did not share their vision were ready for the next stage of a carefully planned counterattack.

After Nathaniel Gorham presented the report of the Committee of the Whole on June 13, the delegates agreed to reassemble the following day as a formal Convention—with Washington in the chair—to consider the items in the report. That next day's session would be an extraordinarily brief one. When the Convention opened its business on June 14, William Paterson of New Jersey immediately announced his intention to block the nationalists' plans to overhaul the Articles of Confederation. Addressing the delegates, Paterson announced that "it was the wish of several deputations" to present a "purely federal" alternative to the Virginia Plan. He promised the delegates he would have an alternate proposal ready by the following day, requesting that the Convention adjourn "in order that leisure might be given for the purpose." The delegates agreed to the early adjournment, giving Paterson and his allies the "leisure" to put the finishing touches on their rebuttal to the Virginia Plan.[34]

Paterson had been preparing to launch his attack on the principles embodied in the Virginia Plan from the moment Randolph presented them to the Convention on May 29. In the private notes he made that day, Paterson took aim at the proposal for proportional representation, observing that "this is the Basis upon which the larger States can assent to any Reform." Convinced that the Virginia Plan's intent was to undermine the sovereign power of the states, he succinctly summarized the motivation behind Randolph's resolutions. "We ought to be one Nation." Paterson could not imagine a system of divided sovereignty. Either the states should possess ultimate sovereign power or they would be forced to yield it to a central government. His own position was unambiguous. In its ultimate, "integral" sense, sovereignty should reside with the state governments.[35]

Paterson's misgivings about both the specific issue of proportional representation and the location of sovereign power within the proposed new government found full expression on June 15, when he presented to the Convention a plan that "several of the deputations wished to be substituted in place of that proposed by Mr. Randolph."[36]

Paterson's proposals, which the delegates frequently referred to as the New Jersey Plan, had been cobbled together by a coalition of small-state delegates, including Paterson and David Brearley of New Jersey, Roger Sherman of Connecticut, and Luther Martin of Maryland, joined by John Lansing of New York. The New Jersey Plan opened with a restatement of the original charges to the Convention from the Annapolis Convention and the Confederation Congress—that "the Articles of Confederation ought to be so revised, corrected, and enlarged, as to render the federal Constitution adequate to the exigencies of Government, and the preservation of the Union." Unlike the Virginia Plan, with its call for a supreme national government, the New Jersey Plan proposed a government distinctly "federal" and then explicitly enumerated the limited and specific areas in which the powers of that government should be expanded, the most important of which involved the power to levy taxes on goods imported into the country and the power to regulate trade and commerce.[37]

Paterson's primary motive in presenting an alternative to the Virginia Plan was to protect the power of the smaller states, but his plan made no mention either of the composition of the Congress or of the method of apportioning representation in that Congress. His intent, however, was clear. By couching his plan as a set of specific amendments to the Articles of Confederation, without mentioning the composition and apportionment of the federal Congress, he was reaffirming the principle that the individual states would continue to be represented as they had been in the past, with each state sending as many delegates to the Congress as it wished, but with each state delegation having only one vote in that Congress.

James Wilson of Pennsylvania had proposed direct election of the nation's chief executive as a means of creating an American president who would serve as a powerful representative of the people of the nation as a whole. James Madison also favored a powerful chief executive, but he wanted the president to be selected by those virtuous and knowledgeable few in the national legislature. Paterson's conception, which drew much of its inspiration from the Articles of Confederation, was distinctly provincial. In Paterson's plan, the individual states represented in Congress would elect a "federal executive" consisting of an unspecified number of persons—unspecified, but presumably plural. Those serving in the executive office would be given the narrow charge of "execut[ing] the federal acts." Moreover, they would be removable by the Congress "on application by a majority of the Executives of the several States." The architects of the New Jersey Plan plainly intended the executive to be a creature of the Congress and the Congress, in turn, to be a creature of the individual state governments.[38]

Not surprisingly, Madison was appalled by what he considered the retrograde character of the New Jersey Plan. But Delaware's John Dickinson, certainly one of the wisest and most experienced delegates in the Convention, believed that Madison and his uncompromising nationalist allies had brought some of the difficulties they were about to experience on themselves. Dickinson, though a resident and representative of Delaware, had built his professional career in Pennsylvania. He was well situated to see the merits of both the large-state and the small-state positions. Though he sympathized with Madison's desire for a stronger central government, he had, earlier in the Convention, given a compelling speech in which he had "compared the proposed national system to the solar system, in which the states were the planets, and ought to be left to move freely in their proper orbits." In constructing that analogy, Dickinson grasped an important idea that few of his fellow delegates, including Madison, had yet comprehended. He was suggesting a government that was part national and part federal, one that mixed federal and state powers in a system of divided sovereignty. But Madison had brushed Dickinson's comments aside, accusing him of "contradictory" reasoning.[39]

Now, after Paterson finished presenting the New Jersey Plan, Dickinson confronted Madison. "You see the consequence of pushing things too far," he said. "Some members of the small states wish for two branches in the General Legislature, and are friends to a good national Government; but we would sooner submit to a foreign power, than submit to be deprived of an equality of suffrage, in both branches of the legislature, and thereby be thrown under the domination of the large states." Madison was unrepentant, refusing to yield an inch. For a full month following the introduction of the New Jersey Plan, the Convention would find itself nearly paralyzed by the deadlock between the large-state nationalists and the defenders of small-state interests. The success of the Convention was very much in jeopardy.[40]

CHAPTER NINE

"WE ARE NOW AT FULL STOP"

WHATEVER PERSONAL INSECURITIES may have plagued him, James Madison had full confidence in his powers of reason. And his experience in the Continental Congress and in the planning leading up to the Constitutional Convention had demonstrated that his skills as a practical politician were also formidable. But Madison's dismissal of John Dickinson's cautionary words in the aftermath of the introduction of the New Jersey Plan, combined with his insistence on a system of proportional representation in both houses of Congress—although based on sound reason and a logically consistent commitment to a government founded on the will of the American people—would lead the Convention into some of its most difficult days.

The eighteen days between the introduction of the New Jersey Plan on June 15 and the Convention's temporary recess at the end of the day on July 2 to celebrate the anniversary of independence were the most confusing, contentious, and unproductive of the summer. Over the course of those eighteen days, Madison and Edmund Randolph of Virginia, James Wilson and Gouverneur Morris of Pennsylvania, Rufus King of Massachusetts, and Charles Pinckney of South Carolina would all deride the New Jersey Plan as merely a patched-up version of the Articles of Confederation. While William Paterson, New York's John Lansing and Robert Yates, Gunning Bedford of Delaware, and Luther Martin of Maryland led the charge against the Virginia Plan, the Connecticut delegates—Roger Sherman, Oliver Ellsworth, and William Samuel Johnson—sought a middle ground, proposing on several occasions that representation in the lower house be apportioned according to population and in the upper according to the principle of equality of representation for each state. But as the days passed and the heat and humidity in the room climbed, few were willing to settle on that middle ground. The Constitutional Convention, called together to deliberate on the future of the American union, was increasingly taking on the tone of a rancorous, partisan debate.

ENTER COLONEL HAMILTON

Three days after William Paterson presented the New Jersey Plan, the lone nationalist delegate from New York, Alexander Hamilton, presented his own plan. Rising to his feet on the morning of June 18 and continuing until midafternoon, when the exhausted delegates moved for an adjournment, the lean and intellectually intense Hamilton indulged in an extraordinary exegesis of his political philosophy. Hamilton's plan would have little influence on the subsequent proceedings of the Convention, and, indeed, it no doubt tried the patience of many of the delegates. But it provides important insight into the philosophical and political assumptions of one of the most influential statesmen of the early republic.

Hamilton was thirty years old when he offered his observations to the Convention. He stood about five feet seven, had reddish brown hair, "deep blue, almost violet" eyes, a fair complexion, and fine, even delicate, features. His friends referred to him as the "Little Lion," not because of his size but because of his erect posture and skill in intellectual combat. William Pierce of Georgia, observing Hamilton's performance at the Convention, found his manner disagreeable, describing it as "tinctured with stiffness and sometimes with a degree of vanity." Pierce's disapproval notwithstanding, few who encountered the young New Yorker could dispute that, along with his handsome figure, he displayed uncommon intellectual brilliance.[1]

In spite of humble beginnings and a mediocre early education on the West Indies island of Nevis, Hamilton had a genius that was quickly recognized by some of the leading residents of the island, who sponsored his journey to New York in the fall of 1772. He gained admission to

The "Little Lion" combined formidable intellect with formidable ambition. Portrait of Alexander Hamilton by Charles Willson Peale, circa 1790–95, courtesy of Independence National Historical Park.

King's College (later Columbia University) the following year and quickly distinguished himself as a young man of extraordinary intellect. By the spring of 1776, he had received a commission as commander of an artillery company in New York and within a year had so impressed the commander in chief of the Continental army, General Washington, that he promoted Hamilton to the rank of lieutenant colonel and made him one of his aides-de-camp. By late 1780, the young upstart had managed to persuade the family of Elizabeth Schuyler, the daughter of the enormously wealthy and politically powerful Hudson River manor lord Philip Schuyler, to allow him to take her hand in marriage. Elizabeth was better known for her wealth than her beauty, but Hamilton—despite some spectacular sexual indiscretions during their married life—was, in his own way, devoted to her. Most important, the marriage would, along with Washington's patronage, propel Hamilton into positions of power and influence greater than anything that a young lad from Nevis might ever have contemplated.[2]

It is difficult to know what to make of Alexander Hamilton, either on the basis of his performance during the Constitutional Convention or during his tragically short career as a public servant. His personal manner, which at times bordered on arrogance, and his political philosophy, which was at its core fundamentally elitist and contemptuous of the abilities of the common man, elicited extravagantly positive and negative reactions in his own time and continue to do so. John Adams, referring to the irregular circumstances surrounding Hamilton's birth in the West Indies, called him the "bastard brat son of a Scots peddler," and he forever nurtured the belief that Hamilton's character was at best treacherous and at worst treasonous.[3]

Thomas Jefferson—who clashed bitterly with Hamilton over issues of domestic and foreign policy while they served together in President Washington's cabinet during the early 1790s—despised Hamilton, believing that his financial policies and constitutional principles would lead to America's ruin. Jefferson believed that Hamilton was at the head of a group of British sympathizers who preferred "the calm of despotism to the boisterous sea of liberty." In later years, the Virginian would become sufficiently alarmed that he planted a series of unflattering articles in the press accusing Hamilton of aristocratic and monarchical leanings.[4]

By contrast, another of Hamilton's contemporaries, the wily French minister Talleyrand, himself skilled in the arts of palace intrigue and diplomatic duplicity, believed Hamilton to be the greatest of the eighteenth-century American statesmen, declaring that "he had never known one . . . equal to him." And Hamilton's biographers typically praise him lavishly, often referring to him as a "genius" who pointed America toward its modern liberal capitalist future.[5]

Hamilton began his oration the morning of June 18 by acknowledging that his ideas on government were "dissimilar" from those held by most of the members of the Convention, but, he insisted, "the crisis . . . which now marks our affairs" was so serious that he was compelled to speak his mind. "I am obliged therefore," he announced, "to declare myself unfriendly to both [the Virginia and New Jersey] plans." The former, though preferable to the New Jersey version, seemed to Hamilton like "pork still, with a little change of the sauce."[6]

Hamilton proceeded to aim most of his fire at the New Jersey Plan, though. All of his experience as an officer in the Revolutionary War and as an official in the Confederation government had persuaded him that only a purely national government would satisfy the needs of the country. He believed, with a fervor edging toward contempt, that anything resembling a "merely federal government" would be hopelessly inadequate.

Drawing on his extensive knowledge of the history of governments both ancient and modern, as well as on a profoundly pessimistic view of the inherently selfish character of human nature, Hamilton listed five "essential principles necessary for the support of government." The first of these was "an active and constant interest" in supporting a government. Nearly the opposite was the case in the government under the Articles of Confederation; the individual state governments, Hamilton contended, "constantly pursue internal interests adverse to those of the whole."

The second motivating condition was the "love of power," a natural human tendency that, again in the case of the Confederation government, worked in direct opposition to the support of a national government. Those holding the reins of power in the state governments "hate[d] the control of the general government" and did everything within their power to thwart it. The third condition was the "habitual attachment of the people" to that closest to them and "immediately before the[ir] eyes," an impulse that fostered provincialism and led to the fragmentation, rather than the harmony, of the nation's interest. The fourth—and probably the most important in Hamilton's view—was the simple fact of "force"—the "coercion of laws or coercion of arms." Remembering the fiscal irresponsibility in Rhode Island and the rebelliousness of Massachusetts farmers, Hamilton believed that the states possessed both too little and too much of that "force"—too little to enforce order within their boundaries but too much to allow for the larger interest of a strong union to prevail. Finally, there was influence—a "dispensation of those regular honors and emoluments, which produce an attachment to the government." Once again looking to the British government as his model, Hamilton believed that patronage—the ability to reward one's friends and win over one's enemies either through flattery or with offers of lucrative jobs and contracts—was the lubricant that made governments operate smoothly. All five of these natural human tendencies, Hamilton concluded, worked "on the side of the states, and must continue so as long as the states continue to exist."[7]

Only a strong national government, Hamilton argued, would be capable of counteracting the "principles and passions" of those committed to the supremacy of the state governments. The New Jersey Plan was hopelessly inadequate, for it would have precisely the opposite effect. It would allow individual state governments to continue to aggrandize their power and influence. Hamilton's focus was to do away with the state governments altogether. "They are not necessary for any of the great purposes of commerce, revenue, or agriculture," and, he declared, "If they were extinguished, I am persuaded that great economy might be obtained by substituting a general government."[8]

If Hamilton's preference for abolishing the state governments made many in his audience uneasy, then his prescription for a stronger central government could only have increased their anxiety. "The British government," he declared, "is the best in the world, and I doubt much whether anything short of it will do in America." The British House of Lords, Hamilton continued, was "a most noble institution," and no "temporary senate"—its members elected for limited terms as was proposed under both the New Jersey and Virginia plans—could match the stability and independence of mind and the ability to withstand "popular passions" of a body whose members served for life.[9]

The same antidemocratic impulse shaped Hamilton's view of the executive. Indeed, Hamilton believed that "no good [executive] . . . could be established on republican principles," for an executive serving a limited term and dependent on either the people or the legislature for his election, would inevitably be too weak to carry out the duties of his office. Again, he praised the "English model"—the monarchical model that Thomas Jefferson had so roundly denounced in the Declaration of Independence and against which Americans had fought in the Revolution—as "the only good one on this subject." Hamilton proclaimed that "the hereditary interest of the King was so interwoven with that of the nation, and his personal emoluments so great" that he was unlikely to be corrupted by either the love of money or the need to grasp for power. Yet Hamilton was not prepared to argue for a *hereditary* monarch. He still believed that while America should follow "republican principles" as much as possible, "stability and permanency demanded that at least one branch of the legislature, as well as the chief executive, should hold their offices for life."[10]

Hamilton next laid out the specifics of his plan. The government should have a bicameral legislature, with the lower house elected directly by the people for a term of three years and the upper house chosen by electors selected by the people and to serve "during good behavior," which, in the common understanding of that term, meant for life. Consistent with his desire to weaken the power of the states, his plan apportioned representation in the Senate according to population, with the states divided into electoral districts for that purpose. Like the Virginia Plan, Hamilton's plan called for proportional representation. But by proposing that the states be divided into electoral districts based on population, Hamilton went a step further, rendering the states nearly irrelevant in the selection of senators.

Hamilton's executive, who would be chosen by electors in districts essentially similar to those choosing the Senate, would have extraordinary powers, including an absolute veto on any laws passed by the legislature and sweeping control over the departments of finance and foreign affairs—the two areas of governance in which the failure of the Confederation had been most conspicuous. Perhaps most telling, Hamilton's plan stipulated that "all laws of the particular states contrary to the Constitution or to the laws of the United States [would] be utterly void; and the better to prevent such laws being passed, the governor or president of each state shall be appointed by the general government and shall have a negative upon the laws about to be passed in the state of which he is governor or president."[11]

Hamilton's plan displayed his profound revulsion at "the amazing violence and turbulence of the democratic spirit" prevailing in the state governments, a distinct distrust of popular election of government officials, and a preference for insulating most of those serving in the government from the necessity of frequent elections. It was also a plan that, if it did not obliterate the state governments altogether, made them wholly subordinate to the central government, going so far as to make the chief executives of those state governments mere pawns of the central government.[12]

As Hamilton wrapped up his five- to six-hour speech, he was greeted with a deafening silence. Not a single delegate rose to comment on it, and certainly no one was inclined to second it and accord it the stature of being brought to a vote. They simply and immediately adjourned for the day.

Hamilton's views strayed so far from mainstream republican principles that they appeared not to merit a response. In fact no one even rose to dispute them. Although the delegates' views on executive power may have varied widely, none of them was prepared to create the sort of "elected monarch" envisioned by Hamilton. And though the delegates may have differed in their views of where the balance of power between the state and continental governments should rest, few would have gone so far as to abolish the state governments altogether. Three days later, William Samuel Johnson of Connecticut would review the merits of the various plans presented to the Convention. "The gentleman from New

York," Johnson noted, had "been praised by every body," but was "supported by none."[13]

THE NATIONALISTS REGROUP

As Madison took his scrupulous notes on Hamilton's epic speech, he may have felt some unease. At best, Hamilton's speech amounted to a diversion from the main issues separating the large- and small-state delegates. At worst, its antidemocratic elements and contempt for the governments of the states ran the risk of alienating those delegates whose loyalties were wavering between the Virginia and New Jersey plans. He knew that he would have to take some action.[14]

The next morning, Tuesday June 19, Madison seized the floor. In a speech nearly as long as Hamilton's, he dissected the New Jersey Plan piece by piece. He began by reminding the delegates of the two essential goals for which the Convention had been called: the preservation of the union and "to provide a government that will remedy the evils felt by the states both in their united and individual capacities." He then posed—and answered—a series of questions aimed at demonstrating that the New Jersey Plan was a woefully inadequate solution to those two grand goals. Would it prevent the "violations of the law of nations and of treaties" that had so embarrassed the Confederation government? Would it prevent the states from encroaching on federal authority? Would it prevent "trespasses of the states on each other?" And, evoking the specter of Shays' Rebellion, "Will it secure the internal tranquility of the states themselves?"[15]

Madison admitted that "the great difficulty lies in the affair of representation; and if this could be adjusted, all others would be surmountable." But at this stage at least, he would not budge an inch. He insisted that both the legitimate interests of the larger states and the very principle of a government based on the sovereign will of the people, as opposed to the states, demanded that the new Constitution be founded on the principle of proportional representation.[16]

When Madison finished his oration, his Massachusetts ally Rufus King put the question squarely before the delegates. Should the Convention proceed on the understanding that "Mr. Randolph's resolutions should be adhered to as preferable to those of Mr. Paterson?" When confronted with that either/or proposition, seven states, Massachusetts,

Pennsylvania, Virginia, North Carolina, South Carolina, Georgia, and, somewhat surprisingly, Connecticut (for its delegates were on record as favoring neither alternative), endorsed the Virginia Plan; three, Delaware, New Jersey, and New York, supported the New Jersey Plan; and the Maryland delegation was divided. The New Jersey Plan was dead. But everyone in the room knew that a bare majority of seven of thirteen states in favor of the Virginia Plan was an insufficient foundation for a durable union.[17]

SEARCHING FOR A MIDDLE GROUND

On Wednesday June 20, George Washington took his place at the front of the room and resumed his role as chair of the Convention. Aside from the two days on June 14 and 15 when the delegates assembled themselves as a Convention in order to take formal receipt of William Paterson's New Jersey Plan, they had operated as a Committee of the Whole for the entire period from May 30 through June 19. Nathaniel Gorham, who had been presiding while the delegates were operating as a Committee of the Whole, returned to his seat along the north wall of the Assembly Room with his fellow Massachusetts delegates. By moving back into the more formal mode of a Convention, perhaps the delegates were signaling that it was time to begin making some binding decisions.

As the Convention opened its business that day, Oliver Ellsworth of Connecticut, seeking to bridge the gap between the nationalists and the small-state advocates, proposed that the initial resolution of the Virginia Plan be amended such that it retained the idea of a "supreme" legislative, executive, and judiciary but dropped the word "national."[18] He pointed out that when the proposed Constitution was sent to the states for ratification, it would fare much better if it were presented as an amendment to the Articles of Confederation, rather than as a means of dissolving the Confederation. The deletion of the word "national," Ellsworth argued, would serve to ease fears on that score.[19]

This concession to state pride, if not to state power, was apparently something the nationalists could live with, for none of them registered opposition. But mere fiddling with the language—as opposed to the substance—of the constitutional structure was not going to satisfy those who remained concerned more with protecting state power than pride. John Lansing and Robert Yates of New York remained implacable in their determination to protect New York's favored position within the existing structure of government. Lansing brushed aside Ellsworth's change of wording as meaningless. The "true question," he observed, "was whether the Convention would adhere to or depart from the foundation of the Confederacy." He then launched another full-fledged assault on the principles underlying the Virginia Plan. Whereas the opposition of many of the small states' delegates to the Virginia Plan amounted to nothing more than a predictable attempt to gain advantage in the ultimate decision on how representation would be apportioned, Lansing's attack represented a thorough rejection of the nationalist conception of union. The only union Lansing desired was a confederation of independent and sovereign states. Toward that end he introduced a motion stipulating that "the powers of legislation be vested in the United States in Congress," a change of language that would have made the new government a government of "we the states," not "we the people."[20]

Over the course of the next week, a parade of delegates rose both to defend the interests of their individual states and to articulate their differing visions of the relationship between the continental government and the state governments. For all of the impressive rhetorical firepower unleashed over the course of that week, the rate of progress toward a resolution of the issue was negligible.

Throughout all the disputation, the delegates remained true to their vow of secrecy. William Samuel Johnson, though right in the thick of the battle over representation, wrote to his sons at home with only the news that "there is great diversity of sentiment, which renders it impossible to determine what will be the result of our deliberations." George Mason wrote to Governor Beverly Randolph of Virginia and, invoking the rule of secrecy, revealed only that "things are now drawing to that point on which some of the fundamental principles must be decided," without revealing what those principles might be.[21]

Although they were still outnumbered, the anti–Virginia Plan forces were gaining strength. In order to test their strength, they asked for a formal vote on a proposal by John Lansing stipulating that legislative power be vested not in a "national legislature," but in the "united states in Congress"—in other words that the Congress would be the agent of the *states* and not the *people* of the nation. The nationalists still had a preponderance of votes on their side, but their support appeared to be slipping. The familiar coalition of Massachusetts, Pennsylvania, Virginia, North Carolina, South Carolina, and Georgia opposed the proposal, but this time Connecticut joined New York, New Jersey, and Delaware in supporting it, with Maryland still divided.[22]

The Connecticut delegates, meanwhile, continued to push for compromise. On June 21—a humid, sultry day interrupted by thundershowers—William Samuel Johnson attempted to bridge the gap between the opposing sides. The words most commonly used to describe Johnson were "dignified" and "gentlemanly," and he was, by all accounts, one of the most impressively educated men at the Convention, with a bachelor's degree from Yale, a master's degree from Harvard, and an honorary doctorate from Oxford. Although he proved to be a highly constructive delegate at the Convention, Johnson never enjoyed himself in Philadelphia. He complained constantly not only about the unhealthy environment, but also about a chronic shortage of funds that left him living hand to mouth during his three-and-a-half-month stay in the city. To make matters worse, just as he was settling into his lodgings at City Tavern, Johnson fell ill with an intestinal disorder and had to be treated by a local doctor.[23]

Like his Connecticut colleagues Oliver Ellsworth and Roger Sherman, Johnson sought some middle ground between the Virginia and New Jersey plans. Attempting to undo any damage to the Virginia Plan resulting from Alexander Hamilton's extremist speech, he was careful to distinguish between the two. The Virginia Plan, though it did place the states in a subordinate position, was not intended to destroy the "individuality" of the states altogether; by contrast, Hamilton's proposal "boldly and decisively contended for the abolition of the state governments." Johnson did not believe that the current draft of the Virginia Plan offered the states sufficient protection for their individuality, but he was prepared to support it if some means might be found by which the states could be guaranteed to retain some portion of their sovereignty.[24]

Try as they might, at this stage the Connecticut delegates were unsuccessful in persuading a sufficient number of delegates on either side of the question to accept their notion of a divided sovereignty between state and nation. Though Johnson's conciliatory remarks on June 21 may have laid the groundwork for eventual compromise, most delegates were not yet ready to give in. Wilson and Madison, in their responses to Johnson, took pains to express their respect for his good intentions, but they were unyielding in their belief, in Madison's words, that "there was less danger of encroachment from the general government than from the state government" and that "the mischief from encroachments would be less fatal if made by the former, than if made by the latter."[25]

THE BOMBASTIC LUTHER MARTIN

Madison may justly be accused of clinging too dogmatically to his nationalist vision for the union, but his defense of this vision was always cogent and most often presented in a spirit of moderation. The same cannot be said about one of his principal antagonists in the debate over representation, Luther Martin of Maryland, who was occasionally cogent, but rarely either moderate or conciliatory.

Martin's career had begun auspiciously enough. After graduating with honors from Princeton in 1766 and working as a schoolteacher for three years, he began a career in law that had, by the beginning of the American Revolution, grown into a lucrative practice, first in Virginia and then in Maryland. He was appointed attorney general of Maryland in 1778, and in 1785, at the age of thirty-seven, he served as a delegate to the Continental Congress. He was, undeniably, a smart, able attorney.[26]

A man "of medium height, broad-shouldered, near-sighted, absent-minded, shabbily attired, harsh of voice . . . with a face crimsoned by the brandy which he continually imbibed," Martin had a fondness for drink that has become the stuff of legend. His fellow Baltimoreans loved to tell the story of the time he bumped into a cow on the main street of the town, elaborately bowed and apologized to the animal, and then stumbled along his way. Supreme Court Justice Roger Taney, who frequently observed Martin, claimed he was "often intoxicated" in court. Taney described Martin with a combination of affection and horror, as having "an utter disregard of good taste and refinement in his dress and language and his mode of argument. He was as coarse and unseemly at a dinner-table, in his manner of eating, as he was in everything."[27]

Martin was, however, far from stupid, and on those occasions when he bothered to exercise a modicum of self-discipline, he could be a formidable opponent. Arriving in Philadelphia on June 9, Martin quickly made it known that he did not approve of the direction the Convention was taking. On June 20, he launched into a long, rambling speech in which he endorsed the principle of "confederation," contending, with history on his side, that "at the separation from the British Empire, the people of America preferred the establishment of themselves into thirteen separate sovereignties instead of incorporating themselves into one." The confederated government they created was intended for strictly limited purposes—"to defend the whole against foreign nations in case of war, and to defend the lesser states against the ambition of the

The brilliant but bombastic Luther Martin of Maryland. Portrait
by William Shaw Tiffany, after Cephus Thompson, courtesy
of Independence Historical National Park.

larger." In granting those limited powers, Martin insisted, the people
did not mean to betray the very principle—independence for the thirteen independent states—for which the Revolution had been fought.[28]

Some have speculated that Martin was intentionally selected by the
small-state advocates to present their case because of his reputation as an
excellent courtroom litigator, but whatever his talents in the courtroom,
they were not on their best display in the Pennsylvania State House on
June 27. According to Madison, whose notes on Martin's speech betray
his exasperation at the Marylander's long-windedness, Martin "contended at great length and with great eagerness" that the only purpose of
a central government was to help protect and preserve the state governments. It was emphatically not, however, designed to govern individuals
within the states. That was the responsibility of the states themselves. Relying heavily on citations of European political theorists—from John
Locke to Joseph Priestly to Emmerich de Vattel—Martin maintained that
the people of the states had entered into a state of nature at the moment
of their declaration of independence from Great Britain and had explicitly delegated authority to their state governments, not to a central government. When the Continental Congress adopted the Declaration of
Independence, those ideas moved from the realm of theory to practice,

and, Martin contended, nothing short of a removal back to that state of
nature could justify the central government in absorbing the powers given
by the people to their state governments. Martin argued his case with im-
peccable logic, but during the course of what amounted to an extended
harangue, he continually returned to his primary—and essentially self-
interested—concern: to guarantee his home state of Maryland adequate
weight within any central government. At one point he threatened that
should the three largest states—Virginia, Pennsylvania, and Massachusetts—insist on proportional representation, then the remaining ten
states "should league themselves together" against them.[29]

As the time for adjournment on June 27 approached, James Madison
recorded in his notes that Martin had announced himself "too much exhausted . . . to finish his remarks" that day, and then, with obvious
weariness, added that Martin had informed the Convention that "he
should tomorrow resume them." True to his word, Martin picked up
where he had left off the next morning, speaking for more than half the
day on June 28. At this point, Madison didn't even make an effort to keep
track of the argument, devoting roughly a paragraph in his notes to a
summary of Martin's speech and characterizing it as follows: "This was
the substance of the residue of his discourse which was delivered with
much diffuseness and considerable vehemence."[30]

Even his allies lost patience with Martin's bombastic performance.
Robert Yates, who strongly supported Martin's position, noted in his
summary of Martin's June 27 speech that "his arguments were too diffuse and in many instances desultory; it was not possible to trace him
through the whole, or to methodize his ideas into a systematic or argu-
mentative arrangement." Oliver Ellsworth, Martin's former Princeton
classmate and an opponent of the Virginia Plan in its current form, was
more pointed in his condemnation of the inappropriateness of the performance. Writing to Martin several months later, Ellsworth rebuked his
colleague, saying that the speech very likely "might have continued two
months, but for those marks of fatigue and disgust you saw strongly expressed on whichever side of the house you turned your mortified
eyes."[31]

Martin's prodigious thirst for liquor may have had some influence
on his performance, for he was known to drink even more heavily in
hot weather "to supply the amazing waste of perspiration." We do not
know whether Martin was actually drunk during the two days of his
speech or whether he merely appeared to be.[32]

Some historians have argued that Martin's miserable performance on June 27 and June 28 set back the cause of the antinationalist and small-state delegates immensely, causing them to be on the defensive in the Convention from that time forward. This point of view perhaps invests too much power—for good or ill—in oratory as a decisive force in the deliberations. Martin's declamations were no doubt tedious to some and downright obnoxious to others, but the business of reconciling the conflicting views and interests of the delegates was not going to be achieved by speech making, no matter how eloquent or prolix. That business was going to be settled by a combination of behind-the-scenes maneuvering and the sheer fatigue of those delegates who, whatever their views on representation in the legislature, were anxious to get on with the rest of the business of the Convention.[33]

DR. FRANKLIN, RELIGION, AND THE AMERICAN CONSTITUTION

Late in the day on June 28, the venerable Dr. Franklin, observing the evident disgust of his colleagues at Martin's intemperate performance, attempted to diffuse some of the hostility in the Assembly Room. For the first time feeling well enough to deliver a speech himself, he reflected that "the small progress we have made after five weeks close attendance and continual reasonings with each other is methinks a melancholy proof of the imperfection of the human understanding. We indeed seem to feel our own want of political wisdom, since we have been running in search of it." The delegates had "gone back to ancient history for models of government, and examined the different forms of those Republics which having been formed with the seeds of their own dissolution now no longer exist." They had also examined the "modern states" existing in Europe, "but find none of their Constitutions suitable to our circumstances." We are, he lamented, "groping as it were in the dark to find political truth, and scarce able to distinguish it when presented to us."[34]

This introduction made obvious the delegates' dilemma. What should they do next? Franklin's solution, coming as it did from one of the world's most celebrated deists, no doubt confounded many of the assembled delegates. "How has it happened," Franklin asked, "that we have not hitherto once thought of humbly applying to the Father of lights to illuminate our understandings?" He recalled that the members of the Continental

Congress, when confronting the crisis of the Revolution against Great Britain, "had daily prayer in this room for divine protection," and, indeed, "our prayers . . . were heard, and they were graciously answered." Turning to address General Washington, he averred, "I have lived, Sir, a long time, and the longer I live, the more convincing proofs I see of this truth—that God Governs in the affairs of men. And if a sparrow cannot fall to the ground without his notice, is it probable that an empire can rise without his aid?" In most of his speculations on religion, Franklin tended to use words like "Providence" or "Destiny" rather than God, but this speech was an exception. What's more, he actually underscored the word "God" twice in his handwritten copy of the speech.[35]

Having reminded his colleagues of the power and utility of the deity, he proposed in a formal motion "that henceforth prayers imploring the assistance of Heaven, and its blessings on our deliberations, be held in this Assembly every morning, before we proceed to business, and that one or more of the clergy of this city be requested to officiate in that Service." Roger Sherman quickly seconded Franklin's motion. An embarrassed silence followed.

Finally, Alexander Hamilton, the first to speak, tried as tactfully as possible to brush Franklin's proposal aside. He complimented Franklin by saying that his suggestion would have been useful had it been implemented at the beginning of the Convention's proceedings, but by coming "at this late day," Hamilton feared that it might "lead the public to believe that the embarrassments and dissensions within the Convention had suggested this measure." That, however, was precisely Franklin's point, and indeed, in answer to Hamilton, Franklin and Sherman noted the sounding of an "alarm out of doors that might be excited for the state of things within, would, at least be as likely to do good as ill." At this point, Hugh Williamson of North Carolina, in a rare intervention in the debates up to that point, conjured a more practical reason to oppose Franklin's proposal. "The true cause of the omission [of prayers] could not be mistaken. The Convention had no funds" with which to compensate the clergy who might be called in to lead them. This no doubt seemed highly implausible to many, including Franklin, for surely there were many members of the clergy who would have volunteered their services.[36]

Edmund Randolph stepped in to help Franklin save face. He proposed "that a sermon be preached at the request of the Convention on the 4th of July, the anniversary of Independence; and thenceforward prayers be used in the Convention every morning." Franklin seconded

Randolph's motion, but this motion failed as well, and the Convention adjourned after what had been a long, frustrating, and inconclusive day.[37]

From the time America's constitutional experiment first began until the present moment, historians, politicians, and theologians have been inclined to invoke the deity—or some form of divine intervention—when describing the work of the Founding Fathers in Philadelphia that summer of 1787. James Madison, as committed a rationalist as could be found in late-eighteenth-century America, would nevertheless proclaim just a few months after the Convention adjourned, that "it is impossible for the man of pious reflection not to perceive in [the Constitution] a finger of that Almighty hand which has been so frequently and signally extended to our relief in the critical stages of the revolution." Benjamin Rush, speaking in the Pennsylvania ratifying convention in November of 1787, echoed Madison, declaring that he believed "the hand of God was employed in this work, as that God divided the Red Sea to give a passage to the children of Israel." Nearly one hundred years later, when the historian George Bancroft completed his monumental *History of the Formation of the Constitution of the United States of America* in 1882, he described the framers of the Constitution as acting under divine guidance and pointed to the Constitution itself as proof of "the movement of the divine power which gives unity to the universe, and order and connection to events."[38]

In point of fact, the document produced that summer is remarkably secular. While the other great American founding document, the Declaration of Independence, begins with the invocation of "the Laws of Nature and of Nature's God" and concludes with an appeal to a "firm Reliance on the Protection of divine Providence," the only substantive mention of religion in the body of the Constitution is aimed quite explicitly at separating religion and government. Introduced first by Charles Pinckney in mid-August and eventually incorporated into Article VI, the framers provided that "no religious test shall ever be required as a Qualification to any office or public Trust under the United States." Although the prohibition of religious tests for public office did not amount to an explicit articulation of the principle of separation of church and state (that would await the adoption of the First Amendment in the federal Bill of Rights in 1791), it did point the way toward a secular conception of the American state.[39]

That there was no attempt to invoke divine providence in the debates and decisions in the Convention or in the document itself is not altogether surprising. The Declaration of Independence was intended to serve multiple purposes, but first and foremost it is an exhortatory document, meant to uplift and inspire citizens to action. Toward that end it used a combination of law, history, logic, rhetoric, and religion to accomplish the task. The United States Constitution was meant to be—and is, resolutely—a legal document, drafted in an age when the substance of the law was becoming more secular and when its leading practitioners were consciously purging their profession from legal imperatives derived from anything hinting of divine sanction. Although it remained the case that a few New England states persisted in attempting to maintain the connection between government, public order, morality, and religion, on the whole the independent American states were deliberately moving in the opposite direction.

The delegates themselves were representative of an era in which political leaders were unlikely to invoke divine intervention, or indeed, any religious basis for the "science" of government and politics. As Frank Lambert has observed, the delegates in Philadelphia were "concerned primarily with 'temporal freedom'—specifically, the problem of how to allocate and restrain power in a way that best assured liberty. The pursuit of 'eternal truth' they left to individuals and churches."[40]

This is not to say they weren't religious. Virtually all of the Founding Fathers would have characterized themselves as Christians. With the exceptions of Daniel Carroll of Maryland and Thomas Fitzsimons of Pennsylvania, who were Roman Catholics, the delegates were Protestants of one form or another, with nearly 70 percent of them affiliated with the Episcopal Church.[41]

From the evidence we have available, the churchgoing habits of the delegates varied considerably while they were in Philadelphia. William Samuel Johnson, a devout Episcopalian, attended one of Philadelphia's several Episcopal churches nearly every Sunday that he was in the city that summer. George Washington, by contrast, was more likely to spend his Sundays enjoying the fresh air of the countryside. During his four months in Philadelphia, he attended church a total of three times—once at a High Mass at St. Mary's Catholic Church, another time at Christ Church, the city's largest Episcopal church, and on July 4 he listened to patriotic oration at a German Lutheran church (which he mistakenly referred to as a "Calvanast" church). Washington, like Franklin, was more comfortable talking about "Providence" than God, and, as far as we know, he did not take Communion at any time during his adult life. To be sure, some of the framers, whatever their denominational preferences, were men of great piety—men for whom the practice of the Christian religion was an active and important part of their daily lives. But whatever their private beliefs, the vast majority of the Founding Fathers operated on the assumption that temporal and spiritual aspects of public life should be kept separate.[42]

Was his speech then merely a ploy to defuse what was becoming an increasingly acrimonious debate? Perhaps it was, but there is no doubting the seriousness with which he made his suggestion for divine guidance. At the conclusion of the day's session in which the delegates rejected his suggestion, he scrawled a note at the bottom of the speech he had written expressing his incredulity. "The convention, except three or four persons, thought prayers unnecessary!"[43]

FRANKLIN'S CALL TO PRAYER, alas, did not temper the discord among the delegates. For the next several days, the mood among them seemed only to grow more vitriolic. The diehards from the small states continued to argue, with ever greater vehemence, for a single-house legislature with equality of representation. The larger number of them, recognizing they would never get delegates from the large states to agree, fell back to defending various versions of the compromise Connecticut's Roger Sherman and Oliver Ellsworth had proposed in early June—proportional representation in the lower house and equality of representation in an upper house. With the benefit of hindsight, it is easy to see that the Connecticut delegates' proposal was the only way out of the stalemate, but the delegates from Virginia, Pennsylvania, and Massachusetts—Madison, Wilson, Gouverneur Morris, and Rufus King being the most vocal and obdurate—continued to resist the obvious compromise.

Despite the vehemence of debate and sour mood in recent days, Friday, June 29, actually began in promising fashion. Connecticut's William Samuel Johnson, addressing the persistent division between those who wanted to defend state sovereignty at all costs and those who insisted on supremacy for the central government, observed that "in some respect the states are to be considered in their political capacity, and in others as districts of individual citizens." These two ideas, he contended, "instead of being opposed to each other, ought to be combined: that in one branch, the people ought to be represented; in the other, the states."

This was similar to the formulation of the doctrine of "divided sovereignty" that James Madison would articulate six months later in *The Federalist*, but on that day in June, Madison was impervious to Johnson's logic. He responded with what was for him an exceptionally combative speech, denouncing the irresponsibility of the state governments and mocking the naiveté of those who persisted in believing that those state governments could somehow transform themselves into "vigorous and high toned governments."[44]

From that point forward things went downhill, with each side dogmatically repeating the familiar arguments. Massachusetts's Elbridge Gerry, although unpredictable on many subjects, remained firmly allied with Madison and the nationalists on the question of representation. The acerbic Gerry joined Madison in ridiculing the idea that state sovereignty was somehow sacred. He had supported an equal vote for the states in the Continental Congress only because of the "public danger, and the obstinacy of the lesser states," and he had no intention of making the same mistake twice. As he concluded his speech, he may, for a moment, have regretted his belligerence. "Instead of coming here like a band of brothers, belonging to the same family, we seemed to have brought with us the spirit of political negociators."[45]

The mood of the Convention did not improve on Saturday June 30—another hot, cloudy, humid day. Wilson and Madison continued to resist compromise. Wilson led off. If the small states were not prepared to join the union on the terms of proportional representation, he implied, then so be it. The large states, combined in a powerful union, could survive perfectly well; the small states, left outside the union, would be the ones to suffer. Madison was in an equally contentious mood. No doubt recalling the way in which Rhode Island had injured the welfare of the country as a whole by its refusal to allow the Confederation government to impose import taxes, he insisted that there was far less danger that the large states would combine to pass laws harmful to the small states than there was in the possibility that the small states, if given equal representation, would combine to "injure the majority of the people." Like Wilson, Madison was not willing to let go of the notion that the new government must be a government of "we the people of the United States," and not one merely of "the united states."[46]

In the course of his defense of the original components of the Virginia Plan, Madison made a truly profound observation in attempting to respond to the frequently voiced fear that the large states would somehow combine to undermine the interests of the smaller. The principal divisions of interests within the country, he observed, would never "lie between the large and small states." Rather, "it lay between the Northern and Southern" and arose principally "from the effects of their having or not having slaves."[47] Unfortunately, Madison chose to undercut this important moment with a cheap shot at the Connecticut delegation, singling out Connecticut as proof of the way in which the self-interested behavior of one state could stand in the way of the broader good of the people at large. Looking across the center aisle toward the front of the room where the Connecticut delegates were seated, Madison acidly noted, "The party claiming from others an adherence to a common engagement ought at least to be guiltless itself of a violation." But, "of all the states," he charged, Connecticut should be the last to make that claim, for by her refusal to comply with congressional requisitions for revenue contributions to the war effort, she had worked directly to undermine the public good.[48]

Oliver Ellsworth, one of the principal proponents of the compromise, was a man of a patient and conciliatory nature, but this charge infuriated him. He rose angrily to answer Madison, and, looking straight ahead at General Washington, appealed to the presiding officer to set the record straight. "The muster rolls," Ellsworth claimed, "will show that [Connecticut] had more troops in the field than even Virginia. We strained every nerve to raise them; and we neither spared money nor exertions to complete our quotas." The effort, Ellsworth admitted, had "greatly distressed and impoverished" his state, leading to an accumulation of debts. But, he challenged, "We defy any gentleman to shew that we ever refused a federal requisition."[49]

Benjamin Franklin tried once again to lead the delegates toward common ground. He opened by acknowledging the legitimacy of the small states' fears of marginalization, but at the same time he sympathized with the large states' desire for a system of representation that adequately reflected their constituents. "When a broad table is to be made," Franklin observed, "and the edges of planks do not fit, the artist takes a little from both, and makes a good joint. In like manner here both sides must part with some of their demands in order that they may join in some accommodating proportion." With that image in mind, he tried his own version of compromise, proposing a complicated system by which the states would have equal representation in the upper house of the legislature in most matters, but that in matters relating to salaries of government officials, allowances for public services, and in all decisions to raise and spend government monies, the "delegates of the several states shall have suffrage in proportion to the sums which their respective states do actually contribute to the treasury." It was almost certainly an unworkable scheme. Moreover, tempers were by this time too frayed for Franklin's proposal to blunt much of the animosity that was starting to show on both sides. Once again, the delegates politely ignored Franklin's intervention.[50]

Gunning Bedford of Delaware filled the breach with one of the most ill-tempered and bellicose speeches of the Convention. Like Madison and Wilson, Bedford refused to see any middle way between a "perfect consolidation and a mere confederacy of the states," but as a passionate defender of Delaware's sovereignty, he flatly ruled "the first out of the question." He then launched into an all-out assault on the "ambition," "interest," and "avarice" of the large states, which, he was convinced, would inevitably work to "aggrandize themselves at the expense of the small." His eyes sweeping across the room to confront the delegates from Massachusetts, Pennsylvania, and Virginia, Bedford thundered, "I do not, gentlemen, trust you. If you possess the power the abuse of it could not be checked; and what then would prevent you from exercising it to our destruction?" He then issued a direct challenge: "We have been told with a dictatorial air that this is the last moment for a fair trial in favor of a good government," but, he declared, this was nonsense. "The large states dare not dissolve the Confederation. If they do, the small ones will find some foreign ally of more honor and good faith, who will take them by the hand and do them justice." In saying this, Bedford threatened not only that the small states would refuse to join a union on the nationalists' terms, but, indeed, that they might seek other suitors—perhaps even some foreign power—for an alternative union. Clearly, if there had been more in the Convention like Bedford, for whom the idea of an "American" union was only one of many alternatives, the United States of America, as we know it, might have looked very different.[51]

Rufus King of Massachusetts leaped to his feet, declaring himself deeply offended by the "intemperance . . . of the honorable gentleman from Delaware." It was the overagitated Bedford, King averred, not he, "that had uttered a dictatorial language. . . . It was not he, who with a vehemence unprecedented in the House, had declared himself ready to turn his hopes from our . . . common Country, and court the protection of some foreign hand. This too was the language of the honorable member himself!" On that sour note, the Convention adjourned for a much-needed Sunday respite.[52]

The next day, Gouverneur Morris walked the three-and-a-half blocks from his residence to that of his friend and business mentor, Robert Morris, where he found further confirmation of the despair that had gripped the Convention. Robert Morris and his houseguest, General Washington, both expressed their profound sense of dejection at the "deplorable state of things in the Convention." Gouverneur Morris would later describe what the three men believed to be a moment of crisis. "Debates had run high, conflicting opinions were obstinately adhered to, animosities were kindling, some of the members were threatening to go home, and, at this alarming crisis, a dissolution of the Convention was hourly to be apprehended."[53]

Were things as bad as Morris described them? Indeed, some of the delegates were leaving, and at least a few of those departures would have a profound effect on the events to come. William Few and William Pierce of Georgia headed north, to New York. As was the case with several delegates, they were their states' representatives in the Continental Congress. As a result the Congress had limped along without a quorum for much of the time the Constitutional Convention was in session. In the coming week, important legislation that might be favorable to Southern interests was likely to come to a vote in the Congress, and the two Georgians, joined by William Blount of North Carolina, made the decision to attend Congress that week in the hopes of obtaining both a quorum and a necessary majority in favor of those interests.[54]

Though he did not actually leave town, another Southern delegate, Maryland's Daniel of St. Thomas Jenifer, chose to absent himself from Monday's proceedings, though he never gave an explanation for his absence. An elderly, wealthy bachelor and a supporter of the nationalist position, Jenifer's votes had often offset those of Luther Martin in the balloting within the Maryland delegation. His absence would have fateful consequences.[55]

When the delegates reconvened on Monday July 2, Oliver Ellsworth again pushed for his delegation's compromise proposal giving to each state a single vote in the upper house. As the state delegations were polled, it was clear that Ellsworth's proposal would once again fall short of a majority. The result caused particular discomfort to James Madison, who now realized that the balance of power was beginning to shift. As expected, Massachusetts, Pennsylvania, Virginia, North Carolina,

and South Carolina—all holding out for some form of proportional representation in the Senate—voted against the measure. Voting for the
measure—as expected—were Connecticut, New York, New Jersey, and
Delaware. But there were two surprises. Maryland, whose delegation at
that stage was composed only of the ardent antinationalist Luther Martin
and the mild nationalist Daniel of St. Thomas Jenifer, had been recorded
as "divided" on most of the earlier votes on representation. But because
of Jenifer's mysterious absence from the gathering that morning, when
the vote was taken, Luther Martin was the only Maryland delegate voting, thus putting Maryland in the "yes" column in favor of Ellsworth's
resolution. The Georgia delegation, believing the future growth of the
state's white and slave populations would soon result in a system of proportional representation that worked to their advantage, had also consistently sided with the large states. But the absence of Pierce and Few
changed the equation. One of the two remaining Georgia delegates,
William Houstoun, voted against the Ellsworth resolution, just as he had
done when similar proposals had been put forward by the Connecticut
delegates. But the other delegate, Abraham Baldwin, this time voted in
favor of Ellsworth's proposal for equal state representation in the Senate,
leaving the Georgia delegation divided on the question. The vote on
Ellsworth's proposal thus stood five states in favor, five opposed, and one
divided.[56]

There has been a good deal of speculation about Abraham Baldwin's
motives in voting with the small-state delegations. The son of a self-
educated blacksmith, he was born and had spent all but the last three
years of his life in Connecticut. By all accounts he had a brilliant, penetrating mind, so much so that this blacksmith's son not only studied theology at Yale, but at the age of thirty-one he was offered a professorship
there. He turned instead to the law and seemed to be well on his way to a
successful career as a lawyer in Connecticut when he abruptly moved his
law practice to the backcountry of Georgia in 1784. It did not take him
long to win a reputation among the middling farmers of western Georgia as a man of uncommon ability. In 1787, Baldwin was the acknowledged leader of Georgia's delegation to the Constitutional Convention,
speaking only rarely, but serving on four of the six most important committees formed during the final eight weeks of the Convention.[57]

Some historians, citing Baldwin's Connecticut connections and, in
particular, his friendship with Roger Sherman, have suggested that he
may have made some sort of arrangement with the delegates from the

state of his birth, perhaps a deal involving the willingness of the Connecticut delegates to include in the Constitution protections against any attempt to undermine the institution of slavery. It is more likely, however, that Baldwin was operating from both a more pragmatic and more principled point of view. As a Westerner, he knew that a stronger central government was essential to the protection of the Georgia frontier in the ongoing warfare between Indians and the state's rapidly expanding European population. Baldwin's nationalism owed more to that concern than it did to the theoretical perspectives of men like Madison and Wilson. Equally important, he recognized more clearly than Madison and Wilson that if the large-state nationalists pushed too hard for proportional representation, the small states might well walk out of the Convention, dooming the opportunity to strengthen the government.[58]

And what of the absence of Maryland delegate Daniel of St. Thomas Jenifer? Following a long tradition in a family where nearly all of the males were named Daniel, Jenifer had been given the unusual moniker of Daniel of St. Thomas to differentiate himself from his brother, Daniel Jenifer. Unlike the Georgians Pierce and Few, Jenifer was not on his way to New York. In fact, he was loitering not far from the Pennsylvania State House and, immediately after the vote was taken, he ambled back into the proceedings to join his delegation. Jenifer had gone on record as favoring a system of proportional representation, but, like Baldwin, he may have realized that the insistence of the large-state nationalists on proportional representation in both houses might spoil any chance for a successful outcome for the Convention. He may have concluded that his temporary absence would help ease the way toward compromise and thus keep the Convention alive.[59]

The small states had somehow prevented Madison and his coalition from steamrolling them into submission. And with the delegates deadlocked on the issue of representation in the Senate, the Convention was no closer to a solution that would enable it to get on with the rest of its business. Charles Pinckney, still supporting the idea of proportional representation in the Senate, urged the implementation of the device that he had included in his original plan for the government. He again proposed that the states be grouped into three electoral districts and that representation within those districts be apportioned according to population. Not only did this seem unworkable, but the small-state delegates, now seeing that the tide was turning in their favor, were in no mood to give way.

At this point, Pinckney's cousin, General Charles Cotesworth Pinck-

ney, proposed that a Grand Committee be formed consisting of one delegate from each state to try to work toward a compromise solution. Luther
Martin was immediately on his feet, suspicious that the forming of a committee might be designed to push through some form of unacceptable
fiat. "You must give each state an equal suffrage," he insisted, "or our
business is at an end." Roger Sherman had a cooler head. He summed up
the situation, somberly declaring, "We are now at full stop." He urged the
delegates to go ahead with the appointment of the committee, for it may
well be the last hope "to set us right."[60]

One by one, a wide assortment of delegates began slowly to coalesce
around the idea of appointing a committee charged with settling the
issue of representation once and for all. Gouverneur Morris of Pennsylvania, Edmund Randolph of Virginia, Caleb Strong of Massachusetts,
Hugh Williamson of North Carolina, John Lansing of New York, and Elbridge Gerry of Massachusetts all rose to speak, with varying degrees of
enthusiasm and logic, in favor of creating the committee. Williamson
perhaps best summed up the rationale. "If we do not concede on both
sides, our business will soon be at an end. . . . As a Committee would be
a smaller body, a compromise would be pursued with more coolness."
The only two to oppose this logic, and to oppose it vehemently, were
Madison and James Wilson. Wilson opposed it because the very method
of its composition—one delegate from each state—stood in opposition
to the principle of proportional representation for which he and the
other nationalists were fighting. Madison no doubt shared those
objections—and many more—but the only reason he gave for opposing
was that "he had rarely seen any other effect than delay coming from
such committees in Congress." When the delegates voted on the question, ten states were in favor and only one, Pennsylvania, opposed. Madison knew that any recommendation that might come from such a
committee would only dilute his formula for proportional representation, but he could not even persuade his fellow Virginians to side with
him. The remainder of his delegation had gone over to the side of those
who were looking for conciliation.[61]

The most ominous portent from Madison and Wilson's point of view
was the actual composition of the committee. By the rules of the Convention, all committees were to be appointed by ballot of the state delegations
present. In this case, the delegates were electing one committee member
from each state, and it is likely that each delegation caucused to designate
its representative on the committee. The results of the ballot seemed to

doom any hope that Madison and Wilson might have for a recommendation favorable to their designs. The committee had an overwhelming antinationalist cast: from Maryland, the bilious Luther Martin; from New Jersey, William Paterson; from New York, the committed defender of state sovereignty, Robert Yates; from Delaware, the man who had gone so far as to threaten an alliance with a foreign power if the large states did not yield, Gunning Bedford; from Connecticut, Oliver Ellsworth, who, along with his colleague Roger Sherman, was the foremost proponent of compromise; and from Georgia, Abraham Baldwin, who had cast a crucial vote in favor of Ellsworth's proposal for equality of representation in the Senate. Even the three most aggressively nationalist states—Massachusetts, Pennsylvania, and Virginia—were to be represented by three of their most diffident supporters of the large-state position. Massachusetts was represented by the dyspeptic Elbridge Gerry, Pennsylvania by Franklin, and Virginia by George Mason, who had already shown signs of deserting the nationalist camp altogether.[62]

Once the committee was chosen, the delegates adjourned—with the understanding that the committee would use at least part of the upcoming Independence Day holiday to hammer out a compromise. As the delegates left the State House that Monday afternoon of July 2, James Madison could see his base of support crumbling, and he returned to Mary House's boardinghouse with a distinct sense of foreboding.

CHAPTER TEN

THE FOURTH OF JULY, 1787

PHILADELPHIA WAS ABUZZ WITH EXCITEMENT. It would be the first time since the epochal day in 1776 that so many distinguished Americans would be gathered at the birthplace of independence. Although cities such as Boston, Philadelphia, and Charleston had already begun to commemorate the decision for independence as early as 1777 (in 1783, Philadelphians had honored General Washington on July 4 by awarding him an honorary degree from the University of Pennsylvania), the celebration in Philadelphia in 1787 was more elaborately orchestrated and enthusiastically attended than any of the previous celebrations of the event.[1]

The delegates themselves carried powerful memories not only of the importance of the events of July 1776, but also of the extraordinary sacrifices and acts of heroism set in motion by those events. Although only eight of the fifty-five men serving in the Convention had been among the group of fifty-six who signed the Declaration of Independence, the lives of virtually all of the men gathered in the Pennsylvania State House in 1787 had in one way or another been directly affected by the act of declaring independence.

Thirty of the fifty-five men serving in the Convention had engaged in active military service during the Revolutionary War. Washington was of course the paragon of the self-sacrificing soldier-citizen, but a number of his fellow delegates had compiled impressive military records during the struggle. Five delegates—Alexander Hamilton of New York, James McHenry of Maryland, Thomas Mifflin of Pennsylvania, Charles Cotesworth Pinckney of South Carolina, and Edmund Randolph of Virginia—had served at various points in the war as an aide-de-camp to the general.[2]

Alexander Hamilton's service in that capacity not only won Washington's respect but helped propel his subsequent political career. James McHenry, in addition to his service as Washington's aide, performed heroically as a surgeon during the war, spending at least part of his time with Washington tending to the sick during the ordeal at Valley Forge. Mifflin, who eventually rose to the rank of major general, saw action in Long Island, Trenton, and Princeton, and he spent much of the war serving as the army's quartermaster general. Edmund Randolph served only briefly as Washington's aide in 1775, after which he returned to Virginia to serve first as attorney general and then as governor. However, the other Southerner serving as aide-de-camp to Washington, Charles Cotesworth Pinckney, compiled a genuinely distinguished military record, rising to the rank of general and performing bravely in the defense of Charleston in 1776, in the battles of Germantown and Brandywine, and in the brutal warfare carried out all over the South in 1779 and 1780.

Six of the delegates—Washington, Hamilton, Mifflin, David Brearley and Jonathan Dayton of New Jersey, and William Pierce of Georgia—had endured all or part of the brutal winter at Valley Forge. Four—Pierce, and William Davie, Hugh Williamson, and Richard Dobbs Spaight of North Carolina—had seen significant service in the bloody campaigns in the South during the period 1779–81. Davie, Pierce, and James McClurg of Virginia had been present with Washington and Hamilton at the climactic moment at Yorktown when the British finally surrendered to the combined French and American army.[3]

To be sure, there were a handful in the Convention—Robert Morris, John Dickinson, James Wilson, and William Samuel Johnson—who had initially wavered at the moment of decision regarding independence, but they recovered from their temporary hesitation and went on to assume important responsibilities in the continental government during the years between 1776 and 1787. Indeed, one of the most notable features of the body of men who served in the Constitutional Convention was the extent to which they had served in the continental government during the most trying times of the Revolution. Fully forty-two of the fifty-five delegates had served at one time or another in the Continental Congress, an experience that gave them a sharp perspective on the challenges—and the frustrations—involved in fighting a war and holding a fragile American union together.[4]

The Revolutionary experience of these continental-minded American leaders served therefore not only as a source of pride among them, but also as a powerful reminder of the gravity of the task in which they had been engaged thus far that summer. As the delegates prepared to celebrate the anniversary of their hard-fought and well-earned independence, they were acutely aware of what was at stake in their deliberations—and of the consequences to the union should they fail to reconcile the differences over representation that had paralyzed the Convention.

But on July 4, 1787, most of the delegates were able to set aside—at least for a moment—their concerns about the fate of the union. Paeans of praise to America's destiny could be heard from every quarter in the city, with the ringing of bells and an elaborate observance by the combined forces of the city's elite Light Horse Brigade, artillery, light infantry, and a battalion of militiamen. They assembled in the State House yard and, "after performing various revolutions, etc., they tried a *feu de joie* [gun salute]." The artillery brigade "then fired twelve rounds in honor of the day." Later in the day, all of the militiamen, together with members of the Society of the Cincinnati, marched to the German Lutheran Church on Race Street where they joined General Washington for more solemn observances. In addition to these formal celebrations, the citizens of Philadelphia ate and drank with gusto at taverns and outdoor picnics all around the city.[5]

In orations in the churches and taverns alike, Philadelphia's leading citizens rose to make optimistic proclamations about America's divine destiny as a beacon of liberty and opportunity for the rest of the world. At one gathering, held at "Mr. Preston's Tavern" several blocks north of the State House, the celebrants drank toasts to the success of the Convention, to George Washington, Benjamin Franklin, and the Marquis de Lafayette, to the "immortal memory of those gallant men who fell in defence of their country," and, lastly, "May Rhode Island be excluded from the Union until they elect *honest* men to rule them." The day was capped off by "a very beautiful set of fire works," which, perhaps for the first time, the citizens saw launched into the air.[6]

Most of the delegates took part in at least some of the celebration.

Washington, joined by several others, attended the oration at the German Lutheran Church by a young law student, James Campbell. Campbell's speech, ironically, was bursting with optimism. "Is the science of government," he asked, "so difficult that we have not men among us capable of unfolding its mysteries and binding our states together by mutual interests and obligations? Methinks, I already see the stately fabric of a free and vigorous government rising out of the wisdom of a Federal Convention."[7]

Washington also attended to other business during the break in the Convention's activities. In the morning on July 3 he dressed in the blue and buff uniform of the First Virginia Regiment, which he had commanded during the French and Indian War, and began sitting for a portrait by Charles Willson Peale, a painting ultimately entitled *His Excel: G: Washington Esq: LLD. Late Commander in Chief of the Armies of the U.S. of America & President of the Convention of 1787.*[8]

GENERAL WASHINGTON'S RESPITE

George Washington's strong sense of duty guaranteed that he would attend to the business of the Constitutional Convention with the same diligence and strength of character that marked all of his activities on the public stage. He had a flawless record of attendance at the Convention. He did not miss a single day, perhaps not a single hour, during the entire summer. More important, he carried with him all that summer the convictions that the fate of the union depended upon the success of the Convention, and that responsibility for its success or failure rested in large measure on his broad, but aging, shoulders.

However much Washington was motivated throughout his life by a sense of duty, he also enjoyed the companionship of friends and the pleasure of convivial gatherings. He still took pride in his abilities as a dancer and a conversationalist, and though he frequently made mild protests against the lavish compliments heaped upon him in private and public gatherings alike, he relished the attention and was flattered by the encomiums that came his way.

From the moment he arrived in Philadelphia, Washington had been showered with invitations to dinners, teas, and fancy dress balls. And although he tried to set aside Saturday nights for club dinners either at City Tavern or at Robert Morris's country estate with some of the Con-

vention delegates, rarely an evening went by that he wasn't being entertained by one of Philadelphia's worthies. Upon arriving in the city, he
had spent his first night dining with Robert Morris and his family, the
next dining with the Society of the Cincinnati, and the third dining at
Dr. Franklin's, and then, on May 17, he enjoyed a late afternoon dinner
with Philadelphia mayor Samuel Powel and his wife, Elizabeth, and
stayed on with them into the evening to have tea.[9]

Washington had formed a close relationship with the Powel family in
1775 while serving in the Second Continental Congress, and that relationship became even closer over the years. Samuel Powel was a Philadelphia merchant of considerable means who owned a handsome mansion
on Third Street between Spruce and Walnut streets. More important, his
handsome and highly intelligent wife, Elizabeth, would prove to be an
utterly charming companion for the general. Over the course of the summer, Washington spent fifteen evenings in the company of the Powels—
often simply with Elizabeth—at either their house in the city or their
country estate. He no doubt shared her company on many other occasions at the homes of other prominent neighbors, such as the Morrises,
the Merediths, and the Binghams, all of whom were part of the social circle in which the Powels were regularly entertained.[10]

Samuel Powel was a member of one of the oldest and wealthiest families in Pennsylvania. Although he had converted to Anglicanism, his
grandfather and father—both also named Samuel Powel—were members of the city's Quaker elite, steadily increasing their fortunes in the
mercantile trade and by timely real estate speculation. By the time
Samuel Powel came of age, he was one of the wealthiest citizens in
Philadelphia; he was also an Anglophile, as well—the result of considerable time spent in England and Europe during his young adulthood.
Powel was—first and foremost—a businessman, described by one of his
contemporaries as "minutely attentive to whatever Business he under-
takes." By the time of independence, he had ascended to the position of
mayor of Philadelphia, although the fact that he and Elizabeth would remain in their luxurious home in the city during the British occupation
suggests that his loyalties in the Revolution were ambiguous at best. The
French aristocrat, the Marquis de Chastellux, traveling through
Philadelphia in November of 1780, met Powel at a dinner party and commented that "his attachment to the common cause . . . appeared rather
equivocal."[11]

The famously vivacious Elizabeth Powel boasted a family lineage at

*A gracious hostess with a sharp intellect, Elizabeth Powel and her husband
Samuel frequently entertained General Washington during the summer of
1787.* Portrait attributed to Matthew Pratt, circa 1793, courtesy of
Pennsylvania Museum of Fine Arts.

least as distinguished as that of her husband. Her older brother, Thomas
Willing, joined Robert Morris in creating the most powerful mercantile
firm in Philadelphia. Her older sister, Mary, married William Byrd II,
perhaps the most prominent and ostentatious member of the Virginia
planter gentry, thus joining the Pennsylvania and Virginia aristocracy in
a powerful union. When Elizabeth and Samuel Powel were married in
1765, she was twenty-two and he was twenty-seven. Nearly everyone
who commented on the union was struck by the contrast between the
stolid manner of the husband and the spiritedness of the wife. The Marquis de Chastellux, when he first met Elizabeth, noted that "contrary to
American custom, she plays the leading role in the family." He noted
that for all of her husband's European travel it was Elizabeth who "has
wit and a good memory, speaks well and talks a great deal." In spite of
never having traveled to Europe herself, she would go on to become one
of the most impressive *salonistes* of Philadelphia, convening frequent
gatherings of men and women at her home for evenings of convivial but

also intensely intellectual exchange. Elizabeth's sisters—more inclined toward traditional female roles—commented with at least a hint of disapproval that "when in society she will animate and give a brilliancy to the whole Conversation; you know the uncommon command she has of Language and her ideas flow with rapidity."[12]

For Washington, as for many other visitors to the Powel mansion, Elizabeth was the main attraction, not her husband. Eleven years younger than the fifty-five-year-old Washington, and certainly more outgoing and sophisticated than the absent Martha Washington, Elizabeth may well have been one of the few people in the city during that summer of enforced secrecy in whom Washington felt free to confide. He genuinely enjoyed her company. Whether at a formal dinner at the Powel mansion in the presence of her husband or on the many occasions when he and Elizabeth had tea together or went for a stroll, it seems clear that she was a bright light in what was often a taxing summer.[13]

Washington would spend the evening with the Powels on both July 3 and July 4. As the summer wore on, he and Elizabeth spent more and more time together, sometimes simply taking walks around the city or a carriage ride into the country. There is nothing to suggest any impropriety in their friendship, but there was certainly no one in Philadelphia, either among the delegates or among the city's leading citizens, whose company Washington enjoyed more.[14]

Looking back on the summer of 1787 and on her role as hostess for the Convention delegates, Elizabeth spoke of her pride in having been "associated with the most respectable, influential Members of the Convention that framed the Constitution, and that the all important Subject was frequently discussed at our House." Elizabeth did not hold back on giving her own views on that "important subject." Indeed, she made it clear to those in her circle that she was both proud and unafraid of engaging Washington and other Convention delegates about the seminal topic of that summer. We have no record of her contributions to those conversations and, indeed, such was her discretion that she would have considered it a breach of honor to have revealed any of what was said around her table. But based on the later Federalist political allegiances she openly expressed as a leading Philadelphia saloniste during the 1790s, we can imagine that, as one who later became an outspoken supporter of the Federalist Party, she almost certainly would have sided with the large-state nationalists in preferring a system of proportional representation. Moreover, given her admiration for the general and her stead-

fast defense of his actions during his presidency, she was likely an advocate of a strong chief executive.[15]

Elizabeth would continue her close association with Washington for
many years, visiting Mount Vernon on several occasions with her husband. And when Washington found himself back in Philadelphia after
the new government had moved there from New York in 1790, she continued to see him regularly. Sometime in the fall of 1792 Washington
confessed to her that he was considering stepping down from the presidency after his first term. After hearing this news, Elizabeth took the extraordinary step—for a woman in her position—of writing to him in
boldly political language. "Your resignation," she wrote,

> wou'd elate the Enemies of good Government. . . . They
> would say that you were actuated by Principles of self-Love
> alone—that you saw the Post was not tenable with any
> Prospect of adding to your Fame. The antifederalists would
> use it as an argument for dissolving the Union, and would
> urge that you, from Experience, had found the present
> System a bad one, and had, artfully, withdrawn from it that
> you might not be crushed under its Ruins.

Elizabeth did not stop there. In an extraordinarily long and passionate
letter, she listed the reasons why Washington—and Washington alone—
had all of the "Abilities and Integrity" necessary for the job. You are, she
insisted, "the only Man in America that dares to do right on all public
Occasions." Among his attributes she listed his refusal "to be intoxicated
by Power or misled by Flattery," his well-known "circumspection," and,
perhaps most important in Elizabeth's view, his legendary self-control.
"You have," she wrote, "demonstrated that you possess an Empire over
yourself."[16]

Far from taking umbrage at her bold letter, Washington continued to
cherish Elizabeth's friendship for many years thereafter. On the occasion
of Elizabeth's fiftieth birthday, he sent a lengthy and flowery poem to her
extolling all of her virtues. Inscribed "Lines, by a Friend, addressed to
Mrs. Elizabeth Powel on her Birth Day of Fifty Years," the poem was apparently written by the poet Elizabeth Graeme Ferguson and copied for
Washington by his personal secretary, Tobias Lear. But the sentiments
expressed in it obviously captured some of the general's admiration for
Elizabeth.

Like Mira, Virtue's Self possess
Let her adorn your Mind
For Virtue in a pleasing dress
Has Charms for all Mankind

Her spotless Mantle shall be shown
When its blest Owner flies
The flaming Chariot make it known

When soaring to the Skies.[17]

Elizabeth Powel was not the only charming and outspoken woman Washington visited during those early days in July. On Monday, July 2, after a particularly grueling day during which the wrangling over representation in the Convention had begun to try everyone's patience, Washington had tea at the home of William and Anne Bingham. As was the case with Samuel and Elizabeth Powel, one suspects that the chief attraction that evening was the remarkable Anne rather than her pompous and overbearing husband, William.[18]

An extraordinarily wealthy banker and merchant, William Bingham had spent most of the period of the American Revolution abroad, where he continued to enhance his fortune. Upon his return to Philadelphia, he built what everyone agreed was the finest mansion in the city. Located on Third and Spruce streets, adjacent to the Powel's home, the Bingham mansion was modeled after that of the Duke of Manchester in London. By Philadelphia standards, it was immense. It boasted a large walled garden, numerous outbuildings, a large central hall of marble with pedestals on which sat the busts of Voltaire, Rousseau, Franklin, and other Enlightenment luminaries, two formal parlors, and, upstairs, a grand ballroom. More than any home in the Northeast, and perhaps in all of America, it reflected its owners' devotion to the finest attributes of European culture, from the British and French furniture to the Old World sculpture and paintings.[19]

Anne Willing was sixteen years old when she married the twenty-eight-year-old William Bingham in 1780. The daughter of the extraordinarily wealthy and powerful Thomas Willing and the niece of Elizabeth Powel, she was by many accounts the most ravishingly beautiful young woman in America. Abigail Adams, who could be as sharp-tongued and censorious toward other women as her husband, John, could be toward other men, first saw her in London and commented that "her elegance and beauty attracted more admiration than perhaps was willingly expressed in the old Court of George III." Anne and her husband then went on to France, where she made the same impression at the court of Louis XVI. John Adams, seated next to Anne at a dinner in Paris, was struck by her boldness in engaging him in "something of a political conversation." But he readily admitted that she had "more ideas on the subject" than he would have expected of a still very young American woman. Moreover, he confessed, she had "a corrector judgment" about those matters than he ever could have imagined.[20]

Like her older aunt, Elizabeth Powel, this daughter of a powerful Willing would succeed where their wealthy husbands would not. They created an atmosphere in which the delegates to the Convention could not only relax and unwind, but where they could also bend just a bit the strict rules of secrecy that governed their proceedings. Washington visited the Bingham mansion on formal occasions at least six times and described the evening meals himself as filled with "great splendour." Anne Bingham proudly displayed her French formal dinnerware of 350 pieces and drinking glasses numbering 206. The Binghams, like the Powels, spared no expense in entertaining as many delegates as they could gather over the course of that summer, although Washington was always the prize guest at any of these Philadelphia gatherings. Anne, like Elizabeth Powel, was fearless in speaking her mind about any and all of the issues confronting the new nation.[21]

Not all of the delegates enjoyed the lavish hospitality that Washington did after the exhausting proceedings of the second of July. James Madison's Independence Day was considerably less festive. In his notes on the Convention on Monday, July 2, he remarked somewhat sourly that the delegates were to adjourn until Thursday in order that "such as chose to attend the celebrations on the anniversary of Independence" could do so. Madison apparently did not attend any of the celebrations, nor did he write any letters over the course of the break. It seems most likely that he spent the time working on his notes on the Convention. That task was, he confided to Jefferson a few weeks later, sheer "drudgery," but his devotion to his duty would ultimately elevate his stature greatly among the pantheon of Founding Fathers. One also suspects that the introspective Madison spent much of the independence anniversary brooding on the future of the Convention, which, from his perspective at that moment, did not look good.[22]

CHAPTER ELEVEN

COMPROMISE:
LARGE STATES, SMALL STATES,
SLAVE STATES, AND FREE STATES

THE INDEPENDENCE DAY BREAK would provide no respite for the members of the Grand Committee. On the evening of July 2, its members—composed of one delegate from each of the states present at the Convention at that point—met for dinner at Benjamin Franklin's house. Once again playing the role of convivial host and conciliator, Franklin had invited them in hopes that his hospitality might facilitate a workable compromise on the vexing issue of representation in the legislature.[1]

But was conciliation possible? A few among the eleven—Luther Martin of Maryland and Elbridge Gerry of Massachusetts—had already distinguished themselves for their disputatiousness. Two of the small-state delegates—Paterson of New Jersey and Bedford of Delaware—were among the most determined defenders of small-state interests. And Robert Yates of New York remained deeply suspicious of any attempt at significant constitutional revision. But among the others—Franklin, Oliver Ellsworth of Connecticut, George Mason of Virginia, William Davie of North Carolina, John Rutledge of South Carolina, and the gentle Abraham Baldwin of Georgia—there appeared to be a genuine desire to reach a compromise. Perhaps, just perhaps, conciliation was possible.

The eleven men first engaged in a "lengthy recapitulation" of the arguments for and against the Virginia and New Jersey plans. We can speculate that at least some of the acrimony that might have accompanied this exercise was softened by the effects of Franklin's unerring ability to provide good food, good humor, and, perhaps most important, ample liquor. The next day, members of the Grand Committee continued their discussions in the more formal setting of the State House. Once they finished covering familiar ground, Franklin presented his one truly substantive contribution to the Convention, proposing a plan similar to that of the Connecticut delegates but with concessions designed to win over large-state delegates.[2]

Like the Connecticut plan, Franklin's called for representation in the House of Representatives to be apportioned according to population. Each state would be allowed one member in the House for every forty thousand inhabitants, a formula consistent with the provisions of the Virginia Plan and the proposals of the Connecticut delegates. In a small concession to the large states, Franklin's proposal gave the lower house sole authority to originate bills for raising or apportioning money and for fixing the salaries of government officials. Finally, and crucially, Franklin allied himself with the Connecticut delegates in proposing that each state should have "an equal vote" in the Senate.[3]

The proposal left some important issues unresolved. Franklin's formula for representation in the lower house referred vaguely to counting "inhabitants," a word susceptible to different definitions by Northern and Southern delegates. Most members of the Grand Committee certainly believed that the three-fifths ratio, tentatively endorsed by the Convention on June 11 as the formula for representing those "other persons" among America's inhabitants, should be part of any proposal on apportioning representation. Franklin's failure to mention the three-fifths ratio was likely the result of his desire to extricate himself from an embarrassing position within his home state. On the same day members of the Grand Committee were dining at Franklin's house, Tench Coxe, secretary of the Pennsylvania Society for Promotion of the Abolition of Slavery, of which Franklin was president, presented to Franklin a petition from the society asking the delegates to take steps to put an end to the slave trade as a first step toward the elimination of slavery altogether. Franklin, realizing that the political climate in the Convention with regard to slavery was already tense, declined even to present the petition, suggesting to Coxe that it be left to "lie over for the present." However much Franklin may have expressed his public disapproval of slavery, he was not about to let that issue further roil the waters.[4]

And what was meant by an "equal vote" in the Senate? Did it mean that each state would have one vote? Or did it mean that each state would be entitled to an equal number of senators, with the precise number of those senators yet to be determined? The latter alternative would have allowed each senator to make independent decisions about how to cast a vote, rather than acting merely as an agent of a state government. In spite of this vagueness, Franklin's proposals came close enough to being a "conciliatory adjustment" that the members of the Grand Committee ended their session on July 3 by agreeing to take them to the Convention once the Independence Day holiday ended. There were almost certainly a few—Paterson, Bedford, and perhaps Luther Martin—who believed that equal representation in the Senate did not go far enough to protect the small states. But even those stalwart small-state holdouts were probably beginning to realize that some version of Franklin's scheme was the best they were likely to get.

The Grand Committee's compromise would come not a moment too soon judging by some of the letters written by a few delegates to friends and family back home. George Mason, writing to Beverly Randolph, Virginia's acting governor in Edmund Randolph's absence, noted that "things . . . are now drawing to that point on which some of the fundamental principles must be decided, and two or three days will probably enable us to judge—which is at present very doubtful—whether any sound and effectual system can be established or not." Writing to his confidant and relative by marriage, David Stuart, General Washington vented his consternation at what he saw as the obstinacy of the defenders of state power and state sovereignty. "Whilst independent sovereignty is so ardently contended for, whilst the local views of each State and separate interests by which they are too much govern'd will not yield to a more enlarged scale of politicks," Washington complained, the outcome of the Convention would remain in doubt. "Every body wishes—every body expects something from the Convention—but what will be the final result of its deliberation," he noted gloomily, "the book of fate must disclose."[5]

Alexander Hamilton had left the Convention to return to New York on June 30. His departure was prompted by a combination of hurt feelings over the cool reception to his June 18 speech praising the British Constitution and the realization that he was doomed to be outvoted on any important question by his two antinationalist New York colleagues, Yates and Lansing. On his way to New York he wrote a letter to Washington filled with pessimism. "I own to you Sir that I am seriously and deeply distressed at the aspect of the Council which prevailed when I left Philadelphia. I fear that we shall let slip the golden opportunity of rescuing the American empire from disunion, anarchy and misery." Washington's response to Hamilton was equally gloomy.

> The state of the Councils which prevailed at the period you left this city [are] . . . now, if possible, in a worse train than ever; you will find but little ground on which the hope of a good establishment can be formed. In a word, I almost despair of seeing a favourable issue to the proceedings of the Convention, and do therefore repent having had any agency in the business.[6]

For most of his life Washington was able to avoid personalizing the conflict that came his way, but on this occasion he allowed himself to rail against those who "oppose strong & energetic government" as "Narrow-minded politicians" who were entirely "under the influence of local views." The general's public demeanor—controlled, impartial, even magisterial—was in this private communication giving way to anger and frustration.[7]

Not long after Hamilton's departure, his two antinationalist colleagues, Yates and Lansing—tired of the proceedings and convinced that the nationalists were plotting to "consolidate" the government—also bolted from the Convention. Although Hamilton would return to the Convention at the very end, in time to sign the Constitution, New York would lack its required quorum of delegates for the remainder of the summer. Yates and Lansing's departure would strengthen the hand of the nationalists in the Convention, removing as it did two of the most implacable opponents of a strengthened government. Their departure would, however, also serve as a warning sign that any proposed Constitution, once it was presented to the people of New York for their approval, might well face tough sledding.

THE GRAND COMMITTEE REPORTS

When the Convention reassembled on the morning of July 5, Massachusetts's Elbridge Gerry rose and presented the Grand Committee's proposals diffidently, noting that many of the members of the committee "were of different opinions" and had agreed to the report "merely in order that some ground of accommodation might be proposed." Those opposed to the equality of votes in the upper house, he noted, "have only assented conditionally." Nevertheless, most members of the Convention probably realized that the proposal coming from the Grand Committee was their best—and possibly last—hope for compromise on an issue that had paralyzed the Convention for the better part of a month.[8]

Still, a few diehard large-state nationalists would not yield. Madison delivered a passionate speech in which he defended proportional representation as the hallmark of a truly representative government and exhorted the delegates not to "depart from justice in order to conciliate the smaller states." South Carolina's Pierce Butler echoed Madison, calling the compromise proposal "evidently unjust."[9]

Predictably, Gouverneur Morris of Pennsylvania proved the most defiant and inflammatory in defense of the large-state nationalist position. He began on a note of grandiosity. Brandishing his cane, he proclaimed, "I came here as a representative of America . . . I came here in some degree as a representative of the whole human race; for the whole human race will be affected by the proceedings of this Convention." Surely, he continued, a truly just government would not be one in which "we were assembled to truck and bargain for our particular States," but, rather, one in which the people of those states would be equitably represented. This was, he concluded, only "reasonable and right," and "all who have reasonable minds and sound intentions will embrace it." But then Morris's tone turned truculent. Should the larger states see the justice of this and "the smaller refuse," the consequences would be devastating. The country, Morris thundered, "must be united," and if "persuasion does not unite it, the sword will." He then painted a gruesome picture of the "scenes of horror attending [the] civil commotion" that would follow. "The stronger party will make traytors of the weaker; and the gallows and halter will finish the work of the sword."[10]

Delegates from the small states were infuriated by Morris's belligerence. New Jersey's William Paterson complained of the contemptuous manner in which Morris and the other large-state delegates had treated the small states. Gunning Bedford repeated his haunting threat that states like Delaware might be forced to turn to other nations in order to protect their security if Morris's views were to prevail.[11]

SLAVERY INTRUDES ONCE AGAIN

From the moment the delegates first began their discussions of representation, it became clear that there were not one but two issues of contention. The most persistent and combative was that of proportional versus equal representation, but once the discussion turned to proportional representation, it became impossible to avoid the question of who among America's inhabitants was to be represented. Gouverneur Morris had long believed that property, as well as the number of inhabitants, ought to be taken into the estimate of the weight to be given to each state, and, immediately following his speech defending proportional representation, he reaffirmed that belief. When Morris spoke of including property in the formula for representation, he was referring to *all* forms of property, but, while he may not have intended it, his suggestion had the effect of emboldening some Southern delegates to escalate their demands for representing slaves in the proposed new Congress. John Rutledge immediately rose and agreed with Morris that "property was certainly the principal object of society."[12]

By the next day, Morris retreated, perhaps realizing that his insistence on including property in the formulation for representation might cause further conflict among the delegates. He opened the proceedings on July 6 by proposing that the Convention move forward to fix the precise number of representatives each state would have on the basis of the Grand Committee's recommendation of one representative for every forty thousand inhabitants. Most delegates agreed that the one to forty thousand ratio was a reasonable one, but since the young nation had never conducted a census, the actual allocation of representatives under that formula was more guesswork than science. After further debate on the relative merits of using property versus population as the means of apportioning representation, the delegates elected a committee—composed of Gouverneur Morris, Nathaniel Gorham, Rufus King, Edmund Randolph, and John Rutledge—to bring back a recommendation on the specific allocation of representatives for each state. It is significant to note that all the committee members were from large states and one of them, John Rutledge, was the Convention's most persistent and effective defender of slavery.[13]

Three days later, on Monday, July 9, the committee—chaired by Morris—presented its report, apportioning a total of fifty-six members of the House of Representatives among the states. The allocation was as follows: New Hampshire, two; Massachusetts, seven; the absent Rhode Island, one; Connecticut, four; New York, five; New Jersey, three; Pennsylvania, eight; Delaware, one; Maryland, four; Virginia, nine; North Carolina, five; South Carolina, five; and Georgia, two. Although Morris had earlier proposed the one-to-forty-thousand-inhabitants ratio as the formula for allocating representatives, when the committee deliberated on the matter, it had instead used an unspecified combination of population and property as the basis for its recommendations. Morris admitted that the committee's report amounted to "little more than a guess" about the relative property valuations in each state, but in making that guess, he factored in to the equation "the number of blacks and whites with some regard to supposed wealth."[14]

It was a hopelessly confused report and immediately prompted objections from delegates anxious to gain advantage for their states. George Read of Delaware complained that his state, with a population of about sixty thousand, received only one representative, while Georgia, whose population exceeded Delaware's by only twenty thousand, received two. Hugh Williamson of North Carolina thought that the western lands in his state had been undervalued.[15]

William Paterson, still unhappy about any formula involving proportional representation, attacked the report from every angle. Although his opposition to the committee's report was founded primarily on his persistent defense of New Jersey's interests, his critique had a powerful logic. Paterson objected to the general idea of including property in the formula for representation, but he reserved special scorn for any attempt to represent slave property. He regarded "negroe slaves in no light but as property. They are not free agents, have no personal liberty, no faculty of acquiring property, but on the contrary are themselves property, and like other property entirely at the will of the master." Taking aim at the Virginians, Paterson noted that neither free inhabitants nor slaves were included in the formula for representation in *their* state legislature. In the Virginia House of Delegates, each county in the state sent two representatives regardless of population.

Paterson also opposed the inclusion of slaves in the formula for representation on the grounds that such a step would prove "an indirect encouragement of the slave trade," pointedly observing that in the initial proposal to the Continental Congress suggesting the three-fifths ratio as the basis for apportioning state requisitions, the delegates to that Congress "had been ashamed to use the term 'slaves' and had substituted a description." The implication was clear. The advocates of the Virginia Plan were guilty of the same hypocrisy.[16]

There is some irony in Paterson, a slave owner from one of only two Northern states that had not yet moved to abolish slavery, being the one to reignite a debate over the three-fifths ratio. Madison tried to defuse the issue by reintroducing his proposal for counting slaves fully in one house of the legislature and not at all in the other. It was a move doomed to failure, for by this time most of the delegates had come to the conclusion that there would be equality of state representation in the upper house, making Madison's "compromise" proposal irrelevant.[17]

Rufus King of Massachusetts now attempted to play the role of conciliator. In a speech asking the delegates to reaffirm their earlier support of the three-fifths ratio, King echoed Madison's pivotal assessment that the principal "differences of interests did not lie . . . between the great and small States, but between the Southern and Eastern." King's candid affirmation of this point represented a clear public concession by an "Eastern" leader that the different regions had distinct and potentially conflicting political and economic interests that needed to be protected in creating the Constitution. King urged his Northern colleagues to provide the necessary protection by taking the middle ground and endorsing the three-fifths ratio. As King analyzed the situation, the Northern commercial states would benefit most from a more powerful national government's ability to promote and regulate trade—as proposed by a new Constitution. And in return for ceding that advantage to the North, the South had a right to expect some representation for their slave wealth.[18]

Some have argued that the adoption of the three-fifths clause was an insidious bargain between pragmatic Northerners and aggressively proslavery Southerners. Indeed, King's rationale for ceding some advantage to the South in the matter of slave representation does taste of a bargain, but it was a bargain that recognized the hard, unchangeable facts of political life. Immediately following King's speech, General Washington—recognizing that the report from Morris's committee had managed to stir up still more unease among the delegates—used his authority as presiding officer to appoint another committee. This time it was a "committee of eleven," composed of one member from each of the state delegations then present at the Convention, whose charge was to make another attempt at enumerating the size of each state's delegation in the House of Representatives. Perhaps not coincidentally, Rufus King was appointed chair of the committee.[19]

We have no record of the King committee deliberations, but it is clear they chose to base their recommendations on the formula of one to forty thousand free inhabitants and "three-fifths of all other persons." The committee's report, delivered by King the next day, increased the total number of representatives from fifty-six to sixty-five, but it did not appreciably change the ratio of Northern to Southern delegates. In the Morris committee proposal, the Northern states had thirty delegates and the Southern states had twenty-six. In the King committee proposal, the Northern states had thirty-five delegates and the Southern states had thirty. In the absence of a reliable census—an initiative that would only occur in 1790, once the new government had commenced operation— the recommendations from King's committee were subjected to the same kind of second-guessing as those from Morris's committee. This jockeying for position among the states was perhaps to be expected, but the tone of the debate, already inflamed over the issue of proportional versus equal representation, was beginning to turn even nastier, this time along North-South lines.[20]

The Southern delegates in particular believed that Morris's earlier report had been more favorable to them than the King committee report. They argued that New Hampshire, which was allotted three delegates, had been treated too generously and that the committee had underestimated the rapidly growing populations of North Carolina, South Carolina, and Georgia in allocating representatives to those states. King, who had already run the risk of censure from some Northern colleagues because of his acquiescence to the three-fifths ratio, was plainly annoyed that the Southern delegates were pushing for even greater advantage. Their aggressiveness, he warned, threatened a "gross inequality," which would make union impossible.[21]

In response, a parade of Southern delegates rose to complain that if the Northern states were initially given a clear majority of representatives in the new government they would assuredly do everything within their power to perpetuate that advantage. In particular, South Carolina's General Pinckney criticized the Committee of Eleven report as a step backward, claiming that its allocation of representatives further undermined the power of the South, removing those states "farther [from a position of equality] than they were before." After the speech making had ended, the Convention delegates voted to approve the King committee's proposal for the apportionment of representatives using the three-fifths standard by a vote of nine states in favor, two opposed. That the two states standing in opposition were South Carolina and Georgia signaled more trouble ahead.[22]

The trouble was not long in coming. On July 11, in the midst of a long debate on the method by which the new government should conduct a periodic census, Pierce Butler and Charles Cotesworth Pinckney reopened the question of the weight to be given slaves in apportioning representation, insisting "that blacks be included in the rule of representation *equally* with the Whites." In their view, the terms of the debate had shifted since James Wilson and Charles Pinckney had initially proposed the three-fifths ratio back on June 11. At that point, they claimed, slaves had been classified as "persons," but now, even Pennsylvanian Gouverneur Morris was regarding them as "property." If that were the case, General Pinckney and Butler argued, then "the labor of a slave in South Carolina was as productive and valuable as that of a freeman in Massachusetts. Since "wealth was the great means of defence and utility to the nation," then it was only appropriate that slave property be counted equally in apportioning representation.[23]

Pinckney and Butler's aggressive attempt to aggrandize the power of the lower South was too much even for some Southern delegates. George Mason stood and acknowledged that the Pinckney-Butler proposal would work in Virginia's favor, but he questioned its fairness. However valuable slaves might be, he cautioned, "I cannot regard them as equal to freemen and cannot vote for them as such." Mason closed his brief speech with an afterthought that brought into sharp relief the dilemma that all the delegates—North and South—were facing as they grappled with the three-fifths issue. Mason thought it "worthy of remark that the Southern States have this *peculiar species of property* over and above the other species of property common to all the States." It was becoming clearer as the debate over the three-fifths issue dragged on that the real sticking point was the ambivalence of many delegates about how to regard that "peculiar species."[24]

The main effect of the Pinckney-Butler proposal was to further irritate Northern delegates who were already uneasy about accepting the three-fifths ratio. Later that day, Rufus King, who earlier had taken the lead in voicing his willingness to bend the interests of the North to accommodate those of the South on the issue of counting slaves in the formula for representation, reversed field. Claiming that any form of representation of slaves "along with Whites would excite great discontents among the States having no slaves," he now announced his opposition to the three-fifths clause. Gouverneur Morris, who had helped ignite the controversy by stating his preference for using property as a basis of representation, now came out strongly against the notion that only one form of property—slave property—should be so privileged.

Morris, like King, predicted that the citizens of his state would "revolt at the idea of being put on a footing with slaves." In the end, Morris was left with the "dilemma of doing injustice to the Southern States or to human nature." When forced to make that choice, Morris declared, he was compelled to do injustice to the South, for "he could never agree to give such encouragement to the slave trade as would be given by allowing them a representation for their negroes."[25]

Pennsylvania's James Wilson, an original cosponsor of the three-fifths compromise, began to have second thoughts about his own proposal. "Are slaves to be admitted as Citizens? Then why are they not admitted on an equality with White Citizens? Are they admitted as property? Then why is not other property admitted into the computation?" Wilson was a man who placed a high value on logical consistency, and the murky combination of citizenship and property that went into the three-fifths formula defied all logic. Moreover, Wilson shared Gouverneur Morris's concern that the "blending of blacks with whites" in the three-fifths formula would "give disgust to the people of Pennsylvania."[26]

As the time for adjournment for the day neared, it became clear that the earlier consensus was in danger of collapsing. When General Washington called a vote on whether "to include 3/5 of the blacks" in apportioning representation, only four states supported the formula, with six opposed. The four yes votes came from Connecticut, which continued to try to play the role of mediator; Virginia and North Carolina, whose interests were reasonably well served by the compromise; and Georgia, which voted in favor of compromise in spite of the fact that it eventually would have benefited from a more militantly proslavery position. The no votes comprised a curious combination of states—a mixture of North and South, large and small. The vote in the Massachusetts delegation was probably not unanimous, because Nathaniel Gorham had already indicated that he reluctantly supported the compromise. But Rufus King must have ended up joining Elbridge Gerry in voting in the negative. Although James Wilson may have persuaded himself that he could live with the illogic of the three-fifths ratio, a majority of his fellow delegates sided with Gouverneur Morris, putting Pennsylvania in the no column. Delaware and New Jersey, both of which were consistently voting no on any issue that had anything to do with the principle of proportional representation, did so again on this occasion. Maryland's delegates did not record their views during the debate, so it is difficult to say whether the state's no vote was an expression of its "small-state" or of its "slave-state" interests. And finally, South Carolina, in spite of Charles Pinckney's early support of the three-fifths ratio, voted no in order to register its support of full representation for slave property.[27]

July 12 saw the delegates trying to put some of the pieces back together. It started well enough. Putting aside for a moment the confusion and contention over the three-fifths clause, the delegates first discussed a proposal from Gouverneur Morris that any formula for apportioning representation should be applied in the same manner as apportioning taxation. There was some confusion about what sorts of "taxation" might fall under that proviso, so Morris amended it to read that "direct taxation ought to be proportioned to representation," and with that change, the delegates unanimously agreed to Morris's proposal. The decision to apply to the three-fifths ratio to direct taxation as well as to representation was clearly intended to make the three-fifths ratio more palatable to Northern states. In fact, most of the Convention delegates knew from prior experience that taxes on imports, and not direct taxes, would be the usual source of government revenues. Nevertheless, this was a modest step forward, for even if the delegates seemed unable to agree on a formula for representation, they had at least agreed that once they did reach agreement, the formula for direct taxation should mirror that for representation.[28]

But then controversy erupted once again. William Davie of North Carolina, proclaiming that "it was high time now to speak out," did so with a stridency bordering on paranoia. He could now see what was afoot. "It was . . . meant by some gentlemen to deprive the Southern states of any representation for their blacks." If that step were taken, Davie declared, "the business [of the Convention] was at an end."[29]

In fact, the number of "gentlemen" prepared to go to the mat and refuse any representation of Southern slaves was very few. One of those few, Gouverneur Morris, was by this time in a state of high dudgeon. He shot back at Davie, saying that if the Southern states were willing to enter into a compact of union on reasonable terms, all to the good, but if not, then so be it. The "Eastern States" would go ahead in a union without those from the South. He concluded by insisting that "the people of Pennsylvania will never agree to a representation of negroes."[30]

Morris's outburst may have been good for his psyche, but it only served to fan the fires among the more extreme proslavery delegates. The South Carolinians quickly renewed their calls for full representation of slaves. Even Virginia's Edmund Randolph, who had been among the moderates on the issue, joined the fray, expressing for the first time his fear that a "de-

sign was entertained by some of excluding slaves altogether" in the calculation of representation. It was essential, he argued, that "security ought
to be provided for including slaves in the representation."[31]

Once again it was the Connecticut delegates—this time Oliver
Ellsworth and William Samuel Johnson—who tried to lead the delegates
to a middle ground. Johnson addressed the still-unresolved conceptual
issue of whether representation was to be based on population alone or
on some combination of population and wealth. While agreeing with
men like Gouverneur Morris that wealth and population together were
the "true, equitable basis of representation," he made the commonsense
observation that "population" was probably as good an index of wealth as
the delegates were likely to find. Therefore, he reasoned, the "two principles resolved themselves into one." While he did not express his own
view on whether slaves should be counted fully or according to the
three-fifths ratio, he was able at least to persuade the delegates to abandon the idea of basing representation on a census that used wealth as
one of the criteria. Johnson's colleague Oliver Ellsworth supported his
position, but Ellsworth specifically endorsed the three-fifths ratio as a
reasonable formula for calculating the weight given to persons of "every
other description."[32]

The delegates had by this point apparently exhausted themselves, for
there followed a series of quick votes on an earlier motion by Edmund
Randolph that contained two essential components: the taking of a periodic census and the apportionment of representation and taxation using
the calculation "recommended by Congress in their resolution of April 18,
1783," (that is to say, on the basis of "all free persons and three-fifths
of all other persons"). After a couple of false starts, the delegates agreed
to take the initial census six years after the government commenced operation and every ten years thereafter. The South Carolinians made one
last effort to substitute the words "persons of every description and condition" for the April 18, 1783, formulation, but that effort was turned
back by the usual wide margin, with only South Carolina and Georgia
supporting it. Finally, the delegates endorsed what was in its essentials
the identical formula proposed by James Wilson and Charles Pinckney
more than a month earlier—apportioning representation and direct taxation based on all white inhabitants and three-fifths of the slave inhabitants. The vote was six in favor, two opposed, and two divided. The two
no votes were New Jersey and Delaware, both registering their continuing, and futile, protest against any form of proportional representation.
The two divided delegations were Massachusetts and South Carolina. In

Massachusetts, Elbridge Gerry, consistent with his earlier positions, no doubt refused to assent to any representation for slaves; his colleagues Caleb Strong and Nathaniel Gorham probably favored the more conciliatory approach; and, finally, it is difficult to determine how Rufus King voted on the issue, for he had been on both sides of the question during the debate. In South Carolina, Pierce Butler and Charles Cotesworth Pinckney were almost certainly the delegates who held most tenaciously to the idea of full representation for the slave population, with Charles Pinckney and John Rutledge acquiescing to the three-fifths formula.[33]

The Convention adjourned for the day immediately following the vote. The next day, a Friday the thirteenth, brought more bickering among the delegates about the timing of the taking of the first census, about distinctions between "population" and "wealth," about the uncertain balance of power between North and South, and about the dangers posed to the small states by *any* formula based on the principle of proportional representation. As had been the case since the slavery issue first came to the floor, the divisions between Northern and Southern delegates on the three-fifths ratio were both confused and exacerbated by the still-unresolved issue of proportional versus equal representation for the states. For most delegates, the slavery issue was less important than a successful resolution of the question of proportional versus equal representation, but as the delegates moved closer to settling that latter issue, some of the emotion and vitriol engendered by the question of how slaves were to be counted diminished.[34]

Just before the Convention adjourned for the day on July 13, Edmund Randolph presented an amended version of his earlier resolution affirming that representation would be predicated on a periodic census based on the "number of whites and three-fifths of the blacks." In an attempt to clarify once and for all the question of *what* was being represented, the amended version specifically deleted "wealth" as a part of the calculation. Finally, Randolph's resolution stipulated that the same calculations would apply to states admitted to the union in the future. The vote was called, and nine of ten states supported Randolph's amended resolution, with only a few delegates from Delaware steadfastly resisting. The battle over the three-fifths formula had come, temporarily, to a close.[35]

IN REVIEWING THE CONTROVERSY over the three-fifths clause, one comes away with a depressing sense of the near-total absence of anything resembling a moral dimension to the debate. The three-fifths compromise was, fundamentally, about states' individual interests, not the morality of slavery. Those few Northerners like Gouverneur Morris, Rufus King, or Elbridge Gerry who voiced unhappiness with the idea of counting the slave population in apportioning representation did so either out of a fear that Northern interests were being sacrificed to those of the South or, as James Wilson phrased it, the "disgust" that their white constituents may have felt about being considered even in the same category as slaves. The disgust that white Pennsylvanians like Franklin and other members of the Pennsylvania Abolition Society felt was occasioned in part by their moral objections to the institution of slavery, but many Northern delegates were merely uncomfortable with the idea of being associated in *any* way with slaves. That uneasiness was generated at least as much by a deeply seated racism as by any humanitarian concern about the plight of enslaved Africans.

While the absence of a moral component to the delegates' infighting may seem shocking when viewed through a modern day lens, both Northerners and Southerners were primarily concerned about *power* when the issue of slavery came into play. Southerners had little to gain by opening a full-scale debate into their moral right to own slaves. And while some have argued that Northern acquiescence to the three-fifths formula amounted to a *victory* for the South, one could equally argue that the Northern refusal to acquiesce to the demands of the South Carolinians that slaves be counted fully in the apportionment of representation was a defeat for the aggressive proslavery forces.

As the historian Jack Rakove has observed, the adoption of the three-fifths formula was neither an explicit endorsement of a racial hierarchy nor a precursor to the militant proslavery ideology that was to emerge in the nineteenth century. Rather, it was indicative of the extent to which all of the delegates agreed that two of the important functions of government were to protect the rights of property ownership and to distribute and balance power in as fair and equitable a fashion as possible. It should therefore not surprise us that the debate over the way in which slaves would be counted in apportioning representation and taxation would turn on issues of property and power.[36]

Yet one cannot help but long for at least something hinting at a moral sense in the debate. Delaware's John Dickinson had remained wholly silent during the debates over the three-fifths clause. But on July 9, in the midst of the most acrimonious exchanges between Northerners and Southerners, Dickinson set down in a notebook his private thoughts on the subject.

Acting before the World, What will be said of this new principle of founding a Right to govern Freemen on a power derived from Slaves, . . . [who are] themselves incapable of governing yet giving to others what they have not. The omitting [of] the WORD will be regarded as an Endeavour to conceal a principle of which we are ashamed.

Dickinson's astute moral assessment, which even he chose to keep to himself, was, alas, recognized by few others sitting that summer in the Assembly Room of the Pennsylvania State House.[37]

SLAVERY AND THE NORTHWEST ORDINANCE

In what probably was not a coincidence, the delegates to the Confederation Congress, meeting ninety-one miles to the north in New York City, brought to closure another issue involving slavery on the day the delegates in Philadelphia came to an accord on the three-fifths compromise.

When America signed its Treaty of Peace with Great Britain, it also gained a vast western empire stretching all the way to the Mississippi River. Those western lands were a tremendous source of future wealth—and also a source of great contention among private individuals, rival land companies, and the several states. The state of Maryland, with limited claims to western lands, nevertheless went so far as to hold up ratification of the Articles of Confederation for two years in its quest to gain some advantage on the western land issue. The western lands logjam was broken when Virginia ceded to the central government all of its claims lying northwest of the Ohio River. In March 1784, Thomas Jefferson, acting as chair of a committee appointed by Congress, drafted a plan to organize all of the territory north and south of the Ohio River into fourteen future states. Although Jefferson's plan never came to fruition, it contained many of the essentials of what would become the plan for the northwestern portion of those western lands, ultimately comprising five states. The most important elements of Jefferson's plan were an explicit and fair process for laying out the boundaries of new territories carved from the vast western domain, provision for self-government within each territory as settlement progressed, and a process by which a territory would, when its population warranted it, apply for statehood and be admitted to the confederated government on an equal footing. Jefferson's effort to prohibit slavery in all those territories—North and South—after the year 1800 failed by a narrow margin.[38]

A combination of suspicion between North and South over the political effects of creating a large number of new states, a more generalized Eastern disdain for the "rudeness" of the West and many of its settlers, and, perhaps most important, incessant lobbying and maneuvering by private land speculators, made it extremely difficult for a fair and even-handed plan like Jefferson's to make much headway. After more than two years of disaccord, a congressional committee including Rufus King, William Samuel Johnson, and Charles Pinckney introduced a bill into the Confederation Congress proposing that at least the territories north of the Ohio River be organized roughly along the lines that Jefferson had proposed. This so-called Northwest Ordinance was debated in fits and starts by the Confederation Congress. As we have seen, the Congress was barely functioning. It had gone seventy-two consecutive days without a quorum in late 1786 and early 1787. The indolence of Congress would have slowed the progress of the ordinance in any case, but the behind-the-scenes machinations of private land speculators made the process even more difficult. Finally though, on July 13, 1787, a sufficient number of delegates from the eight states that were at the time represented in New York made their appearance. The decision of Convention members William Few and William Pierce of Georgia and William Blount of North Carolina to journey from Philadelphia to New York at that moment to attend the Congress allowed it to assemble a long-overdue quorum, and on that date, it unanimously agreed to the Northwest Ordinance. It appears quite likely from the circumstances of their trip that the Georgia and North Carolina members traveled to New York for the express purpose of providing a quorum in Congress so that the ordinance could be adopted.[39]

The Northwest Ordinance spelled out in great detail the conditions under which the territories in that region would be organized, but the section of the ordinance that has attracted the most attention is Article VI, which stipulates that "there shall be neither slavery nor involuntary servitude in the said territory, otherwise than in the punishment of crimes whereof the party shall have been duly convicted." For antislavery advocates of subsequent generations, this language constituted the new nation's one clear achievement in combating the institution of slavery. In the words of Salmon Chase, one of the leaders of the antebellum antislavery movement, that section of the Northwest Ordinance constituted "the last gift of the congress of the old confederation to the country . . . a fit of consummation of their glorious labors."[40]

Given the near simultaneity of the passage of the three-fifths compromise and the Northwest Ordinance, and given the fact that three Convention delegates from the South chose that moment to go to New York to provide additional Southern support for the ordinance, some historians have suggested that its passage was another part of a "grand bargain" between North and South over the issue of slavery, one that included Northern acquiescence to the three-fifths compromise in return for Southern support of the antislavery provision of the ordinance. The facts, however, do not entirely support this contention. Although there may well have been a bargain between North and South on the ordinance, it did not involve the three-fifths compromise. As historian George Van Cleve has argued, Southerners in the Continental Congress and in the Convention were deeply concerned about ongoing negotiations with the Spanish that would have resulted in the surrender of navigation rights of the Mississippi River to Spain for a period of thirty years. It was the concession of Northerners to abandon that position that caused Southerners in the Continental Congress to come around to support the Northwest Ordinance.[41]

Moreover, one should not overstate the extent to which the Northwest Ordinance constituted a landmark in the history of antislavery legislation in the United States. Although it did provide a gradualist approach for limiting the expansion of slavery in a carefully delineated portion of the northwestern part of the country, its endorsement of other aspects of the existing slave system are equally striking. It is likely that there was an informal understanding that the slavery prohibition in the Northwest Ordinance would not be applied to western territories south of the Ohio River, which quickly began to be organized by Congress after the Constitution was adopted. And the final wording of Article VI of the Northwest Ordinance—that which contains the prohibition on slavery—did not provide the unequivocal victory for the cause of antislavery that some have suggested. The full text of Article VI reads,

> There shall be neither slavery nor involuntary servitude in the said territory, otherwise than in the punishment of crimes, whereof the party shall have been duly convicted: provided always, that any person escaping into the same, from whom labour or service is lawfully claimed in any of

the original states, such fugitive slaves may be lawfully reclaimed, and conveyed to the persons claiming his or her labour or service as aforesaid.

While the Northwest Ordinance took the important step of moving toward the prohibition of slavery in what became the five new states north of the Ohio River, it also meant that the Constitution itself could avoid directly confronting the ongoing expansion of slavery to the West and could lay the groundwork for what would eventually become the fugitive slave clause in the United States Constitution.[42]

LARGE STATES AND
SMALL STATES COMPROMISE—GRUDGINGLY

With the nasty business of the apportioning of slaves in the formula for representation dispatched, the Convention continued its business on July 14, a Saturday morning on which the temperature stood at only sixty-one degrees, unusually cool for a midsummer day in Philadelphia. Maryland's Luther Martin, anxious to move the small states' agenda forward, began the proceedings by calling the question on the Report of the Grand Committee. Although he claimed still to dislike any change in the traditional formula of a one-house legislature based on the principle of equality of representation, he conceded that "he was willing . . . to make trial of the plan, rather than do nothing." James Wilson of Pennsylvania immediately responded, repeating his familiar refrain, and claiming that any step away from proportional representation in either house would constitute a violation of "the essential principles of justice." Martin shot back defiantly, "I would rather there should be two Confederacies, than one founded on any other principle than an equality of votes in the second branch at least." And back and forth it went, with each side repeating the familiar arguments, each side defending the self-interest of their states by invoking high principle.[43]

Charles Pinckney of South Carolina tried one last time to push yet another version of a compromise proposal. He proposed that the apportionment of representation in the Senate be based on a sliding scale, running from one for very small states such as Delaware and Rhode Island up to five for the most populous state, Virginia. This would not give the large states the full weight they would have achieved under a system of true proportional representation, but it was at least a move in that direction. James Wilson, with only modest enthusiasm, seconded Pinckney's motion, and Madison, with even greater reluctance—as well as the realization that he was not likely to achieve anything better—endorsed it as "reasonable." But there it died. The small-state delegates, knowing that the recommendations of the Grand Committee had swung the weight of opinion in the Convention toward a solution more favorable to their interests than Pinckney's proposal, were not about to yield. The delegates rejected Pinckney's proposal six states to four, with Massachusetts joining the small states in voting no. On that depressing note, the Convention adjourned for the remainder of the weekend.[44]

The long, painful, and, for the most part, intellectually barren debate over representation in the legislature would conclude on July 16. The end came quickly, anticlimactically. Luther Martin's proposal "for agreeing to the whole Report [of the Grand Committee] as amended and including the equality of votes in the second branch" passed in the affirmative, with five states voting yes, four no, and Massachusetts divided. The breakdown of the vote was hardly surprising. Because New York's delegates were absent, the five positive votes came from four small states—Connecticut, New Jersey, Delaware, and Maryland—joined by North Carolina. Pennsylvania, Virginia, South Carolina, and Georgia rejected the compromise. Massachusetts was divided, with Elbridge Gerry and Caleb Strong reluctantly supporting the measure and the two nationalists Rufus King and Nathaniel Gorham voting against it.[45]

The one significant shift from the previous votes on the issue was that of North Carolina. Some part of the explanation may lie in the fact that William Blount, who had sided with Madison and other large-state delegates previously, was absent, having traveled to New York to serve in the Continental Congress. It is also likely that Hugh Williamson, certainly the most distinguished member of the North Carolina delegation, had come around to see that compromise on the issue of representation in the Senate was essential to the success of the Convention. Earlier that month, on July 2, speaking in support of creating a committee to arrive at a compromise on the matter, Williamson had warned that "if we do not concede on both sides, our business must soon be at an end." Writing to North Carolina governor Richard Caswell after the fact, he commented on "how difficult a part has fallen to the share of our state in the course of this business," going on to conclude that his state's actions on the critical business of the Convention may well "have contributed to the happiness of millions." Whether through Williamson's powers of persuasion or through a common recognition that compromise was essential, three of North Carolina's delegates—Williamson, William Davie, and Alexander Martin—voted in favor of the compromise, with only Richard Dobbs Spaight opposing it.[46]

Although North Carolina's vote did tip the balance, it can hardly be considered decisive. After all, during the weeks since Edmund Randolph had first presented the Virginia Plan on May 29, the Convention delegates had recorded dozens of votes, many of them decided by only the narrowest of margins. By the rules of the Convention, however, any vote taken was subject to reconsideration if a delegate requested it. The delegates had availed themselves of that privilege frequently, going back to discuss and reconsider a wide range of issues. The question now confronting the delegates—particularly those who found themselves on the short end of the July 16 vote—was whether to acquiesce to the will of the bare majority of five states that had supported the Connecticut Compromise or to demand further consideration of the subject.

Edmund Randolph was one of those most devastated by the defeat. Later in the afternoon of July 16, he rose and announced his profound unhappiness at the outcome of the vote. For Randolph, it represented a fatal undermining of the principles of the Virginia Plan, which was, in his view, "founded on the supposition that a proportional representation was to prevail in both branches of the legislature." He deplored the obduracy of the small states on the issue, but given that outcome, and considering that if New York had been "present [it] would have been on the same side," he admitted that there was probably little point in discussing the matter further. Nevertheless, he believed that any decision of this importance that rested on just "a bare majority on either side" was not likely to be sufficient to allow a union of the states to succeed. For that reason, "he wished the Convention might adjourn, that the large states might consider the steps proper to be taken in the present solemn crisis of the business." He concluded by suggesting, petulantly, "that the small states might also deliberate on the means of conciliation."[47]

For a moment, it looked as if everything would fall apart. William Paterson, who in his heart still wished for a government with a single legislature identical to that under the Articles of Confederation, agreed with Randolph "that it was high time for the Convention to adjourn, that the rule of secrecy ought to be rescinded, and that our constituents should be consulted." But lest he be misunderstood to agree with the motive be-

hind Randolph's motion for adjournment, he insisted that "no conciliation could be admissible on the part of the smaller states on any other
ground than that of an equality of votes in the second branch."[48]

Charles Cotesworth Pinckney, fearful that the Convention was disin-
tegrating, quickly interposed, asking Randolph if he really meant for the
Convention to adjourn permanently, or whether he merely intended it to
adjourn for the remainder of the day to allow the delegates to compose
their thoughts. At that point Randolph retreated, assuring the delegates
that he only meant for a temporary adjournment "in order that some
conciliatory experiment might if possible be devised." He added though,
"that in case the smaller states should continue to hold back, the larger
might then take such measures . . . as might be necessary." On that ominous note, the Convention adjourned for the day.[49]

Sometime before ten o'clock the next morning a caucus of members
from the large states met in the State House in order to discuss how to
respond to the unfavorable outcome of the previous day's vote. It was in
no sense a closed caucus, for several delegates from the small states also
attended, although they apparently remained silent. The prime movers
of the meeting were the die-hard large-state nationalists—Madison,
Randolph, Wilson, Gouverneur Morris, and Rufus King. It is not clear
what they hoped to accomplish. Did they really think they could come
up with an alternative proposal that would be acceptable both to them
and to the delegates from the smaller states? Given the repeated failure
of all efforts at achieving a meaningful consensus on the matter in the
past, it is hard to imagine what alternative existed. Or were they seriously
thinking of leaving the Convention, and abandoning the attempt at a
strengthened union altogether?[50]

We may never know their initial intentions, but the organizers of the
caucus soon discovered that they had overestimated the extent to which
other large-state delegates shared their dismay over the outcome of the
July 16 vote. Madison gloomily reported that "the time was wasted in
vague conversation on the subject, without any specific proposition or
agreement." He discovered much to his chagrin that only a handful of
delegates felt as strongly about the issue as he did, and no one was willing to risk the outcome of the Convention on it. He concluded his report
on that final, unsuccessful attempt to push his cause forward by finding
at least a small silver lining in the cloud of his defeat. He observed that at
least one result of the "consultation" on the morning of July 17 was to
satisfy "the smaller states that they had nothing to apprehend from a

union of the larger." As much as he disliked the way the votes had fallen, the support of the small states would prove essential to the success of his larger plan for a stronger union.[51]

In fact, the vote on the compromise—5-4-1—was not as narrow as it appeared. Had New York delegates Yates and Lansing been present, they would have sided with the small states, for they had done so at every stage in the debate before they left the Convention. New Hampshire, which did not get around to sending delegates to the Convention until July 23, would certainly have sided with the small states. And though Georgia had sided with Virginia, Pennsylvania, and South Carolina in opposing the compromise, one suspects that Abraham Baldwin, if he had believed his vote against the compromise would have doomed it, probably would have switched sides and voted with the small-state delegates, just as he had done on the crucial vote on the report from the Grand Committee on July 2. And of course, Rhode Island, which was sufficiently suspicious of being dominated by large states in a consolidated government that it never sent delegates to the Convention, would certainly have sided with the small states and, indeed, may have been even more obstinate about joining the union if they had not gotten their way on the issue.

With the benefit of hindsight, we can see that the delegates from the small states exaggerated the dangers to their interests posed by a phalanx of large-state representatives in either house of the proposed Congress. Although Madison may have clung too stubbornly and too long to his position, his disdain for the worries expressed by the small-state delegates was in some measure justified. Madison had, correctly, pointed to the triviality of the small states' concerns in his speech on June 30, when he predicted that the principal difference of interest that would appear in the new union would occur not "according to size" but, rather, "from the effects of having or not having slaves." Once the new government commenced operation, there would never be a significant instance in which representatives aligned themselves along the lines of large states versus small states. The most frequent cause of those divisions would indeed be sectional, involving differences not only between North and South, but involving the West as well. And, with increasing frequency, the issue of slavery would play an important role in shaping the character of those divisions.

To the extent that the large-state–small-state conflict within the Convention was generated by the delegates' provincial, though exaggerated, fears about the balance of *power* between the states—rather than the institution of slavery—it would seem that much of the turmoil that had deadlocked the Convention was unnecessary. But even though most of the delegates were motivated by self-interested calculations of their states' relative power within the new government, there were at least some whose views were shaped by considerations that transcended petty squabbling over imagined threats to state power. While it is no doubt true that some of James Madison and James Wilson's insistence on proportional representation in both houses was motivated by the fact that they lived in the most populous states in the union, the more critical reason for their insistence was their belief that the very foundation of representative government demanded proportionality in representation. They held the principled view that it was wrong to give *any* state government, be it a large state or a small one, too much weight and authority within the new national government. The only way to avoid that injustice was to represent the people according to their numbers.

The most passionate spokesmen for the other extreme—steadfast defenders of equality of representation for each state such as Gunning Bedford of Delaware, William Paterson of New Jersey, and Luther Martin of Maryland—were first and foremost vigilant watchdogs for the interests of their particular states. But their attachment to the idea of individual states as the original and indispensable units of political society was genuine. While they may have been willing to cede substantial state power to the central government, the defenders of equal representation for the states were nevertheless sincerely committed to a conception of the states as entities with an inherent autonomy and legitimacy.

The compromise ending the deadlock between large- and small-state delegates was the product of a Grand Committee composed of delegates from all of the states present at the Convention, and it was formally presented to that committee by a Pennsylvanian—the venerable Dr. Franklin. Yet there is some justification for the appellation by which it has come to be known—the Connecticut Compromise. It was the Connecticut delegates—Roger Sherman, Oliver Ellsworth, and William Samuel Johnson—who argued most consistently for the necessity of compromise on the issue. They argued for compromise not merely as a pragmatic necessity in order to avoid a complete collapse of the Convention, but, equally important, they were able to articulate a principled defense of the grounds for compromise. In a June 29 speech, William Samuel Johnson sketched out the essential point of division between men like James Madison on the one hand and William Paterson on the other, while at the same time providing a reasonable alternative. "Those on one side," he observed, considered the states merely "as districts of people comprising one political society," while those on the other side insisted on the states as distinct political societies. But, he argued, those "two ideas embraced on different sides, instead of being opposed to each other, ought to be combined." While the states did indeed "exist as political societies," and therefore deserved to be "armed with some power of self-defence," it was equally the case that the people of the nation as a whole deserved to be recognized as an entity with a power and legitimacy of their own. What could be more logical, Johnson argued, than "in one branch the *people* ought to be represented, in the other, the *states*."[52]

Political scientist Clinton Rossiter observed some forty years ago that if the political accommodation that we call the Connecticut Compromise "had been simply an exercise in political arithmetic, it would never have stood up under the pressure of later events." It has stood the test of time, Rossiter concluded, because it "was indeed a projection, crude, but effective, of the large facts of life in the new republic. The Great Compromise, in sum, was the longest constitutional step ever taken in the process of creating a new kind of compound nation."[53]

One great irony in this long "constitutional step"—the creation of a compound republic whose constituent parts were "part national," and "part federal"—is that the man who would become most closely associated with the new concept of divided sovereignty was the individual who opposed the Connecticut Compromise most strenuously—James Madison. In "Federalist No. 39," justly one of his most celebrated pieces of political writing, Madison pointed to the "divided" character of representation in the two houses of the federal Congress as precisely one of those unique features of a government that was capable of being at one and the same time part *national* and part *federal*.

It was, however much Madison may initially have resisted it, an ingenious solution. But it was not a foolproof solution. Sovereignty is a concept, not a formula for governance. Governments are the entities that exercise sovereign political power. When the central and state governments find themselves in conflict, representatives of those governments must find a political means of resolving their disagreement or run the risk either of open defiance on the part of the governmental entity that feels most aggrieved or the coerced submission of one entity to the superior will of the other. That was precisely what happened in the American Civil War—nearly six hundred thousand Americans lost their lives before that coerced submission could be achieved. The very ambiguity of the part-national/part-federal solution the delegates had reached on July 17, together with the cloud of slavery hovering on the far horizon, meant that the Connecticut Compromise may actually have contributed to the war by distorting the sectional balance of power in Congress for decades and by allowing both sides of the war to portray their political claims to sovereignty as legitimate. In reality, the delegates had deferred rather than solved the problem of political sovereignty. But most of the delegates, at that moment in mid-July 1787, thought they had achieved the best solution possible if union were to be achieved, and they were relieved to be able to move on to other parts of their important business.

CHAPTER TWELVE

BEYOND THE CONNECTICUT COMPROMISE

THOSE CONVENTION DELEGATES who read the Pennsylvania *Packet*—Philadelphia's only daily newspaper—on Wednesday, July 18, received a sharp reminder of the thin line that separated an enlightened society bound by the rule of law from one fueled by violence and superstition. The *Packet* reported that an elderly German woman, known in the city as Widow Korbmacher, had died of the wounds she received at the hands of an "ignorant and inhuman mob," who suspected her of being a witch. The editors of the *Packet* expressed their outrage. "It must seriously affect every humane mind," they wrote, "that in consequence of the barbarous treatment lately suffered by the poor old woman, called a Witch, she died on Wednesday last."[1]

Widow Korbmacher's tragedy began to unfold just a few days after James Madison first arrived in town to prepare for the Convention. On May 5, she was viciously attacked by a mob just a few blocks from the Pennsylvania State House. According to the report printed in the *Packet* on May 11, she had "long . . . laboured under suspicions of sorcery, and was viewed as the pest and night-mare of society in those parts of the town where she has . . . lived." As punishment, "according to ancient and immemorial custom," the mob administered a severe cut on her forehead. The *Packet* deplored the incident, editorializing that "the absurd and abominable notion of witchcraft and sorcery" had no place in "an empire like ours that has emancipated itself from the superstitions of authority."

The belief in witchcraft, the *Packet* noted, was a remnant of the "old world," and had no place in the "free and civilized parts" of independent America.[2]

But superstition died hard. On July 10, as the delegates were struggling to reach a compromise on the matter of representation in the national legislature, the temper of the mob bent on punishing Widow Korbmacher for her suspected sorcery frayed and snapped. This time an even larger mob attacked her and carried her through the streets, where the citizens of the City of Brotherly Love shouted insults and pelted her with stones. Eight days later, she died of the wounds she received at the hands of the angry mob.[3]

Poor Korbmacher's travail provides a sobering reminder that while our Founding Fathers were for the most part farseeing men living in an age of Enlightenment, the year in which they carried out their deliberations, 1787, was more closely linked in time to 1692—the year of the Salem witchcraft trials and executions in Massachusetts—than it is to our own era.[4]

On Thursday, July 19, the delegates reading the *Packet* were greeted with more uplifting news. The report, most likely planted in the *Packet* by Benjamin Franklin, proclaimed that "so great is the unanimity that prevails in the Convention, upon all great subjects, that it has been proposed to call the room in which they assembled Unanimity Hall." But reality, of course, was somewhat less than harmonious, and the coming weeks would help determine whether the delegates could overcome the discord caused by the debate over representation and forge a durable consensus on other vital features of the new Constitution.[5]

DEFINING THE EXTENT OF FEDERAL POWER

Resolution Six of the Virginia Plan gave Congress the power "to legislate in all cases to which the separate States are incompetent" and asserted that legislation enacted by the Congress should take precedence over any conflicting legislation enacted by the individual states. Although the delegates debated the resolution briefly during the weeks before July 16, they chose to defer action until they were able to settle the contentious issue of representation. During the morning of July 17, Delaware's Gunning Bedford, who had been so foul-tempered during the debate on representation, rose and introduced a resolution that essentially endorsed the language of Resolution Six of the Virginia Plan. Pennsylvania's Gouverneur Morris, who had locked horns with Bedford in the debate over representation, now saw that the small-state stalwart was changing his tune and seized the opportunity for conciliation, quickly seconding Bedford's motion. The motion passed easily, eight states to two, with only South Carolina and Georgia dissenting.

It is notable that four of the small states—Connecticut, New Jersey, Delaware, and Maryland—supported the expansion of congressional power. James Madison, looking back on the aftermath of the Connecticut Compromise late in his life, recalled that the delegates from the small states "exceeded all others in zeal" for a strong central government once they had achieved their victory on the subject of representation.[6]

Interestingly, the delegate who dissented most vehemently from Bedford's resolution was the man who had originally presented Resolution Six, Edmund Randolph. While the language of the Bedford resolution did not differ significantly from that in Randolph's resolution, Randolph, appearing increasingly agitated, denounced it, calling it a "formidable idea indeed" and arguing that such an open-ended grant of power to the Congress would "violat[e] all the laws and constitutions of the states."[7]

The second section of the Virginia Plan's original Resolution Six—that giving Congress the power to veto any state laws it considered to conflict with the laws of the central government—had been included in an attempt to add muscle to the more general wording of the first section. Madison fervently believed that this constituted the heart and soul of his plan for a new government, for it would guarantee once and for all federal supremacy over the irresponsible actions of the state legislatures. Surprisingly, Madison's usually staunch ally Gouverneur Morris now stood to oppose the move to give Congress a veto power over state legislation, predicting that it would turn many states who might otherwise support it against the proposed Constitution. He also believed that it would be unnecessary if "sufficient legislative authority" were given to the federal Congress. More predictably, Roger Sherman and Luther Martin opposed it not only as too sweeping in its grant of federal power, but also as excessively cumbersome. As Martin put it, "Shall the laws of the states be sent up to the general legislature before they shall be permitted to operate?" Indeed, although Martin was not always a paragon of good judgment, his concern on this score had merit. Had Congress been given authority to veto state laws, much of its time may well have been spent in conflict and negotiation with each of the individual state legislatures rather than tending to the business of the nation at large.[8]

As the debate continued that morning of July 17, Madison sought to counter Martin's argument by insisting that the congressional veto was "essential to the efficacy and security of the general government," but he was fighting a losing battle. Charles Pinckney was one of the few delegates to support Madison's position, although, one suspects, for different reasons. While Madison's position was fueled by his deep distrust of misconduct by state legislatures, Pinckney's was born of a confidence that he could produce a constitution that would guarantee South Carolina would play a key role in any decision made by the Congress.[9]

When General Washington called the question, only Massachusetts, Virginia, and North Carolina supported a congressional veto over state legislation. Luther Martin, no doubt enjoying being on the winning side on at least one vote in the Convention, immediately followed, offering as a substitute to Madison's congressional veto the convoluted language of the New Jersey Plan: "that the Legislative acts of the U.S. made by virtue & in pursuance of the articles of Union, and all treaties made & ratified under the authority of the U.S. shall be the supreme law of the respective States . . . and that the . . . States shall be bound thereby in their decisions." That language pointedly did not include a congressional veto over state legislation and in some senses amounted to a restatement, though in different language, of the principles embodied in Gunning Bedford's resolution that supported an expansion of congressional power. Without indicating whether that resolution was meant to supersede the Bedford resolution or merely to complement it, the delegates endorsed it unanimously.

All in all, the debate on "federal supremacy" was an extraordinarily confusing and, in many senses, unproductive one. The only certain outcome of that debate was that the Convention had decisively rejected the notion of a congressional veto over state legislation. Although the relationship between the resolutions of Delaware's Bedford and Maryland's Martin was unclear at that moment on July 17, by the end of the Convention the delegates would decide to ignore both Bedford's and Martin's resolutions and instead provide for a specific enumeration of those instances in which the powers of the Congress would be "supreme."[10]

THE FRUSTRATING AFTERNOON OF JULY 17

With barely a pause, General Washington, in his role as presiding officer, raised the unresolved issues involving the executive branch. Though

Washington never uttered a word about his own opinions on the subject, his very presence, sitting in the ornate chair on the raised dais at the front of the room, would ultimately have a profound effect on the outcome of those discussions. More than a month had passed since the delegates had last debated the character of the executive in early June, and although they had reached tentative agreement on a few features at that time, most of the important issues relating to the mode of election and the character of the president's power remained in dispute. While the issue of representation in the legislature had produced bitter conflict among contending interests in the Convention, the alternatives facing the delegates on that issue were relatively straightforward—equal representation for each state, representation according to population, or some combination of the two. The debate on the character of the American presidency, while less openly contentious, would prove more challenging. The weight of America's history as a dependent colony governed by a powerful and sometimes tyrannical monarch, combined with the delegates' still-hazy understanding of the role of the doctrines of separation of powers and checks and balances in their new constitution, rendered the debate over the executive branch confusing in the extreme. Then, as today, the nature of presidential power was among the most confounding subjects they faced all summer.

Resolution Nine of the amended Virginia Plan stipulated

> that a National Executive be instituted to consist of a single person, to be chosen by the Natl. Legislature for the term of seven years, with power to carry into execution the national laws, to appoint to offices in cases not otherwise provided for—to be ineligible a second time, & to be removable on impeachment and conviction of malpractices or neglect of duty—to receive a fixed stipend by which he may be compensated for devotion of his time to public service to be paid out of the national treasury.[11]

The ten state delegations unanimously reaffirmed their June 13 decision that the executive branch should consist of a single person. But in one important case, that unanimity was deceptive, for Virginia's Edmund Randolph had already protested the idea of a single executive as the "foetus of monarchy," and he remained adamant in his opposition.[12]

Relatively few delegates shared Randolph's fear of a single executive, but the next item—the method of selecting the president—proved to be more contentious. The delegates had voted by a margin of eight states to two on June 2 to give the national legislature the power to choose the president, and they had reaffirmed that position on June 26 by a vote of seven to three. In fact, though, there were many delegates even among the states voting yes who believed that mode of election would render the executive excessively dependent upon the legislature, thus repeating the mistakes made in many of the state constitutions.

As the delegates continued to debate the method of electing the executive they split along the same lines they had in June. Pennsylvania's Gouverneur Morris and James Wilson continued to argue for an independent executive who would serve as the sole representative of the people of the nation rather than being the "mere creature" of the legislature. Roger Sherman of Connecticut once again stood at the other extreme, advocating presidential selection by the Congress so that the president would exist primarily as an agent for carrying out Congress's will. Moreover, he continued to worry about the ability of common citizens to make intelligent political decisions. The "people at large," he argued, "will never be sufficiently informed to make a wise choice." He was convinced that voters would invariably cast their ballots for a person from their own state, an outcome that would consistently work in favor of larger, more populous states. Charles Pinckney joined Sherman in preferring election by the Congress, but his preference had less to do with any desire for the Congress to dominate the executive than it did with his instinctive elitism. Pinckney worried that "a few active and designing men" could easily dupe an uninformed populace, and, like Sherman, he feared that the most populous states might be able to combine to promote a candidate who would work to serve their interests alone.[13]

Virginia's George Mason, increasingly discomfited by the tone of the debate, noted wryly that "one side appeared to have unbounded confidence in the Congress" and to be willing to give it unlimited power, while the other depicted the legislature as "governed by intrigue and corruption, and [not] to be trusted at all." Mason did not propose a solution of his own, but neither did he make an effort to hide his disdain for James Wilson's proposal for direct, popular election of the president. That, Mason said, "would be the equivalent of "refer[ring] a trial of colors to a blind man." Mason, unlike Pinckney, did have some respect for the basic intelligence of ordinary citizens, but like the vast majority of delegates, he was convinced that "the extent of the country renders it impossible that the people can have the requisite capacity to judge of the respective merits of the candidates."[14]

Mason's concerns were not misplaced. The American landscape—all 890,000 square miles of it—was as large as Great Britain, Ireland, France, Germany, and Italy combined. Yet the vast majority of Americans were settled in only a small sliver of that land lying between the Atlantic Ocean and the Appalachian Mountains, and they remained resolutely provincial, forging their identities in their own localities, whether that be in a town in western New England, numbering no more than a few hundred souls, or a county in the backcountry of North Carolina, where there were few towns even worthy of the name. Indeed, in many parts of America it was difficult to persuade even qualified voters to perform their civic duty on election day, for the ten- or twenty-mile ride to the polling place often seemed too arduous to be worth the effort.[15]

Although he knew he was outnumbered, James Wilson pressed for a vote on the proposition that the president be elected by the people. He was able to persuade a majority of the members of the Pennsylvania delegation to support it, including the avowedly elitist Gouverneur Morris, but that was it. The proposal was defeated nine to one. A few of the delegates—among them Elbridge Gerry of Massachusetts and Pierce Butler of South Carolina—no doubt opposed Wilson's proposal because of their fundamental distrust of the inherent abilities of ordinary citizens to make a wise choice. But by far the greater number of delegates opposed it because of their fear that America's vast expanse would make it difficult for voters, whatever their wisdom, to make an informed decision—that local rather than national considerations would guide citizens in their voting.[16]

During the debates in June, when it had become clear he did not have sufficient votes to support a provision for direct election by the people, Wilson came forward with a proposal for the indirect election of the president by "electors" who would themselves be elected by the people. The proposal gained little favor in June, but Luther Martin attempted to offer a variation on Wilson's proposal on July 17, calling for the electors to be appointed by the state legislatures rather than to be elected by the people. This method, Martin believed, would not only place responsibility for the selection in the hands of more knowledgeable and capable men, but it would also recognize the individual states as important parties to the presidential selection process. Martin's proposal attracted no more favor than Wilson's; it went down to defeat by a vote of eight to two, with only Delaware and Maryland in the affirmative. At that point, more out of weariness than conviction, the delegates unanimously endorsed the original proposal in the Virginia Plan—election of the president by the Congress. While that may have appeared to be progress, a significant number of delegates continued to feel uneasy about any system that might cause the president to be unduly dependent on the Congress. It remained to be seen whether even a unanimous endorsement of that mode of presidential selection would survive subsequent votes.[17]

The July 17 session had been an exceptionally long and taxing one, but the delegates made one more effort to settle the related issues of the length of the president's term and re-eligibility for office beyond a single term before they adjourned for the day. Although they had expressed a preference for limiting the president's service to one term in early June, by the end of the day on July 17 the delegates were sufficiently confused about nearly all aspects of the executive branch that they reversed themselves, narrowly supporting the right of a president to serve more than one term. At that point, Virginia's James McClurg rose to offer what was perhaps his only meaningful contribution to the debates in the Convention. A distinguished scientist and perhaps the finest physician in his home state, McClurg had virtually no prior political experience. He was only selected to be a delegate after Patrick Henry refused to serve, and, indeed, given the wealth of political talent in Virginia, it is a wonder that he was selected to serve at all.[18]

McClurg proposed that the president serve not for seven years, but "during good behavior"—effectively, for life. He believed that by making the president eligible for reelection in a system in which the Congress would make the selection, the delegates were only increasing the president's dependence on that body. These two provisions, operating together, he argued, would require the president to curry favor with the legislature in order to gain reelection. Although it is not clear whether McClurg was motivated by purely tactical considerations or by his own elitist impulses, Gouverneur Morris enthusiastically seconded McClurg's motion. "This," Morris exclaimed, is "the way to get a good government."[19]

Given the pervasive fear of excessive executive power, most delegates were no doubt horrified by McClurg's proposal, but it had the useful effect of forcing members to examine their assumptions about the independence of each of the branches of government. Madison, in a long and thoughtful response to McClurg's proposal, seemed to reexamine his earlier preference for election of the executive by the Congress. While he opposed McClurg's scheme because he thought it would be difficult to find an appropriate tribunal capable of determining when an executive had failed to serve "in good behavior," he was beginning to realize that a "union between the executive and legislative powers" would be dangerous. In an about-face from his original proposal in the Virginia Plan, he now concluded that it was "absolutely necessary to a well-constituted republic that the two should be kept distinct and independent of one another."[20]

While Madison dealt with McClurg's proposal politely, George Mason dismissed it out of hand. Like Madison, he thought it would be impossible to define misbehavior and, moreover, "perhaps still more impossible to compel so high an offender holding his office by such a tenure to submit to a trial." For Mason, allowing the president to serve during good behavior was tantamount to allowing him to serve for life, and from there, he argued, "the next logical step would be an hereditary monarchy." Should McClurg's proposal be adopted, Mason predicted, the country would soon be engulfed in another revolution against monarchical rule.[21]

McClurg's proposal went down to a narrow defeat, four states in favor, six opposed. Unlike the votes on representation, in which states divided according to either size or region, the division on McClurg's proposal, like virtually all of those on the executive branch, defied any characterization based on either region or "interest." New Jersey, Pennsylvania, Delaware, and Virginia voted yes, with Massachusetts, Connecticut, Maryland, North Carolina, South Carolina, and Georgia voting no. Those voting in favor of the proposal probably did so not because they actually wanted to give the president an indefinite term, but as a way of signaling their opposition to any scheme that would make the executive overly dependent upon the legislature for his election and continuance in office. Madison, in an aside in his notes on the debates that day, opined that many of those who voted for McClurg's proposal "had it chiefly in view to alarm those attached to a dependency of the executive on the legislature." The immediate effect of McClurg's resolution was to throw the questions of the mode of electing the president and the length of term he should serve up for grabs. And with that step backward, the Convention adjourned for the day.[22]

AFTER THE CONVENTION finished on July 17, William Paterson wrote to his wife, Euphemia, that although the business of the Convention was "difficult," he believed that the delegates would "eventually agree upon and adopt a system that will give strength and harmony to the Union, and render us a great and happy people." In spite of those optimistic sentiments, Paterson was one of those delegates who couldn't wait to get out of town, and he was already planning an early exit sometime by the first of August. In addition to his dislike of the city, he was running out of cash. In a telling admission of the bankruptcy of his own state government, he asked his wife to send him twelve pounds, the equivalent of about sixty dollars in today's money, in "hard money" in order that he might pay his bills in Philadelphia. "It is no end for me to draw on the Jersey treasury," he lamented, "as it contains nothing but paper money, which few people will take."[23]

George Washington, who would remain in the chair as presiding officer of the Convention for the remainder of the summer, was among the many delegates anxious for respite after a long day's work. On the evening of the seventeenth, he joined a large group for a club-style dinner—with ample quantities of alcohol—at Mary House's boardinghouse. As the Convention unfolded, those staying at Mrs. House's constituted a decidedly mixed cast of characters—Madison, the most resolute of the large-state nationalists; Read and Dickinson of Delaware, who had supported the New Jersey Plan unreservedly; James McHenry, whose mild nationalism had served to moderate the strident antinationalism of his voluble Maryland colleague Luther Martin; and Charles Pinckney, who tended to agree with his nationalist colleague Madison on many issues but likely harbored intense resentment at the extent to which the Virginian's proposals had occupied center stage. On that particular evening, those regulars at Mrs. House's were joined by the Connecticut delegates, who had played such an important role in brokering the rapprochement that ended the deadlock on representation. Washington lent dignity to any gathering, and his presence served to ensure that others in the group would be on their best behavior.[24]

It was precisely dinners such as these—whether at Mary House's or City Tavern or the Indian Queen—that proved so important in soothing hurt feelings or nudging delegates toward a common understanding of the complex issues with which they were wrestling. The Founding Fathers lived in an age when men of high social station appreciated the benefits of lubricious conviviality. While that evening at Mary House's may not have led to a breakthrough on the thorny issues surrounding the American presidency, it did help to restore some of the collegiality that would be necessary if the delegates were going to resolve the remaining issues still confronting them.

THE DEBATE OVER THE NATIONAL JUDICIARY

One of the issues that still confronted the delegates was that involving the national judiciary, a subject that had taken a backseat to other issues throughout most of the Convention. Few delegates felt as passionate about the character of the judicial branch of the government as they did about the need to protect their state interests in the contest for representation or about the prospects and perils of a strong chief executive. The subject had first come before the Convention back on June 4, when the delegates reached unanimous agreement on the general proposition that there should be a national judiciary and that it should "consist of one supreme tribunal and one or more inferior tribunals."

The delegates could not agree at that time, however, on how the judiciary should be chosen. The issue at stake was a familiar one—the relative power of each of the branches of government and the degree of separation that should exist among them. The original resolution in the Virginia Plan had called for the appointment of judges by the national legislature, but James Wilson, consistent with his vision of a strong executive, thought it more appropriate for the president to appoint judges. With no consensus in sight, Benjamin Franklin had weighed in on June 5 with an extraordinary proposal. He recommended the "Scotch mode" of selecting judges, a method by which that country's lawyers voted among themselves and selected the "ablest of the[ir] profession in order to get rid of him, and share his practice among themselves." This way, Franklin argued, the self-interest of the lawyers would induce them "to make the best choice." In twenty-first-century America—where the ratio of lawyers to citizens is three times higher than in Great Britain, nine times higher than in France, and forty times higher than in Japan— it's hard to imagine how the nation's lawyers would gather together to select the members of the highest court in the land.[25]

As was the case with many of Franklin's speeches, this one was greeted politely, but with silence. During the second week in June, the delegates debated various features of the judiciary sporadically and inconclusively. The revised report of the Committee of the Whole on June 13 had placed the power of judicial appointment with the Senate, but there were few who were comfortable with that resolution of the issue.

The delegates returned to the subject of the judiciary on the morning of July 18, driven less by any great enthusiasm for the topic than by the realization that the previous afternoon's discussion of the executive branch had become so hopelessly muddled that they had best turn to some other less contentious subject. The delegates immediately and unanimously reaffirmed their earlier decision that a national judiciary be established and then moved on to the more difficult issue of judicial selection. As had been the case in early June, the delegates were nearly evenly divided between those who favored selection by the Congress and those who favored presidential selection. On the whole, the debate was a civil, even subdued one, with the notable exception of Luther Martin's contribution. Still committed to a definition of federalism that would allow the states to retain as much power as possible, he unleashed an unnecessarily combative argument in favor of appointment by the Senate on the grounds that that body would best serve the interests of the individual states and would be "most capable of making a fit choice." Martin was fast proving himself capable of speaking passionately on almost any issue—even if it involved the timing of temporary adjournments to use the privy on the grounds of the State House—but however much his fulminations may have annoyed many of the delegates, his determination to defend state power at any cost was yet another sign of the persistence of provincial loyalties among at least some of the Convention delegates.[26]

The delegates dropped the issue of the judiciary for a few days, but it would reappear in different form on July 21. James Wilson and Madison had hoped that the president and members of the judiciary could be combined in a council of revision that would have the power to review laws passed by Congress and the state legislatures, and although their attempt to include that provision in the Constitution had been soundly defeated in an earlier vote, the two men hoped to revive it. They persisted in large measure because of their oft-stated concern—indeed, contempt—for the way in which state legislatures had overreached their powers and competencies. Such a council, they believed, was one other means by which the new government might assert its supremacy.[27]

In answer to Wilson and Madison, Nathaniel Gorham of Massachusetts observed that judges did not possess any special expertise in matters of public policy that would qualify them to exercise a veto power over legislation. While judges might have a legitimate "constitutional" role in reviewing the legality of measures passed by legislatures, the mixing of the policy judgments of an executive with the legal judgment of a court seemed to confuse the functions of those two different branches of government. Luther Martin observed, with unusual brevity and perspicuity, that "a knowledge of mankind, of legislative affairs cannot be presumed to belong in a higher degree to the judges than to the legislature. And, as to the constitutionality of laws, that point will come before the judges in their proper official character." John Rutledge of South Carolina agreed with Martin, insisting that "judges ought never to give their opinion on a law till it comes before them."[28]

Madison and Wilson convinced three states—Connecticut, Virginia, and Maryland—to endorse their plan, but, happily for our constitutional system, their persistent efforts to create a council of revision failed.[29]

Madison would make one more effort to persuade the delegates to create a council of revision later in the summer, but having lost that round on July 21, he moved back to discuss the best means of appointing members of the national judiciary. In an earlier discussion of that issue on July 18, Nathaniel Gorham had suggested a middle ground between legislative and executive appointment—appointment by the president with the "advice and consent of the Senate." At that point, no one really knew what "advice and consent" meant, but Gorham's proposal seemed to find some favor among the delegates. On July 21, Madison, still eager to give the executive as much power as possible, suggested a modification of Gorham's proposal. He proposed that judicial appointments by the executive should take effect unless two-thirds of the members of the Senate opposed the appointment, a provision that would have made it very difficult for the Senate to overrule the president. Madison was badly out of touch with the sentiment of the Convention on the matter, for no one rose to support him.

Although there seemed to be substantial support for Gorham's proposal, the delegates concluded their discussion of judicial selection on July 21 by reaffirming the original language of the revised Randolph Resolutions that had been presented on June 13—that the national judiciary be appointed by the Senate alone. The framers may have believed they were moving forward at that point, but, at least on this particular issue, they had actually taken a step back.[30]

The delegates had made scant progress in defining the national judiciary. They continued to struggle with the relationship of the judiciary to the other branches of government. Much of the difficulty lay in the framers' still-fuzzy conception of the relationship between the principle of separation of powers on the one hand and that of checks and balances on the other. As was the case with so many other features of their proposed new government, the framers wished to create an independent judiciary but at the same time wanted to install some checks to ensure that it did not become too independent or too powerful. The challenge of finding the proper balance between independence and excessive power would have been difficult under any circumstance, but it was made even more formidable by the delegates' failure to resolve many of the issues relating to the powers of the president and his relationship to the people and to the other branches of government. Until the delegates were able to reach agreement on the character of the American presidency, a host of other issues would remain unresolved.

CHAPTER THIRTEEN

"THE PEOPLE ARE THE KING"

THE DEBATE ON THE PRESIDENCY RESUMES

When the convention delegates sent James McClurg's proposal that the president be elected for a period of good behavior down to defeat at the end of the day on July 17, the debate had been so confused and conflicted that when the delegates reconvened the following day they decided to postpone further discussion of the executive branch and move on to other matters. But beginning on Thursday, July 19, and continuing until July 26, they would have another go at it.

As the session opened on July 19, Luther Martin attempted to revive the discussion of whether the president should be eligible to serve more than one term, but a frustrated Gouverneur Morris seized the floor. In a long, wide-ranging speech, he implored the delegates to rise above the specific details of the mode of selection, the length of term, and the number of terms and to "take into one view all that relates to the establishment of the executive." If the delegates could agree on the general principles of what sort of president they desired, then agreement on specific features of the executive branch would, Morris hoped, come more easily.

To Morris's dismay, the delegates ignored his plea, and immediately after he concluded his speech, they plunged right back into specifics, presenting a dizzying array of suggestions as to how the presidents' electors should be appointed. Connecticut's Oliver Ellsworth proposed election of the president by electors chosen by the state legislatures, using a formula that would have given small- and medium-sized states disproportionate advantage. Elbridge Gerry was ever fearful of the masses and preferred presidential electors appointed by the governors of the several states. Gerry's method aimed not only to ensure that only the most able and informed would choose the president, but also that it would render him beholden to the interests of the states those governors represented. By the end of the day on July 19 a substantial majority seemed to favor Ellsworth's proposal to give state legislatures the power to select presidential electors, but the delegates failed to agree on a formula for how the electors would be distributed among the states.[1]

Luther Martin, not to be deterred, reintroduced a resolution making the executive ineligible to serve a second term. Hugh Williamson of North Carolina supported Martin, expressing his lack of confidence in the ability of the electors to make a wise choice. Citing a concern that would be echoed by many others over the course of the next week, Williamson predicted that the electors would not "be the most respectable citizens," and, moreover, would be "liable to undue influence." Martin's resolution making the executive ineligible for reelection was roundly defeated, with only two states in favor and eight opposed. On the question of whether the president should be elected to a term of seven years, a question that many had thought was long ago settled, the delegates once again reversed themselves, voting three yes, five no, and two states divided. The delegates toyed with other alternatives covering a wide range of possibilities, and toward the end of the day on July 19 and for no apparent reason, endorsed a six-year term—with nine states in favor and only Delaware opposing.[2]

This tendency of the delegates to bounce back and forth between alternatives—supporting one position one day, then rejecting it and embracing another the following day—was in some sense typical of their behavior at this stage in the Convention. In the absence of a strong consensus on any aspect of the presidency, the delegates had, perhaps unconsciously, settled on taking a series of straw votes on each of the issues in the hopes that some sort of consensus would emerge. In the case of the six-year presidential term, that strong consensus, the nine-to-one vote notwithstanding, was obviously not present.

The following day, Saturday, July 20, the delegates took up the subject of how a president might be removed from office. That issue—impeachment—was intimately bound up with the question of the executive's relationship to the legislature and to the people. Charles Pinckney, Rufus King, and, initially, Gouverneur Morris opposed any provision for impeachment. They believed that the periodic election of the president, whether by the legislature, electors, or the people themselves, would be sufficient defense against "malpractice or neglect of duty." The fact that neither the mode of election nor the term of service of the president had been resolved made it difficult for the delegates to imagine whether those who argued against the need for an impeachment provision were correct. But, in general, the delegates were inclined to believe that it was at least possible that a president might commit some crime or act of "malpractice" that would require immediate action.[3]

But what constituted an impeachable offense? James Madison suggested "incapacity, negligence or perfidy" as a standard. Edmund Randolph spoke presciently of the opportunities an executive would have for "abusing his power, particularly in time of war when the military force, and in some respects the public money, will be in his hands." Gouverneur Morris, admitting that his initial opinion had been changed by the arguments of delegates like Madison and Randolph, came around to support the idea of impeachment, listing "bribery, treachery, corrupting his electors, and incapacity" as grounds for removal. Some of these offenses, Morris continued, should be punishable not only by removal from office, but by criminal trial as well; the others, however, would be "punished only by degradation from his office." Morris, despite being one of the Convention's strongest advocates for a powerful president, reminded the delegates that "This magistrate is not the King, but the prime-Minister. The people are the King."[4]

Virtually all of the delegates shared that sentiment, but it led them no closer to agreement on either the method or the grounds for impeachment. By an eight-to-two margin, they reaffirmed the necessity of some sort of procedure for removing a president, but they were not prepared to be more specific about what that procedure might be. On that inconclusive note, they adjourned for the day.[5]

THE NEW HAMPSHIRE DELEGATES
JOIN THE CONVENTION

On Monday, July 23, sixty days into the Convention, New Hampshire's delegates finally arrived. The New Hampshire legislature had elected one slate of delegates in January 1787. But when those elected refused to serve, the legislature was forced to elect a new delegation in late June, a month after the Convention had begun. They selected four men, John Pickering, Benjamin West, John Langdon, and Nicholas Gilman. True to its unmatched record for parsimony in matters of government expense—a record that persists to this day—the New Hampshire legislature refused to pay the expenses of the delegates, with the result being that it took nearly another month for any of the elected to agree to serve. When Langdon and Gilman finally did show up—Pickering and West never made it—they did so because Langdon, a wealthy merchant from Portsmouth, had agreed to pay the delegation's expenses himself.[6]

It has been said that Langdon was chosen to attend the Convention because he was one of the most affluent and politically powerful men in the state and that Gilman was selected because he came from a distinguished family and, perhaps more important, because he was one of the few people in the state who seemed willing to take the trouble to go to Philadelphia. Certainly New Hampshire's reputation for stinginess, as well as its isolation from the workings of the continental government, combined to cause some of the state's delay in sending delegates. However, that explanation raises as many questions as it answers. The same combination of attitudes was present to a greater or lesser extent in every state, and in some cases—most notably that of Patrick Henry in Virginia—it had the same effect. Of all of the reasons for New Hampshire's long absence from the Convention, it was perhaps apathy that operated most forcefully. It is difficult in retrospect to comprehend why any state—or any individual from any state—would consciously choose to be absent from one of the most important gatherings in modern history. But, as we have already seen from the tardy beginnings of the Convention, few at the time recognized the epochal quality of the gathering in Philadelphia.[7]

"WE THE PEOPLE . . . DO ORDAIN
AND ESTABLISH THIS CONSTITUTION"

Because of the rule of secrecy, when the New Hampshire delegates first arrived in Philadelphia sometime during the weekend of July 21–22, they likely knew little about the events that had occurred inside the State House throughout the previous eight weeks. And after their first full day on the job on Monday, July 23, they may have come away with an overoptimistic sense of the state of affairs at the Convention. With one brief exception, the delegates avoided discussion of the executive branch that day, and instead they turned to other important issues on which at least tentative agreement seemed possible. They began by endorsing the need for a mechanism to add "future amendments to the Articles of Union." Nearly all of those present recognized that one of the fatal flaws of the Articles of Confederation was its requirement that any amendment receive unanimous approval of the state legislatures. It was obvious to nearly all that some other formula for amendment would be necessary, even if the delegates were not ready to agree on specifics.[8]

The delegates also attended to an important omission from the Connecticut Compromise on that day. Although they had fashioned a grudging consensus around the principle of equality of representation in the upper house, they had neglected to specify the number of representatives that each state would send to the Senate. The delegates all agreed that the Senate should be a small, elite body of virtuous and deliberative men, but in the July 23 debate they went back and forth about whether each state should send two or three delegates, finally agreeing on two.[9]

But even this was not without controversy. The wording of the resolution on which the delegates voted read, "the second branch to consist of two members from each State and to vote per capita." But what did "per capita" mean? Luther Martin suspected that the supporters of the proposal intended "per capita" to mean that each of the two senators from a state would vote individually, rather than having each state vote as a single unit. For Martin, it was not enough that each state had received equal representation in the Senate; he believed that each state needed to vote as a unit if the Senate were to be truly representative of the sovereign power of the those states. For that reason, Martin believed that the per capita provision constituted a departure from the idea that *states* rather than *individuals* were being represented in the Senate.[10]

If the delegates had intended states to vote as a single unit, then they probably would have given each state three, rather than two senators in order to avoid a deadlock within a state's senatorial delegation. The use of "per capita" was indeed confusing and would eventually be deleted, but the very fact that Martin was inclined to make a fuss about it suggests that there were at least some in the Convention who believed the proposed new government should be primarily responsible to the states, rather than to the people.

In the midst of that busy day, the delegates began to consider the essential question of how the proposed Constitution, once completed, would become the law of the land. The nineteenth of the Randolph Resolutions, as restated on June 13, offered a cryptic formula by which the "amendments" proposed by the Convention would, "after the approbation of Congress," be submitted to an "Assembly or Assemblies recommended by the several Legislatures to be expressly chosen by the people to consider and decide thereon." The delegates held widely varying ideas about what this meant. Hugh Williamson of North Carolina thought it should be interpreted to mean that the Constitution might be submitted either to the state legislatures or to conventions recommended by the legislatures. Although he tended to prefer conventions on the grounds that they would be more likely to attract "the ablest men in the states," he could live with either method. Oliver Ellsworth and William Paterson, still clinging to the view that the legislatures were the embodiments of the will of the people of their states, thought the state legislatures should pass judgment on any proposed revision to the Articles of Confederation. Citing past precedent, Ellsworth noted that the Confederation Congress had applied to the state legislatures, not to the people, when it sought to increase its power, and since the Confederation government's authority rested on the consent of those legislatures, so too should any amended form of government under a new Constitution.[11]

Most other delegates who spoke on the matter dissented vigorously. Virginia's George Mason believed that only the people, through specially elected conventions, could give the new Constitution legitimacy. The state legislatures, by contrast, were mere creatures of their state constitutions, competent to act within the sphere dictated by those constitutions, but not beyond. Nathaniel Gorham, supporting Mason, homed in on the other, purely practical reason for keeping the state legislatures out of the decision on whether to accept the proposed Constitution: "Men chosen by the people for the particular purpose, will discuss the subject more candidly than members of the legislature who are to lose the power which is to be given up to the general government." Gorham, like most everyone in the Assembly Room, knew that to ask the state legislatures to approve the particulars of a revolution whose effect would be to reduce substantially their power and autonomy would almost certainly undo all of the work of the Convention.[12]

Not surprisingly, James Madison, who had expressed his contempt for the irresponsibility of state legislatures on so many occasions, supported Gorham's position. Yet his support of the idea of popular ratifying conventions also rested on solid theoretical ground. He drew a sharp distinction between a "league or treaty" and a true constitution. He considered the Confederation government a "league," created by a treaty among the states, whereas he understood full well—for that is what he had intended—that a true constitution was and could only be created by a sovereign act of the people themselves.[13]

Those in favor of submitting the completed Constitution to state conventions chosen by the people had both logic and numbers on their side. That method was endorsed by a vote of nine to one, with only Delaware opposed. Though Delaware's delegates gave no reason for their dissent, it is possible that the leader of the Delaware delegation, George Read, may have felt more confident of his ability to control his state legislature than a popularly elected ratifying convention.

In a crucial omission, however, the delegates had not yet spoken about the *number* of those assemblies of the people that would be necessary to make the new government a legitimate one. It was clear to all that the existing formula prevailing under the Articles of Confederation—unanimous consent—would doom all of their efforts to failure. But none were ready yet to take up the delicate matter of how many states it would take to compose a true union of the "United States."[14]

CREATING A COMMITTEE OF DETAIL

At the end of the day on July 23, Elbridge Gerry placed before the Convention a proposal that would greatly affect the Constitution's final form. Gerry suggested that all of the decisions made thus far "be referred to a committee to prepare and report a Constitution conformable thereto."[15]

Gerry's proposal was not unexpected and, indeed, was probably offered with the full knowledge and consent of his fellow delegates. After nearly two months in session, it was clearly time to begin the task of drafting a coherent statement of the new government's form and structure. Many of the delegates had been discussing such a committee privately for several days before Gerry made his motion. Hugh Williamson was one of the few delegates to bend, if not actually break, the rule of the Convention with respect to secrecy, communicating from time to time with his North Carolina friend James Iredell about the general drift of business in the Convention. On July 22 he wrote to Iredell—overoptimistically and misleadingly as it would turn out—that "after much labor the Convention have nearly agreed on the principles and outlines of a system, which we hope may fairly be called an *amendment* of the Federal Government." The system of government, he told his friend, would be "referred to a small committee, to be properly dressed, and if we like it when clothed and equipped, we shall submit it to Congress; and advise them to recommend it to the hospitable reception of the States."[16]

The delegates immediately and unanimously adopted Gerry's motion, after which they briefly debated the appropriate number to serve on the committee. After debating various proposals, they agreed on a small five-person committee, which came to be known as the Committee of Detail. The next day the state delegations, each casting ballots according to the rules of the Convention, voted to determine the members of the committee. They selected John Rutledge, Edmund Randolph, Nathaniel Gorham, Oliver Ellsworth, and James Wilson to serve on it. Although there is nothing in the Convention record indicating why those five were the ones chosen, the committee, with its unassuming and somewhat misleading title, and the five men who composed it—not all of them obvious choices—would play a vitally important role in moving the business of the Convention forward.[17]

THE DELEGATES HAD MADE so little progress in clarifying aspects of the American presidency up to that point that they specifically excluded the matter from the charge of the Committee of Detail. In the hope that they might reach agreement on at least some features of the executive branch before they adjourned at the end of the day on July 26, they continued their debates on that vexed subject. On July 24, the Convention considered again the proposal that the president be elected by the Congress. At this point there was nothing that anyone in the Convention could say about the advantages and disadvantages of this method of selection that had not already been said, yet that did not stop many delegates from going over the same ground. Elbridge Gerry, who had opposed election by the legislature from the beginning, noted that should the delegates decide to grant Congress the power to elect the president, it should also vote to bar the president from serving more than one term in order that the president not be placed in a position of trying to please the legislature.[18]

Hugh Williamson of North Carolina seemed to be making the same point, proposing that the Convention return "to the original ground" of the Virginia Plan—election by the national legislature for one seven-year term. Yet, in virtually the same breath, he proposed a radically different alternative. He confessed that his true preference was to have "Executive power to be lodged in three men taken from three districts into which the States should be divided." Pointing to the differing interests of the Northern and Southern states, he thought the best way to prevent one section's interests from being sacrificed to those of another would be to create a three-person executive as a broker among the various sections of the country. Williamson's other objection to a single executive was similar to that expressed so often by Edmund Randolph and others, namely that the president would become an "elective King, and feel the spirit of one." In a powerful testimony to the way in which the very idea of monarchy invoked both fear and resignation among Americans, Williamson predicted that "it was pretty certain . . . that we should at some time or other have a King, but he wished no precaution to be omitted that might postpone the event as long as possible."[19]

Hugh Williamson was not given to paranoia. Extraordinarily able and thoughtful, he had graduated first in his class from the College of Philadelphia. His early career was vigorous and varied. He studied theology and earned a license to preach in Connecticut, taught college-level math for a few years, studied medicine in Edinburgh and Utrecht, practiced medicine in Philadelphia for four years, and then traveled around Europe for another three. At the age of forty-one, with his impressive education and wealth of worldly experience, Williamson moved to North Carolina to begin a career as a merchant. During the Revolution he served as surgeon general of the North Carolina army, and beginning in 1782 he entered politics, running successfully for a seat in the North Carolina legislature. A strong nationalist who nevertheless felt bound to defend Southern interests within a stronger union, he possessed a cosmopolitan view of America's place in the world more pronounced than any other Convention delegate except Benjamin Franklin. Perhaps it was that cosmopolitanism—a familiarity with the vices that had beset governments all over the world—that made Williamson so pessimistic about the young country's ability to stave off monarchy.[20]

The best way to prevent, or at least to delay the return of monarchy, Williamson argued, was to limit the president to one term. If that provision were included, then he was prepared to support a much longer term for the president—as much, perhaps, as twelve years.[21]

From Williamson's advocacy of a tripartite executive serving a single, exceptionally long term the discussion next veered elsewhere. Elbridge Gerry proposed a preposterously complicated procedure by which, in the first instance, the state legislatures would vote by ballot for the president, with each state receiving between one and three votes depending upon some rough approximation of its population. Since it was unlikely that this balloting would produce a majority for any candidate, the election would next be referred to the Congress, where the House of Representatives would choose two out of the four candidates having the most votes, and then, out of those two, the Senate would make the final selection.[22]

Rufus King seconded Gerry's proposal, but he was met with deafening silence. And then it was back to square one. The delegates voted once again on the original motion for election of the president by the national legislature. And, once again, the motion passed, seven in favor, four opposed. But seven to four, with dissenters in many of the delegations voting in favor, was not sufficient. Many delegates, led by Gerry and Luther Martin, persisted in linking the issue of a second term to that of the method of selection, insisting that they could not support election by the national legislature if the executive were to be eligible for reelection by that same legislature.[23]

The discussion was threatening to spiral out of control. Luther Martin proposed a single term of eleven years. Gerry suggested fifteen years. Rufus King suggested twenty years, noting that "this is the medium life of princes." (The ever-serious Madison merely commented in his notes that "this might possibly be meant as a caricature of the previous motions in order to defeat the object of them.")[24]

James Wilson, aiming to restore some order, pointed out that the ridiculous extremes to which the discussion had run were the result of giving Congress the power to select the president. If the president were to be independent of the legislature, some other method of election would have to be found.[25]

Wilson followed his analysis with a proposal that was even less practical than any of the proposals that preceded it and, indeed, that seemed to run counter to his preferred method of direct popular election of the president. He suggested that the president be elected for a six-year term by a small number, not more than fifteen, of the members of Congress. These fifteen legislators would be selected not by ballot, but by lot. Once the lucky legislators had been selected, they would "retire immediately and make the election." The advantages of that method, he suggested, were that "intrigue might be avoided" and "dependence [on the Congress] would be diminished." It was, in truth, one of the least plausible proposals presented, and perhaps recognizing this, Wilson admitted that "this was not . . . a digested idea and might be liable to strong objections."[26]

The delegates' ability to comprehend the merits of various alternatives before them was rapidly diminishing. Nevertheless, they pressed ahead to consider Wilson's ill-conceived proposal. Elbridge Gerry, who did not always speak sensibly, did so on this occasion, observing that Wilson's proposal "commit[ted] too much to chance." The delegates then indulged themselves in an ill-informed discussion of the laws of probability, expressing a wide range of opinions of varying plausibility about the extent to which chance rather than wisdom would determine the outcome if Wilson's proposal were implemented. In the midst of the discussion, Wilson made it clear, for the record, that the absurd method he had proposed was far from ideal. That a man of Wilson's acumen in matters of statecraft would even float a proposal like the one he had just offered suggests the degree of desperation the delegates were feeling on the subject of presidential selection. But they were not that desperate. Wilson finally recommended that the delegates call a halt to the debate, a suggestion that was gratefully accepted.[27]

JULY 25—a day of steady rain and cooler-than-average temperatures— they began anew. The delegates no doubt welcomed the respite from the heat, and the city's residents welcomed the cleansing effects of the rain, which washed all of the blood, excrement, and detritus from the roadways into the Dock Street Creek.

Oliver Ellsworth of Connecticut once again sought to play the role of mediator. In his view, the challenge facing the delegates was to find a way to vest members of Congress with the power to elect the president— they were, after all, likely to be the brightest and most knowledgeable citizens—while at the same time freeing the president from an excessive dependence on the Congress. Ellsworth proposed that the executive be appointed by the legislature for his first term, and, should he wish to continue in office, the decision for reelection would be made by electors appointed by the state legislatures. The practical difficulties with this were almost too numerous to catalogue, and the delegates did not even try. Ellsworth's proposal died immediately. Elbridge Gerry then returned to push for his latest idea—election of the president by the governors of the several states—but this method seemed altogether too far removed from the people to satisfy anyone other than the most antidemocratic members of the Convention.[28]

Madison now rose to give a cogent summary and analysis of the strengths and weaknesses of the various methods that had been proposed. In the end, he could see only two viable alternatives: direct election either by the people or by electors chosen by the people. Of the two, he claimed that he preferred direct election by the people (or, as he put it, "the qualified part of them," by which he meant free, white, property-owning men). Madison continued to worry that the instinctive parochialism of America's citizens would make it likely that most voters would cast ballots only for candidates from their own states. This, he believed, would work to the disadvantage of the less-populous states. Moreover, in one of the few instances in which he identified himself in the Convention as a defender of Southern, rather than American, interests, Madison feared that the North would inevitably have more qualified voters, thus placing the Southern states at a disadvantage. This left Madison with only one alternative—some form of indirect election of the president by electors chosen by the people. Unfortunately, Madison noted, "this mode . . . had been rejected so recently and by so great a majority that it probably would not be proposed anew."[29]

Madison had indeed identified the two most plausible options, but he understood that neither option was likely to command enough support to settle the issue, so he did not bother to put either in a formal motion. Rather, the delegates next voted on Ellsworth's impractical proposal, defeating it by a vote of seven to four. Charles Pinckney then proposed an equally elaborate system by which Congress would elect the president with the proviso that the person elected would not be eligible for more than six of any twelve years. George Mason and Elbridge Gerry seemed to like that proposal, but Gouverneur Morris skewered it, predicting that it would lead to disruptive and abrupt changes in policy. Citing his home state as an example of a political system in which such rotation in office was mandatory, he noted that the provision did nothing whatsoever to minimize "intrigue and dependence on the legislature."[30]

Hugh Williamson next stepped forward with a proposal that was at least as outlandish as his previous one. To give Williamson his due, he was struggling to come up with a plan that would allow for direct election by the people without the attendant parochialism that most people feared would result from that method. His solution was that each citizen vote for three candidates, but that two of the three must come from outside the voter's state. Thus, while voters would likely cast one of their ballots for someone from their home state, the other two would reside in some other state, and, in his view, "as probably a small as a large one." Gouverneur Morris, having temporarily taken leave of his senses, tried a variation on that same theme. He suggested "that each man should vote for two persons one of whom at least should not be of his own state." Madison caught some of the enthusiasm, noting that "the second best man in this case would probably be the first, in fact." He then started to have second thoughts, worrying that citizens would throw away their second votes "on some obscure citizen of another state, in order to ensure the object of their first choice."[31]

John Dickinson, like Madison, Morris, Wilson, and Williamson, was groping for a way in which to allow for direct popular election of the executive while at the same time negating the parochialism that would subvert the outcome. Dickinson's solution was to embrace the voters' provincialism, to require that the people of each state vote for the "best citizen" in their respective states, and, of the thirteen names put forward, allow either the Congress or electors appointed by Congress to choose the president.[32]

Men like Williamson, Morris, Wilson, Dickinson, and Madison were among the most sophisticated political thinkers in the Convention, yet all of them found themselves going to great—and occasionally ridiculous—lengths to get around their concern about the inherent provincialism of the people for whom they were creating a new government. Even as they sought to create a "national" government, they realized that the loyalties of most citizens remained with their towns, counties, or states, not with the nation. They needed to find some extraordinary means by which they could mitigate those state loyalties.

Elbridge Gerry, dyspeptic as usual, repeated his opposition to popular election as a "radically vicious" idea, pointing once again to the "ignorance of the people," a condition that would allow a small group of influential men to connive to manipulate their votes. Facing General Washington—the president not only of the Convention but also of the Society of the Cincinnati, the fraternity of Revolutionary War officers—Gerry denounced the very existence of "such a society of men [as] existed in the Order of Cincinnati." He predicted that precisely because they were "respectable, united, and influential . . . they will in fact elect the chief magistrate in every instance if the election be referred to the people." Knowing Washington's legendary sense of self-control, it is likely that nothing on his visage—neither his facial expression, nor body language, nor even his eyes—betrayed any sense of either discomfort or annoyance at Gerry's attack. But discomfited and annoyed he must have been.[33]

Gerry, though hardly a paragon of tact or politeness, no doubt meant no disrespect either to Washington or to individual members of the Society. But in just a few short sentences he revealed the two fears that guided much of his conduct during the Convention—a fear of both the ignorance and cupidity of the people at large and the way in which small, self-interested groups of men might manipulate the multitude to their own ends. Gerry was an archetypal "old republican"—intensely fearful of concentrations of power in the hands of just a few but at the same time convinced that ordinary citizens lacked either the intelligence or the virtue to govern themselves responsibly.

There were so many alternatives, but none of them was altogether attractive. At the end of the day, the delegates nevertheless tried to take stock of where opinion was falling by a series of votes on some—but not all—of the proposals that had surfaced over the course of the day. The outcome was depressingly predictable. None of the proposals was endorsed by a majority of delegates. Then two rather different propositions came before the Convention. The first, proposed by Charles Pinckney, requested that members of the Committee of Detail, which was soon to meet, be furnished with copies of all of the proceedings of the Convention from the opening day up to that point so that they could have the information necessary to do their job. This passed easily with only South Carolina, inexplicably, voting in the negative. Luther Martin next requested that *all* of the members of the Convention be given copies of the proceedings, a motion the delegates rejected. Their rejection of Martin's motion came out of a concern for maintaining the rule of secrecy, but Martin took the rejection as an affront to his honesty and discretion. In his later opposition to the Constitution in the Maryland ratifying convention, he inveighed against

> the same spirit which caused our doors to be shut, our
> proceedings to be kept secret—our journals to be locked
> up, and every avenue, as far as possible to be shut to public
> information, prevailed also in this case . . . precluding even

the members themselves from thee necessary means of
information and deliberation on the important business in
which they were engaged.[34]

A LAST EFFORT
ON THE EXECUTIVE BRANCH BEFORE RECESS

On July 26, the delegates looked forward to two weeks off, during which
time the Committee of Detail would do its work. Some had already given
up on making any headway on the matter of the executive branch and
were content to allow the Committee of Detail to try to grapple with that
issue as well as all the others that had come before the Convention. Others, James Wilson in particular, thought the matter too important to be
turned over to a five-person committee. So the delegates made one last
attempt at finding common ground before they recessed. George Mason
began the day's proceedings with a long speech in which he summarized
with admirable clarity the dizzying array of alternatives that had been
placed before the Convention and the principal objections raised to each.
Upon completing his summary, Mason was led all the way back to square
one. "After reviewing all these various modes," he said, "I am led to conclude that an election by the national legislature as originally proposed,
is the best." He emphasized that the original proposal stipulated that the
executive would *not* be eligible for reelection. That, he believed, was a
sound recommendation, for it was an "essential point, as the very palladium of civil liberty, that the great officers of the state, and particularly
the executive, should at fixed periods return to that mass from which
they were at first taken." After a brief intervention from Benjamin
Franklin, who agreed with Mason about the importance of public servants returning to the ranks of the citizenry, the delegates voted on
Mason's motion. Once again, and by pretty much the same margin—
seven in favor, three opposed, one absent—the delegates endorsed the
proposal to elect the president by the national legislature for a single
term of seven years. In a subsequent vote, the delegates considered the
whole of Resolution Nine respecting the executive

> that a National Executive be instituted—to consist of a
> single person—to be chosen by the Natl. Legislature—for
> the term of seven years—to be ineligible a 2d time—with

power to carry into execution the natl. laws—to appoint to offices in cases not otherwise provided for—to be removable on impeachment & conviction of mal-practice or neglect of duty—to receive a fixt compensation for the devotion of his time to the public service, to be paid out of the National Treasury.

The whole resolution passed—six states in favor; three, Pennsylvania, Delaware, and Maryland, opposed; and one state, Virginia, divided. In spite of the generally positive vote on the resolution, there was almost no individual item in it capable of commanding a solid consensus among the delegates. They continued to disagree about both the length of the executive's term and the issue of his re-eligibility, few were content with the vagueness of "malpractice or neglect of duty" as the grounds for impeachment, and, although the margin in favor of having the national legislature select the president was about the same as it had been on most previous votes on the subject, it was clear that there were many even among those voting in the affirmative who had grave misgivings about the intermingling of executive and legislative power. Did the positive vote on the resolution represent progress toward a solution to the myriad issues of executive selection and executive power? Few believed that it did.[35]

WHO SHALL HAVE THE RIGHT TO VOTE AND TO SERVE?

About noon on the final day before the Convention recessed, George Mason requested that the committee be instructed to consider a clause requiring "certain qualifications of landed property and citizenship" as a condition for serving in the Congress. Moreover, he proposed that people "having unsettled accounts" or those who were indebted to the continental government or the states, be disqualified from serving in the Congress. Mason was particularly concerned about reports that some members of state legislatures had used their public office to escape paying their debts. Gouverneur Morris seized on Mason's recommendation to push forward two of his own agendas. On the one hand, some of his closest political associates, including his mentor, Robert Morris, had at one time or another found themselves in debt to the government, and as a consequence Gouverneur was adamantly opposed to that part of

Mason's motion. But he really wished to make a different point. He was, he observed, far less concerned about corruption among elected officials than he was about the corrupting effects of an ignorant and irresponsible electorate. Joined by that persistent critic of democracy, Elbridge Gerry, Morris expressed his preference for the imposition of property qualifications on voters, rather than on those standing for election to office.[36]

The confusing debate that followed revealed the delegates' ambivalence about political equality. Some delegates, like Morris, wished to create a uniform, federally imposed property qualification for voting, but most others struggled to find some way to keep "bad men" out of office without the necessity of exclusionary voting qualifications. In the end, the delegates voted on the two parts of an amended version of Mason's original proposal separately. The first part imposing a qualification "of property and citizenship" (the original wording of "landed property" was removed in recognition of the fact that there were many forms of wealth other than land) for people serving in the Congress passed, eight states in favor, three opposed. In a series of votes, the provisions excluding from office individuals indebted to the state or continental governments or those with "unsettled accounts" were eviscerated, no doubt because there were many among the delegates who might well fall into one or both of those categories. That whole section of Mason's resolution went down to defeat, nine states opposing, only two supporting the exclusion.

As confused as the debate may have been, there was no doubt that most members of the Constitutional Convention believed that ownership of property was an essential requirement for anyone who aspired to public service. Although this provision would ultimately disappear from the final draft of the Constitution, with the delegates deciding to leave the question of voting qualifications to the individual states, the delegates' distrust of democratic processes would continue to influence debate during the remainder of the Convention. Although the Founding Fathers genuinely believed that their new government should be founded upon the will of the people, their belief that "the people are the king" stopped short of giving to all of those people a full, active role in the day-to-day business of politics.[37]

The delegates had struggled mightily, and inconclusively, with the question of who might be qualified to serve in office and, even more futilely, with the full range of issues relating to the executive branch. They foundered as they tried to create an American president who was, on the one hand, strong and independent, and, on the other, answerable not only to the people of America but also to the wiser and more knowledgeable representatives in Congress and in the legislatures in the states.

The twists and turns of James Madison's thinking about the American presidency best exemplify the intractability of the problem. Madison admitted at the Convention's outset that he had "scarcely ventured to form my own opinion either of the manner in which [the executive branch] ought to be constituted or of the authorities with which it ought to be clothed." Over the course of the summer, he struggled to bring his views on a wide range of subjects—his desire for a more powerful central government, his desire to strengthen the executive and judicial branches as a counterweight to what he considered to be the fickle and excessively powerful legislatures, his ambivalence about the wisdom and constancy of popular majorities, his respect for principles of separation of powers—into some degree of consistency with his conception of the American presidency.

As the Convention prepared to recess on July 26, Madison had not made much progress in resolving in his own mind many of the crucial aspects of the presidential selection process or about the relationship of the president to the other branches of government. The Convention had emphatically rejected his proposal that the president and some members of the national judiciary combine in a council of revision. On the last day before the recess he had been one of the members of a divided Virginia delegation to vote against election of the president by the national legislature—a proposal that had initially appeared in his own Virginia Plan. There was little in his speech making during the previous ten days, however, that suggested he was convinced that any other alternative was preferable. Indeed, the tentative support he had given to some of the more improbable proposals floated during those ten days—such as that of Hugh Williamson's suggesting multiple nominations by the Congress—suggests that Madison was as much at sea on the question as anyone.[38]

James Madison never voiced disappointment that he was not among those chosen to serve on the Committee of Detail, which would occupy center stage (although in utter secrecy) for the next two weeks. Perhaps it is just as well he did not serve. The intellectually ambitious Virginian would use the intervening two weeks to enjoy some rare leisure and to sharpen his understanding of the work that lay ahead.

CHAPTER FOURTEEN

FASHIONING A FIRST DRAFT
OF THE CONSTITUTION:
JULY 27–AUGUST 6

UNREALISTIC EXPECTATIONS

At the end of the day on July 25, the Convention delegates gathered to submit the collection of proposals and resolutions to the Committee of Detail. The realists among them knew that their work was far from complete. Nevertheless, with the announcement of the temporary adjournment of the Convention at the end of the day on July 26, people outside the walls of the Assembly Room began to receive optimistic reports. The local newspapers, reporting on the recess, declared that a committee was putting the "finishing touches" on the Constitution. On July 28, the Pennsylvania *Herald* reported that the delegates had already "resolved upon the measures necessary to discharge their important trust," and that all that was left to do was "to arrange and systemize the materials which that honourable body had collected." That bit of misinformation would spread far beyond the confines of the city. Bishop William White, a Philadelphia cleric with close ties to many of the delegates, wrote to Richard Price in London on July 31 that "it is now well known that [the delegates] have settled the principles of the Plan . . . and the body has lately adjourned for a short time, leaving a Committee to digest and arrange the business." By August 4, the Massachusetts *Centinel* was reporting that "the Convention . . . have unanimously agreed on a system for the federal government of the United States—which will speedily be laid before the several legislatures for their acceptance."[1]

Amid this climate of optimism, a few began for the first time to take aim at the one state noticeably absent from the proceedings. Black Beard, writing under his pseudonym in the Pennsylvania *Packet*, spoke approvingly of the "twelve states" that would form the new American nation and proposed that the new nation "consider Rhode Island as Europe considers the states of Barbary." "We should," Black Beard suggested, "surround her by land, and consider her in the same class as the pirates of Algiers."[2]

With the exception of Hugh Williamson's cavalier reference to the mere need to "properly dress and clothe" a nearly completed Constitution, most delegates who had been paying attention to the proceedings were less optimistic in their private assessments. James Madison remained adamant about adhering to the rule of secrecy even when responding to his father's earnest inquiries about the state of things. He did, however, caution his father that the Convention had much work still ahead and predicted that it was a long way from completing its business. George Washington, writing to his confidant Henry Knox, ruefully remarked that the Convention was making some progress, but "by *slow*, [and] I wish I could add, *sure* movements" toward success. With typical discretion, Washington concluded, "When [the Convention] will end, or what will be the result, is more than I dare venture to do and therefore shall hazard no opinion thereon."[3]

ADJOURNMENT AND RECESS

Friday, July 27, the first day of the Convention's adjournment, was cool and pleasant, with clear skies and temperatures reaching the midseventies by the afternoon. With the exception of the five delegates elected to the Committee of Detail, the members of the Convention would enjoy a ten-day vacation. Several of the delegates living in neighboring states, and a few from further afield, used the recess as an opportunity to escape Philadelphia and return to their homes.

Some had even left the Convention before the temporary recess. Virginia delegate George Wythe had left only ten days into the Convention in order to attend to his dying wife. Wythe's Virginia neighbor James McClurg, who had never felt comfortable among the notables at the Convention, had been casting "longing looks toward Richmond" almost from the beginning of the Convention, and he used the recess as an excuse to decamp for home.[4]

New Jersey's William Churchill Houston attended the Convention only for a week and then went home suffering from a fatal case of tuberculosis. His colleague William Paterson, who had made his dislike of the city life of Philadelphia plain to everyone who cared to listen, left the Convention on July 23, shortly after the adoption of the Connecticut Compromise. He did not turn up again until the final day of the Convention so that he could sign his name to the completed document.[5]

Like many of the delegates, Connecticut's William Samuel Johnson and Roger Sherman were desperately eager to return to their families. They made the trip home during the recess, leaving their colleague Oliver Ellsworth in Philadelphia to labor on the Committee of Detail. Sherman paid a price for his decision to make the quick trip home; he was violently seasick during his passage from New York to New Haven across Long Island Sound.[6]

Elbridge Gerry, one of many delegates who complained about "the foul air of Philadelphia," met his wife, Ann, in New York City. Nearly the entire Georgia delegation—William Blount, William Pierce, and William Few—and Pierce Butler of South Carolina headed for New York as well, to attend the Continental Congress. Butler had brought his family north with him while he was attending the Convention, but, like many delegates, he judged Philadelphia to be "not so healthy," so he chose to locate them in New York.[7]

William Pierce had attended the Convention with a cloud looming over him. His mercantile business back in Georgia was in dire straits, and his personal finances were in shambles. All of this caught up with him in New York as he was confronted by one of his creditors, John Auldjo, who accused him of defaulting on a debt. Pierce, following the Southern code of a gentleman, promptly challenged Auldjo to a duel. As it turned out, Auldjo was a client of Alexander Hamilton's, who, having returned to New York, acted as an intermediary and successfully interceded to calm Pierce down enough to prevent the duel from taking place. Had he not done so, it is possible that Pierce might have become the third member of the Constitutional Convention—the other two being Hamilton and Richard Dobbs Spaight—to be killed in a duel. Although Pierce avoided the duel, he did not escape the consequences of his financial misadventures; he would be mired in debt until his untimely death in 1789.[8]

Although Philadelphia's reputation for high heat and humidity during the summer months was hardly unique on the eastern seaboard, the unavoidably rank air and pestilence made it even harder to bear. Given those conditions, it's hardly surprising that many of the delegates who did not go home during the recess found ways to take as many excursions outside the city as possible. And, indeed, the respite may have done many of them good, for when the Convention did reconvene on August 6 the delegates appeared to approach their task with renewed vigor.

General Washington was one of those who thoroughly enjoyed his vacation from the daily routine of the Convention. As the summer had dragged on, Washington, growing ever more weary of the heat and stench of the city and the claustrophobic atmosphere of the Assembly Room of the State House, had seized nearly every opportunity to take leave of the city. His usual destination was Springsbury, one of the country manors set aside by William Penn for his family members, located just north of the city. In all, Washington made twenty-three trips outside the city that summer, dining "in club" at Springsbury on at least eight occasions. Thus it was no surprise that he would make good use of his time during the temporary recess of the Convention.

He spent some of his time during the recess indulging one of his sporting passions—fishing. On Monday, July 30, he set off with Gouverneur Morris to a country estate that had a special meaning for him, as it was located in Upper Merion Township in a tract that had once been a part of the general's Valley Forge encampment. After fishing for trout without much success on Monday and part of Tuesday, he rode around the camp where his army had been encamped during the winter of 1777 through 1778. Viewing the scene in the full bloom of summer for the first time, he visited all of the fortifications and camps built during that terrible winter. He found the fortifications "in Ruin" and the encampments now obscured by the thick woods that had been allowed to grow up around them. Ever guarded, he only recorded the bare details of the visit in his diary, but he must have experienced painful nostalgia as he remembered the suffering of his troops, some justifiable measure of pride at his ability to hold his army together during the long war, and perhaps some glimmer of optimism as he contemplated the outcome of the Convention. Maybe, just maybe, America's experiment in liberty—and its union—would endure.[9]

Washington returned from his fishing trip on Wednesday morning but tried his luck again two days later, this time with both Robert Morris and Gouverneur Morris, staying at the home of Colonel Samuel Ogden near Trenton, where he stayed through Sunday evening. He returned to

Philadelphia at about nine o'clock in order to be present the following morning for the reopening of the Convention.[10]

Washington may have embarked on his fishing trips outside the city with a mixture of anticipation and regret, for on the morning of his departure on July 30 he wrote a note to Elizabeth Powel that was, for him, remarkably unguarded. Elizabeth had invited him to join her at a performance of Richard Sheridan's *The School for Scandal* on the evening of the day he was to accompany Gouverneur Morris on the fishing trip. In expressing his regrets to her, he lamented the fact that things had "turned out so unluckily," for he had so much wanted to receive from her "a lesson in the School for Scandal."[11]

While Washington was entertaining himself with fishing parties and lavish dinners, James Madison, neither an outdoorsman nor a bon vivant, was worrying. Madison never commented, either publicly or privately, on his feelings about not being included as a member of the Committee of Detail, but he certainly had, as much as any delegate, a great deal invested in the outcome of their deliberations. Nevertheless, he appears to have made no attempt to intrude on their business. Some of Madison's worries were no doubt assuaged by his confidence that most of the members were generally well disposed toward his own nationalist views. This was particularly true of James Wilson, who, more than any other delegate in the Convention, agreed with Madison on most issues.

As the days passed, and as delegates and townspeople alike speculated about what members of the Committee of Detail might be doing, Madison remained silent about the state of the proceedings. He was so scrupulous that on July 29, in response to an inquiry from his father, he wrote, "I am sorry that I cannot gratify your wish to be informed of the proceedings of the Convention. An order of secrecy leaves me at liberty merely to tell you that nothing definitive is yet done."[12]

But the delegates' commitment to secrecy would occasionally have a negative effect on the public confidence. Although most politicians back home in their respective states seemed content to remain in a state of apathetic ignorance about the proceedings (Patrick Henry, for example, never showed, at least publicly, the slightest curiosity about what his Virginia colleagues were up to in Philadelphia), a few, such as Governor Richard Caswell of North Carolina, began to show their impatience about the absence of any reliable information regarding the state of the Convention's proceedings.[13]

In at least one case, the absence of news contributed to the circulation of a wildly inaccurate rumor. Some time in late July an anonymous pamphleteer in Fairfield, Connecticut, spread the rumor that the delegates were considering sending to England for the "Duke of Osnaburgh," the second son of George III, "to have him crowned King over this continent." The writer implied that the framers of the Constitution had not found anyone among themselves capable of governing the new nation, and therefore it would be necessary "to tread back the wayward path" and to return to a monarchy. Two of George Washington's former military aides, Alexander Hamilton and David Humphreys, tried to track down the rumor and find out who was spreading it, but to no avail. The pamphleteer's charges were patent nonsense, and it is unlikely that many Connecticut residents gave the pamphlet much credence. Still, in the absence of real news about the Convention, rumors like this one did have the potential to reawaken latent American fears about the return of monarchy.[14]

They were fears that would hardly have been allayed by the indiscreet letters home from New Hampshire delegate Nicholas Gilman, who indulged himself in confident pronouncements in spite of the fact that he had only been attending the Convention for four days before the recess. Writing to his cousin Joseph Gilman, he claimed that "vigorous minds" in the Convention were "advocat[ing] a high-toned monarchy." In another letter to his brother, Gilman reported—with stupendous inaccuracy—that since "secrecy is not otherwise enjoined than as prudence may dictate to each individual," he was free to spill the beans about what was happening in the Convention. He then sketched out many of the general principles, without specifics, of "the plan of national Government."[15]

WHILE WASHINGTON WAS FISHING, Madison was worrying, and Gilman was gossiping, the five members of the Committee of Detail were hard at work drafting a provisional constitution. Beginning on July 27 and continuing through the weekend of August 4 and 5, the five delegates elected to the Committee of Detail sorted through all of the resolutions, amendments, qualifications, and failed proposals presented to the Convention during the previous two months and sought to bring some order to the chaos. If the committee had been vested with the power to settle any of the remaining and contested issues in the Convention, rather than as a small "board of editors," the delegates probably would have enlarged it to include representatives from each of the states. But the committee's charge was not to plow new ground; rather they were to bring some form and shape to the ground already covered. That job, the delegates understood, could be better accomplished by a more compact group.

The divisions of the early summer seem to have played no part in the selection of the members of the Committee of Detail. Acceptance of the Connecticut Compromise by the large-state delegates had apparently made that issue a thing of the past. Of the members of the Committee of Detail, Oliver Ellsworth, for example, was the only one who came from a relatively small state (Connecticut ranked eighth overall among the thirteen in terms of population), and, as we have seen, during the previous month he had been a broker of compromise rather than a partisan defender of either small- or large-state interests.

Though imbalanced in terms of state size, the membership of the Committee of Detail did display a rough geographical balance, with Nathaniel Gorham representing northern New England, Ellsworth representing lower New England, James Wilson representing the middle states, Edmund Randolph representing the upper South, and John Rutledge representing the lower South. With the large-state small-state division out of the way, it was becoming increasingly clear that differing sectional and regional interests were likely to be the greatest impediment to consensus, so it is likely that a concern for geographical balance did play a role in the election of committee members.

Certainly there were others serving in the Convention whose talents as constitutional theorists and draftsmen were at least as impressive as those of Gorham, Ellsworth, Wilson, Randolph, and Rutledge. Madison, Gouverneur Morris, Alexander Hamilton, and, perhaps, Charles Pinckney come to mind. But one can also think of reasons why those individuals might have been passed over. However well regarded Madison may have been, not only were his nationalist views well known, but some delegates may also have seen them as inflexible. Gouverneur Morris, however brilliant, was mercurial and capable of antagonizing those with whom he disagreed. Hamilton, though perhaps the most brilliant of the bunch, had already expressed constitutional views at variance with nearly everyone at the Convention, and, with the departure of his New York colleagues Yates and Lansing on July 10, Hamilton's attendance at the Convention was erratic. He was probably back in New York during the recess. As for Pinckney, he may well have believed that this was yet another occasion on which his talents were undervalued, but, in truth,

John Rutledge was certainly his intellectual equal and was the senior statesman of the South Carolina delegation in the bargain.

Nathaniel Gorham of Massachusetts had played an important role in the Convention up to that point, earning widespread respect among the delegates for the skill and fairness with which he served as chair of the Committee of the Whole. Like his Massachusetts colleague Rufus King, Gorham was a moderate nationalist, and nearly all of his speeches in the Convention reflected both his moderation and his good sense. He would not play a decisive role in the deliberations of the Committee of Detail, but he was almost certainly a steady, moderating influence.

Oliver Ellsworth was perhaps the only member of the committee whose commitment to a national—rather than a purely federal—government remained unclear, but he had played a consistently conciliatory role in bringing the conflicting interests of large and small, Northern and Southern states into a semblance of harmony. Forty-two years old in 1787, Ellsworth was the product of a solidly middle-class Connecticut family. Educated by a Calvinist tutor, he was sent by his father to Yale to study theology, in hopes that he would become a minister. Neither Yale nor theology was to Ellsworth's liking, and after spending two years at Yale he transferred to Princeton. He was one of nine Convention delegates to have graduated from Princeton—an astonishing number considering that the school only graduated about twenty students per year during the pre-Revolutionary period.[16]

Ellsworth spent a few years teaching school back in Connecticut and then turned to the study of law. His legal career was helped greatly by his marriage to the sixteen-year-old Abigail Wolcott, who came from one of the most affluent families in Connecticut. From that point on he began to build a highly successful career in law and politics, and by the time the Revolution began he was probably the most successful lawyer in Connecticut. He served as a Connecticut delegate to the Continental Congress between 1777 and 1783, and in 1785 he became a judge on the Connecticut Superior Court. Ellsworth had a tendency to talk to himself—often animatedly—and he was a snuff addict of prodigious proportions. His daughter recalled that "when he was more than ordinarily engaged in thinking . . . he would take out his box at frequent intervals and go through the form of taking a pinch, and would then drop most of the snuff in little piles on the carpet near him." His family sometimes "judged . . . the intensity and depth of his meditations by the number of the piles of snuff around his chair."[17]

Of the five members of the committee, James Wilson was the most dedicated supporter of a truly national government and the least protective of the interests of any particular state or region. Moreover, in the absence of Madison, he was the one member of the committee who could claim a deep and complex understanding both of political theory and of the history of governments, ancient and modern. Indeed, Madison must have slept easier knowing that Wilson, whose intellectual weight and orientation were equal and similar to his own, was there. Madison's confidence was well placed; Wilson's contributions to the work of the committee would prove invaluable.

Edmund Randolph's role in the Convention at this stage was becoming more and more puzzling. Along with Madison, he had been among the most earnest in working to initiate a "general convention" that would undertake a radical overhaul of the Articles of Confederation. Perhaps even more than Madison, he had been instrumental in persuading George Washington to cast aside his doubts and attend the Convention. As the delegate who first presented the Virginia Plan to the Convention, he certainly *appeared* to other delegates as one of the most steadfast of nationalists. But however much Randolph continued to wish for a stronger central government, his commitment to specific features of the evolving constitution was wavering. Whereas nationalists like Madison, Gouverneur Morris, and Wilson believed that a single executive was an essential part of a vital and effective government, Randolph had grown more vehement in his belief that a strong executive would inevitably morph into an "elective monarch." Nor was it executive power alone that Randolph feared. As early as May 31, he had expressed concerns about the extent to which his own Virginia Plan might give excessive power to the national legislature at the expense of the state governments. On July 17, Randolph had denounced Gunning Bedford's proposal that the government should be able to legislate "in all cases of general interest of the union and also in those to which the separate states are incompetent," saying that it would allow the federal government to intervene in the business of the states whenever it pleased.[18]

Randolph was nearly as upset by the Connecticut Compromise as Madison, but unlike Madison, whose commitment to proportional representation was part of a consistent philosophical position, Randolph seemed to have been much more aggrieved at the diminution of Virginia's power in the upper house than he was about any inconsistencies in the theoretical basis of the new union. In that sense, Randolph's qualified nationalism was much closer to that of delegates like the Pinckneys

"Dictator John" Rutledge was the most powerful politician in South Carolina. Portrait by John Trumball, courtesy of Yale University Art Gallery.

and John Rutledge—as he desired a strengthened central government in which his state would play a leading role. As the Committee of Detail began its deliberations, it remained to be seen whether Randolph's thoughts on the Constitution would more closely resemble those of his South Carolina colleagues on another important, unresolved issue—the status of slavery within the union.

The fifth member of the committee, and the man designated as its chair, could be counted on to take an active part in protecting the interests of his state on the issue of slavery. While Charles Pinckney was the most active and actively self-promoting member of the South Carolina delegation, John Rutledge was far and away its most powerful and respected member. He was sometimes referred to as Dictator John because of the extraordinary degree of power he had exercised while serving as South Carolina's chief executive in the early days of the Revolution, but that sobriquet was often used with a combination of affection and respect.[19]

John Rutledge was only eleven when his father died, and he was raised by his uncle, Andrew Rutledge, an influential Charleston lawyer. Like many of the members of the planter and mercantile elite in Charleston, Rutledge studied at Oxford, returning to Charleston in 1761 with a law degree and the distinction of having been admitted to practice before the Inns of Court in London.[20]

Rutledge combined careers in law and rice planting as the means to his positions of wealth and power. He was a phenomenally successful Charleston lawyer and claimed never to have lost a case in twenty-six years of practice. As his legal career advanced, he steadily invested in land and slaves. Owning five plantations in the South Carolina low country and more than two hundred slaves, Rutledge was well on his way to becoming one of the richest men in South Carolina on the eve of the Revolution. As the war approached, Rutledge became the leader of the South Carolina delegation to the Continental Congress and a confidant of George Washington. Nevertheless, he was one of those delegates who counseled moderation and hoped that some sort of reconciliation with Great Britain could be achieved. Yet when the moment of decision came, Rutledge was firmly in the Patriot camp. After South Carolina had drafted and implemented its state constitution, he became the first "president" of the independent state. (South Carolina, in common with a few other states, called their chief executive a president, rather than governor, but there was no meaningful distinction between the two.) With Charleston under heavy siege by the British, the South Carolina Assembly, in February 1779, passed a resolution "herewith delegating to John Rutledge . . . power to do everything that to him . . . appears necessary to the public good."[21]

Dictator John was well used to exercising political power forcefully, confident that his own judgment and well-being were wholly compatible with the public good of his state. His experience as president of South Carolina nurtured in him not only a self-confidence about his own use of political power, but also a keen sense of the weaknesses of the government of the Articles of Confederation. While these feelings shaped Rutledge's preference for a stronger central government, his nationalism, like that of Charles Pinckney and Charles Cotesworth Pinckney, tended to be refracted through a distinctly South Carolinian prism. He would, true to his nature and experience, act forcefully within the arena of both the Committee of Detail and the Convention more generally to promote the interests of his state, and while no one among that assemblage of notables could get away with dictatorial behavior, John Rutledge was, as we will see, a strong champion of the interests of South Carolina, and of the slave-owning South in general.

One of the factors working to reinforce and broaden Rutledge's nationalism was his friendship with and respect for James Wilson. The two had first met while serving in the First Continental Congress in the fall of 1774, and they quickly developed a close friendship. They possessed strikingly different personalities—the scholarly, sometimes standoffish Wilson and the gregarious, more practical-minded Rutledge—but their friendship would persist for the remainder of their lives. When Rutledge arrived in Philadelphia on May 18 to attend the Constitutional Convention, Wilson sent a messenger to the wharf with a letter explaining that the gathering of delegates was causing an "unprecedented tax on the facilities of our excellent taverns" and invited Rutledge to stay at his home. It was among the finest homes in the city and boasted a garden on one side as well as a stable equipped to accommodate eight horses. Rutledge gratefully accepted Wilson's offer. When Rutledge's wife, Elizabeth, arrived in Philadelphia three weeks later, the two moved into a suite of rooms at the Indian Queen tavern, but Rutledge and Wilson would remain close companions and colleagues throughout the summer.[22]

As the Committee of Detail began its work on the morning of Friday, July 27, its five members knew that they faced certain challenges—chief among them those relating to the executive branch—that could not be resolved by skillful editing alone. Moreover, there was one other issue lurking in the wings. On the day the Convention formally agreed to appoint the Committee of Detail, Charles Cotesworth Pinckney rose to warn the Northern delegates that if there were any shenanigans in the committee that might serve to threaten Southern interests, the consequences would be severe. General Pinckney left no doubt as to the subject most on his mind. "If the Committee should fail to insert some security to the Southern states against an emancipation of slaves, and taxes on exports, I will be bound by duty to my state to vote against their report." Pinckney had no reason for concern on the first score, for the very nature of the part-national, part-federal compact the framers were crafting would leave the fate of slaves entirely in the hands of those states that permitted the institution. But Pinckney's concern about taxes on exports and, more important, about other central government uses of the commerce power to weaken the institution of slavery would prove to become sources of contention after the Committee of Detail made its report.[23]

The primary basis on which the Committee of Detail carried out its work was the amended set of resolutions first introduced by Edmund Randolph as part of the Virginia Plan, but the committee was also instructed to take into account the much-neglected "propositions submitted to the Convention by Mr. C. Pinckney," as well as any appropriate parts of the New Jersey Plan presented in mid-June by William Paterson. Although the effort at pulling all of these disparate strands together was a collective one, Edmund Randolph was given the task of producing a rough draft for the committee's perusal. Randolph's skills as a constitutional draftsman were probably not equal to those of Wilson, and perhaps a few others on the committee, but it is not difficult to see why he was chosen to make a first pass at producing a compendium of the delegates' work. He was, after all, the person who first introduced the Virginia Plan to the Convention. And the set of resolutions composing that plan, which most delegates referred to as the Randolph Resolutions, had formed the primary focus of discussion for the previous two months.

As he set about producing that initial draft, Randolph laid down two principles that, while they never appeared in the final report of the committee, seem extraordinary in their wisdom and foresight more than two centuries later. They were

1. to insert essential principle only, lest the operations of government should be clogged by rendering those provisions permanent and unalterable, which ought to be accommodated to times and events, and

2. to use simple and precise language, and general propositions, according to the example of the constitutions of the several states. (For the construction of a constitution of necessarily [sic] differs from that of law.)[24]

One cannot help but be impressed by the extent to which the framers remained true to those two principles, which in a sense contain the essential divide in contemporary constitutional debates. The first of his principles gives support to the arguments of contemporary jurists and constitutional scholars who argue that ours is a "living constitution" that must be interpreted in the light of changing times and circumstances. The second of Randolph's principles speaks to those contemporary jurists and scholars who argue for an "originalist" interpretation of our Constitution, claiming that the only way to remain true to the vision of the Founding Fathers is to interpret the precise words of the Constitution in the manner in which they would have been understood by eighteenth-century Americans. Of the two principles, however, the second would prove much more difficult to uphold. It was one thing to aspire to "simple and precise language," but, as the delegates continued to disagree about both the substance and the subtleties of much of the constitutional language they were drafting, the "simple meaning" of their words—to use a phrase much admired by the proponents of originalism—would often prove confounding.

The other notable aspect of Randolph's approach to the task of constitution writing was his insistence that a lengthy preamble similar to that contained in the Declaration of Independence was not necessary. He considered the Constitution to be a legal, rather than a philosophical, document, and by his reasoning, "a preamble seems proper not for the purpose of designing the ends of government and human polities." Randolph believed that elaborate displays of theory, though perhaps necessary in the drafting of the state constitutions, were inappropriate to the task now at hand. For Randolph, the business of constitution making was not an excursion back to fundamental principles or an articulation of the natural rights of man. Rather, it was a matter of taking those fundamental principles and natural rights already articulated in the Revolutionary state constitutions and interweaving them with the delegated powers written into a federal constitution. If there were to be any preamble at all, he argued, then it should confine itself to a brief declaration of why the Confederation government was insufficient and an assertion of the necessity of having a "supreme legislative, executive and judiciary." Although what we call the "preamble" to our present United States Constitution went through several different transformations between the time Randolph expressed his views in his draft of the Report of the Committee of Detail and the closing day of the Convention, in the end, the framers of the Constitution supported Randolph's fundamental premise.[25]

The preamble to the committee's report began prosaically.

> We the people of the States of New Hampshire, Massachusetts, Rhode Island and Providence Plantations, Connecticut, New-York, New-Jersey, Pennsylvania, Delaware, Maryland, Virginia, North-Carolina, South-Carolina, and Georgia, do ordain, declare and establish the following Constitution for the Government of Ourselves and our Posterity.

The inclusion of Rhode Island and Providence Plantations was more of a wish than a statement of reality, but as things turned out, it was probably wise for the framers to reject the advice of Black Beard and to assume that their Rhode Island neighbors would come around.[26]

The members of the Committee of Detail were as scrupulous in maintaining secrecy in their work as were the delegates in the Convention itself. As a consequence, we know relatively little about the dynamic and division of labor among the five committee members. They probably carried out their work in a variety of settings—sometimes in the State House itself, at other times in the home of James Wilson, and yet others at the Indian Queen. Once Randolph pulled together a rough draft of what he thought the delegates had agreed to, James Wilson produced several revised drafts, with John Rutledge adding marginal comments on each of the drafts as they were produced. Although Randolph provided the organizing principles for the report, the handwriting in most of the subsequent drafts suggests that it was Wilson and Rutledge who gave the final product its shape and substance.[27]

Given the continuing disagreements among the delegates on some important issues, it is to the credit of the committee that the final draft emerged with as much coherence and clarity as it did. It laid out in intelligible fashion the organization and functioning of the two branches of the legislature, right down to the minimum age for representatives and senators, the staggering of terms of senators, and the scheduling of its meeting times. The committee also seemed finally to have settled on a name for what most delegates had previously called "the second branch." Perhaps reflecting some of the influence of Charles Pinckney's draft on their deliberations, the upper house of the legislature became the "Senate," a term that would stick.[28]

The committee sought to move forward in clarifying some of the less-controversial aspects of the office of chief executive. The chief executive became the "president." That president was instructed, from "time to time, [to] give information to the Legislature on the state of the Union." He was also given authority to "appoint officers in all cases not otherwise provided for by this Constitution," a provision that opened the way for the modern-day cabinet. The committee also laid out the process by which the president might veto acts of Congress and the circumstances under which the Congress might override that veto. It stuck with the language of the most recent of the multitudinous recommendations on the election and term of service of the executive—election by the national legislature for one term of seven years only. The committee went beyond the recommendations of the Convention in stipulating the means of removing the president from office; it proposed that removal should occur upon impeachment by the House of Representatives and conviction by the Supreme Court. Neither that formula nor the grounds for impeachment suggested by the committee—"treason, bribery or corruption"— was destined to find its way into the final draft of the Constitution.[29]

The character and extent of judicial power in the proposed new government had been badly muddled in the original Virginia Plan, and the delegates' understanding of the extent of judicial power had remained vague throughout most of the summer leading up to July 26. The Committee of Detail would define the jurisdiction of the federal judiciary more precisely. The committee's report also ventured into some territories in which the delegates had not yet been able to make up their minds. Whereas some eastern delegates like Gouverneur Morris and Elbridge Gerry wished to limit the number of new states that might be admitted to the union for fear of being overwhelmed by "less civilized" regions of the West, the committee's report stipulated that new states should be admitted on an equal basis with the original states. The committee also proposed specific allocations of representatives in the House of Representatives for each state until their populations could be determined in some more precise manner by a subsequent census. The committee proposed that the ratio of representatives to "inhabitants" be set at one for every forty thousand "according to the provisions hereinafter made." That language would later prove a source of contention. Not only did many of the delegates believe that the one-to-forty-thousand ratio would create congressional districts that were too large to ensure a close connection between representatives and constituents, but, more important, the use of the word "inhabitants" rather than "citizens" or "free inhabitants" threatened to reopen the debate over the way in which the slave population would be figured within the new body politic.[30]

The committee's report reflected earlier disagreements among the delegates with respect to qualifications for both voting and serving in public office. It left the matter of qualifications for those voting for members of the House of Representatives to the states, suggesting that those qualifications mirror those for the lower houses of the state legislatures.[31]

In one significant instance, the Committee of Detail went well beyond its authorization from the larger body of the Convention to make a fundamental structural change in the body of the Constitution. In the days leading up to the temporary adjournment, the delegates had continued to disagree over the scope of general authority of the Congress and, in particular, over the relationship of congressional power to that of the state legislatures. The wording of the final resolution on that subject, passed by a margin of eight to two on July 17, had given to the national legislature the power to "legislate in all cases for the general interests of the Union, and also in those to which the States are separately incompetent." It was that resolution that had provoked from Edmund Randolph a warning that such a broad grant of power would give to the central government the ability to violate "all the laws and constitutions of the States, and of intermeddling with their police."[32]

When Randolph was given the opportunity to prepare the rough draft of the Committee of Detail report, he deleted that broad, general grant of power to the Congress. He inserted in its place a list of some eighteen specifically enumerated powers of Congress—among them the power to raise money by taxation, to make treaties of peace, to coin money, to establish post offices, etc. Randolph's initial list was refined over several drafts, and at some point in the process still another item was added—most likely by James Wilson, who continued to prefer a general grant of power to the Congress, rather than specifically enumerated ones. The additional clause would come to assume enormous importance in the evolution of the power of America's national government. It gave to Congress the power "to make all Laws that shall be necessary and proper for carrying into execution the foregoing powers, and all other powers vested by this Constitution in the government of the United States, or in any department or officer thereof." The "necessary and proper" clause, as it came to be interpreted once the new government commenced operation, would serve as a powerful engine of congressional power and, by extension, a powerful means of extending the power of the federal government.[33]

Following the decision on July 17 to give to Congress the power to legislate "in all cases for the general interest of the Union," nationalists like Madison and Wilson had also attempted to secure for the government the power to "negative" any state laws that threatened to undermine the federal Constitution's powers. Most delegates thought this was going too far; the proposal fell by a vote of seven to three. Madison and Wilson were able to recoup some of their loss in the Committee of Detail report, for it listed specific instances in which the states were forbidden to act—as in the printing of paper money, the laying of duties on imports, the keeping of "troops or ships of war in time of peace," or the making of separate treaties on their own authority. Although the Confederation government had also attempted to limit the states' authority in some of those areas, it had largely proven ineffectual in doing so, and the members of the Committee of Detail no doubt hoped that this more explicit prohibition would strengthen the central government's power vis-à-vis the state governments.[34]

There was one notable feature of the Committee of Detail report that, far from resolving previous controversies among the delegates, would only inflame them. As the committee prepared its report, its members no doubt remembered Charles Cotesworth Pinckney's warning about the consequences of putting anything in their document that might weaken the institution of slavery or that might open the way to taxing Southern agricultural exports. And at least some of the committee's members—no doubt led by John Rutledge—were prepared to accommodate Pinckney. Not only was the committee report explicit about those powers the new Congress *should* possess, it also devoted a separate section to those powers the Congress *should not* possess. Article VI, Section 4 of the Committee of Detail report explicitly prohibited Congress from taxing exports and from placing any restrictions—either through taxation or outright prohibition—"on the migration or importation of such persons as the several States shall think proper to admit." The "persons" being referred to, of course, were slaves. Finally, in a move that was almost certainly aimed at further protecting Southern interests, the committee also stipulated that any "navigation" acts—which is to say, any law that sought to regulate foreign commerce through tariffs, quotas, or the like—could not be passed unless two-thirds of the members of both houses assented to them. While there were a few Northern delegates who were also wary of allowing a mere majority in Congress to pass laws regulating foreign trade, this provision, like the provisions explicitly exempting exports from taxation and prohibiting any regulation of the slave trade, represented an aggressive attempt by the Southern members of the committee—and Rutledge in particular—to defend Southern interests.[35]

One recent account of the Convention has claimed that Rutledge, perhaps with the acquiescence of his longtime friend James Wilson, "hijacked the Constitution" by his aggressive defense of Southern interests in the Committee of Detail report. While Rutledge was an extraordinarily effective promoter of Southern interests throughout the summer of 1787, it is implausible to believe either that he was sufficiently clever or that the other delegates were sufficiently gullible as to allow him to subvert the will of the Convention. The Committee of Detail report did have a pro-Southern tilt that reflected some of Rutledge's influence in the committee. But the report's recommendations would be subject to rigorous scrutiny once the Convention reassembled. To the extent that the final draft of the Constitution represented a victory for men like Dictator John, the delegates from the North and the upper South must be judged equally responsible.[36]

On Friday, August 3, the committee turned the report over to John Dunlap and David Claypoole, the publishers of the Pennsylvania *Packet*, and asked them to print a sufficient number of copies for each of the delegates when the Convention reconvened on Monday, August 6. Dunlap and Claypoole carried out this task with remarkable discretion; the pages of the *Packet* during the period immediately before and after the printing of the report are utterly devoid of any news relating to the committee's deliberations. In our own age, the most likely source of any leak about the contents of a document as important as the Report of the Committee of Detail would be one (or more!) of the delegates themselves, but the men gathered in the Assembly Room operated by a different code. Not a single delegate allowed any hint of the content of the report to leak out to the general public. In that atmosphere of mutual trust and confidentiality, the delegates would take their seats on August 6 to consider the form and shape of what was beginning to look like a proper constitution.[37]

CHAPTER FIFTEEN

REVISING THE CONSTITUTION: AUGUST 6–AUGUST 31

AS THE DELEGATES ASSEMBLED on Monday, August 6, they expected to begin discussion of the Report of the Committee of Detail, but finding that only eight states with a quorum of delegates had made it back to town on time, they decided merely to acknowledge receipt of the report and then adjourn and try again at eleven the following morning.[1]

By Tuesday, the delegations from Delaware and Georgia had wandered back into town, but the New Jersey delegates, though all they needed to do was to make a short journey across the Delaware River, remained truant. Charles Pinckney began the proceedings by asking that the Report of the Committee of Detail be discussed in the Committee of the Whole. This move would allow for more give-and-take in the discussions, but it also ran the risk of slowing the Convention's proceedings, since any votes taken in the Committee of the Whole were subject to reconsideration. Several delegates immediately objected to Pinckney's suggestion, arguing that such a move would "likely produce unnecessary delay." Seven of the ten states present—anxious to move the business along as quickly as possible—agreed, deciding that Washington should remain in the chair and continue to preside over the Convention in his formal capacity.[2]

From August 7 through August 31 the delegates doggedly worked through every one of the twenty-three articles and their various sections and subsections in the Committee of Detail report. This was tedious but

important work, for the process of both refinement of language and reconciliation of differing points of view required a combination of patience, persistence, and flexibility. More than a few delegates simply
were not up to the task. In addition to those delegates who had already
departed by July 26, Oliver Ellsworth of Connecticut, William Pierce
and William Houstoun of Georgia, William R. Davie and Alexander
Martin of North Carolina, Luther Martin of Maryland, John Mercer of
Virginia, and Caleb Strong of Massachusetts all left the Convention before it had completed its work.[3]

Many of those who did persist were not always good humored about
it. James Madison, writing to his father during the second week in August, complained that it was hard to "determine the period to which the
Session will be spun out," predicting that it would be many weeks, and
possibly months, before the Convention finished its business. Washington, writing to his friend and confidant Henry Knox, scrupulously adhered to the rule of secrecy but noted with some sarcasm that if "some
thing good does not proceed from the [Convention] the defects cannot
with propriety be charged to the hurry with which the business has been
conducted." Some of the delay, Washington believed, resulted from the
fact that some parts of the document were "not well digested," but a
large measure of it was brought about by the "contrariety of sentiments
with which such a body is pervaded."[4]

David Brearley of New Jersey was in a particularly sour mood, both
because of the slow pace of deliberation and because his fellow delegate
William Paterson had already bolted from Philadelphia and was comfortably back home in Trenton. "Every article is again argued over, with
as much earnestness and obstinacy as before it was committed." He concluded by imploring his absent colleague to rejoin the New Jersey delegation in Philadelphia, but such was Paterson's dislike of the city that he
did not return to the Convention until the very last day, just in time to
sign the completed Constitution.[5]

As the delegates began to go through the Report of the Committee of
Detail item by item, they quickly approved the preamble and Articles I
and II. As Randolph had recommended, the preamble was not a philosophical treatise, but rather a simple affirmation that "We the people" of
the specifically named states "do ordain, declare and establish the following Constitution for the Government of Ourselves and our Posterity." Article I declared simply that "The Stile of this Government shall
be 'the United States of America,' " a modest, but perhaps significant

change from the Articles of Confederation, which stated that "the stile of this *confederacy* shall be 'The United States of America.'" Article II re-iterated the message of the original May 30 resolution introduced by Gouverneur Morris, stipulating that the government would possess "supreme legislative, executive, and judicial powers."[6]

From that point on, the Committee of Detail report received intense scrutiny. Article III, vesting the legislative power in a two-house Congress, was only four lines long, but the delegates managed to spend nearly half a day debating the meaning of "legislative acts" and the frequency and desired season of the Congress's meetings before agreeing to a version with only slightly altered wording.[7]

Article IV of the report stipulated that the qualifications for voting for members of the House of Representatives should be the same as those for electing members of the legislature in each of the respective states, a departure from the tentative agreement reached by the delegates on July 26, when they endorsed a "qualification of property and citizenship." Gouverneur Morris, consistent with his oft-stated belief that property was an indispensable element of full citizenship, proposed that the right to vote for members of the House of Representatives be limited to freeholders only—those who owned a sufficient quantity of property. John Dickinson, speaking in support of Morris's proposed amendment, articulated the traditional rationale for restricting the vote to property owners. Only freeholders, Dickinson claimed, could provide adequate "defense against the dangerous influence of those multitudes without property and without principle."[8]

Morris, responding to the charge that such a restriction would give the government an aristocratic tilt, retorted that he was not at all alarmed by "the sound of Aristocracy." Indeed, Morris claimed, if there was any danger of a real aristocracy coming into being, that danger lay in a House of Representatives elected by the propertyless masses. "Give the votes to the people who have no property," Morris warned, "and they will sell them to the rich who will be able to buy them." He predicted that the time would soon come when the nation would "abound with mechanics and manufacturers who will receive their bread from their employers" and warned that "the ignorant and the dependent can be as little trusted with the public interest" as small children, who were, quite properly, denied the right to vote.[9]

Delegates with a more generous appraisal of the inherent abilities of the people rose to answer Morris and Dickinson's arguments. George

Mason, James Madison, Hugh Williamson, Oliver Ellsworth, Pierce Butler, and, most notably, Benjamin Franklin weighed in on the other side. Franklin's argument against a property qualification for voting was simple and from the heart. It was, he observed, "of great consequence that we should not depress the virtue and public spirit of our common people, of which they displayed a great deal during the war, and which contributed principally to the favorable issue of it."[10]

By the end of the day, the delegates had embraced Franklin's more optimistic assessment of the virtues of ordinary citizens, rejecting Morris's proposal to impose federal property qualifications higher than those imposed by the individual state governments by a vote of only one state in favor (Delaware), seven opposed, and one (Maryland) divided. However, the antidemocratic instincts of many of the framers resurfaced a few days later when the delegates took up requirements for members of either house of the legislature.

It was one thing to allow a free white male without property to *vote* for a representative, but should he actually be able to serve in public office? Many delegates viewed that prospect with horror. Charles Pinckney, thinking that the proposal in the Report of the Committee of Detail did not go far enough, proposed specific property qualifications for officeholders. He thought the minimum requirement for the president should be the astronomical sum of one hundred thousand dollars—which, in today's dollars, would have amounted to well over two million dollars—and that judges and members of Congress should have a property requirement of fifty thousand dollars. These were sums of money that would have disqualified more than 99 percent of the population from serving in federal office.[11]

The debate on Pinckney's proposal was spread out over three days, and on August 10 Benjamin Franklin had the last word, forcefully rebuking those inclined to make public service the preserve only of the wealthy. He stoutly opposed "every thing that tended to debase the spirit of the common people" and insisted that honesty and virtue had never been the exclusive property of the wealthy. Indeed, he noted, "some of the greatest rogues I was ever acquainted with, were the richest rogues." Immediately following Franklin's interjection, the delegates emphatically rejected Pinckney's proposal. They rejected it not so much because they embraced Franklin's egalitarian sentiments, but because they could not agree on what the requisite qualification should be. The commentary on the issue of property qualifications for voting and public service from many of the most ardent supporters of the new government—Gouverneur Morris, Charles Pinckney, John Rutledge, and, on occasion, Madison—displays in striking fashion the fear and distrust with which many of the Founding Fathers regarded the common people. They believed that they were creating a republic, not a democracy, and most of the wealthy and privileged men serving in the Convention were convinced that true republican government depended on a virtuous, property-owning citizenry. However much the Founding Fathers *wished* to believe that America's citizens would retain their virtue, their experience during the tumultuous years of the Revolution had often taught them otherwise. Not only did self-sacrifice and virtue seem to be giving way to wartime profiteering and the unbridled pursuit of self-interest, but a new class of men, previously unschooled in the arts of governance, began to displace more "respectable" citizens in state and local political offices. As New Yorker John Jay derisively put it, "Effrontery and arrogance . . . are giving rank and Importance to men whom Wisdom would have left in obscurity." One of the great fears motivating them as they crafted a new continental government was that a tyrannical majority of propertyless citizens might combine to render the rights of property insecure.[12]

On Wednesday, August 8, the delegates turned to the article dealing with citizenship requirements for those serving in the House and Senate. The original version had stipulated that members of the House be citizens for three years and members of the Senate citizens for four. George Mason, Gouverneur Morris, Roger Sherman, and Pierce Butler (who was born in Ireland) complained that such a short citizenship requirement would open the government up to foreign influence. Mason claimed that he favored "opening a wide door for emigrants," but in the same breath insisted that it was improper to "let foreigners and adventurers make laws for us." He conjured up the notion of Great Britain sending "over her tools who might bribe their way into the legislature for nefarious purposes." John Rutledge had other worries. He argued not only that there should be a longer national citizenship requirement, but also that any member of the Congress should reside at least seven years in the state from which he was elected. Rutledge was convinced that "an emigrant from New England to South Carolina or Georgia would know little of its affairs and could not be supposed to acquire a thorough knowledge in less time."[13]

Madison and Franklin both protested the "illiberality" of longer citizenship requirements, but a majority of delegates, when confronted with demands from men like Gouverneur Morris to raise the citizenship requirement to as high as fourteen years, compromised by raising the requirement to seven years for members of the House and nine years for members of the Senate, provisions that remain in the Constitution to this day.[14]

Continuing their review of the Report of the Committee of Detail on August 8, the delegates squabbled in predictable fashion over Article IV, Section 3, which parceled out specific numbers of representatives to each state until a proper census could be taken. But in the end, the recommendations of the committee were allowed to stand. That was not the case with the language of Article IV, Section 4, which prescribed that the ratio of representatives to inhabitants be permanently set at one for every forty thousand, a formula that if in place today would produce a House of Representatives with some seventy-five hundred members. Madison had the foresight to see that the one-to-forty-thousand ratio might cause problems in the future. "The future increase of population," Madison objected, would, "if the union should be permanent, render the number of representatives excessive." Nathaniel Gorham immediately responded with incredulity. "It is not to be supposed that the government will last so long as to produce this effect. Can it be supposed that this vast country . . . will 150 years hence remain one nation?" The fact that Madison, a primary architect of the union, would preface his remarks with "if," and Gorham, a strong supporter of union, would regard the likelihood of its lasting 150 years with incredulity speaks volumes about the fragility of the new union the framers were struggling to create. Fortunately, in the matter immediately at hand, the delegates agreed to accept an amendment by Madison changing the wording of Article IV, Section 3 to read "*not exceeding*" one for every forty thousand inhabitants.[15]

Beginning on that same Wednesday, and continuing into the following week, the delegates engaged in an acrimonious debate over Article IV, Section 5, which not only gave the House of Representatives exclusive power over initiating money bills, but also stipulated that the Senate would have no power to amend legislation coming out of the House. Those delegates with the most pronounced antidemocratic fears argued for a stronger Senate role in the origination of money bills; those with greater faith in the popular branch wanted to retain the language of the Report of the Committee of Detail. George Mason was among those who supported the exclusive privilege of the House to originate money bills, doing so not only because he believed that any legislation affecting the pocketbooks of the citizens ought to originate in the body whose members were elected directly by those citizens, but also because that provision was an essential part of the Connecticut Compromise. To strike out the section was to "unhinge the compromise of which it made a part." In the end, Madison and John Dickinson found an appropriate middle ground, retaining the language that gave the House the sole power to originate money bills, but deleting the clause that prevented the Senate from any role in altering or amending such bills as they emerged from the House.[16]

In the course of articulating his position on the relationship between the House and the Senate, John Dickinson, in one of the most memorable speeches of the Convention, gave voice to the essential conservatism that shaped his views on government and society—views shared by nearly all those delegates gathered in the Assembly Room. "Experience," Dickinson noted,

> must be our only guide. Reason may mislead us. It was not Reason that discovered the singular and admirable mechanism of the English Constitution. It was not Reason that discovered or ever could have discovered the . . . absurd mode of trial by jury. Accidents probably produced these discoveries, and experience has given sanction to them. This then is our guide. And has not experience verified the utility of restraining money bills to the immediate representatives of the people. . . . All the prejudices of the people would be offended by refusing this exclusive privilege to the House of Representatives. . . . And these prejudices should never be disregarded by us when no essential purpose was to be served.

What is remarkable about Dickinson's speech is that he, as much as any man in the Convention, valued reason as one of the highest virtues. He had on more than one occasion exalted the English House of Lords as a particularly impressive repository of virtuous, rational statesmen, and by that reasoning, one would expect him to give more power to the Senate—the closest American equivalent to the House of Lords—as the repository of the greatest wisdom when it came to money bills. But the essence of Dickinson's conservatism was that he understood that the

John Dickinson, a carefully modulated voice of moderation during the Convention. Portrait by Charles Willson Peale, courtesy of Independence National Historical Park.

tide of political sentiment in America was running in a different direction. Whatever his own ideological preferences, he saw that it was necessary to rely on America's historical experience rather than his own fallible powers of reason to dictate the proper course on this particular question. There were many similar-minded men in the Convention—Madison, Gouverneur Morris, and James Wilson come to mind—who no doubt shared many of Dickinson's elitist assumptions. But they too came to understand that they needed to frame a constitution consistent with America's historical experience if that constitution was to be a durable one.[17]

THE SEAT OF GOVERNMENT

Article IV, Section 8, which dealt primarily with the coordination of times of adjournment between the House and Senate, mentioned only vaguely the "place" at which the Congress, and by implication, the seat of government, should be located. As the delegates took up this oversight in the committee report, they were well aware that New York was currently serving as the seat of the continental government. To designate New York as the permanent capital would be to locate the seat of government far to the north of the geographic center of the country. Moreover, all of the delegates, whatever their sectional loyalties, were mindful that the frequent changes that had occurred in the meeting place of the Continental Congress—which over the course of its short life had met in Philadelphia, Trenton, Princeton, Lancaster, York, Annapolis, and, finally, New York—were emblematic of the sense of instability in the continental government. While Northern and Southern delegates predictably expressed their preferences for cooler or warmer climes depending on their state of residence, they all understood they would need to ensure that the new government would operate from a reasonably central location and that such a location should not be in the same place as any of the state capitals. To do otherwise would run the risk of causing the politics of the national government and of a particular state to become too closely intertwined.

The delegates fumbled ineffectively for several weeks before sorting out the matter. Finally, on September 4, they agreed on a provision that would give Congress the power, after a state had ceded territory for that purpose, to designate an area "not exceeding ten miles square" as the seat of the government. This left the question of *where* the new government would be located up in the air, but it did at least make clear that, wherever it might be located, the "ten mile square" area would not be part of any existing state. In retrospect, this has proven to be a wise decision, but our hindsight should not blind us to the intense fear that many delegates harbored about concentrations of power in any one body or any one place. Indeed, the decision to create a "federal district" was one of the factors that would turn George Mason against the proposed Constitution. When debating the document in the Virginia ratifying convention, Mason railed against the separate existence of a "federal territory" predicting that it would become a "sanctuary of the blackest crimes." If any of the members of the new national government "should attempt to oppress the people or to perpetrate the blackest deed," Mason argued, "he has nothing to do but to get into the ten mile square."[18]

Luther Martin, already beginning his campaign against the proposed Constitution before the Convention had finished its business, saw an even darker prospect for the goings-on within the "ten miles square." It would, he predicted, become a "seat of empire"—a powerful empire of the sort that had oppressed people the world over for centuries. Over-stated, polemical language was Martin's stock in trade, so perhaps we can discount his predictions of tyranny and oppression. But we must also give him some credit for prescience. One of the results of the creation of the American Constitution, with its vastly increased powers, was the cre-ation of a formidable seat of empire. It is unlikely that the decision to lo-cate the nation's capital in an area ten miles square rather than in one of the existing states rendered that empire any more powerful or its poten-tial for oppression any greater, but in the two-and-a-quarter centuries since Martin issued his warning, the concentration of power in Amer-ica's seat of empire has grown ever more formidable.[19]

The suspicions voiced by Mason and Martin over the proposed fed-eral district signaled that the dispositions of at least some of the delegates were turning sour as the summer wore on, but amidst the grumblings, the work of the delegates went on. On August 14 they took up the provi-sion in Article VI, Section 10 providing that "members [of the Congress] be paid by their respective States." It seemed a relatively minor matter, but many considered it a question of great significance. In the first in-stance, there were still some delegates who continued to believe that rep-resentatives should not be paid at all for fear that the lure of financial gain would stimulate an unhealthy pursuit of public office. Those delegates believed that the best way to ensure that the legislature would contain only the most virtuous men would be to foreclose any opportunity for monetary gain while serving in office. No doubt their concern for ensur-ing the republican virtue of American public servants was genuine, but the other consequence of an insistence that government officials serve without compensation would have been to make it impossible for ordi-nary citizens to devote their time to public service.

Equally important, many delegates opposed having the states, rather than the national government, pay the salaries and expenses of legisla-tors. Some pointed to the varying degrees of generosity or parsimony prevailing within the various state governments. With some justification, they objected to a system in which there might be embarrassing dispari-ties of compensation for those serving in the national government. When it came to matters of the parsimony of state legislatures, John Langdon of New Hampshire spoke from the bitter experience of one who had to pay both his own and Nicholas Gilman's expenses at the Convention. Langdon rose to protest payment by the states, noting that states distant from the capital would bear a disproportionate share of the expense.[20]

Langdon's concern was not a trivial one, and the nationalists in the Convention shared his desired outcome—albeit for a different reason. They wanted to do everything possible to render the members of the national Congress independent of the state governments. This principle had already been compromised by the provision allowing state legislatures to elect United States senators, but to render representatives dependent upon the states for their salaries would further subject them to the "prejudices, passions and improper views" of the state legislatures. The members of the Committee of Detail who had drafted this particular proposal stayed out of the debate, and, in the end, the delegates voted by a nine-to-two margin to amend the report by providing that members of the Congress would be paid from the "National Treasury."[21]

At this stage in the Convention's deliberations the question of payment of salaries and expenses was hardly an abstract one for most delegates. Aside from Philadelphia's summer climate, unpleasant odors, and aggressive pestilence, the most consistent source of private complaint from the delegates was the poor state of their remuneration while toiling in the Assembly Room. Pennsylvania, whose delegates all came from the immediate Philadelphia vicinity, paid its delegates absolutely nothing for their nearly four months' worth of work—neither salary nor expenses. Delegates from the other eleven states attending the Convention received no salary but were compensated for a small portion of their expenses—ranging from four dollars per day for the New Jersey delegates to about six dollars per day for those from Delaware. And many states were slow in paying expenses. As the weeks dragged into months, the North Carolina delegates wrote to their governor complaining that they were running out of money. Finding themselves with only a few depreciated North Carolina dollars left, they asked for an additional two months' worth of expense money. William Samuel Johnson had received a lump sum of about nine hundred dollars from the Connecticut treasury before leaving for the Convention, but as the summer wore on, he realized that it would not be enough to see him through to the end of the Convention. By mid-July he had moved out of his lodgings at City Tavern to more modest quarters at a boardinghouse run by Silas Wilson, several blocks north of the area where most of the delegates were staying, to save money. That economy was not sufficient, however, and at the conclusion of the Convention he had to borrow one hundred dollars to clear his debts.[22]

Nathaniel Gorham of Massachusetts was in the same boat as Johnson;

his home state of Massachusetts failed to reimburse him, forcing him to borrow money from Robert Morris to pay his board bill and to purchase passage for his trip back home. Even Virginia gentry like George Mason, though richly endowed in land and slaves, faced a perennial cash crunch. Mason, who was always loathe to leave his beloved Gunston Hall to perform public service, was forced to remind acting governor Beverly Randolph several times that he had only agreed to attend on the understanding that he would be given a cash advance. Mason was among those cash-strapped delegates whose good humor could not have been improved as the summer dragged on.[23]

The Confederation government was in even greater financial distress than the state governments, and it made only minimal contributions to meet the expenses of the Convention over and above those of the individual delegates. The total amount expended by the continental government on the unparalleled gathering of the Founding Fathers between May 25 and September 17 was $1,586, primarily for the salaries of the doorkeeper, messenger, stationer, and printers. The first three of those individuals had to wait until three days after the Convention had adjourned to get their salaries, and the two printers, Robert Dunlap and David Claypoole, did not collect their debt from the continental government until March 1793.[24]

"NECESSARY AND PROPER"

On August 16 the delegates began to debate the specific enumeration of the powers of Congress. The Committee of Detail, in moving from a general and exceptionally broad grant of power to specifically enumerated powers, had gauged the mood of the Convention correctly. In spite of the nationalists' strong support for a broad, *general* grant of power to the Congress, no one rose to question the wisdom of the committee's action. Indeed, the delegates seemed disinclined even to raise questions about most of the specifically enumerated powers. They spent four days discussing the specific wording of some of the provisions in Article VII, Section 1. But, surprisingly—given subsequent contention over the extent and limits of congressional power—with just a few exceptions the discussion provoked little controversy.[25]

On August 18, James Madison and Charles Pinckney each proposed additional enumerated powers. Madison's list, numbering ten in all, included such things as regulating Indian affairs, granting charters of incorporation, securing copyright protection to authors, establishing a university, and encouraging by "premiums and provisions the advancement of useful knowledge and discoveries." Pinckney's eleven additional proposals overlapped quite a bit with Madison's, but they also included items such as the granting of patents and regulating stages on post roads. The similarity between Madison's and Pinckney's lists was sufficiently great that the delegates felt comfortable simply referring them back to the Committee of Detail, which would continue to meet informally, for further refinement and possible integration into the original list of enumerated powers.[26]

The single provision in Article VII, Section 1 that would have the most profound effect on expanding congressional and, by extension, federal government power was the one giving Congress the power "to make all laws necessary and proper for carrying into execution the foregoing powers, and all other powers vested, by this Constitution, in the Government of the U.S. or any department or officer thereof." Just a few years after the Constitution was adopted, Alexander Hamilton and Thomas Jefferson would articulate sharply contrasting definitions of the meaning of the words "necessary and proper" as they debated whether Hamilton's proposal for a federally chartered Bank of the United States was constitutionally permissible, with Hamilton arguing for a "broad construction" of the meaning (for example, "needful," "useful," or "conducive to") and Jefferson arguing for a "strict construction" (for example, an "invincible necessity").[27]

The division over the meaning of the phrase "necessary and proper" would resound for decades after. The line of constitutional division between Jefferson and Hamilton would form a portion of the underpinning for an entirely novel invention in the history of American politics—the emergence of the Hamiltonian Federalist and Jeffersonian Republican parties, which would help transform the American republic into a *democratic* republic. And, as the sectional conflict between North and South gained momentum in the nineteenth century, Southern politicians would increasingly rely on strict-constructionist arguments to protect their slave-based economy, with their Northern opponents countering them with broad constructionist arguments. The constitutional underpinning for Southern secessionist doctrine was firmly grounded in the strict-constructionist position, and while the terrible war that followed Southern secession had as its fundamental cause the deep division within the country over both the economics and the morality of slavery, the constitutional division between North and South on the meaning of the necessary and proper clause was another important source of conflict.

Yet when the delegates debated that final item in the list of specifically enumerated congressional powers on Monday, August 20, not a word of protest was raised. In an attempt to make more explicit Congress's power to create additional government agencies as it saw fit, James Madison unsuccessfully tried to insert the words "establish all offices" between the words "laws" and "necessary." This was quickly dismissed as being redundant, and the necessary and proper clause, as reported from the Committee of Detail, passed unanimously.[28]

Perhaps the delegates had been influenced by John Rutledge's remarks the previous Saturday on the "impatience of the public and the extreme anxiety of many members of the Convention to bring the business to an end." Rutledge was certainly among those impatient to "bring the business to an end." He accompanied his complaint with the suggestion, adopted by the Convention, that the delegates move up the pace of their proceedings by beginning their sessions no later than ten o'clock in the morning and extending them from the customary three o'clock time of adjournment to four, with the added stipulation that "no motion to adjourn sooner [would] be allowed."[29]

RUMBLINGS OF DISSENT

John Rutledge's impatience at the slowness of the proceedings may have been exacerbated by an outburst by Elbridge Gerry on August 17. Gerry heatedly objected to the item in Article VII, Section 1 giving to Congress the power to "subdue a rebellion in any state on the application of its legislature." Although some historians have argued that the hidden agenda behind these powers was to guard against possible slave insurrections, in reality, the event uppermost in the minds of the delegates was Shays' Rebellion, which had frightened Elbridge Gerry out of his wits. Ignoring the proviso that the legislature of the state so affected would need to request the presence of federal troops, Gerry unleashed an attack on the very notion of "letting loose the myrmidons of the United States on a state without its own consent." "More blood," he contended, would have been spilt in Massachusetts in the late insurrection, if the general authority had intermeddled."[30]

Gouverneur Morris was plainly annoyed by Gerry's belligerence, noting, "We are acting a very strange part. We first form a strong man to protect us, and at the same time wish to tie his hands behind him." The following day Gerry took up the cudgel again, this time protesting that there was no restriction in the Constitution on the proposed government's ability to keep standing armies in times of peace. Both Gerry and Luther Martin of Maryland favored explicit limitations on the size of the army in peacetime. They feared that if there were too large a national standing army, the states would then create their own armies in order to ward off invasion by the central government.[31]

And how, Gerry asked, was this army to be trained? Would the federal government command the states to act as "drill seargents"? Gerry regarded any plan by which the state militia system was to be replaced by a single, national army as a formula for despotism that would lead inevitably to the destruction of the state governments as independent entities. Indeed, he predicted that a national army would pave the way for "the introduction of a king," and, with the king and army in alliance with one another, the states would be powerless to prevent America's return to a despotic monarchy.[32]

Gerry's alienation from the proceedings had personal as well as ideological sources. Although his young wife, Ann, had been with him during the early stages of the Convention, she had returned to Marblehead during the recess in late July, and by the end of August Gerry was not only angry at his fellow delegates but also missing his new bride. "I am as sick of being here as you can conceive," he wrote to her on August 21, adding that "entre nous, I do not expect to give my voice to the measure." The "measure" to which he was referring was the completed Constitution.[33]

At about this time Gerry began to participate in private evening meetings with other potentially dissident delegates. The object of their meetings, according to Maryland delegate James McHenry, was to scrutinize the Report of the Committee of Detail line by line and "to give our opinions thereon." Luther Martin, who was part of the group until he left the Convention and returned to Maryland on September 4 to begin a campaign against the still-uncompleted Constitution, reported that the delegates taking part in the meeting included George Mason, the delegates from Connecticut and New Jersey, Martin's fellow delegates from Maryland, John Mercer, Daniel Carroll, and McHenry, and at least one delegate each from Delaware, South Carolina, and Georgia.

It was a loose and largely inchoate collection of men with a wide assortment of concerns about particular features of the Constitution, and it hardly constituted a serious mobilization capable of halting the Convention's progress toward the revolution in government that James Madison had launched three months earlier. While a few historians have suggested that one of the primary purposes of the meetings was to achieve an accommodation regarding slavery, the evidence for this is not compelling. The primary effect of the meetings, it seems, was to make the often-inebriated Luther Martin even more inebriated, and the often-dyspeptic Elbridge Gerry even more dyspeptic.[34]

By the fourth week of August the slow pace and tedium of the deliberations had reached the point where even the tireless James Madison was beginning to show signs of fatigue. His notes on debates became noticeably shorter as the weeks in August rolled by, and the tone of his comments on speeches by dissenting delegates such as Gerry and Luther Martin began to betray his impatience. But the delegates continued to wrangle. On Thursday, August 23, Charles Pinckney attempted to resurrect the provision giving Congress the power to veto any laws passed by state legislatures that might conflict "with the general interests and harmony of the union." At various times over the course of the summer that provision had won the support of a majority of state delegations, but it had also excited enough opposition to cause the delegates to remove it from the approved list of Randolph Resolutions during the week before the Committee of Detail got down to work. James Wilson spoke strongly in favor of Pinckney's proposal, saying that he "considered this as the key stone wanted to complete the wide arch of Government we are raising." John Rutledge was as adamantly opposed to the provision as his South Carolina colleague Charles Pinckney was in favor of it. "If nothing else," Rutledge averred, "this alone would damn and ought to damn the Constitution." In the ensuing debate, it was clear that the delegates were nearly evenly divided, with passionate feelings on each side of the question. However much the supporters of a *supreme* national government would have liked to have seen the provision included, it was becoming clear that its inclusion would doom the Constitution to defeat, so Pinckney reluctantly withdrew his proposal.[35]

Although it may not have seemed like it, the delegates were making progress. Bit by bit, as they worked through every item in the Committee of Detail report, they came closer to a consensus on a completed product on which they might take a final, official vote. The delegates continued to complain about the slowness of the pace, and they continued to be obsessed with the secrecy of their proceedings. William Paterson, writing to Oliver Ellsworth from the comfort of his home in New Jersey but being kept informed of the proceedings by his colleague David Brearley, noted with a condescension unbecoming a delegate who had scurried out of town a full month earlier, "Full of Disputation and noisy as the Wind, it is said, that you are afraid of the very Windows, and have a Man planted under them to prevent the Secrets and Doings from flying out."[36]

ON AUGUST 30 AND 31, the delegates turned to a subject vital to the success or failure of their efforts. Article XXI of the Report of the Committee of Detail simply stated, "The ratification of the Conventions of States shall be sufficient for organizing this Constitution." While the delegates had earlier reached tentative agreement that ratification of the proposed Constitution should be decided by specially elected state conventions rather than by state legislatures, they had not agreed on how many states needed to approve the Constitution before it could go into effect. If the document had merely been an amendment to the Articles of Confederation, then the rule stipulated by the Articles for amendments was clear—unanimous approval of the states. While no one in the room seriously believed that the document before them was merely a collection of amendments to the Articles of Confederation, a few delegates insisted on unanimous approval by the states. Once again, antinationalist stalwart Luther Martin led the charge. Joined by his fellow Maryland delegates James McHenry and Daniel Carroll, he not only argued that ratification should be unanimous among all thirteen states but also tried to reverse the earlier decision that state conventions, rather than the state legislatures, be the ratifying bodies. Although on other occasions Martin had invoked the dangers of the proposed Constitution to the liberties of the people, he now reversed himself, citing "the danger of commotions from a resort to the people."[37]

Elbridge Gerry jumped on the Maryland bandwagon, complaining that the proposed Constitution was already "full of vices" and insisting that it would be improper to destroy the Confederation government without the unanimous consent of the states that had created it. George Mason, less deliberately and belligerently intent on scuttling the effort for a new Constitution but nevertheless increasingly skeptical, was not ready to commit himself to any decision about how to put the Constitution into effect. Confronting the nationalists in his own Virginia delegation, Mason proclaimed, "I would sooner chop off my right hand than put it to the Constitution as it now stands." Mason insisted on seeing "some points not yet decided brought to a decision, before being compelled to give a final opinion" on the mode of ratification. Gouverneur Morris, in a fit of pique, bellowed, "I too am ready for a postponement. I have long wished for another Convention that will have the firmness to provide a vigorous government, which we are afraid to do." Morris was no stranger to hyperbole, and this occasion was certainly one of the times when his temper got the better of him. Once he cooled down, he must have realized that he and his nationalist colleagues had worked too hard and achieved too much to abandon the effort at this point.[38]

Aside from the relatively few delegates who argued for unanimous approval as a means of sinking the whole enterprise, the views of most delegates on the question fell within a reasonable range, with James Wilson contending for approval by seven states—a bare majority of the thirteen—and Roger Sherman arguing that the approval of at least ten states would be necessary to give the new government sufficient legitimacy. After a day and a half of discussion involving a wide variety of alternatives, including one extraordinarily complicated one by Madison that would have provided for ratification by any seven or more states entitled to "thirty-three members at least in the House of Representatives," the delegates agreed on the number of nine, or roughly two-thirds of the states. Only the antinationalist stalwarts from Maryland voted in the negative, and many of them would soon be heading home.[39]

The vote marked yet another decisive step. The decision to allow the proposed new government to begin its operations with the support of only nine—rather than all thirteen—of the original parties to the Articles of Confederation violated at least the spirit of the resolution from the Confederation Congress authorizing the Convention. If one considers the Articles of Confederation to be America's first "constitution," then the framers' decision to ignore that compact, abandon the government formed under its authority, and propose an altogether new kind of centralized union in its place might be viewed as an illegal act.

Citing the ambivalence, and in some cases outright antipathy, of many of the nationalist delegates toward the popular excesses they believed plagued many of the state governments, some historians have gone so far as to argue that the framers of the Constitution were creating not a revolution but, rather, a counterrevolution. Nearly all of the delegates—be they large-state or small-state men, Northerners or Southerners, supporters of a strong national government or defenders of state sovereignty—expressed at one time or another significant doubts about the wisdom of allowing ordinary citizens too extensive a role in the affairs of government. Our Founding Fathers, whatever their views on the specific powers of the central government vis-à-vis the state governments, were not necessarily the progenitors of America's democratic future.[40]

Yet the charge that the framers were committing an illegal act when they proposed that the Constitution would go into effect with the assent of only nine—rather than thirteen—states rests on dubious reasoning. The frame of government under the Articles of Confederation was not, in truth, a proper constitution. It was, as many of its authors always insisted, a "league of friendship," a treaty of "amity and commerce" among separate and sovereign states. And, as Otto von Bismarck famously said, treaties are made to be broken once their purposes are no longer relevant to conditions at hand. Moreover, all of the Founding Fathers' actions up through August 31 and beyond remained only their *opinion* until the people of the states passed judgment on their handiwork. In that sense, it did not matter whether the framers had decided that their government should go into effect unless five or seven or nine or thirteen states had added their assent. The people of the states would ultimately be given their own opportunity to pass on the wisdom of that formulation, as well as all of the other proposals put forward by the framers over the course of the long summer.

By setting the bar at nine states, and by deciding to use the device of specially elected conventions rather than state legislatures as the bodies that would approve or reject their handiwork, the delegates had certainly made ratification of the Constitution easier. But there was still much to be done, not the least of which was to deal with the great beast that had been lurking in the Assembly Room of the Pennsylvania State House ever since the Convention temporarily adjourned at the end of the day on July 26—the American presidency.

CHAPTER SIXTEEN

THE "GENERAL WELFARE" AND THE PRESIDENCY

THE DELEGATES MADE SUBSTANTIAL PROGRESS refining the Report of the Committee of Detail during the weeks in early August, in large part because they had sidestepped the question of the presidency. On August 15 they would return to the question of presidential authority, but—once again—they would spend much of their time spinning their wheels.

In the aftermath of a discussion of the power of the Senate to approve treaties, James Madison, unbidden, tried to resurrect his plan for a council of revision. His plan this time called for a complicated procedure by which all legislation from Congress would be submitted to both the executive and judicial branches. If either of those branches should object, the agreement of two-thirds of the members of each House would be required to override the veto; if both the executive and judicial branches should object, then a three-fourths vote in each house would be necessary to override. Elbridge Gerry, losing patience, complained that Madison was simply wasting their time. Most of the delegates appeared to agree. Madison's proposal was summarily rejected by a vote of three states in favor, eight opposed.[1]

Gouverneur Morris tried another route by which to rein in congressional power. The Committee of Detail report proposed allowing the Congress to override a presidential veto by a two-thirds vote in both houses, but Morris now pushed for an absolute veto for the executive.

James Wilson supported Morris, lecturing the delegates that their "prejudices against the executive" resulted from a misapplication of the lessons of the Americans' experience with George III. The American president, he argued, would be not an unelected tyrant but a representative of the people. This reasoning might have been unassailable if the people directly elected the president, but since the delegates had not yet decided how they were going to elect their president, and, indeed, had specifically rejected Wilson's proposal for direct popular election, his arguments floundered.[2]

John Rutledge, having grown increasingly exasperated by the meandering quality of the debate over the executive, rose and snarled that he was heartily sick of the "tediousness of the proceedings," suggesting that if the delegates didn't get on with their business they might well spend the remainder of the year in Philadelphia. Rutledge's prodding produced at least a small, if temporary, victory for the proponents of executive power. The delegates endorsed a motion by Hugh Williamson to require three-quarters rather than two-thirds of each house to override a presidential veto, with six states in favor, four opposed, and one divided.[3]

THE COMMITTEE ON POSTPONED PARTS

Still stalled on the presidency, the delegates moved on to other business for most of the remainder of August. At the close of their session on August 31, having made significant progress on many of the items in the Report of the Committee of Detail, the delegates endorsed a proposal from Roger Sherman to "refer such parts of the Constitution as have been postponed" to a committee consisting of eleven members elected by each of the state delegations then represented in the Convention. Sherman's proposal was prompted at least in part by the increasingly vocal dissatisfaction of delegates such as Luther Martin, Elbridge Gerry, and George Mason about individual clauses of the Constitution. Sherman no doubt hoped that a smaller body might be able to forge a consensus on at least some of these items, thereby reducing the volume of dissent within the Assembly Room. The Committee on Postponed Parts, whose members were selected by ballot in each of the state delegations, was a solid group. Chaired by David Brearley of New Jersey, it also included Sherman, Gouverneur Morris, John Dickinson, and James Madison.[4]

The committee got down to work immediately, taking on some of the least controversial so-called postponed parts first. On Saturday, September 1, it made recommendations that were quickly adopted by the Convention on such matters as ineligibility of members of Congress to serve in other government offices, full faith and credit to be given in each state to acts and judicial proceedings in other states, and the power of Congress to establish uniform laws with respect to bankruptcies.[5]

The delegates continued to make progress on September 3 and 4, unanimously endorsing an amendment to Article I, Section 8, adding to the provision giving Congress the power to lay and collect taxes the words "to pay the debts and provide for the common defence and general welfare of the U.S." We have no record of why the committee proposed the change, and there was no debate on the matter, but, like the necessary and proper clause, the addition of the so-called general welfare clause would provide an opening for an extraordinary expansion in the power of the federal government in years to come.[6]

Some forty-three years later, James Madison reflected back on that moment. He acknowledged that he had included the phrase "general welfare" in his original version of the Virginia Plan on May 29, but by 1830 he had become a staunch opponent of nationalist politicians and jurists who were using the general welfare clause as a means of expanding federal government power—particularly in the area of economic regulation. Writing to Virginia representative Andrew Stevenson, he admitted that there were many "variations and vicissitudes" in the meanings given by the delegates to the clause, a fact he attributed to "differences of opinion" among them. But Madison insisted that his use of the phrase "general welfare" in the Virginia Plan "was nothing more than a mere copying of the similar phrase contained in the Articles of Confederation."[7]

Considering that Madison had vigorously supported a proposal that would have given a "supreme" national government the power to veto any state laws not to its liking, his cavalier dismissal of the importance of the general welfare clause in 1830 seems disingenuous. He was no doubt correct in pointing to the widely varying opinions among the delegates about the precise meaning of "general welfare." Moreover, few in the Convention could have predicted what the consequences of including the phrase in the finished Constitution might be. The original meaning of that phrase was contested in 1787, and there is no small irony in the fact that even so devoted a nationalist as Madison would come to change his mind about what he had originally intended by the use of the term.

One thing, however, is certain. The interpretations that successive generations of Americans have given to the term, particularly in connection with the power of taxation, have been highly elastic, allowing for a growth of central government power beyond the imagination of any of the Founding Fathers.[8]

One possible explanation for the lack of concern with which the delegates endorsed the general welfare clause was their anticipation of what would come next. Immediately following their casual endorsement of the general welfare provision, the delegates debated the recommendations of the Committee on Postponed Parts with respect to the American presidency.

According to testimony from John Dickinson, written fifteen years later, the committee had not had an easy time of it. Dickinson, who had been ill during much of late August and early September, missed some of the committee's meetings, but he joined the group in the Library Room on the second floor of the State House at just the moment that they appeared ready to endorse once again a proposal to have the Congress elect the president. Dickinson immediately registered his alarm. He reminded his colleagues that the "powers which we have agreed to vest in the President were so many and so great," that the people would never agree to a constitution containing such a provision "unless they themselves would be more immediately concerned in [the President's] election."

Gouverneur Morris, seeing the committee's consensus dissolve before him, invited the committee members to "sit down again, and converse further on this subject." At that point, according to Dickinson's recollection, James Madison "took out a Pen and Paper, and sketched out a Mode of Electing the President" that might bring the people more fully into the process. Madison's solution, already much discussed and frequently ignored, was to rely on the device of presidential electors. This intervention by Dickinson and the subsequent responses by Morris and Madison probably constitute the most decisive moment in the creation of the American electoral college.[9]

The committee's recommendation on the mode of election of the president, like the final provision in the Constitution on that subject, was mind-numbingly complex. The committee recommended that the president should

> hold his office during the term of four years, and together
> with the Vice-President, chosen for the same term, be

elected in the following manner, viz: Each State shall appoint in such manner as its Legislature may direct, a number of electors equal to the whole number of Senators and members of the House of Representatives, to which the State may be entitled in the Legislature. The Electors shall meet in their respective State and vote by ballot for two persons, of whom one at least shall not be an inhabitant of the same State with themselves; and they shall make a list of all persons voted for, and of the number of votes for each. The Person having the greatest number of votes shall be the President, if such a number be a majority of that of the electors; and if there be more than one who have such a majority, and have an equal number of votes, then the Senate shall immediately choose by ballot one of them for President: but if no person has a majority, then from the five highest on the list, the Senate shall choose by ballot the President. And in every case after the choice of the President, the person having the greatest number of votes shall be Vice-President.[10]

The dense prose of the committee's resolution deserves close scrutiny, for it represented real progress. The idea of presidential electors had been on the table before, but some delegates feared that electors would be too parochial and that the cost of assembling them too expensive. The committee's recommendation calling for the selection of electors finessed the question of *who* should select the electors, stipulating merely that they should be chosen "in such manner as [each state] Legislature may direct." This left open the possibility that electors would not be selected by direct popular vote, but by individuals—such as state legislators—who might be better informed about the possible field of candidates and less provincial in their outlook. As an impediment to the tendency of electors to vote for candidates from their own states, the proposal stipulated that of the two ballots cast by the electors, one must be for someone living outside of their own states. Finally, by having the electors cast their ballots within their respective states it mitigated significantly the issue of expense.

But what to do if no candidate received a majority of electoral votes? Most of the delegates in the Convention were reasonably confident that the first presidential election would produce a clear winner—provided that General Washington would agree to be a candidate. But few could imagine what might happen next. The provision allowing each elector to cast two votes was designed to increase the likelihood that a candidate might receive a sufficient number of votes, but many delegates continued to fear that the expanse of the country and the parochialism of the electors would make it difficult for any candidate to receive a majority of electoral votes. To avoid this difficulty, the committee inserted the provision that one of the branches of Congress would make the selection from among the five "highest on the list" in case no one received a majority of electoral votes. By the end of the Convention, the delegates would decide to place that authority in the hands of the House of Representatives and not the Senate. Were it not for the unexpected and entirely novel development of a two-party system that has focused the attention of the voters on just a few rather than multiple candidates in most elections, it is likely that the power to elect the American president would have devolved to the Congress and not the people themselves through their electors. That outcome would have caused our system to resemble more closely that of England, where Parliament, rather than the people themselves, select their prime minister.

In another resolution presented on the same day, the Committee on Postponed Parts inserted a provision stipulating that the president had to be a natural-born citizen of the United States "or a citizen of the United States at the time of the adoption of this Constitution." It was in some respects an odd decision, since several of the members of the Convention themselves had been born outside the United States, but it was dictated in large measure by the delegates' fears of the corrupting effects of European society. It also added the provision, without defining the specifics, that allowed the chief executive, "with the advice and consent of the Senate," to make treaties, appoint "ambassadors, and other public Ministers, Judges of the Supreme Court, and all other Officers of the U.S." Finally, the committee resolved to give responsibility for impeachment to the House of Representatives, giving to the Senate the power to hear the case and vote for either conviction or acquittal. The grounds for impeachment—only for "treason or bribery"—were in this iteration phrased in terms that many delegates would find far too narrow.[11]

Given the previous discord among the delegates about the nature of the presidency, it is not surprising that their opinions about the committee's recommendations varied widely. Gouverneur Morris was the first of many to predict that Congress would elect most presidents; he repeated his fear of the inevitable "intrigue and faction" that would dictate the outcome. George Mason predicted that if the committee's recommendation on the method of election were accepted in its present form, "nineteen times in twenty the President would be chosen by the Senate," which, because it was elected by the state legislatures and not directly by the people, he thought a wholly "improper body for the purpose." Georgia's Abraham Baldwin had a slightly more optimistic and, as it turned out, realistic view. He predicted that "the increasing intercourse among the people of the states, would render important characters less and less unknown" and, therefore, that the Senate would consequently be less likely to be in a position to make the selection.[12]

It was left to James Wilson, the only man in the Convention to argue consistently for direct popular election of the president, to help the delegates find a more comfortable middle ground between that of direct popular election on the one hand and election by the Congress or, even less democratically, the Senate alone on the other. Wilson acknowledged that "this subject has greatly divided the [Convention] and will also divide people out of doors. It is in truth the most difficult of all on which we have had to decide." Admitting his own ambivalence about all of the alternatives proposed, he came around to support, with modifications, the proposal offered by the Committee on Postponed Parts. Wilson agreed with Baldwin that the number of "Continental characters will multiply as we more and more coalesce," thus making the electoral college system more likely to be a workable one.[13]

Wilson had another reason for supporting the idea of an electoral college. One of the other unresolved issues relating to the office of the chief executive was whether to permit the president to serve more than one term. Most of the discussions on the presidency had been confounded by the fact that the issue of eligibility for reelection had been tied to that of the president's election by the national legislature, with the fear being that if one allowed the president to serve more than one term with that mode of selection in place, he would forever be currying the favor of the legislators. Wilson believed that if the primary power for presidential selection was taken out of the hands of Congress, that would "clear the way . . . for a discussion of the question of re-eligibility on its own merits." Those "merits," as the delegates saw them, ran both ways. Allowing for reeligibility might lead to an excessive concentration of power in the hands of one, long-serving executive. On the other hand, the delegates were reluctant to impose term limits on an able executive who had gained the respect of the people.[14]

Wilson made one important recommendation for amending the committee's proposal—ultimately endorsed by the delegates—that the House of Representatives, not the Senate, be responsible for electing the president should the electoral college not provide a majority of votes for a candidate. Not only did members of the House owe their election to the people, but the frequency of elections for the House would "free [it] from the influence and faction to which the permanence of the Senate may subject that branch." Wilson was moving the delegates closer to consensus, but many still remained convinced that, with the unique exception of Washington, the electoral college would never manage to produce a majority of votes for any candidate. Consequently, the delegates fell to bickering once again about the relative advantages and disadvantages of an appointment by either of the houses of Congress. Edmund Randolph, echoing concerns expressed by Charles Pinckney and George Mason, argued that if the Senate made the choice, the result would be to "convert that body into a real and dangerous aristocracy." It was clear by this time—late in the day on September 5—that the tide of opinion was turning against the Senate, but when Wilson's proposal for an alternative election by the House of Representatives came up for a vote, it too was defeated, only three states in favor, seven opposed, and one divided.[15]

With the failure of the delegates to agree on either of those methods, the delegates began to search for other alternatives—but with distinctly unsatisfactory results. Madison and North Carolina's Hugh Williamson proposed that the requirement for election as president be lowered from a majority to only a third of the electoral votes. Elbridge Gerry proposed that a combination of six senators and seven representatives chosen by joint ballot of both houses make the choice should a candidate fail to receive the required majority of electoral votes. George Mason suggested that instead of choosing the president from the top five electoral vote getters, the number be reduced to three, to which Roger Sherman replied that he would "just as soon give up the plan. He would prefer seven or thirteen." Mason's proposal, which would eventually be written into the final draft of the Constitution, was at this point voted down overwhelmingly, two states in favor and eight opposed.[16]

The session on September 5 concluded on a dispiriting note. George Mason, unhappy with the provision allowing the Senate to elect the president and worried that giving that body too wide a latitude in making their selection would allow just a few individuals to conspire to make the selection, announced that "he would prefer the Government of Prussia" to one with such a defective mechanism for selecting the executive.

James McHenry of Maryland, who had begun to keep brief notes on the proceedings of the Convention, simply recorded in his journal, "Sept. 5— The greatest part of the day spent in desultory conversation on that part of the report respecting the mode of chusing the President—adjourned without coming to a conclusion."[17]

From the perspective of the Pennsylvania state legislature it was particularly unfortunate that the day had produced so little progress. September 5 was the day that body was due to begin its session, and their normal meeting place was the Assembly Room, now occupied by disputatious Convention delegates. The Pennsylvania assemblymen agreed to move upstairs to the grand hallway of the State House until the delegates could finish their business. When that might be, no one was certain.[18]

The next day the delegates continued to argue over whether the House or the Senate should select the president if no one received a majority of electoral votes. Such was the state of frustration in the room that Pennsylvania's two staunch nationalists found themselves in bitter disagreement on the question. Gouverneur Morris continued to argue for selection by the Senate, while James Wilson—still believing in the link between authority and popular consent—argued with equal fervor that the popularly elected House of Representatives should make the choice. In the midst of these differences, the one thing on which most delegates seemed to agree was that the expanse of the American landscape and the diversity of its people and their interests would, as Madison had phrased it earlier in the debate, cause "local considerations" to take precedence over the "general interest," thus making it difficult for anyone other than Washington to gain a majority of electoral votes.[19]

It seemed as if the delegates would never reach a consensus on anything relating to the American presidency. Then, suddenly, toward the end of the day on September 6, Roger Sherman proposed to amend the committee report by stipulating that the House of Representatives, and not the Senate, be the alternative body for selecting the president should no candidate receive a majority of electoral votes. His proposal contained the proviso that each state delegation in the House, no matter what its size, would have only one vote in that decision.

Miraculously, the delegates coalesced around Sherman's formulation, with ten states in favor and only Delaware opposed. That coalescence probably did not occur spontaneously, for the delegates had balloted— and rejected—similar proposals on numerous occasions. It seems likely that the delegates—no doubt at one of their club dinners or in a more informal gathering at City Tavern or the Indian Queen—had worked through all of the possibilities and reluctantly agreed that Sherman's was the best of an imperfect lot. It attracted the support not only of those who thought the Senate too small and aristocratic a body to be trusted with the election but also those delegates from the small states who may have mildly preferred election by the House rather than the Senate but who were afraid that the formula of proportional representation in the House would put their states at a disadvantage. By placing authority for election in the House, but stipulating that each state delegation would receive only one vote, Sherman had hit upon a formula that, though perhaps satisfying no one entirely, satisfied nearly everyone enough to forge the consensus.[20]

"THE MOST INSIGNIFICANT OFFICE"

During the next few days the delegates spent what seemed to many like an eternity trying to sort out a few more details respecting the executive. The delegates seemed implicitly to agree that some provision needed to be made for an orderly succession should the president either die or become incapacitated, and the creation of the office of vice president seemed a useful way of doing that. But what, aside from waiting for the president to die or become incapacitated, was a vice president supposed to do? John Adams, while he was serving as Washington's vice president, derisively called it "the most insignificant office that ever the invention of man contrived or his imagination conceived," and a good many delegates admitted that the office was essentially one without a function. The Committee on Postponed Parts had proposed that the vice president preside over the Senate, and though this seemed innocuous enough to most delegates, Elbridge Gerry and George Mason—the two who most fretted about concentrations of executive power—feared that this would give the executive branch an unhealthy influence over the deliberations of the Senate. Connecticut's Roger Sherman once again came to the rescue. He reminded the delegates that if the vice president did not preside over the Senate, "he would be without employment" altogether. He also noted that the vice president would only cast a vote in the Senate in case of a tie, "which would be but seldom." Sherman apparently convinced the delegates that the office of the vice presidency was indeed an inconsequential one and therefore not worth wasting any more of their time

over. The Convention endorsed Sherman's motion that the vice president also serve ex officio as president of the Senate by a vote of eight
states in favor, two opposed.[21]

The delegates nailed down the requirement that the president would
need the advice and consent of *two-thirds* of the senators in order to enter
into treaties with foreign nations. They also listened to, but ultimately rejected, George Mason's insistent proposal that the president operate in
conjunction with a "council of state," or "privy council." Mason's idea
for an executive council was very different from that of our modern conception of a presidential "cabinet," for in Mason's plan the men serving
in that council would act as a check on presidential power, rather than as
the direct agents of that power. Benjamin Franklin, who had remained
silent for most of the debate over the executive, sided with Mason on this
occasion. Franklin remained a fan of the Pennsylvania Constitution, and
as the sitting president of his state, he was aided by the sort of executive
council that Mason was advocating. In Pennsylvania, the president was
nothing more than the chair of a body of nearly equal councillors, and
Franklin believed that a similar council for America "would not only be
a check on a bad president but be a relief to a good one." Though the delegates greeted Franklin's intervention respectfully, they were not about
to render the president merely a "first among equals" in a multiple presidency.[22]

"HIGH CRIMES AND MISDEMEANORS"

The delegates took up one other important matter respecting the presidency on September 8—that of the grounds for removing the president
from office. No one was particularly happy with the narrow phraseology
of the Report of the Committee of Detail. Surely there might be other
misdeeds beyond "bribery and treason" that would warrant removal of a
president from office. George Mason, again seconded by his unlikely
ally, Elbridge Gerry, thought that "maladministration" ought to be
added to the list along with bribery and treason, but Madison objected,
noting that "so vague a term will be equivalent to a tenure during the
pleasure of the Senate." Mason grasped for other language, finally coming up with "other high crimes and misdemeanors." "Other high
crimes," while vague, at least had the ring of something serious to it;
"misdemeanors," however, seemed not only to be vague, but also to sug-

gest that a president might be removed for trivial offenses. But the delegates' energies were flagging, and, with little serious reflection, they adopted Mason's new language by a vote of eight states to three.[23]

There were still other issues—important issues—yet to be resolved. The delegates had not yet agreed upon a process for amending their Constitution. And, although most of the delegates would prefer to brush the matter aside, they would have to consider, however briefly, the matter of a bill of rights. But as their session on the afternoon of September 8 was coming to a close, the two things that most occupied the delegates' minds were that they were tired and they wanted to go home. So as its last deed on September 8 the Convention created yet another committee "to revise the stile and arrange the articles which had been agreed to by the House." Perhaps, just perhaps, the Convention would manage to finish its work before the summer ended.[24]

CHAPTER SEVENTEEN

"THE PARADOX AT THE NATION'S CORE"

DURING THE MONTH OF AUGUST, the delegates had checked off most of the items in the Report of the Committee of Detail. However, the crucial matter of the place of slavery in the new American republic remained. In mid-July, an apparent settlement on one aspect of that issue had been reached in the context of representation. According to the terms of the Connecticut Compromise, a slave would be counted as three-fifths of a person in apportioning representation in the House of Representatives, and this seemed to bring some measure of peace among Northern and Southern delegates. But the delegates had yet to confront other issues relating to the continuation of the African slave trade and the security of slave property, and, as the summer wore on, several delegates from the lower South appeared prepared to reignite the debate over representation and slavery as well.

THE FOUNDING FATHERS AND SLAVERY

The men who wrote the American Constitution lived in a world where slavery was commonplace. When George Washington rode into Philadelphia on May 13 to receive "the acclamations of the people," he had left his wife, Martha, behind, but he was accompanied by three of his more than one hundred slaves. Few in the crowd that greeted him would have considered the presence of those slaves in Washington's company as anything unusual. Nor was Washington the only Convention delegate to bring one or more of his slaves with him to Philadelphia. Nearly all of the delegates to the Constitutional Convention were men of substantial wealth and property, but many of the delegates owed much of their wealth to a special kind of property. Twenty-five of the fifty-five delegates attending the Convention owned slaves, and at least some of them decided that the inconvenience of being without one or more personal servants during their stay in Philadelphia was too much to bear.[1]

General Charles Cotesworth Pinckney had roughly two hundred slaves at his Charleston home and multiple outlying plantations, and therefore he was fully accustomed to the convenience of having servants at his beck and call. The general, an avid horseman, had purchased at least a few thoroughbred racehorses that summer, and his need for someone to care for his horses made it only natural for him to bring a groom along with him. Further, he had a new wife (his first wife had died three years earlier), and he and Mary viewed their stay in Philadelphia as a kind of delayed honeymoon. They would have required one or more domestics to make their Philadelphia home comfortable.[2]

Among the Southern delegates, there were two in particular for whom slave ownership presented a particular dilemma. George Mason, owner of one of the grandest plantations in Virginia—with a corps of more than three hundred slaves—brought at least two of them with him to Philadelphia to tend to his needs.[3]

James Madison did not bring any of his nine slaves to the Convention. But Madison had already experienced the incompatibility of slavery with life in a society dedicated to liberty. While serving in the Continental Congress, Madison had brought his manservant, Billy, to the city. Enjoying unprecedented freedom of movement in a city in which free blacks overwhelmingly outnumbered slaves, Billy ran away in 1782. He was quickly recaptured and returned to service, but Madison recognized that his taste of freedom in Philadelphia had "too thoroughly tainted" him "to be a fit companion for fellow slaves in Virginia." As a consequence, when it was time for Madison to return home, he resolved that he would leave Billy behind, though not without regaining as much of his value as possible. The problem was that Pennsylvania law prevented Madison from selling Billy for more than a seven-year term of service— the maximum term permitted for white indentured servants. Faced with that restriction, Madison grumbled that "I do not expect to get near the worth of him." Although he grumbled, his conscience prevented him from shipping Billy back to Virginia, or, worse, selling him to a new master further south, where he could have recouped his investment. Madison, to his credit, concluded that it would be unfair to punish Billy "merely for coveting that liberty for which we have paid the price of so much blood, and have proclaimed so often to be the right . . . of every human being."[4]

Of the Pennsylvania delegates, Robert Morris, Thomas Fitzsimons, and James Wilson each owned at least one slave. Benjamin Franklin, who by 1787 had become president of the Pennsylvania Society for the Abolition of Slavery, waited until 1785 to emancipate his one remaining slave, George. Franklin had come to believe by 1787 that slavery was an "atrocious debasement of humans," but, on the other hand, his immediate reason for freeing his slave owed more to the "bother" associated with keeping a slave. At least a few other Northern delegates—William Samuel Johnson of Connecticut and William Paterson of New Jersey for certain—owned household slaves.[5]

Southerners and Northerners, whatever their moral qualms about the institution, recognized slavery as a fact of life. At the time of the Constitutional Convention, slaves constituted about 20 percent of the population of the American nation. The slave population was of course not spread evenly either across the nation or, indeed, across the states of the South. In New England, the slave population numbered about 3,700 out of a total population of more than 900,000. Alone among those states, Massachusetts enacted legislation that eliminated the institution entirely by 1787. There were some 36,000 slaves living in the Mid-Atlantic states—less than 3 percent of the population of that region—with by far the greatest number of those, 21,000, living in New York. Although Delaware was technically a "Southern" state, its slave population in 1787 was slightly less than 9,000—less than one-sixth of its population of just under 60,000.

From Maryland southward, however, the demography of slavery looked strikingly different. The number of slaves in Maryland and Virginia alone exceeded 400,000, constituting just under 40 percent of the population. In North Carolina, slaves constituted just over one-quarter of that state's population of nearly 400,000. South Carolina's slave population was something over 100,000, out of a total population of around 240,000. Those numbers understate the importance of slaves in the politics and economy of South Carolina. Most of South Carolina's political leaders lived in the low-country parishes, situated in an expanse of land generally lying at or below sea level within about thirty miles of the coast and extending into the barrier islands off the coast. And in those parishes slaves often outnumbered whites by a margin of four or five to one. The population of Georgia may have reached 75,000 by 1787, of which some 30,000 were slaves. As was the case in South Carolina, the political ruling class of Georgia lived in the low country, where the concentration of slaves was much higher. Perhaps most important, virtually all of Georgia and South Carolina's political leaders were convinced that their state's potential for growth was directly dependent on the future importation of slaves.

And so, it is easy to see why the South, and the lower South in particular, pushed so strongly to have their slave property calculated in the formula for representation in the new government. The other area of potential expansion of slavery was the American frontier. Already by 1787 the territory of Kentucky was populated by 12,000 slaves—about a sixth of the population. As Americans continued to push westward toward the Mississippi, those numbers seemed certain to increase.[6]

Therefore, on the one hand, slavery was part of the normal fabric not only of American life, but of life as most humans on the earth had known it. On the other hand, by 1787 it was also an institution increasingly under attack. The dissonance between the promises of liberty and equality contained in Thomas Jefferson's preamble to the Declaration of Independence and the denial of liberty and equality to African slaves was too loud—and too grating—to ignore entirely. Between 1776 and 1787 most Northern states, with the exceptions of New York and New Jersey, took steps to abolish slavery. In the New England states, abolition and emancipation came quickly. In the Mid-Atlantic, the process was more gradual. Although the Pennsylvania legislature passed a law abolishing slavery in 1780, it added language that provided that any child born into slavery after the law went into effect would have to serve for up to an additional twenty-eight years before achieving freedom.[7]

The inclination toward gradual rather than immediate emancipation was born of both a genuine theoretical dilemma and a more obvious instinct toward the protection of economic interests. In the Lockean triad of natural rights that served as the bedrock justification for America's leap toward independence, "life, liberty, and property" were seen as inseparable. An attack on one would inevitably leave the others equally vulnerable. How could a state take action to divest citizens of their slave property without at the same time threatening their liberty? Only one state—Massachusetts—was prepared to resolve the issue by interpreting its Constitution as giving primacy to liberty over property, going so far as to divest citizens of their slave property even while the owners of that property were still alive. Most Northern states found a far more comfortable resolution of the issue in a form of emancipation that did not deprive slave owners of their property during their lifetimes, but that mandated the emancipation of the slave's children after a lengthy term of service.

It is surely no surprise that the Northern states with the fewest slaves moved toward a more immediate form of emancipation, while those that opted for the gradualist approach had larger amounts of slave property at stake. The tension between liberty and property was rooted not merely in theory, but also in reality.[8]

If the Northern states took gradual, but nevertheless meaningful, steps toward eliminating slavery, progress in the South was much more modest. Delaware, in whose economy slavery had only ever played a modest role, outlawed importation of slaves in 1776. Although Delaware did not abolish slavery outright until the 1860s, it is notable that none of the state's delegates to the Constitutional Convention owned slaves in 1787. Further south, the contradiction between liberty and slavery remained stark, though there were harbingers of change. Virginia and Maryland passed laws in the wake of the Revolution that made it easier for masters to free their slaves. Every Southern state except Georgia enacted some sort of prohibition or at least inhibition on the continued importation of slaves from Africa. Yet in most areas of the South, the combination of theoretical and tangible impediments to the elimination of slavery overpowered any of the mild antislavery impulses Southern citizens may have felt.[9]

Patrick Henry, himself the owner of more than fifty slaves, exemplified the contradiction between Patriot rhetoric about liberty and the continuing commitment to the slave system. In a 1771 letter to the Quaker antislavery activist Robert Pleasants, Henry expressed his amazement that "this abominable practice has been introduced in the most enlightened ages." He was particularly aggrieved that slavery was tolerated in Virginia, "a Country above all others fond of Liberty." Yet even in Virginia,

> when the Rights of Humanity are defined & understood
> with precision . . . we find Men professing a Religion the

most humane, mild, meek, gentle, & generous; adopting a principle as repugnant to humanity as it is inconsistent with the bible and destructive to Liberty.

And then came the punch line. "Would anyone believe I am the master of slaves of my own purchase! I am drawn along by the general inconvenience of living here without them." Indeed, that inconvenience apparently was too great a burden to Henry even after he had taken his last breath, since, unlike many of his Revolutionary contemporaries, including Washington, he made no provision for freeing his slaves upon his death.[10]

As the Southern colonies had taken the fateful steps toward independence, the contradictions in their proclamations about liberty and equality and the reality of their social and economic systems had become ever more apparent. Perhaps nothing better symbolizes the warring elements of nobility, irony, and tragedy inherent in the Southern embrace of the libertarian ideals of the American Revolution than the language of one of America's most important founding documents, the Virginia Declaration of Rights. Drafted in June 1776 by George Mason, it served as a powerful inspiration to Thomas Jefferson when he was composing the Declaration of Independence. It would subsequently serve as an important model both for other states' bills of rights and for the Bill of Rights added to the United States Constitution in 1790.

The first article of Mason's original draft of the Virginia Declaration of Rights read that

> All men are by nature equally free and independent, and have certain inherent rights, of which they cannot by any compact deprive or divest their posterity; namely, the enjoyment of life and liberty, with the means of acquiring and possessing property, and pursuing and obtaining happiness and safety.

As the debate on Mason's draft began, several of Mason's colleagues immediately voiced their concern that such an open-ended grant of liberty and equality would apply to slaves. Clearly, the overwhelming majority of the members of Virginia's revolutionary Convention believed that this should not be the intent of their Declaration of Rights, so, with no discussion or dissent, they added just a few words—"when they enter into a state of society"—to the document so that it would exclude those unfortunate souls who had not been allowed entrance into that "state of society." How remarkably easy it was, with a simple turn of phrase, to ignore the paradox at Virginia's—and the nation's—core.[11]

Virginia's revolutionary Constitution makers embodied the divided mind not only of Southern slave owners, but of most Americans with respect to the institution of slavery. On the one hand, the logic of American Revolutionary ideology made it difficult to ignore the contradictions inherent in a commitment both to liberty and to an institution of involuntary and perpetual servitude. On the other hand, two sets of conditions caused Americans, and Southerners in particular, to divert their attention from those contradictions. The first condition was of course economic interest, which operated with ever-greater force as one moved farther south. Yet an even more powerful deterrent was the instinctive, unthinking attachment to a belief in Africans' fundamental inferiority—to the notion among whites in both the North and South that a people so physically and culturally different from themselves could never function responsibly as equal citizens in a free republic.

The word "racism" is one used so loosely and in so many contexts in our twenty-first-century world that we often have difficulty separating its meaning from that of other less pervasively pernicious sets of attitudes and fears. But the culture of virtually all eighteenth-century Europeans, including those living in both the Northern and Southern parts of America, was one in which racism—the belief that one (or more) races of human beings was fundamentally inferior to another—was widespread. Where opinion differed was over whether such differences were inherent, or whether they were the product of oppressive, hierarchical social institutions such as slavery. But acceptance of the idea that the legal and social system should be engineered in a way that reflected those differences as long as they existed (just as it was engineered to reflect differences in wealth) was even more deeply rooted than the emerging ideas of liberty and equality.[12]

This consensus on the inferiority of people different from themselves—be they African American or Indian—made it highly unlikely that the delegates gathered in Philadelphia in 1787, whether Northern or Southern, would move decisively to abolish slavery in the American states. It made it even less likely that the delegates would take steps to enforce principles of equal protection and due process for all African Americans, slave or free. Nevertheless, by 1787 there was a consensus among even the most affluent slave owners of the upper South that America already had too many

slaves. Those in Virginia and Maryland and some in North Carolina recognized that an overreliance on tobacco—a labor-intensive crop, subject
to market booms and busts, that also depleted the soil in the bargain—
was not in their economic self-interest. Looking just a few miles northward to Pennsylvania, where the residents were using free labor to grow
wheat and raise livestock to supply an ever-growing and lucrative market,
it was easy to imagine a future in which slave labor was not an essential
component of prosperity. By 1787, George Washington had converted
much of his acreage at Mount Vernon from tobacco production into a di-
versified operation involving the cultivation of wheat and the raising of
livestock, and he enthusiastically promoted agricultural diversification as
a means of freeing Virginians from overreliance on a single staple. As
much, however, as Virginians like Washington may have wished to free
themselves of dependence on slave labor, it was also the case that as much
as one-third of the wealth of the state was invested in slaves, a fact that
made most Virginians reluctant to endorse any scheme of emancipation
unless they could be assured of recouping the value of their slaves.[13]

Only South Carolina and Georgia had a strong economic incentive to
promote the expansion of slavery. One source of that incentive was in-
digo—a labor-intensive crop well suited to slave labor from which a beautiful blue dye, a product highly prized in the expanding English textile
industry, was extracted. Even more important, rice—the cultivation of
which was first introduced by Africans who had produced the crop in
their homelands—would prove to be a major source of wealth for planters
in the South Carolina and Georgia low country. South Carolina's first
Revolutionary governor, Rawlins Lowndes, remarked on the continuing
need for slaves. "Without negroes, this state is the most contemptible in
the Union. . . . Negroes [are] our wealth, our only natural resource."
South Carolina and Georgia planters built their fortunes and their political careers on rice, and the delegates from those two states—alone among
the delegates to the 1787 Constitutional Convention—were determined
to protect not only their livelihoods, but also their way of life.[14]

SECOND THOUGHTS ON THE THREE-FIFTHS COMPROMISE

The large states' acquiescence to the Connecticut Compromise on
July 17 had appeared to put to rest the issue of how slaves should be

counted in the apportioning of representation in the House of Representatives. But when the delegates reconvened on August 7 to review the Report of the Committee of Detail, they encountered several items in the
report touching on the issue of slavery that would excite further controversy. In rephrasing the Convention's prior agreements on the three-fifths
clause, the committee had simply stated that the rule of representation
would be made according to "the provisions hereinafter made," a choice of
words that seemed the very opposite of the "simple and precise language"
that was supposed to mark the committee's work. In the course of debate
on August 8, North Carolina's Hugh Williamson seized on this vagueness
and asked that the report make a more direct reference to the three-fifths
principle. The delegates agreed to make the change, but the necessity of
spelling out the terms of the concession clearly rankled at least a few
Northern members. Rufus King of Massachusetts, unhappy about both
the Connecticut Compromise and the three-fifths formula, responded
that the "admission of slaves was a most grating circumstance to my
mind," and he predicted that it would prove to be equally irritating to "a
great part of the people of America." Roger Sherman—still playing the
role of conciliator—intervened, asserting that he too found the slave
trade "iniquitous." But then he reminded King that "the point of representation having been settled after much difficulty and deliberation,"
there was nothing to be gained by agitating the issue yet again.[15]

Sherman's intervention seemed to end the matter, for the delegates
went on to discuss other aspects of the report. Later that day, however,
Gouverneur Morris, still smarting over the Connecticut Compromise
and annoyed by the unwillingness of his Northern colleagues to stand up
to the Southerners in the debate over representation of the slave population, launched the first full-scale attack on the immorality of slavery
to be heard at the Convention. It was, Morris declaimed, "a nefarious
institution— It was the curse of heaven on the states where it prevailed."
Not content to denounce slavery, he went on to compare the "rich and
noble cultivation" that marked the societies of the free states with the
"misery and poverty which overspread the barren wastes of Virginia,
Maryland, and the other states having slaves."

The demand to include slaves in the formula for representation, he
claimed, came down to a simple fact that

the inhabitant of Georgia and South Carolina who goes to
the Coast of Africa, and in defiance of the most sacred laws

of humanity tears away his fellow creatures from their dearest connections and damns them to the most cruel bondages, shall have more votes in a government instituted for the protection of the rights of mankind, than the citizen of Pennsylvania or New Jersey who views with a laudable horror so nefarious a practice.

Morris correctly perceived that the decision to count slaves in the apportionment of representation would only give added incentive to the Southern states to continue to "import fresh supplies of wretched Africans," with the effect being not only to burden the entire nation with the expense of providing for the defense against slave insurrections, but also to degrade the national honor. "I would," Morris thundered, "sooner submit myself to a tax for paying for all the Negroes in the United States than saddle posterity with such a Constitution."[16]

There was, to be sure, an element of bombast in Morris's outburst, for there was no one in the room, North or South, who would have been willing to tax themselves to compensate for the value of slaves in the South—an amount that would have roughly doubled the national debt. But his outrage over the three-fifths clause was nevertheless real, and consistent with his long-held antipathy toward the institution of slavery. Nor was this the first time that he had voiced such views. Slaves had always been an important part of the labor force at the Morris family manor, Morrisania, and at the time of independence New York was the largest slaveholding state in the North. Yet Morris had freed the only slave he had inherited from his family, and in 1776 he argued eloquently for the abolition of slavery in New York, claiming that

every human being who breathes the air of this state [should] enjoy the privileges of a freeman. . . . The rights of human nature and the principles of our holy religion loudly call on us to dispense the blessing of freedom to all mankind.

Morris's fellow New Yorkers would not heed that call until 1799, when they finally passed legislation that would gradually abolish slavery.[17]

An overwhelming number of the delegates who heard Morris's speech—Northern and Southern—ignored it entirely. James Wilson, perhaps because of his friendship and alliance with John Rutledge, made a point of distancing himself from his Pennsylvania colleague's remarks. The Southern delegates, knowing that they were already ahead in the game, remained silent, with only Charles Pinckney commenting that he would answer some of Morris's charges "if the occasion were a proper one."[18]

ALTHOUGH THE CONVENTION DELEGATES preferred to ignore Morris's fiery speech, other issues affecting the future of slavery arose soon after that would force them to confront its substance. The Committee of Detail had included in Article VII, Section 4 language that would have prohibited taxes on exports as well as any tax or limitation on the importation of slaves. The discussion, which began on August 21, first focused on exports, with South Carolina's Pierce Butler weighing in to oppose export taxes as "unjust and alarming to the staple states." Butler and his Southern colleagues—whether from tobacco-exporting Virginia and North Carolina or from the rice-and-indigo-exporting states of South Carolina and Georgia—had reason to complain, for the Southern economy was disproportionately dependent on the export of staple crops, and any tax on exports would hit them particularly hard. Everyone in the Assembly Room knew that any tax that threatened the Southern economy also constituted a threat to slavery—an institution that provided not only the labor to grow those staple crops, but also a fundamental building block of Southern society itself.

Predictably, Gouverneur Morris, who strongly supported the general principle of an invigorated taxation power for the new government and who had already demonstrated that he was not reluctant to step on the toes of Southern delegates, brushed the Southerners' objections aside. Morris cavalierly predicted that a tax on exports would not fall as heavily on the Southern states as their delegates feared, and, moreover, he argued, "local considerations ought not to impede the general interest."[19]

James Wilson, who also believed that the general interests of the American people were more important than the particular interests of any one state, supported Morris's position, noting that to take from the government the power to tax exports would be "to take from the common government half the regulation of trade." A few New England delegates—John Langdon of New Hampshire and Oliver Ellsworth and Roger Sherman of Connecticut—were far more conciliatory to their Southern colleagues, siding with them in opposing export taxes.[20]

James Madison searched for a compromise on the subject of export taxes. Hoping to offer the Southern states some protection against unfair taxation but at the same time determined to grant the government new powers to regulate commerce and levy taxes, he proposed that a two-thirds vote of the Congress be required for levying export taxes. His proposal was narrowly defeated. Five states, New Hampshire, Massachusetts, New Jersey, Pennsylvania, and Delaware, voted in favor; and six states, Connecticut, Maryland, Virginia, North Carolina, South Carolina, and Georgia, opposed. Madison was outvoted within his delegation on the issue, and Connecticut was the only Northern state to side with those of the South in demanding a complete prohibition on export taxes.[21]

Following the defeat of Madison's compromise proposal, the delegates voted on the original version of that part of Article VII, Section 4 prohibiting export taxes. The outcome was even more decisively in favor of those advocating the prohibition—seven states in favor and four opposed. Massachusetts and Connecticut, whose shipping interests were profiting handsomely from carrying rice and other Southern staple crops to overseas markets, joined the Southern delegates in supporting the provision, and once again Madison was outvoted by his Virginia colleagues.[22]

It fell to Luther Martin to bring the subject of slavery directly to center stage. The prohibition of export taxes was a clear victory for the economic interests of the Southern, slave-owning states, but the second part of Article VII, Section 4 of the Committee of Detail report, which prohibited any tax or limitation on the slave trade, amounted to a clear statement of intent to perpetuate the institution of slavery indefinitely. Martin jumped into the fray, arguing that Congress should be permitted to tax or prohibit the importation of slaves. Martin may have been cantankerous, but his logic was unassailable. He complained that the three-fifths compromise, in combination with a constitutional guarantee that the slave trade would be continued, would encourage that trade. Referring to the provision in the Committee of Detail report that committed the federal government's resources to putting down domestic insurrections, he maintained that "slaves weakened one part of the Union which the other parts were bound to protect." He concluded his attack on the slave trade by insisting that it was "inconsistent with the principles of the revolution and dishonorable to the American character to have such a feature in the Constitution."[23]

Martin owned six slaves at the time he uttered those words, but his abhorrence of the institution was probably genuine. A few years later he became one of the founding members of the Maryland Society for the Abolition of Slavery, and all of his recorded statements, if not his actions, suggest that he was deeply disturbed by the contradictions inherent in America's commitment to liberty on the one hand, and the protection of the slave system on the other.[24]

Martin's proposal ignited the most emotionally charged debate of the summer. John Rutledge was the first to answer him. Angrily brushing aside talk of potential slave insurrections, he noted that the only insurrection since the Revolution had occurred not among the slaves of the South, but among the farmers of Massachusetts. He addressed the morality of the slave trade in equally cavalier fashion. "Religion and humanity had nothing to do with the question. Interest alone is the governing principle with nations." He then issued the challenge starkly. The question before the Convention was "whether the Southern states shall or shall not be parties to the Union."[25]

Charles Pinckney pushed the brinksmanship still further, warning that "South Carolina can never receive the plan if it prohibits the slave trade." Pinckney and Rutledge's commitment to a strong national government was far greater than that of their two South Carolina colleagues, Pierce Butler and Charles Cotesworth Pinckney, but they sent a clear message to the assembled delegates that they were not willing to sacrifice the interests of their state to those of the nation. As a way of offering at least a whiff of reassurance to his Northern nationalist colleagues, Pinckney added that if the states were given the "liberty" to make their own decisions about the continuation of the slave trade, South Carolina might "by degrees" take steps to limit it. On that mildly pacific note, the Convention adjourned for the day.[26]

The debate picked up the following morning where it had left off, and the man to answer Rutledge and Pinckney was none other than George Mason, the Virginia planter from Gunston Hall and the owner of three hundred slaves. Mason launched a full-scale attack on both the slave trade and the institution of slavery itself. The "infernal traffic" in slaves, he asserted, "originated in the avarice of British merchants." He went on to claim, with only half of the truth on his side, that "the British government constantly checked the attempts of Virginia to put a stop to it." Had one of those British merchants been present, he might well have noted that it takes two parties to make a sale, and that the Virginians, for most of the eighteenth century, were willing parties to the bargain.[27]

*Author of the Virginia Declaration of Rights and an outspoken op-
ponent of the continuation of the slave trade, George Mason felt
keenly the absence of a bill of rights in the proposed new Constitution.*
Portrait is a copy of D. W. Boudet after John Hesseilus, courtesy
of Independence National Historical Park.

Responding to John Rutledge's casual dismissal of the potential for
slave insurrections, Mason noted that it was only the ineptitude of the
Tories that prevented the slaves of America from being "dangerous in-
struments" in the hands of the British during the Revolution. As one of
those Virginians who had been terrified when Virginia's royal governor,
Lord Dunmore, offered freedom to all those slaves who deserted their
masters to fight on the side of the British, Mason spoke from direct experience.

He then moved to the present. Maryland and Virginia had already
prohibited further importation of slaves, and North Carolina was moving rapidly in that direction. "All this," he argued,

> would be in vain if South Carolina and Georgia be at
> liberty to import. The western people are already calling
> out for slaves for their new lands; and will fill that country
> with slaves if they can be got through South Carolina and
> Georgia.

He closed with an impassioned commentary on the effect of the institution of slavery on the American character and offered a dire warning.

> Slavery discourages arts and manufactures. The poor despise labor when performed by slaves. They prevent the immigration of Whites, who really enrich and strengthen a country. They produce the most pernicious effect on manners. Every master of slaves is born a petty tyrant. They bring the judgment of heaven on a country. As nations can not be rewarded or punished in the next world they must be in this. By an inevitable chain of causes and effects providence punishes national sins, by national calamities. I lament that some of our Eastern brethren had from a lust of gain embarked in this nefarious traffic. As to the states being in possession of the right to import, this was the case with many other rights, now to be properly given up. I hold it essential in every point of view that the general government should have power to prevent the increase of slavery.[28]

This was not the first occasion on which Mason had spoken out against slavery. His very first piece of political writing, a pamphlet condemning Parliament for enacting the Stamp Act, published in December 1765, began not with a recitation of the principle of "no taxation without representation" but with a denunciation of the pernicious effects of slavery. In a passage strikingly similar to his speech in the Constitutional Convention twenty-two years later, he passionately lamented his colony's failure to implement a policy aimed at encouraging the immigration of free white Europeans rather than relying on the importation of slaves. Had Virginia taken that course, Mason argued, "we should not at this Day see one Half of our best Lands in most Parts of the Country remain unsettled & the other cultivated with Slaves; not to mention the ill Effect such a Practice has upon the Morals and Manners of our People." In 1773, in a longer essay on the state of his colony, he went even further.

> That slow Poison . . . is daily contaminating the Minds & Morals of our People. Every Gentleman here is born a petty Tyrant. Practiced in Acts of Despotism & Cruelty, we become callous to the Dictates of Humanity, & all the finer

feelings of the Soul. Taught to regard a part of our own Species in the most abject & contemptible Degree below us, we lose that Idea of the dignity of Man which the Hand of Nature had implanted in us, for great & useful purposes.[29]

Mason's rhetorical aversion to slavery would remain a constant throughout his life, yet he never moved beyond rhetoric. He made no attempt to halt the expansion westward of slavery in his own colony, nor did he free his own slaves. The same man who spoke of every slave owner being born a petty tyrant showed little discomfort with his own role as master of his own self-contained world supported by the three hundred slaves in his possession.[30]

It is easy enough to explain this inconsistent behavior with the single word "hypocrisy," but the matter was far more complex than that. Mason, like another deeply conflicted Virginian, Thomas Jefferson, was simultaneously repelled by the inequities of the institution of slavery and by the presence of blacks in his society. As much as Mason may have wished to rid his state—and his country—of slavery, his inability to imagine free blacks as equal citizens left him paralyzed. Thus, in the Constitutional Convention and at other times, he was ferocious in his determination to impede the *spread* of slavery by abolishing the slave trade, but there his activist impulses stopped.[31]

With only a few exceptions, Mason's cri de coeur was met with astonishing indifference. John Dickinson briefly brought his public utterances into line with his private thoughts on the subject, agreeing with Mason that it was "inadmissible on every principle of honor and safety that the importation of slaves should be authorized to the States by the Constitution." Rufus King sided with Mason, avoiding any moral judgments, but at the same time issued a warning to the South Carolina and Georgia delegates. Their threats to reject the Constitution unless they received explicit protections for slavery were sure to be met with an equal determination from the Northern states not to accept a document that contained those protections. In fact, King's assessment of the balance of power in the Convention was sadly inaccurate. South Carolina and Georgia cared far more about protecting the slave trade than the other states cared about abolishing it. Moreover, they were prepared to carry out their threats in a way that delegates from Massachusetts or Pennsylvania were not, because public opinion in Massachusetts and Pennsylvania was largely indifferent to the slavery issue. Indeed, the citizens of the North were no more able to imagine living with large numbers of blacks as equal citizens than were George Mason and Charles Pinckney.[32]

The delegates from the lower South calmly and emphatically rejected Mason's, Dickinson's, and King's arguments. Answering Mason on August 22, Charles Pinckney offered the lone attempt to defend slavery as a positive good, observing only that "if slavery be wrong, it is justified by the example of all the world." Citing examples from ancient Greece and Rome as well as from France, England, Holland, and "other modern states," he observed with some exaggeration that "in all ages one half of mankind have been slaves." The other delegates from the lower South were for the most part content to make it clear that their interest in perpetuating the slave trade was one on which they were simply unwilling to compromise. If the delegates from the North and upper South insisted on abolishing the slave trade, then they could forget about including the states from the lower South in the new union. As John Rutledge put it, "If the Convention thinks that North Carolina, South Carolina, and Georgia will ever agree to the plan, unless their right to import slaves be untouched, the expectation is vain." Charles Cotesworth Pinckney agreed and proceeded to impugn the motives of the Virginia delegates who opposed the slave trade. Virginia already had a surplus of slaves, he noted, and with the abolition of the slave trade, her slaves would only rise in value due to the increased demand for them from the lower South and Southwest. He added, defiantly, "I do not think South Carolina will stop her importations of slaves in any short time, but only stop them occasionally."[33]

The Connecticut delegates chose this moment to intervene in the quarrel among the Southern delegates. Oliver Ellsworth blandly declared that "as he had never owned a slave, [he] could not judge of the effects of slavery on character." Then, taking aim at George Mason and his three hundred slaves, he observed that if the issue were "to be considered in a moral light we ought to go farther and free those already in the country." Ellsworth knew that that was politically impossible, and, moreover, he probably believed that it was undesirable unless some means of compensating slave owners for the value of their property could be found. Indeed, most Northerners, whatever their modest moral qualms about slavery, were as concerned as Southerners about the need to preserve the principle of the sanctity of private property—whether that property be in the form of land, a horse, or a slave. Ellsworth came to the defense of the states of the lower South by noting that in Virginia and Maryland, where life expectancies were longer, it was cheaper to breed slaves than it was to import them, "whilst in the sickly rice swamps foreign supplies are necessary."[34]

In his closing remarks, Ellsworth revealed the full extent of both his indifference toward and his miscomprehension of the institution of slavery. "Let us not intermeddle. As population increases, poor laborers will be so plenty as to render slaves useless. Slavery in time will not be a speck in our country." Ellsworth's sentiments were echoed by his colleague Roger Sherman. He registered a perfunctory disapproval of the slave trade, but he nevertheless concluded that "it was better to let the Southern states import slaves than to part with them, if they made that a sine qua non."[35]

During the debate on the slave trade on August 22, Gouverneur Morris, who had up to that point been among the most vehement about the evils associated with slavery, rose and asked that the "whole subject"— meaning not only the issue of prohibitions on the slave trade but also any clauses relating to taxes on imports and exports—be referred to a committee. "These things," he suggested, "may form a bargain among the Northern and Southern States." Although he did not explicitly state the terms of the bargain, what he had in mind was that by acceding to the lower South's desire to continue the slave trade, the Northern states could win the support of the lower South on more general issues relating to Congress's power to regulate commerce.[36]

Edmund Randolph supported Morris's motion, hoping that "some middle ground might, if possible, be found," but he also noted that "I could never agree to the clause as it stands. I would sooner risk the constitution." Randolph offered his own diagnosis of the dilemma facing the delegates. To perpetuate the slave trade would on the one hand "revolt the Quakers, the Methodists, and many others in the states having no slaves. On the other hand, two states might be lost to the union." Randolph thought some form of compromise was essential in order to prevent either eventuality. Although there were some on both sides of the question who wanted to resolve the issue then and there, most delegates were content to let a smaller group hammer out a compromise. In two separate votes toward the end of the day on August 22, one decided by a seven-to-three margin and the other by nine to two (with neither vote following any discernible sectional pattern), the delegates agreed to refer both the issue of the slave trade and all issues relating to navigation acts to an eleven-person committee consisting of one delegate from each of the states present.[37]

According to the testimony of Luther Martin, who served as Maryland's representative, the delegates on the committee made short work of their task. Martin discovered that

> the Eastern States notwithstanding their aversion to slavery, were very willing to indulge the Southern States, at least with a temporary liberty to prosecute the slave trade, provided the Southerners would, in their turn, gratify them by laying no restriction on navigation acts; and after a very little time the committee, by a very great majority, agreed on a report by which the general government was to be prohibited from preventing the importation of slaves for a limited time, and the restrictive clause relative to navigation acts was to be omitted.[38]

The committee presented a draft of its report on Friday, August 24. Phrased in euphemisms, it proposed that the importation of "such persons as the several States . . . shall think proper to admit" should not be prohibited by Congress prior to 1800. It permitted "such persons" to be taxed at a rate not exceeding the average tax rate for all other imports. Perhaps most important from the point of view of those delegates who favored strengthening the central government's power over the regulation of commerce, it amended an item from the Report of the Committee of Detail that required a two-thirds majority in each house of Congress in order to pass any navigation act; the revised proposal would allow such acts to be passed by a simple majority. This was precisely the bargain that delegates like Gouverneur Morris, James Madison, and James Wilson—all of whom remained silent during the subsequent debate on the slave trade—had hoped for.[39]

When the committee's report was debated in full the following day, Charles Cotesworth Pinckney, aiming to buy some extra time for his state's trade in Africans, proposed to change the date on which Congress would be permitted to legislate on the slave trade from 1800 to 1808. Though willing to bend his principles on the slave trade in order to secure for the Congress the power to regulate commerce by a simple majority, James Madison was clearly annoyed. "Twenty years," Madison complained, "will produce all the mischief that can be apprehended from the liberty to import slaves." There was a plaintive quality to his protest. He knew that Pinckney's proposal would allow for the importation of tens of thousands of additional slaves, a result he sincerely believed would "dishonor" the new republic. And he knew the South Carolinians would get their way. The proposal to permit the trade until 1808 passed, seven in favor and four opposed. New Jersey, Pennsylvania, Delaware, and, notably, Virginia were in the negative.[40]

Gouverneur Morris, clearly aggrieved, now sought to deprive the lower South of any ambiguity about what had happened, asking that the proposal be amended to speak plainly of "the importation of slaves into North Carolina, South Carolina, and Georgia." On one level, Morris's motion was an attempt to point a finger of blame at the delegates from the lower South—to make it clear to all what was being done and why it was being done. One other important consequence of his suggestion, had it been adopted, would have been to bar slave imports into the western territories. While some of the delegates may have been inclined to support Morris's proposal to explicitly identify the states most ardent in the defense of the slave trade, nearly everyone was anxious to avoid opening a debate over the expansion of slavery into the West, so Morris, having made his point, withdrew his motion.[41]

After a bit more fine-tuning, the much-amended resolution on the slave trade was adopted by the same seven-to-four vote as in the August 25 session. "The migration or importation of such persons as the several States now existing shall think proper to admit, shall not be prohibited by the Legislature prior to the year 1808." Once again, a coalition of New England and lower South states constituted the majority. The United States Constitution, without ever having mentioned the nature of the trade they were sanctioning, would permit the overseas traffic in human beings for another twenty years. Luther Martin, in a lengthy critique of the Constitution penned during the debate over ratification in Maryland, captured the essence of it all. In crafting the clause respecting the slave trade, Martin noted, the committee "anxiously sought to avoid the admission of expressions which might be odious in the ears of Americans, although they were willing to admit into their system those things which the expressions signified."[42]

It would take until August 29 for the delegates to reach agreement on the other half of the compromise, relating to a simple, rather than a two-thirds, congressional majority in order to pass acts regulating overseas commerce. If the relaxing of prohibitions on the slave trade was indeed part of a "bargain" between New Englanders and the delegates from the lower South in order to gain Southern support for the right to pass navigation laws, then at least a few of the parties to that bargain behaved rather badly in the debate over the navigation provision. When the proposal to allow navigation acts to be passed by a simple majority came up for discussion, Charles Pinckney immediately attempted to amend it back into its earlier form of a two-thirds majority. He was concerned that the superior numerical power of the North would prove "oppressive . . . if no check to a bare majority should be provided." With remarkable gall, he contended that "the power of regulating commerce was a pure concession on the part of the Southern states," who, after all, "did not need the protection of the Northern states at present." Charles Cotesworth Pinckney chimed in to support his cousin's contention that "it was the true interest of the Southern states to have no regulation of commerce." Then, whether in recognition of the fact that a bargain was, after all, a bargain, or out of more generous motives, he went on to note that "considering the loss brought on the commerce of the Eastern states by the revolution [and] their liberal conduct toward the views of South Carolina . . . I think it proper that no fetter should be imposed on the power of making commercial regulations."[43]

Madison, in his marginal notes on Charles Cotesworth Pinckney's speech, clearly interpreted Pinckney's reference to the "liberal conduct towards the views of South Carolina" as meaning "the permission to import slaves," and he went on to elaborate that "an understanding on the two subjects of *navigation* and *slavery* had taken place between those parts of the Union, which explains the vote on the Motion, as well as the language of General Pinckney and others."[44]

Nearly all of the delegates from North Carolina, South Carolina, and Georgia who spoke on the subject of navigation laws agreed in principle with Charles Pinckney's preference for a two-thirds majority. But with the exceptions of Charles Pinckney and Hugh Williamson of North Carolina, the Southern delegates who had been most adamant about extending the slave trade kept their part of the bargain, using the rationale provided by Charles Cotesworth Pinckney for supporting the Northern position. Pierce Butler, for example, while asserting that "he considered the interests of [the Southern States] and of the Eastern States to be as different as the interest of Russia and Turkey," averred that he was nevertheless "desirous of conciliating the affections of the East," and on those grounds he would support the Northern desire for a simple majority for navigation laws.[45]

The delegates who felt themselves the clear losers on each side of the bargain were those from the upper South. Luther Martin, Hugh Williamson, George Mason, and Edmund Randolph all wished to require at least a two-thirds majority for navigation laws, and, indeed, Randolph was so upset that he revealed that "there were features so odious in the Constitution as it now stands, that I doubt whether I shall be able to agree to it." It is not surprising that the only delegate from the upper South who spoke in favor of a simple majority for navigation laws was Madison, who tried, unsuccessfully, to convince his Virginia colleagues that the Southern states would benefit as much as the Northern states from a vigorous exercise of congressional power over overseas commerce, arguing that by putting an end to existing commercial rivalries among the states and by strengthening the security offered to overseas commerce in general, the South, as well as the North, would derive an "essential advantage."[46]

In a vote to continue discussion of Charles Pinckney's proposal for a two-thirds majority requirement, four states—Maryland, Virginia, North Carolina, and Georgia—voted yes, while South Carolina (presumably with Charles Pinckney dissenting) joined all of the Northern states in voting no. Following that vote, the delegates finally agreed, with no recorded opposition, to the provision granting Congress the power to pass navigation laws by a simple majority.[47]

THE SAME WEEK the bargain over the slave trade and the congressional power over the regulation of commerce was consummated, Pierce Butler and Charles Pinckney fired another salvo in support of the protection and perpetuation of the institution of slavery. Article XV of the Report of the Committee of Detail had stipulated the obligations of states to "deliver up" any person charged with treason, felony, or a high misdemeanor to that state where the crime had been committed. On August 28 Butler proposed to insert a phrase that would "require fugitive slaves and servants to be delivered up like criminals." James Wilson issued a mild dissent relating to the expense that states might incur in complying with that provision. Roger Sherman—like Wilson more concerned about expense than morality—asked why there was "more propriety in the public seizing and surrendering a slave or servant, than a horse." Butler asked to withdraw the motion until he could do some fine-tuning of it, and then, immediately after the vote on the right of Congress to pass navigation laws by a simple majority was approved on

August 29, he reintroduced a slightly different version. The revised version was no longer part of Article XV of the Committee of Detail report but instead was set off as a separate section of the proposed Constitution. It read,

> If any person bound to service or labor in any of the U. States shall escape into another State, he or she shall not be discharged from such service or labor, in consequence of any regulations subsisting in the State to which they escape, but shall be delivered up to the person justly claiming their service or labor.

The Convention delegates unanimously embraced Butler's revised version, without a single delegate raising his voice in protest.[48]

The fugitive slave clause of the United States Constitution was not merely a provision that passively countenanced slavery, but, rather, it was one that required those states where slavery had been abolished to be actively complicit in keeping slaves in bondage. As the fugitive slave clause was enforced with increasing vigor after the passage of the Compromise of 1850, it would become one of the focal points of Northern opposition to slavery, helping to transform abolitionism from the political fringes into the mainstream. Perhaps more than any other provision of the Constitution, it would infect and pollute the document's libertarian purity, giving credence to William Lloyd Garrison's oft-repeated assertion that the Constitution was a "covenant with death."[49]

THE DEBATE OVER THE PLACE of the African slave trade had been nearly as contentious as that involving the ratio by which slaves would be counted in representation in both the Congress and the electoral college. Like the earlier debate, it was for the most part about *self-interest*. With only a few exceptions—Madison perhaps being the most notable—every delegate from every state carefully calibrated his state's interest and spoke and voted accordingly.

There was, however, one significant difference between the debate over the three-fifths clause and that over the slave trade. The former was intimately bound up in the protracted debate between the large states and small states over representation. But because there were nearly equal numbers of large and small states in the North and South, there was no way for any of the defenders of any of those sets of interests—large states, small states, slave-owning states and non-slave-owning states—to enter into workable alliances with one another as a way of advancing their interests. That was not the case with respect to the issues of commerce and the slave trade. As the subsequent history of the new nation would prove, the Northern states did have a stronger interest in securing for Congress the power to regulate and tax overseas commerce than did the states of the South. And, of course, the states of the lower South, whose slave-based economies were still expanding, had a strong desire to continue the international slave trade because it assisted that expansion. In those calculations of interest, there were only two states that decided to play their hands with ferocious tenacity—to go for broke in their willingness to sacrifice all of the benefits of union to protect their so-called peculiar institution.

Were the delegates from the lower South really prepared to sacrifice the advantages of union to gain a temporary extension of the slave trade? Most of those delegates—the South Carolinians in particular—came into the Convention as strong nationalists. Deeply troubled by the weaknesses of the Articles of Confederation, they had a strong stake in a successful outcome to the Convention. Moreover, they had a great deal to lose if a strengthened union were to go forward without them.

But the nationalism of the delegates from the lower South was of a decidedly different flavor from that of men like Gouverneur Morris and James Wilson of Pennsylvania or of Madison and, more silently, Washington in Virginia, who believed that the common good of the people of the nation as a whole should in all cases be paramount to the interests of any particular state. Nowhere was this more apparent than in Madison's support of a simple majority for enacting navigation laws. He knew that such a provision might work against the short-term interests of his state, and he knew as well that when the finished document was submitted to Virginians for ratification, the inclusion of that provision would make it more difficult to secure their assent. But he fought for the provision because he believed it was essential to creating a central government adequate to the needs of the country.

By contrast, the South Carolina delegates, though steadfast in their desire to strengthen the central government, never made the conceptual break from the idea of a confederation of states to that of a truly national government charged with the task of serving the public good of the people of the nation as a whole. Their commitment to nationalism always stopped at the point where a proposal to strengthen the power of the central government threatened to work against their state's interests. In this regard, the differences between Charles Pinckney's initial draft for a Constitution and Madison's are noteworthy. Madison's draft scrapped the structure of the Confederation government altogether and created a government founded primarily upon "we the people" of the nation. Pinckney's draft, though it contained language and specific proposals for augmenting central government power, nevertheless took the form of a series of amendments to the Confederation government, not of a transformation of that government. Pinckney's initial draft called for the strengthening of Congress's power over the regulation of commerce, but it specified that power as one that could only be exercised by a two-thirds—not a simple—majority. In that sense, Pinckney's behavior at the close of the debate on the linked issues of the slave trade and the power to regulate navigation was consistent with the position he had taken when he composed his initial draft.

Some historians have argued that had the Northern delegates—the New Englanders in particular—called the bluff of the delegates from the lower South on the slave trade, those Southern delegates would have ultimately yielded—that, in the end, the compromise on the slave trade was an unnecessary one. Legal historian Paul Finkelman has written that "the delegates from the Deep South did not need to be lured into the Union, because they were already deeply committed to the Constitution by the time the slave trade debate occurred." But perhaps we should not overestimate the commitment of the lower South delegates to the union. We will of course never know whether the South Carolina or Georgia delegates were really willing to take the risk of walking out of the Convention and remaining outside a union of the American states. But we do know that the Northern delegates were not willing to call their bluff.[50]

We are left to wonder about the speedy, even collegial, adoption of the fugitive slave clause. The Articles of Confederation had included a guarantee that escaped criminals would be returned to the states in which they had committed crimes, and it was assumed that this could also be applied to escaped slaves. As a dispute between Massachusetts and South Carolina in 1784 had demonstrated, however, the weakness of the Articles made it difficult for slave owners to enforce their rights. Notably, the Northwest Ordinance, passed by the Confederation Congress in the midst of the Convention debates on slavery, did contain a fugitive slave provision, at least in part as a way of buying Southern support for the ordinance. But still, the silence of the Convention delegates on this issue is not merely puzzling, but deeply disturbing. Unlike the bargain involving the extension of the slave trade and the grant of congressional power to regulate commerce, there was nothing the Northern states received in return for their support of a fugitive slave clause. Perhaps the Northern delegates were simply weary of sectional strife. Perhaps if they had objected they would have had to deal once again with Southern threats— this time with threats from both the upper and lower South—to defeat the Constitution.[51]

It is also important to note that although not all of the delegates in Philadelphia were indifferent to the moral dimension of the slavery issue, even those who regarded slavery as an evil tended to regard it as a "necessary evil" rather than a "radical evil," as nineteenth-century abolitionists like William Lloyd Garrison would define it. The delegates were somehow able to live with a "necessary evil" in the name of the imperatives of creating a durable union. In the absence of a moral sense that might cause them to define slavery as a radical evil, the Founding Fathers found it relatively easy to add their assent to a provision that would require generations of Americans to be actively complicit in holding the slave system in place.[52]

THERE ARE NO MORAL HEROES to be found in the story of slavery and the making of the American Constitution. There were a few notable moments when delegates actively challenged the morality of the institution and its compatibility with their project, but those moments were fleeting, and none were prepared to match words with deeds. It is tempting as well to try to identify a few villains—the most obvious candidates being men like the Pinckneys or John Rutledge or Pierce Butler of South Carolina—who pushed the proslavery agenda the hardest. But in fact they were only doing what other delegates were doing—defending the interests of their states and their free white constituents as ably as they could.

The delay in abolishing the international slave trade would have enduring consequences. Between 1788 and 1808, the number of African slaves imported to the United States numbered something in excess of two hundred thousand, only about fifty thousand fewer than the total number of slaves imported to America in the preceding 170 years. As the slave population of America exploded due to natural increase in subsequent years, the impact of the decision to extend the African slave trade resonated all the more forcefully. The two hundred thousand slaves imported during the years 1788–1808 would find themselves and their descendants entrapped in bondage for generations to come. Moreover, the dramatic increase in slave numbers, in conjunction with the operation of the Constitution's three-fifths provision, further strengthened the political power of the slave-owning South, making a political solution to the problem of slavery in the United States all the more difficult.[53]

If we should be reluctant to assign blame to particular individuals, we cannot avert our eyes from the magnitude of the evil sanctioned by the Founding Fathers. If there is a villain in this story it is the collective *indifference* of the Founding Fathers to the inhumanity of the institution to which they gave sanction. It was an indifference born both of their sense of innate superiority over African Americans and of their preoccupation with protecting *property rights*, even if that meant accommodating themselves to a "necessary evil." The Founding Fathers were also aware that many non-slave-holding Americans, such as John Adams, believed that large-scale emancipation would cause significant social disruptions, including life-threatening poverty, theft, and violence. They were unwilling to require their white counterparts in the slave states to endure such disruptions as part of the price of union, as their acceptance of federalism as a central organizing principle for slavery's relation to government shows.[54]

The Constitutional Convention of 1787, far from giving forward momentum to some Americans' wish to rid themselves of slavery, served instead to slow that momentum and, in some parts of the country, to make it even more difficult to effect any meaningful change in the plight of slaves. Even in states like Virginia, where the economic advantages of slavery were rapidly diminishing, attempts at abolishing slavery failed. They failed, as Thomas Jefferson was to lament, because "the public mind would not bear the proposition."[55]

Perhaps the outcome of the debates over slavery in the Constitutional Convention was preordained, unavoidable. After all, the American Revolution was fought to defend liberty *and* property. Indeed, owners of slave property like Jefferson, Washington, Pinckney, and Rutledge were all an integral part of that Revolution, risking their lives in that struggle at least in part to *protect* their right to own slaves. Nor perhaps should we be surprised by the unwillingness of these late-eighteenth-century Convention delegates to attempt to resolve any tension that may have existed between abstract notions of liberty and the continuation of an institution that later generations would come to regard as reprehensible. Virtually none of the delegates in Philadelphia, whether from the North or the South, was prepared to live with the social disruption they saw as inevitable should large numbers of whites and free blacks find themselves living together. Those among our Founding Fathers who later roused themselves to champion some form of gradual emancipation of slaves usually tied their proposals for emancipation with schemes to repatriate the freed slaves back to Africa.

Seen through the lenses of these late-eighteenth-century Americans, the outcome seems somehow inevitable, and our Founding Fathers seem somehow to have been prisoners of the prevailing economic forces and social attitudes of their time. Given those forces and attitudes, how could we ever expect that they might be able to create a durable union among the states and at the same time make even modest progress in granting a measure of justice for enslaved blacks?

But it was one thing to bow reluctantly to the reality of slavery's existence and quite another to take positive steps to give to that institution even greater standing within the new national edifice. The Convention delegates, whether from a combination of guilt and duplicity or from wishful thinking, twisted themselves into linguistic knots to avoid admitting what they had done. Luther Martin seemed to come down on the side of guilt and duplicity when he attributed the absence of the words "slave" or "slavery" in the Constitution to the fact that the delegates "anxiously sought to avoid the admission of expressions which might be odious in the ears of Americans," even while admitting "into their system those things which the *expressions* signified." John Dickinson, more thoughtful and restrained than Martin, nevertheless came to the same conclusion, regarding the omission as "an endeavor to conceal a principle of which we are ashamed."[56]

Abraham Lincoln, debating his opponent, Stephen A. Douglas, in his 1858 campaign for the United States Senate, took a more optimistic view. The omission of the words "slavery" and "slave," and the substitution of "covert language" in their place, was, Lincoln argued, "full of significance." The substitution was made, Lincoln believed, in order that

> our Constitution . . . should be read by intelligent and patriotic men, after the institution of slavery had passed from among us—[in a way that] there should be nothing on

the face of the great charter of liberty suggesting that such a thing as negro slavery ever existed among us. This is part of the evidence that the fathers of the Government expected and intended the institution of slavery to come to an end.[57]

The delegates debating the issue of slavery in the Pennsylvania State House that summer were probably motivated by a combination of the cynicism, shame, and hope implied in Martin's, Dickinson's, and Lincoln's assessments. Mere intentions, whether cynical, self-interested, or high-minded, are not in themselves sufficient. The Founding Fathers failed to face up to the paradox of slavery within a constitutional system dedicated to securing the blessing of liberty. Some three-quarters of a century later, the new nation would pay heavily in blood and treasure to set things right.

CHAPTER EIGHTEEN

A FRAGILE CONSENSUS:
SEPTEMBER 10–SEPTEMBER 15

MONDAY, SEPTEMBER 10—with the contentious issue of slavery settled, the delegates could sense that they were finally entering the home stretch. New Jersey's Jonathan Dayton, bending the rule of secrecy, wrote home to his father Elias and told him that "we have happily so far finished our business, as to be employed in giving it its last polish and preparing it for public inspection." But there was still work to be done. After a brief period of clear, sunny, and cool weather, the summer heat and humidity returned with a vengeance, with the temperature moving back into the eighties and nineties. There was barely a breath of air in the cramped Assembly Room. At the end of the day on September 8, the Convention members had appointed a "Committee of Stile and Arrangement" charged with the task of assembling a final draft of the Constitution. The members of that committee—William Samuel Johnson, Alexander Hamilton, Gouverneur Morris, James Madison, and Rufus King—had to do double duty. After spending the day on the Convention floor participating in discussions of a host of still-unresolved and contentious issues, they would spend their off-hours during the next week editing a document that changed daily.[1]

AMENDING THE CONSTITUTION

Among the Articles of Confederation's fatal weaknesses had been its lack of a workable method for amendment. Initially the Committee of Detail seemed destined to repeat the mistake. It proposed that amendments could be put forth only by calling a "convention" into being with the consent of two-thirds of the state legislatures. Objections sprang up from all directions. Elbridge Gerry, with dubious logic, protested that the provision would result in a further weakening of the power of the state governments. Alexander Hamilton, who had returned to the Convention after several weeks' absence, argued that the only amendments likely to be favored by state legislatures would be those "with a view to increase their own powers." Hamilton believed it was imperative that Congress be empowered to issue the call for a convention.[2]

In an ironic turnabout, considering the extent to which they had exceeded their instructions from the Continental Congress, some delegates raised important questions about how they would limit the scope of any convention created for the purpose of amending the Constitution. How could one limit its actions and what would be "the force of its acts"? These questions, coming from different directions, were enough to cause the delegates to reject the Committee of Detail proposal. Madison, hoping to satisfy these concerns, quickly drafted language providing multiple routes toward amendment. He proposed,

> The Legislature of the U.S., whenever two thirds of both Houses shall deem necessary, or on the application of two thirds of the Legislatures of the several States, shall propose amendments to this Constitution, which shall be valid to all intents and purposes as part thereof, when the same shall have been ratified by three fourths at least of the Legislatures thereof, or by Conventions in three fourths thereof, as one or the other mode of ratification may be proposed by the Legislature of the U.S.

There was still more bickering over details. John Rutledge, ever vigilant in protecting the interests of slave owners, added language prohibiting any amendments that might affect slave property prior to 1808. With this further concession to slave interests, Madison's proposal passed overwhelmingly.[3]

Madison's formulation gave equal power to the state legislatures and the Congress in proposing amendments; but it gave state legislatures final authority to ratify proposed amendments, setting a high bar by requiring that three-fourths of those legislatures approve any amendment.

Madison hoped at all costs to avoid the calling of additional constitutional conventions, for he feared that such conventions might well undo the work they were doing in Philadelphia, and, for the same reasons, he wished to use state conventions as an alternative means of ratifying—but not proposing—amendments. In the end, Madison won only a partial victory, for the version of the section in the Constitution that ultimately emerged from the Committee of Style included, as an alternative to either the Congress or the state legislatures proposing amendments, the calling of a general convention of the states for the purpose of proposing amendments.[4]

As things have turned out, the delegates made wise choices about the amendment process. The United States Constitution has only been amended when a decisive percentage of the populace has agreed that an amendment was of sufficient importance to justify changing the language of the Constitution. As a consequence, the American Constitution remains a model of concision. The original document consisted of only four handwritten pages, and if its twenty-seven amendments were written in the same hand, it would be about seven pages long. By contrast, those responsible for crafting America's state constitutions have viewed the amendment process more capaciously—so much so that the Constitution of the State of California, for example, is now 350 pages long. The "founders" of the European Union, as they struggle with their conception of a federal union among an ever-expanding cohort of nations in Europe, have thus far produced a draft of a constitution running to 855 pages, with no end in sight.

RATIFYING THE CONSTITUTION

Although the delegates seemed to have agreed on August 31 that ratification of the Constitution would be contingent on the approval of at least nine of thirteen state conventions, Elbridge Gerry, having settled comfortably into his obstructionist role, raised the topic again on September 10. He demanded that both the Confederation Congress and the states approve the Constitution before it could go into effect. He protested against "the indecency and pernicious tendency of dissolving in so slight a manner, the solemn obligations of the Articles of Confederation. If nine out of thirteen can dissolve the compact, six out of nine will be just as able to dissolve the new one hereafter." By this time Gerry may have been looking for a way to provoke a wholesale reconsideration of all the work the delegates had accomplished that summer, and requiring the approval of the Continental Congress might well have produced that result.[5]

For the second time that day, Alexander Hamilton found himself in odd alliance with Gerry. He proposed a three-step process by which the Confederation Congress would initially approve the document, then send it to the state legislatures, who would then refer it to state conventions, with the concurrence of nine of those conventions being sufficient to put the Constitution into effect. Hamilton no doubt thought prior approval by the Confederation Congress would help rather than hurt the chances of getting the requisite number of states to approve the Constitution. However, as most other delegates understood, the twin problems of chronic absenteeism in the Congress and the tendency of representatives still serving in that body to be protective of the old government would, at best, slow their momentum or, at worst, defeat their efforts altogether. The effect of requiring the Confederation Congress's approval, James Wilson argued, would be to allow that Congress to debate the document to its death.[6]

Edmund Randolph, though not as irretrievably disaffected as Elbridge Gerry, was moving in that direction. He complained that because the Convention had "irreconcilably departed from . . . the Republican propositions" that had marked his original proposal, he now believed that when the new Constitution was presented to the state conventions, those conventions should be allowed to offer amendments to it. The revised Constitution, with the multitude of amendments likely to be proposed by the various state conventions, would then be submitted to a "second general convention" charged with the task of sorting things out. Most of the delegates realized that Randolph's plan would be the equivalent of an arrow straight to the heart of their hard work that summer. However much they may have disagreed about particulars, nearly all of the delegates understood that the only way the new Constitution could win approval was by an up or down vote, not by a complicated process of successive amendments.[7]

Gerry's, Hamilton's, and Randolph's suggestions provoked a flurry of debate, but their overall effect was to cause the delegates to acknowledge that a simpler ratification process was more likely to assure that the proposed Constitution would get an expeditious hearing. In the end, they reaffirmed the principle of ratification by nine state conventions, limiting the role of the Confederation Congress to that of receiving and transmitting the document to the states.[8]

The delegates would continue to tinker with the balance of power between the president and the Congress right up to the end. In the first item of substantive business on September 12, Hugh Williamson, who had earlier supported a three-quarters majority in both houses of Congress to override a presidential veto, now feared that this gave the president too much power, suggesting that it be reduced to two-thirds. Roger Sherman, Elbridge Gerry, George Mason, Edmund Randolph, and, perhaps more surprising, Charles Pinckney supported Williamson's proposal that the number be reduced to two-thirds. On the other side, Gouverneur Morris, Alexander Hamilton, and Madison continued to support the three-fourths formula. George Washington, though he did not speak on the subject, sided with the proponents of a stronger president. The vote was close—six states supporting Williamson's proposal, four opposing, with New Hampshire divided. The close vote provided one more piece of evidence attesting to the wide range of opinion among the delegates on the extent and limits of presidential power. But in spite of the closeness of the vote, this time the decision of the Convention would stick. The final form of the Constitution would allow two-thirds of the Congress to override a presidential veto.[9]

THE OMISSION OF A BILL OF RIGHTS

On that same day, George Mason raised an issue that would profoundly impact the proposed Constitution's chances for popular approval by the people of the states. Mason expressed his wish that "the plan had been prefaced with a Bill of Rights." It would, he said, "give great quiet to the people and, with the aid of the state declarations, a bill might be prepared in a few hours."

Mason's suggestion stemmed in part from pride of authorship. As the principal draftsman of the Virginia Declaration of Rights, he believed that the articulation of fundamental rights should be a part of any proper constitution. Elbridge Gerry, who was by now closely bonded to Mason on almost every issue, immediately put Mason's rumination forward as a formal motion. Roger Sherman, who had so often occupied the middle ground, dissented. He argued that since there was nothing in the proposed Constitution that ran counter to the provisions in the bills of rights that were a part of many state constitutions, there was no need to duplicate them by adding a bill of rights to it.[10]

Mason disagreed emphatically. He had become increasingly concerned about states' rights, and in particular was worried that laws passed by the new Congress would override provisions in the states' bills of rights." A federal bill of rights, modeled on those of many of the states, would offer a guarantee that the new federal government could not encroach on those fundamental liberties—freedom of speech, press, religion, trial by jury—offered by the states' bills of rights. When the matter was put to a vote, and after a discussion lasting no more than a few moments, with a glib unanimity that seems shocking in retrospect, not a single state delegation in the Convention supported the idea of a federal bill of rights.[11]

That decision, arrived at hastily and casually, would prove to be one of the most serious mistakes made by the Founding Fathers. When Thomas Jefferson—still serving as ambassador in Paris—received a copy of the Constitution along with a long letter from his friend James Madison some three months after the Convention had adjourned, he found much that he did not like. Although Madison was his most trusted friend and intellectual soul mate, Jefferson was taken aback by the extent to which the proposed new government had assumed powers previously exercised by the states. He confided to Madison, "I own I am not a friend to a very energetic government. It is always oppressive." He was deeply concerned and dismayed about the absence of a bill of rights. "The omission of a bill of rights, providing clearly and without the aid of sophisms, for freedom of religion, freedom of the press, protection against standing armies, restriction against monopolies, the eternal and unremitting force of the habeas corpus laws, and trials by jury in all matters of fact, triable by the laws of the land and not by the law of Nations," was, Jefferson believed, an appalling mistake. Writing to his friend Alexander Donald in the midst of the ratification debates, Jefferson would go further. Out of loyalty to Madison, he expressed the hope that the necessary nine states would ratify the new Constitution, but he added that "I equally wish, that the four latest conventions . . . may refuse to accede to it, till a declaration of rights is annexed." Listing the same fundamental liberties he had recited to Madison in his earlier letter, Jefferson described them as "fetters against doing evil, which no honest government should decline." Even after the Constitution had been ratified and the new government was commencing operation, Jefferson was still mystified by the oversight. Persisting in his objections, he noted to Francis Hopkinson that "the enlightened part of Europe have given us the greatest credit for inventing this instrument of security for the rights of the people, and have been not a little surprised to see us so soon give it up."[12]

One of the enduring lessons of the American Revolution was that in the absence of written constitutions laying out not only the powers that governments might exercise but also those they may not, liberty would always be endangered. Most of the American states, in the aftermath of the Revolution, had incorporated into their constitutions bills of rights enumerating the fundamental rights of their citizens in order to erect those protections to liberty.

How could the delegates have ignored the lessons of the Revolution and not created a bill of rights for their proposed plan of union? The delegates failed to address that question at that moment in early September, but later, in the debate over ratification, they were pressed to defend their inaction. James Wilson, defending the absence of a bill of rights in the Pennsylvania ratifying convention on November 28, 1787, would argue that the proposed federal government was concerned with "objects of a general nature," and to attempt to replicate the bills of rights of the individual states would have been not only redundant but also potentially dangerous. "Who will be bold enough," Wilson asked, "to undertake to enumerate all the rights of the people? And when the attempt to enumerate them is made, it must be remembered that if the enumeration is not complete, everything not expressly mentioned will be presumed to be purposely omitted."[13]

James Madison was equally cavalier in discounting the need for a federal bill of rights. He dismissed the state bills of rights as mere "parchment barriers," which the various state governments disregarded whenever it suited their needs. Madison echoed Wilson's argument, insisting that the federal government was one of "limited powers," and the "jealousy of the subordinate governments" would "afford a security" against the invasion of the citizens' rights. Within that single sentence was the essence of the contradictory logic both Madison and Wilson had embraced. On the one hand, they insisted the new government they had created was one of limited powers. Yet on the other, Madison acknowledged the "subordinate" condition of the state governments, a condition that opened at least the possibility that the federal government might invade those fundamental rights guaranteed in the state bills of rights. Given that possibility, how could a federal constitutional guarantee of fundamental rights be merely "redundant?"[14]

Perhaps the real reason for the failure of the delegates to add this vital feature to the nation's new frame of government was more prosaic than the reasons given by Wilson and Madison. They were desperately weary and hot in the stuffy Assembly Room and profoundly anxious to avoid anything that would prolong the Convention. Although Mason had suggested that "a bill might be prepared in a few hours," the delegates knew better. It would be a difficult, arduous task, filled with contention. So, looking longingly homeward, they took a pass. They would, however, pay the price for their impatience in the ensuing months.

SUMPTUARY LAWS

During the war for independence, Americans, seeking to demonstrate that they were more virtuous than their European counterparts, had made a self-conscious effort to abstain from conspicuous consumption of luxury items such as fancy lace clothing or fine dinnerware of the sort manufactured in Europe. As the emotional fervor of the Revolution waned, however, this self-restraint began to fade. And so it was on Thursday, September 13, that George Mason started the day by trying to revive another of his pet projects, a provision in the Constitution giving the government power to enact sumptuary laws—laws that were designed to restrain luxury or extravagance in personal consumption. Mason had become deeply disturbed by what he saw as "the extravagance of our manners [and] the excessive consumption of foreign superfluities," and he wished to do something to put a stop to that trend. The Convention agreed to appoint a committee to consider the matter, though some were certainly bemused by the fact that Mason—in most other matters among those most fearful of government encroachments on the personal liberties of the people—would be the one to insist on laws restricting the consumer habits of the citizenry. His own consumer choices could hardly be considered a model of republican austerity and simplicity. Indeed, his home at Gunston Hall in particular suggested nearly the opposite. Surrounded by elaborate landscaping and set majestically overlooking the Potomac River, it featured ornate carved woodwork throughout, a grand entrance hall, spacious rooms with high ceilings, and furnishings of the highest quality—many of them imported from Europe.[15]

Nothing would come of Mason's proposal, but it offers a window into some of the tensions that existed not only in Mason's thought and behavior, but in the American Revolutionary psyche more generally. Many Americans believed not only that their Revolution was waged against a tyrannical king and Parliament, but that it was also a struggle of virtue against vice, of republican simplicity against the dissipation that extravagance and frivolity inevitably encouraged. Yet America's prosperity flowed from its integration into an expansive capitalist economy in which part of the meaning of "liberty" extended to the purchase of consumer goods that might well undermine the republican simplicity of which men like Mason were so nostalgically fond. One could see signs of the contradictions between an ideology of republican simplicity and material extravagance in the behavior of nearly all of those upper-class Americans who, with very few exceptions, composed the delegations to the Constitutional Convention in Philadelphia.[16]

WHILE THE DELEGATES were trying to settle the myriad issues relating to amending and ratifying the Constitution, the relationship between congressional and executive power, and the desirability of a bill of rights and sumptuary laws, the Committee of Style, most often working in the evening, was working to provide the "last polish" to the document.

Four of the five men elected to the committee in the ballot of each of the state delegations—King, Johnson, Gouverneur Morris, and Madison—were obvious choices, all having served in the Convention continuously and with considerable distinction from the beginning. Three of those four had been advocates of a strong national government from the start, with William Samuel Johnson joining his Connecticut colleagues in playing the role of compromiser. The final member, Alexander Hamilton, is a more puzzling choice. He was frequently absent from the Convention, and his contributions when he was present had been of dubious value and were colored by his consistent elitism. Moreover, when he returned to the Convention in early September after a lengthy absence during the month of August, he announced that "he had been restrained from entering into the discussion by his dislike of the scheme of the government in general." This could not have endeared him to those who had labored so hard in his absence to craft the document. His unhappiness with the Constitution was of a different nature than that of vigorous defenders of state power such as Elbridge Gerry and Luther Martin. He wished for a constitution that went much further in augmenting central government power at the expense of the states, and he was still smarting from the indifference with which the delegates had greeted his June 18 suggestions for a constitution based more on the English model.

Why was Hamilton chosen to serve on such an important committee despite his spotty record and anglophilic politics? In all likelihood the delegates realized that, whatever his shortcomings, the vain young colonel was a brilliant thinker and an accomplished stylist. He might therefore be useful in adding the necessary "polish" to the document.[17]

The committee worked from sometime after dinner on September 8 through the evening of September 11. Although William Samuel Johnson was the nominal chair of the committee, he apparently delegated much of the initial writing to Gouverneur Morris. Writing to Massachusetts congressman Timothy Pickering some twenty-seven years later, Morris proudly affirmed that the "instrument was written by the fingers which write this letter." Writing to the historian Jared Sparks in 1831, James Madison observed that Morris, like Hamilton, was never "incline[d] to the democratic side," but he gave Morris full credit for "the *finish* given to the style and arrangement" of the Constitution. All in all, Madison believed that "a better choice could not have been made, as the performance of the task proves."[18]

The committee hammered out a general outline on September 8, further refined the language and added detail on the ninth and tenth, and then did some final polishing on September 11. The Convention stood in temporary recess on the eleventh, waiting for the Committee of Style to complete its work, and on Wednesday, September 12, William Johnson, on behalf of the Committee of Style, presented a digest of the plan to the Convention. The Convention ordered that Messrs. Dunlap and Claypoole—the same individuals who had shown such discretion in providing the delegates with the Report of the Committee of Detail—prepare printed copies for each of the delegates so they could begin to debate it in earnest the following day.[19]

FROM SEPTEMBER 13 through September 15 the delegates reviewed the Report of the Committee of Style. Although Morris and his fellow committee members had not substantially reduced the number of words in their document, they had taken the twenty-three articles in the Committee of Detail report and, by combining and editing, reduced the total number to seven more artfully worded articles.[20]

The draft constitution, as it emerged from the Committee of Style, brought clearly into view the important differences between the proposed new federal Constitution and both the state constitutions and the Articles of Confederation. The men who drafted the Revolutionary state constitutions had intended them not only to replace the old colonial charters, but also to serve as Revolutionary manifestos explicitly announcing the separation of each state from the mother country. Most important, the structure of those state constitutions had reflected Americans' intense fear of monarchical power. Concerns about checks and balances and separation of powers seemed far less important to the state constitution makers than the need to limit executive power. As a consequence, most of the state constitutions, with the exception of that of Massachusetts, were heavily weighted toward legislative power, rendering the executive and judicial branches distinctly subordinate to the legislative branch.[21]

The new Constitution's contrast with the Articles of Confederation was even more striking. At best, a league of friendship among independent and sovereign states, the Articles of Confederation made it clear that "each state retains its sovereignty, freedom, and independence, and every power, jurisdiction, which is not by this Confederation expressly delegated to the United States, in Congress assembled." With that concession to the sovereign power of the states, there was little need to devote much attention to questions relating to the balance of power between the state and continental governments. Similarly, there was little need to devote much attention to the question of the separation of powers within the Confederation government, for nearly all of the power within that government was given to a Congress in which each sovereign state was to have an equal vote.[22]

One of the most important changes in the version of the Constitution produced by the Committee of Style occurred right up front. Whereas the Committee of Detail report had begun with a brief preamble announcing that "we the people of the states of New Hampshire, Massachusetts, Rhode Island and Providence Plantation, Connecticut, New-York, New-Jersey, Pennsylvania, Delaware, Maryland, Virginia, North-Carolina, South-Carolina, and Georgia do ordain, declare and establish the following Constitution," the Committee of Style report contained a lengthier preamble, but a more concise and powerful definition of the source of the document's legitimacy.

> We the *People* of the United States, in order to form a more perfect union, to establish justice, insure domestic tranquility, provide for the common defence, promote the general welfare, and secure the blessing of liberty to ourselves and to our posterity, do ordain and establish this Constitution for the United States of America.

That preamble, almost certainly written by Gouverneur Morris, came as close to literary elegance as the Constitution would achieve. But the importance of the preamble extended well beyond matters of style. The deliberate omission of the mention of the individual states would have a profound effect in subsequent interpretations of the power of the federal government vis-à-vis that of the state governments. Whereas the Committee of Detail report placed authority for establishing the new government in the hands of the people of the individual *states*, the Committee of Style report placed that authority in the hands of "the people of the United States." It was a fine point perhaps, but it was the point on which the constitutional argument leading to the Civil War would turn. Was this a government created by people acting in their capacity as citizens of the individual states, or was it created by people acting in their capacity as citizens of a new entity, a nation called the United States? The preamble to the Articles of Confederation made it clear that the states retained sovereign power. The preamble in the Committee of Detail report suggested that it was the people, acting through the agency of their respective states, who possessed sovereign power. Gouverneur Morris's preamble, though not definitive in its articulation, seemed to suggest that the people of the *nation* possessed that sovereign power. It is likely that not all of the Convention delegates understood the meaning of the phrase in that way, but it was certainly the way in which nationalists like Morris, Madison, and James Wilson wished for it to be understood.[23]

The particular order of the reorganization of the Committee of Detail's twenty-three articles into seven gave a clear signal about the priorities of the framers of the Constitution. Article I, containing ten sections and in some of those sections as many as eighteen subclauses, dealt in exhaustive and specific ways with the structure and powers of the Congress. However much some of the nationalist delegates may have wished to strengthen the executive branch, even the most dedicated among them realized that the power of the Congress would constitute the heart and soul of the new government. In most instances, Article I is extraordinarily specific in defining those powers, although, as we have seen, the casual insertion of the "necessary and proper" clause, no doubt inserted at the tail end of Article I, Section 8 by James Wilson, would have profound consequences in creating a more open-ended legislative power.

The language of Article II, Section 1 reflects the delegates' torment as they wrestled with the questions of how to give to the president *sufficient* power without giving him *excessive* power, as well as how to free him from excessive dependence on the legislature while at the same time assuring that he did not become an "elective monarch." The Report of the Committee of Detail simply stated that the president would be "elected by ballot by the legislature," whereas the Committee of Style report reflected the tortuous path by which the framers decided that the president should be chosen by an electoral college. Most sections of the Constitution (with the notable exceptions of the circumlocution in every section dealing with the issue of slavery) are straightforward and concise, but the language of Article II, Section 1 relating to the election of the president is so complicated that even today intelligent adults are often unable to read that section and fully understand it.

The items in Article II respecting the president's specific powers are both concise and maddeningly vague. Article II, Section 1 merely states that "executive power shall be vested in a president of the United States of America," without defining what executive power is. Article II, Section 2 stipulates that the president will act as "commander in chief of the army and navy of the United States and of the militia of the several States" but does not mention any specific presidential powers in time of war. Article I, Section 8, paragraph 1 gives to Congress the power "to declare war," but there is little in either Article I or Article II that speaks to the division of congressional and executive power in the actual waging of war. The framers did, in giving the Congress power over the purse, give it the power to control military appropriations, as well as the power to "make rules for the government and regulation of the land and naval forces." Those specific grants of power to the Congress suggest at the very least that the framers intended for the legislative and executive branches to share in decisions about the actual waging of war, but the vagueness of both Article I and Article II reminds us that the framers were ultimately divided and, indeed, perhaps confused about the relationship between congressional and executive power.

Finally, Article II, Section 4, which dealt with impeachment and conviction for "treason, bribery, or other high crimes and misdemeanors" was also remarkably vague. If the thirty-nine delegates who eventually signed the Constitution had been asked to list their definitions of "high crimes and misdemeanors" it is likely that they would have given thirty-nine different answers.

Article III, which created a federal judiciary and defined its jurisdiction, had traveled a long way since James Madison's initial and muddled proposals for combining executive and judicial authority in the form of a council of revision. The language of Article III was clear in creating both a single supreme court and "such inferior courts as the Congress may from time to time ordain and establish." It was also reasonably clear in defining the federal judiciary's jurisdiction in all cases arising under the Constitution, under laws and treaties of the United States, in all cases of admiralty and maritime jurisdiction, and in controversies between two or more states or in cases in which the United States was a party. Even in the absence of a federal bill of rights, Article III did at least stipulate that "trial of all crimes except that of impeachment, shall be by jury." What was not resolved, however, was whether the federal judiciary had the power to hold a law passed by a state legislature or by the Congress unconstitutional. There were certainly many delegates in the Convention—perhaps most of them—who believed that the United States Supreme Court should possess ultimate jurisdiction in those cases, but the resolution of that issue was left uncertain in the language of Article III.

Article IV defined the relationship between the federal government and the states. It provided for "full faith and credit" to be given in each state to the public acts of other states, guaranteed to citizens of each state all of the "privileges and immunities" of the citizens in the other states, and gave to Congress the important authority to admit new states to the union and make necessary rules and regulations for new territories within the United States. Article IV, Section 2, paragraph 3 contained the most odious of the compromises with slavery made by the delegates, guaranteeing that persons "held to service or labour in one state, escaping into another, shall . . . be delivered up on claim of the party to whom such service or labour may be due."

The delegates had reached tentative agreement on the means by which the Constitution might be amended on September 10, but the Committee of Style, in what now became Article V, inserted an alternative means of proposing amendments. The final draft allowed "on Application of the Legislatures of two-thirds of the several States," a convention of the states, and Congress, to propose amendments. The provision for ratifying amendments—approval of three-fourths of the state legislatures—remained the same.[24]

Article VI ensured that "all debts contracted . . . before the adoption of this Constitution shall be as valid against the United States under this Constitution." While it was clear from that wording that the debts contracted by the Confederation government would be honored by the new government, it left unclear whether the government of the United States possessed either the power or the obligation to pay the debts of individual states. This vagueness would explode into a bitter and divisive debate within the new government in 1790, when Alexander Hamilton, serving as secretary of the treasury, would propose that the federal government take over responsibility for those state debts. The debate was resolved in Hamilton's favor, with those who wished to see a strong central government with sweeping powers over matters of public finance adding another arrow to their quiver.[25]

The other noteworthy feature of Article VI was its provision that "this constitution, and the laws of the United States . . . shall be the supreme law of the land; and the judges in every state shall be bound thereby." While subject to a multitude of interpretations, the inclusion of this article certainly pleased the initial cohort of Virginians and Pennsylvanians who had come together before the Convention began to create a "supreme" national government. And although the word "national" had dropped out of the text of the Constitution as the summer wore on, the "supremacy clause" would enable the nationalists to keep their vision of a national government alive.[26]

Finally, Article VII simply stated that the Constitution would go into effect after conventions in nine states had added their assent.

The Committee of Style included in its report a letter of transmission to the Confederation Congress, written in the hand of Gouverneur Morris. We might be inclined to pass off the letter as a mere formality, a small bow to the Congress that had authorized the gathering in Philadelphia, but, in fact, the letter was intended for at least three rather different audiences. To the members of the Philadelphia Convention themselves, who had suffered through the contention of the summer, the letter represented the first attempt to justify their actions. To the members of the Confederation Congress, meeting in New York on the periphery of the political action, the letter sought to enlist them in the cause of constitutional reform. And finally, although most Americans no doubt went about their daily lives that summer largely oblivious to what was going on in the Pennsylvania State House, there were certainly many—particularly those serving in the legislatures of the individual states—who were likely to be taken aback by the boldness of the Convention's actions. The delegates knew that when the people of the states began to debate the merits of the proposed Constitution, the words on the printed page would not speak for themselves; they would need to be explained and defended by a host of politicians and pamphleteers who were urging its acceptance. Even before the proposed Constitution was submitted to the states, the delegates to the Confederation Congress, and through them the people of the states they represented, needed at least some general description and justification of the revolutionary actions that had occurred in Philadelphia.[27]

As if anticipating that some in the Confederation Congress would charge that the Convention had gone too far, Morris aggressively defended the magnitude of the change the delegates were proposing. The true "Friends of our Country," the letter declared "have long seen and desired that the Power of making war Peace and Treaties, that of levying Money & regulating Commerce, and the correspondent executive and judicial Authorities should be fully and effectually vested in the general Government of the Union." To achieve those ends, the letter continued, the nation required "a different Organization" altogether. Noting the impossibility of giving "all rights of independent Sovereignty" to each of the states while at the same time providing for the "interest and safety of all," Morris asserted that "Individuals entering into society must give up a Share of Liberty to preserve the Rest." Acknowledging the difficulty of "draw[ing] with Precision the Line between those Rights which must be surrendered and those which may be reserved," Morris noted that the problem the delegates faced was made all the more difficult because of the "difference among the several States as to their Situation, Extent, Habits and particular Interests." Perhaps stepping over the line separating his own views from those of the Convention as a whole, Morris insisted that "our Prosperity, Felicity, Safety, [and] perhaps our national Existence" depended upon the "consolidation of our union."[28]

Writing some thirty-seven years later, James Madison ruefully noted that the use of the terms "consolidation" and "national" in the letter of transmittal was "meant to give strength and solidity to the union of the States." But then referring with obvious distaste to the expansive use of the implied powers doctrine by the Supreme Court under the leadership of John Marshall during the first decades of the nineteenth century, he went on to add that "in its current and controversial application it means a destruction of the States by transferring their powers into the government of the union." The issue that troubled Madison those many years later had been a point of confusion and contention for the delegates throughout that summer of 1787, and it would continue to dominate the debate over the Constitution once it was submitted to the people for ratification. The "original intent" of the framers on the question of whether they had created a consolidated national government or one that was part national and part federal remained muddled.[29]

Some of the most vocal dissidents in the Convention—men like Luther Martin, John Lansing, and Robert Yates—had already left Philadelphia precisely because they feared that the end result of the Convention would be a "consolidated government." Many of the moderates in the Convention—among them Roger Sherman and his Connecticut colleagues—would stay around to support the Constitution because they believed their efforts had brought the balance of power between the proposed government and the states more closely into equilibrium. Nationalists like James Wilson and Gouverneur Morris, on the other hand, preferred to give as much vitality as possible to the new government even if that meant a substantial reduction in the power of the states. Madison, who had been firmly in the nationalists' corner at least at the beginning of the Convention, may in subsequent years have backed away from his earlier position, but he gave no sign of dissenting from the essential thrust of Morris's letter of transmittal when Morris composed it.

FURTHER FINE-TUNING

The Convention spent nearly all of the days from September 13 to September 15 discussing particular features of the Report of the Committee of Style. One of the important powers to be given to Congress as part of Article I, Section 8 was that of appointing a treasurer. On the one hand, giving Congress that power made sense, for that body possessed important powers over the purse. On the other hand, those who desired a stronger executive noted that the function of a treasurer was to help the president in executing the laws and therefore the treasurer should be appointed by the president. The decision went to those who favored presidential rather than congressional authority. It seemed like a minor matter at the time, and, indeed, most of the delegates from the Massachusetts, Pennsylvania, and Virginia delegations preferred that the power of appointment remain with the Congress, but during Alexander Hamilton's term of service as President Washington's secretary of the treasury, Americans of all political persuasions would come to appreciate the importance of the treasury secretary as an agency of executive power.[30]

George Mason, by this point alert to any possibility that the new government would assert its power at the expense of the people's liberties, reiterated his concern about limiting the power of the government to maintain a standing army in peacetime. Conceding that it was impractical to impose an outright prohibition on such armies, he proposed instead that the delegates add a preface to the clause in Article I, Section 8 providing for the organizing of state militias. That preface would include the cautionary words, "and that the liberties of the people may be better secured against the danger of standing armies in time of peace." The majority of delegates, believing that Mason's language was both unnecessary and unnecessarily insulting to the "military class of Citizens," defeated the amendment. It was just one more indignity for Mason to add to his growing list of grievances. Perhaps more important, it was one more step away from America's revolutionary commitment to a citizens' army, which would be called into being only in time of war.[31]

At the end of the day on September 14, the delegates were in a celebratory mood, even though their work was not yet complete. The First Troop of the City Light Horse, the same elite group of militiamen who had greeted George Washington upon his arrival to the city on May 13, staged a party in honor of the general, and many of the delegates joined in the festivities. The fifty-five gentlemen present at the dinner consumed fifty-four bottles of Madeira, sixty bottles of claret, fifty bottles of "old stock," copious quantities of porter, beer, and cider, and some large bowls of rum punch. Apparently the food, drink, and merriment enjoyed by the gentlemen got out of control, for along with the bill for the food and drink, the management of City Tavern took the unusual step of presenting the First Troop with an additional bill for "breakage."[32]

September 15, the penultimate day of the Convention, would be a long one, with the delegates continuing their business until after six in the evening. It began with Daniel Carroll of Maryland proposing that the Convention prepare a general address to the people of the United States explaining their actions. The delegates must have greeted Carroll's proposal with silent groans. Gouverneur Morris's letter transmitting the Constitution to the Confederation Congress had already satisfied some of that need, and the delegates were loathe to engage in a long, drawn-out debate on the fine points of a defense of their Constitution at this late stage. John Rutledge, in what was becoming a familiar refrain from him, "objected on account of the delay it would produce," a sentiment shared by nearly everyone present.[33]

Much of the remainder of the morning was spent on various self-interested attempts to increase the number of representatives that individual states would have in the House of Representatives. John Langdon of New Hampshire proposed adding a member to the delegations of North Carolina and Rhode Island. Charles Pinckney supported the proposal to increase North Carolina's representation, but not that of Rhode Island. Gunning Bedford of Delaware wanted to increase both Delaware's and Rhode Island's representation. All of these attempts were beaten back, and the delegates moved on to a few important final matters.[34]

About midday, Roger Sherman made a final effort to tilt the balance of power between the federal government and the states a bit more toward the states. In particular, he wanted to add further safeguards to the rights of the smaller states. Sherman proposed that the safeguards extended to the Southern states with respect to the importation of slaves ought to be extended to smaller states in two areas. First, he wanted an absolute guarantee that the states would have control over their own "internal police," by which he meant that federal armies in no case be allowed to march into a state unless specifically requested to do so by that state. Most important, Sherman wanted guarantees that the provision guaranteeing equal representation for each state in the Senate would not be changed by subsequent constitutional amendment. Gouverneur Morris, attempting to placate Sherman, agreed to add to Article V the language, "No state, without its consent shall be deprived of its equal suffrage in the Senate." Madison, editorializing in his notes, commented, "This motion being dictated by the circulating murmurs of the small States, was agreed to without debate, no one opposing it."[35]

THREE VOICES OF DISSENT

This was pretty much the end of any tinkering with the finished product, but the sound and fury were yet to come. Edmund Randolph was the first to speak out. His primary concern was the "indefinite and dangerous power given by the Constitution to Congress"—a puzzling complaint given the fact that aside from the explicit enumeration of powers championed by Randolph himself in the Committee of Detail report, the powers of Congress in the completed Constitution were not notably greater than those contemplated in the Virginia Plan. Randolph then announced that his minimum requirement for signing the Constitution would be the inclusion of an amendment providing for the calling of a second general convention to consider amendments proposed by the state ratifying conventions.[36]

George Mason was next, agreeing with Randolph "on the dangerous power and structure of the government," predicting that "it would end

either in monarchy or a tyrannical aristocracy." Mason's language during the final weeks of the Convention had become increasingly over-
heated, bordering on paranoia. He was among that generation of "old
republicans" who, having experienced the threat to liberty posed by the
British during the Revolution, were inclined to invoke similar fears of
aristocracy and monarchy when confronted with *any* form of energetic
government. Less able than many of his younger counterparts to envision the difference between the potency of a government founded on
popular consent and one founded on the principle of the divine right of
kingship, Mason instinctively feared the ill effects of too much, rather
than too little, government.[37]

Had these denunciations come from a blustering Luther Martin, the
delegates would probably have simply ignored them, but Mason and
Randolph were prestigious and influential members of the Convention's
most powerful state delegation. Charles Pinckney responded, acknowledging that the objections from delegates "so respectable" as Randolph
and Mason "give a peculiar solemnity to the present moment." He admitted that he too had misgivings about aspects of the document. He
disliked what he described as "the contemptible weakness and dependence of the executive," and, with South Carolina's slave-based agricultural interest in mind, he wished as well that more than a mere majority
in Congress would be required for bills regulating commerce. But he
then reminded his colleagues of the dire alternative. "Apprehending the
danger of a general confusion, and an ultimate decision by the sword, I
shall give the plan my support." As for Randolph and Mason's proposal
for a second general convention to consider amendments proposed by
the state ratifying conventions, Pinckney thought that such a method
would prove disastrous, with "nothing but confusion and contrariety"
arising from the measure.[38]

The last speech of the day was given by the Convention's most consistently ornery delegate. If the already departed Luther Martin was the
most bombastic delegate in Philadelphia that summer, Elbridge Gerry
was the most consistently contrary. Gerry listed eleven objections "which
determined him to withhold his name from the Constitution." These
ranged from relatively minor issues such as the length of senators' terms
to the power of Congress over determining the places of election and setting the compensation of its members. Gerry also believed that "Massachusetts has not a due share of representation allotted to her." Reiterating
an objection he had frequently voiced, he strongly opposed the provision

that "three-fifths of the blacks are to be represented as if they were freemen." Gerry gave no sign that his concern about the three-fifths clause had anything to do with morality. He simply believed that if slaves were considered to be property, then other forms of property ought to be counted in apportioning representation as well.[39]

All of those objections, Gerry asserted, were secondary to his primary concern that the Constitution rendered the "right of the citizens . . . insecure." The most serious threat in his view was the "necessary and proper" clause in Article II, Section 8—including the unlimited power of the government to raise armies and the provision to try some civil cases without juries. Gerry concluded by joining Mason and Randolph in calling for a second general convention.[40]

Having had their say, the three dissenting delegates found themselves isolated from the rest of their colleagues. As the long day wound to a close, the delegates first voted on Randolph's proposal for a second convention. "All the states answered—no." However much many of the delegates may have wished for changes in some particular features of the proposed Constitution, they were solidly and emphatically opposed to the prospect of yet another convention that would reopen all of the questions they had spent the long summer debating. The second vote, recorded simply in Madison's notes, stated that "on the question to agree to the Constitution, as amended. All the States Ay." The Constitution was then ordered to be engrossed on parchment in preparation for signing. On that note, the delegates adjourned for the day.[41]

Having already indulged in a full-fledged blowout the night before, the delegates may have relished the prospect of spending the remainder of the weekend peacefully before their final meeting on Monday. General Washington spent a quiet evening at Robert Morris's on Saturday and then a relaxing day on Sunday with the Morris family at their country estate. William Samuel Johnson recorded in his diary—"Dinner at City Tavern, 6 O'Clock." James Madison, no doubt eager to see all of his hard work brought to a successful conclusion on the coming Monday, dealt with a more practical concern that weekend. He had run out of money. Since he was due to return to New York as one of Virginia's delegates to the Confederation Congress once the Convention had adjourned, he managed to borrow one hundred dollars from his Virginia colleague John Blair.[42]

One little-known figure in the history of the Constitution was busy for the remainder of that weekend. Jacob Shallus, assistant clerk to the

Pennsylvania legislature, was given the job of engrossing the completed document on parchment. He began immediately, using quill pens made from large goose feathers and ink made from oak galls, iron, and gum Arabic. He first drew guidelines along the parchment using a pale brown crayon, and then, working from a revised and expanded copy of the Report of the Committee on Style, he set to work. The result—four elegant parchment pages of text—was ready for the delegates by the time they reassembled on Monday, September 17.[43]

CHAPTER NINETEEN

SEPTEMBER 17:
DAY OF DECISION

MONDAY, SEPTEMBER 17, brought a crystal clear sky that grew into a deep blue as the sun rose higher. The temperature—barely in the fifties—made it feel more like late fall. But it was a beautiful, invigorating day, and with the exception of the three holdouts—Randolph, Mason, and Gerry—the delegates made their way to the Pennsylvania State House from their private homes and boardinghouses with feelings of anticipation, pride, and profound relief. Forty-one out of the original fifty-five delegates present at one time or another during that summer were in attendance.[1]

The session began with the Convention's secretary, William Jackson, reading aloud the full text of the Constitution. The preamble specifically affirmed that this was indeed a constitution—a statement of fundamental principles of government and not merely a collection of articles in a treaty defining the terms under which the sovereign states would enter into a union. By the standards of most constitutions, that of the United States is remarkably short. But after nearly four months, the task of listening to every word of every article, section, subsection, and clause— many of them debated and amended many times over—may have seemed an unnecessarily time-consuming one, clocking in at thirty-two minutes. Each of the delegates had his copy of the Report of the Committee of Style and, depending on his diligence over the course of the previous few days, could compare handwritten emendations with those read aloud.[2]

That task completed, "Doctor Franklin rose with a speech in his hand," which, Madison noted, "he had reduced to writing" in order that he could choose his words carefully. Franklin had spent at least some of the weekend composing the speech. His vanity—a minor vice cheerfully acknowledged in his autobiography—may have led him to hope that his would be the final words spoken at the Convention. Whatever his own impulses, it is also likely that Franklin's Pennsylvania colleagues—especially James Wilson and Gouverneur Morris, but perhaps Virginia's Madison as well—may have approached Franklin and encouraged him to give the Convention's valedictory.[3]

Franklin's very presence at the Convention, along with Washington's, had given the gathering a weight and legitimacy that it otherwise would have lacked. Washington, who had not delivered a single speech during the formal proceedings in the Assembly Room throughout the entirety of the summer, nevertheless played a crucial role as president of the Convention—guiding the deliberations and making important decisions about whom to recognize and whom to ignore in the give-and-take of debate. In spite of his poor health, Franklin had attended virtually every session from May 28 onward; he had been fully engaged with the proceedings and had spoken frequently. He had gone to the mat on several important occasions, as when on June 30 he presented a version of what would become the Connecticut Compromise, defending it with a wonderful combination of Franklinian insight and simplicity. But he had also allowed himself more than a few moments of self-indulgence, discoursing off the point or offering historical examples not always germane to the issue at hand. His fellow delegates respected and admired him, but at times they must have rolled their eyes heavenward as he launched into one of his digressions.

Franklin rose but then handed the speech to James Wilson, who would read it for his friend and senior colleague. Looking back over the nearly four months of debate, disagreement, and occasional outbursts of ill temper, Franklin observed that whenever "you assemble a number of men to have the advantage of their joint wisdom, you inevitably assemble with those men all their prejudices, their passions, their errors of opinion, their local interests, and their selfish views. From such an assembly can a perfect production be expected?" The wonder of it all, Franklin asserted, was that the delegates had somehow managed to create a system of government "approaching so near to perfection as it does."[4]

Franklin acknowledged there were "several parts of this Constitution which I do not at present approve," but, he added, "the older I grow the more apt I am to doubt my own judgment and pay more respect to the judgment of others." And in that spirit, Franklin announced, "I agree to this Constitution with all its faults, if they are such, because I think a general government necessary for us. . . . I doubt too whether any other Convention we can obtain may be able to make a better Constitution."

Franklin then appealed to the delegates' sense of humility and fallibility. "If every one of us," he warned, "in returning to our constituents were to report the objections he has had to it, and endeavour to gain partisans in support of [those objections], we might prevent it being generally received, and thereby lose all the salutary effects and great advantages resulting naturally in our favor . . . from our real or apparent unanimity." He then asked that "every member of the convention who may still have objections to [the Constitution] would, with me, on this occasion doubt a little of his own infallibility—and to make manifest our unanimity—by putting his name to this instrument."

Franklin's appeal to the delegates concluded with a formal proposal that "the Constitution be signed by the members [in] . . . a convenient form, viz. Done in Convention, by the unanimous consent of *the states* present the 17th of September. . . . In Witness whereof we have hereunto subscribed our names."[5]

The "convenient form" Franklin proposed—that of asking each delegate to sign the Constitution in recognition of the "unanimous consent of the states present"—was a ploy conceived by Gouverneur Morris "in order to gain the dissenting members." The dissenting members were not being asked to signal their own approval of the Constitution, but merely to acknowledge that their state delegations had approved it. Morris hoped that this strategy, "put into the hands of Doctor Franklin," might be sufficient to produce at least the appearance of unanimity.[6]

If the script for the Constitutional Convention had been conceived and directed by a Hollywood filmmaker, Franklin's speech would have been the final one of the Convention, with perhaps a few gracious closing words from Washington. But this was real life, and so other voices—some supportive and others dissonant—would have to be heard before the Convention could be done with its business. Nathaniel Gorham now rose with a note of apology in his voice—as if he were aware of the inappropriateness of intruding on Dr. Franklin's moment—and asked if it might lessen objections to the Constitution if the clause setting the ratio of representation from one to forty thousand was changed to one to thirty thousand. After his motion was seconded by Rufus King of Massachusetts and Daniel Carroll of Maryland, George Washington rose and, incredibly, made the only substantive speech he is known to have made during the whole of the Convention.

He noted that his role as presiding officer had "hitherto restrained him from offering his sentiments on questions depending in the House," and admitted that the same principle "ought now to impose silence on him." He nevertheless chose on this sole occasion to speak in support of Gorham's resolution to reduce the ratio of representation. Washington's speech was neither eloquent nor forceful. He merely "acknowledged that it [the one to forty thousand ratio] had always appeared to himself among the exceptionable parts of the plan." Like many in the Convention, he believed that smaller congressional districts would ensure a closer relationship between representatives and their constituents, and he hoped that the proposed change might reduce the number of those opposing the Constitution.

Whatever the personal opinion of the delegates on the relative merits of the two formulas for representation, this was hardly a moment when anyone wanted to pick a fight with General Washington! Gorham's amendment passed unanimously. It seems unlikely that any of the delegates—even the most disaffected—would vote against Washington on the only occasion on which he had voiced an opinion.[7]

We are still left with the question of why Washington would choose to break his silence on this particular issue. The only plausible answer is that he knew this would be his last chance to speak on a matter on which his words might elicit unanimity among the delegates. He did not want to see the Convention end before seizing that one last opportunity.

But so much for unanimity. Edmund Randolph, plainly uncomfortable about rebuffing Franklin's conciliatory speech, "apologized for refusing to sign the Constitution, notwithstanding the vast majority and venerable names that would give sanction to its wisdom and worth." He left open the possibility that he might, in the end, support its adoption during the ratification debates, but for the moment, he would refuse to sign because he believed that the people of the states would not accept the Constitution in its present form.[8]

Gouverneur Morris rose to answer Randolph, reminding the delegates that they were being asked to sign the document not as an affirmation of their own individual appraisal but of the unanimity existing among the state delegations present. Echoing Franklin, he admitted that "I too have objections, but considering the present plan as the best that was to be attained, I should take it with all its faults." The alternative, Morris argued hyperbolically, was the onset of a "general anarchy" across the nation.[9]

The extent of Morris's reservations about the completed draft remains a point of uncertainty. He is said later to have commented that "I not only took it as a man does his wife, for better, for worse, but what few men do with their wives, I took it knowing all its bad qualities." That retrospective assessment no doubt contained a measure of truth, but it is likely that at that moment he felt considerable pride at the magnitude of his accomplishment.[10]

Hugh Williamson and Alexander Hamilton echoed Morris in asking the discontented few to put aside their misgivings in favor of unanimity. Hamilton actually had no technical right to sign the Constitution, because the absence of his two naysaying New York colleagues, Yates and Lansing, meant that New York was not even entitled to vote on the document. This did not, however, stop him from making his own speech urging all of the delegates to sign and, when the time came, stepping forward and affixing his name to the document. Hamilton warned ominously that a "few characters of consequence by opposing or even refusing to sign the constitution, might do infinite mischief." Acknowledging his position at the far right of the political spectrum, he reminded the delegates that "no man's ideas were more remote from the plan than his own were known to be; but it is possible to deliberate between anarchy and convulsion on the one side, and the chance of good to be expected from the plan on the other."[11]

At least one delegate, William Blount of North Carolina, was brought into line by the strategy conceived by Morris and articulated by Franklin. Following Hamilton's speech, Blount announced that though he had not intended to sign the document, "I am relieved by the form proposed and will without committing myself, attest to the fact that the plan was the unanimous act of the states in the Convention."[12]

Randolph, Mason, and Gerry would stand their ground. Randolph was obviously torn, and possibly repentant. As Madison recorded Randolph's final words on that day, "In refusing to sign the Constitution, I take a step which might be the most awful of my life, but it is [a step] dictated by my conscience, and it is not possible for me to hesitate, much less, to change." Elbridge Gerry, though admitting "the painful feelings of his situation," was more combative in reiterating his objections. Gerry, along with Mason, was still clinging to his old classical republican fears. With the tumult of Shays' Rebellion still in mind, he continued to worry "that a Civil War may result from the present crisis of the United States." The source of that crisis, Gerry believed, was the clash of two opposing parties, "one devoted to democracy, the worst of all political evils, the other as violent in the opposite extreme." It was for these reasons that he had supported the idea of a Convention, but he now concluded that the final result of the Convention combined some of the worst elements of each of the two extremes. Unlike Randolph, who seemed genuinely pained not to join Franklin (not to mention his fellow Virginian, George Washington, whom he had literally begged to come to the Convention), Gerry appeared to resent Franklin's remarks, commenting acidly that "I cannot . . . but view them as leveled at myself and the other gentlemen who meant not to sign."[13]

Franklin's speech had accomplished as much as it could, but no more. It had brought William Blount into the camp of those willing to sign the Constitution, but two South Carolina delegates, Charles Cotesworth Pinckney and Pierce Butler, "disliked the equivocal form of the signing" proposed in Franklin's motion. On that note of mild discord, the delegates voted on Franklin's motion. "Done in Convention by the unanimous consent of *the States* present the 17th of September . . . In Witness thereof we have hereunto subscribed our names." Franklin's motion passed, with ten states in favor and South Carolina divided.[14]

Before proceeding to the formal signing, the delegates spent several minutes trying to decide what to do with the official journals of the Convention that were kept, however haphazardly, by William Jackson. The delegates' fear, as Rufus King expressed it, was that "if suffered to be made public a bad use would be made of them." The two suggestions put forward were either to destroy them—a decision that would have made the scanty Convention record even scantier—or to deposit them in the custody of the president of the Convention. The delegates agreed to the latter scheme by a vote of ten states to one, with the Maryland delegates objecting because they had been explicitly instructed by their legislature to report the proceedings of the Convention back to their state.[15]

This left the "president," General Washington, in a bit of a quandary. What was he supposed to do with the Convention papers, and what if members of the Convention asked him for copies? The delegates ultimately decided that Washington should hold the papers under conditions of strict secrecy until a "Congress, if ever formed under the Constitution," could give him further instructions. Washington would officially convey the journals of the Convention to the Department of State in December 1796, just before he left office as president, and the Congress continued to impose a prohibition against publishing them until 1818.[16]

Left unresolved was what the other delegates would do with their materials from the Convention. Nearly all of the delegates had, with varying degrees of diligence, retained copies of the various drafts and reports that had been produced by the Convention, and several had made notes along the way. The most thorough of these were produced by Madison, who had taken extraordinary pains to record the proceedings. Remarkably, given the size of the egos and the diversity of personalities present at the Convention, the delegates who had kept their own diaries and notes during the Convention kept their resolve as well, waiting until the Congress lifted its ban on their publication. From that time forward, bit by bit, various delegates—or their descendants—began to make portions of their notes public.[17]

Again, Madison presents the most interesting case. He began to review his notes and make revisions, entering into an active correspondence with a number of key figures, soon after the Convention journals were published in 1819. However, he remained true to a pledge he had made to himself—to withhold the publication of his notes until after his death, in 1836.[18]

"THE MEMBERS THEN PROCEEDED TO SIGN THE INSTRUMENT"

With those simple words, Madison recorded the epochal event of the Constitutional Convention. At about three in the afternoon, beginning with the New Hampshire delegates, moving southward to Massachusetts, then progressing down the eastern seaboard, and ending with Georgia, the delegates moved to the table at the center of the east wall of the Assembly Room where Washington had presided, picked up the goose quill pen, dipped it in ink, and signed their names to the document. All of those who stepped forward to sign the fourth of the parchment sheets shared in varying degrees the same tentativeness and diffidence so eloquently (and cleverly) described by Franklin in his speech earlier in the day. They all believed they had framed a document that would create "a more perfect union," but no one believed that they had achieved perfection.[19]

Among the ardent nationalists, Gouverneur Morris still believed that too much authority had been left with the state governments and too much power within the new government had been given to the small states. Alexander Hamilton was of much the same mind. He no doubt thought the Constitution too republican and insufficiently British in its inspiration.

The two Connecticut delegates still present at the Convention, Roger Sherman and William Samuel Johnson, had considerable cause for pride. Their intervention helped produce the compromise between large and small states, and they had successfully moderated some of the more extreme impulses of the most zealous nationalist delegates. For better or for worse, they had played a key role in brokering the compromise that provided protection for the slave states of the lower South. Yet Sherman, who had consistently argued for an executive authority that would merely be the agent of the legislature, must have still harbored fears about the overly powerful presidential role created by the Constitution.

William Paterson had left the Convention on July 23, and in spite of entreaties by his fellow New Jersey delegates to return, he had resolutely refused. He managed, however, to summon up the energy to make the short trip across the Delaware River from Trenton to Philadelphia in time to sign the document on September 17. Although he had grudgingly abandoned his attachment to his own New Jersey Plan and voted in favor of the Connecticut Compromise, he was still not wholly reconciled to the diminution of state equality and power inherent in the Constitution. As a testimony to how time, and success, can change one's perspective, Paterson would deliver orations just a few years later in which he would take pride in his role in drafting the Constitution and praise it as "the ark of safety and the palladium of our liberties."[20]

As the delegates from the slave-owning states moved forward to the president's table, they were hardly of one mind about the virtues and imperfections of the Constitution. Many delegates from both the upper and lower South continued to worry that Congress's power to regulate commerce by a mere majority vote would work to the disadvantage of the agricultural-staple-producing states. But whatever misgivings individual delegates from the slave-owning states may have harbored, most of them had spoken consistently on the side of a stronger federal union. Moreover, the South Carolina and Georgia delegates—with help from some of their colleagues to the North—had managed to write into the Constitution protections for slavery that would work decisively to their advantage for years to come.

The two most prominent Virginia signers—James Madison and George Washington—were reserved in their assessments of the finished product. At the end of his life, looking back on the events of that summer, Madison would characterize the conduct and outcome of the Convention in extravagant terms, claiming that "collectively and individually . . . there never was an assembly of men, charged with a great and arduous trust, who were more pure in their motives or more exclusively or anxiously devoted to the object committed to them than were the members of the Federal Convention of 1787."[21]

Yet at the moment Madison stepped forward to sign the Constitution, his pride in his accomplishment was almost certainly tempered by the sting of at least a few defeats. He was disappointed that the feature giving the federal government a negative on state laws had been deleted from the Constitution, and he continued to feel deeply aggrieved about the compromise that had given the smaller states equal representation in the Senate. He persisted in believing that the Connecticut Compromise was a serious blow to the fundamental principle that the new government was to be directly representative of the people of the nation and not of the states. He was acutely aware that he had not achieved all that he had wished when he first set out to launch his revolution in government. But those misgivings notwithstanding, the real wonder is that he had achieved as much as he did.[22]

George Washington, though a member of the Virginia delegation, had, as president, been the first to sign. His diary entry for September 17 tells us less about his feelings about the Constitution itself than about the arduousness of the process. After the Convention adjourned, he dined with the delegates at City Tavern and then returned to his lodgings, where, after receiving the Convention papers from William Jackson, he "retired to meditate on the momentous work Which had been executed, after not less than five, for a large part of the time six, and sometimes 7 hours sitting every day [except] Sunday . . . for more than four months."[23]

DR. FRANKLIN WOULD, after all, have the last word. As the line of delegates waiting to sign the Constitution was nearing its end, the old philosopher-statesman looked up at the Chippendale-style chair Washington had occupied during that summer. Fashioned by a local cabinetmaker, John Folwell, it had a red leather seat and a high back—on the center of which was carved a half-sunburst—and was topped by a Phrygian Liberty cap on a pike, an ancient Roman symbol of freedom. As the final delegate—Abraham Baldwin of Georgia—added his name to the list of signers, Franklin's attention turned to that sunburst.[24]

Although too frail to rise from his chair, Franklin spoke in his own words on this occasion. He confided to the delegates that he had, "in the course of the session, and the vicissitudes of my hopes and fears as to its issue," gazed at the sunburst on the back of the president's chair "without being able to tell whether it was rising or setting." With a note of deep satisfaction, Franklin announced that "now at length I have the happiness to know that it is a rising and not a setting sun."[25]

"At length I have the happiness to know that it is a rising and not a setting sun." Close-up photo of Rising Sun Chair, courtesy of Independence National Historical Park.

CHAPTER TWENTY

THE PEOPLE'S CONSTITUTION: "FEDERALISTS" SEIZE THE INITIATIVE

WHEN THE CONVENTION ADJOURNED shortly past three o'clock on Monday, September 17, the delegates went off to City Tavern to dine and, in Washington's words, "took a cordial leave of each other." Unlike the boisterous affair a few nights earlier, this dinner was subdued, with most of the delegates making an early evening of it.[1]

Few of the delegates in Philadelphia wasted time leaving town. General Washington departed sometime in the late afternoon of September 18. That morning he paid his respects to "those families in which I had been most intimate." He shared a final meal with the Morris family and then set off in his carriage for Mount Vernon. Robert Morris rode with him as far as Gray's Ferry, at which point Washington's fellow Virginia delegate John Blair joined him for the ride the rest of the way to Mount Vernon.[2]

No fewer than ten of the delegates present at the Philadelphia Convention on September 17—Langdon and Gilman of New Hampshire, Gorham and King of Massachusetts, William Samuel Johnson of Connecticut, James Madison, William Blount of North Carolina, Pierce Butler of South Carolina, and William Few and William Pierce of Georgia—were preparing to move northward to attend the meetings of the Confederation Congress in New York. James Madison, ever diligent, remained in Philadelphia for several days, editing and adding to the voluminous notes he had taken of the Convention's proceedings. He might have stayed even longer, but he received a message from his Virginia colleague Edward Carrington urging him to travel to New York without delay in order to prevent a few of the members of the Virginia delegation to the Congress—Richard Henry Lee and William Henry Grayson in particular—from sabotaging the proposed Constitution before it could even be given a fair hearing.[3]

THE CONTEST OF INTERESTS AND IDEAS

As the Convention adjourned, in the early evening of September 17, the words engrossed on the four sheets of parchment were nothing more than opinion. They lacked the sanction of the Confederation Congress, of the state governments, and of the people of the nation at large. Nine years later, James Madison, looking back on the process of constitution making, observed,

> Whatever veneration might be entertained for the body of men who formed our Constitution, the sense of that body could never be regarded as the oracular guide in expounding the Constitution. As the instrument came from them it was nothing more than the draft of a plan, nothing but a dead letter, until life and validity had been breathed into it by the voice of the people, speaking through the several State Conventions.[4]

The delegates who had labored that summer in Philadelphia knew the next step in the process of constitution making would be far from easy. The story of how the "framers' Constitution" became the "peoples' Constitution" is not one story, but thirteen, with varying plots, subplots, and a highly disparate cast of characters.

The quality and tone of the debate over the Constitution in the Assembly Room of the State House during the summer of 1787 was in part a product of the intellect, talent, and experience represented in that body. But it was also given substantial encouragement by the manner in which the Convention proceeded—with the delegates' deliberations occurring away from the glare of the public eye and with a set of rules that allowed them to remain flexible in the positions they took from one day to the next. This was not the case in the debate on ratification. The ratification of the United States Constitution featured an unprecedented degree of popular involvement in deciding a fundamental political question before the nation. Unlike state or local political campaigns of the past, where multiple candidates and issues often rendered the meaning of any outcome confusing, the decision facing Americans during ratification was starkly straightforward—a simple yes or no.

Both the supporters and the opponents of the Constitution would use all of the tricks at their disposal to effect an outcome in their favor. The ability of each side to reach people with their arguments across the vast expanse of America would be crucial in the contest, and in this regard, the supporters of the Constitution had a decisive advantage. News of the proposed Constitution circulated quickly. A copy of the document was first published in the Pennsylvania *Packet,* which devoted its entire issue on September 19 to reproducing the text. That edition of the *Packet* was quickly circulated to newspapers across the country.[5]

FIRST STOP

The first stop for the proposed Constitution was the Confederation Congress, which had done very little business that summer. It was, however, unlikely to remain somnolent now. The Congress formally received a copy of the Constitution on September 20, and copies began to appear in the New York newspapers the same day. By September 20, nine states had a quorum of their delegates present in New York. Within a few days eleven states were represented, with only Maryland and Rhode Island still missing. Since some members who had been delegates to the Philadelphia Convention had not yet arrived, the Congress set September 26 as the day on which discussion of the document would begin.[6]

As the Confederation Congress gathered that day, they found that ten of the thirty-three delegates present had been members of the Convention in Philadelphia, which seemed to bode well for speedy and affirmative action. But endorsement of the Constitution by the Congress was by no means a foregone conclusion, for there were at that point at least a few Americans who were familiar with the Constitution and disliked it, and they were preparing a modest counterattack. The bitterness of George Mason of Virginia over the proposed Constitution had only increased during the last weeks of the Convention, and it seemed to intensify in the days immediately after adjournment. On September 15, after it had become clear that the Constitution was going to be approved by the

Convention, Mason began to write out his "Objections to This Constitution of Government" on the blank pages of his copy of the Report of
the Committee of Style. It was a detailed critique. He began by lament-
ing the absence of a bill of rights, then moved on to complain that the
House of Representatives was too small and would provide "the shadow
only of representation." He complained that the executive branch, together with the Senate, possessed altogether too much power. He concluded with the gloomy prediction that "this government will set out
(commence) a moderate aristocracy; it is at present impossible to foresee
whether it will, in its operation, produce a monarchy, or a corrupt, tyrannical (oppressive) aristocracy; it will most probably vibrate some years
between the two, and then terminate in the one or the other." As soon as
the Convention adjourned, Mason began to circulate his ruminations,
first to a few of his close Virginia political allies and later in printed form.
Two who received it were Richard Henry Lee and William Henry
Grayson, the two Virginia members of the Congress whose opposition
James Madison most feared.[7]

Richard Henry Lee, who along with Patrick Henry had declined to
serve in the Philadelphia Convention, was among the first to object to
the new Constitution when the Congress began its discussion of the document on September 26. The Convention had, Lee believed, committed
a "constitutional impropriety" in scrapping the Articles of Confederation. He then presented an elaborate set of amendments that, in addition
to a declaration of rights, included a proposal for a council of state, similar to those existing in several states, that would simultaneously advise
and restrain the president. Lee's critique was supported by New Yorkers,
like Robert Yates and John Lansing, who, after leaving the Convention
early, were now, according to James Madison's informant, Edward Carrington, "active in spreading the seeds of opposition."[8]

Although the supporters and opponents of the Constitution in the
Congress skirmished during the sessions on September 26 and 27, the
supporters, who had begun to call themselves Federalists, had the numbers on their side. Late in the day on September 28, the Congress passed
a resolution that read, "Having received the report from the Convention
lately assembled in Philadelphia, Resolved Unanimously that the said report, together with the resolutions and letter accompanying the same, be
transmitted to the several state legislatures." The reference to unanimity
referred only to the willingness—grudging on the part of many—to
transmit the "report" to the states. The resolution even omitted the word
"constitution" in referring to the Convention's work.[9]

Richard Henry Lee would become a leader of the still-inchoate group of people who would later become known as Antifederalists. Unhappy that Congress had agreed even to transmit the Constitution to the states, Lee objected both to the "greatness of the powers" of the new government and also to "the coalition of monarchy men, military men, aristocrats, and drones" who, he believed, were certain to control the affairs of this "consolidated government." Lee's denunciation of monarchy, aristocracy, and excessive concentrations of power followed closely those of his Virginia neighbor, George Mason. Lee, even more than Mason, was a slave-owning, planter-gentry man whose manner of living strongly mirrored the cultural norms of the British aristocracy. As embodiments of Virginia's "natural aristocracy," their denunciations of monarchy and hereditary aristocracy were no doubt sincere, but certainly a part of their opposition to the proposed Constitution was shaped by their desire to protect the political autonomy of their home state—and all of the privileges that they and many other planter gentry enjoyed.[10]

THE FEDERALIST ADVANTAGE

By succeeding in getting the Confederation Congress to release the proposed Constitution to the state legislatures on the terms proposed in the Convention, the supporters of the Constitution had capitalized on one of the factors working most decisively in their favor—momentum. The Philadelphia Convention had been called because political leaders and opinion makers in many parts of the country believed that all was not well with the Confederation government, a belief given added urgency by the threat—real or perceived—posed by Shays' Rebellion. During the four months that the delegates were cloistered in secrecy that sense of unease only increased. Although the newspapers across the country were as much in the dark about what was going on inside the Pennsylvania State House as any of America's citizens, most of the publishers of those newspapers were temperamentally and professionally inclined to reinforce the sense of crisis and to advocate a stronger central government to set things right.[11]

As the delegates emerged from their secret conclave, they recognized the importance of maintaining their momentum as they approached their state ratifying conventions. Their investment of four months of debate and disputation inside the State House would make them formidable adversaries. Many of the objections they would confront in the coming months had been raised, debated, and resolved over the course of the summer.

To be sure, there were naysayers among them. Of the three men who had refused to sign the Constitution, two—Mason and Gerry—would try to rally Antifederalist forces. And a few more who had bolted from the Convention early—especially Lansing and Yates of New York and Luther Martin of Maryland—were better prepared than most to marshal arguments against the Constitution. But the small band of dissidents from the Convention was no match for those who would lead the effort to secure ratification. From New England to the lower South, the advocates of the Constitution were able to mobilize those members of the Convention with real intellectual firepower—Rufus King, Roger Sherman, Alexander Hamilton, James Wilson, John Dickinson, James Madison, John Rutledge, and Charles Pinckney—who were capable of convincing people in their home states that the document was a worthy one. As one Antifederalist complained, in nearly every state ratifying Convention, the opponents of the Constitution "were browbeaten by many of those Ciceros as they think themselves and others of Superior rank." Finally, even though General Washington and the wise Dr. Franklin did not actively involve themselves in the ratification struggle, their well-publicized support of the document proved an invaluable asset.[12]

Not only did the Federalists have the intellectual advantage, but they also enjoyed substantial control over the means of disseminating their points of view and rebutting the arguments of their opponents. Of the hundred or so newspapers in circulation in America at the time, only a few actively supported the Antifederalist side. One Antifederalist grumbled that newspaper editors, "afraid to offend the great men," closed their columns to opposition writers. As historian Gordon Wood has observed, the "Antifederalists were not so much beaten as overawed."[13]

The Constitution's advocates also enjoyed another critical advantage. They had a specific object for their advocacy—the Constitution itself. Madison in particular recognized the importance of this advantage. For that reason, he fiercely resisted any attempt by the Constitution's opponents to initiate discussions aimed at amending individual portions of the document, for he realized that such debates could prove nearly endless. To a remarkable extent, the Federalists were successful in demanding that the proposed Constitution be voted up or down, and this would play a significant role in its ultimate fate. Even some of the most severe critics of the Constitution were not in favor of maintaining the status quo as it existed under the Articles of Confederation. The tactics of the Constitution's supporters, together with the near impossibility of gaining the necessary unanimity among the states to amend the Articles of Confederation, put those critics on the defensive, leaving them to argue against the Constitution as it was presently written but hindered in their ability to present a preferable alternative in a timely fashion.[14]

The fact that the advocates of the Constitution self-consciously depicted themselves as agents of change and their opponents as defenders of the status quo opened up another opportunity for the Federalists. When Madison and his Pennsylvania colleagues launched their revolution in late May, they had explicitly argued that a "merely federal" government would not be sufficient to the nation's needs—that what was required was a truly "national" government, with a "supreme legislative, judiciary, and executive." By mid-July, however, in the wake of the Connecticut Compromise, they were more often than not referring to their brainchild as a "federal" government, and in the debate over ratification, they were successful in appropriating—or, perhaps more accurately, *expropriating*—the name "Federalists" for themselves. Their opponents, who believed in a confederation of sovereign states in which specifically enumerated powers might be delegated to the central government, were the true federalists in the traditional meaning of the term, but they were stuck with the unattractive and singularly negative-sounding designation of "Antifederalists."

The greatest challenge facing these self-described Federalists was to maintain their momentum in the face of attempts by Antifederalists either to impede or at least to stall their progress toward ratification. Since the language of the Constitution stipulated that the ratification of nine states was necessary to put the new government into operation, theoretically each state—no matter what its size—carried equal weight in the ratification process. In reality the contest over ratification in Pennsylvania, Massachusetts, and Virginia would have a decisive effect on the actions of many other states.

THE CONTEST IN PENNSYLVANIA

The order by which states considered the proposed Constitution was left entirely up to the legislatures of the individual states, who were responsible for calling the ratifying conventions. The Pennsylvania General Assembly, which had been pushed upstairs into the grand hallway on the second floor for the final twelve days that the Constitutional Convention continued in session, received a copy of the Constitution immediately after the Convention adjourned. Because of that accident of timing, the state of Pennsylvania would provide the most important initial test of the Constitution's popularity.

The politics of Pennsylvania had been tumultuous from the moment that its radically democratic Constitution had been adopted in 1776. But at the moment of the adjournment of the Philadelphia Convention, a group of relatively conservative and on the whole nationalistic legislators—closely connected to the Pennsylvania Convention delegates themselves—enjoyed a healthy majority in the Assembly. It didn't hurt either that Benjamin Franklin, the current "president" of Pennsylvania, was closely identified with the document that had emerged from the summer's deliberations.

The strongly Federalist-leaning Assembly was eager to act on the proposed Constitution immediately, but it had to wait for the official submission of the Constitution to the legislature from the Confederation Congress. Moreover, the legislature was due to adjourn on September 29. Facing the prospect of sitting helplessly while the legislature adjourned and then having to wait several months for it to reconvene in order to initiate the ratification process, the supporters of the Constitution in the Assembly jumped the gun. After waiting ten days with no word from the Congress in New York, Federalists in the Pennsylvania legislature passed resolutions laying out the rules for electing delegates to a state ratifying convention. The official authorization from the Congress arrived in Philadelphia by special courier late in the day on September 28, but the Federalist majority in the legislature could not act that day because nineteen Antifederalist members had deliberately absented themselves, thus preventing a quorum from being present. When the Assembly reconvened on September 29, the last day on which it would be in session, the nineteen members were still absent. At that point the exasperated Federalists recruited a gang of men to search the city to find the missing delegates. The exuberant gang approached their task with relish, and with just a few hours remaining before the Assembly was to adjourn, they found two of the delegates—James McCalmont of Franklin County and Jacob Miley of Dauphin County—hiding in their boardinghouses and dragged them back to the State House.[15]

The jeering, jubilant group of Philadelphia artisans and mechanics who had formed the search party jammed into the Assembly room, spilled out into the hallways, and clamored for the Assembly to vote. McCalmont and Miley, infuriated by their treatment but anxious to extricate themselves, offered to pay a fine for their absence rather than being forced to attend under such humiliating circumstances. But it wasn't to be. They were thrust into their seats and counted as present. With the necessary quorum, the Federalist majority immediately voted to call a ratifying convention, setting the date for elections to the convention for the first Tuesday in November, with the convention set to begin on November 21.[16]

Not only was the Pennsylvania Federalists' haste prompted by the impending recess and their desire to maintain momentum for constitutional change, but it was also a means of further undercutting the power of the supporters of the Pennsylvania Constitution of 1776. Most Federalists believed that the Pennsylvania state Constitution, with its annually elected single-house legislature and weak executive, had given too much power to the legislature and swung too far toward a democratic extreme.

Between September 29 and the opening of the Pennsylvania ratifying convention on November 21, the state's Federalists and Antifederalists engaged in a war of words, seeking to swing the unconverted over to their side. In Pennsylvania, as in subsequent state ratifying contests, attitudes toward the federal Constitution did not fall into the neat categories that a yes or no vote on the Constitution required. While Federalists like James Wilson led the charge, giving unequivocal support to the Constitution, many others ended up supporting it in spite of grave reservations.

There were similar variations of sentiment toward the Constitution in the camp of those who opposed ratification. Samuel Bryan, writing as "Centinel," had been an active supporter of Pennsylvania's democratic Constitution of 1776. Writing a day after the publication of George Mason's "Objections" in the Philadelphia newspapers, Centinel denounced the "wealthy and ambitious, who, in every community think they have the right to lord it over their fellow creatures." Echoing Mason, Bryan predicted that the adoption of the Constitution would lead to the creation of "a permanent aristocracy." He castigated the Federalists for demanding that the people rush to a judgment on the Constitution's merits, giving them "no alternative between adoption and absolute ruin."[17]

Bryan's Centinel essays gained unusually wide circulation, running in newspapers all over the country. They appealed openly to class antagonisms, arguing that the "wealthy and ambitious" were likely to be those most intent on "domination." The proposed Constitution, he argued, was precisely the sort of instrument that would enable those wealthy few to consolidate government power in their hands. Bryan's feelings were echoed in earthier terms by a humble tenant farmer from Carlisle, Pennsylvania. William Petrikin denounced the "destable [sic] Fedrall conspiracy" that had produced the document, claiming that it was a plot hatched by the "well-born" and "money men" who wished to impose aristocratic government on the ordinary people of America.[18]

More moderate Pennsylvania Antifederalists such as George Bryan or William Findley, on the other hand, avoided raising the specter of class warfare in their critique of the Constitution, focusing instead on the accomplishments of their own state government under the 1776 Constitution and questioning the need for the sort of radical overhaul envisioned by the proposed Constitution.[19]

The Federalists were more than prepared to meet the Antifederalists' objections. Although less powerful in Pennsylvania's backcountry, where support for the 1776 state Constitution and skepticism about *any* form of centralized government were strongest, the Federalists launched a powerful counterattack. James Wilson was by far the most articulate and outspoken of the advocates of the Constitution. He was joined in his advocacy by Tench Coxe, a particularly articulate Philadelphia businessman and politician and the young lexicographer Noah Webster. Interestingly, Gouverneur Morris, who was so active during the Convention, had turned back to his business affairs with a vengeance, apparently deciding that four months was more than enough time to devote to matters of state.[20]

As would be the case in every contest, the Pennsylvania Federalists' main challenge was to prevent their opponents from opening up a wide-ranging debate that would slow their momentum and allow proposals for delay and amendment to take hold. As another Federalist supporter, Thomas McKean, put it, though the supporters of the Constitution had an obligation "not to preclude, but to promote a free and ample discussion of the federal plan," they nevertheless needed to insist that the ultimate vote would be on the single question of whether to vote yes or no on the draft of the Constitution as presented.[21]

While it is not surprising that the Federalists' arguments would find the greatest support among the urban professional classes of Philadelphia, they were also embraced by many of the artisans and tradesmen of the city, for whom issues of social class may have been less important than the common desire for a government that would promote trade and commerce. In the lead-up to the election of delegates to the Pennsylvania ratifying convention, to be held on November 6, a large mob gathered outside the boardinghouse of Major Boyd, which lodged many of the Antifederalist delegates who had refused to attend the Pennsylvania Assembly sessions of September 28 and 29. "Here the damned rascals live who did all the mischief," cried out one of the gang members, and with that the mob began banging on the doors of Major Boyd's establishment, smashing the windows and creating general mayhem.[22]

Even James Wilson regarded this incident with mixed feelings, for he could not have failed to remember the time ten years earlier when an angry mob suspecting him of Toryism had assaulted his own house. Wilson would have preferred to engage the citizens of Philadelphia in a sophisticated philosophical debate. Nonetheless, on October 6 he found himself addressing a large crowd at a raucous public meeting in the State House yard. Standing before the crowd, he delivered a passionate but tightly reasoned defense of the handiwork of the Philadelphia framers. It was a magical moment. For perhaps the first time in the nation's history, a large crowd of ordinary citizens listened to a discourse not on the destruction of an empire—the subject of impassioned and often loosely reasoned speeches in the months leading up to independence—but on the fundamental principles on which America's new government should be founded. The speech was so well received that it was reprinted all across America.[23]

The Antifederalists knew they needed to respond immediately, and they did their best to paint Wilson as an elitist "tainted with the spirit of *high aristocracy*." But in spite of the efforts to use the language of social class against Wilson and the Constitution's supporters, working-class support of the Constitution in and around Philadelphia remained strong, so much so that Federalist candidates outpolled Antifederalists by about seven to one within Philadelphia and Philadelphia County. The Federalists' large margin there, combined with surprisingly strong showings in some of the western counties, gave the Federalists nearly a two-to-one advantage when the Pennsylvania ratifying convention opened its business on November 21.[24]

On November 21, the delegates to the Pennsylvania ratifying convention gathered in the same room in which the delegates to the Philadelphia Convention had spent the previous summer. Within the cramped quarters of the Assembly Room, the sixty-nine elected delegates arranged themselves according to their political allegiances, with Federalists and

Antifederalists facing one another. Unlike the Constitutional Convention, the Pennsylvania ratifying convention was open to the public, with spectators—often raucous—crowding their way through the open doors, trying to get a glimpse of the proceedings.[25]

After electing Frederick Muhlenberg, a strong supporter of the Constitution, as presiding officer of the convention, the delegates got down to business the following day, November 22. Faced with a decisive numerical disadvantage, the Antifederalists tried to use various procedural devices to delay the pace of the proceedings as much as possible so that they could better organize their forces. In a key tactical move, Antifederalist leaders like William Findley and John Smilie tried to widen the discussion to include the introduction of necessary amendments to the proposed Constitution. They demanded that upon all questions in which "yeas and nays were called, any member might insert the reason of his vote upon the Journals of the Convention." Because the debate over ratification was open for all to see, the Antifederalists wished to use every device possible to have their arguments inserted in the public record. Since the newspapers were avidly reporting on the debates, the Antifederalists hoped the reports would "produce a change in the minds of the people and incline them to new measures."[26]

Much of the first few days of the Convention were consumed by procedural bickering between Federalists and Antifederalists, but on November 24 James Wilson rose to give a speech that would frame the debate for the remainder of the Convention. Looking directly at his Antifederalist opponents, he claimed that the delegates to the Philadelphia Convention confronted three alternatives—to abolish the state governments and create a single consolidated government, to divide the country into "thirteen separate, independent commonwealths," or to create a "comprehensive Federal Republic." Wilson's description and defense of that comprehensive federal republic was every bit as impressive as the extended defense of the same concept articulated by James Madison, Alexander Hamilton, and John Jay in *The Federalist,* the series of essays that were beginning to appear at about the same time in the New York newspapers. Addressing the thorny issue of whether the new government would displace the state governments or leave their sovereignty intact, Wilson insisted that there was a third alternative. "In truth," Wilson argued, final authority rested not with either a central or a state government, but, rather, "remains and flourishes with the people. . . . That the supreme power, therefore, should be vested in the people, is in my judgment the great panacea of human politics. It is a power paramount to every constitution, inalienable in its nature, and indefinite in its extent." By that logic, Wilson concluded, the principles underlying the new government were "purely democratical." When assessing the "streams of power that appear through this great and comprehensive plan," he assured his audience, "we shall be able to trace them all to one great and noble source, THE PEOPLE."[27]

The Federalists' two-to-one advantage among Pennsylvania's citizenry would have permitted them to demand an immediate vote on the Constitution, but instead they chose to allow their opponents to speak as long and loudly against the proposed Constitution as they wished, although, notably, they did everything possible to prevent their opponents' arguments from appearing either in the Journal of the Convention or in the public press. And they continued to resist any attempt by the Antifederalists to amend the proposed Constitution to death. Nevertheless, they gave their opponents full license to express their views before bringing the matter to a vote. As a consequence, the debate on the Constitution in the Pennsylvania ratifying convention provided a good preview—and a primer—for the debates that would follow in other states.

The principal opponents of the Constitution in the Pennsylvania convention, led by western politicians such as John Smilie and William Findley, countered Wilson's democratic nationalism with a rhetoric of grassroots populism that was well suited to their backcountry constituencies. Historian Forrest McDonald has described Smilie and Findley as "a pair of Scottish bumpkins from the back country, [who] picked their noses and talked through them," but he also recognized that they were enormously skillful politicians. Though they did not have sufficient numbers on their side to block ratification of the Constitution, their language of populist democracy represented the future of American politics much more than the lofty, cerebral tone of Wilson's.[28]

As the Pennsylvania ratifying convention moved into its fourth week and the debate bogged down in minutiae and repetition, even the Antifederalists realized that it was time to vote. The Federalists, in informal meetings among themselves, had agreed that Wednesday, December 12, would be the day on which they would move for a final vote on the Constitution. James Wilson was among the last to speak on that final afternoon. Distilling the essence of his thoughts on the new federal government, he compared the construction of a "free government" to that of a pyramid.

It is laid on the broad basis of the people; its powers
gradually rise, while they are confined, in proportion as they
ascend, until they end in that most permanent of all forms.
When you examine all its parts, they will invariably be found
to preserve that essential mark of free governments, a chain
of connection with the people.[29]

William Findley and his followers would close on a shrill note. Findley predicted that "if this constitution is adopted I look upon the liberties of America as gone until they shall be recovered by arms." But those
rhetorical excesses aside, the Pennsylvania ratifying convention had allowed for a full airing of the arguments from both sides. Few, if any,
minds had been changed (the final vote on ratification was forty-six in
favor and twenty-three against, nearly exactly the predicted division
when the body first convened), but overall, the debate had been spirited
and serious.[30]

The day after the vote the jubilant Federalists staged an elaborate victory procession around the blocks surrounding the State House. Benjamin
Franklin, acting in his capacity as president of the state of Pennsylvania,
led the procession, which included the "members of Congress, the faculty
of the University, the magistrates and militia officers of the city." When
the throng reached Market Street, the resolution affirming Pennsylvania's
ratification of the Constitution was read from the balcony of the courthouse at Second and Market streets to what the *Packet* described as "a
great gathering." After the formalities were concluded, the crowd retired
to Epple's Tavern to drink celebratory toasts.[31]

QUICK VICTORIES IN DELAWARE AND NEW JERSEY

Pennsylvania was the first state to launch its drive to ratify the Constitution, but it would not be the first state to give its official assent to the
document. The citizens of Delaware, like those of Pennsylvania, learned
of the content of the proposed Constitution almost immediately after
the Convention had adjourned. The Delaware legislature was not in session at the time, but when it did convene on November 7 it voted unanimously to hold elections for a ratifying convention just three weeks
later. Delaware's delegates to the Convention—particularly George
Read and John Dickinson—were firmly in control, and when the

Delaware ratifying convention met in early December it quickly dispatched its business. On December 7, after only five days of discussion, the thirty delegates to the convention voted unanimously to ratify the Constitution, thus giving Delaware the right to put "The First State" on its license plates forevermore.[32]

New Jersey was the third state in the immediate vicinity of Philadelphia to add its assent to the Constitution. When the New Jersey legislature met in late October, its members unanimously agreed to set the fourth Tuesday in November as the date for elections to a ratifying convention to be held two weeks later. Having won the concession of equal representation in the Senate, New Jersey's political leaders put aside their concerns about being overwhelmed by the large states and rallied solidly behind ratification of the Constitution. Moreover, many of New Jersey's citizens looked to a strengthened federal union as a form of protection against the predatory and protectionist taxation policies of their more powerful neighbors, Pennsylvania and New York. As a consequence, the New Jersey state convention, which stayed in session for only one week during mid-December, also ratified the Constitution unanimously.[33]

GAINING MOMENTUM IN GEORGIA AND CONNECTICUT

As the year ended, the Federalists could congratulate themselves on having achieved ratification in three states—two unanimously and one with considerable contention. Their forward momentum continued into the new year. On January 2, Georgia voted unanimously in favor. George Washington, following the course of events from Mount Vernon, assessed the reasons for the enthusiasm of the Georgia delegates. Writing to his friend Samuel Powel, Washington offered the opinion that Georgia was "a weak State with the Indians on its back and the Spaniards on its flank." If they could "not see the necessity of a General Government there must I think be wickedness or insanity in the way."

The Spanish were a vague though omnipresent threat, but the Creek Indians, who had been gearing up for an attack at precisely the time the ratifying convention was preparing to meet, posed imminent danger. The history of both federal and state government relations with the Indian tribes on America's frontier during the period of the early republic is one about which the American nation cannot be proud, but the political reality in January 1788 was that the white settlers of Georgia felt that they would be much safer if they had the military backing of a stronger central government.[34]

Connecticut was next, ratifying the Constitution on January 4, 1788, by a vote of 128 to 40. The Connecticut legislature issued a call for elections to a ratifying convention on October 29, and in late December citizens gathered in special town meetings to elect delegates. It was not readily apparent whether the people selected were supporters or opponents of the Constitution, for many of the towns that elected the delegates did not issue formal instructions to those delegates stipulating how they should vote on the Constitution. But the Federalists had a clear advantage in the propaganda wars preceding the Connecticut state convention. All of the principal newspapers in the state were strongly pro-Federalist, which meant that the Antifederalist message was circulated primarily at the local level by individuals disconnected from the larger political debate across the nation. One Connecticut Antifederalist, Hugh Ledlie, complained that the Federalists "have got almost all the best Writers (as well as speakers) on their side." The Federalists made it clear that anyone who opposed the Constitution could not expect to receive any favors once the new government commenced operation, and, in general, Ledlie lamented, the whole affair was carried out with a "high hand," with those of "Superior rank" using their influence to dampen Antifederalist sentiment.[35]

The principal source of the Federalists' strength in Connecticut rested less on their control of the communications media than on the prestige and ability of the Constitution's principal defenders—Convention delegates Roger Sherman, Oliver Ellsworth, and William Samuel Johnson. Though Sherman, Johnson, and Ellsworth had all objected to some features of the Constitution over the course of the summer in Philadelphia, by the time they returned home to Connecticut they had become enthusiastic supporters. Ellsworth in particular wrote a series of thirteen influential "Letters from a Landholder" that ran in the Connecticut newspapers in November and December. The letters aptly displayed Ellsworth's command of the issues that the delegates had debated throughout the summer. Such was their intellectual weight that they continued to circulate in other New England states even after Connecticut had ratified.[36]

The other key factor influencing the outcome in Connecticut related to a provision in the Constitution that would have eliminated the power of states like New York and Massachusetts to levy state import duties on goods that came through their ports but were ultimately bound for other states like Connecticut. The proponents of the Constitution devoted as much of their speech making to its economic advantages as they did to abstract arguments about state versus federal government power. Many of those speaking against the Constitution criticized relatively minor sections of the document for the most part and acknowledged that they would vote in favor of the Constitution in spite of their reservations. Once again, the Federalist tactic of insisting on an up or down vote on the Constitution and blocking all attempts to amend or alter specific parts of it resulted in victory.[37]

When Connecticut voted affirmatively on January 4, it became clear that the Federalists' strategy, at least for the moment, was paying off. Their opponents were not yet sufficiently organized to articulate either a coherent critique of the Constitution or a plausible alternative to the weaknesses of the Articles of Confederation. Equally important, as one state after another agreed to the Constitution, the terms of the debate subtly changed. In the first state ratifying conventions, the central question was whether to accept the proposed plan of union or not. As more and more states ratified the Constitution, it became more likely that the new union would indeed go forward. As it became more likely that there would be a new form of union under a new Constitution, delegates in those states that had not yet considered the matter were faced with a new question. Were they prepared to leave their states outside of a federal union in which most of their neighbors were members?

But the battle was not yet done. The contest over the Constitution was about to move to states known to have proud traditions of resistance to central authority.

CHAPTER TWENTY-ONE

ACHIEVING
A MORE PERFECT UNION:
THE FEDERALISTS PREVAIL

BOSTON, JANUARY 9, 1788

Three hundred fifty-five delegates, elected by their town meetings, gathered with the knowledge that five states had already voted to ratify. The planned venue, the Massachusetts State House, proved too small to hold the throng of delegates, so they moved to the larger Brattle Street Congregational Church. Unfortunately, the acoustics in the cavernous church made it impossible to hear, so they moved, briefly, back to the State House. Again, the cramped quarters proved intolerable, so, finally, on January 17 they moved to the Long Lane Congregational Church, capable of accommodating not only the 355 delegates, but also a packed gallery of between six hundred and eight hundred spectators. As the Massachusetts ratifying convention began its business that day, most delegates would have agreed that the eventual outcome was too close to call.[1]

Two factors would make the Massachusetts ratifying convention unusual and affect the course of its proceedings. First, the state's two most visible and powerful political figures—Governor John Hancock and the popular leader of Revolutionary resistance Samuel Adams—had not attended the Convention in Philadelphia. They would, however, attend the ratifying convention, and their views on the proposed Constitution, though not implacably hostile, were known to be skeptical at best.

The second factor was the continuing hangover from Shays' Rebellion. While many saw it as proof of the need for a stronger central government, by January 1788 there was at least as much sympathy for the grievances of the insurgent farmers identified with the rebellion—if not their methods—as there had been alarm. And so the debate over the Constitution in Massachusetts, more than in the states that preceded it, turned on issues of social and economic conflict. Rufus King, now a delegate to the convention, wrote to Madison in exasperation.

> Their objections are not directed against any part of the constitution, but their opposition seems to arise from an Opinion, that is immoveable, that some injury is plotted against them, that the System is the production of the Rich, and ambitious; that they discern its operation, and that the consequence will be, the establishment of two Orders in the Society, one comprehending the Opulent & Great, the other the poor and illiterate.

Typical of this sentiment were the laments of Amos Singletary, an Antifederalist delegate from Sutton, Massachusetts, near Worcester, who complained of "these lawyers, and men of learning, and moneyed men, that talk so finely, and gloss over matters so smoothly, to make us poor little people swallow down the pill."[2]

In spite of these complaints, the Massachusetts ratifying convention would offer the opponents of the Constitution a greater opportunity to voice their misgivings than had been afforded to Antifederalists at the conventions that had preceded it. Recognizing the need to counter the idea that the powerful were ignoring the voices of the poor and less privileged, Federalist leaders introduced a motion proclaiming that the Constitution was to "be discussed and considered with moderation, candor, and deliberation," inviting their opponents to debate the document "by paragraphs, until every member shall have an opportunity to express his sentiments." As a further olive branch, the Federalists agreed to a request to give Elbridge Gerry a seat in the convention, even though Gerry had not been elected a delegate, in order that he might explain his reasons for refusing to sign the Constitution in Philadelphia.[3]

But Gerry's appearance would do little to help the Antifederalist cause. The rules governing his attendance prohibited him from speaking directly to the delegates. He was invited only to submit written statements or to answer questions from the delegates. He would therefore sit in the Convention for three days "biting the head of his cane" in frustration over his inability to speak his mind. On January 18, a delegate asked Gerry to speak to an issue relating to the apportionment of representation and taxation, but when Gerry rose to respond, he was told that he could not speak, but, rather, could only submit a written answer. The following day, in response to another question, Gerry tried once again to speak, and when prevented from doing so, he erupted in rage. At this point Federalist delegate Francis Dana called out that Gerry was out of order, prompting a bitter argument that soon escalated into a full-scale fistfight. Delegates from both sides separated the two men, but the angry Gerry never again appeared on the floor of the convention, complaining all the while that he had been denied the opportunity to communicate "important truths" to the representatives of the people of Massachusetts. By this time, Gerry's behavior had become so incorrigibly hostile as to alienate delegates who may otherwise have been inclined to vote against ratification.[4]

As the debates unfolded, the Federalists appeared to make little headway in converting the stance of their opponents, but they continued to hope that by persisting in their strategy of discussing every line and paragraph of the Constitution, they could eventually wear down some of the opposition. In contrast to the dynamic in other state conventions, in Massachusetts it was the opponents of the Constitution, and not the Federalists, who seemed to be losing patience and who wished to press forward with a vote on the document as a whole.

As the debate dragged into a third week, the Federalists made two crucial strategic decisions. First, although their counterparts in other states had steadfastly resisted allowing a discussion of possible amendments to the Constitution, the Massachusetts Federalists proposed that ratification be coupled with recommendations for *future* amendments. This was a dangerous game, for any discussion of future amendments would inevitably lead some to demand the adoption of amendments as a *precondition* to ratification. But the Federalists realized that they would have to make this concession if they were going to win ratification.[5]

Their second strategic action would involve reaching out to John Hancock and Samuel Adams in the hope that the concession on considering amendments might bring the two influential delegates into their camp. Hancock, suffering from a recurrence of his chronic gout, did not attend the convention until January 30, but during some negotiations behind closed doors he indicated his interest in pursuing a compromise solution involving "recommendatory amendments." He may also have been interested in the prospect—held out to him by Rufus King, Henry Knox, and others—that they would support not only his reelection as governor, but also his candidacy for the vice presidency of the new nation if the Constitution were adopted. Indeed, if Virginia should choose not to ratify, then it was not out of the question, King and Knox coyly suggested, that Hancock might be headed for the presidency.[6]

Meanwhile, the hard-core opponents, in a reversal of their strategy in other states, objected vehemently to discussions of possible amendments. William Widgery of New Gloucester insisted that "the Convention did not meet for the purpose of recommending amendments, but to adopt or reject the Constitution." His protest was echoed by General Samuel Thompson of Topsham, who proclaimed, "We have no right to make amendments. It was not . . . the business we were sent for." The Federalists, now using the logic of their opponents in other states, protested that "if we have a right . . . to receive or reject the Constitution, surely we have an equal authority to determine in what way this right shall be exercised."[7]

By the end of January, Hancock had changed sides. When he finally made an appearance at the convention late in the afternoon on January 30, bundled up in flannel, he announced—in carefully nuanced and qualified language—his willingness to support the Constitution so long as it was accompanied by a proposal for amendments.[8]

Hancock's decision to support the Constitution put the ball in Samuel Adams's court. Adams, who considered Elbridge Gerry a close friend and political ally and shared at least some of Gerry's misgivings about the threat of an excessively powerful central government, was by this time feeling considerable pressure from his own primary political constituency. The artisans and mechanics of Boston, like their counterparts in Philadelphia, had come out strongly in favor of the Constitution. And the promise of the possibility of subsequent amendments went at least part of the way toward easing his misgivings about the Constitution.[9]

On the morning of January 31, before a packed gallery, Federalist William Heath urged adoption of the Constitution, along with a series of recommended future amendments. The convention then recessed for a noontime break, though the spectators in the gallery, anxious not to lose their seats, stayed on. When the delegates reassembled, Governor Hancock—his feet wrapped in bandages—rose, endorsed ratification, and proposed nine *future* amendments to the Constitution. One of the proposed amendments bore a close resemblance to what would eventually become the Tenth Amendment to the Constitution, declaring that all powers not expressly delegated to Congress were reserved to the states. Another called for the addition of a requirement that any trial for a capital offense be preceded by an indictment by a grand jury, a recommendation that would later find its way into the Fifth Amendment.[10]

At this point, Samuel Adams publicly expressed his support for ratification and for Hancock's proposed amendments. The debate over the next several days revealed the extent to which the Antifederalists—never a cohesive group—were by no means of one mind about how to respond to the compromise proposal for future amendments. On February 5, Gilbert Dench of Middlesex County tried to delay a vote on the Constitution by asking for an adjournment, but even moderate opponents of the Constitution thought this a bad idea, voting down the proposal by a three-to-one margin. On February 6, after an impressive closing speech by John Hancock urging ratification, the vote was called, and the convention approved the Constitution, together with the proposed amendments, by a narrow vote of 187 to 168.

After the final vote was taken, a steady parade of delegates who had voted no pledged their support for the new government. Benjamin Randall and Benjamin Swain, who were the last two delegates to speak, struck a conciliatory tone. Randall announced that "he had been uniformly opposed to the Constitution. He had . . . fought like a good soldier, but, as he was beaten, he should sit down contented, hoping the minority disappointed in their fears." Swain had the last word, declaring that

> the Constitution has had a fair trial and that there had not . . . been any undue influence exercised to obtain the vote in its favor; that many doubts which lay on his mind had been removed, and that, although he was in the minority, he should support the Constitution as cheerfully and as heartily as though he had voted on the other side of the question.[11]

These closing words by the Antifederalists in Massachusetts were not merely gracious. They portended well for the future of the American republic. The debate in Massachusetts had been an emotional and closely contested one, but, in the end, after good-faith concessions by the Federalists, the losers were willing to accept the legitimacy of the outcome and to pledge their support of the new government for their republic, whatever form it might ultimately take.

RESISTANCE IN NEW HAMPSHIRE

One week later, on February 13, delegates in New Hampshire met in Exeter to begin their deliberations. Federalists in Massachusetts thought their influence and the weight of their arguments would cause New Hampshire to quickly follow suit, but they had not reckoned on the combination of apathy and independent spirit that had long been the hallmark of the state's political behavior. The Federalist John Langdon had been cautiously optimistic when the 113 delegates to the New Hampshire convention gathered in the First Congregational Church meeting house in Exeter. He knew that the vote would be close, but he hoped that when the delegates from "remote communities" learned of Massachusetts's ratification they might swing the balance in favor of ratification. He would be disappointed. Although we do not have a record of the debate that unfolded over the course of the next ten days, the end result was confusion. The Federalists, apparently fearing defeat, proposed that the convention adjourn without taking action. They hoped that once disaffected delegates learned of the support for the Constitution in other states they would change their tune. With that ambiguous ending, the convention adjourned without taking action.[12]

DEFIANCE IN RHODE ISLAND

Thus far, six states were in favor, with one unresolved. Rhode Island provided little cheer for the Federalists. The perennially dissenting Ocean state, resolutely absent in Philadelphia, would make short work of its consideration of the Constitution. Meeting in February 1788, the Rhode Island legislature refused even to call a ratifying convention, instead asking the state's citizens to express their views in what turned out to be chaotic town meetings. Less than two-thirds of the usual number of voters turned out at the town meetings, and the large towns of Providence and Newport essentially boycotted the popular referendum. The final popular vote on the Constitution in Rhode Island was a resounding 2,708 opposed to calling a convention and 235 in favor.[13]

Rhode Island Federalists made four other attempts to call a convention in the state between March 1788 and January 1790. In March, October, and December of 1788 and in June of 1789, the Rhode Island legislature rebuffed their efforts. It would not be until January 1790, after the new government had gone to work, that the Rhode Island legislature grudgingly bowed to the inevitable, called a convention, and ratified the Constitution.[14]

Rhode Island's obstinate refusal to have anything to do with the federal Constitution is, at least on the surface, puzzling. The Constitution's protections—designed to improve the representation of small states—should have satisfied many who feared that their state would not have an adequate voice in the new government. Moreover, many of the commercial provisions written into the Constitution that aimed at promoting economic development in those states whose economies were closely tied to the import/export trade would almost certainly have worked to the benefit of Rhode Island. Explanations of Rhode Island's behavior are to be found not in calculations of political or economic self-interest but, rather, in the state's political culture. Dating back from its early-seventeenth-century establishment, when the renegade Puritan Roger Williams left Massachusetts to found the colony, and continuing through the early 1780s, when the state legislature steadfastly resisted attempts to strengthen the Articles of Confederation, Rhode Islanders had displayed an extraordinary suspicion of central authority and a fierce protectiveness of their own autonomy. While the citizens of Rhode Island would eventually recognize that it was not in their interest to exist outside of a union of the twelve other states, they joined with the greatest reluctance. But in February 1788, with Rhode Island's initial refusal even to consider the Constitution, the count in favor of ratifying the Constitution stood at six in favor, one opposed, and one unresolved.

THE SOUTHERN CAMPAIGN: MARYLAND

The Southern states were the next to deliberate. On April 26, 1788, the Maryland ratifying convention approved the Constitution by a vote of sixty-three to eleven. The Federalists controlled the process from beginning to end, but that did not prevent Luther Martin from unleashing a torrent of sound and fury in the run-up to the convention. Martin had settled into a position of implacable opposition to the Constitution; he had from the moment of his departure from Philadelphia campaigned tirelessly against ratification. According to Daniel Carroll, a reluctant signer of the Constitution in Philadelphia, Martin indulged himself in "tavern harangues" in which he claimed that at least twenty members of the Philadelphia Convention had expressed themselves in favor of a "Kingly Government." John Mercer joined Martin in these charges, claiming, falsely, that John Langdon of New Hampshire had expressed a willingness to crown Washington "despot of America."[15]

Daniel Carroll would claim that when the voters of Maryland went to the polls to choose their delegates, there was "a wildness . . . and many show'd they were really frightened." Some of this fright likely existed only in Carroll's imagination, but some of it may have been generated by Luther Martin's predictions of "consolidation" and "tyranny." Martin's over-heated rhetoric notwithstanding, public opinion in Maryland was solidly on the side of the Federalists. Supporters of the Constitution outpolled opponents by about two to one, putting the Federalists in control of the ratifying convention from the outset. Although Luther Martin continued to thunder against the evils of consolidation, the threat of the destruction of the state governments, and the dangers of an incipient monarchy, the Federalists patiently waited until his energy was exhausted and then, after only five days in session, called for a vote. The convention continued for another three days while the delegates, following the Massachusetts example, proposed twenty-eight wide-ranging amendments—eventually whittled down to thirteen more narrowly framed changes—that they hoped would be considered once the government had commenced operation.

The Maryland Federalists, enjoying their large majority and impatient with the posturing of Martin, rejected all thirteen proposed amendments and then pushed through a motion to adjourn. Twenty-seven members opposed the motion to adjourn, most likely because they were in favor of some if not all of the amendments and because they were uneasy about the high-handedness with which the Federalists had operated. Whatever ill will the Maryland Federalists may have generated, however, they prevailed.[16]

THE SOUTHERN CAMPAIGN: SOUTH CAROLINA

By the time the South Carolina legislature had met in its regular session, arranged for elections to a ratifying convention, and, finally, gathered the delegates to that convention together in May 1788, the general outlines of the debate—sketched out in other state ratifying conventions and in scores of newspaper articles and pamphlets—were pretty clear. But South Carolina would be the first state where the issue of slavery was paramount to the debate. (Georgia had similar interests with respect to slavery, but in that state the issue of defense against the Spanish and Indians had proven to be of more urgent importance.)

The South Carolina legislature did not convene in regular session until mid-January of 1788, and, as things turned out, the battle over the Constitution in the legislature turned out to be more significant than that in the ratifying convention itself. Some legislators, including the state's former governor, Rawlins Lowndes, attempted to block the calling of a convention altogether. A majority in the legislature finally agreed to issue a call for a convention, but they took their time about it, setting the date for elections for April 11 and 12, and for a convention to meet the first week in May.[17]

The Federalists' greatest support came from the low-country parishes in and around Charleston—precisely the areas where men like the Pinckneys and John Rutledge had their bases of power. Historian Forrest McDonald suggests that the swollen egos of South Carolina's planter elite played a large role in the positive vote on the Constitution. "The Constitution pleased Carolina planters' vanity," McDonald claims, "for in a broad sense it was, in considerable measure, their own handiwork; nearly half the 149 men who voted for ratification were related, directly or indirectly, through blood or marriage, to the Rutledges and Pinckneys who had sat in the Philadelphia Convention."[18]

It is no doubt true that there were few people anywhere in America who could match the vanity of the South Carolina planter elite, but the more important reason for South Carolina's support of the Constitution was the success of her delegates to Philadelphia in writing into it fundamental protections for South Carolina's way of life. The constitutional ban on export taxes constituted a huge victory for the staple-crop-producing states and, of course, even more important were the constitutional protections for South Carolina's "peculiar species of property."

Rawlins Lowndes, whose devotion to South Carolina interests was such that one contemporary described him as having "not one federal idea in his head nor one that looks beyond the Pedee River," tried to exploit South Carolinians' fear of the North, predicting that "the interest of the Northern states would so predominate as to divest us of any pretensions to the title of the republic." The Pinckneys countered Lowndes's fearmongering effectively, for their experience in the Convention in

Philadelphia had given them a solid basis on which to argue that precisely the opposite was the case. Charles Cotesworth Pinckney acknowledged that the South Carolina delegates "had to contend with the religious and political prejudices" of the eastern and middle states, as well as those of Virginia, with respect to the slave trade. Nevertheless, whether on the matter of slave representation, the continuation of the slave trade, or the capture and return of escaped slaves, the South Carolinians had come out on top.[19]

To appease a few of the doubters, the South Carolina Federalists followed the lead of Massachusetts, proposing four amendments that did not substantially alter the balance of power proposed by the Constitution. As had been the case with Massachusetts's proposed amendments, the most important was a rather clumsily worded version of what would later become the Tenth Amendment. It asserted that "no Section of the said Constitution warrants a construction that the States do not retain every power not expressly relinquished by them." With relatively little discussion of those amendments, South Carolina approved the Constitution by a vote of 149 to 73.[20]

A CLIFF-HANGER IN VIRGINIA

The Virginia ratifying convention began its work on June 2, 1788, just a few days before the New Hampshire delegates tried for a second time to resolve their inconclusive deliberations on the Constitution. In fact, the New Hampshire convention ratified the Constitution on June 21, a few days before Virginia made its decision, thus becoming the ninth, and decisive, vote in favor of the new government. But the delegates to the Virginia convention were not aware of the timing of New Hampshire's deliberations, and they went into the debate believing that their decision on the Constitution might well determine its ultimate fate. Virginians were well aware of their status as citizens of the most powerful, populous state in America, the home of the man who was virtually certain to be the first president of the United States should Virginia join the union. Virginia was of course also the home of the most deeply informed and articulate defender of the Constitution—James Madison.

But the forces arrayed against the Constitution in Virginia were more formidable than those anywhere in America. Two of the three nonsigners of the Constitution—the reluctant and internally conflicted Edmund

Randolph and the adamant George Mason—both played active roles in the Virginia ratifying convention. Unlike their irascible counterpart in Massachusetts, Elbridge Gerry, Randolph and Mason were respected and well liked by nearly all of their colleagues in Virginia. They would be joined by the most powerful man in the state—the "son of thunder," Patrick Henry—who was geared up for the political fight of his life.

When Washington's contemporaries called him the "Father of his Country," there was no doubt in their minds that the country being referred to was America. Patrick Henry—far more than Jefferson, Madison, Mason, or Randolph—was the acknowledged political leader of *his* country. And his country was the independent, sovereign state of Virginia.

Washington had been the first person to show Henry a copy of the Constitution. Perhaps anticipating Henry's objections, he admitted that he "wished it had been more perfect." When Henry saw the draft, he was aghast at the extent to which it repudiated the principles of the Articles of Confederation and created in its stead a "consolidated" government. Mindful of the requirements of civility toward America's first citizen, his reply was polite. But he was genuinely aggrieved, telling Washington that his distress over the document was "really greater than I am able to express." From that moment on, Henry would work tirelessly to prevent the adoption of the Constitution in his home state.[21]

At the start of the Convention, the outcome was too close to call. Madison, ever the worrier, attributed the strong current of opposition to the combined influence of Henry and Mason. Henry, Madison claimed, was disposed "to aim at disunion." Mason, he believed, "was growing every day more bitter and outrageous in his efforts to carry his point; and will probably in the end be thrown by the violence of his passions into the politics of Mr. Henry." On balance, Madison felt that "the business is in the most ticklish state that can be imagined. The majority will certainly be very small on whatever side it may finally lie; and I dare not encourage much expectation that it will be on the favorable side."[22]

In general, the delegates from the longer-settled regions of Virginia's Tidewater and Northern Neck, the home of the state's most prestigious and well-established gentry, tended to be in the Federalist camp. The voters in the Virginia Piedmont and backcountry, where Patrick Henry's influence among the state's middling planters and small farmers was greatest, tended to be opposed. It was likely that the outcome would turn on the votes of delegates from Virginia's far western regions and, in particular, on the eleven votes from the delegates from present-day Kentucky. Many of those delegates were largely uninformed about the merits of the arguments on either side of the question at the time they arrived in Richmond for the convention, so their votes remained very much in doubt.[23]

As the Convention opened, Madison and the supporters of the Constitution already had one trick up their sleeve. George Washington, anxious to appear above partisan battle, had chosen not to attend the convention, but both he and Madison had been working quietly to bring Edmund Randolph around. Washington's effort was crucial, perhaps due to the power of his persona or the fact that as the likely president he would be appointing the nation's first attorney general—who, it turned out, would be none other than Edmund Randolph. On June 4, the first full day of debate, Randolph rose in the convention and, in a speech that would cause George Mason thereafter to refer to him as "the young Arnold," announced that he would support the Constitution. Certainly Madison's and Washington's powers of persuasion, in combination with Randolph's ambition, had something to do with the change of heart. But perhaps the best explanation for Randolph's reversal is the one he offered to the delegates at the Virginia Convention. Virginia was populous and powerful, but could the state really make a go of it alone in the face of a consolidated phalanx of the other states of America? As Randolph put it in his closing speech in the Convention,

> I went to the federal Convention with the strongest affection for the Union; . . . I acted there in full conformity with this affection; . . . I refused to subscribe, because I had, as I still have, objections to the Constitution, and wished a free inquiry into its merits; [but] the accession of eight states reduced our deliberations to the single question of *Union or no Union.*

Faced with that difficult choice, Randolph chose union.[24]

Randolph's defection was important to the outcome, but the Antifederalists would also contribute to their own demise. Although allied in their opposition, Henry and Mason often worked at cross-purposes during the Convention. At the beginning of the Convention, Mason insisted on "the freest discussion, clause by clause" of the Constitution before a final vote was to be taken. Perhaps to Mason's surprise, Madison readily agreed, for he was fully prepared to carry out a defense on those terms. Frequently to the annoyance of his fellow delegates, Mason engaged in extended discussions of even the minutest details of the Constitution, the effect of which was often mind-numbing to those forced to listen to his recitation. Moreover, Madison, ably supported by Randolph and the Convention president, Edmund Pendleton, was usually well prepared with a rebuttal.

Patrick Henry, by contrast, was not a man to get bogged down in details. His strategy was to mount a full-scale assault on the principles underlying the new government. Henry spoke on all but five of the twenty-two days that the Virginia ratifying convention was in session, often several times in the course of a day. In one memorable session he spoke for seven hours without a stop.

If Henry could have confined his argument against the Constitution to a single hour, he might have made a greater impact, for his essential concerns about the Constitution resonated powerfully with many of the delegates. His very first point went to the core of his provincial beliefs. Why was it, he asked, that such a radical change in government was necessary, given the "general peace and . . . universal tranquility" that already prevailed in Virginia? Henry was particularly displeased that the members of the Philadelphia Convention, and Madison in particular, would effect such a radical change in the locus of sovereignty without informing the people beforehand. Had he known that such a change was being contemplated, he surely would have raised his voice in protest. Henry, echoing Luther Martin's objections in the Philadelphia Convention, argued that the new Constitution would produce "consolidation." "This government," he exclaimed "is not a Virginian, but an American government. Is it not, therefore a consolidated government?"[25]

The only occasions on which Henry approached the heights of the oratory that had made him the firebrand of the Revolution in Virginia were those on which he departed from his assault on the document itself and appealed instead to his fellow delegates' sense of pride and history. At one point he asked the delegates to think back to the Revolution, when

> the Genius of Virginia called on us for liberty—called us from our beloved endearments, which, from long habits, we were taught to revere. . . . On this awful occasion did you want a federal government? Did federal ideas lead you to the most splendid victories? I must again repeat the favorite idea, that the genius of Virginia did, and will again, lead us to happiness. To obtain the most splendid prize you

did not consolidate. You accomplish the most glorious ends
by the assistance of our country.

It was the message of a provincial politician, for Henry's "country"
was indubitably Virginia, not America. But it was a message that resonated with particular force in the Old Dominion.[26]

Patrick Henry and George Mason had not initially agreed on the best
means of opposing the Constitution. Their failure to agree was reflected
in part on their different oratorical strategies, but there was a more fundamental issue at the root of their differences. Henry detested the Constitution and believed that Virginia should reject it outright. Mason was
still wedded to the views he and Randolph had voiced at the end of the
Convention—that the states, and Virginia in particular, should have an
opportunity to suggest amendments as a *prior condition* to ratification.
Randolph had already deserted Mason and was now supporting the
Constitution with the hope that amendments to his liking would be
added subsequently. It took awhile for Mason to convince Henry that
their best hope was to demand that a specific set of amendments be
adopted as a prior condition to Virginia's ratification, but when Henry
came around to support Mason's strategy, he did so with enthusiasm.[27]

Altogether, Mason, Henry, and their Antifederalist colleagues proposed
forty amendments. The first twenty restated the individual liberties guaranteed in Virginia's Declaration of Rights. The other twenty—which were
far more controversial—aimed at tilting the balance of power back to the
states. Some of the amendments, such as those relating to the compensation of legislators and judges and the annual publication of the journals of
the Congress, constituted only minor bits of fine-tuning, but several others contemplated substantive changes. One of the amendments, for example, would have required the consent of two-thirds of the members of
Congress for the passage of any navigation law, and another would have
imposed conditions on the ability of the federal government to impose direct taxes or collect excises.[28]

As Mason and Henry prepared these amendments, they were in direct
communication with Antifederalist stalwarts in New York. Their hope
was that if Virginia and New York *together* insisted on the amendments as
a prior condition to ratification, the other states would have to fall into
line. James Madison remained adamantly opposed to any amendments,
including even those that were aimed at protecting individual liberties,
but he also recognized that the only way to secure ratification would be

to acquiesce to them as *suggestions* for possible subsequent action. Thus, the final battle in the Virginia ratifying convention was fought over the question of prior or subsequent amendments.[29]

Going into the final vote on the Constitution, neither side had a clear idea of how the issue would be resolved. In a conciliatory gesture crafted by Edmund Pendleton, supporters of the Constitution introduced a set of resolutions calling for adoption of the Constitution but also that the First Federal Congress under the new government consider "whatsoever amendments may be deemed necessary." Henry and his forces immediately moved to amend the motion. They stipulated that the states submit a wide-ranging set of amendments as a prior condition to ratification. The vote, taken on June 25, 1788, was close. Henry's amendment was defeated, eighty in favor, eighty-eight opposed. Pendleton's original motion then passed, nearly equally narrowly, eighty-nine in favor, seventy-nine opposed.[30]

Spencer Roane, soon to become one of the new government's most bitter critics, described the somber mood prevailing at the time of ratification. There was, he noted,

> no rejoicing on account of the vote of ratification—it would not be prudent to do so; and the federalists behave with moderation and do not exult in their success. . . . The decision has been distressing and awful to great numbers; and is generally believed will be so received by the people.

Apparently a group of disappointed Antifederalists met immediately after the vote to explore ways to block the new government. They approached Henry for his support, but they were rebuffed. Henry had, in his final words to the convention, accepted his defeat gracefully, promising that "I will be a peaceable citizen. My head, my hand, and my heart, shall be at liberty to retrieve the loss of liberty and remove the defects of that system in a constitutional way." Henry would work vigorously to secure amendments to the new Constitution once it went into effect, but, true to his promise, he did so "in a constitutional way."[31]

BRINKMANSHIP IN NEW YORK

With Virginia and New Hampshire's ratification, the adoption of the new Constitution was certain. Moreover, Virginia's ratification made it likely that once a new government was formed, George Washington, as the likely first president, would give added legitimacy to the government. But New York's attitude toward the new Constitution continued to pose a threat to the effectiveness and durability of the new union. Among the most populous and commercially powerful states, New York alone had displayed unremitting hostility to the Constitution during the Convention in Philadelphia. When New York's deliberations on the Constitution began on June 17, Virginia had not yet ratified the Constitution. Opponents had been pinning their hopes on a defeat of the Constitution in Virginia, for, they reasoned, rejection of the Constitution in two of America's most powerful states would cause others to reconsider as well.

New York City was a cosmopolitan urban center with abundant intellectual talent on both sides of the question and with a multitude of ambitious printers willing to publicize their arguments within the city and beyond. Moreover, because the state was one of the last to take up ratification, the people of New York were better informed about the merits and demerits of the Constitution than the people of any other state.[32]

Of the sixty-five delegates elected to the New York ratifying convention, forty-six opposed the Constitution in varying degrees. Moreover, the man elected as president of the convention, Governor George Clinton, had been the person most responsible for Robert Yates' and John Lansing's opposition to the Constitution in Philadelphia. Clinton was an extraordinarily canny politician who enjoyed nearly unrivaled power in his state. As governor of a state that enjoyed substantial revenues from customs duties imposed by its own government, he was able to pass along the tax savings from those revenues to his constituents in the rural regions of the state. While there was relatively robust support for a stronger central government among the commercial and professional classes of New York City, most of the political leaders of upstate New York, men of more modest wealth and social standing, provided a solid base for Clinton's political power and a sympathetic audience for Clinton's Antifederalist views.[33]

Between June 17 and July 2, the date on which New Yorkers heard the news of Virginia's decision to ratify the Constitution, New York's delegates witnessed an epic debate between Alexander Hamilton, who had already honed his arguments under the pseudonym "Publius" in *The Federalist,* and Antifederalist Melancton Smith, who had ably articulated his views in the press as the "Federal Farmer." The Antifederalist majority in the convention allowed the debate to take place because they felt certain they had enough votes to carry the day in the convention and because they were hopeful that a double defeat for the Constitution in Virginia and New York would be decisive in reversing the outcome in other parts of the nation. But news of Virginia's ratification took much of the wind out of the New York Antifederalists' sails. The Federalists, who had spent the previous two weeks earnestly debating each section of the Constitution, were now content to sit back and see how the Antifederalists would respond.[34]

The Antifederalists were not of one mind about what to do next. With a few exceptions, most of them had given up on an outright rejection of the Constitution. Instead, they debated a bewildering array of fifty-five possible amendments. They then adjourned and divided those amendments into three categories. Some of the amendments were to be considered as "conditional." In other words, they should be considered as a prior condition for New York's ratification. Others were to be considered as "recommendary"—to be recommended for subsequent adoption once the Constitution took effect. And, to make matters still more confusing, there was yet another category of amendments, which included a bill of rights, that were to be considered as "explanatory"—essentially an attempt by New York's Antifederalists to suggest the way particular features of the Constitution should be interpreted in the future. Whether an explanatory amendment would in practice turn out to be a conditional one was not altogether clear, but one thing seems certain. The New York amendments, both in their extent and in their complexity, would have turned ratification—and subsequent constitutional interpretation—into a nightmare.

The Federalist minority in the New York convention knew they would have to give some ground on the matter of amendments, but on July 11 John Jay made it clear that so-called conditional amendments were unacceptable. Jay proposed that the Constitution be adopted without any conditions, but, as an olive branch to the Antifederalists, he added language asking that parts of the Constitution whose meaning was unclear be explained and that any amendments that a majority of delegates approved be recommended to the First Federal Congress of the new government. Nationalists like Jay and Hamilton considered this a substantial concession, but it was not enough to satisfy their opponents.

On July 11, Melancton Smith proposed an idea that he and other New York Antifederalists had been discussing with Patrick Henry and other Antifederalists in Virginia: that New York "conditionally" ratify the Constitution with the understanding that a second general constitutional convention would be called to propose amendments. This was a version of what Edmund Randolph had proposed at the tail end of the Philadelphia Convention, and it was no more acceptable to the Federalists in New York than it had been to the delegates in Philadelphia.[35]

At this point, the political and semantic maneuverings in New York began to turn comical. Between July 14 and July 24, a group of Federalists and Antifederalists—including Jay, Hamilton, Lansing, and Smith—tried to hammer out a compromise in which the words "upon condition nevertheless" would be replaced by the phrase "in full confidence nevertheless," thus making the conditional amendments somewhat less conditional. By this time Melancton Smith, though he still considered the Constitution in its present form "defective," had been persuaded that those defects could be corrected through the amendment process laid out in the Constitution. The decision of Smith and other moderate Antifederalists to soften their opposition may have been due less to their impulses toward compromise than to fear of the consequences of doing otherwise. Although the evidence on this point is contested, it appears that Hamilton and Jay, privately and discreetly, let it be known that if New York did not assent to the Constitution, they would lead New York City in a secessionist movement from the state, thus allowing the city to be part of the new union and leaving the rest of the state to fend for itself. On July 25, after more behind-the-scenes maneuvering, the New York ratifying convention adopted the Constitution by a vote of thirty to twenty-seven. The vote in favor of ratification was accompanied by a host of explanatory, anticipatory (the new word in place of "conditional"), and "recommendatory" amendments. To make matters more confusing, Hamilton and John Jay, two of the Constitution's staunchest supporters, joined with Robert Lansing and Melancton Smith in drafting a letter asking for another convention to consider the various amendments proposed by the states. All in all, it was a messy affair, but New York was now in the "win" column.[36]

NORTH CAROLINA HOLDS OUT—FOR A WHILE

The fight was over by the time Virginia and New York added their assent, but it was treated as anything but a settled question by the citizens of the Tar Heel state. While North Carolina's delegates in Philadelphia had been moderately sympathetic to the nationalist vision of the Constitution, their constituents back home were far more concerned by the threat of consolidation posed by the new government.

The North Carolina legislature, overwhelmingly composed of men whose instincts were provincial rather than national, sought to buy time to build support for their arguments. They delayed even discussing a ratifying convention until early December of 1787 and, after acrimonious debate, set a date for elections the following March, with the ratifying convention itself not to assemble until July 21, 1788—long after all of the states other than Rhode Island would have made their decisions. When the convention met in late July, Antifederalists enjoyed a majority of more than two to one.

The debates in the North Carolina ratifying convention were extraordinarily intense, even abusive; the Antifederalists assaulted nearly every aspect of the proposed Constitution and made highly personal attacks against the Federalists. Before long each side was throwing insults at the other, including charges of "horrid ignorance" and "indecent scurrility," and at least one shouting match that nearly shut down the convention. As Antifederalist Timothy Bloodworth noted ruefully, the intellectual merits of the arguments presented by both sides tended to "have gone in at one ear, and out at the other."[37]

At the core of the Antifederalist objections was the notion already articulated so forcefully by Patrick Henry: that the Philadelphia Convention had violated its charge by scrapping the Articles of Confederation and proposing an altogether new form of government. Antifederalists in North Carolina believed that by asserting in the Constitution's preamble that "we the people" rather than "we the states" were the source of sovereign power, the framers had acted illegally. Like their neighbor Henry, North Carolinians thought of their "country" as North Carolina, not America, and they believed that their only true representatives could be North Carolinians. Indeed, when they spoke of representatives of the United States government, they most often spoke of "them," a distant, alien people who could not appreciate the needs of North Carolinians.[38]

This hearty distrust of central authority was deeply entrenched in the politics of North Carolina, dating at least to the so-called Regulator movements of the 1760s, when North Carolina backcountry citizens rebelled against a combination of corrupt local leadership and an unresponsive central authority. On August 2, 1788, the North Carolina ratifying convention rejected the proposed Constitution by a vote of 184 to 83. The intensity of opposition to the proposed union in North Carolina, as in Rhode Island, suggests just how far many of the citizens of the "United States" had to travel before they would truly consider themselves citizens of a single nation.[39]

North Carolina accompanied its outright rejection with proposals for no fewer than forty-six amendments, twenty to be included in a bill of rights and twenty-six aimed at changing specific features of the government that the Antifederalist delegates particularly disliked. But with dubious reasoning, the two final resolutions presenting the amendments stated that "this Convention has thought proper neither to ratify nor reject the Constitution" and made provision for "a law for collecting a[n] impost on goods imported into this state, and appropriate the money arising therefrom to the use of Congress." In other words, though the Antifederalists in North Carolina had clearly indicated their disapproval of the Constitution, they had somehow convinced themselves, or at least *wished* to convince themselves, that they could remain within the union even though they had not ratified the Constitution.[40]

More than a year would pass before North Carolinians bowed to the inevitable. By that time, the future enactment of a limited bill of rights would seem inevitable. Moreover, the new government had been successfully launched with the revered Washington at its head and without any apparent ill effects to the liberties of the people. The Antifederalists were left with few compelling arguments to continue their resistance.

THE INTELLECTUAL FOUNDATIONS OF "A MORE PERFECT UNION"

With ratification of the Constitution by Virginia, New York, and North Carolina, the Federalists' victory in the people's debate over the Constitution was assured. Some measure of their success owed to their superior preparation and organizational abilities; they had seized the initiative and swung a largely uninformed populace over to their side. But the ratification contests also produced an impressive body of political writing, some of it rising above its primary purpose of political persuasion and achieving enduring intellectual importance.

Between late September 1787 and the fall of 1788, several hundred pamphlets and newspaper essays appeared on the subject of the Constitution, the largest outpouring of opinion on any subject in the young country's history. In fact, the effect of all that verbiage on the outcome of the contests in the various states is unclear, for circulation of Federalist and Antifederalist writings was inconsistent, and much of it only appeared after many of the states had already voted on the question. Nevertheless, the content of those writings deepens our understanding of the issues most on Americans' minds as they contemplated the prospect of a new and stronger union.[41]

The most influential political writings on the Constitution were of course the eighty-five essays written by Alexander Hamilton, James Madison, and John Jay, appearing under the combined pseudonym "Publius" in the New York City newspapers between October 1787 and May 1788. Although they did not circulate much beyond New York before the spring of 1788, they have by now achieved the status of a canonical text of the American government and constitutionalism.

The essays were written in haste, with more than 175,000 words flowing from the pens of their authors during the hectic months of their composition. Hamilton took the initiative in organizing the project. Although he was not pleased with some aspects of the final document, by the time the Constitutional Convention adjourned he recognized that it represented the one and only chance Americans would have to energize their government. He would first attempt to recruit Gouverneur Morris as a collaborator, but Morris declined because of his business commitments. Hamilton then turned to Jay and, subsequently, to Madison, who recalled later in life that he was asked to "join him [Hamilton] and Mr. Jay in carrying it into effect." In all, Hamilton wrote fifty-one of the essays; Madison, twenty-nine; and Jay, five.[42]

The essays were for the most part written independently, with little collaboration or coordination among the three authors. Indeed, they were written under such pressure of time that there was usually no time for review or revision. A number of commentators, looking back from the period of the 1790s, when Hamilton and Madison found themselves locked in combat over the new government's constitutional authority, have talked about the "split personality," or even the "schizophrenia" of *The Federalist*, but in fact, the essays demonstrate a remarkable coherence. Madison focused for the most part on general issues of government and politics—on republicanism and representation in particular. His most famous essay, "Federalist No. 10," which argued for the virtues of an "extended republic," owed heavily to his essay on the "Vices of the Political System," which he had composed in April 1787 in anticipation of the Philadelphia Convention. Hamilton tended to focus on specific issues such as taxation or the construction of the executive and judiciary. Since he was defending the specific language of the Constitution on those issues rather than articulating his own views about the nature of government, any differences he may have had with Madison were less apparent.[43]

The Federalist would grow more influential over time and come to be considered an essential means of understanding the intent of the framers of the Constitution. In the period between 1790 and 1800, when leaders of the new republic were facing the challenge of creating a government that conformed to the precepts of their new Constitution, *The Federalist* was cited in Supreme Court opinions only once. In the whole of the nineteenth century, the essays were cited 58 times. In the first half of the twentieth century they were cited 38 times, but in the last half of that century they were cited no fewer than 194 times. This increasing tendency to regard the hurried, even frenzied political arguments of Publius as sacred text has not followed any discernible ideological lines. Liberal and conservative justices, strict constructionists and broad constructionists, originalists and advocates of a "living constitution" have all found something to like in *The Federalist*.[44]

However much the essays may on some occasions rise to the level of high-minded political theory, they were, first and foremost, political propaganda aimed at persuading undecided voters to support the Constitution. The case that perhaps best illustrates this tension between *The Federalist* as high-minded theory and political propaganda is the justly celebrated "Federalist No. 39," in which Madison sings the praises of a government that would be "part national" and "part federal." Pointing to the constitutional provisions providing proportional representation in the House and equal representation for the states in the Senate, as well as the requirements for ratifying and amending the Constitution, Madison argued,

> In its foundation it is federal, not national; in the sources
> from which the ordinary powers of government are drawn,
> it is partly federal and partly national; in the operation of
> those powers; it is national, not federal; in the extent of
> them, again it is federal, and not national; and, finally, in
> the authoritative mode of introducing amendments, it is
> neither wholly federal nor wholly national.

Madison avoided the question of whether it would be the state or national government that could claim ultimate authority in the case of a conflict between the two. But, more important, "Federalist No. 39" is notable for the way in which Madison was able to turn what he believed to be two major defects of the Constitution as it emerged from the Convention into virtues. He had argued up to the very end of the Convention for a provision giving to the central government the power to negative state laws, but he was thwarted. Madison also remained opposed to the notion of equal representation for the states in the Senate, complaining in a letter to Jefferson shortly after the Convention adjourned that such an arrangement "unbalanced" the government. Yet it was that very compromise that allowed Madison in "Federalist No. 39" to argue for the part-national and part-federal character of the new government.[45]

It is difficult to tell whether Madison's intellectual conversion experience in "Federalist No. 39" was genuine. During the Virginia ratifying convention, Patrick Henry made it clear that he for one was not convinced. In his denunciation of consolidated government, Henry mocked Madison's argument in "Federalist No. 39," calling it an amusing "treatise of political anatomy." Caricaturing Madison's argument, Henry mused that "in the brain it [the government] is national; the stamina are federal—some limbs are federal—others national." Henry felt that he could see through all of this, for, in the end, "to all the common purposes of legislation it is a great consolidation of government."[46]

There was no single set of Antifederalist writings that matched *The Federalist* either in their immediate impact or in their influence on subsequent generations. Antifederalist writers nonetheless managed to produce an impressive body of work, publishing more than two hundred pamphlets and broadsides, many of them having been reprinted and recirculated thirty or forty times.[47]

Two of the most coherent Antifederalist critiques were the *Letters from a Federal Farmer,* written by New York's Melancton Smith, and the essays addressed to "The Citizens of the State of New York" written under the pseudonym "Brutus," probably the work of Abraham Yates, a relative of the discontented New York delegate Robert Yates who had bolted from Philadelphia early in the proceedings.

Although not the most widely circulated of the Antifederalist writers, Brutus provided one of the most cogent summaries of Antifederalist concerns about the proposed Constitution. Appearing in sixteen installments in the New York *Journal* between mid-October 1787 and late spring of 1788, Brutus wrote of the dangers of consolidation, the concentration of power in the hands of a government too distant from the people and from the previously independent and sovereign states. He sounded that theme in his very first essay on October 18, predating, and no doubt acting as a stimulus for, Publius. The "first question," Brutus asked, was whether the states "shall be reduced to one great republic, governed by one legislature, and under the direction of one executive and judicial, or whether they should continue thirteen confederated republics." Then followed what would come to be the standard Antifederalist bill of complaint against the Constitution—the dangers of the "necessary and proper" and federal supremacy clauses and, perhaps most important, the "unlimited" power of the new government over taxation. Brutus identified the power over taxation as the "most important of any power that can be granted; it connects with almost all other powers," and it had the greatest potential to become "the great engine of tyranny and oppression."[48]

Brutus and the Federal Farmer feared that Congress would become the primary engine of oppression, not only because of the extent and vagueness of its powers, but also because of the small number of representatives relative to the population and expanse of the country. This concern about the ratio of representation and the extent of the country may have been prompted in part by an attachment to principles of locally based democracy, but it was also rooted in a much more traditional set of political beliefs. Nearly all of America's political leaders were familiar with the writings of the Baron de Montesquieu, who had argued persuasively that a successful republican government could only rule over a small territory. Though James Madison had proposed a brilliant refutation of Montesquieu's conception of republicanism in "Federalist No. 10," arguing that "extensive republics" were better suited to serving the broader public good, most Antifederalists did not buy it.[49]

The one other recurring theme in the Antifederalist critique was the absence of a bill of rights. Try as the Federalists might to argue that a bill of rights was redundant or that it might run the risk of unintentionally omitting some of the essential natural rights of mankind, the Antifederalists understood that the public at large simply would not be persuaded by that argument. The omission of a bill of rights was one clear instance in which the Founding Fathers misjudged the state of public opinion. As the ratification fight demonstrated, they nearly paid a high price for that misjudgment. It is entirely possible that the Constitution would not have been ratified had the Federalists remained unwilling to yield to Antifederalist demands to add a bill of rights to the document. Moreover, continuing Antifederalist pressure to assure that the Federalists kept their promise was the decisive factor in the drafting of a bill of rights by the First Federal Congress under the new Constitution.[50]

The Antifederalists' warnings of the dangers of an overly powerful, consolidated central government too far removed from the great mass of the American people, was fully consonant with the historical experience of all Americans who had rebelled against British rule. And, as the history of the United States has unfolded since 1787, Americans have been presented with ample evidence of the ways in which the federal taxation power, buttressed by the Sixteenth Amendment giving Congress the power to levy an income tax, has been used not only to promote the "general welfare" but also to expand the role of government in ways that the founders had not anticipated. One of the great ironies of the debate over the Constitution was the extent to which James Madison, who had been so influential in both drafting and then defending the Constitution, would himself become alarmed at the way those in control of the newly created government would use the power of the purse to expand its powers.

In the end, the Federalists won the contest over ratification not only because of their superior tactics, but also because their arguments were stronger and more coherent than those of their opponents. That this was the case owed less to superior wisdom or foresight than to the fact that so many of the principal advocates of the Constitution had spent that long summer in Philadelphia examining all of the weaknesses of the Confederation government and crafting the remedies for those weaknesses. The Antifederalists, geographically dispersed and often forced to formulate their objections to the Constitution in haste and in isolation from one another, never coalesced into a unified opposition. Moreover, the Federalists, upon emerging victorious from the ratification struggle, were able to control the future agenda and to deprive their opponents of the opportunity to fashion their own alternative brand of federalism.

But none of this was inevitable. In 1796, James Madison wrote that it was the state ratifying conventions, and not the Convention in Philadelphia, that had breathed "life and validity" into the Constitution. One of the reasons he was inclined at that moment to downplay the role of the framers of the Constitution in Philadelphia was that he had by that time come around to embrace views closer to those of the Antifederalist critics of the Constitution than of extreme nationalists like Hamilton. But, in fact, it was neither the framers nor the hundreds of delegates who debated the Constitution in the state ratifying conventions who breathed life into that document. As historian Bernard Bailyn has noted, "the whole thing was merely words on paper until implemented" by the new government under George Washington. "Washington knew," Bailyn has observed, "how malleable the situation was; he understood that every move he and his administration made would be precedent that would shape the actuality of the Constitution."[51]

One might go further. The framers in Philadelphia may be fairly credited with creating the initial plan. Those voting in the state ratifying conventions may be justly credited with giving the people's sanction to that plan. George Washington is deservedly honored as the "indispensable man" who launched the plan. But that plan—the United States Constitution—remained a work in progress. The Founding Fathers had indeed created a more perfect union, but the true character of that union was yet to be revealed.

EPILOGUE

"A REPUBLIC, IF YOU CAN KEEP IT"

THERE IS AN OFT-TOLD anecdote about an encounter between Benjamin Franklin and Elizabeth Powel. They met, so the story goes, as Franklin was leaving the Pennsylvania State House shortly after the Constitutional Convention had adjourned. According to Maryland delegate James McHenry, who claimed to have overheard the conversation, the "lady asked Dr. Franklin, Well, Doctor, what have we got a republic or a monarchy?" Franklin's reply: "A republic, if you can keep it."[1]

Franklin's response was technically accurate, but insufficient as a full explanation of what the framers had wrought. The Constitution that emerged from the Convention in Philadelphia during the summer of 1787 was in many respects unmistakably republican. It emphatically rejected notions of hereditary monarchy and aristocracy, and while it stopped well short of creating a *democratic* republic, including as it did an indirectly elected Senate and president, it did recognize "we the people" of the nation as the ultimate source of political authority. But the debates in the Assembly Room of the State House during the summer of 1787 and those in the individual states during the battle over ratification had revealed widely varying understandings of the way in which America's new republican government should operate. As the new federal government commenced operations in March of 1789, Americans continued to disagree over such vitally important issues as the proper division of power between the state and federal governments, the nature and extent of executive power, and whether their new nation should be a genuinely democratic republic. Over the course of the next twelve years, as presidents George Washington and John Adams attempted to construct a solid national edifice around the spare and sometimes-ambiguous framework provided by the Founding Fathers, those disagreements would erupt again and again and, in the process, would transform America's Constitution in fundamental ways.

HOPE, DESPAIR, AND FAREWELL

On April 14, 1789, Charles Thomson, secretary of the new Federal Congress, appeared at George Washington's door at Mount Vernon and informed the general that he had received every one of the sixty-nine votes cast by the electors in the nation's first presidential election. Within two days of Thomson's visit, Washington embarked on his journey from Mount Vernon to the nation's temporary capital in New York. He was acutely aware of the formidable task that awaited him. The struggle over ratification had made it abundantly clear that many Americans remained apprehensive about the dangers inherent in a strong central government, and in a strong chief executive in particular. And that chief executive would be faced with the unresolved problems of the Confederation government—a substantial government debt, continuing jealousies among the states, and formidable challenges in dealing with the nations of Europe, most of which remained contemptuous of America's weakness.[2]

But as Washington made his journey from Mount Vernon to New York City, he was deeply touched by the thousands of people lining the roads all along his route, jostling just to get a glimpse of their hero and cheering him every mile of the way. It was an extraordinary outpouring of affection—all the more touching because of its spontaneity.

His formal inauguration as president was a relatively modest affair. Washington took his oath of office on April 29, 1789, before an assembly of members of both houses of the new Congress, who were gathered together in the Senate chamber of Federal Hall in New York City. In America's first inaugural address, Washington expressed the same humility as when he was elected president of the Constitutional Convention. "No event," he began, "could have filled me with greater anxiety" than the awesome responsibility of serving as the nation's first president. As he had on previous occasions, he accepted his new post with diffidence, acknowledging his "inferior endowments" and inexperience "in the duties of civil administration." Most observers believed his modesty to be genuine, but few shared his fears.[3]

Over the course of the next eight years, Washington would establish the legitimacy not only of the American presidency, but also of the American state. Although acutely conscious of the dangers of the abuse of power, he was nevertheless a decisive and powerful chief executive—as decisive and as powerful as any man who has occupied the office since. In the process, however, he would find himself thrust into an often-bitter debate over what the Constitution actually meant—over the very nature of America's federalist and republican system of government. Washington's willingness to assert the power of his office in defending and executing his vision of the Constitution when necessary would be the source of his greatness as a president, but it would also cause him greater anguish than he had experienced at any other time in his life.[4]

As Washington neared the end of his second term in office, he should have felt enormous pride in his accomplishments. He created the institution of the presidential cabinet and built the essential infrastructure of the executive branch. He established important precedents with respect to the relationship between Congress and the executive branch, helping to define the separation of power between those branches that had been sketched out only vaguely by the framers of the Constitution. With the help of his treasury secretary, Alexander Hamilton, he restored the nation's credit both at home and abroad. And in agreeing to a necessary, but highly controversial, commercial treaty with Great Britain, he took the initial, often difficult steps in building respect for America on the world stage. But his mood as he left office was marked by feelings more of torment than of triumph. He felt more urgently than ever that "ease and retirement" were "indispensably necessary" to him. As he contemplated leaving the public stage forever on a final ride back to Mount Vernon, Washington felt compelled to prepare some form of "valedictory address," a statement to the people of America aimed not only at vindicating his eight years of service as president but, more important, at articulating his hopes and fears for the country in the years and decades to come.

Washington's Farewell Address began with customary humility, with expressions of his inadequacy to the task he had been called to perform and of gratitude to the people for their confidence in him. But the commander in chief then abandoned humility as a rhetorical tool. "Here then," he wrote, "perhaps I should stop. But a solicitude for your welfare which cannot end but with my life, and the apprehension of danger . . . urge me . . . to offer to your solemn contemplation and to recommend to your frequent review, some sentiments which are the result of much reflection, of no inconsiderable observation, and which appear to me all-important to the permanency of your felicity as a people." Washington's advice to his people was shaped in some measure by the most urgent subject on his mind—the treacherous waters of foreign affairs and foreign intrigue the new nation had been forced to navigate during his final years in office. His second term had been consumed by the difficulties of finding an independent path for America in the ongoing wars between England and France, and the best-remembered part of his address is his caution against "connecting ourselves with the politics of any nation." The only certain guide to managing America's relations with Europe, Washington cautioned, was a clearheaded calculation of its own national interest.

Washington's admonition has been interpreted through the ages either as a defense of isolationism or as the first American expression of a "realist" foreign policy, but it ultimately spoke to a larger subject: the duty of all Americans to work diligently to hold their fragile union together. Washington had watched, anguished, as Americans succumbed to a "party spirit," pitting supporters of France against supporters of Great Britain, Southerners versus Northerners, and Easterners versus Westerners. The true salvation of America's republican liberty, Washington believed, lay in the union itself. The American government was

> the offspring of our own choice, uninfluenced and unawed, adopted upon full investigation and mature deliberation, completely free in its principles, in the distribution of its powers, uniting security with energy, and containing within itself a provision for its own amendment, has a just claim to your confidence and support. Respect for its authority, compliance with its laws, and acquiescence to its measures are duties enjoined by the fundamental maxims of true liberty.[5]

Washington's farewell to his countrymen was more an expression of hope than of certainty. During the final years of his presidency, he had endured bitter attacks from an increasingly well-organized "Republican" political party. In signing the controversial commercial treaty with Great Britain negotiated by his Federalist colleague John Jay, Washington had opened himself up to charges that he had sold out America's independence to the country's former foe and that he was the dupe of British aristocrats and monied interests. To make matters worse, it seemed that his former friends and allies, Thomas Jefferson and James Madison, were behind some of the attacks. As he began his retirement, he turned once again to his dear friend and companion during the summer of 1787, Elizabeth Powel, for consolation. In his message to Elizabeth, he predicted that the attacks might well continue long after he had departed the earth. His only hope, he joked, was that he would outlive his enemies. He vowed to do everything he could to live into the next century in order to get the better of his adversaries. He fell just short of that goal.[6]

When, in the late evening of December 14, 1799, Washington succumbed to a bacterial infection and passed quietly from the world, the political environment in his country was anything but quiet. "Party spirit," acrimonious enough while he occupied the presidency, exploded during the administration of his prickly successor, John Adams. Although Adams and his vice president, Thomas Jefferson, had vowed when they took office to do everything possible to subdue the partisan rancor, their vow barely lasted the month. By the time of Washington's death, members of the emerging Jeffersonian Republican party, now in open revolt against the foreign policies of the Adams administration, were threatening to fight on the side of France should the United States government's warlike posture toward that country result in open hostilities. Adams and his supporters in Congress, in retaliation against what they considered to be their adversaries' disloyal behavior, had enacted the Alien and Sedition Laws, punishing with fines or jail sentences anyone who "wrote or spoke, falsely or maliciously" against the officers of the federal government. Thomas Jefferson, by now a vice president in exile, worked with James Madison to promote a series of resolutions in the Virginia and Kentucky legislatures declaring the Alien and Sedition Laws unconstitutional and threatening to defy any attempt to enforce them. Extreme Federalists reacted by threatening to march troops into Virginia and Kentucky to impose the government's will.[7]

How had it come to this? Had Washington been alive, his mind may well have turned to that moment in the fall of 1786, when he received anguished reports from his friends and Revolutionary War compatriots about the impending breakup of the fragile American union in the aftermath of Shays' Rebellion. Was America's new experiment in republican liberty doomed to follow the path that had brought about the demise of the Confederation government? Was the tumult across America proof of what Washington had so long feared—"that mankind, when left to themselves, are unfit for their own government"?

THE REVOLUTION OF 1800

The presidential election of 1800, pitting the incumbent president, John Adams, against his now-rebellious vice president, Thomas Jefferson, was one of the vilest and most mean-spirited elections ever to occur in America. The full story of that election makes for compelling reading, but its immediate importance for our purposes is that it brought into bold relief the inadequacies of the electoral system devised by the framers. Jefferson received seventy-three electoral votes and Adams sixty-four, but that was not the end of it. The framers of the Constitution had neither reckoned on the emergence of organized political parties, nor imagined that each of those parties would organize a presidential *ticket*, consisting not only of a presidential nominee, but a vice-presidential nominee as well. By the extraordinarily complicated terms of Article II, Section 1 of the Constitution, each elector was "to vote by ballot for two persons," with the person receiving the greatest number of votes to be designated president and the recipient of the next highest number of votes to be designated vice president. The Republican electors had faithfully cast their votes for *both* Thomas Jefferson and his vice-presidential running mate, Aaron Burr, with the result being that Burr received the same number of electoral votes as Jefferson. Since the Constitution provided no means of distinguishing a presidential from a vice-presidential vote, the election would now be decided by the House of Representatives.

Had Aaron Burr been a self-sacrificing and loyal Jeffersonian, he no doubt would have bowed out gracefully, conceding the presidency to Jefferson and assuming his place as vice president. But the combination of Burr's ambition and the Federalists' fear and fury at the prospect of Jefferson's election made subsequent developments in the House of Representatives anything but gracious or serene. The nation found itself with a full-fledged constitutional crisis on its hands.

It took thirty-six ballots in the House of Representatives, but Jefferson finally emerged victorious. Both sides were inclined to label Jefferson's election as "the revolution of 1800," an event in many ways as momentous as the throwing off of British rule in 1776. Jefferson's supporters breathed a sigh of relief and began making plans to dismantle much of what the Federalists had constructed during the first twelve years of the government's operation. The revolution of 1800 would, they hoped, reestablish the true principles of republicanism. Not only would it amount to a repudiation of a foreign policy that rendered America subservient to Great Britain, but, equally important, it would signify a return to an earlier constitutional understanding of the concept of "federalism," one in which the power and autonomy of the state governments was paramount. Many Federalists believed that Jefferson would do exactly what some of his most enthusiastic supporters were hoping for. The consequence, in their view, would be disintegration of America's experiment in republican union into disorder and anarchy.[8]

THE INAUGURATION OF Thomas Jefferson as America's third president was the first to occur in America's new capital, the District of Columbia. The physical condition of the capital city hardly foretold a nation destined for greatness. The grand design of the capital's architect, Pierre L'Enfant, was barely discernible. The principal avenues of the city, confusing to visitors even today, were even more confounding to those attending Jefferson's inauguration in the spring of 1801. Perpetually flooded in the swampland on which the city was being constructed, the muddy streets would abruptly end, awaiting the construction of government buildings that may have existed on L'Enfant's drawing board but not in reality. One could easily forgive a stranger for concluding that he had arrived not at the seat of government of a great nation but rather at a dilapidated country town in some unknown wilderness.[9]

Jefferson took his oath of office in the senate wing of the Capitol building, but the Capitol too seemed more a vain hope than a vigorous reality. Only the north wing of the building—the Senate chamber—had been completed by the spring of 1801. The south wing had reached a height of about twenty feet. Constructed within the south wing was an oval brick building, derisively called "the Oven," which was to serve as the temporary meeting place of the House of Representatives. The center part of the Capitol, from which the great dome today rises, was nothing more than a bare foundation.[10]

John Adams, the retiring president, was notably absent from the inauguration of his successor. As Adams's great-grandson, Henry Adams, noted, "Perhaps the late President was wise to retire from a stage where everything was arranged to point a censure upon his principles, and where he would have seemed, in his successor's opinion, as little in place as George III would have appeared at the installation of President Washington."[11]

John Adams, in one of his last acts as president after losing the election to Jefferson, had appointed John Marshall, Jefferson's longtime political rival in Virginia, as chief justice of the Supreme Court. It was Marshall who stood before Jefferson in the Senate chamber to administer the oath of office. Marshall and Jefferson were opposites in every way except one. Marshall was a man of easy informality, a self-confident ladies' man who enjoyed his convivial pleasures. He had been intensely loyal to George Washington and remained committed to upholding an expansive view of the powers granted to the federal government under the Constitution. Jefferson, though polished in manners, was often awkward in the social settings that Marshall so much enjoyed. Jefferson and Washington had drifted apart, primarily because of the latter's embrace of Hamiltonian doctrines. The one thing both Jefferson and Marshall had in common was high intelligence, but that attribute would only intensify their rivalry.[12]

Standing by Jefferson's side as Marshall administered the oath of office was Aaron Burr. At that moment it would have been difficult to judge which of the two men Jefferson despised more—his longtime Virginia rival or the erstwhile running mate who had so recently connived with the Federalists to deprive him of his election. The Jefferson-Burr combination was the nation's first example of a "balanced ticket," a Southerner paired with a Northerner, a man of strict constructionist constitutional principles paired with a man of no discernible principles. It would not be a happy partnership.[13]

That was the scene as Jefferson looked out upon his audience and began his inaugural address. He began in the same diffident rhetorical mode that had been the hallmark of George Washington's speeches on similar occasions. He professed his "sincere consciousness that the task is above my talents" and acknowledged "those anxious and awful presentments which the greatness of the charge and the weakness of my own powers so justly inspire." But then, far more eloquently than Washington ever could have described it, he shared his vision of the nation's future.

A rising nation, spread over a wide and fruitful land,
traversing all the seas with the rich productions of their
industry, engaged in commerce with nations who feel
power and forget right, advance rapidly to the destinies
beyond the reach of mortal eye. . . . Kindly separated by
nature and a wide ocean from the exterminating havoc of
one quarter of the globe; too high-minded to endure the
degradations of the others; possessing a chosen country,
with room enough for our descendants to the thousandth
and thousandth generation.

Given the humbleness—and the backwardness—of the setting in
which he was speaking, it was an ambitious, even an audacious vision.[14]

Jefferson next acknowledged the bitter "contest of opinion through
which we have passed." Although he could have chosen that moment to
announce his agenda for reversing the course of Federalist policy, he
chose instead to hold out the olive branch. Noting that "every difference
of opinion is not a difference of principle," Jefferson spoke the most
memorable words of his inaugural address.

We are all Republicans, we are all Federalists. If there be
any among us who would wish to dissolve this Union or to
change its republican form, let them stand undisturbed as
monuments of the safety with which error of opinion may
be tolerated where reason is left free to combat it.[15]

George Washington's Farewell Address and Thomas Jefferson's first
inaugural had two important themes in common. In 1776, the "common
cause" of Americans' struggle against Great Britain had served as the
unifying force within thirteen states aspiring to independence. As the
immediacy of that common cause faded with time, Americans discovered they needed something other than a common enemy to hold them
together. Whatever their differences of opinion on the proper *interpretation* of the Constitution, Washington and Jefferson had both come to believe that the United States Constitution was the instrument that not
only held a political entity—the union—together, but also that which
helped define Americans as one people.

If both men had come to appreciate the transcendently important role
the Constitution would play in defining the character of the young

American nation and its people, they also shared an acute sense of the fragility both of the document itself and of the union it had created. Their addresses expressed both hope and trepidation. In the same breath that Washington extolled "the unity of Government, which constitutes you one people," he worried about the "pains [that] will be taken, the many artifices employed, to weaken in your minds the conviction of this truth." Jefferson, while praising the Constitution as "the world's best hope," had also recognized impulses to abandon it in the heat of partisan battle. For both Washington and Jefferson, America's experiment in constitutional union was one that needed to be carefully tended.

"THE TIMELESS CONSTITUTION AND THE LIVING CONSTITUTION"

From Jefferson's time forward, Americans have argued about the best means of nurturing and protecting their Constitution. Throughout most of our history, Americans have proven themselves a remarkably forward-looking people, largely unconcerned about looking back on their past and resolutely, optimistically, looking toward the future. Yet we have adopted a reverential attitude toward the wisdom of those men who over two hundred years ago framed our Constitution. We regard the product of their labors as timeless. James Madison, *an* author if not *the* author of the Constitution, changed his mind about many of its features during the course of the Philadelphia Convention. Moreover, his original intentions about the powers of the new government underwent even more dramatic change in the decades to come, as he came to embrace a strict constructionist interpretation of the powers granted under the Constitution. Yet, as historian Jack Rakove has emphasized, Madison was profoundly respectful of history and of tradition. In "Federalist No. 49" he wrote approvingly of "that veneration which time bestows on every thing, and without which perhaps the wisest and freest governments would not possess the requisite stability."[16]

Madison's close friend and political ally, Thomas Jefferson, was of a different temperament. In a remarkable letter written to Madison just before he returned from France in 1789, Jefferson took up the question of "whether one generation of men has a right to bind another." Jefferson answered in the negative. "The earth belongs to the living; . . . the dead have neither power nor right over it." Applying that belief to the durability and immutability of constitutions, Jefferson asserted that "no society can make a perpetual constitution or perpetual law. The earth belongs always to the living generation. They may manage it then, and what proceeds from it, as they please."[17]

However much Madison may have respected the intellect of his Virginia neighbor, he was not ready to jettison history and tradition so casually. Responding to Jefferson, he acknowledged that his friend's argument might have some merit in theory, but that "it seems liable in practice to some very powerful objections." "A Government so often revised," Madison objected, would "become too mutable to retain those prejudices in its favor which antiquity inspires, and which are perhaps a salutary aid to the rational Government in the most enlightened age." Madison feared that constant revisions in the form of the government, depending merely on the whims of public opinion in a particular age, would "engender pernicious factions that might not otherwise come into existence." It would be far preferable, Madison thought, if the Constitution were more firmly rooted in the "prejudices" of those wise men with whom he had gathered in Philadelphia in the summer of 1787.[18]

But Jefferson stuck to his guns. Writing some twenty-five years later, he reiterated his skepticism about the permanency of constitutions. "Some men," Jefferson noted,

> look at constitutions with sanctimonious reverence, and deem them like the ark of the covenant, too sacred to be touched. They ascribe to the men of the preceding age a wisdom more than human, suppose what they did to be beyond amendment. I knew that age well; I belonged to it, and labored with it. It deserved well of its country. . . . But I know, also that laws and institutions must go hand and hand with the progress of the human mind. As that becomes more developed, more enlightened, as new discoveries are made, new truths disclosed, and manners and opinions change with the change of circumstances, institutions must advance also, and keep pace with the times.[19]

Madison had participated in nearly every minute of the deliberations of the Constitutional Convention in Philadelphia. He had witnessed the bitter disagreements, the displays of personal ambition and pettiness, and he knew well the vast diversity of opinion among the members of that Convention as to the meanings of the words written on those four parchment pages. Madison's Constitution was certainly no divinely inspired text delivered directly from heaven. Nevertheless, he believed to the very end of his life that the Constitution created that summer, though imperfect, was the best that any group of men at any time could have achieved. Perhaps influenced by his pride in his own authorial role and by his veneration of tradition, Madison continued to defend the timeless quality of his achievement.

THERE IS A MIDDLE course between Madison's timeless Constitution and Jefferson's protean one. We would be devaluing the extraordinary accomplishment of the Founding Fathers if we did not accord their Constitution the veneration that such a time-tested document deserves. But, in the egalitarian and democratic spirit of Jefferson, we must have faith in the wisdom of citizens of our own age to guide our continuing political experiment down paths that will ensure that we fulfill the promise of our other great Revolutionary document, the Declaration of Independence. Jefferson came to appreciate the achievement of those who created the constitutional revolution of 1787; he saw it as an important step—but just a step—toward securing the blessings of liberty promised by the Revolution of 1776. In the Jeffersonian sense, the revolution of 1787, like that of 1776, continues even today.

ACKNOWLEDGMENTS

I HAVE SPENT the past forty years thinking about this book, and the last four years writing it. During this time my understanding of the issues and personalities central to the making of the American Constitution has been shaped and enriched by the work of hundreds of scholars who have worked on aspects of this subject over the past two centuries. I have made a conscientious effort to acknowledge in the extensive Notes section my debt to those scholars.

Several of my history and political science colleagues have read drafts of this book at various stages. My good friend and history colleague at Penn, Bruce Kuklick, read two different drafts of the manuscript, offering useful advice every step of the way. Dr. George Van Cleve of the University of Virginia, who has just completed a path-breaking work on slavery and the Constitution, read all of the sections of the book dealing with the Founding Fathers and slavery. Although we may differ on some points of interpretation, his expertise and sound advice were invaluable in sharpening my understanding of that vexed subject. Professor Pauline Maier, who is completing what is certain to be the definitive study of the ratification of the Constitution, read my chapters on ratification and was extraordinarily generous in sharing some of her insights with me. Professor John R. Vile, author of the monumental *The Constitutional Convention of 1787: A Comprehensive Encyclopedia of America's Founding*, read the entire manuscript and offered exceptionally useful advice on matters of both fact and interpretation. Moreover, he was extraordinarily gracious in his responses as I pestered him with dozens of e-mailed questions about subjects both large and small. The irrepressible Professor Billy G. Smith of Montana State University provided me with invaluable information, some of it suitable for family audiences, on aspects of social and economic life in Philadelphia during the era of the Constitutional Convention.

I have spent nearly all of my professional career working in the city in which the Declaration of Independence and the Constitution were born. It has been my good fortune to have benefited from the help of the talented staff of the National Park Service at Independence National Historical Park. Anne Coxe Toogood, Independence Park historian, answered literally hundreds of questions I posed about the physical site in and around Independence Hall, always with good cheer. Karen Stevens, archivist and librarian at Independence Park, helped me find some of the treasures in that wonderful facility. And Andrea Ashby Leraris went out of her way to help me locate many of the images that I have used in the illustrations for the book.

Tim Bartlett, senior history editor at Random House, has been a vital part of this project from the beginning. He worked through at least four different rounds of editing of the manuscript, always giving sound, supportive advice. He not only has superb intellectual judgment, but he is a Philadelphia Phillies fan—a perfect combination. Paula Cooper Hughes did a superb job of copyediting the manuscript. Indeed, the phrase "copyediting" does not describe the level of historical insight, literary grace, and craft that she brought to her task. Lindsey Schwoeri and Patricia Nicolescu at Random House provided timely and highly competent support in the final stages of production of the book.

I had never had a literary agent before embarking on this project and, frankly, had no idea what an agent did other than taking a portion of any profits that a book might generate. My agent, John Wright, has taught me more than I ever could have imagined about how to conceive, organize, and write a book intended for that elusive "general" public. John has been with me every step of the way, encouraging me, reading many drafts of portions of the book, and serving as my on-call psychotherapist at those moments when I seemed to be losing my way.

Although I have taught the subject of the United States Constitution to students at the University of Pennsylvania for forty years, it was not until I began my association with the National Constitution Center, a true treasure of a museum located on Independence Mall in Philadelphia, that I began to think about writing a book that would convey my knowledge of the Constitution to a wide audience. I am enormously grateful to the staff of the Constitution Center, and to its extraordinarily talented leader, Joseph Torsella, for providing me with some of the inspiration to write *Plain, Honest Men.*

My wife, Mary Cahill, has had the difficult job of playing the role of "intelligent general reader." She has read many drafts of many chapters of this book. If I have succeeded in engaging her attention with it, I hope I may be able to engage the attention of others as well.

Finally, I owe a mixed debt of gratitude to my golden retriever puppy, Abigail Adams. During the final year of writing this book, I have spent nearly every waking hour at my computer. At ninety-minute intervals, Abby would saunter up to my desk with a Frisbee in her mouth and begin to whine. At which point we would go outside, in all kinds of weather, and play. This ritual unquestionably slowed my progress on the book, but it improved my Frisbee toss slightly and her catching skills to championship levels. And it helped clear my foggy brain in the bargain. As much as I would like to hold Abby responsible for any errors of fact or interpretation in this book, I'm afraid that I will have to assume that burden.

APPENDIX 1

Full List of Delegates to the Constitutional Convention of 1787

CONNECTICUT
Oliver Ellsworth*
William Samuel Johnson*
Roger Sherman*

DELAWARE
Richard Bassett*
Gunning Bedford, Jr.*
Jacob Broom*
John Dickinson**
George Read*

GEORGIA
Abraham Baldwin*
William Few*
William Houstoun
William Pierce

MARYLAND
Daniel Carroll*
Luther Martin
James McHenry*
John Mercer
Daniel of St. Thomas Jenifer*

MASSACHUSETTS
Elbridge Gerry
Nathaniel Gorham*
Rufus King*
Caleb Strong

NEW HAMPSHIRE
Nicholas Gilman*
John Langdon*

NEW JERSEY
David Brearley*
Jonathan Dayton*
William Churchill Houston
William Livingston*
William Paterson*

NEW YORK
Alexander Hamilton*
John Lansing, Jr.
Robert Yates

NORTH CAROLINA
William Blount*
William R. Davie
Alexander Martin
Richard Dobbs Spaight*
Hugh Williamson*

PENNSYLVANIA
George Clymer*
Thomas Fitzsimons*
Benjamin Franklin*
Jared Ingersoll*
Thomas Mifflin*
Gouverneur Morris*

Robert Morris*
James Wilson*

SOUTH CAROLINA
Pierce Butler*
Charles Pinckney*
Charles Cotesworth Pinckney*
John Rutledge*

VIRGINIA
John Blair*
James Madison*
George Mason
James McClurg
Edmund Randolph
George Washington*
George Wythe

*Signed the Constitution
**Instructed George Read to sign the Constitution in his absence

APPENDIX 2

U.S. Constitution (September 17, 1787), Article I–VII

WE THE PEOPLE OF THE UNITED STATES, in Order to form a more perfect Union, establish Justice, insure domestic Tranquility, provide for the common defence, promote the general Welfare, and secure the Blessings of Liberty to ourselves and our Posterity, do ordain and establish this Constitution for the United States of America.

ARTICLE. I.

SECTION. 1.

All legislative Powers herein granted shall be vested in a Congress of the United States, which shall consist of a Senate and House of Representatives.

SECTION. 2.

The House of Representatives shall be composed of Members chosen every second Year by the People of the several States, and the Electors in each State shall have the Qualifications requisite for Electors of the most numerous Branch of the State Legislature.

No Person shall be a Representative who shall not have attained to the Age of twenty five Years, and been seven Years a Citizen of the United States, and who shall not, when elected, be an Inhabitant of that State in which he shall be chosen.

Representatives and direct Taxes shall be apportioned among the several States which may be included within this Union, according to their respective Numbers, which shall be determined by adding to the whole Number of free Persons, including those bound to Service for a Term of Years, and excluding Indians not taxed, three fifths of all other Persons. The actual Enumeration shall be made within three Years after the first Meeting of the Congress of the United States, and within every subsequent Term of ten Years, in such Manner as they shall by Law direct. The Number of Representatives shall not exceed one for every thirty Thousand, but each State shall have at Least one Representative; and until such Enumeration shall be made, the State of New Hampshire shall be entitled to chuse three, Massachusetts eight, Rhode-Island and Providence Plantations one, Connecticut five, New-York six, New Jersey four, Pennsylvania eight, Delaware one, Maryland six, Virginia ten, North Carolina five, South Carolina five, and Georgia three.

When vacancies happen in the Representation from any State, the Executive Authority thereof shall issue Writs of Election to fill such Vacancies.

The House of Representatives shall chuse their Speaker and other Officers; and shall have the sole Power of Impeachment.

SECTION. 3.

The Senate of the United States shall be composed of two Senators from each State, chosen by the Legislature thereof for six Years; and each Senator shall have one Vote.

Immediately after they shall be assembled in Consequence of the first Election, they shall be divided as equally as may be into three Classes. The Seats of the Senators of the first Class shall be vacated at the Expiration of the second Year, of the second Class at the Expiration of the fourth Year, and of the third Class at the Expiration of the sixth Year, so that one third may be chosen every second Year; and if Vacancies happen by Resignation, or otherwise, during the Recess of the Legislature of any State, the Executive thereof may make temporary Appointments until the next Meeting of the Legislature, which shall then fill such Vacancies.

No Person shall be a Senator who shall not have attained to the Age of thirty Years, and been nine Years a Citizen of the United States, and who shall not, when elected, be an Inhabitant of that State for which he shall be chosen.

The Vice President of the United States shall be President of the Senate, but shall have no Vote, unless they be equally divided.

The Senate shall chuse their other Officers, and also a President pro tempore, in the Absence of the Vice President, or when he shall exercise the Office of President of the United States.

The Senate shall have the sole Power to try all Impeachments. When sitting for that Purpose, they shall be on Oath or Affirmation. When the President of the United States is tried, the Chief Justice shall preside: And no Person shall be convicted without the Concurrence of two thirds of the Members present.

Judgment in Cases of Impeachment shall not extend further than to removal from Office, and disqualification to hold and enjoy any Office of honor, Trust or Profit under the United States: but the Party convicted shall nevertheless be liable and subject to Indictment, Trial, Judgment and Punishment, according to Law.

SECTION. 4.

The Times, Places and Manner of holding Elections for Senators and Representatives, shall be prescribed in each State by the Legislature thereof; but the Congress may at any time by Law make or alter such Regulations, except as to the Places of chusing Senators.

The Congress shall assemble at least once in every Year, and such Meeting shall be on the first Monday in December, unless they shall by Law appoint a different Day.

SECTION. 5.

Each House shall be the Judge of the Elections, Returns and Qualifications of its own Members, and a Majority of each shall constitute a Quorum to do Business; but a smaller Number may adjourn from day to day, and may be authorized to compel the Attendance of absent Members, in such Manner, and under such Penalties as each House may provide.

Each House may determine the Rules of its Proceedings, punish its Members for disorderly Behaviour, and, with the Concurrence of two thirds, expel a Member.

Each House shall keep a Journal of its Proceedings, and from time to time publish the same, excepting such Parts as may in their Judgment require Secrecy; and the Yeas and Nays of the Members of either House on any question shall, at the Desire of one fifth of those Present, be entered on the Journal.

Neither House, during the Session of Congress, shall, without the Consent of the other, adjourn for more than three days, nor to any other Place than that in which the two Houses shall be sitting.

SECTION. 6.

The Senators and Representatives shall receive a Compensation for their Services, to be ascertained by Law, and paid out of the Treasury of the United States. They shall in all Cases, except Treason, Felony and Breach of the Peace, be privileged from Arrest during their Attendance at the Session of their respective Houses, and in going to and returning from the same; and for any Speech or Debate in either House, they shall not be questioned in any other Place.

No Senator or Representative shall, during the Time for which he was elected, be appointed to any civil Office under the Authority of the United States, which shall have been created, or the Emoluments whereof shall have been encreased during such time; and no Person holding any Office under the United States, shall be a Member of either House during his Continuance in Office.

SECTION. 7.

All Bills for raising Revenue shall originate in the House of Representatives; but the Senate may propose or concur with Amendments as on other Bills.

Every Bill which shall have passed The House of Representatives and the Senate, shall, before it become a Law, be presented to the President of the United States: If he approve he shall sign it, but if not he shall return it, with his Objections to that House in which it shall have originated, who shall enter the Objections at large on their Journal, and proceed to reconsider it. If after such reconsideration two thirds of that House shall agree to pass the Bill, it shall be sent, together with the Objections, to the other House, by which it shall likewise be reconsidered, and if approved by two thirds of that House, it shall become a Law. But in all such Cases the Votes of both Houses shall be determined by yeas and Nays, and the Names of the Persons voting for and against the Bill shall be entered on the Journal of each House respectively. If any Bill shall not be returned by the President within ten Days (Sundays excepted) after it shall have been presented to him, the Same shall be a Law, in like Manner as if he had signed it, unless the Congress by their Adjournment prevent its Return, in which Case it shall not be a Law.

Every Order, Resolution, or Vote to which the Concurrence of the Senate and House of Representatives may be necessary (except on a question of Adjournment) shall be presented to the President of the United States; and before the Same shall take Effect, shall be approved by him, or being disapproved by him, shall be repassed by two thirds of the Senate and

House of Representatives, according to the Rules and Limitations prescribed in the Case of a Bill.

SECTION. 8.

The Congress shall have Power To lay and collect Taxes, Duties, Imposts
and Excises, to pay the Debts and provide for the common Defence and
general Welfare of the United States; but all Duties, Imposts and Excises
shall be uniform throughout the United States;

To borrow Money on the credit of the United States;

To regulate Commerce with foreign Nations, and among the several
States, and with the Indian Tribes;

To establish an uniform Rule of Naturalization, and uniform Laws on
the subject of Bankruptcies throughout the United States;

To coin Money, regulate the Value thereof, and of foreign Coin, and fix
the Standard of Weights and Measures;

To provide for the Punishment of counterfeiting the Securities and
current Coin of the United States;

To establish Post Offices and post Roads;

To promote the Progress of Science and useful Arts, by securing for
limited Times to Authors and Inventors the exclusive Right to their respective Writings and Discoveries;

To constitute Tribunals inferior to the supreme Court;

To define and punish Piracies and Felonies committed on the high
Seas, and Offences against the Law of Nations;

To declare War, grant Letters of Marque and Reprisal, and make Rules
concerning Captures on Land and Water;

To raise and support Armies, but no Appropriation of Money to that
Use shall be for a longer Term than two Years;

To provide and maintain a Navy;

To make Rules for the Government and Regulation of the land and
naval Forces;

To provide for calling forth the Militia to execute the Laws of the
Union, suppress Insurrections and repel Invasions;

To provide for organizing, arming, and disciplining, the Militia, and for
governing such Part of them as may be employed in the Service of the
United States, reserving to the States respectively, the Appointment of
the Officers, and the Authority of training the Militia according to the
discipline prescribed by Congress;

To exercise exclusive Legislation in all Cases whatsoever, over such
District (not exceeding ten Miles square) as may, by Cession of Particu-

lar States, and the Acceptance of Congress, become the Seat of the Government of the United States, and to exercise like Authority over all Places purchased by the Consent of the Legislature of the State in which the Same shall be, for the Erection of Forts, Magazines, Arsenals, dock-Yards, and other needful Buildings;—And

To make all Laws which shall be necessary and proper for carrying into Execution the foregoing Powers, and all other Powers vested by this Constitution in the Government of the United States, or in any Department or Officer thereof.

SECTION. 9.

The Migration or Importation of such Persons as any of the States now existing shall think proper to admit, shall not be prohibited by the Congress prior to the Year one thousand eight hundred and eight, but a Tax or duty may be imposed on such Importation, not exceeding ten dollars for each Person.

The Privilege of the Writ of Habeas Corpus shall not be suspended, unless when in Cases of Rebellion or Invasion the public Safety may require it.

No Bill of Attainder or ex post facto Law shall be passed.

No Capitation, or other direct, Tax shall be laid, unless in Proportion to the Census or Enumeration herein before directed to be taken.

No Tax or Duty shall be laid on Articles exported from any State.

No Preference shall be given by any Regulation of Commerce or Revenue to the Ports of one State over those of another; nor shall Vessels bound to, or from, one State, be obliged to enter, clear, or pay Duties in another.

No Money shall be drawn from the Treasury, but in Consequence of Appropriations made by Law; and a regular Statement and Account of the Receipts and Expenditures of all public Money shall be published from time to time.

No Title of Nobility shall be granted by the United States: And no Person holding any Office of Profit or Trust under them, shall, without the Consent of the Congress, accept of any present, Emolument, Office, or Title, of any kind whatever, from any King, Prince, or foreign State.

SECTION. 10.

No State shall enter into any Treaty, Alliance, or Confederation; grant Letters of Marque and Reprisal; coin Money; emit Bills of Credit; make any Thing but gold and silver Coin a Tender in Payment of Debts; pass any Bill of Attainder, ex post facto Law, or Law impairing the Obligation of Contracts, or grant any Title of Nobility.

No State shall, without the Consent of the Congress, lay any Imposts or Duties on Imports or Exports, except what may be absolutely necessary for executing it's inspection Laws: and the net Produce of all Duties and Imposts, laid by any State on Imports or Exports, shall be for the Use of the Treasury of the United States; and all such Laws shall be subject to the Revision and Controul of the Congress.

No State shall, without the Consent of Congress, lay any Duty of Tonnage, keep Troops, or Ships of War in time of Peace, enter into any Agreement or Compact with another State, or with a foreign Power, or engage in War, unless actually invaded, or in such imminent Danger as will not admit of delay.

ARTICLE. II.

SECTION. 1.

The executive Power shall be vested in a President of the United States of America. He shall hold his Office during the Term of four Years, and, together with the Vice President, chosen for the same Term, be elected, as follows:

Each State shall appoint, in such Manner as the Legislature thereof may direct, a Number of Electors, equal to the whole Number of Senators and Representatives to which the State may be entitled in the Congress: but no Senator or Representative, or Person holding an Office of Trust or Profit under the United States, shall be appointed an Elector.

The Electors shall meet in their respective States, and vote by Ballot for two Persons, of whom one at least shall not be an Inhabitant of the same State with themselves. And they shall make a List of all the Persons voted for, and of the Number of Votes for each; which List they shall sign and certify, and transmit sealed to the Seat of the Government of the United States, directed to the President of the Senate. The President of the Senate shall, in the Presence of the Senate and House of Representatives, open all the Certificates, and the Votes shall then be counted. The Person having the greatest Number of Votes shall be the President, if such Number be a Majority of the whole Number of Electors appointed; and if there be more than one who have such Majority, and have an equal Number of Votes, then The House of Representatives shall immediately chuse by Ballot one of them for President; and if no Person have a Majority, then from the five highest on the List the said House shall in like Manner chuse the President. But in chusing the President, the Votes shall be taken by States, the Representation from each State having one Vote; A quorum for this purpose shall consist of a Member or Members from two thirds of the States, and a Majority of all the States shall be necessary to a Choice. In every Case, after the Choice of the President, the Person having the greatest Number of Votes of the Electors shall be the Vice President. But if there should remain two or more who have equal Votes, the Senate shall chuse from them by Ballot the Vice President.

The Congress may determine the Time of chusing the Electors, and the Day on which they shall give their Votes; which Day shall be the same throughout the United States.

No Person except a natural born Citizen, or a Citizen of the United States, at the time of the Adoption of this Constitution, shall be eligible to the Office of President; neither shall any Person be eligible to that Office who shall not have attained to the Age of thirty five Years, and been fourteen Years a Resident within the United States.

In Case of the Removal of the President from Office, or of his Death, Resignation, or Inability to discharge the Powers and Duties of the said Office, the Same shall devolve on the Vice President, and the Congress may by Law provide for the Case of Removal, Death, Resignation or Inability, both of the President and Vice President, declaring what Officer shall then act as President, and such Officer shall act accordingly, until the Disability be removed, or a President shall be elected.

The President shall, at stated Times, receive for his Services, a Compensation, which shall neither be increased nor diminished during the Period for which he shall have been elected, and he shall not receive within that Period any other Emolument from the United States, or any of them.

Before he enter on the Execution of his Office, he shall take the following Oath or Affirmation:—"I do solemnly swear (or affirm) that I will faithfully execute the Office of President of the United States, and will to the best of my Ability, preserve, protect and defend the Constitution of the United States."

SECTION. 2.
The President shall be Commander in Chief of the Army and Navy of the United States, and of the Militia of the several States, when called into the

actual Service of the United States; he may require the Opinion, in writing, of the principal Officer in each of the executive Departments, upon any Subject relating to the Duties of their respective Offices, and he shall have Power to grant Reprieves and Pardons for Offences against the United States, except in Cases of Impeachment.

He shall have Power, by and with the Advice and Consent of the Senate, to make Treaties, provided two thirds of the Senators present concur; and he shall nominate, and by and with the Advice and Consent of the Senate, shall appoint Ambassadors, other public Ministers and Consuls, Judges of the supreme Court, and all other Officers of the United States, whose Appointments are not herein otherwise provided for, and which shall be established by Law: but the Congress may by Law vest the Appointment of such inferior Officers, as they think proper, in the President alone, in the Courts of Law, or in the Heads of Departments.

The President shall have Power to fill up all Vacancies that may happen during the Recess of the Senate, by granting Commissions which shall expire at the End of their next Session.

SECTION. 3.

He shall from time to time give to the Congress Information of the State of the Union, and recommend to their Consideration such Measures as he shall judge necessary and expedient; he may, on extraordinary Occasions, convene both Houses, or either of them, and in Case of Disagreement between them, with Respect to the Time of Adjournment, he may adjourn them to such Time as he shall think proper; he shall receive Ambassadors and other public Ministers; he shall take Care that the Laws be faithfully executed, and shall Commission all the Officers of the United States.

SECTION. 4.

The President, Vice President and all civil Officers of the United States, shall be removed from Office on Impeachment for, and Conviction of, Treason, Bribery, or other high Crimes and Misdemeanors.

ARTICLE. III.

SECTION. 1.

The judicial Power of the United States shall be vested in one supreme Court, and in such inferior Courts as the Congress may from time to time ordain and establish. The Judges, both of the supreme and inferior Courts, shall hold their Offices during good Behaviour, and shall, at stated Times, receive for their Services a Compensation, which shall not be diminished during their Continuance in Office.

SECTION. 2.

The judicial Power shall extend to all Cases, in Law and Equity, arising under this Constitution, the Laws of the United States, and Treaties made, or which shall be made, under their Authority; —to all Cases affecting Ambassadors, other public Ministers and Consuls; —to all Cases of admiralty and maritime Jurisdiction; —to Controversies to which the United States shall be a Party; to Controversies between two or more States; between a State and Citizens of another State; —between Citizens of different States; —between Citizens of the same State claiming Lands under Grants of different States, and between a State, or the Citizens thereof, and foreign States, Citizens or Subjects.

In all Cases affecting Ambassadors, other public Ministers and Consuls, and those in which a State shall be Party, the supreme Court shall have original Jurisdiction. In all the other Cases before mentioned, the supreme Court shall have appellate Jurisdiction, both as to Law and Fact, with such Exceptions, and under such Regulations as the Congress shall make.

The Trial of all Crimes, except in Cases of Impeachment, shall be by Jury; and such Trial shall be held in the State where the said Crimes shall have been committed; but when not committed within any State, the Trial shall be at such Place or Places as the Congress may by Law have directed.

SECTION. 3.

Treason against the United States, shall consist only in levying War against them, or in adhering to their Enemies, giving them Aid and Comfort. No Person shall be convicted of Treason unless on the Testimony of two Witnesses to the same overt Act, or on Confession in open Court.

The Congress shall have Power to declare the Punishment of Treason, but no Attainder of Treason shall work Corruption of Blood, or Forfeiture except during the Life of the Person attainted.

ARTICLE. IV.

SECTION. 1.

Full Faith and Credit shall be given in each State to the public Acts, Records, and judicial Proceedings of every other State. And the Congress may by general Laws prescribe the Manner in which such Acts, Records and Proceedings shall be proved, and the Effect thereof.

SECTION. 2.

The Citizens of each State shall be entitled to all Privileges and Immunities of Citizens in the several States.

A Person charged in any State with Treason, Felony, or other Crime, who shall flee from Justice, and be found in another State, shall on Demand of the executive Authority of the State from which he fled, be delivered up, to be removed to the State having Jurisdiction of the Crime.

No Person held to Service or Labour in one State, under the Laws thereof, escaping into another, shall, in Consequence of any Law or Regulation therein, be discharged from such Service or Labour, but shall be delivered up on Claim of the Party to whom such Service or Labour may be due.

SECTION. 3.

New States may be admitted by the Congress into this Union; but no new State shall be formed or erected within the Jurisdiction of any other State; nor any State be formed by the Junction of two or more States, or Parts of States, without the Consent of the Legislatures of the States concerned as well as of the Congress.

The Congress shall have Power to dispose of and make all needful Rules and Regulations respecting the Territory or other Property belonging to the United States; and nothing in this Constitution shall be so construed as to Prejudice any Claims of the United States, or of any particular State.

SECTION. 4.

The United States shall guarantee to every State in this Union a Republican Form of Government, and shall protect each of them against Invasion; and on Application of the Legislature, or of the Executive (when the Legislature cannot be convened), against domestic Violence.

ARTICLE. V.

The Congress, whenever two thirds of both Houses shall deem it necessary, shall propose Amendments to this Constitution, or, on the Application of the Legislatures of two thirds of the several States, shall call a Convention for proposing Amendments, which, in either Case, shall be valid to all Intents and Purposes, as Part of this Constitution, when ratified by the Legislatures of three fourths of the several States, or by Conventions in three fourths thereof, as the one or the other Mode of Ratification may be proposed by the Congress; Provided that no Amendment which may be made prior to the Year One thousand eight hundred and eight shall in any Manner affect the first and fourth Clauses in the Ninth Section of the first Article; and that no State, without its Consent, shall be deprived of its equal Suffrage in the Senate.

ARTICLE. VI.

All Debts contracted and Engagements entered into, before the Adoption of this Constitution, shall be as valid against the United States under this Constitution, as under the Confederation.

This Constitution, and the Laws of the United States which shall be made in Pursuance thereof; and all Treaties made, or which shall be made, under the Authority of the United States, shall be the supreme Law of the Land; and the Judges in every State shall be bound thereby, any Thing in the Constitution or Laws of any State to the Contrary notwithstanding.

The Senators and Representatives before mentioned, and the Members of the several State Legislatures, and all executive and judicial Officers, both of the United States and of the several States, shall be bound by Oath or Affirmation, to support this Constitution; but no religious Test shall ever be required as a Qualification to any Office or public Trust under the United States.

ARTICLE. VII.

The Ratification of the Conventions of nine States, shall be sufficient for the Establishment of this Constitution between the States so ratifying the Same.

Done in Convention by the Unanimous Consent of the States present the Seventeenth Day of September in the Year of our Lord one thousand seven hundred and eighty seven and of the Independence of the United States of America the Twelfth In witness whereof We have hereunto subscribed our Names,

Attest William Jackson Secretary
G. Washington
Presidt and deputy from Virginia

DELAWARE
Geo: Read, Gunning Bedford jun, John Dickinson, Richard Bassett, Jaco: Broom

MARYLAND
James McHenry, Dan of St. Thos. Jenifer, Danl Carroll

VIRGINIA
John Blair, James Madison Jr.

NORTH CAROLINA
Wm. Blount, Richd. Dobbs Spaight, Hu Williamson

SOUTH CAROLINA
J. Rutledge, Charles Cotesworth Pinckney, Charles Pinckney, Pierce Butler

GEORGIA
William Few, Abr Baldwin

NEW HAMPSHIRE
John Langdon, Nicholas Gilman

MASSACHUSETTS
Nathaniel Gorham, Rufus King

CONNECTICUT
Wm. Saml. Johnson, Roger Sherman

NEW YORK
Alexander Hamilton

NEW JERSEY
Wil: Livingston, David Brearley, Wm. Paterson, Jona: Dayton

PENNSYLVANIA
B Franklin, Thomas Mifflin, Robt. Morris, Geo. Clymer, Thos FitzSimons, Jared Ingersoll, James Wilson, Gouv Morris

A NOTE ABOUT QUOTATIONS

Much of what we know about the deliberations inside the Assembly Room of the Pennsylvania State House during the summer of 1787 comes from just one source—James Madison's notes on the debates in the Convention. That extraordinary document is a compilation of Madison's own diligent note-taking and drafts of speeches given to Madison by many of the participants in the Convention. Those notes, extensively revised by Madison before they were published posthumously in 1840, are not always consistent in their spelling, capitalization, punctuation, and abbreviations. In quoting speeches from Madison's notes, I have modernized some spellings, capitalizations, punctuation, and abbreviations for the sake of clarity. I have also, where appropriate, changed speeches reported by Madison from the third person to the first person, and from the past to the present tense. In no case have I altered the substance of the speeches recorded by Madison or by any of the other delegates who took notes on speeches.

In quoting from the principal resolutions and proposals presented in the Convention—for example, the Virginia Plan, the New Jersey Plan, the Report of the Committee of Detail, etc.—I have retained the original spelling and punctuation. I have also retained the original language in quoting from letters, newspaper reports, diaries, and other contemporaneous sources relating to the Convention.

ABBREVIATIONS
OF FREQUENTLY CITED WORKS

Cultural Landscape Report   Anne Coxe Toogood, "Cultural Land-
scape Report," Independence Square, Historical Narrative, Volume 1,
Independence Hall Block, and Blocks 1–4 surrounding Independence
Hall, National Park Service, 2004.

Daybooks   Constitutional Convention Daybook Files, Independence
National Historical Park Archive, Philadelphia, Pa.

DHRC   Merrill Jensen, John Kaminski, and Gaspare Saladino, eds.,
The Documentary History of the Ratification of the Constitution, 21 vols.
(Madison, Wis.: State Historical Society of Wisconsin, 1976–).

Elliot, *Debates*   Jonathan Elliot, *The Debates in the Several State Conventions, on the adoption of the Federal Constitution* . . . 2nd ed., 5 vols.
(Washington, D.C.: U.S. Congress, 1836).

Farrand   Max Farrand, ed., *The Records of the Federal Convention of
1787*, 4 vols., rev. ed. (New Haven, Conn.: Yale University Press,
1937, repr. 1966).

The Federalist   Jacob E. Cooke, ed., *The Federalist* (Middletown, Conn.:
Wesleyan University Press, 1961).

GW Diary   Donald Jackson and Dorothy Twohig, eds., *The Diaries of
George Washington*, 6 vols. (Charlottesville, Va.: University Press of
Virginia, 1976–79).

GW Papers, C.S.   W. W. Abbot, Dorothy Twohig, et al., *The Papers of
George Washington*, Confederation Series, 6 vols. (Charlottesville, Va.:
University Press of Virginia, 1992–).

GW Papers, P.S.   W. W. Abbot, Dorothy Twohig, et al., *The Papers of*

George Washington, Presidential Series, 11 vols. (Charlottesville, Va.: University Press of Virginia, 1987–).

Hamilton Papers Harold C. Syrett and Jacob Cooke, eds., *The Papers of Alexander Hamilton,* 27 vols. (New York: Columbia University Press, 1961–87).

Jefferson Papers Julian Boyd et al., *The Papers of Thomas Jefferson,* 17 vols. (Princeton, N.J.: Princeton University Press, 1950–).

Madison Papers William T. Hutchinson, William M. E. Rachal, Robert A. Rutland, et al., *The Papers of James Madison,* 19 vols. (Chicago and Charlottesville, Va.: University of Chicago Press and University Press of Virginia, 1961–).

Supplement James H. Hutson, *Supplement to Max Farrand's The Records of the Federal Convention of 1787* (New Haven, Conn.: Yale University Press, 1987).

WMQ William and Mary Quarterly, 3rd ser. (1944–).

1787 David Dutcher, Anna Coxe Toogood, et al., *1787: The Day-to-Day Story of the Constitutional Convention* (New York: Exeter Books, 1987).

NOTES

PREFACE

1. Washington to the Marquis de Lafayette, Sept. 18, 1787, in W. W. Abbot, Dorothy Twohig, et al., *The Papers of George Washington*, Confederation Series, 6 vols. (Charlottesville, Va.: University Press of Virginia, 1992–), vol. 5, 334.

2. Washington to Lafayette, Feb. 7, 1788, in *GW Papers*, C.S., vol. 6, 95.

3. Catherine Drinker Bowen, *Miracle at Philadelphia: The Story of the Constitutional Convention, May to September, 1787* (Boston: Little, Brown, 1966), vii. Bowen's book has had more influence on popular understandings of the Constitutional Convention than perhaps any book written on the subject, but the number and variety of books written on the Convention are vast. Among the most notable general accounts are Max Farrand, *The Framing of the Constitution of the United States* (New Haven, Conn.: Yale University Press, 1913); Charles Warren, *The Making of the Constitution* (Boston: Little, Brown, 1928); Carl Van Doren, *The Great Rehearsal* (New York: Viking Press, 1948); Clinton Rossiter, *1787: The Grand Convention* (New York: Macmillan Company, 1966); Christopher Collier and James Lincoln Collier, *Decision in Philadelphia* (New York: Random House, 1986); Richard B. Morris, *Witnesses at the Creation* (New York: Holt, Rinehart & Winston, 1985). More recent brief accounts are Carol Berkin, *A Brilliant Solution: Inventing the American Constitution* (New York: Harcourt, 2002); David Stewart, *The Summer of 1787* (New York: Simon & Schuster, 2007). Although not a traditional narrative account of the making of the Constitution, Jack Rakove, *Original Meanings: Politics and Ideas in the Making of the Constitution* (New York: Knopf, 1996) is a masterful study of the ideological underpinnings of the Constitution. From a political scientist's perspective, Calvin Jillson, *Constitution Making: Conflict and Consensus in the Federal Convention of 1787* (New York: Agathon Press, 2003) is an insightful analysis of political alignments in the Convention. John R. Vile, *The Constitutional Convention of 1787: A Comprehensive Encyclopedia of America's Founding*, 2 vols. (Santa Barbara, Calif.: ABC-CLIO, 2005) is a treasure trove of useful information about the Convention. Standing in a class by itself and less an analy-

sis of the events of the Convention than of the economic motives of the framers is Charles Beard's landmark study, *An Economic Interpretation of the Constitution of the United States* (New York: Macmillan, 1913). Beard's work launched a debate that continues to this day. Among Beard's critics are Robert E. Brown, *Charles Beard and the Constitution* (Princeton, N.J.: Princeton University Press, 1956); and Forrest McDonald, *We the People: The Economic Origins of the Constitution* (Chicago: University of Chicago Press, 1958). The most recent study of the constitutional era that supports Beard's economic analysis of the Constitution is Woody Holton, *Unruly Americans and the Origins of the Constitution* (New York: Hill and Wang, 2007).

4. Jared Sparks, *The Life of Gouverneur Morris; with Selections from His Correspondence and Miscellaneous Papers*, 3 vols. (Boston, Gray & Bowen, 1832), vol. 1, 291–92. The usually reliable Max Farrand, ed., *The Records of the Federal Convention of 1787*, 4 vols., rev. ed. (New Haven, Conn.: Yale University Press, 1937, repr. 1966), vol. 3, 242–43, mistakenly attributes the quote to Robert, rather than Gouverneur Morris. Farrand based his attribution on a passage from Catherine Keppele Meredith, "Sketch of the Life of Gouverneur Morris," *Pennsylvania Magazine of History and Biography II* (1878), 191–92, but, in fact, Meredith, following Sparks, attributed the quote to Gouverneur Morris.

5. Interestingly, the first person to use the word "demigods" to describe the assemblage in Philadelphia was Thomas Jefferson, a man among the least likely to ascribe the work of the framers of the Constitution to divine intervention. Thomas Jefferson to John Adams, Aug. 30, 1787, in Julian Boyd et al., *The Papers of Thomas Jefferson*, 17 vols. (Princeton, N.J.: Princeton University Press, 1950–), vol. 12, 69.

6. Gordon S. Wood, *Revolutionary Characters: What Made the Founders Different* (New York: Penguin Press, 2006), esp. 8–12.

CHAPTER ONE

1. Much of this account of what came to be called the Newburgh Conspiracy is based on the excellent study by Richard H. Kohn, *Eagle and Sword: The Federalists and the Creation of the Military Establishment in America, 1783–1802* (New York: Free Press, 1975), 17–39; and Kohn, "The Inside History of the Newburgh Conspiracy: America and the Coup d'Etat," *William and Mary Quarterly* 27, 3rd ser. (1970), 187–220; Washington to Alexander Hamilton, March 12, 1783, in Harold C. Syrett and Jacob Cooke, eds., *The Papers of Alexander Hamilton*, 27 vols. (New York: Columbia University Press, 1961–87), vol. 3, 286–87.

2. Pauline Maier, *American Scripture: Making the Declaration of Independence* (New York: Knopf, 1979), 156.

3. For a description of the soldiers' condition and their disillusionment, see Charles Royster, *A Revolutionary People at War: The Continental Army and American Character, 1775–1783* (Chapel Hill, N.C.: University of North Carolina Press, 1979), 190–94 and passim. The New Building was also called the Temple of Virtue, signifying the intention to use the structure as not only a general meeting place, but also a house of worship. I am grateful to Michael J. Clark, historic site manager of the New Windsor Cantonment Historic Site, for providing me with descriptions of both the landscape and the New Building.

4. Kohn, *Eagle and Sword*, 31.

5. Washington's dramatic speech is recounted in Douglas Southall Freeman, *George Washington: A Biography*, 7 vols. (New York: Charles Scribner's Sons, 1948–57), vol. 5, 433–35.

6. Ibid., 435.

7. Kohn, *Eagle and Sword*, 32–33.

8. John Adams to Abigail Adams, Sept. 29, 1774, in Lyman H. Butterfield, ed., *The Adams Family Correspondence*, 2 vols. (Cambridge, Mass.: Harvard University Press, 1963), vol. 1, 163.

9. For an excellent discussion of the ideological context and the specifics of the drafting of the Articles of Confederation, see Jack Rakove, *The Beginnings of National Politics: An Interpretive History of the Continental Congress* (New York: Knopf, 1979), 136–91.

10. Ibid., 275–399. The best discussion of the politics of finance during the Confederation period is E. James Ferguson, *The Power of the Purse: A History of American Public Finance, 1776–1790* (Chapel Hill, N.C.: University of North Carolina Press, 1961), esp. 1–69.

11. Robert Morris to Benjamin Franklin, Nov. 27, 1781, in Leonard Labaree, Whitfield J. Bell, Jr., Barbara Oberg, et al., eds., *The Papers of Benjamin Franklin;* 37 vols. (New Haven, Conn: Yale University Press, 1959–) vol. 36, 160.

12. Clarence L. Ver Steeg, *Robert Morris: Revolutionary Financier* (Philadelphia: University of Pennsylvania Press, 1954), 3–6.

13. Edmund Cody Burnett, *The Continental Congress* (New York: Macmillan, 1941), 514, 529, 535, 601–3; Richard Henry Lee to Henry Laurens, Aug. 1, 1779; Lee to Ralph Wormley Carter, June 3, 1783, in James C. Ballagh, ed., *The Letters of Richard Henry Lee*, 2 vols. (New York: Macmillan, 1911–14), vol. 2, 99, 282.

14. Burnett, *Continental Congress*, 492–514; Forrest McDonald, *E Pluribus Unum: The Formation of the American Republic, 1776–1790* (Boston: Houghton-Mifflin, 1965), 44, 49–50.

15. McDonald, *E Pluribus Unum*, 49–57; Ver Steeg, *Robert Morris*, 65–110.

16. Quoted in Ferguson, *Power of the Purse*, 153.

17. Quoted in ibid., 158.

18. Ibid., 164–71.

19. Farewell Orders to the Armies of the United States, Nov. 2, 1783, in John C. Fitzpatrick, ed., *Writings of George Washington*, 39 vols. (Washington, D.C.: U.S. Government Printing Office, 1931–39), vol. 27, 223.

20. Freeman, *George Washington*, vol. 5, 474, 475–78. See also James Thomas Flexner, *George Washington: The Indispensable Man* (Boston: Little, Brown, 1969), 178.

21. Freeman, *George Washington*, vol. 6, 1–2; Washington to Lafayette, Feb. 1, 1784, in W. W. Abbot, Dorothy Twohig, et al., *The Papers of George Washington*, Confederation Series, 6 vols. (Charlottesville, Va.: University Press of Virginia, 1987–), vol. 1, 87–88.

22. When the Continental Congress initially proposed its Requisition Plan of 1783, it included a number of different provisions, including mandatory state contributions to the Confederation government treasury. By 1786, only the impost proposal survived. My account of the collapse of the Confederation government in the preceding paragraphs is based on Ferguson, *Power of the Purse*, 220–50; McDonald, *E Pluribus Unum*, 227–31, 338–42; and Rakove, *Beginnings of National Politics*, 333–59.

23. The most up-to-date account of Shays' Rebellion is Leonard J. Richards, *Shays's Rebellion: The American Revolution's Final Battle* (Philadelphia: University of Pennsylvania Press, 2002). See also David P. Szatmary, *Shays' Rebellion: The Making of an Agrarian Insurrection* (Amherst, Mass.: University of Massachusetts Press, 1980).

24. Gary B. Nash, *The Unknown American Revolution: The Unruly Birth of Democracy and the Struggle to Create America* (New York: Viking, 2005), 448; Richards, *Shays's Rebellion*, 5–7, 26–27.

25. Szatmary, *Shays' Rebellion*, 71, 72, 74.

26. Donald Jackson and Dorothy Twohig, eds., *The Diaries of George Washington*, 6 vols. (Charlottesville, Va.: University Press of Virginia, 1976–79), vol. 5, 61. Henry Lee to Washington, Oct. 17, 1786, in *GW Papers*, C.S., vol. 4, 295. Washington to Henry Lee, Oct. 31, 1786, *GW Papers*, C.S., vol. 4, 318–19.

27. Henry Lee to Washington, Oct. 17, 1786, in *GW Papers*, C.S., vol. 4, 295; Madison to James Madison, Sr., Nov. 1, 1786, in William T. Hutchinson, William M. E. Rachal, Robert A. Rutland, et al., *The Papers of James Madison*, 19 vols. Chicago and Charlottesville, Va.: University of Chicago Press and University Press of Virginia, 1961–), vol. 9, 154.

28. Richards, *Shays's Rebellion*, 28–29; McDonald, *E Pluribus Unum*, 254–55.

29. *Report of the Annapolis Convention*, Sept. 14, 1786, in *Hamilton Papers*, vol. 3, 686–90.

30. Burnett, *Continental Congress*, 669.

31. Ibid., 669–79; Irving Brant, *James Madison*, 6 vols. (New York: Bobbs-Merrill, 1941–61), vol. 2, 400–402.

32. *Journal of the Continental Congress*, Feb. 21, 1787, in Max Farrand, ed., *The Records of the Federal Convention of 1787*, 4 vols., rev. ed. (New Haven, Conn.: Yale University Press, 1937, repr. 1966), vol. 3, 13–14.

CHAPTER TWO

1. Madison to Randolph, April 15, 1787, in William T. Hutchinson, William M. E. Rachal, Robert A. Rutland, et al., *The Papers of James Madison*, 19 vols. (Chicago and Charlottesville, Va.: University of Chicago Press and University Press of Virginia, 1961–), vol. 9, 379, Ralph Ketcham, *James Madison: A Biography* (New York: Macmillan, 1971), 190.

2. Madison to Jefferson, May 15, 1787, in *Madison Papers*, vol. 9, 415. Some indication of the delegates' slow progress from their homes to Philadelphia can be gleaned from Donald Jackson and Dorothy Twohig, eds., *The Diaries of George Washington*, 6 vols. (Charlottesville, Va.: University Press of Virginia, 1976–79), vol. 5, 153–55. Diary of William Samuel Johnson, July 20–22, 1787, transcript at Independence National Historical Park archive. For a contemporary description of the state of the roads of America in 1789, see Christopher Colles, *A Survey of the Roads of the United States of America, 1789* (Cambridge, Mass.: Harvard University Press, 1961); and John R. Stilgoe, *The Common Landscape in America* (New Haven, Conn.: Yale University Press, 1982), 128–32.

3. Pennsylvania *Herald*, May 16, 1787.

4. National Park Service, "Cultural Landscape Report" (2004) for Independence Hall Block, and Blocks 1–4 surrounding Independence Hall, 44–45. See also Ketcham, *Madison*, 190–95; and Irving Brant, *James Madison*, 6 vols. (New York: Bobbs-Merrill, 1941–61), vol. 2, 16–17.

5. Brant, *Madison*, vol. 2, 283–87, presents a good account of Madison's infatuation with Kitty Floyd. For aspects of Madison's physical appearance, see Ketcham, *Madison*, 107–8; Jack N. Rakove, *James Madison and the Creation of the American Republic* (New York: Longman, 2002), 3–5, 33–34; Forrest McDonald, *E Pluribus Unum: The Formation of the American Republic, 1776–1790* (Boston: Houghton-Mifflin, 1965), 263–64. My description of Madison's appearance is based primarily on the portraits of him painted by Charles Wilson Peale in 1792 and James Sharples ca. 1796–97.

6. Jefferson to Madison, April 14, 1783, in Julian Boyd et al., *The Papers of Thomas Jefferson*, 17 vols. (Princeton, N.J.: Princeton University Press, 1950–), vol. 6, 261–62; Madison to Jefferson, April 22, 1783, in *Madison Papers*, vol. 6, 481–82.

7. Brant, *Madison*, vol. 2, 285–87; Madison to Randolph, July 28, 1783, in *Madison Papers*, vol. 7, 257.

8. Madison to Jefferson, Aug. 11, 1783, in *Madison Papers*, vol. 7, 268–69; Jefferson to Madison, Aug. 31, 1783, in *Jefferson Papers*, vol. 6, 335–36. It would be another ten years before Madison ventured into the dangerous terrain of romance once again, and this time, older and wiser, he wasted little time in persuading Dolly Todd to marry him before she could have second thoughts.

9. Fisher Ames to George Minot, May 18, 1789, quoted in Brant, *Madison*, vol. 3, 261–62.

10. Rakove, *Madison*, 1–4, provides a brief but perceptive account of Madison's early childhood and education. See also Ketcham, *Madison*, 17–23.

11. Ketcham, *Madison*, 23–33; Rakove, *Madison*, 3–4.

12. Madison to William Bradford, Nov. 9 1772, in Gaillard Hunt, *The Writings of James Madison*, 9 vols. (New York, G.P. Putnam's Sons, 1900–10), vol. 1, 10–11; Rakove, *Madison*, 4–5, 9–16; Ketcham, *Madison*, 51–87.

13. Rakove, *Madison*, 12.

14. Ibid., 17–20.

15. Ibid., 49–52. See also Lance Banning, *The Sacred Fire of Liberty: James Madison and the Founding of the Federal Republic* (Ithaca, N.Y.: Cornell University Press, 1995), 115. Madison's notes on "Ancient and Modern Confederacies" are printed in full in *Madison Papers*, vol. 9, 3–22; his treatise on "Vices" is in *Madison Papers*, vol. 9, 345–57.

16. *Madison Papers*, vol. 9, 345–57.

17. *Madison Papers*, vol. 9, 345–57. See also Rakove, *Madison*, 52–60, for an excellent analysis of Madison's treatise.

18. "Vices," in *Madison Papers*, vol. 9, 352, 354–57. Madison's thoughts on the relative advantages of small and large republics were certainly influenced by the writings of David Hume, which he had first encountered as a student at Princeton; his argument in this section of "Vices" anticipated the argument that he would make in "Federalist No. 10" on the advantages of an "extended republic."

19. Ibid., 357.

20. Ibid.

21. *GW Diary*, vol. 5, 155; Douglas Southall Freeman, *George Washington: A Biography*, 7 vols. (New York: Charles Scribner's Sons, 1948–57), vol. 6, 87–88; Pennsylvania *Packet*, May 14, 1787.

22. Washington to Henry Lee, Oct. 31, 1786, in W. W. Abbot, Dorothy Twohig, et al., *The Papers of George Washington*, Confederation Series, 6 vols., (Charlottesville, Va.: University Press of Virginia, 1992–), vol. 4, 319.

23. Rakove, *Madison*, 46; Madison to Washington, Nov. 8, Dec. 7, 1786, in *Madison Papers*, vol. 9, 166, 199; Edmund Randolph to Washington, Dec. 6, 1786, Jan. 4, 1787, John Jay to Washington, Jan. 7, 1787, in *GW Papers*, C.S., vol. 4, 445, 501; 502–4; Randolph to Washington, March 11, 1787, Henry Knox to Washington, March 19, 1787, in *GW Papers*, C.S., vol. 5, 83–84, 96.

24. Joseph J. Ellis, *His Excellency, George Washington* (New York: Knopf, 2005), 149–50,

presents a sensitive account of the effects of aging on Washington. Washington to Henry Knox, Feb. 3, 25, April 1, 1787, in *GW Papers*, C.S., vol. 5, 7–9, 52–53, 119–20; Washington to the Society of the Cincinnati, Oct. 31, 1786, in *GW Papers*, C.S., vol. 4, 316–17.

25. See, for example, Washington to David Humphreys, Dec. 26, 1786, Washington to Knox, Dec. 26, 1786, Humphreys to Washington, Jan. 20, 1786, in *GW Papers*, C.S., vol. 4, 477–80, 481–83, 526–30; Washington to Knox, Feb. 3, 25, March 8, April 2, 1787, in ibid., vol. 5, 7–9, 52–53, 75–76, 119–20.

26. Washington to Randolph, March 28, 1787, Randolph to Washington, April 2, 1787, in ibid., vol. 5, 112–14, 122.

27. Washington to Madison, March 31, 1787, in ibid., vol. 5, 115; Madison to Washington, April 16, 1787, in *Madison Papers*, vol. 9, 382–87.

28. "Notes on the Sentiments on the government of John Jay, Henry Knox, and James Madison," April, 1787, in *GW Papers*, C.S., vol. 5, 163–66.

29. Franklin to Washington, April 3, 1787, Robert Morris to Washington, April 23, 1787, Washington to Morris, May 5, 1787, in ibid, vol. 5, 122, 153, 171.

30. Edward Moyston to Washington, April 24, 1787, in ibid., vol. 5, 125.

31. *GW Diary*, May 13, 1787, vol. 5, 155. The description of the Morris mansion is from Cultural Landscape Report, 56–58. Ellis, *His Excellency*, 40, 44–45, 49, presents a revealing sketch of Washington's opulent lifestyle.

32. Ellis, *His Excellency*, 44, 46, 79. For detailed analyses of Washington's complicated relationship with the institution of slavery, see Dorothy Twohig, " 'That Species of Property': Washington's Role in the Controversy Over Slavery," in Don Higginbothom, ed., *George Washington Reconsidered* (Charlottesville, Va.: University of Virginia Press, 2001), 114–38; and William Wiencek, *An Imperfect God: George Washington, His Slaves, and the Creation of America* (New York: Farrar, Straus, and Giroux, 2003).

33. *GW Diary*, May 13, 1787, vol. 5, 155; Walter Isaacson, *Benjamin Franklin: An American Life* (New York: Simon & Schuster, 2003), 177, 203.

34. Richard Norton Smith, *Patriarch: George Washington and the New American Nation* (Boston: Houghton-Mifflin, 1993), 273–75.

35. The anecdote about the two-headed snake is from the still-classic biography of Franklin by Carl Van Doren, *Benjamin Franklin* (New York: Viking Press, 1938), 554. While the Constitutional Convention was under way, Franklin displayed the snake and told the fable to the Reverend Manasseh Cutler, who was visiting the city. Franklin was about to make a comparison to certain divisions that had surfaced in the Convention when, according to Cutler, delegates who were in the room with them stopped him, reminding him of "the secrecy of Convention matters." William Parker Cutler and Julia Perkins Cutler, *Life, Journals, and Correspondence of Rev. Manasseh Cutler, L.L.D.*, 2 vols. (Cincinnati: Robert Clark and Co., 1888), vol. 1, 268–69.

36. Two excellent accounts of Franklin's career in Paris, and his comfortable life there, are Isaacson, *Franklin*, 325–435; and Stacy Schiff, *The Great Improvisation: Franklin, France, and the Birth of America* (New York: Henry Holt, 2005).

37. Quoted in Isaacson, *Franklin*, 352.

38. Ibid., 437; Franklin to David Hartley, Oct. 27, 1785, Jared Sparks, ed., *The Works of Benjamin Franklin*, 10 vols. (Boston: Whittemore, Viles, and Hall, 1840), vol. 10, 235–36.

39. Gordon Wood, *The Americanization of Benjamin Franklin* (New York: Penguin Press,

2004), 213–15. Wood's book, though not a comprehensive biography, is perhaps the most insightful study of the evolution of Franklin's thought and behavior over the course of a long life. For the turbulence of Pennsylvania politics during this period, see Robert L. Brunhouse, *The Counter-Revolution in Pennsylvania, 1776–1790* (Harrisburg, Pa.: Pennsylvania Historical and Museum Commission, 1942).

40. For a good account of Franklin's pique at his shabby treatment by the Continental Congress, see Wood, *Americanization*, 221–26. See also Franklin to Charles Thomson, Nov. 29, 1788, in Sparks, *The Works of Benjamin Franklin*, vol. 10, 368–78.

CHAPTER THREE

1. Donald Jackson and Dorothy Twohig, eds., *The Diaries of George Washington*, 6 vols. (Charlottesville, Va.: University Press of Virginia, 1976–79), 156–57; Madison to Jefferson, in William T. Hutchinson, William M. E. Rachal, Robert Rutland, et al., *The Papers of James Madison*, 19 vols. (Chicago and Charlottesville, Va.: University of Chicago Press and University Press of Virginia, 1961–), vol. 9, 415.

2. Max Farrand, ed., *The Records of the Federal Convention of 1787*, 4 vols., rev. ed. (New Haven, Conn.: Yale University Press, 1937, repr. 1966), vol. 3, 587–90. Richard Barry, *Mr. Rutledge of South Carolina* (New York: Duell, Sloan, and Pearce, 1942), 315; Marty D. Matthews, *Forgotten Founder: The Life and Times of Charles Pinckney* (Columbia, S.C.: University of South Carolina Press, 2004), 40.

3. John J. Reardon, *Edmund Randolph: A Biography* (New York: Macmillan, 1964), 4–8, 96.

4. Mason to George Mason, Jr., May 20, 1787, in Farrand, vol. 3, 22; the most recent biography of Mason is Jeff Broadwater, *George Mason: Forgotten Founder* (Chapel Hill, N.C.: University of North Carolina Press, 2006).

5. Farrand, vol. 3, 24; Constitutional Convention Daybook Files, Independence National Historical Park Archive, Philadelphia, Pa., cabinet 2, drawer 2, folder 52; Broadwater, *Mason*, 159–60.

6. Mason to George Mason, Jr., May 27, 1787, in Farrand, vol. 3, 28.

7. E. James Ferguson, *The Power of the Purse: A History of American Public Finance, 1776–1790* (Chapel Hill, N.C.: University of North Carolina Press, 1961), 171–74; Clinton Rossiter, *1787: The Grand Convention* (New York: Macmillan Company, 1966), 102–3.

8. James J. Kirschke, *Gouverneur Morris: Author, Statesman, and Man of the World* (New York: St. Martin's Press, 2005), 5. Other recent biographies of Morris are William Howard Adams, *Gouverneur Morris: An Independent Life* (New Haven, Conn.: Yale University Press, 2003); Richard Brookhiser, *Gouverneur Morris: The Rake Who Wrote the Constitution* (New York: Free Press, 2003).

9. Kirschke, *Morris*, 4–14; Brookhiser, *Morris*, 11–12, 59–61, 64–65.

10. Kirschke, *Morris*, 15–18, 29–31.

11. Ibid., 69–70; Adams, *Morris*, 121–25.

12. Kirschke, *Morris*, 116–18.

13. Ibid., 121–58; Daybooks, May 26, 1787, cabinet 1, drawer 3, folder 4; William Pierce, "Character Sketches," in Farrand, vol. 3, 92.

14. Kirschke, *Morris*, 118–19, 208–12, 219, 231, 263–65; John Jay to Robert Morris, Sept. 16, 1780, in Richard B. Morris, ed., *The Papers of John Jay*, 2 vols. (New York: Harper and Row, 1975) vol. 1, 821; Brookhiser, *Morris*, 61–62.

15. The story of Morris's "liberty" with General Washington has come down to historians

from the nineteenth century to the present day, but we do not have a contemporary eyewitness account of the incident. Kirschke, *Morris*, 185–86, is inclined to believe that Morris had too much respect for Washington to take the liberty. On the other hand, the combination of Morris's extraordinary self-confidence and sense of humor suggests that the event is highly plausible. One other testimony supporting the plausibility of the story is James Madison's assessment of Morris as a man with a "fondness for saying things . . . that no one else would," in Farrand, vol. 3, 534.

16. Farrand, vol. 3, 92.
17. Adams, *Morris*, 148; Kirschke, *Morris*, xxi; Charles Page Smith, *James Wilson, Founding Father, 1742–1798* (Chapel Hill, N.C.: University of North Carolina Press, 1956), 217; Farrand, vol. 3, 565–67; Jacob C. Parsons, ed., *Extracts from the Diary of Jacob Hiltzheimer* (Philadelphia Press of W. F. Fell, 1893), 111–12.
18. Smith, *Wilson*, 217.
19. Ibid., 3–21.
20. Ibid., 21–31, 54–62.
21. Ibid.
22. Ibid., 116–17, 149–68.
23. Forrest McDonald, *E Pluribus Unum: The Formation of the American Republic, 1776–1790* (Boston: Houghton-Mifflin, 1965), 263; Farrand, vol. 3, 91–92.
24. Franklin to Thomas Jordan, May 20, 1787, in Sparks, *The Works of Benjamin Franklin*, vol. 10, 304–5.
25. Mason to George Mason, Jr., May 20, 1787, in Farrand, vol. 3, 23–24.
26. Ibid.; there is some disagreement among historians about both the timing and the venue of these informal meetings among the Virginians and the Pennsylvanians. David Stewart, *The Summer of 1787* (New York: Simon & Schuster, 2007), 37–38, asserts that there were "Virginians only" sessions at Mrs. House's boardinghouse in the morning and meetings with the Pennsylvanians at three o'clock in the afternoon in the State House. The evidence does not support this assertion. If the morning meetings were at Mrs. House's, then Charles Pinckney of South Carolina and George Read of Delaware, who also boarded there, would have not only known about them but also would have resented their exclusion from them. According to Washington's diary, the Virginians and Pennsylvanians gathered at the State House on May 14 and May 15 at eleven in the morning and then moved their meetings back the following day to one o'clock, but still at the State House. There is no mention of the delegates meeting at Mrs. House's, and, judging from George Mason's testimony, it is more likely that they met in the afternoon at the Indian Queen.
27. Farrand, vol. 1, 10–11.
28. Farrand, vol. 1, 10–11; Madison to Washington, April 16, 1787, in *Madison Papers*, vol. 9, 387.
29. Ibid.
30. Mason to George Mason, Jr., May 20, 1787, in Farrand, vol. 3, 23–24; Jack Rakove, *Original Meanings: Politics and Ideas in the Making of the Constitution* (New York: Knopf, 1996), 255.
31. Washington to Arthur Lee, May 20, 1787, in W. W. Abbot, Dorothy Twohig, et al., *The Papers of George Washington*, Confederation Series, 6 vols. (Charlottesville, Va.: University Press of Virginia, 1992–), vol. 5, 191.

32. See for example George Read to John Dickinson, May 21, 1787, and Rufus King to Jeremiah Wadsworth, May 24, 1787, in Farrand, vol. 3, 25–26.

CHAPTER FOUR

1. Madison to Edmund Pendleton, May 27, 1787, William T. Hutchinson, William M. E. Rachal, Robert A. Rutland, et al., *The Papers of James Madison,* 19 vols. (Chicago and Charlottesville, Va.: University of Chicago Press and University Press of Virginia, 1961–), vol. 10, 12. Although historians and popular commentators on the Constitutional Convention have routinely asserted that the summer of 1787 in Philadelphia was unbearably hot, in fact the summer was noticeably cooler than usual. The manuscript diaries of William Samuel Johnson, a transcript of which is in the Independence National Historical Park Archive, provide details of some of the day-to-day weather conditions, but perhaps the most comprehensive account is from Peter Legaux, a French farmer living just outside Philadelphia. They are printed in James H. Hutson, *Supplement to Max Farrand's Records of the Federal Convention of 1787* (New Haven, Conn.: Yale University Press, 1987), 327–38, and, along with Johnson's less systematic observations, will be used as the main source for my observations on Philadelphia weather during the summer.

2. Max Farrand, ed., *The Records of the Federal Convention of 1787,* 4 vols., rev. ed. (New Haven, Conn.: Yale University Press, 1937, repr. 1966), vol. 3, 586–90.

3. Ibid.

4. Ibid.

5. Ibid. Rufus King to Jeremiah Wadsworth, May 24, 1787, in ibid., vol. 3, 26. For the situation in New Hampshire, see Clinton Rossiter, *1787: The Grand Convention* (New York: Macmillan Company, 1966), 81.

6. Farrand, vol. 3, 586–90; "Instructions of the State of Maryland to Its Delegates," in Merrill Jensen, John Kaminski, and Gaspare Saladino, eds., *The Documentary History of the Ratification of the Constitution,* 21 vols. (Madison, Wis.: State Historical Society of Wisconsin, 1976–), vol. 1, 222; also in Farrand, vol. 3, 586.

7. The best description and history of Independence Hall is Charlene Mires, *Independence Hall in American Memory* (Philadelphia: University of Pennsylvania Press, 2002), 4–8.

8. The eight men serving in the Constitutional Convention who were also among the fifty-six delegates to sign the Declaration of Independence were Robert Morris, James Wilson, Benjamin Franklin, and George Clymer of Pennsylvania; Elbridge Gerry of Massachusetts; Roger Sherman of Connecticut; George Read of Delaware; and George Wythe of Virginia.

9. Mires, *Independence Hall,* 4–8, 27–30, 61–62, 229–31. As Mires suggests, the painting "Congress Voting Independence" by Edward Savage (based on early work by the artist Robert Edge Pine and completed in the early 1780s) gives us our best glimpse of the interior of the Assembly Room of the State House as it existed in 1787.

10. Constitutional Convention Daybook Files, Independence National Historical Park Archive, Philadelphia, Pa., March 27, 1787, cabinet 1, drawer 3, folder 13.

11. Negley K. Teeters, *The Cradle of the Penitentiary: The Walnut Street Jail at Philadelphia, 1773–1835* (Philadelphia, Temple University Press, 1955), 28. *Journal of Manasseh Cutler,* July 13, 1787, vol. 1, 263.

12. Daybooks, March 27, 1787, cabinet 1, drawer 3, folder 14; Washington to Samuel

Vaughan, Nov. 12, 1787, *The Papers of George Washington,* Confederation Series, 6 vols. (Charlottesville, Va.: University Press of Virginia, 1992–), vol. 5, 432–33.

13. Cultural Landscape Report. Independence Square, (2004), INHP, 53–54.

14. Daybooks, cabinet 2, drawer 2, folder 35 (Experience—National Politics), Independence National Historical Park Archive, Philadelphia, Pa. See also Clinton Rossiter, *1787: The Grand Convention* (New York: W. W. Norton, 1966), 145, 148.

15. Daybooks, cabinet 2, drawer 2, folders 44, 45, 46 (Education), Independence National Historical Park Archive, Philadelphia, Pa. See also Rossiter, *Grand Convention,* 146–47.

16. The classic statement about the way in which economic interests motivated the framers of the Constitution is Charles A. Beard, *An Economic Interpretation of the Constitution of the United States* (New York: Macmillan, 1913). Beard's argument that the framing of the Constitution was engineered by a group of men whose assets were disproportionately invested in "personalty"—especially public securities and commercial pursuits—has been widely attacked and, for the most part, proven to be erroneous. Yet his essential contribution—his assertion that decisions about political structures and policies are never entirely divorced from economic interests—retains considerable power. That argument is strongly reinforced in a recent work by Woody Holton, *Unruly Americans and the Origins of the Constitution* (New York: Hill and Wang, 2007). Beard's most effective critic, and the historian who has done the most thorough analysis of the economic interests of the framers, is Forrest McDonald, *We the People: The Economic Origins of the Constitution* (Chicago: University of Chicago Press, 1958). My generalizations about the professional and economic interests of the framers rely on the work of McDonald and, to a lesser extent, Rossiter, *Grand Convention,* 142–43.

17. The subjects of slave ownership and its relationship to the deliberations in the Convention on the subject of slavery are covered fully in Chapter Seventeen of his book.

18. Farrand, vol. 1, 3.

19. Ibid.

20. Donald Jackson and Dorothy Twohig, eds., *The Diaries of George Washington,* 6 vols. (Charlottesville, Va.: University Press of Virginia, 1976–79), vol. 5, 162; Farrand, vol. 1, 3–4.

21. Farrand, vol. 1, 4; Walter Isaacson, *Benjamin Franklin: An American Life* (New York: Simon & Schuster, 2003), 419–20.

22. William Jackson to General Otto William, April 26, 1787, in Daybooks, April 24, 1787, cabinet 1, drawer 3, folder 15; Jackson to Washington, ca. April 20, 1787, in W. W. Abbot, Dorothy Twohig, et al., *GW Papers,* C.S., vol. 5, 150–51; Farrand, vol. 1, xi. The delay in the publication of the Journal was the consequence of the Convention's decision, made on the final day of deliberations, to bar publication of the Journal "subject to the order of Congress"—that prohibition being lifted by an act of Congress in 1818.

23. Farrand, vol. 3, 559–60. See also DHRC, vol. 1, 196–98.

24. Farrand, vol. 3, 574–75; DHRC, vol. 1, 203.

25. Pierce, "Sketches," Farrand, vol. 3, 93. One can piece together aspects of Read's career from John Munroe, "Delaware and the Constitution: An Overview of Events Leading to Ratification," *Delaware History* 22 (1987): 219–38; William T. Read, *Life and Correspondence of George Read* (Philadelphia: Lippincott, 1870); and Daniel Terry Boughner, *George Read and the Founding of Delaware State* (Washington, D.C.: n.p., 1968), 68–71.

26. Read to John Dickinson, Jan. 17, 1787, in Read, *Life and Correspondence,* 438.

27. Farrand, vol. 1, 2.

28. Ibid., vol. 1, 2; vol. 2, 328, 399. As the summer wore on, some delegates, John Rutledge of South Carolina in particular, prodded their colleagues to pick up their pace and to extend their deliberations from three o'clock in the afternoon to four.

29. Billy G. Smith, ed., *Life in Early Philadelphia: Documents from the Revolutionary and Early National Periods* (University Park, Pa.: Pennsylvania State University Press, 1995), 3–14.

30. Ibid., 18; Mary Maples Dunn, "The Founding, 1681–1701," and Randall Miller, "The Federal City, 1783–1800"; in Russell Weigley et al., *Philadelphia: A 300-Year History* (New York: Norton, 1982), 1–32; Gary B. Nash, *The Urban Crucible: Social Change, Political Consciousness, and the Origins of the American Revolution* (Cambridge, Mass.: Harvard University Press, 1979), 54–55, 107–8, 194–95, 313–15; "Diary of James Allen, Esq. of Philadelphia," *Pennsylvania Magazine of History and Biography* 9 (1885): 185.

31. Smith, *Life in Early Philadelphia*, 5–10.

32. Miller, "Federal City," 174–75.

33. Ibid., 191.

34. For an excellent description of the High Street Market, and of the sights and smells of the city generally, see Billy G. Smith, "*The Lower Sort": Philadelphia's Laboring People, 1750–1800* (Ithaca, N.Y.: Cornell University Press, 1990), 7–39.

35. Ibid., 34–36.

36. *Pennsylvania Archives*, 8th series, 6: 5384–85; Pennsylvania *Gazette*, Aug. 27, 1783.

37. *Pennsylvania Archives*, 8th series, 6: 5384–85.

38. Smith, *Lower Sort*, 30; Erastus Walcott to the governor and General Assembly of Connecticut, May 15, 1787, in Hutson, *Supplement*, 3–4.

39. Peter Thompson, *Rum Punch & Revolution: Taverngoing & Public Life in Eighteenth-Century Philadelphia* (Philadelphia: University of Pennsylvania Press, 1999), 2–3, 259–60.

40. Cultural Landscape Report (Delegates' Residences).

41. I am indebted to Professor Billy G. Smith of Montana State University for providing me with information relating to dining in late-eighteenth-century Philadelphia. See, for example, Pennsylvania *Gazette*, Oct. 8, 1788, May 18, 1791, July 4, 1792, Jan. 13, 1796.

42. David Dutcher, Anna Coxe Toogood, et al., *1787: The Day-to-Day Story of the Constitutional Convention* (New York: Exeter Books, 1987), 37–38.

43. One can follow Washington's busy social schedule in *GW Diary*, vol. 5, 156–86.

44. *GW Diary*, vol. 5, 163; Washington to George Augustine Washington, May 27, 1787, in W. W. Abbot, Dorothy Twohig, et al., *GW Papers*, C.S., vol. 5, 196–99.

45. Farrand, vol. 1, 7.

46. Isaacson, *Franklin*, 446, 560–61n. The most elaborate description of Franklin's arrival is in Catherine Drinker Bowen, *Miracle at Philadelphia: The Story of the Constitutional Convention, May to September, 1787* (Boston: Little, Brown, 1966), 33–34. Bowen's account has been disputed by L. A. Leo Lemay, "Recent Franklin Scholarship with a Note on Franklin's Sedan Chair," *Pennsylvania Magazine of History and Biography* 76 (2002), 339–40. Lemay insists that there is not evidence supporting the claim that Franklin was ever carried to the Convention in a sedan chair. Isaacson presents evidence from an unpublished letter from Franklin's granddaughter, Sally, that Franklin did use the chair. Moreover, Isaacson argues, given the poor state of his health at the opening of the Convention, it is likely that he would have used the chair as transport.

47. Farrand, vol. 3, 91.

48. Surprisingly, no one left behind a record of the seating arrangements in the Assembly Room for the deliberations on either the Declaration of Independence or the Constitution. The historians at Independence National Historical Park, after careful study, have instructed their guides to present the seating arrangements in the room as being clustered according to state delegations, with the counterclockwise South-to-North arrangement. That the delegates in 1787 were seated by state delegation seems not only logical but necessary, as those delegations needed to caucus on a daily basis—sometimes several times a day—in order to cast their votes. The arrangement suggested by the Independence Park historians is consistent with the arrangement of state delegations in the Continental Congress, as reported by Charles Thomson while the Congress was meeting in Philadelphia. See the "Report of the Secretary of Congress," May 18, 1782, in Edmund C. Burnett, *Letters of Members of the Continental Congress*, 8 vols. (Washington, D.C.: U.S. Government Printing Office, 1921–36), vol. 6, 349.

49. The best description of Wythe's career and background is Joyce Knight Blackburn, *George Wythe of Williamsburg* (New York: Harper and Row, 1975); Bowen, *Miracle at Philadelphia*, 35.

50. Blackburn, *Wythe*, 115; Farrand, vol. 1, 9.

51. Farrand, vol. 1, 10–13, 17.

52. Ibid., 13.

53. Most of King's letters to those individuals have not survived, but that he wrote them to keep them informed can be gleaned from the responses to his letters. See Nathan Dane to King, May 31, June 19, July 5, Aug. 12, 1787, Henry Knox to King, June 8, July 15, 1787, in Charles R. King, ed., *Life and Correspondence of Rufus King*, 6 vols. (New York: G. P. Putnam's Sons, 1894–1900), vol. 1, 220–22, 225–29, 256–58. Robert Ernst, *Rufus King: American Federalist* (Chapel Hill, N.C.: University of North Carolina Press, 1968), gives a valuable perspective on King's role in the Convention.

54. Jared Sparks, Journal, April 19, 1830, in Farrand, vol. 3, 479; Mason to George Mason, Jr., June 1, 1787, Farrand, vol. 3, 33.

55. Jefferson to Adams, Aug. 30, 1787, in Julian Boyd et al., *The Papers of Thomas Jefferson*, 17 vols. (Princeton, N.J.: Princeton University Press, 1950–), vol. 12, 69; Farrand, vol. 3, 76; Virginia Statute of Religious Liberty, in W. W. Hening, ed., *Statutes at Large of Virginia*, 13 vols. (Richmond: Samuel Pleasants, 1809–23), vol. 12, 84–86.

56. Farrand, vol. 1, xi–xxv provides a good summary of the various firsthand reports of the Convention that are extant. Hutson, *Supplement*, xv–xxvi provides additional information and also gives a useful evaluation of the trustworthiness of some of those sources. Pinckney's proposal is in Farrand, vol. 1, 17.

57. Madison, "Preface to the Debates in the Convention of 1787," in Farrand, vol. 3, 550.

58. Farrand, vol. 3, 550.

CHAPTER FIVE

1. Max Farrand, ed., *The Records of the Federal Convention of 1787*, 4 vols., rev. ed. (New Haven, Conn.: Yale University Press, 1937, repr. 1966), vol. 1, 18–19, 23–24.

2. Madison to John Tyler, ca. Oct., 1833, in ibid., vol. 3, 525. Irving Brant, *James Madison*, 6 vols. (New York: Bobbs-Merrill, 1941–61), vol. 2, 23, asserts that "the [Virginia] Plan was undoubtedly written by Madison," implying that few others, including Randolph, had any meaningful role in crafting it. John J. Reardon, *Edmund Randolph: A Biography*

(New York: Macmillan, 1964), 96–97, is inclined to give Randolph somewhat more credit. Catherine Drinker Bowen, *Miracle at Philadelphia: The Story of the Constitutional Convention, May to September, 1787* (Boston: Little, Brown, 1966), 36–37, and Clinton Rossiter, *1787: The Grand Convention* (New York: Macmillan Company, 1966), 60–61, are vague on the identity of the discussants, but they agree that Madison was the prime mover. The likelihood that the Pennsylvanians—particularly the two Morrises and James Wilson—were active participants in the formulation of the plan is suggested by three factors. First, we know they engaged in direct conversation (and disagreement) with Madison on the question of the method of apportioning voting in the Convention. Second, their views of how to strengthen the executive branch were more fully developed than Madison's, and those views made their way into the Virginia Plan. Third, next to Madison himself, and far more than many of the Virginians, Wilson and Morris were the two strongest supporters of the Virginia Plan in the Convention.

3. Farrand, vol. 1, 20–22. For most of the Convention, the delegates continued to refer to a "national legislature," although many delegates also referred to that branch of government as the "Congress." Since the legislative branch ultimately came to be called a "Congress," I use the two terms interchangeably in this narrative.

4. Ibid.

5. Randolph's expressions of concern about the "democratic parts of our constitutions" were recorded not by Madison, but by James McHenry of Maryland, in ibid., vol. 1, 26–27.

6. Ibid., 20–22.

7. Ibid.

8. Ibid., 23.

9. The tale of Henry refusing to attend the Convention because "I smelt a rat" has been repeated by nearly every historian of the Convention, but if he ever uttered the phrase at all, it was certainly long after the Convention had concluded and he had realized his mistake in *not* attending. The two most recent scholarly biographies, Richard R. Beeman, *Patrick Henry: A Biography* (New York: McGraw-Hill, 1974), 137–38, 141–42, and Henry Mayer, *A Son of Thunder: Patrick Henry and the American Republic* (New York: Franklin Watts, 1986), 370–76, both believe that Henry, who had just retired from yet another term as governor, was eager to return to his estate and put public affairs out of his mind for a while. The source of the statement that Henry "smelt" a rat is the highly unreliable Hugh Blair Grigsby, *The History of the Virginia Federal Convention of 1788 with Some Account of the Eminent Virginians of That Era Who Were Members of the Body,* 2 vols. (Richmond, Va.: Virginia Historical Society, 1890–91), vol. 1, 32.

10. Beeman, *Henry,* 148–63; Madison to Jefferson, Dec. 9, 1787, in William T. Hutchinson, William M. E. Rachal, Robert A. Rutland, et al., *The Papers of James Madison,* 19 vols. (Chicago and Charlottesville, Va.: University of Chicago Press and University Press of Virginia, 1961–), vol. 9, 311–12; Madison to Jefferson, Feb. 19, April 22, 1788, in ibid., vol. 10, 519–20, vol. 11, 27–29.

11. Farrand, vol. 1, 23.

12. It is surprising, given the significance of Pinckney's career—and the controversy surrounding it—that there has not been a full-scale biography of the South Carolinian. However, a recent effort, Marty D. Matthews, *Forgotten Founder: The Life and Times of Charles Pinckney* (Columbia, S.C.: University of South Carolina Press, 2004), esp., 1–38, provides a partial remedy.

13. Ibid., 39–40; Farrand, vol. 3, 96.
14. I am indebted to Christopher Collier and James Lincoln Collier, *Decision in Philadelphia* (New York: Random House, 1986), esp. 87–101, for first bringing the case of Pinckney's possible authorship of the Constitution to my attention. Although they may in the end overstate the case for his authorship, their analysis of the issue is illuminating. The Colliers rely heavily on two important but often-overlooked articles on the subject: S. Sidney Ulmer, "Charles Pinckney: Father of the Constitution?" *South Carolina Law Quarterly* 10 (1958), 225–47, and S. Sidney Ulmer, "James Madison and the Pinckney Plan," *South Carolina Law Quarterly* 9 (1957), 416–43. I am grateful to Professor Ulmer for sharing copies of these essays with me.
15. Farrand, vol. 3, 514–15. Brant, *Madison*, vol. 2, 29, uses Madison's reference to the fact that he and Pinckney were "familiar in conversation when Mr. Pinckney was preparing his plan" as the basis for his assertion that once Pinckney learned of Madison's thoughts on the Virginia Plan at Mrs. House's, he then plagiarized Madison's principal ideas and presented them to the Convention as his own. Given the facts that Pinckney had already devoted considerable time to thinking about amendments to the Articles of Confederation and the pronounced differences between the Virginia Plan and the various drafts of the Pinckney Plan, this assertion is simply not plausible.
16. Read to Dickinson, May 21, 1787, in Farrand, vol. 3, 23–27. See also William T. Read, *Life and Correspondence of George Read* (Philadelphia: Lippincott, 1870), 443–44. Read's copy of the plan is in the Pennsylvania Historical Society.
17. The text of Pinckney's *Observations*, printed in pamphlet form first in New York and reprinted in the *State Gazette* of South Carolina between October 29 and November 29, 1787, is in Farrand, vol. 3, 106–23.
18. Ibid.
19. Pinckney to John Quincy Adams, Dec. 30, 1818, in ibid., vol. 3, 427–28.
20. During the spring and summer of 1831, Madison systematically analyzed the various Pinckney drafts and became convinced that the draft Pinckney had sent to Adams bore little resemblance to the draft he presented to the Convention on May 29. Madison to J. K. Paulding, April, 1831, June 6, 1831, June 27, 1831, Madison to Jared Sparks, June 27, 1831, in ibid., vol. 3, 501–15.
21. Madison to Jared Sparks, June 27, 1831, Nov. 25, 1831, in ibid., vol. 3, 514–15.
22. At the beginning of the twentieth century, two distinguished American historians, J. Franklin Jameson and Andrew C. McLaughlin, undertook systematic analyses of the various Pinckney drafts of the Constitution. They concluded that the draft he sent to John Quincy Adams was *not* the draft he presented at the Convention and, moreover, that in the years following the Convention Pinckney had made excessive claims for his role in drafting the Constitution. At the same time, however, they were persuaded that Pinckney's various draft proposals did constitute "a noteworthy contribution" to the Constitution. J. Franklin Jameson, "Portions of Charles Pinckney's Plans for a Constitution, 1787," *American Historical Review* 8 (1903): 117–20; Andrew C. McLaughlin, "Sketch of Charles Pinckney's Plan for a Constitution, 1787," *American Historical Review* 9 (1904): 735–41.
23. Forrest McDonald, *We the People: The Economic Origins of the Constitution* (Chicago: University of Chicago Press, 1958), 43–44. See also Rossiter, *Grand Convention*, 171. David

Stewart, *The Summer of 1787* (New York: Simon & Schuster, 2007), 54, disparages Gorham's abilities by repeating a speculation made more than a century ago that Gorham had become so panicked by Shays' Rebellion that he had written Prince Henry of Prussia asking if he would be willing to assume "regal powers" over the dis-united states. There is no evidence to support this speculation, and, moreover, such a panic-stricken response seems wholly out of character for Gorham.

24. Farrand, vol. 1, 33.
25. Ibid., 33–34, 39.
26. Ibid., 34.
27. Ibid., 35.
28. Ibid., 34–36.

CHAPTER SIX

1. Max Farrand, ed., *The Records of the Federal Convention of 1787*, 4 vols., rev. ed. (New Haven, Conn.: Yale University Press, 1937, repr. 1966), vol. 1, 35–36, 49–50. Lawrence Goldstone, *Dark Bargain: Slavery, Profits and the Struggle for the Constitution* (New York: Walker and Company, 2005), 102–3, has been the most insistent in arguing that the defense of slave interests lay at the heart of the struggle for the Constitution. See also Paul Finkelman, *Slavery and the Founders: Race and Liberty in the Age of Jefferson* (Armonk, N.Y.: M. E. Sharpe, 1996). For a powerful critique of the tendency of twenty-first-century historians to place slavery and race at the center of all aspects of the Revolutionary and constitutional eras, see Gordon Wood, "Reading the Founders' Minds," *New York Review of Books*, 54 no. 11 (2007), 63–66. An outstanding recent study of the debates and decisions in the Convention on the way in which slaves should be counted in apportioning representation is George Van Cleve, "A Slaveholders' Union: The Law and Politics of American Slavery, 1770–1821" (PhD diss., University of Virginia, 2008). I am exceptionally grateful to Dr. Van Cleve for his helpful critique of my discussions of slavery and the Constitutional Convention.
2. Farrand, vol. 1, 36. For a description of King, see Robert Ernst, *Rufus King: American Federalist* (Chapel Hill, N.C.: University of North Carolina Press, 1968), 36–37, 407.
3. Farrand, vol. 1, 36.
4. Ibid.
5. Ibid.
6. Ibid.
7. Ibid.
8. W. R. Dave to James Iredell, May 30, 1787, William Dobbs Spaight to Governor Caswell, June 12, 1787, in Farrand, vol. 3, 31, 46.
9. Washington to Jefferson, May 30, 1787, in W. W. Abbot, Dorothy Twohig, et al., *The Papers of George Washington*, Confederation Series, 6 vols. (Charlottesville, Va.: University Press of Virginia, 1992–), vol. 5, 203–8; Donald Jackson and Dorothy Twohig, eds., *The Diaries of George Washington*, 6 vols. (Charlottesville, Va.: University Press of Virginia, 1976–79), vol. 5, 164.
10. Farrand, vol. 1, 48.
11. George Billias, *Elbridge Gerry: Founding Father and Republican Statesman* (New York: McGraw-Hill, 1976), 1–99.

12. Farrand, vol. 3, 88; Billias, *Gerry*, 7. Billias's study of the conflicting strains in Gerry's personality and ideology is unusually perceptive, placing it among the very best of the biographies of the framers of the Constitution. I draw heavily on Billias's insights for my own generalizations about Gerry, although I ultimately dissent from his more favorable assessment of Gerry's contributions to the Convention.

13. Gerry to Ann Gerry, May 30, 1787, in James H. Hutson, *Supplement to Max Farrand's Records of the Federal Convention of 1787* (New Haven, Conn.: Yale University Press, 1987), 33–34; William Parker Cutler and Julia Perkins Cutler, *Life, Journals and Correspondence of Rev. Manasseh Cutler, L.L.D.*, 2 vols. (Cincinnati, Robert Clarke & Co., 1888) July 13, 1787, vol. 1, 255; Billias, *Gerry*, 147.

14. Billias, *Gerry*, xiv–xvi, 103–6, 149–52, 155.

15. Farrand, vol. 1, 48.

16. Ibid., 50. Unfortunately, relatively few of Butler's personal papers have survived. Lewright B. Sikes, *The Public Life of Pierce Butler, South Carolina Statesman* (Washington, D.C.: Rowman and Littlefield, 1979), provides some useful information on Butler's life. More helpful is S. Sidney Ulmer, "The Role of Pierce Butler in the Constitutional Convention," *Review of Politics* 22 (1960): 361–74.

17. Farrand, vol. 1, 35, 48.

18. Christopher Collier, *Roger Sherman's Connecticut: Yankee Politics and the American Revolution* (Middletown, Conn.: Wesleyan University Press, 1971), 5–8. Collier's study of Sherman is excellent.

19. Ibid., 18–23. The position of inspector of pennies was not as trivial as it may sound. In 1785, the state licensed a private mint in New Haven to turn out copper pennies, which turned out over $185,000 worth of the coins between 1785 and 1787.

20. Ibid., 138–236; Rossiter, *Grand Convention*, 91.

21. Farrand, vol. 3, 88–89; Adams's assessment is quoted in Collier, *Roger Sherman's Connecticut*, 129. Bernard Bailyn, *To Begin the World Anew: The Genius and Ambiguities of the American Founders* (New York: Knopf, 2003), 28–30, constructs a brilliant portrait of Sherman.

22. Farrand, vol. 3, 88–89; Collier, *Roger Sherman's Connecticut*, 94.

23. Jeremiah Wadsworth to Rufus King, June 3, 1787, in Farrand, vol. 3, 34.

24. Ibid., vol. 1, 50.

25. Ibid., 48–49.

26. Ibid., 49.

27. Ibid., 50.

28. The most recent and comprehensive account of the origins of the United States Senate is Daniel Wirls and Stephen Wirls, *The Invention of the United States Senate* (Baltimore: Johns Hopkins University Press, 2004), esp. 28–31, 71–134.

29. Ibid., 51–52.

30. Ibid., 21.

31. Ibid., 53–54.

32. Ibid., 54.

CHAPTER SEVEN

1. Gordon Wood, *The Creation of the American Republic, 1776–1787* (Chapel Hill, N.C.: University of North Carolina Press, 1969), provides an excellent discussion of the creation

of state constitutions in the immediate aftermath of the Revolution. See also Marc Kruman, *Between Authority and Liberty: State Constitution-Making in Revolutionary America* (Chapel Hill, N.C.: University of North Carolina Press, 1997). On the operation of the Committee of the States within the Confederation government, see Jack Rakove, *The Beginnings of National Politics: An Interpretive History of the Continental Congress* (New York: Knopf, 1979), 180, 336, 351, 356–57. The Articles of Confederation can be conveniently accessed at http://www.yale.edu/lawweb/avalon/artconf.htm. That website is part of Yale Law School's Avalon Project, an outstanding source for primary documents relating to early American constitutionalism.

2. Madison, "Vices of the Political System of the United States," in William T. Hutchinson, William M. E. Rachal, Robert A. Rutland, et al., *The Papers of James Madison*, 19 vols. (Chicago and Charlottesville, Va.: University of Chicago Press and University Press of Virginia, 1961–), vol. 9, 348–57.

3. Max Farrand, ed., *The Records of the Federal Convention of 1787*, 4 vols., rev. ed. (New Haven, Conn.: Yale University Press, 1937, repr. 1966), vol. 1, 64–65.

4. Ibid.

5. Ibid.

6. Ibid., 66.

7. Surprisingly, few historians of the Convention—or of the American presidency—have remarked on the powerful, if unspoken, influence of Washington on the creation of the executive branch. One notable exception is Clinton Rossiter, *1787: The Grand Convention* (New York: Macmillan Company, 1966), 221–24.

8. Max Farrand, vol. 1, 65, 66, 68, 69.

9. Clarence C. Brigham, *Bibliography of Early American Newspapers* (Worcester, Mass.: American Antiquarian Society, 1923), remains the best general guide to early American newspapers. See also Merrill Jensen, John Kaminski, and Gaspare Saladino, eds., *The Documentary History of the Ratification of the Constitution*, 21 vols. (Madison, Wis.: State Historical Society of Wisconsin, 1976–), vol. 1, 48–50.

10. Pennsylvania *Gazette*, May 30, 1787.

11. Pennsylvania *Packet*, June 1, 1787.

12. Quoted in Charles Page Smith, *James Wilson, Founding Father, 1742–1798* (Chapel Hill, N.C.: University of North Carolina Press, 1956), 202.

13. Ibid., 78–89, 107–15.

14. Ibid., 116–33.

15. Ibid., 133–36; John K. Alexander, "The Fort Wilson Incident of 1779: A Case Study of the Revolutionary Crowd," *William and Mary Quarterly*, 3rd ser. (1974) 41: 589–612, presents a picture of the incident far more sympathetic to the militiamen and more hostile to Wilson.

16. Smith, *Wilson*, 136–39.

17. Farrand, vol. 1, 76–114.

18. Ibid., 97.

19. Ibid., 80, 81, 132, 137–38.

20. Ibid., 80.

21. Ibid., 81.

22. Ibid., 69.

23. Ibid., 21–22.

24. The scholarly writing on *Marbury v. Madison* and its historical antecedents is vast. However, there does seem to be an emerging consensus among scholars that most of the delegates to the Convention probably did assume that the federal judiciary would have some power of judicial review, however hazily defined. The most detailed study is William E. Nelson, *Marbury v. Madison: The Origins and Legacy of Judicial Review* (Lawrence, Kans.: University of Kansas Press, 2000). Akhil Reed Amar, *America's Constitution: A Biography* (New York: Random House, 2005), 60–61, 121–22, 179–81, makes a persuasive case that the function of judicial review was not seen by the framers as residing in one specific branch of government alone.
25. Farrand, vol. 1, 98. Wilson had no objection to giving the judicial branch an absolute negative over legislation as well, but he did not believe that they should be intermingled in the same branch or office of the government.
26. Ibid., 81–85.
27. Ibid., 99.
28. Ibid., 98–100.
29. Ibid., 99–100.
30. Ibid., 103–4.
31. Ibid., 104.
32. Ibid., 85.
33. Ibid., 85, 86.
34. Ibid., 87.

CHAPTER EIGHT

1. Pennsylvania *Herald*, June 8, 1787.
2. Max Farrand, ed., *The Records of the Federal Convention of 1787*, 4 vols., rev. ed. (New Haven, Conn.: Yale University Press, 1937, repr. 1966), vol. 1, 164.
3. Ibid., 165–68.
4. Ibid., vol. 1, 167–68, vol. 3, 92; John Munroe, *Federalist Delaware, 1776–1815* (New Brunswick, N.J.: Rutgers University Press, 1954), 105–6; John P. Nields, *Gunning Bedford, Jr.* (Wilmington, Del.: 1907).
5. Farrand, vol. 1, 168.
6. Ibid., 175, 177–79. For a full biography of the extraordinary Luther Martin, see Paul Clarkson and R. Samuel Jett, *Luther Martin of Maryland* (Baltimore: Johns Hopkins University Press, 1970).
7. John E. O'Connor, *William Paterson: Lawyer and Statesman, 1745–1806* (New Brunswick, N.J.: Rutgers University Press, 1979), 7–43, 103–11; Farrand, vol. 3, 90.
8. O'Connor, *Paterson*, 16, 18–20, 49–67.
9. Ibid.
10. Farrand, vol. 1, 178. The Massachusetts commission is reprinted in *Farrand*, vol. 3, 584–85, and in Merrill Jensen, John Kaminski, and Gaspare Saladino, eds., *The Documentary History of the Ratification of the Constitution*, 21 vols. (Madison, Wis.: State Historical Society of Wisconsin, 1976–), vol. 1, 205–6.
11. Farrand, vol. 1, 178–79.
12. Ibid., 179–80.
13. Ibid., 196.
14. Ibid., 355, 461, 469–70.

15. Ibid., 197–200.

16. Ibid.

17. Ibid., 200.

18. Ibid., 196, 200–201.

19. Ibid., 201.

20. Charles Page Smith, *James Wilson, Founding Father, 1742–1798* (Chapel Hill, N.C.: University of North Carolina Press, 1956), 367.

21. The literature—and scholarly contention—on the so-called three-fifths compromise is vast. Much of it is either overly protective of the reputation of the framers or polemically presentist in the imputation of a "dark bargain" between Northern and Southern delegates. Among the most useful discussions of the compromise are Paul Finkelman, "Slavery and the Constitutional Convention: Making a Covenant with Death," in Richard R. Beeman et al., *Beyond Confederation: Origins of the Constitution and American National Identity* (Chapel Hill, N.C.: University of North Carolina Press, 1987), 188–225; Howard Ohline, "Republicanism and Slavery: Origins of the Three-Fifths Clause in the United States Constitution," *William and Mary Quarterly*, 3rd ser. (1971) 28: 563–84; Earl Maltz, "The Idea of a Pro-Slavery Constitution," *Journal of the Early Republic* (1997) 17: 38–59; William W. Freehling, "The Founding Fathers and Slavery," *American Historical Review* (1972) 77:81–93; William C. Wiecek, *The Sources of Antislavery Constitutionalism in America, 1760–1848* (Ithaca, N.Y.: Cornell University Press, 1977), 62–83. The account that is most unrelentingly critical of the Founding Fathers on this issue is Lawrence Goldstone, *Dark Bargain: Slavery, Profits and the Struggle for the Constitution* (New York: Walker and Company, 2005), esp. 100–144. The most balanced, full account is George Van Cleve, "A Slaveholders' Union: The Law and Politics of American Slavery, 1770–1821" (PhD diss., University of Virginia, 2008), esp. 176–210. Van Cleve's essential argument is that "morality" played little part in the debate over the three-fifths formula, or, indeed, in the debates on any issues involving slavery. For Van Cleve, the "3/5 clause was the explicitly chosen political security foundation for the constitutional bargain protecting the political economy of the southern states."

22. Read to Dickinson, May 21, 1787, in Farrand, vol. 3, 25; Ohline, "Origins of Three-Fifths Clause," 569.

23. Farrand, vol. 1, 201, 208.

24. Ibid., 201.

25. Ibid., 201–2.

26. For a perceptive analysis of this subject, see Drew McCoy, "James Madison and Visions of American Nationality in the Confederation Period," in Beeman et al., *Beyond Confederation*, 226–58.

27. The best example of Maryland's jealousy over Virginia's size and power was Maryland's refusal to ratify the Articles of Confederation because of her competition with Virginia over western land claims. See Peter Onuf, *The Origins of the Federal Republic: Jurisdictional Controversies in the United States, 1775–1787* (Philadelphia: University of Pennsylvania Press, 1983), 88, 94.

28. Clinton Rossiter, *1787: The Grand Convention* (New York: Macmillan Company, 1966), 93–96; John P. Kaminski, *George Clinton: Yeoman Politician of the Early Republic* (Madison, Wis.: University of Wisconsin Press, 1993), 113–20.

29. Farrand, vol. 1, 235–37. Luther Martin of Maryland was one of those delegates who were incensed at the extent to which the revised report reflected a triumph for nationalist aims.

He was particularly upset that neither Washington nor Franklin, the two most illustrious members of the Convention, stepped in at that point to try to bring some balance to the report. See Martin's testimony in Farrand, vol. 3, 178.

30. Farrand, vol. 1, 235–37.
31. Ibid., 236.
32. Ibid., vol. 3, 86–87.
33. Ibid.
34. Ibid., vol. 1, 240.
35. Ibid., 27–28.
36. Ibid., 242.
37. Ibid., 242–45; Rossiter, *Grand Convention*, 175; O'Connor, *Paterson*, 145–51.
38. Farrand, vol. 1, 244.
39. Ibid., 152–54.
40. Ibid., 242n.

CHAPTER NINE

1. Harry MacNeill Bland and Virginia Northcott, "The Life Portraits of Alexander Hamilton," *William and Mary Quarterly*, 3rd ser. (1955) 12: 187–98; Max Farrand, ed., *The Records of the Federal Convention of 1787*, 4 vols., rev. ed. (New Haven, Conn.: Yale University Press, 1937, repr. 1966), vol. 3, 89.
2. The details of Hamilton's early life can be found in any of a number of excellent biographies of Hamilton, including Broadus Mitchell, *Alexander Hamilton*, 2 vols. (New York: Macmillan, 1957–62); John C. Miller, *Alexander Hamilton and the Growth of the New Nation* (New York: Harper and Row, 1964); Jacob E. Cooke, *Alexander Hamilton: A Biography* (New York: Scribner's, 1979); Forrest McDonald, *Alexander Hamilton: A Biography* (New York: Norton, 1979); Nathan Schachner, *Alexander Hamilton* (New York: Appleton-Century, 1946); and, most recently, Ron Chernow, *Alexander Hamilton* (New York: Penguin Press, 2004).
3. The Adams characterization is quoted in Chernow, *Hamilton,* 522.
4. Jefferson's and Hamilton's biographers have taken predictable sides in the ongoing conflict of personalities and principles between Hamilton and Jefferson. See, for example, McDonald, *Hamilton*, 212–17, 237, 239, 242–43, 251–53, 260–61, 270–83; and Dumas Malone, *Jefferson and His Time*, 6 vol.; (Boston: Little, Brown, 1948–81), vol. 3, 14–26, 74–76, 253–56.
5. As one recent biographer, Ron Chernow, has written, "We are indisputably the heirs to Hamilton's America, and to repudiate his legacy is in many ways to repudiate the modern world." Chernow, *Hamilton*, 6, 466.
6. Farrand, vol. 1, 283–301. The day following the formal presentation of the New Jersey Plan, Saturday, June 16, the delegates reconstituted themselves as a Committee of the Whole so that they would have more freedom to express their opinions on the various plans thus far offered. This gave Hamilton the license to embark on his extended exegesis. The Convention would remain in that mode through Tuesday, June 19.
7. Ibid., 284–86.
8. Ibid., 287.
9. Ibid., 287–88.

10. Ibid., 289.

11. Ibid., 291–93.

12. See Yates's notes on Hamilton's speech in Farrand, vol. 1, 294–301.

13. Ibid., 363.

14. Madison apparently went to great lengths to assure that he had captured the essential elements of Hamilton's speech in his notes. See Farrand, vol. 1, 293, n. 9.

15. Ibid., 314–22.

16. Ibid., 321–22.

17. Ibid., 322.

18. Ibid., 335.

19. Ibid.

20. Ibid., 336–38.

21. Ibid., vol. 3, 49–50.

22. Ibid., 344.

23. Just two months after the Constitutional Convention adjourned, Johnson would accept the presidency of Columbia University, in Farrand, vol. 3, 88. George C. Groce, Jr., *William Samuel Johnson: A Maker of the Constitution* (New York: Columbia University Press, 1937) provides only a sketchy account of Johnson's services in the Convention. Elizabeth P. McCaughey, *From Loyalist to Founding Father: The Political Odyssey of William Samuel Johnson* (New York: Columbia University Press, 1980), 211–37, is somewhat more helpful. Clinton Rossiter, *1787: The Grand Convention* (New York: Macmillan Company, 1966), 89–90, provides a brief overview of Johnson's impressive educational background. For his illness, see William Samuel Johnson Diary, June 3–5, 1787.

24. Farrand, vol. 1, 355.

25. Ibid., 356.

26. Paul Clarkson and R. Samuel Jett, *Luther Martin of Maryland* (Baltimore: Johns Hopkins University Press, 1970), 33–71. The year of Martin's birth is disputed, with estimates ranging from 1744 to 1748. Clarkson and Jett make a convincing case for 1748.

27. Ibid., 203–4, 311–12.

28. Farrand, vol. 1, 340–41.

29. Ibid., 437–38; Christopher Collier and James Lincoln Collier, *Decision in Philadelphia* (New York: Random House, 1986), 159; Clarkson and Jett, *Luther Martin*, 99.

30. Farrand, vol. 1, 438, 445.

31. Ibid., 439; Oliver Ellsworth to Martin, Feb. 1788, in ibid., vol. 3, 272.

32. Collier and Collier, *Decision in Philadelphia*, 160.

33. Ibid., 159–63.

34. Farrand, vol. 1, 451.

35. Ibid.

36. Ibid., 452.

37. Ibid.

38. James Madison, "Federalist No. 37," in Jacob E. Cooke, ed., *The Federalist* (Middletown, Conn.: Wesleyan University Press, 1961), 238. Rush's speech is quoted in Jon Meacham, *God, the Founding Fathers, and the Making of a Nation* (New York: Random House, 2006), 91; George Bancroft, *History of the Formation of the Constitution of the United States of America*, 2 vols. (New York: Appleton, 1882), vol. 2, 284.

39. Farrand, vol. 2, 342, 468. There are in fact two other references in the Constitution that have at least some religious connotation, although they seem casual and perfunctory rather than purposeful. Article I, Section 7 stipulates that the president will have only ten days, "Sundays excepted," in which to decide whether to veto a bill, and in the final words of Article VII, the delegates included the phrase, "the Seventeenth Day of September in the Year of our Lord one thousand seven hundred and eighty-seven."

40. Frank Lambert, *The Founding Fathers and the Place of Religion in America* (Princeton, N.J.: Princeton University Press, 2003), 247. For a contrary view, see James Hutson's passionate rebuttal in *Religion and the Founding of the American Republic* (Washington, D.C.: Library of Congress, 1998).

41. Historians' identifications of the religious affiliations of the framers have varied, but the most comprehensive compilation of information can be found in Constitutional Convention Daybook Files, Independence National Historical Park Archive, Philadelphia, Pa., cabinet 2, drawer 2, folder 40 (Religion).

42. Donald Jackson and Dorothy Twohig, eds., *The Diaries of George Washington*, 6 vols. (Charlottesville, Va.: University Press of Virginia, 1976–79), vol. 5, 156–86; William Samuel Johnson Diary, June–Sept. 1787, transcript at Independence Historical National Park Archive, Philadelphia, Pa. For an excellent, brief discussion of Washington's religious beliefs, see Joseph J. Ellis, *His Excellency, George Washington* (New York: Knopf, 2005), 45, 151, 269. The number of books devoted to the subject of Washington's religion is staggering. Among the most recent are Michael and Jane Novak, *Washington's God: Religious Liberty and the Father of Our Country* (New York: Basic Books, 2000); Peter Lillack, *George Washington's Sacred Fire* (New York: Providence Forum Press, 2006); and Frank Grizzard, *The Ways of Providence: Religion and George Washington* (New York: Mariner, 2003).

43. Farrand, vol. 1, 452. Walter Isaacson, *Benjamin Franklin: An American Life* (New York: Simon & Schuster, 2003), 19–20, 32–33, 44–45, 84–88, 92–94, 107–11, 467–69, has insightful analyses of the evolution of Franklin's religious beliefs.

44. Farrand, vol. 1, 461–62, 463–65.

45. Ibid., 467.

46. Ibid., 482–87.

47. Ibid., 486.

48. Ibid., 485–86.

49. Ibid., 487, 497–98.

50. Ibid., 488–89.

51. Ibid., 490–92, 500–2. Both Madison and Robert Yates took extensive notes of Bedford's speech, but Yates's notes seem to capture more of the passion of Bedford's feelings on the subject.

52. Ibid., 493.

53. Quoted in Christopher Collier and James Lincoln Collier, *Decision in Philadelphia* (New York: Random House, 1986), 168.

54. Ibid., 168–69.

55. Ibid., 169–70.

56. Farrand, vol. 1, 510.

57. My account of Baldwin's background and activity in the Convention follows closely that of Collier and Collier, *Decision in Philadelphia*, 170–71.

58. Forrest McDonald, *E Pluribus Unum: The Formation of the American Republic, 1776–1790* (Boston: Houghton-Mifflin, 1965), 283; Clinton Rossiter, *1787: The Grand Convention* (New York: Macmillan Company, 1966), 187; and Collier and Collier, *Decision in Philadelphia,* 171–72.

59. Collier and Collier, *Decision in Philadelphia,* 169–70, provide the most plausible explanation.

60. Farrand, vol. 1, 510–11.

61. Ibid., 511–16.

62. Ibid., 516.

CHAPTER TEN

1. Though somewhat light on empirical detail and heavy on postmodern analysis, the most recent and comprehensive account of the early history of Independence Day celebrations is Len Travers, *Celebrating the Fourth: Independence Day and the Rites of Nationalism in the Early Republic* (Amherst, Mass.: University of Massachusetts Press, 1997), esp. 31–68. See also the less scholarly Diana Karter Appelbaum, *The Glorious Fourth: An American Holiday, An American History* (New York: Facts-on-File, 1989) esp. 16–26.

2. Clinton Rossiter, *1787: The Grand Convention* (New York: Macmillan Company, 1966), 145.

3. Constitutional Convention Daybook Files, Independence National Historical Park Archive, Philadelphia, Pa., cabinet 2, drawer 2, folder 53 (Military Experience).

4. Rossiter, *Grand Convention,* 145; Daybooks, cabinet 2, drawer 2, folder 35 (Experience—National Politics).

5. Pennsylvania *Packet,* July 6, 1787; Pennsylvania *Herald,* July 7, 1787.

6. Ibid.

7. Ibid.

8. Donald Jackson and Dorothy Twohig, eds., *The Diaries of George Washington,* 6 vols. (Charlottesville, Va.: University Press of Virginia, 1976–79), vol. 5, 173–74.

9. Ibid., 155–58.

10. Ibid., 155–86. I am grateful to Mr. David Maxey for sharing with me at an early stage the material from his extended essay, now published as *A Portrait of Elizabeth Willing Powel (1743–1830)* (Philadelphia: American Philosophical Society, 2006), esp. 30–32.

11. Maxey, *A Portrait of Elizabeth Willing Powel,* 21, 26.

12. Ibid., 18–21, 26, 29.

13. Unfortunately, we know virtually nothing about any confidences that Washington may have shared with his wife, Martha, during that summer, for none of his correspondence with her during the summer of 1787 has survived.

14. *GW Diary,* vol. 5, 173–74.

15. Maxey, *Elizabeth Willing Powel,* 30–31. See also Susan Branson, *Those Fiery Frenchified Dames: Women and Political Culture in Early Philadelphia* (Philadelphia: University of Pennsylvania Press, 2001), 133. The speculations on her conversation are my own.

16. Elizabeth Powel to Washington Nov. 17, 1792, in W. W. Abbot, Dorothy Twohig, et al., *The Papers of George Washington,* Presidential Series, 11 vols. (Charlottesville, Va.: University Press of Virginia, 1987–), vol. 11, 395–97.

17. Washington to Elizabeth Powel, Feb. 1793, in ibid., vol. 12, 239–42.

18. *GW Diary,* vol. 5, 173.

19. For descriptions of William Bingham and his mansion, see Robert C. Alberts, *The Golden Voyage: The Life and Times of William Bingham, 1752–1804* (Boston: Houghton-Mifflin, 1969), 157–64; and Branson, *Fiery Frenchified Dames,* esp. 135–36.

20. Daybooks, cabinet 1, drawer 3, folder 16, May 23, 1787; Branson, *Fiery Frenchified Dames,* 134, 137–38; Alberts, *William Bingham,* 153–55, 161–62.

21. Branson, *Fiery Frenchified Dames,* 135–36; *GW Diary,* vol. 5, 159, 169, 173, 175, 181–82.

22. Madison to Jefferson, July 18, 1787, in William T. Hutchinson, William M. E. Rachal, Robert A. Rutland, et al., *The Papers of James Madison,* 19 vols. (Chicago and Charlottesville, Va.: University of Chicago Press and University Press of Virginia, 1961–), vol. 10, 105.

CHAPTER ELEVEN

1. Our knowledge of the Grand Committee's deliberations comes from the notes made by Robert Yates, a member of the committee. There is no evidence that Madison participated in the deliberations, although, theoretically, other delegates could have joined the committee as observers. Max Farrand, ed., *The Records of the Federal Convention of 1787,* 4 vols., rev. ed. (New Haven, Conn.: Yale University Press, 1937, repr. 1966), vol. 1, 522–23, vol. 3, 278–79. For Franklin's role, see David Waldstreicher, *Runaway America: Benjamin Franklin, Slavery, and the American Revolution* (New York: Hill and Wang, 2004), 234.

2. Farrand, vol. 1, 526.

3. Ibid.

4. Waldstreicher, *Runaway America,* 234. See also Joseph Ellis, *Founding Brothers: The Revolutionary Generation* (New York: Knopf, 2001) 110–11.

5. Farrand, vol. 3, 50, 51.

6. Hamilton to Washington, July 3, 1787, Washington to Hamilton, July 10, 1787, in W. W. Abbot, Dorothy Twohig, et al., *The Papers of George Washington,* Confederation Series, 6 vols. (Charlottesville, Va.: University Press of Virginia, 1992–), vol. 5, 257.

7. Ibid.

8. Farrand, vol. 1, 527.

9. Ibid., 527–29.

10. Ibid., 529–30.

11. Ibid., 531–34.

12. Ibid., 533, 534.

13. Ibid., 540, 542.

14. Ibid., 559, 560–61.

15. Ibid.

16. Ibid., 561–62.

17. Ibid., 562.

18. Ibid., 562, 566.

19. Ibid., 562.

20. Ibid., 566.

21. Ibid., 566–68.

22. Ibid., 570.

23. Ibid., 580–81.

24. Ibid., 581.
25. Ibid., 581–83.
26. Ibid., 587.
27. Ibid., 588.
28. Ibid., 591–93.
29. Ibid., 593.
30. Ibid.
31. Ibid., 594.
32. Ibid., 593, 594.
33. Ibid., 597. In his later years, Rufus King lamented the fact that he had acquiesced to the three-fifths compromise in the Convention, but we have no record of how he voted on this particular occasion.
34. Ibid., 600–5.
35. Ibid., 603–6. In fact, most delegates would have agreed with James Wilson that there was most likely a 1:1 relationship between population and wealth, so that the distinction was not a very important one. The deletion of wealth from the resolution, however, did at least serve to bring greater clarity to the issue.
36. Jack Rakove, *Original Meanings: Politics and Ideas in the Making of the Constitution* (New York: Knopf, 1996), 73–74, 92–93. The best and most comprehensive treatment of the debate and decisions respecting the three-fifths clause is George Van Cleve, "A Slaveholders' Union: The Law and Politics of American Slavery, 1770–1821" (PhD diss., University of Virginia, 2008), esp. 176–211. Van Cleve, while disagreeing with Rakove on some particulars, does view the debate over the three-fifths clause as primarily involving a contest for power, with the end goal being the protection of property. Van Cleve's study is the most illuminating analysis of the combination of economic interest and ideology that drove the discussion over slavery in the Convention. Though Van Cleve is inclined to give more weight to matters of state economic interest—and to issues of economic development more generally—than I would, his insights into all aspects of the slavery issue in the Convention have proven enormously helpful.
37. James H. Hutson, *Supplement to Max Farrand's The Records of the Federal Convention of 1787* (New Haven, Conn.: Yale University Press, 1987), 158. Dickinson had apparently written out these thoughts in his notebook, intending to deliver them on the Convention floor, but he never did so.
38. The scholarly literature on the Northwest Ordinance and its connection to the slavery debates in the Constitutional Convention is nearly as extensive as that on the more general subject of slavery and the Convention. The most important early work to connect the Northwest Ordinance and the creation of a "pro-slavery" Constitution was Staughton Lynd, "The Compromise of 1787," *Political Science Quarterly* 81 (1966), 225–50 and, subsequently, Staughton Lynd, *Class Conflict, Slavery, and the United States Constitution* (Indianapolis: Bobbs-Merrill, 1967). See also Peter Onuf, *Statehood and Union* (Bloomington, Ind.: University of Indiana Press, 1987); Paul Finkelman, "Slavery and the Northwest Ordinance: A Study in Ambiguity," *Journal of the Early Republic* 6 (1986), 343–69; and Lawrence Goldstone, *Dark Bargain: Slavery, Profits and the Struggle for the Constitution* (New York: Walker and Company, 2005), 132–33, 136–41. My own account of the connection between the Northwest Ordinance and the Conven-

tion debates on slavery relies on the excellent analysis of Van Cleve, "A Slaveholders' Union," 233–60.

39. Van Cleve, "A Slaveholders' Union," 233–60.

40. Finkelman, "Slavery and the Northwest Ordinance," 343.

41. Those arguing most explicitly that there was a "grand bargain" are Lynd, "Compromise of 1787"; Goldstone, *Dark Bargain*, 132–33, 136–41. David Stewart, *The Summer of 1787*, (New York: Simon & Schuster, 2007), 127–49, argues, unconvincingly, that the principles in the bargain were western land speculators and Southern slave owners. My account, which rejects the conspiracy theory approach to the ordinance, follows that of Van Cleve, "A Slaveholders' Union," esp. 240–51.

42. Finkelman, "Slavery and the Northwest Ordinance," esp. 344–49.

43. Farrand, vol. 2, 4.

44. Ibid., 5–11.

45. Ibid., 15.

46. Ibid., vol. 1, 515, vol. 3, 70–71. Walter A. McDougall, *Freedom Just Around the Corner: A New American History, 1585–1828* (New York: HarperCollins, 2004), 300–301, argues that Williamson's intervention was crucial, "quite possibly sav[ing] the United States from death in the cradle." See also Daniel Wirls and Stephen Wirls, *The Invention of the United States Senate* (Baltimore: Johns Hopkins University Press, 2004), 89–101.

47. Farrand, vol. 1, 17–18.

48. Ibid., 18.

49. Ibid.

50. Farrand, vol. 2, 19–20.

51. Ibid.

52. Ibid., vol. 1, 461–62.

53. Clinton Rossiter, *1787: The Grand Convention* (New York: Macmillan Company, 1966), 193. Some historians and political scientists have argued that the Connecticut Compromise, far from saving and strengthening the union, fundamentally undermined its democratic character. It may well be that the facts of life of America's eighteenth-century republic are no longer as relevant to the challenge of governing the United States in the early twenty-first century. The states have lost some of their distinctiveness as discrete political entities, and the disproportionate power that smaller states wield in the United States Senate and, to a lesser extent, in the electoral college, has struck at least some commentators as antithetical to principles of democratic governance. In that sense, men like James Madison and James Wilson may have had logic and democratic principle on their side. But judged by the realities of that summer in 1787, the Connecticut Compromise, however much it may have owed more to pragmatic necessity than to principle, was essential if the union was to move forward. Rakove, *Original Meanings*, 54–83, implies that the "Great Compromise" constituted one of the serious weaknesses, rather than strengths, of the new Constitution. For a robust critique of the antidemocratic character of the decision to allow equal state representation in the Senate, see Robert Dahl, *How Democratic Is the American Constitution?* (New Haven, Conn.: Yale University Press, 2003), esp. 7–40.

CHAPTER TWELVE

1. The Pennsylvania *Herald* and the *Packet* printed essentially similar accounts of the incident: Pennsylvania *Packet*, July 18, 1787, Pennsylvania *Herald*, July 14, July 21, 1787. Ed-

mund S. Morgan, "The Witch & We, the People," *American Heritage* (August/September 1983), 6–11, presents an excellent account of the whole affair.

2. Pennsylvania *Packet,* May 11, 1787.

3. Ibid.; Pennsylvania *Herald,* July 14, July 21, 1787.

4. I am grateful to Morgan, "The Witch & We, the People," 6, for this insight.

5. Pennsylvania *Packet,* July 19, 1787.

6. Max Farrand, ed., *The Records of the Federal Convention of 1787,* 4 vols., rev. ed. (New Haven, Conn.: Yale University Press, 1937, repr. 1966), vol. 2, 26–27; Madison to Martin Van Buren, May 13, 1828, in Farrand, vol. 3, 477; and Clinton Rossiter, *1787: The Grand Convention* (New York: Macmillan Company, 1966), 196. The two negative votes on Bedford's resolution were most likely influenced by the feelings of South Carolina's Charles Pinckney and John Rutledge, who, when the original resolution was first discussed back on May 31, objected to the vagueness of the word "incompetent" and expressed a preference for a specific enumeration of the powers of the new Congress.

7. Farrand, vol. 2, 26.

8. Ibid., 27.

9. Ibid., 27–28.

10. Ibid., 28–29.

11. Ibid., vol. 1, 230.

12. Ibid., 66, vol. 2, 29.

13. Ibid., vol. 2, 29–30.

14. Ibid., 31.

15. For a vivid description of the challenges posed by the American landscape, see Rossiter, *Grand Convention,* 23–40.

16. Ibid., 32.

17. Ibid.

18. Rossiter, *Grand Convention,* 123, makes the tongue-in-cheek suggestion that perhaps the Virginia delegates feared falling ill and being subjected to "Philadelphia medicine" and thus wanted to bring their own physician with them. In fact, the state of medical practice in Philadelphia was significantly better than that in Virginia.

19. Farrand, vol. 2, 32–33.

20. Ibid., 33–35.

21. Ibid., 35.

22. Ibid., 36.

23. Although exchange rates varied widely from state to state, as a general rule, a British pound was worth about five dollars. See John McCusker, *How Much Is That in Real Money?* (New Castle, Del.: Oak Knoll Press, 2001).

24. Donald Jackson and Dorothy Twohig, eds., *The Diaries of George Washington,* 6 vols. (Charlottesville, Va.: University Press of Virginia, 1976–79), vol. 5, 176.

25. Farrand, vol. 1, 120.

26. Ibid., vol. 2, 41.

27. Ibid., 73–80.

28. Ibid.

29. Ibid., 80.

30. Ibid., 44, 83.

CHAPTER THIRTEEN

1. Max Farrand, ed., *The Records of the Federal Convention of 1787*, 4 vols., rev. ed. (New Haven, Conn.: Yale University Press, 1937, repr. 1966), vol. 2, 57–59.
2. Ibid., 58–59.
3. Ibid., 64–65.
4. Ibid., 65–69.
5. Ibid., 69.
6. Ibid., 87; Clinton Rossiter, *1787: The Grand Convention* (New York: Macmillan Company, 1966), 81–92.
7. Rossiter, *Grand Convention*, 81–83.
8. Farrand, vol. 2, 87.
9. Ibid., 94.
10. Ibid., 94–95.
11. Ibid., 88–94.
12. Ibid.
13. Ibid., 92–93.
14. Ibid., 94.
15. Ibid., 95.
16. Williamson to Iredell, July 22, 1787, in Farrand, vol. 3, 61.
17. Ibid., 95–96, 106.
18. Farrand, vol. 2, 100, 102.
19. Ibid., 100–101.
20. There is no modern biography of Williamson, but see David Hosack, *A Biographical Memoir of Hugh Williamson* (1820); Rossiter, *Grand Convention*, 127–28; and Walter A. McDougall, *Freedom Just Around the Corner: A New American History, 1585–1828* (New York: HarperCollins, 2004), 300–301.
21. Farrand, vol. 2, 101.
22. Ibid., 99.
23. Ibid., 101.
24. Ibid., 103.
25. Ibid.
26. Ibid.
27. Ibid., 105–6.
28. Ibid., 109.
29. Ibid., 109–11.
30. Ibid., 111–13.
31. Ibid., 113–14.
32. Ibid., 114.
33. Ibid.
34. Ibid., 115; Luther Martin, "Genuine Information Delivered to the Legislature of the State of Maryland," in Farrand, vol. 3, 191.
35. Ibid., vol. 2, 118–21.
36. Ibid., 121–22.
37. Ibid., 122–25.
38. Ibid., 121.

CHAPTER FOURTEEN

1. Pennsylvania *Herald,* July 28, 1787; Constitutional Convention Daybook Files, Independence National Historical Park Archive, Philadelphia, Pa., cabinet 1, drawer 3, folder 18, July 31, Aug. 4, 1787.
2. Pennsylvania *Packet,* Aug. 14, 1787.
3. Williamson to James Iredell, July 22, 1787, in Max Farrand, ed., *The Records of the Federal Convention of 1787,* 4 vols., rev. ed. (New Haven, Conn.: Yale University Press, 1937, repr. 1966), vol. 3, 61; Madison to James Madison, Sr., July 28, 1787, in William T. Hutchinson, William M. E. Rachal, Robert A. Rutland, et al., *The Papers of James Madison,* 19 vols. (Chicago and Charlottesville, Va.: University of Chicago Press and University Press of Virginia, 1961–), vol. 10, 118–19; Washington to Henry Knox, Aug. 19, 1787, in W. W. Abbot, Dorothy Twohig, et al., *The Papers of George Washington,* Confederation Series, 6 vols. (Charlottesville, Va.: University Press of Virginia, 1992–), vol. 5, 297.
4. Joyce Knight Blackburn, *George Wythe of Williamsburg* (New York: Harper and Row, 1975), 115–16; David Dutcher, Anna Coxe Toogood, et al., *1787: The Day-to-Day Story of the Constitutional Convention* (New York: Exeter Books, 1987), 103.
5. Clinton Rossiter, *1787: The Grand Convention* (New York: Macmillan Company, 1966), 318; Farrand, vol. 2, 664; vol. 3, 589.
6. William Samuel Johnson Diary, July 20, 21, 1787, Independence National Historical Park Archive, Philadelphia, Pa.
7. George Billias, *Elbridge Gerry: Founding Father and Republican Statesman* (New York: McGraw-Hill, 1976), 186; Farrand, vol. 3, 587, 589; Pierce Butler to Weedon Butler, Aug. 1, 1787, in ibid., 67.
8. Alexander Hamilton to Auldjo, July 26, 1787, in Farrand, vol. 3, 64; Forrest McDonald, *Alexander Hamilton: A Biography* (New York: Norton, 1979), 105; Dutcher, Toogood, et al., *1787,* 17–18, 67.
9. Donald Jackson and Dorothy Twohig, eds., *The Diaries of George Washington,* 6 vols. (Charlottesville, Va.: University Press of Virginia, 1976–79), vol. 5, 178–79; Douglas Southall Freeman, *George Washington: A Biography,* 7 vols. (New York: Charles Scribner's Sons, 1948–57), vol. 6, 102–3.
10. *GW Diary,* vol. 5, 180.
11. Washington to Elizabeth Powel, July 30, 1787, in *GW Papers,* C.S., vol. 5, 280–81.
12. Madison to James Madison, Sr., July 28, 1787, in *Madison Papers,* vol. 10, 118.
13. Farrand, vol. 3, 63–65, 68, 71–73.
14. Ibid., vol. 2, 333n., vol. 3, 73, 74, 80–81; Carl Van Doren, *The Great Rehearsal* (New York: Viking Press, 1948), 145. Hamilton and Humphries came to suspect that former Tories in Connecticut were behind the rumor, but they could never identify the culprits.
15. Nicholas Gilman to Joseph Gilman, July 31, 1787, in Farrand, vol. 3, 66. The letter to John Taylor Gilman has not survived, but Nicholas mentions it in his letter to his cousin Joseph.
16. William Garrot Brown, *The Life of Oliver Ellsworth* (New York: DaCapo Press, 1970), 12–20.
17. Ibid., 30–52, 341–42.
18. Farrand, vol. 2, 26.
19. The only full-scale biography of Rutledge is the lively, but overwritten, Richard Barry, *Mr. Rutledge of South Carolina* (New York: Duell, Sloan, and Pearce, 1942). See also James

Haw, *John and Edward Rutledge of South Carolina* (Athens, Ga.: University of Georgia Press, 1997). Two accounts overstate Rutledge's influence in the Convention, especially as it relates to the slavery issue. They are David Stewart, *The Summer of 1787* (New York: Simon & Schuster, 2007), 163–75; and Lawrence Goldstone, *Dark Bargain: Slavery, Profits and the Struggle for the Constitution* (New York: Walker and Company, 2005), esp. 96–97, 149–69, 180–81.

20. Barry, *Mr. Rutledge*, 6–14.

21. Ibid., 62–63; Forrest McDonald, *We the People: The Economic Origins of the Constitution* (Chicago: University of Chicago Press, 1958), 79–80.

22. Barry, *Mr. Rutledge*, 315; Charles Page Smith, *James Wilson, Founding Father, 1742–1798* (Chapel Hill, N.C.: University of North Carolina Press, 1956), 203.

23. Farrand, vol. 2, 95.

24. Ibid., 128, 137. The handwriting in the first draft of the Report of the Committee of Detail, which includes the articulation of the principles guiding the committee's report, is Randolph's, although there are a few emendations by John Rutledge.

25. Ibid., 137–38. See also John J. Reardon, *Edmund Randolph: A Biography* (New York: Macmillan, 1964), 111.

26. Farrand, vol. 2, 163–75.

27. One can follow the evolution of the various drafts in the Committee of Detail report in Farrand, vol. 2, 129–75, and it is Farrand's judgment that the final draft of the report owes mainly to the work of Wilson and Rutledge. Stewart, *Summer of 1787*, 170–75, and Goldstone, *Dark Bargain*, emphasize Rutledge's influence on those sections of the report that touch on the slavery issue.

28. Farrand, vol. 2, 183.

29. Ibid., 185–86.

30. Ibid., 186–87, 178.

31. Ibid., 178.

32. Ibid., 26. The idea of a senate, as well as the specific name, goes back at least as far as ancient Greece. See Daniel Wirls and Stephen Wirls, *The Invention of the United States Senate* (Baltimore: Johns Hopkins University Press, 2004), 11–38.

33. Randolph's original formulation of the specific delegates' powers is in Farrand, vol. 2, 142–44. Wilson's and Rutledge's refinement of that formulation is in ibid., 167–68 and 181–82.

34. Ibid., 187.

35. Ibid., 183.

36. This is the view of Stewart, *Summer of 1787*, 163–75, who titles his chapter on this subject, "Rutledge Hijacks the Constitution."

37. Daybooks, cabinet 1, drawer 3, folder 19, Aug. 3, 1787. See also Dutcher, Toogood, et al., *1787*, 110, and Rossiter, *Grand Convention*, 202.

CHAPTER FIFTEEN

1. Max Farrand, ed., *The Records of the Federal Convention of 1787*, 4 vols., rev. ed. (New Haven, Conn.: Yale University Press, 1937, repr. 1966), vol. 2, 176.

2. Ibid., 196.

3. Ibid., vol. 3, 587–90.

4. Madison to James Madison, Sr., Aug. 12, 1787, in William T. Hutchinson, William M. E. Rachal, Robert A. Rutland, et al., *The Papers of James Madison,* 19 vols. (Chicago and Charlottesville, Va.: University of Chicago Press and University Press of Virginia, 1961–), vol. 10, 146; Washington to Henry Knox, Aug. 19, 1787, in W. W. Abbot, Dorothy Twohig, et al., *The Papers of George Washington,* Confederation Series, 6 vols. (Charlottesville, Va.: University Press of Virginia, 1992–), vol. 5, 297.

5. David Brearley to William Paterson, Aug. 21, 1787, in Farrand, vol. 3, 73; Paterson to Oliver Ellsworth, July 23, 1787, in James H. Hutson, *Supplement to Max Farrand's Records of the Federal Convention of 1787* (New Haven, Conn.: Yale University Press, 1987), 236.

6. Farrand, vol. 2, 196.

7. Ibid., 196–200.

8. Ibid., 201–2.

9. Ibid., 202–3.

10. Ibid., 202–5.

11. Ibid., 206, 216, 248–49. Economists and statisticians have come up with widely varying ways of calculating the rate of inflation between the late eighteenth century and the present day. The numbers used in the text are on the low end of those calculations.

12. Ibid., 249–51. For a brilliant analysis of the prevailing fear of the leveling forces unleashed by the Revolution, see Gordon S. Wood, *The Creation of the American Republic, 1776–1787* (Chapel Hill, NC: University of North Carolina Press, 1969), esp. 475–83. The quote from Jay is on p. 477.

13. Ibid., 216–17.

14. Ibid., 236–39.

15. Ibid., 219, 221, 223.

16. Ibid., 224, 276–78, 280.

17. Ibid., 278.

18. Ibid., 505, 506, 509, 510. Robert A. Rutland, ed., *The Papers of George Mason, 1725–1792,* 3 vols. (Chapel Hill, N.C.: University of North Carolina Press, 1970), vol. 3, 1082.

19. Farrand, vol. 3, 195.

20. Ibid., vol. 2, 290–93.

21. Ibid., 292.

22. David Dutcher, Anna Coxe Toogood, et al., *1787: The Day-to-Day Story of the Constitutional Convention* (New York: Exeter Books, 1987), 23; Constitutional Convention Daybook Files, Independence National Historical Park Archive, Philadelphia, Pa., cabinet 1, drawer 2, folder 1 (Pay and Finances); North Carolina delegates to Governor Caswell, in Farrand, vol. 3, 46, 552–54. William Samuel Johnson Diary, transcript, June 7, 1787, Independence National Historical Park Archive, Philadelphia, Pa. The exact date of Johnson's move to Wilson's boardinghouse is uncertain, but he began taking his meals there regularly beginning in late June.

23. Daybooks, cabinet 1, drawer 3, folder 20, September 5, 1787; Mason to Beverly Randolph, June 30, Aug. 11, Sept. 17, 1787, "Account of Federal Convention Expenses," Sept. 28, 1787, all in Robert A. Rutland, ed., *The Papers of George Mason, 1725–1792,* 3 vols. (Chapel Hill, N.C.: University of North Carolina Press, 1970), vol. 3, 918, 954, 994.

24. Dutcher, Toogood, et al., *1787,* 23–24.

25. Farrand, vol. 2, 303–50.

26. Ibid., 324–26. Farrand suggests that though Madison's notes ascribe eleven additional items to Pinckney's list, some of those may have been suggested by Elbridge Gerry, John Rutledge, and George Mason.

27. For useful discussions of the origins and evolution of the "necessary and proper" clause see Jack Rakove, *Original Meanings: Politics and Ideas in the Making of the Constitution* (New York: Knopf, 1996), 84–180; Akhil Reed Amar, *America's Constitution: A Biography* (New York: Random House, 2005), 110–14, 212, 238, 319, 361–62. For a more technical discussion of the evolution of what many legal historians call the "sweeping clause," see William W. Van Alstyne, "The Role of Congress in Determining the Incidental Powers of the President and the Federal Courts: A Comment on the Horizontal Effect of the Sweeping Clause," *Law and Contemporary Problems* 40 (1976), 102.

28. Farrand, vol. 2, 345.

29. Ibid. 328; vol. 3, 71, 73, 137–38.

30. Ibid., vol. 2, 317. For the view that this provision was intended primarily to protect slaveholding interests, see Lawrence Goldstone, *Dark Bargain: Slavery, Profits and the Struggle for the Constitution* (New York: Walker and Company, 2005), 35–42; and Paul Finkelman, "Slavery and the Constitutional Convention: Making a Covenant with Death," in Richard R. Beeman et al., *Beyond Confederation: Origins of the Constitution and American National Identity* (Chapel Hill, N.C.: University of North Carolina Press, 1987), 191.

31. Farrand, vol. 2, 317, 329–30.

32. Ibid., 385, 388. See also George Billias, *Elbridge Gerry: Founding Father and Republican Statesman* (New York: McGraw-Hill, 1976), 192.

33. Gerry to Ann Gerry, Aug. 21, 1787, Hutson, *Supplement*, 233–34.

34. Luther Martin, "Reply to the Landowner," March 14, 1788, in Farrand, vol. 3, 282; Forrest McDonald, *E Pluribus Unum: The Formation of the American Republic, 1776–1790* (Boston: Houghton-Mifflin, 1965), 295–302, presents an elaborate, though largely conjectural, account of what might have occurred in those meetings. Goldstone, *Dark Bargain*, 159–60, suggests, wrongly, that the subject of slavery was the principal focus of the meetings. One can get at least a glimpse into the subject matter of the meetings in James McHenry's notes during that period, in Farrand, vol. 2, 190–92, 209–12, 226.

35. Farrand, vol. 2, 390–92.

36. Paterson to Ellsworth, Aug. 23, 1787, in Hutson, *Supplement*, 236.

37. Farrand, vol. 2, 468, 475–76.

38. Ibid., 478–79.

39. Ibid., 475, 477.

40. Charles Beard, *An Economic Interpretation of the Constitution of the United States* (New York: Macmillan, 1913), was among the first, and by far the most influential, to argue that the federal Constitution was a counter-revolutionary document. For the most recent, and more subtle, restatement of Beard's thesis, see Woody Holton, *Unruly Americans and the Origins of the Constitution* (New York: Hill and Wang, 2007). Many historians who dissent from Beard's overall interpretation, however, would agree that most of the framers of the Constitution possessed a deep skepticism about the virtues of democracy. In particular, see Wood, *Creation of the American Republic*, esp. 471–518; and Gordon S. Wood, *Revolutionary Characters: What Made the Founding Fathers Different* (New York: Penguin Press, 2006), esp. 26–28, 48–49, 149, 258–61.

CHAPTER SIXTEEN

1. Max Farrand, ed., *The Records of the Federal Convention of 1787*, 4 vols., rev. ed. (New Haven, Conn.: Yale University Press, 1937, repr. 1966), vol. 2, 298.

2. Ibid., 299–301.

3. Ibid., 301.

4. Ibid., 481.

5. Ibid., 484–85.

6. Ibid., 497, 499.

7. Madison to Andrew Stevenson, Nov. 17, 1830, in Farrand, vol. 3, 483–90.

8. One of the truly remarkable, if perverse, works of modern scholarship on the subject of Madison's understanding of the original meaning of the general welfare clause is William Winslow Crosskey, *Politics and the Constitution in the History of the United States*, 2 vols., (Chicago: University of Chicago Press, 1953). Crosskey's work, which was much in vogue during the years immediately after the New Deal, argued that Madison's "original understanding" of the extent of the commerce power was an exceptionally broad one, and that he subsequently altered his notes on the Convention in order to create— erroneously—a more narrow construction. On the perils of this kind of effort at discerning the original meaning of the framers, see Jack Rakove, *Original Meanings: Politics and Ideas in the Making of the Constitution* (New York: Knopf, 1996), 3–22.

9. Dickinson to George Logan, Jan. 16, 1802, in James H. Hutson, *Supplement to Max Farrand's The Records of the Federal Convention of 1787* (New Haven, Conn.: Yale University Press, 1987), 300–301.

10. Farrand, vol. 2, 497–98.

11. Ibid., 498–99.

12. Ibid., 500–501.

13. Ibid., 501–2.

14. Ibid.

15. Ibid., 502, 511–13.

16. Ibid., 514.

17. Ibid., 515–16.

18. Hutson, *Supplement*, 168.

19. Farrand, vol. 2, 522–24.

20. Ibid., 527.

21. Ibid., 536–38, 548–49.

22. Ibid., 540–42.

23. Ibid., 550.

24. Ibid., 553.

CHAPTER SEVENTEEN

1. Constitutional Convention Daybook Files, Independence National Historical Park Archive, Philadelphia, Pa., cabinet 2, drawer 2, folder 46 (Composite Data). See also Forrest McDonald, *We the People: The Economic Origins of the Constitution* (Chicago: University of Chicago Press, 1958), 68–85.

2. McDonald, *We the People*, 80; Marvin Zahisner, *Charles Cotesworth Pinckney* (Chapel Hill, N.C.: University of North Carolina Press, 1967), 31, 65, 80, 87–88. For Pinckney's preoccupation with horses while in Philadelphia, see the Diary of Jacob Hiltzheimer,

transcript at Independence National Historical Park Archive, Philadelphia, Pa., original at the American Philosophical Society, Philadelphia, Pa. Hiltzheimer was the stable keeper for many of the delegates, and, in addition to being one of the chroniclers of Philadelphia's weather during the summer of 1787, he also had extensive dealings with General Pinckney in the care and purchase of horses.

3. Jeff Broadwater, *George Mason: Forgotten Founder* (Chapel Hill, N.C.: University of North Carolina Press, 2006), 159.

4. McDonald, *We the People*, 72; Irving Brant, *James Madison*, 6 vols. (New York: Bobbs-Merrill, 1941–61), vol. 2, 48; Ralph Ketcham, *James Madison: A Biography* (New York: Macmillan, 1971), 148–49.

5. Daybooks, cabinet 2, drawer 2, folder 46 (Composite Data); Walter Isaacson, *Benjamin Franklin: An American Life* (New York: Simon & Schuster, 2003), 464.

6. The figures in the previous three paragraphs are based on the United States Census of 1790, which can be conveniently accessed at http://www.census.gov/prod/www/abs/decennial/1790.htm.

7. Orlando Patterson, *Slavery and Social Death: A Comparative Study* (Cambridge, Mass.: Harvard University Press, 1982), viii–ix; David Brion Davis, *The Problem of Slavery in Western Culture* (Ithaca, N.Y.: Cornell University Press, 1966). For the pace of abolition after the Revolution, see David Brion Davis, *The Problem of Slavery in the Age of Revolution* (Ithaca, N.Y.: Cornell University Press, 1975), esp. 23–342; Duncan MacLeod, *Slavery, Race and the American Revolution* (Cambridge: Cambridge University Press, 1974); Ira Berlin, "The Revolution in Black Life," in Ronald Hoffman and Alfred E. Young, eds., *The Radicalism of the American Revolution* (DeKalb, Ill.: Northern Illinois University Press, 1976), 356–59.

8. For the philosophical dilemmas presented by the tension between property rights and human rights, see Davis, *Slavery in Western Culture*, 188–21, and Winthrop Jordan, *White Over Black: American Attitudes Toward the Negro, 1580–1812* (Chapel Hill, N.C.: University of North Carolina Press, 1968), 349–55.

9. Berlin, "Revolution in Black Life," 358–59; Don E. Fehrenbacher, "Slavery, the Framers, and the Living Constitution," in Robert A. Goldwin and Art Kaufman, eds., *Slavery and Its Consequences: The Constitution, Equality, and Race* (Washington, D.C.: American Enterprise Institute, 1988), 6.

10. Patrick Henry to Robert Pleasants, in Roberts Vaux, *Memoirs of the Life of Anthony Benezet* (Philadelphia: James P. Parke, 1817), 55–57.

11. Broadwater, *George Mason*, 84; David John Mays, *Edmund Pendleton: A Biography*, 2 vols. (Cambridge, Mass.: Harvard University Press, 1952), vol. 1, 121–22; Robert A. Rutland, *The Birth of the Bill of Rights, 1776–1791* (Chapel Hill, N.C.: University of North Carolina Press, 1955), 45–47. Ketcham, *James Madison*, 71–72, implies that both Mason and Madison intended the original version of the resolution to contain a broad grant of equal rights to African Americans and landless whites. Given both Mason's and Madison's ownership of slaves, this seems unlikely.

12. For brilliant exposition on the deep roots of racism in Western culture, see Davis, *Slavery in Western Culture*, passim; and Jordan, *White Over Black*, passim.

13. Joseph J. Ellis, *His Excellency, George Washington* (New York: Knopf, 2005), 164–65, 243–44.

14. Lawrence Goldstone, *Dark Bargain: Slavery, Profits and the Struggle for the Constitution* (New York: Walker and Company, 2005), 67–78, offers a brief account of the economy of the lower South. See also Eugene Sirmans, *Colonial South Carolina* (Chapel Hill, N.C.: University of North Carolina Press, 1966); and Robert Weir, *Colonial South Carolina: A History* (Columbia, S.C.: University of South Carolina Press, 1997), 173–93. There is a common misconception that cotton was a mainstay of the economies of the states of the lower South, but cotton did not begin to play a role in those economies until after the invention of the cotton gin in 1793 and did not become a mainstay of the Southern economy until the second decade of the nineteenth century.

15. Max Farrand, ed., *The Records of the Federal Convention of 1787*, 4 vols., rev. ed. (New Haven, Conn.: Yale University Press, 1937, repr. 1966), vol. 2, 219–21. As noted in chapter 11, the most comprehensive discussion of the unfolding of the debates and decisions over the three-fifths clause is George Van Cleve, "A Slaveholders' Union: The Law and Politics of American Slavery, 1770–1821" (PhD diss., University of Virginia, 2008), 176–211.

16. Farrand, vol. 2, 221–23.

17. James J. Kirschke, *Gouverneur Morris: Author, Statesman, and Man of the World* (New York: St. Martin's Press, 2005), 62.

18. Farrand, vol. 2, 223.

19. Ibid., 359–63.

20. Ibid.

21. Ibid., 363. George Washington sided with Madison within the Virginia delegation, but George Mason, Edmund Randolph, and John Blair voted no.

22. Ibid., 363–64.

23. Ibid., 364.

24. McDonald, *We the People*, 70; Paul Clarkson and R. Samuel Jett, *Luther Martin of Maryland* (Baltimore: Johns Hopkins University Press, 1970), 164.

25. Farrand, vol. 2, 364.

26. Ibid., 364–65.

27. Ibid., 370.

28. Ibid.

29. Robert A. Rutland, et al., *The Papers of James Madison*, 19 vols. (Chicago and Charlottesville, Va.: University of Chicago Press and University Press of Virginia, 1961–), vol. 1, 61–62, 173.

30. Helen Hill Miller, *George Mason, Gentleman Revolutionary* (Chapel Hill, N.C.: University of North Carolina Press, 1975), 55–56.

31. Citing the fact that Mason owned more than three hundred slaves and that he gave speeches in the Virginia ratifying convention raising the specter of federal government interference with the institution of slavery, many historians have been inclined to accuse him of simple hypocrisy. See, in particular, Peter Wallenstein, "Flawed Keepers of the Flame: The Interpreters of George Mason," *Virginia Magazine of History and Biography* 93 (1985), 229–60. See also Goldstone, *Dark Bargain*, 55–66, 166–69, 190–91. Hypocrisy may have been a part of the equation, but Mason's thought processes were undoubtedly more complex than hypocrisy alone would explain.

32. Farrand, vol. 2, 372–73.

33. Ibid., 371–73.

34. Ibid., 371. Later, during the debate on ratification, Ellsworth would step up his attack on what he saw as Mason's hypocrisy. Ellsworth, "The Landowner," Dec. 10, 1787, in Merrill Jensen, John Kaminski, and Gaspare Saladino, eds., *The Documentary History of the Ratification of the Constitution,* 21 vols. (Madison, Wis.: State Historical Society of Wisconsin, 1976–), vol. 8, 229–31.

35. Farrand, vol. 2, 371, 374.

36. Ibid., 374. The most vehement assertion of the "dark bargain" thesis is Goldstone, *Dark Bargain,* esp. 161–75, 192–95. See also David Stewart, *The Summer of 1787* (New York: Simon & Schuster, 2007), 173–75. A similar, though less strident, position has been taken by Donald Robinson, *Slavery in the Structure of American Politics* (New York: Harcourt, Brace, Javonovich, 1971), 218. See also Paul Finkelman, "Slavery and the Constitutional Convention: Making a Covenant with Death," in Richard R. Beeman et al., *Beyond Confederation: Origins of the Constitution and American National Identity* (Chapel Hill, N.C.: University of North Carolina Press, 1987), 191; and William W. Freehling, "The Founding Fathers and Slavery," *American Historical Review* (1972), 81, 84. Van Cleve, "A Slaveholders' Union," esp. 211–33, provides the most balanced discussion of the relationship between the debate over the commerce clause and the slave trade.

37. Farrand, vol. 2, 374–75.

38. Ibid., vol. 3, 210–11.

39. Ibid., vol. 2, 400.

40. Ibid., 414–15.

41. Ibid., 415–16.

42. Ibid., 416, vol. 3, 210.

43. Ibid., vol. 2, 449–50.

44. Ibid., 449.

45. Ibid., 451.

46. Ibid., 449–53.

47. Ibid., 453.

48. Ibid., 443, 453–54.

49. Finkelman, in "Slavery and the Constitutional Convention," 191–92, 219, 221–23, was the first historian to emphasize the complicity of the Founding Fathers in not merely sanctioning, but also enforcing, the slave system in the new republic.

50. Ibid., 221.

51. On the Massachusetts–South Carolina conflict, see Van Cleve, "A Slaveholders' Union," chapter 1.

52. I am grateful to Van Cleve, in ibid., 4–5, 17–20, 163–64, 283–88, as well as private communications with the author, for helping to clarify this distinction.

53. Historians have arrived at drastically varying estimates of the number of slaves imported into the United States between 1787 and 1808. The best review of those estimates, and the estimate on which I base my own, is in ibid., 227–29.

54. John Adams to Jeremy Belknap, Oct. 23, 1795, quoted in Van Cleve, "A Slaveholders' Union," chapter 2.

55. Adrienne Koch and William Peden, eds., *The Life and Selected Writings of Thomas Jefferson* (New York: Modern Library, 1944), 51.

56. Farrand, vol. 3, 210; James H. Hutson, *Supplement to Max Farrand's The Records of the Federal Convention of 1787* (New Haven, Conn.: Yale University Press, 1987), 158.

57. Abraham Lincoln, Seventh Debate, Alton, Illinois, Oct., 15, 1858, can be conveniently accessed at http://www.illinoiscivilwar.org/debates.html.

CHAPTER EIGHTEEN

1. Max Farrand, ed., *The Records of the Federal Convention of 1787*, 4 vols., rev. ed. (New Haven, Conn.: Yale University Press, 1937, repr. 1966), vol. 2, 553, vol. 3, 80.

2. Ibid., vol. 2, 557–58.

3. Ibid., 559.

4. The Report of the Committee of Style is in Farrand, vol. 2, 590–603.

5. Ibid., 561.

6. Ibid., 562.

7. Ibid., 563–64.

8. There was no formal vote on this as a separate resolution, but it was included in the Report of the Committee of Style and ultimately accepted without revision.

9. Farrand, vol. 2, 585–87. Hamilton, Morris, and Madison would have preferred an absolute executive veto, but at this stage they were hoping they might at least be able to raise the bar to three-fourths of the members of both houses.

10. Ibid., 587–88.

11. Ibid., 588.

12. Jefferson to Madison, Dec. 20, 1787, Jefferson to Alexander Donald, Feb. 7, 1788, Jefferson to Francis Hopkinson, March 13, 1789, in Julian Boyd et al., *The Papers of Thomas Jefferson*, 17 vols. (Princeton, N.J.: Princeton University Press, 1950–), vol. 12, 439–42, 570–72, vol. 14, 650–51.

13. Farrand, vol. 3, 143.

14. Madison to Jefferson, Oct. 17, 1788, in William T. Hutchinson, William M. E. Rachal, Robert A. Rutland, et al., *The Papers of James Madison*, 19 vols. (Chicago and Charlottesville, Va.: University of Chicago Press and University Press of Virginia, 1961–), vol. 11, 297–300.

15. Farrand, vol. 2, 606; Helen Hill Miller, *George Mason, Gentleman Revolutionary* (Chapel Hill, N.C.: University of North Carolina Press, 1975), 44–45, 47–62.

16. Timothy H. Breen, *The Marketplace of Revolution: How Consumer Politics Shaped American Independence* (New York: Oxford University Press, 2004), rather than seeing the virtues of republican simplicity as standing in tension with the consumption habits of America's upper classes, sees the two as being wholly compatible, part of the "liberty" for which Americans were fighting. The rhetoric of republicanism, as expressed by men like Mason, would, however, suggest otherwise. For that reason, the argument advanced by Edmund S. Morgan, "The Puritan Ethic and the American Revolution," *William and Mary Quarterly* 24, 3rd ser. (1967), 3–43, seems more persuasive. See also Pauline Maier, *The Old Revolutionaries: Political Lives in the Age of Samuel Adams* (New York: Knopf, 1980).

17. Farrand, vol. 2, 524–25.

18. Morris to Timothy Pickering, Dec. 22, 1814, Madison to Jared Sparks, April 8, 1831, in Farrand, vol. 3, 420, 499.

19. Clinton Rossiter, *1787: The Grand Convention* (New York: Macmillan Company, 1966), 224–26.

20. Ibid., 228–29.

21. The two notable exceptions to the revolutionary character of the state constitutions were those of Connecticut and Rhode Island, which were essentially continuations of those states' colonial charters. The most convenient way to view the Revolutionary state constitutions is through the Yale University Law School's Avalon Project, at http://www .yale.edu/lawweb/avalon/states/stateco.htm.

22. The text of the Articles of Confederation is easily accessed through the Avalon Project website.

23. Farrand, vol. 2, 590.

24. The Report of the Committee of Style, on which the preceding paragraphs are based, is in Farrand, vol. 2, 590–603.

25. A useful, brief account of the constitutional and ideological divisions of the 1790s is James Roger Sharp, *American Politics in the 1790s: The New Nation in Crisis* (New Haven, Conn.: Yale University Press, 1993). For a specific, technical discussion of Hamilton's proposal for the assumption of state debts, see E. James Ferguson, *The Power of the Purse: A History of American Public Finance, 1776–1790* (Chapel Hill, N.C.: University of North Carolina Press, 1961), esp. 203–19.

26. For excellent discussions of the federal supremacy clause, see Jack Rakove, *Original Meanings: Politics and Ideas in the Making of the Constitution* (New York: Knopf, 1996), 82–83, 171–77, 180–87, 324–25; and Akhil Reed Amar, *America's Constitution: A Biography* (New York: Random House, 2005), 178–79, 299–303.

27. Morris's letter of transmittal is in Farrand, vol. 2, 583–84.

28. Ibid.

29. Madison to Henry Lee, June 25, 1824, in Farrand, vol. 3, 464.

30. Ibid., vol. 2, 614.

31. Ibid., 616–17.

32. Constitutional Convention Daybook Files, Independence National Historical Park Archive, Philadelphia, Pa., cabinet 1, drawer 3, folder 16, May 14, 1787. See also Donald Jackson and Dorothy Twohig, eds., *The Diaries of George Washington*, 6 vols. (Charlottesville, Va.: University Press of Virginia, 1976–79), vol. 5, 246.

33. Farrand, vol. 2, 622–23.

34. Ibid., 623–24.

35. Ibid., 629–31.

36. Ibid., 631.

37. Ibid., 632.

38. Ibid.

39. Ibid., 632–33.

40. Ibid.

41. Ibid., 633.

42. *GW Diary*, vol. 5, 246; William Samuel Johnson Diary, Sept. 15, 1787, transcript, Independence National Historical Park Archive, Philadelphia, Pa.; David Dutcher, Anna Coxe Toogood, et al., *1787: The Day-to-Day Story of the Constitutional Convention* (New York: Exeter Books, 1987), 187.

43. Arthur Plotnik, *Man Behind the Quill: Jacob Shallus* (Washington, D.C.: National Archives Trust Fund Board, 1987).

CHAPTER NINETEEN

1. It would have been forty-two, but John Dickinson had been suffering from debilitating headaches and went back home to Delaware over the weekend, asking his Delaware colleague George Read to sign the Constitution in his absence. John Dickinson to George Read, Sept. 15, 1787, in Max Farrand, ed., *The Records of The Federal Convention of 1787*, 4 vols., rev. ed. (New Haven, Conn.: Yale University Press, 1937, repr. 1966), vol. 3, 81.

2. Ibid., vol. 2, 641.

3. The account of the circumstances behind Franklin's speech and Morris's role in preparing the resolution following the speech is contained in a letter in Jefferson's handwriting, to an unnamed informant, dated Oct. 11, 1787, in Farrand, vol. 3, 104–5. See the lengthy explanation of the provenance of the letter in Julian Boyd et al., *The Papers of Thomas Jefferson*, 17 vols. (Princeton, N.J.: Princeton University Press, 1950–), vol. 12, 228–34.

4. Farrand, vol. 2, 641–43.

5. Ibid.

6. Ibid., 643.

7. Ibid., 643–44.

8. Ibid., 644–45.

9. Ibid., 645.

10. Richard Brookhiser, *Gentleman Revolutionary: Gouverneur Morris, the Rake Who Wrote the Constitution* (New York: Free Press, 2003), 92.

11. Farrand, vol. 2, 645–46.

12. Ibid., 646.

13. Ibid., 646–47.

14. Ibid., 647. The division in South Carolina came because of Pinckney's and Butler's disapproval of the timidity of Franklin's approach.

15. Ibid., 648.

16. Ibid.

17. Ibid., vol. 1, xi.

18. Ibid., xv–xix.

19. The parchment original copy of the Constitution, housed at the National Archives, begins with the delegates from Delaware, Maryland, Virginia, North Carolina, South Carolina, and Georgia's signatures on the left-hand side of the page, and then continues with the delegates from New Hampshire through Pennsylvania on the right-hand side of the page. The New Hampshire delegates did indeed begin the signing procession, signing their names on the right-hand side of the page, but, when it was discovered that there was no room for all of the signatures on that side of the page, the delegates, beginning with Delaware and moving southward, began signing on the left-hand side of the page. I am grateful to John R. Vile, *The Constitutional Convention of 1787: A Comprehensive Encyclopedia of America's Founding*, 2 vols. (Santa Barbara, Calif., ABC-CLIO, 2005) for these insights about the details of the signing.

20. "Fourth of July Oration," July 4, 1798, quoted in John E. O'Connor, *William Paterson:*

Lawyer and Statesman, 1745–1806 (New Brunswick, N.J.: Rutgers University Press, 1979), 162.

21. James Madison, "Preface to the Debates in the Convention of 1787, ca. 1836," in Farrand, vol. 3, 551.

22. Madison to Jefferson, Oct. 24, 1787, in William T. Hutchinson, William M. E. Rachal, Robert A. Rutland, et al., *The Papers of James Madison*, 19 vols. (Chicago and Charlottesville, Va.: University of Chicago Press and University Press of Virginia, 1961–), vol. 10, 206–19.

23. Donald Jackson and Dorothy Twohig, eds., *The Diaries of George Washington*, 6 vols. (Charlottesville, Va.: University Press of Virginia, 1976–79), vol. 5, 185.

24. David Dutcher, Anna Coxe Toogood, et al., *1787: The Day-to-Day Story of the Constitutional Convention* (New York: Exeter Books, 1987), 192.

25. Farrand, vol. 2, 648.

CHAPTER TWENTY

1. Donald Jackson and Dorothy Twohig, eds., *The Diaries of George Washington*, 6 vols. (Charlottesville, Va.: University Press of Virginia, 1976–79), vol. 5, 185; William Samuel Johnson Diary, September 17, 1787 transcript, Independence National Historical Park Archive, Philadelphia, Pa.; David Dutcher, Anna Coxe Toogood, et al., *1787: The Day-to-Day Story of the Constitutional Convention* (New York: Exeter Books, 1987), 190; Irving Brant, *James Madison*, 6 vols. (New York: Bobbs-Merrill, 1941–61), vol. 3, 161.

2. *GW Diary*, vol. 5, 186.

3. Jeff Broadwater, *George Mason: Forgotten Founder* (Chapel Hill, N.C.: University of North Carolina Press, 2006), 209–37; Clinton Rossiter, *1787: The Grand Convention* (New York: Macmillan Company, 1966), 275; Edward Carrington to Madison, Sept. 23, 1787, in William T. Hutchinson, William M. E. Rachal, Robert A. Rutland, et al., *The Papers of James Madison*, 19 vols. (Chicago and Charlottesville, Va.: University of Chicago Press and University Press of Virginia, 1961–), vol. 10, 172.

4. Max Farrand, ed., *The Records of the Federal Convention of 1787*, 4 vols., rev. ed. (New Haven, Conn.: Yale University Press, 1937, repr. 1966), vol. 3, 374. For an excellent discussion of Madison's views on the sources of legitimacy of the Constitution and the best means of interpreting it, see Jack Rakove, *Original Meanings: Politics and Ideas in the Making of the Constitution* (New York: Knopf, 1996), 339–65.

5. There is at present no single, comprehensive account of the ratification process. The one indispensable set of sources illuminating the debate over ratification is Merrill Jensen, John Kaminski, and Gaspare Saladino, eds., *The Documentary History of the Ratification of the Constitution*, 21 vols. (Madison, Wis.: State Historical Society of Wisconsin, 1976–). Twenty-one volumes have been published to date, with more on the way. The other important collection of primary sources is Herbert Storing, ed., *The Complete Antifederalist*, 7 vols. (Chicago: University of Chicago Press, 1981). Other important secondary works on ratification are Robert Alan Rutland, *The Ordeal of the Constitution: The Antifederalists and the Ratification Struggle of 1787–1788* (Norman, Okla.: University of Oklahoma Press, 1966); Forrest McDonald, *We the People: The Economic Origins of the Constitution* (Chicago: University of Chicago Press, 1958); Saul Cornell, *The Other Founders: Antifederalism and the Dissenting Tradition in America, 1788–1828* (Chapel Hill, N.C.: Uni-

versity of North Carolina Press, 1999); Steven Boyd, *The Politics of Opposition: Antifederalists and the Acceptance of the Constitution* (Millwood, N.J.: KTO Press, 1979); Jackson Turner Main, *The Antifederalists: Critics of the Constitution, 1781–1788* (Chapel Hill, N.C.: University of North Carolina Press, 1961); Michael Allen Gillespie and Michael Lienesch, eds., *Ratifying the Constitution* (Lawrence, Kans.: University Press of Kansas, 1989).

6. Pennsylvania *Packet*, Sept. 19, 1787; Edmund Cody Burnett, *The Continental Congress* (New York: Macmillan, 1941), 694–95; Rakove, *Original Meanings*, 108.

7. DHRC, 1:322. Burnett, *Continental Congress*, 695–702; Robert A. Rutland, ed., *The Papers of George Mason, 1725–1792*, 3 vols. (Chapel Hill, N.C.: University of North Carolina Press, 1970), vol. 3, 991–93; Broadwater, *George Mason*, 210–11.

8. Rakove, *Original Meanings*, 108–9; Rutland, *Ordeal*, 18–19; Burnett, *Continental Congress*, 695; Carrington to Madison, Sept. 23, 1787, in *Madison Papers*, vol. 10, 172.

9. Burnett, *Continental Congress*, 696–97.

10. Cornell, *Other Founders*, 26, 53, differentiates between Lee's brand of "elite Antifederalism" and the "populist Antifederalism" of less affluent critics of the Constitution. See also Rutland, *Ordeal*, 19; and Rakove, *Original Meanings*, 108–13.

11. For the pro-Federalist leanings of the newspapers of the time, see Main, *The Antifederalists*, 201, 204, 210, 214–17. See also Gordon S. Wood, *The Creation of the American Republic, 1776–1787* (Chapel Hill, N.C.: University of North Carolina Press, 1969), 486–87.

12. Quoted in Wood, *Creation of the American Republic*, 486.

13. Ibid., 486–87.

14. See, for example, Madison to Washington, Sept. 30, 1787, in *Madison Papers*, vol. 10, 179–81.

15. For discussions of the tumultuous character of politics in Pennsylvania during the period from 1776 to 1787, and, in particular, the contention surrounding the decision to call a ratifying convention, see Robert L. Brunhouse, *The Counter-Revolution in Pennsylvania, 1776–1790* (Harrisburg, Pa.: Pennsylvania Historical and Museum Commission, 1942), esp. 200–202; Owen S. Ireland, *Religion, Ethnicity, and Politics: Ratifying the Constitution in Pennsylvania* (University Park, Pa.: Pennsylvania State University Press, 1995), esp. 3–108; Rakove, *Original Meanings*, 110–11; George Graham, Jr., "Pennsylvania: Representation and the Meaning of Republicanism," in Gillespie and Lienesch, *Ratifying the Constitution*, 53–55.

16. Brunhouse, *Counter-Revolution*, 200–202; Charles Page Smith, *James Wilson, Founding Father, 1742–1798* (Chapel Hill, N.C.: University of North Carolina Press, 1956), 264.

17. "Centinel No. 1," Philadelphia *Independent Gazeteer*, Oct. 5, 1787, DHRC, vol. 13, 326–37, esp. 330. Eleaszar Oswald, who began publishing the *Independent Gazeteer* in 1782, was the most active Antifederalist publisher in Philadelphia. See Cornell, *Other Founders*, 128–36.

18. Cornell, *Other Founders*, 40–41, 46–48, 99–105. Storing, *Complete Antifederalist*, vol. 3, 197–98, 204–5.

19. Cornell, *Other Founders*, 85–87, 168–71.

20. Smith, *James Wilson*, 264–80; Rakove, *Original Meanings*, 191–93; William Howard Adams, *Gouverneur Morris: An Independent Life* (New Haven, Conn.: Yale University Press, 2003), 166.

21. Quoted in Rakove, *Original Meanings*, 116–17.

22. Smith, *James Wilson*, 267.

23. Ibid., 265–55. See also Graham, "Pennsylvania," in Gillespie and Lienesch, *Ratifying the Constitution*, 59–63.

24. Smith, *James Wilson*, 266; McDonald, *We the People*, 164–65.

25. Ireland, *Ratifying the Constitution in Pennsylvania*, 71–72.

26. Rakove, *Original Meanings*, 117.

27. Graham, "Pennsylvania," in Gillespie and Lienesch, *Ratifying the Constitution*, 64–66; Smith, *James Wilson*, 269–70.

28. Cornell, *Other Founders*, 225–26; Rutland, *Ordeal*, 55–57; Forrest McDonald, *E Pluribus Unum: The Formation of the American Republic, 1776–1790* (Boston: Houghton-Mifflin, 1965), 107.

29. Rutland, *Ordeal*, 56–58; Jonathan Elliot, *The Debates in the Several State Conventions, on the Adoption of the Federal Constitution . . .* , 2nd ed., 5 vols. (Washington, D.C.: U.S. Congress, 1836), vol. 2, 524.

30. DHRC, vol. 2, 592. See also Smith, *James Wilson*, 278.

31. Smith, *James Wilson*, 278–79.

32. For a summary of these events, see John Munroe, *Federalist Delaware: 1775–1815* (New Brunswick, N.J.: Rutgers University Press, 1954), 107–9; and John Munroe, "Delaware and the Constitution: An Overview of Events Leading to Ratification," *Delaware History* 22 (1987), 219–38. See also Gaspare Saladino, "Delaware: Independence and the Concept of a Commercial Republic," in Gillespie and Lienesch, *Ratifying the Constitution*, 40–43. The pertinent documents relating to ratification in Delaware can be found in DHRC, vol. 3, 36–114.

33. McDonald, *We the People*, 123–29. See also Main, *The Antifederalists*, 194–95. The pertinent documents relating to ratification in New Jersey can be found in DHRC, vol. 3, 117–97.

34. Washington to Samuel Powel, Jan. 18, 1788, in W. W. Abbot, Dorothy Twohig, et al., *The Papers of George Washington*, Confederation Series, 6 vols. (Charlottesville, Va.: University Press of Virginia, 1992–), vol. 6, 45–46. McDonald, *We the People*, 129–30; Rutland, *Ordeal*, 87–88. The pertinent documents relating to ratification in Georgia can be found in DHRC, vol. 3, 200–311. The editors of DHRC are inclined to discount the accuracy of Washington's assessment that fear of Indians was the primary cause of Georgia's unanimous ratification, but they do not provide an alternative explanation.

35. Main, *The Antifederalists*, 199; Christopher Collier, *Roger Sherman's Connecticut: Yankee Politics and the American Revolution* (Middletown, Conn.: Wesleyan University Press, 1971), 270–82; McDonald, *We the People*, 136–48; Rutland, *Ordeal*, 83–86; William Garrot Brown, *The Life of Oliver Ellsworth* (New York: DaCapo Press, 1970), 170–76. The pertinent documents relating to the contest in Connecticut are in DHRC, vol. 3, 314–614.

36. Collier, *Roger Sherman's Connecticut*, 275.

37. Ibid., 277–82; McDonald, *We the People*, 139–44.

CHAPTER TWENTY-ONE

1. Merrill Jensen, John Kaminski, and Gaspare Saladino, eds., *The Documentary History of the Ratification of the Constitution*, 21 vols. (Madison, Wis.: State Historical Society of

Wisconsin, 1976–), vol. 6, 3; Jonathan Elliot, *The Debates in the Several State Conventions, on the Adoption of the Federal Constitution . . .* , 2nd ed., 5 vols. (Washington, D.C.: U.S. Congress, 1836) vol. 2, 154–55; Robert Alan Rutland, *The Ordeal of the Constitution: The Antifederalists and the Ratification Struggle of 1787–1788* (Norman, Okla.: University of Oklahoma Press, 1966), 94–95. The full proceedings of the Massachusetts convention, together with notes from many of the delegates, are in DHRC, vol. 6, 1161–1478. After the ratification battle was over, Federalists spread the word that the Antifederalists had a majority when the Convention began, but as Pauline Maier will demonstrate in her forthcoming book on ratification, the evidence does not support what amounted to a post facto boast. I am grateful to Professor Maier for sharing this information with me.

2. King to Madison, Jan. 27, 1788, in William T. Hutchinson, William M. E. Rachal, Robert A. Rutland, et al., *The Papers of James Madison,* 19 vols. (Chicago and Charlottesville, Va.: University of Chicago Press and University Press of Virginia, 1961–), vol. 11, 436–37; Elliot, *Debates,* vol. 2, 32, 68, 102; Jack Rakove, *Original Meanings: Politics and Ideas in the Making of the Constitution* (New York: Knopf, 1996), 119. See also Gordon Wood, *The Creation of the American Republic, 1776–1787* (Chapel Hill, N.C.: University of North Carolina Press, 1969), 486–90.

3. Elliot, *Debates,* vol. 2, 3; George Billias, *Elbridge Gerry: Founding Father and Republican Statesman* (New York: McGraw-Hill, 1976), 1–99, 213.

4. Ibid.

5. Rutland, *Ordeal,* 105–6; Robert Ernst, *Rufus King: American Federalist* (Chapel Hill, N.C.: University of North Carolina Press, 1968), 128–29.

6. Ernst, *Rufus King,* 129–30; Rakove, *Original Meanings,* 119–20.

7. Elliot, *Debates,* vol. 2, 138, 140, 151–52. This discussion closely follows that in Rakove, *Original Meanings,* 120.

8. Ernst, *Rufus King,* 130. See also Harlow Giles Unger, *John Hancock: Merchant King and American Patriot* (New York: John Wiley, 2000), 312–16; and William M. Fowler, *The Baron of Beacon Hill: A Biography of John Hancock* (Boston: Longman, 1980), 268–72.

9. Forrest McDonald, *We the People: The Economic Origins of the Constitution* (Chicago: University of Chicago Press, 1958), 184. See also John K. Alexander, *Sam Adams: America's Revolutionary Politician* (Lanham, Md.: Rowman and Littlefield, 2002), 203–10; and John C. Miller, *Sam Adams: Pioneer in Propaganda* (Boston: Little, Brown, 1936), 376–86.

10. Ernst, *Rufus King,* 130–31; Elliot, *Debates,* vol. 2, 177–78.

11. Elliot, *Debates,* vol. 2, 182–83.

12. Langdon's lament is in Jean Yarbrough, "New Hampshire Puritanism and the Moral Foundation of America," in Michael Allen Gillespie and Michael Lienesch, eds., *Ratifying the Constitution* (Lawrence, Kans.: University Press of Kansas, 1989), 235–36. See also Jere Daniell, "Ideology and Hardball: Ratification of the Federal Constitution in New Hampshire," in Patrick T. Conley and John P. Kaminski, eds., *The Constitution and the States: The Role of the Original Thirteen States in the Framing and Adoption of the Federal Constitution* (Madison, Wis.: University of Wisconsin Press, 1988), 181–200; and Rutland, *Ordeal,* 117–23.

13. Historians have reached slightly different conclusions with respect to the precise vote count. John P. Kaminski, "Rhode Island: Protecting State Interests," in Gillespie and Lienesch, *Ratifying the Constitution,* 379, states the vote as 2,711 to 239. McDonald, *We*

the People, 322, arrives at a slightly different calculation of the vote, 2,708 against and 237 in favor. My figure is based on a methodical calculation by Pauline Maier from her forthcoming book on ratification.

14. Kaminski, "Rhode Island," 378–83.

15. McDonald, *We the People,* 148–50. Martin's extended campaign against the Constitution is summarized in Paul Clarkson and R. Samuel Jett, *Luther Martin of Maryland* (Baltimore: Johns Hopkins University Press, 1970), 138–41. Mercer's and Carroll's charges are cited in Carl Van Doren, *The Great Rehearsal* (New York: Viking Press, 1948), 207.

16. Van Doren, *The Great Rehearsal,* 207; Rutland, *Ordeal,* 156–58. See also Peter Onuf, "Maryland: The Small Republic in the New Nation," in Gillespie and Lienesch, *Ratifying the Constitution,* 171–94.

17. McDonald, *We the People,* 203.

18. Forrest McDonald, *E Pluribus Unum: The Formation of the American Republic, 1776–1790* (Boston: Houghton-Mifflin, 1965), 347.

19. Robert Weir, "South Carolina: Slavery and the Structure of the Union," in Gillespie and Lienesch, *Ratifying the Constitution,* 201–29, esp. 220, has an excellent account of the underlying reasons for South Carolina's support of the Constitution.

20. Ibid., 224.

21. Washington to Patrick Henry, Sept. 24, 1787, Henry to Washington, Oct. 19, 1787, in W. W. Abbot, Dorothy Twohig, et al., *The Papers of George Washington,* Confederation Series, 6 vols. (Charlottesville, Va.: University Press of Virginia, 1992–), vol. 5, 339–40, 384. The pertinent documents relating to the ratifying contest in Virginia can be found in DHRC, vols. 8–10.

22. Madison to Jefferson, April 22, 1788, Madison to Washington, June 13, 1788, *Madison Papers,* vol. 11, 28, 134.

23. Richard R. Beeman, *The Old Dominion and the New Nation, 1788–1801* (Lexington, Ky.: University of Kentucky Press, 1972), 2–4.

24. Elliot, *Debates,* vol. 3, 25–26, 652–55. The italicized words are part of the official record of Randolph's speech.

25. Ibid., 21–22, 55.

26. Ibid., 162. For a full account of Henry's role in the Convention, see Richard R. Beeman, *Patrick Henry: A Biography* (New York: McGraw-Hill, 1974), 148–63; and Henry Mayer, *A Son of Thunder: Patrick Henry and the American Republic* (New York: Franklin Watts, 1986), 396–439. Joseph Ellis, *American Creation: Triumphs and Tragedies at the Founding of the Republic* (New York: Knopf, 2008), 119–26, provides a dramatic, though perhaps overstated, account of the importance of the Virginia ratifying convention and the centrality of Henry and Madison in the debates.

27. Jeff Broadwater, *George Mason: Forgotten Founder* (Chapel Hill, N.C.: University of North Carolina Press, 2006), 234–37; Rakove, *Original Meanings,* 122–24.

28. Elliot, *Debates,* vol. 3, 653–55.

29. Broadwater, *George Mason,* 234–37.

30. Elliot, *Debates,* vol. 3, 653–55.

31. Ibid., 652; Beeman, *Old Dominion,* 10–11.

32. My account of New York's ratification is based on John P. Kaminski, "New York: The Reluctant Pillar," in Stephen Schecter, ed., *The Reluctant Pillar: New York and the Adop-*

tion of the Constitution (Troy, N.Y.: Russell Sage, 1985), 48–117; Cecil L. Eubanks, "New York: Federalism and the Political Economy of Union," in Gillespie and Lienesch, *Ratifying the Constitution*, 300–334; Linda Grant DePauw, *The Eleventh Pillar: New York State and the Federal Constitution* (Ithaca, N.Y.: Cornell University Press, 1966); and Rakove, *Original Meanings*, 125–28. The pertinent documents relating to New York's contentious ratifying contest can be found in *DHRC*, vols. 19–21.

33. On Clinton's role in the New York ratifying convention and in New York politics generally, see John Kaminski, *George Clinton, Yeoman Politician of the New Republic* (Madison, Wis: Madison House, 1993), 131–69.

34. Eubanks, "New York," 318–25; and Kaminski, "Reluctant Pillar," 100–114.

35. Elliot, *Debates*, 2:411; Rakove, *Original Meanings*, 125–27; Eubanks, "New York," 326; Kaminski, "Reluctant Pillar," 100–114.

36. Rakove, *Original Meanings*, 126–27. McDonald, *We the People*, 287–88, makes the strongest assertion about Hamilton's threats of secession and their effect on moderate Antifederalists like Melancton Smith. Robin Brooks, "Alexander Hamilton, Melancton Smith, and the Ratification of the Constitution in New York," *William and Mary Quarterly* 24, 3rd ser. (1979), 339–58, credits Smith with more independence of action in accepting, however reluctantly, the Constitution.

37. Elliot, *Debates*, vol. 4, 143. The most detailed account of the ratification struggle in North Carolina is Louise Irby Trenholme, *The Ratification of the Federal Constitution in North Carolina* (New York: Columbia University Press, 1967), esp. 100–191. I have relied on her work, Michael Lienesch, "North Carolina: Preserving Rights," in Gillespie and Lienesch, *Ratifying the Constitution*, 343–67, and Rakove, *Original Meanings*, 127–28.

38. Lienesch, "North Carolina," 353–58.

39. Ibid., 363–65; Rakove, *Original Meanings*, 128.

40. Rakove, *Original Meanings*, 128.

41. The full magnitude of the outpouring is best seen by perusing the twenty-one volumes to date of Kaminski, DHRC.

42. The best of the numerous editions of Publius's writings is Jacob E. Cooke, ed., *The Federalist* (Middletown, Conn.: Wesleyan University Press, 1961). For an illuminating analysis of the origins and significance of *The Federalist*, see the insightful essay by Bernard Bailyn, *To Begin the World Anew: The Genius and Ambiguities of the American Founders* (New York: Knopf, 2003), 100–130. I am also indebted in my analysis of *The Federalist*, and of the dynamic of the ratification debate generally, to Rakove, *Original Meanings*, 18–20, 155–62, 280–86.

43. Bailyn, in *To Begin the World Anew*, 101–102.

44. Ibid., 104, 127–28.

45. Publius, "Federalist No. 39," in Cooke, *The Federalist*, 257.

46. Elliot, *Debates*, vol. 3, 171.

47. For a list of some of the most influential Antifederalist pamphlets and broadsides, see Appendices I and II in Saul Cornell, *The Other Founders: Anti-federalism and the Dissenting Tradition in America, 1788–1828* (Chapel Hill, N.C.: University of North Carolina Press, 1999), 309–17. See also Herbert Storing, ed., *The Complete Antifederalist*, 7 vols. (Chicago: University of Chicago Press, 1981), passim; and, though still incomplete, the monumental DHRC.

48. Rakove, *Original Meanings*, 183–85. The complete works of Brutus are reprinted in DHRC, vol. 13, 14.

49. Rakove, *Original Meanings*, 148, 181–83.

50. Interestingly, the first ten amendments to the Constitution were not usually referred to as a "bill of rights" at the time, and, for the most part, they remained a relatively unimportant part of American constitutional law until the end of the nineteenth century. The scholarly literature on the ratification debate and the absence of a bill of rights is immense. For excellent, brief summaries of the Antifederalist position and the Federalists' miscalculation on the issue, see Rakove, *Original Meanings*, 147–48, 318–25, 329–30; and Wood, *Creation of the American Republic*, 536–43. Wood perhaps overvalues the Federalists' defense of the "irrelevance" of a bill of rights. For the evolution of the application of the Bill of Rights to American constitutional law, see Akhil Reed Amar, *America's Constitution: A Biography* (New York: Random House, 2005), esp. 43–44, 315–29, 385–91.

51. Bailyn, *To Begin the World Anew*, 106.

EPILOGUE

1. Max Farrand, ed., *The Records of the Federal Convention of 1787*, 4 vols., rev. ed. (New Haven, Conn.: Yale University Press, 1937, repr. 1966), vol. 3, 85.

2. Douglas Southall Freeman, *George Washington: A Biography*, 7 vols. (New York: Charles Scribner's Sons, 1948–57), vol. 6, 157–66.

3. Ibid., 193–95.

4. There are dozens of works dealing with Washington's presidency. Among the most useful are Freeman, *George Washington*, vols. 6, 7; Joseph J. Ellis, *His Excellency, George Washington* (New York: Knopf, 2005), 192–240; and Forrest McDonald, *The Presidency of George Washington*, (Lawrence, Kans.: University of Kansas Press, 1974). The writing on the political controversies of the 1790s that caused Washington such anguish is also vast, but for a good general account, see James Roger Sharp, *American Politics in the 1790s: The New Nation in Crisis* (New Haven, Conn.: Yale University Press, 1993).

5. In fact, Washington never actually delivered his Farewell Address as a speech. Instead, it was distributed to newspapers across the country and printed in the fall of 1796. The fascinating story of the composition and dissemination of Washington's Farewell Address is well told by Ellis, *His Excellency*, 232–34; and Joseph J. Ellis, *Founding Brothers: The Revolutionary Generation* (New York: Knopf, 2001), 120–61. The classic account of the Farewell Address is Felix Gilbert, *To the Farewell Address: The Beginnings of American Foreign Policy* (Princeton, N.J.: Princeton University Press, 1961), esp. 115–47.

6. Martha Washington to Elizabeth Powel, Dec. 17, 1797, in W. W. Abbot, Dorothy Twohig, et al., *The Papers of George Washington*, Presidential Series, 11 vols. (Charlottesville, Va.: University Press of Virginia, 1987–), vol. 1, 520. Although Martha Washington wrote the letter to Elizabeth, the general dictated the passages relating to the political attacks to which he had been subjected.

7. For a useful summary of these events, see Sharp, *New Nation in Crisis*, 187–225; and Stanley Elkins and Eric McKitrick, *The Age of Federalism: The Early American Republic, 1787–1800* (New York: Oxford University Press, 1993), 691–725.

8. The preceding paragraphs draw on many of the excellent accounts of the election of 1800. Among the most recent are John Ferling, *Adams versus Jefferson: The Tumultuous Election*

of 1800 (New York: Oxford University Press, 2005); and Edward Larson, *A Magnificent Catastrophe: The Tumultuous Election of 1800, America's First Presidential Campaign* (New York: Free Press, 2007). See also Sharp, *New Nation in Crisis,* 226–49; and Elkins and McKitrick, *The Age of Federalism,* 726–42.

9. For an evocative description of the unfinished capital city in 1801, see James Sterling Young, *The Washington Community: 1800–1828* (New York: Harcourt, Brace, 1966), 1–10, 41–48. See also the brilliant, if opinionated, assessment of John Adams's great-grandson, Henry Adams, *History of the United States During the Administrations of Thomas Jefferson and James Madison,* 9 vols. (New York: Charles Scribner's Sons, 1890), vol. 1, 1–41, 185–217.

10. Young, *Washington Community,* 44–45.

11. Adams, *History of the United States,* vol. 1, 191.

12. Ibid., 192–94.

13. Ibid., 19–96.

14. "First Inaugural Address," March 4, 1801, in Adrienne Koch and William Peden, eds., *The Life and Selected Writings of Thomas Jefferson* (New York: Modern Library, 1944), 321. Jefferson's inaugural, and many of the most important documents of the periods of the Revolution, Constitution, and early republic, can be found on the admirable website of the Avalon Project, Yale University Law School, at http://www.yale.edu/lawweb/avalon/presiden/inaug/jefinau1.htm.

15. "First Inaugural Address," in Koch and Peden, *Selected Writings,* 321–22.

16. Jack Rakove, *Original Meanings: Politics and Ideas in the Making of the Constitution* (New York: Knopf, 1996), 367, and, more generally, 366–70. I am much in debt to Professor Rakove for his insights on the differing emphases that Madison and Jefferson placed on the roles of tradition and innovation in American constitutional thought. Much of the commentary that follows is informed by those insights.

17. Jefferson to Madison, Sept. 6, 1789, in William T. Hutchinson, William M. E. Rachal, Robert A. Rutland, et al., *The Papers of James Madison,* 19 vols. (Chicago and Charlottesville, Va.: University of Chicago Press and University Press of Virginia, 1961–), vol. 12, 382–87.

18. Madison to Jefferson, Feb. 4, 1790, in *Madison Papers,* vol. 13, 22–25.

19. Jefferson to Samuel Kercheval, July 12, 1816, in Koch and Peden, *Selected Writings,* 674.

INDEX

RICHARD BEEMAN is a professor of history at the University of Pennsylvania and the author of five previous books on the history of revolutionary America; his biography of Patrick Henry was a finalist for the National Book Award. He has received awards from, among others, the Rockefeller Foundation and the National Endowment for the Humanities, and he has served as Harmsworth Professor of American History at Oxford University. He also serves as a trustee and vice-chair of the Distinguished Scholars Panel of the National Constitution Center. Richard Beeman lives in Philadelphia.